658.403　　　　　　　　179408
Cou

Couger.
Introduction to computer-
based information systems.

The Lorette Wilmot Library
Nazareth College of Rochester, N. Y.

INTRODUCTION TO COMPUTER BASED INFORMATION SYSTEMS

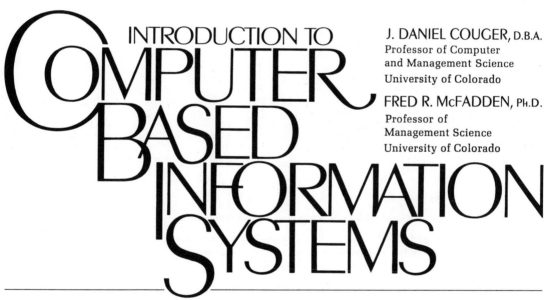

INTRODUCTION TO

COMPUTER BASED INFORMATION SYSTEMS

J. DANIEL COUGER, D.B.A.
Professor of Computer
and Management Science
University of Colorado

FRED R. McFADDEN, Ph.D.
Professor of
Management Science
University of Colorado

JOHN WILEY & SONS, INC.   NEW YORK • LONDON • SYDNEY • TORONTO

LORETTE WILMOT LIBRARY
NAZARETH COLLEGE
DISCARDED

Copyright © 1975, by John Wiley & Sons, Inc.

All rights reserved. Published simultaneously in Canada.

No part of this book may be reproduced by any means, nor transmitted, nor translated into a machine language without the written permission of the publisher.

Library of Congress Cataloging in Publication Data:

Couger, J. Daniel.
  Introduction to computer-based information systems.
  Includes index.
  1. Management information systems. I. McFadden,
Fred R., 1933-   joint author.   II. Title
T58.6.C68   658.4'03   74-28437
ISBN 0-471-17736-9

Printed in the United States of America

10-9 8 7 6 5 4 3 2 1

658.403
Cov

To our wives,
Shirley and Evelyn

PREFACE

More than 800 books have been published on the subject, Introduction to Data Processing, according to the 8th Annual Bibliography of Computer-Oriented Books.[1] However, the curriculum of this field is changing. Schools and colleges are revising courses that previously offered only computing concepts and computer programming to include an introduction to system analysis and design. This trend is evident in the triennial survey of computer curriculum among accredited schools of business (AACSB), conducted by the *Computing Newsletter for Schools of Business* (1967, 1970, 1973). Our textbook is designed for these new courses, and it has been class-tested in four schools.

The Common Database Approach

In addition to the topics mentioned above, this book provides an introduction to computer-based information systems, where systems are integrated through common databases. The integration of systems in this manner is a relatively new concept. Previously, *independent* systems were developed for *interdependent* activities of an organization. Today, progressive organizations are designing systems to provide integration both horizontally and vertically.

The book is intended as a first course for both "users" and "practitioners." Students majoring in the functional areas of the curriculum (for example accounting, public administration, and hospital administration) must be knowledgeable concerning the computer if they are to utilize it effectively in their sphere of responsibility. They need the same foundation course as students who plan to become practitioners in

---

[1]Bibliography published by *Computing Newsletter for Schools of Business*, University of Colorado.

the system design field. With this common background, the user and practitioner will be able to communicate better in order to produce effective systems.

Objectives of the First Course

The core course in data processing usually meets two contrasting objectives:

1. It provides an overview of the computer-based information system, preparing students for the task of managing one of the most important resources of a firm—its information.
2. It provides specific skills, such as computer programming, to enable the student to use the computer as an aid to learning and analysis in subsequent courses.

Until recently, schools considered these objectives to be mutually exclusive; a course was typically designed to meet one but not both objectives. The AACSB survey shows that more and more schools have decided that both objectives should be attained. In the introductory course at these schools, students acquire a computer programming proficiency as well as an understanding of systems analysis and design.

The table on the following page lists the concepts and techniques required of business students today. Achievement levels are defined, depending on whether the student will be a practitioner (I.S. major) or a user (all others). There are three achievement levels.

1. *Knowledge Level.* Acquired through self-study and class attendance.
2. *Understanding Level.* Acquired through completion of problems, exercises, or cases.
3. *Skill Level.* Acquired through completion of projects representative of real-world business situations.

For example, the information system major is expected to acquire skill in the use of file design techniques through a project. Majors in other fields are not required to learn any part of this subject. On the other hand, all students are required to understand computer programming by writing programs in FORTRAN. Information system majors go on to acquire a skill in programming by using a business-oriented language, COBOL or PL/1.

Sequence of Topics

The topics are arranged to provide a sound educational and practical scheduling approach. The consideration of computing concepts early in the course is logical. The discussion of programming before system analysis/design is practical—students need the entire term to write and debug their programs. We also have found that the understanding of computer capabilities acquired through programming facilitates an understanding of the system development task.

The Computing Curriculum Required of All Students

Computing Concepts and Techniques	Achievement Levels					
	Knowledge		Understanding		Skill	
	Majors I.S.	Others All	Majors I.S.	Others All	Majors I.S.	Others All
Systems						
Open and closed systems	X	X				
General systems theory	X					
Cybernetic systems	X					
Man/computer synergism		X	X			
Deterministic/probabilistic sys.		X	X			
System life cycle		X	X			
Management Information Systems						
Planning and control models		X	X			
Management-by-exception		X	X			
Operational/tactical/strategic lev.		X	X			
Programmed decision systems		X	X			
Determining system priorities			X	X		
Common database concept		X			X	
External/internal sources of info.		X			X	
Cost and value of information				X	X	
Computing						
Data representation			X	X		
Software versus hardware concepts		X	X			
Proc. approaches (batch vs OLRT)			X	X		
Multiprocess. and multiprogram.		X	X			
Communication networks		X	X			
Programming						
Algorithmic programming		X			X	
Structured programming					X	
System software		X	X			
Flowcharts/block diagrams				X	X	
Application software						
FORTRAN or BASIC			X	X		
COBOL or PL/1		X			X	
Subroutines and modularity				X	X	
Sorting and file access				X	X	
Debugging and testing				X	X	
Documentation				X	X	
System Analysis (Logical Design)						
System survey techniques		X			X	
Information flowcharts				X	X	
Decision tables				X	X	
Logical design specifications		X			X	
Cost/effectiveness analysis				X	X	
System Design (Physical Design)						
File design techniques					X	
Database design		X			X	
Data management systems					X	
Hardware/software selection		X			X	
Levels of sophistication in design		X			X	
Computer-aided design			X			
Physical design specifications					X	
System optimization techniques			X			
Audit trails		X			X	
Implementation						
Behavioral implications			X	X		
Training approaches			X	X		
Procedure development			X	X		
Implementation techniques			X		X	
Post-implementation audits			X		X	
Determining system performance			X			
Societal Implications						
History of computing	X	X				
Government regulation		X	X			
Technological impact		X	X			
Social impact		X	X			

Instruction Style

The instructor can expect that students have comprehended much of the material in the book prior to class. Self-study is facilitated by three devices: (1) periodic reinforcement questions after each micro module of material, (2) exercises after each macro module of material, and (3) chapter examinations. The chapter examinations require both descriptive and quantitative responses.

An instructor's manual is available, which includes solutions to the chapter examinations and teaching aids.

We are grateful to many people who helped in the preparation of this book. Ken Siler, Ira Weiss, Bill Charlton, and Gene Dolan used the preliminary edition and made an important contribution to the final version. Jim Emery, Joan Hughes, Gerald Wagner, Claudia Plog, Ralph Sprague, Thomas Dock, and George Thomas reviewed the manuscript and provided valuable suggestions. We thank Anne Reints, Lois Morey, Margaret Medina, and Marilyn Mann for the typing. Finally, we thank our students who were our debuggers.

J. DANIEL COUGER

FRED R. McFADDEN

CONTENTS

12 THE PROGRAMMING TASK

13 INTRODUCTION TO FORTRAN AND BASIC

14 INTRODUCTION TO COBOL AND PL/1

19 PHYSICAL SYSTEM DESIGN

20 SYSTEM FEASIBILITY ANALYSIS

21 SYSTEM IMPLEMENTATION

Chapter 1

MANAGEMENT INFORMATION AND THE COMPUTER

Overview

This chapter introduces the student to the major objectives of the textbook:

1. To provide a foundation to enable students to use the computer effectively in their own academic programs.

2. To provide a foundation for a person who plans to become an information analyst, the liaison between the computer department and a department utilizing the computer's services.

3. To provide the prerequisite knowledge for a person who plans to enter a degree program in preparation for becoming a programmer or designer of computer applications.

All-Pervasiveness of Computer Use

Less than 10 years ago, it was rare for an individual to have direct contact with more than three or four computer systems. Typically, payroll was computer processed. Grades were processed and printed on computer forms. Some retail stores had computerized billing systems.

That situation has changed dramatically. It is a rare individual that is not involved today with a wide variety of computer systems. Information about each of us is entered, stored, and processed by computers in schools where we are educated, in the stores where we buy on credit, in the companies that employ us, and in the agencies of local, state and national governments whose citizens we are. In addition, the computer is used by our churches, by organizations where we utilize recreational services, and by our doctors and hospitals. Some person's even use it for selecting dates and prospective spouses.

Today we are affected by computer systems in almost every realm of our lives—education, business, social, service, religious, and recrea-

"En garde, Mr. Benson!"

©Datamation.

tional. We can take either of two attitudes regarding the computer and our involvement with it. One is reflected in the above cartoon.[1]

This attitude is further illustrated in the experience of a firm where one of the authors was employed. A computer system was installed in the manufacturing area, to keep track of each job in production. Workers keyed data concerning the job into a terminal connected to a computer in another building. The first night the system was installed, two of the terminals were destroyed by sledgehammers. For several weeks workers sabotaged the system by keying in erroneous figures or by discarding the punched cards that accompanied each job. They obviously were apprehensive about the computer's effect on their employment, although they had received intensive training on the value of the system.

Five years later, I was in academia and took a class on a tour of the same company. The change in employee's attitude was remarkable. The original system had been replaced by a new one that included attractive visual display units. The workers were proudly bringing their families into the plant on Saturdays to show them how they operated the new terminals.

Although it might appear that the more visually attractive system made employees more responsive, that was not the reason for the change in attitude. The change in attitude resulted from two principal causes. One was a "computer-involvement" program that was instituted by management after the reaction to the first system. Although the employees had been carefully trained concerning the operation of the original system, they had not been involved in its design. When the system was revised, employee representatives were heavily involved in the design. All employees were provided periodic progress reports and opportunities to make comments and suggestions. But they were not able to participate effectively until they knew more about computers. All employees

[1]Cartoon supplied courtesy of Datamation.

2 / MANAGEMENT INFORMATION AND THE COMPUTER

were given a course on computing concepts, capabilities, and limitations.

The second cause of changed employee attitudes occurred not on the job but in activities outside the firm. As we described in the opening paragraphs in this section, each employee was more involved with the computer in nonbusiness activities. The employees were being *formally* educated about the computer on-the-job and *informally* educated through increasing computer involvement in other organizations with which they dealt.

There is no longer a question whether the computer is here to stay. As early as 1964, an editor of *Fortune* magazine wrote a series of articles on the computer field and concluded that "No other technical innovation has changed so many human activities in so short a time. The computer has more beneficial potential for the human race than any other invention in history."[2]

Each of us is confronted, therefore, with the alternative: "fight it or join it." We can take the attitude of the individual in the cartoon—that the computer will replace jobs or that it will lessen the intrinsic value of jobs. Or, we can take the approach demonstrated by the employees in the manufacturing department described above. They chose to stay with the firm, to learn about the computer, and to become involved in the design of systems that affected their jobs.

This book provides the background an individual needs to become an effective computer user. Many schools are requiring students to take an introduction to computing fundamentals, computer programming, and system analysis and design. You may be one of these students, since this textbook is designed for just such a course.

We intend to demonstrate early in this book the value of such a requirement. Most students already have some background in this subject. In common with the employees in the manufacturing division described above, they have been informally educated concerning the computer through their involvement in organizations that have computer systems.

They have been using computer input (punched cards) and computer output (computer-printed bills, bank statements, class schedules, grade reports, even computer-printed Bibles). Now they need to understand what happens between those inputs to and outputs from the computer; that is, the internal processing. With that knowledge they will be able to participate effectively in the design of systems that involve them.

Unfortunately, the opportunity to participate in system design will be provided them only by the firm in which they are employed. Few of the other organizations with which they are involved provide such an opportunity. Nevertheless, the knowledge acquired from completing this textbook will facilitate their dealing with those organizations. When they receive an erroneous bill produced by the computer of a company that has extended credit to them, at least they will be able to deduce what might have caused the error. They will be able to decide what steps to take to produce corrective action, instead of "folding, spindling, or mutilating" the card!

Let us consider an example. Some of the problems of computer use were described in a column published in the *Honolulu Star-Bulletin*.[3]

[2]Gilbert, Burck, *Fortune Magazine*, March, 1964, p. 101.
[3]Courtesy Jim Becker, *Honolulu Star Bulletin*

3 / ALL-PERVASIVENESS OF COMPUTER USE

However, some of the incidents described could not have happened. The columnist either was "pulling-the-leg" of each reader or did not know that some of these situations he described were fallacious. Read the following editorial and try to decide which of the incidents could have happened.

Jim Becker's HAWAII

It had to happen. A mill worker in Naturita, Colo., which sounds like a fictitious place but isn't, worked 40 hours.

His hourly pay rate was fed into a computer which multiplied it by 40, and then began to take out the deductions for income tax, state tax, Naturita tax, social security, pension, medical, parking, credit union, three kinds of insurance and six sorts of miscellany.

And when all the subtraction was done—you guessed it—the fellow broke even, exactly.

The computer reared back and wrote him a check for $000.00 for the week.

At that, I suppose the man should be thankful. He came out even in this machine age.

A fellow in England wasn't so lucky.

He came out even with the gas company because he had been away from home for three months. A bill came for zero.

The man ignored it. The computer billed him again, for zero.

Still ignored, the computer got mad. It began to spin out nasty notices that unless the man paid his bill—of nothing—he would find himself gasless.

Finally, the man sent the computer a check for zero, and solved that.

But—he got his own bank angry at him. "Our computer went up in smoke trying to handle your check for nothing," he was told by an irate bank manager.

These two examples of the machine at work in our troubled times popped out of my Labor Day mail, and seemed appropriate to the season.

So does the story of the man in Albany who was picked up for stealing his own car, thanks to the Police Department computer.

It seems his previous car had been stolen the year before, and wrecked. Only the license plates were saved, and he was allowed to put them on his new car.

Somebody forgot to tell the computer, however, and it put out a call to arrest that man. He finally talked his way out of the mess.

An airman was able to explain his way out of a discharge from the Royal Air Force, too, after its new $2.4 million computer in Gloucester,

England, had advised the authorities that he was pregnant and should be separated from the service.

But no amount of talking could stop a New York publishing house from billing the Chesapeake Public Library for a bill that the library had paid in advance. The publishing house freely and frequently admitted that the bill had been paid, but it said it simply could not get the message across to its computer.

At last report the billing had been going on for 44 months.

It might help if that publishing house computer would meet the man from San Antonio, who fought a computer with a computer.

The man was a computer programmer himself, and he began to receive a series of dunning notices from a book club computer. Pleas failed to right the situation, so he took the book club's computerized statement to his office and key punched it with holes that meant: "Correction needed on account."

The computer got the word.

The cops got the word in New York City when their computer notified a woman in Dolgeville, N.Y., that she had ignored more than 60 city traffic tickets. The woman had never been in New York City in her life.

And so goes life on the billing machine, to which I will add one more story, which comes from a reader via something called Datamation magazine.

The clipping announces something called Autocom, which is an automatic warning device which telephones pre-recorded requests for assistance, according to the magazine, "when a dangerous condition develops." (Whatever that means.)

Apparently this thing can be set up so that if an "unacceptable condition"—let's put that into English for Datamation magazine; they must mean a fire or something—develops, the thing will telephone for help in pre-recorded words.

It can even be arranged to make the machine make a priority call, although it doesn't say what will happen if the machine happens to get another on the line.

And guess who ordered the first one of these things? The Hawaiian Telephone Company, that's who.

"And two bits says it will get the wrong number," wrote the reader, but I think that's a little cruel.

Figure 1–1. A columnist's list of some of the problems in computer use.

The typical student can logically determine that one of these incidents could not have happened, according to our experience in using this editorial in the first class each semester. Through the "informal" education described above, the average person has the knowledge to recognize that the story about the Chesapeake Public Library could not have happened. Even if the original procedures for inputting corrections to the computing system had been lost or destroyed, they could be reconstructed.

5 / ALL-PERVASIVENESS OF COMPUTER USE

How would you respond if you were on the "receiving end" of each of the problems cited in Mr. Becker's column? By the end of this course, you should have the knowledge to determine the cause of each of them. Also, you should be able to determine the best method of getting corrective action.

Objectives in Designing the Textbook

Objective 1   The First Course for an Effective Computer User

The resolving of problems associated with a lay person's use of the computer is one of the objectives for which this textbook was designed.

However, in the business environment of the immediate future all employees need to be much more knowledgeable concerning the computer. To realize the full potential of the computer, in virtually any profession, a person needs a thorough understanding of the inner workings of a computer system.

Where just five years ago a course of this type was taught to seniors, it is now being taught to freshmen and sophomores. The purpose formerly was to educate the student about the applicability of the computer in that student's chosen profession. The purpose today has not changed, but has been enlarged. The course has the added objective of providing the student a capability of using the computer in his or her own academic program. By gaining such a capability at the freshman level, the student can use the computer to gain more depth, to perform more analysis in other courses throughout the academic program.

Therefore, the typical student will be involved in a four-phase computer curriculum. The four-phase curriculum is in existence in the majority of member schools of the American Association of Collegiate Schools of Business, according to a survey by the *Computing Newsletter for Schools of Business*.[4] That curriculum is shown in Figure 1–2.

An individual completing the four-phase curriculum will already be an effective computer user and should be able to utilize the computer's potential in his or her chosen profession. This book provides the background required for Phase I of the four-phase program.

Objective 2   The First Course for an Information Analyst

Other students completing this course will be attracted to a new profession, entitled the "information analyst." This individual will be employed in one of the user areas, such as marketing or hospital administration. The function of this individual is to be a liaison between the

[4]J. D. Couger, "Report on the 3rd Triennial Survey of Computer Uses and Computer Curriculum in Schools of Business," *Computing Newsletter for Schools of Business*, Colorado Springs, October, 1974, p. 1.

1. Coverage of computer fundamentals, programming, system analysis and design through a course required of all students early in their academic program.
2. Coverage of the applications of computers through incorporation of this material into the functional area courses, for example, computer applications in finance in the finance courses, computer applications in marketing in the marketing courses.
3. Coverage of computer capabilities for abetting decision making in a dynamic business environment through computer-oriented business games.
4. Coverage of integration and optimization of computer applications through a course on design and implementation of a sophisticated, computer-based management information system.

Figure 1-2. *Four-phase computer curriculum required of all students.*

using department and the computer department. He or she will determine the informational needs of that organization based on a knowledge of its functions and on interaction with the various managers of that organization. In cooperation with the system designer, those informational needs will be translated into a set of specifications for conversion to the computer.

To prepare to be an information analyst, the student must take four to six computer courses in addition to the courses required in the major field. Most colleges allow more than enough elective credits so that this double major does not lengthen the degree program.

Objective 3   The First Course for a Computer Professional

The individual who is attracted toward a career in the computer field will find that the textbook has fulfilled the computer prerequisite for entry to such a degree program. One of the authors served as chairman of the national committee that designed the undergraduate degree program in information systems. The report of that committee describes degree programs for the information analyst, programmer, and system designer. Individuals interested in a career in these professions can refer to a summary of the program in Appendix I.

Summary

On completion of this book, the reader's perspective in viewing cartoons such as the one on page 2 will be humorous rather than apprehensive. It will be apparent that Mr. Benson of the cartoon need not regard the computer as a threat, but as an ally, if he is properly educated concerning computing concepts, capabilities, and limitations.

7 / OBJECTIVES IN DESIGNING THE TEXTBOOK

We now use another cartoon to summarize our objectives. They are stated by Charlie Brown, below.

(Copyright © 1960 United Feature Syndicate, Inc. Reprinted by permission of United Feature Syndicate)

The graduate of the course for which this book is designed should no longer feel "out of place" in dealing with the computer and with computer professionals. On the contrary, he or she should feel comfortable in use of the computer throughout the academic program and in the chosen profession.

Chapter Examination

1. Who is an effective computer user?_____

_____

_____

_____

2. What comprises the "informal" education that lay people receive about computers? _____

_____

_____

_____

3. What should be provided in a "formal" education concerning the computer? _____

_____

_____

_____

4. What tasks are performed by a person in the new profession, "information analysis?" _____

_____

_____

_____

5. What two categories of knowledge must the information analyst possess to perform the function effectively? _____

_____

_____

_____

6. What brought about the recognition for the need for the new position?

_____

_____

_____

9 / CHAPTER EXAMINATION

7. What constitutes the four-phase computer curriculum required by the majority of schools of business today?

(a) _____

_____

(b) _____

_____

(c) _____

_____

(d) _____

_____

8. Which phase is covered by this book? _____

_____

9. What prerequisite knowledge in the computer area is required of a person who plans to enter a degree program in information systems?

_____

_____

_____

10. Instead of a Charlie Brown feeling of being "out of place," the person who completes this testbook should feel

_____

_____

_____

11. On completion of this book, we shall examine each of the incidents described in the *Honolulu Star-Bulletin* (Figure 1–1) to determine what might have caused the problem. Examine each incident now, below, and suggest what might have caused the problem, based on your present knowledge.

(a) It had to happen. A mill worker in Naturita, Colo., which sounds like a fictitious place but isn't, worked 40 hours.

His hourly pay rate was fed into a computer which multiplied it by 40, and then began to take out the deductions for income tax, state tax, Naturita tax, social security, pension, medical, parking, credit union, three kinds of insurance and six sorts of miscellany.

And when all the subtraction was done — you guessed it — the fellow broke even, exactly.

The computer reared back and wrote him a check for $000.00 for the week.

At that, I suppose the man should be thankful. He came out even in this machine age.

A fellow in England wasn't so lucky.

(b) He came out even with the gas company because he had been away from home for three months. A bill came for zero.

The man ignored it. The computer billed him again, for zero.

Still ignored, the computer got mad. It began to spin out nasty notices that unless the man paid his bill — of nothing — he would find himself gasless.

Finally, the man sent the computer a check for zero, and solved that.

But — he got his own bank angry at him. "Our computer went up in smoke trying to handle your check for nothing," he was told by an irate bank manager.

These two examples of the machine at work in our troubled times popped out of my Labor Day mail, and seemed appropriate to the season.

So does the story of the man in Albany who was picked up for stealing his own car, thanks to the Police Department computer.

(c) It seems his previous car had been stolen the year before, and wrecked. Only the license plates were saved, and he was allowed to put them on his new car.

Somebody forgot to tell the computer, however, and it put out a call to arrest that man. He finally talked his way out of the mess.

11 / CHAPTER EXAMINATION

(d) An airman was able to explain his way out of a discharge from the Royal Air Force, too, after its new $2.4 million computer in Gloucester, England, had advised the authorities that he was pregnant and should be separated from the service.

(e) But no amount of talking could stop a New York publishing house from billing the Chesapeake Public Library for a bill that the library had paid in advance. The publishing house freely and frequently admitted that the bill had been paid, but it said it simply could not get the message across to its computer.

(f) It might help if that publishing house computer would meet the man from San Antonio, who fought a computer with a computer.

The man was a computer programmer himself, and he began to receive a series of dunning notices from a book club computer. Pleas failed to right the situation, so he took the book clubs computerized statement to his office and key punched it with holes that meant: "Correction needed on account."

The computer got the word.

(g) The cops got the word in New York City when their computer notified a woman in Dolgeville, N.Y., that she had ignored more than 60 city traffic tickets. The woman had never been in New York City in her life.

Chapter 2

INTRODUCTION TO COMPUTER BASED MANAGEMENT INFORMATION SYSTEMS

Overview

Chapter 1 discusses the impact of the computer on society and the kind of background an individual needs to feel comfortable in an increasingly computer-oriented society. However, a better objective than "feeling comfortable" is that of actively participating in the development of computer applications that affect the individual.

A synergistic effect can result from such a process. Synergism is the concept that the whole is equal to more than the sum of its parts. Man and computer together can produce more than either can produce alone.

This concept is particularly true in the business world. Providing administrators with a computer-based management information system improves their capability of quick response to a dynamic environment. More important, it provides a capability of better planning to forecast and to diminish the effect of potential problems.

This chapter describes the broad areas of application of the computer. It then concentrates on the objectives in design of computer-based management information systems. Finally, it examines the role of the behavioral sciences in system design—to insure that employee needs are considered in computer use.

What Are Computer Systems?

The term "computer system" is used in the previous chapter in a manner consistent with lay terminology. Actually, the term *computer application* would be more correct. Processing of payroll is an application of the computer. The *computer system* is the set of hardware and software through which the application is processed. As the name implies, hardware is physical equipment, such as the mechanical, electronic and magnetic units in a computer. *Software* is the set of computer programs that cause the computer to produce the desired results.

Jordain provides a good analogy for distinguishing hardware from software: "If a human being were born fully grown physically, he would be analogous to a computer without software: all potential, but no performance. Education (formal or otherwise) enables man to function; software enables computers to function."[1] However, in this chapter we are interested more in providing an overview of computer uses than in defining terms. Only those terms necessary to that objective will be defined.

What Are Business Information Systems?

Although several approaches have been used to categorize the computer field, the most widely used delineation is by area of application. At the top of the hierarchy are three categories: science/engineering, humanities, and business (administrative) applications. The total number of applications has mushroomed, from 300 in 1960 to 2,672 in 1974.[2]

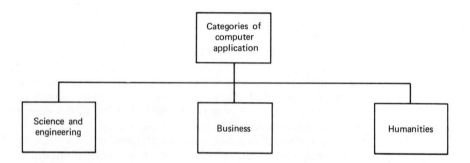

Examples of scientific applications are: airframe stress analysis, guidance and flight control, spectrum analysis, shoreline erosion studies, seismic reading for earthquake detection, matrix inversion, blood count analysis, metal alloy calculations, voice print identification, and solution of differential equations.

Examples of business or administrative applications are: billing and invoicing, accounting, order processing, payroll, stolen automobile identification, church information systems, economic forecasting, garbage truck scheduling, stock market analysis, insurance premium accounting, inventory control, job placement, farm management, college course scheduling, bank check processing, and labor union bargaining strategy analysis.

Examples of applications in the humanities are: artifact classification, computer art design, map reproduction, historical research, language syntax pattern analysis, poetry style analysis, concordance construction, music composition, and harmonics analysis.

[1]Philip B. Jordain, *Condensed Computer Encyclopedia*, 1969, McGraw-Hill Book Company, New York, p. 47.
[2]B. C. Berkeley, *Computer Directory and Buyer's Guide*, 20th Annual Edition, 1974, Berkeley Enterprises, 815 Washington St., Newtonville, Mass., p. 145.

QUESTION: Which application in each category was most surprising to you? Scientific _____, Business _____, Humanities _____.

ANSWER: In the past our students have been most surprised to learn that the computer could: identify voice prints, analyze labor bargaining strategies, and compose music.

Figure 2–1 provides a summary of applications in the two major categories, science/engineering and business. Only 103 applications in the humanities were identified when the survey was taken, therefore these applications are excluded.

QUESTION: Examine Figure 2–1. Which field within each of the major categories has the largest number of applications? Business Applications _____, Scientific Applications _____.

ANSWER: Business Applications: government, 185; Scientific Applications: medicine and physiology, 167

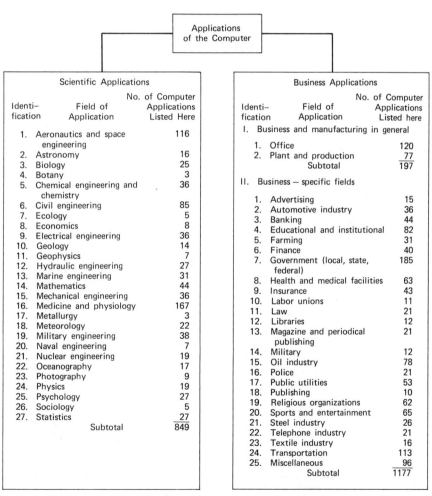

Applications of the Computer	

Scientific Applications

Identi-fication	Field of Application	No. of Computer Applications Listed Here
1.	Aeronautics and space engineering	116
2.	Astronomy	16
3.	Biology	25
4.	Botany	3
5.	Chemical engineering and chemistry	36
6.	Civil engineering	85
7.	Ecology	5
8.	Economics	8
9.	Electrical engineering	36
10.	Geology	14
11.	Geophysics	7
12.	Hydraulic engineering	27
13.	Marine engineering	31
14.	Mathematics	44
15.	Mechanical engineering	36
16.	Medicine and physiology	167
17.	Metallurgy	3
18.	Meteorology	22
19.	Military engineering	38
20.	Naval engineering	7
21.	Nuclear engineering	19
22.	Oceanography	17
23.	Photography	9
24.	Physics	19
25.	Psychology	27
26.	Sociology	5
27.	Statistics	27
	Subtotal	849

Business Applications

Identi-fication	Field of Application	No. of Computer Applications Listed here
I.	Business and manufacturing in general	
1.	Office	120
2.	Plant and production	77
	Subtotal	197
II.	Business — specific fields	
1.	Advertising	15
2.	Automotive industry	36
3.	Banking	44
4.	Educational and institutional	82
5.	Farming	31
6.	Finance	40
7.	Government (local, state, federal)	185
8.	Health and medical facilities	63
9.	Insurance	43
10.	Labor unions	11
11.	Law	21
12.	Libraries	12
13.	Magazine and periodical publishing	21
14.	Military	12
15.	Oil industry	78
16.	Police	21
17.	Public utilities	53
18.	Publishing	10
19.	Religious organizations	62
20.	Sports and entertainment	65
21.	Steel industry	26
22.	Telephone industry	21
23.	Textile industry	16
24.	Transportation	113
25.	Miscellaneous	96
	Subtotal	1177

Figure 2–1. *Categories of applications of the computer (Source. Computer Directory and Buyers' Guide, 1972, p. 137).*

15 / WHAT ARE BUSINESS INFORMATION SYSTEMS?

This book concentrates on business applications. Approximately 65,000 computers were in operation in the United States in 1973,[3] and more than a million persons were employed in the field.[4] As is shown in Figure 2-1, most computers and people are utilized in business applications.

With this background, we are now ready to tackle the question posed in the heading of this section: "What are business information systems?" In one sense, all applications are information systems. A *system* consists of input, processing, and output. Both scientific and business systems have those characteristics. Also, both are processing information. For example, one of the scientific systems that supports space flights is the guidance system. Radar data is continuously collected and fed to the guidance computer system. The data is then processed through the guidance computer program and is compared against the flight plan. The output of the system is automatic correction, to maintain the flight plan. Of course, the system provides for manual override of automatic guidance by the astronauts, when special circumstances arise.

Also associated with the space flights is a vast array of business systems. For example, data are collected on costs, fed into the accounting system, and processed according to the accounting computer program. The output of the system is a series of reports on performance against budget.

In some instances both scientific and business applications share the same input. For example, sensors are attached to the astronauts, primarily to monitor physical condition—a scientific application. However, these same data are collected for later processing in an administrative application, to develop costs associated with providing each astronaut with the proper life-support environment.

QUESTION: Scientific and business applications of the computer have several things in common; both are comprised of _____ _____, and, _____; and both process _____.

ANSWER: input, processing, output; information

Despite similarity in basic characteristics, scientific and business systems generally serve different masters. The output of scientific applications of the computer is oriented toward engineers and scientists of the organization. The output of business application is oriented toward the managers of the organization. Another way of looking at the distinction is in relation to the product of an organization. We might generalize that the scientific applications are used in the design of the product and that the business applications are used to insure that the correct quantity of products is manufactured and that the product gets to the consumer efficiently and economically.

---

[3]*EDP Industry Report*, Vol. 8, No. 12, 60 Austin St., Newtonville, Mass., April 12, 1973, p. 8.
[4]B. Gilchrist and R. E. Weber, "Sources of Trained Computer Personnel—A Qualitative Survey," *AFIPS Conference Proceedings*, Montvale, N.J., 1972, p. 647.

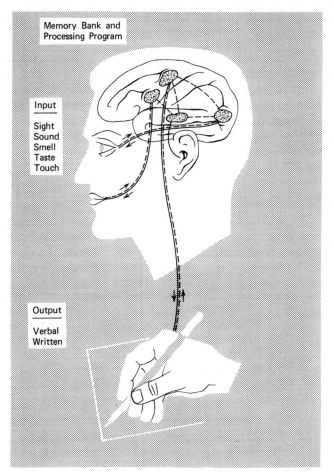

Figure 2–2. *Cybernetic system.*

QUESTION: Scientific applications are used in the _____ of the product and _____ applications are used in the administration of the enterprise.
ANSWER: design, business

Difference Between Systems and Applications

The terms "applications" and "systems" were used interchangeably in the preceding section. Both consist of input, processing, and output. On the other hand, a major distinction exists between systems and applications. Systems existed long before computers were invented. Our oldest recorded history, the Bible, describes many business systems. For example, in the book of Numbers, Moses organized the 40,500 adult Israelites by a numbering system that distinguished warriors (those over 20 years of age) and which established armies within a hierarchy of command.

The previous description also implies that the information processed by systems exists in some physical form. Figure 2–2 illustrates a cybernetic system. The input to that system has no physical form. The external stimulus (input) is processed against the internally stored program. Although the mechanism and procedure for processing are inherent, results vary greatly, depending on the comparison of input data against those in the memory bank. Following on the analogy used earlier in this chapter, if two human beings were born fully grown, the output of their cybernetic systems could be expected to be similar. It is the data in the memory bank that effect the output significantly. A set of data passed through the cybernetic systems of two humans born fully grown should produce essentially the same results—for the first few cycles. Thereafter, only in a completely controlled environment could we be assured of similarity in results. The memory banks of two normally reared adults contain much different data, resulting from different environments. Despite identical input, results would vary significantly.

This situation is not dissimilar to business. Two identical computerized forecasting systems could produce opposite results, depending on the data bank utilized. On the other hand, rarely are systems designed identically. These two reasons account for the great differences in results of computer use in government and industry.

The foregoing should have clarified the concept of a system. Any system can be computerized if the processing rules can be made explicit, even a cognitive system. However, it may not be economically feasible to computerize the system. This book identifies the process of determining when computerization is feasible and also the techniques of computerization. However, it concentrates on business information systems.

QUESTION: (True or False) If managers can make explicit their decision rules, the task of a manager can be computerized. _____.

ANSWER: True. However, many of those decision rules are not explicit, so we are a long way from being able to transfer the manager's task to the computer

Management Information Systems

The popular term for the complete set of business applications for an organization is "management information systems." However, every manager has an information system, whether computerized or not. Augustus Caesar was famous for his organized set of managerial systems for waging war. A major subsystem within this set was his logistics subsystem, a remarkable system for that era. The range of materials, both weapons and foodstuffs, to support 50,000 soldiers was enormous. Yet the highly organized system functioned smoothly. Lack of a system of comparable quality caused the defeat of Alexander the Great.

A more appropriate description for the set of computerized systems that undergird the management process is a *computer-based management information system*. Also, the fact that an organization has a number of business applications does not necessarily mean it has a CBMIS (this abbreviation will be used hereafter). The key concept in design of computer-based management information systems is integration. Figure 2–3 illustrates that the major systems and subsystems are integrated,

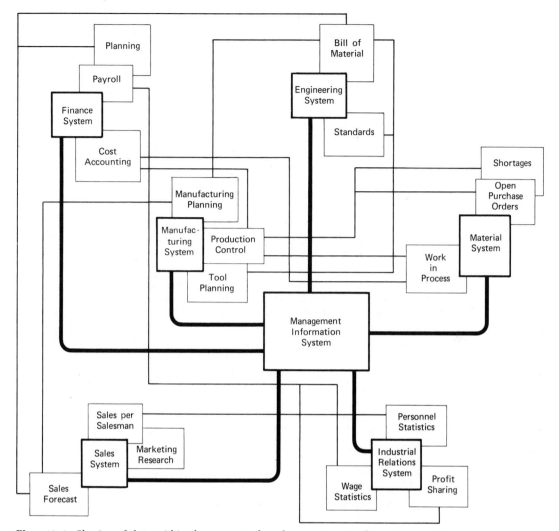

Figure 2–3. *Sharing of data within the computer-based management information system.*

that is, there is sharing of information between systems. Data is captured as close as possible to the point of origin, then is shared with all those systems where it is used.

QUESTION: Study Figure 2–3 as an illustration of the integration concept. The sales forecast is captured and entered to the CBMIS. Information from this subsystem is shared with the following subsystems:

————————, ————————, ————————.

ANSWER: planning, bill of materials, manufacturing planning

How is integration obtained? Integration is assured if the systems designers of each major system area are working on the same set of objectives. The objectives in design of a CBMIS are provided below.

Objectives of a Computer-Based Management Information System
1. To capture or generate all data pertinent to the firm's operations.

2. To process those data in the most efficient and economical manner, utilizing the management science techniques to the fullest extent feasible.

3. To produce concise and timely information, as is required by each level of management.

Objective 1: Capture or Generate All Pertinent Data. There are key phrases in each of these objectives. In the first objective the key phrase is "all data pertinent." Too often the system designer develops a system that inundates the manager with computer output. This point was illustrated in a chemical company where one of the authors served as a consultant. A manager was describing the output of the first 'system designed for his use: "I was excited about the prospect of a comprehensive set of reports," he said. "On Monday of the first week the reports were produced, I told my secretary to try to avoid scheduling any meetings that I could put off until the following week. I wanted to devote full attention to the output of my new system. However, by Friday I was only a little over halfway through the reports. So, when I arrived at work the next Monday and found a new set of reports awaiting me I was somewhat overwhelmed!" His system designers had not met objective one; they had designed the system to produce *all* data, instead of all data *pertinent* to the manager.

Contrast this example with another where a new general manager told his system designers: "I don't know a lot about the electronics business, coming from the wholesale distribution business. Therefore, details are not much value to me at this point. I want a system that produces reports only where there are problems I should know about." He then proceeded to identify the criteria for those reports. For example, he wanted to be informed when any department was ± 5 percent from its budgeted performance. He wanted to know about any customer order that was delinquent more than 10 days. He set up a full list of criteria, insuring that the system designed for his use provided only those data "pertinent" to his decision-making process.

The *management-by-exception* principle is illustrated by the latter manager. He devoted his scarce resource, time, to only those "exceptional" conditions that required his attention. System designers must design a management-by-exception reporting system for the CBMIS, to insure that the firm's executive talents are being utilized properly.

QUESTION: The designers, therefore, meet with the managers for whom the system is being designed, to identify those _____ which are to be isolated and reported by the system.

ANSWER: exceptions

QUESTION: The first objective in design of a computer-based management information system insures that the system captures or generates all data _____ to the firm's operations. Under what circumstances would the admissions officer of a college require that all data on each student's high school transcript be captured and entered into the student file? _____

ANSWER: Pertinent: The admissions officer is concerned only that all requirements have been fulfilled. However, the dean of students might request that data be captured for a system that compared each student's college performance against the high school performance. The objective might be the identification of problems early in the student's college career in hopes of reducing the chance for dropout. Therefore, the admissions officer would be asked to capture those data at the same time the transcript was processed for admission

Objective 2: Utilizing the Management Science Techniques. In the second objective in design of a CBMIS, the key phrase is "utilizing the management science techniques." What are management science techniques? Figure 2–4 lists some of these techniques and shows their area of application within each of the major subsystems of a firm.

QUESTION: Break-even analysis, a technique · covered in your introductory economics courses, is applicable to what major systems:

ANSWER: Marketing and Planning, Finance and Accounting

It is possible to computerize systems without utilizing the management science techniques. However, it is rarely possible to optimize these systems without use of such techniques. For example, consider the linear programming technique that is applicable to every area of the firm as is shown in Figure 2–4. Linear programming is a technique for optimizing assignment of resources. It could be used in the marketing system to analyze brand preferences, in the manufacturing system for machine loading, and in the distribution system to determine optimal warehouse location.

Figure 2–5 illustrates the LP (linear programming) techniques imbedded in the freight-car scheduling system for the Montgomery, New Orleans, and Pensacola division of the Louisville and Nashville Railroad. The track map is shown at the top. The graphic representation and corresponding linear programming (mathematical) representation are shown in the center. One of the series of reports produced by computer allocation of freight cars is shown at the bottom.

QUESTION: Management Science techniques are imbedded in the system to _____ the system.
ANSWER: optimize

QUESTION: The graphic representation of the track map is established to show the relationship of distance and cost. That representation is converted into a _____ representation to produce the optimal assignment of freight cars.
ANSWER: mathematical (linear programming in this case)

Objective 3: Produce Information for Each Level of Management. The key phrase in objective three is "each level of management." However, the previous examples illustrate that the other phrase in this objective is also very important: "to produce concise and timely information."

MANAGEMENT SCIENCE TECHNIQUES \ FUNCTIONAL AREAS	Marketing and Planning	R and D and Engineering	Manufacturing and Q C	Purchasing, Inventory and Distribution	Labor and Industrial Relations	Finance and Accounting	Total Firm
Linear Programming	**********	**********	**********	**********	**********	**********	
Economic Order Quantity				**********			
Economic Lot Quantity	**********		**********				
Breakeven Analysis	**********					**********	
Improvement Curve	**********	**********	**********			**********	
CPM Network Analysis	**********	**********	**********	**********	**********	**********	**********
Time Series Analysis	**********				**********	**********	
Dynamic Programming	**********		**********			**********	
Dimensional Analysis	**********	**********					
Symbolic Logic		**********			**********		
Heuristic Modeling	**********						
Sensitivity Analysis	**********			**********			**********
Decision Theory	**********						
Competitive Modeling	**********		**********	**********	**********		**********
Queuing Theory	**********		**********	**********			
Statistical Quality Control			**********	**********			
PERT Network Analysis	**********	**********	**********	**********	**********	**********	**********
Monte Carlo Theory	**********		**********	**********			
Behavioral Modeling	**********	**********			**********	**********	
Markov Process	**********						
Simulation	**********	**********	**********	**********	**********	**********	**********

Figure 2–4. *Application of Management Science Techniques to Major Systems within the CBMIS.*

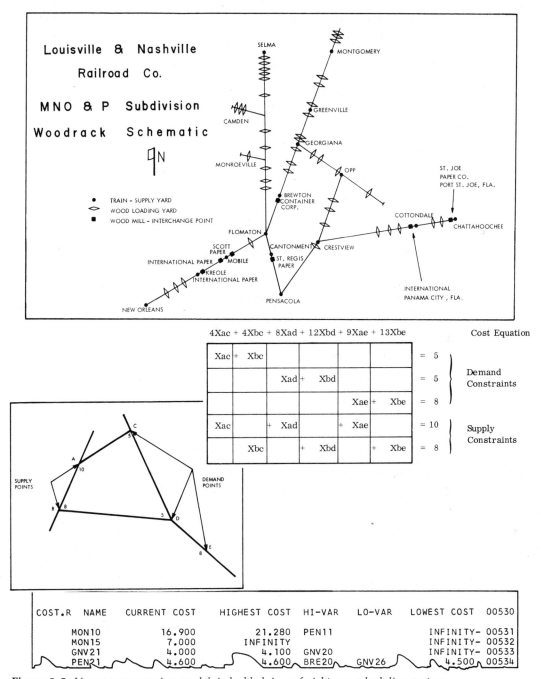

Figure 2-5. *Linear programming model imbedded in a freight-car scheduling system (courtesy IBM).*

The manager in the chemical firm was provided timely information that was *not* concise. His report was too voluminous to be useful. The manager in the electronics firm specified that exceptions be reported from his system, resulting in concise and timely information.

Some systems have met half of objective 3, providing concise and timely information—but only to one level of management. On the other hand, a business application is not necessarily a management application. The payroll application has as its primary purpose a clerical rather than a managerial function. The computerized grade report system in the college is also a clerical system rather than a managerial system. These systems are referred to as *operational level systems*. Both were designed to replace or to improve the clerical operation.

However, the payroll system can be designed to produce managerial information as well as to perform a clerical operation. In the initial system planning process, the designer can provide for sharing payroll information with other systems of the company. Examples of other subsystems that use this information are the accounting and personnel subsystems.

In addition to a horizontal integration, or sharing of data, there should be a vertical integration. In some cases this is a summary process, for example, payroll costs are summarized to be included in the budget performance reports (a middle level management report) and in the balance sheet (a top level management report).

In other cases, management needs information that is not merely a summary of output from operational level systems. For example, top management needs a planning simulation model. Static reports on past performance, such as income statements and balance sheets, are insufficient for managing the firm. Management also needs income statements and balance sheets projected for future years under varying economic conditions. A computer simulation provides that information and permits management the opportunity to vary other factors to forecast the effect on the enterprise; for example, establishing new product lines or building new plants. Figure 2–6 illustrates the vertical/horizontal information concept.

QUESTION: The above description may appear to suggest that planning models are separate systems, unrelated to the integrated set of systems and subsystems. How are top-level management systems related to the other systems within the CBMIS? Use Figure 2–6 for assistance in answering this question: _____

_____

_____

_____ .

ANSWER: Although some data for the planning system must come from external sources (e.g., economic and industry data), a large amount of the input is derived from the data-base of existing systems. Therefore, the planning system is integrated with the operational and middle management level systems within the CBMIS.

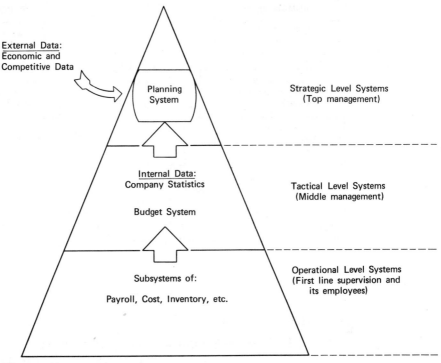

Figure 2–6. *Vertical/horizontal information concept.*

Behavioral Concepts Related to the CBMIS

While a company may meet all three objectives in design of the CBMIS, success is not assured. There exist more than a few examples of beautifully designed systems that were unsuccessful because improper attention was paid to implementation.

Chapter 1 provided an example of a manufacturing firm where the system design-process included participation of the employees who would be operating the new computer system. Both management and computer professionals need to be knowledgeable concerning behavioral principles. To illustrate, we analyze the job satisfaction needs that are threatened when a system is designed and implemented without employee participation. Figure 2–7 identifies the four levels of human needs as classified by Abraham Maslow.[5] Examine the left side of the illustration, which portrays Maslow's Hierarchy of Human Needs.

Employee Needs. The first level of need is the physiological level. Most jobs provide for meeting the need for survival, food, clothing, and shelter. The higher level needs are met to a lesser extent, depending on the individual, the job, and management.

QUESTION: For manual systems, it is the responsibility of _____ to insure that employee needs are fulfilled to the greatest extent possible.

[5]A. H. Maslow, *Motivation and Personality*, 1954, Harper and Brothers, New York, Chapter 5.

25 / BEHAVIORAL CONCEPTS RELATED TO THE CBMIS

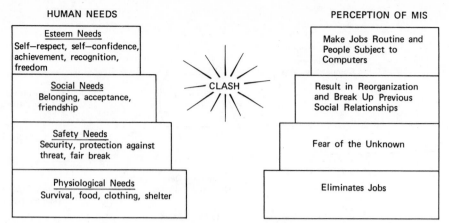

Figure 2–7. The threat of a computer system to employee need fulfillment (courtesy of Donald Warrick, University of Colorado, Colorado Springs, Colorado).

ANSWER: management

Perceived Threat to Employee Needs. The right side of Figure 2–7 lists the threats to fulfillment of human needs, as might be perceived by the employee. As is shown in the illustration, these perceptions clash with human needs. The threat may be real or imagined. The probability that an employee will perceive such a threat is much higher when that employee has not participated in the development and implementation of a system related to his/her job.

QUESTION: The first level need is threatened by a perception that the new computer system might _____.
ANSWER: eliminate the employee's job

The employee's perception may be correct. However, many firms have established a policy that none of their employees will lose employment because of a computer application. The job may be eliminated, but the employee will have the opportunity for another job in the organization.

QUESTION: Informing the employees of such a policy should remove their fear that basic physiological needs will not be provided. However, another need will be threatened by such a policy, the social need. Why?

_____.

ANSWER: The employee may be transferred, breaking up established social patterns (belonging, acceptance, friendship)

It is rarely possible to change all employee perceptions about the threat of computers, even if management establishes policies to reduce the threat to a minimum. Nevertheless, those perceptions will be based on facts, rather than conjecture, if employees participate in the system design and implementation.

On the other hand, it is not feasible to include all employees. Employee representatives can participate in the full cycle of development and can provide periodic reports to the remainder of employees on the approach and intent of the system. By soliciting employee comments during these sessions, all employees should become less apprehensive about the system.

QUESTION: For computerized systems, it is the responsibility of _____ to insure that employee needs are fulfilled to the greatest extent possible.

ANSWER: Management—not the system designer (Did we throw you a curve on that one? Management must not relinquish these responsibilities to the system designer. However, cooperative action by the manager and system designer can insure that employee views and needs are properly considered.)

Summary

The two broad categories of computer application are scientific and business. Scientific applications might be considered as those related to research and development activities of an organization. Business applications are those related to planning, production, and distribution of the product or service. Therefore, business applications are prepared to facilitate *administration*—of a hospital, of a governmental department, of a nonprofit or religious organization, as well as a business.

Since the managerial task involves many activities that cannot be computerized, the appropriate term for the set of computer applications designed for management's use is a "computer-based management information system." Many of the data needed for decision-making can be provided through an integrated approach to designing the various systems within the CBMIS. Capturing data at the point of origin for sharing among systems is a key concept in the CBMIS approach, because it facilitates integration of systems.

Another facet of the CBMIS approach is the provision for horizontally oriented systems and vertically oriented systems. Horizontally oriented systems are called operational systems because they handle the basic operations of the organization, for example, a checking account system (demand deposit accounting). Vertically oriented systems are called management systems because they provide information as needed by each level of management, for example, a market forecasting system for the bank's executive committee.

The CBMIS approach provides for integration of both horizontal and vertical systems. For example, a customer profile can be automatically produced from the demand deposit accounting system as an input to the higher-level market forecasting system. The demand deposit accounting system also shares data horizontally, with subsystems such as the basic accounting system of the bank.

To realize the potential of the CBMIS, the manager must actively participate in the design and implementation of the system. The manager can then be assured that the managerial-level system meets his/her needs and that the operational-level system meets the needs of the employees. However, employees should be actively involved in design and implementation of a system that affects their jobs.

Therefore, both managers and employees need to be knowledgeable about the computer—concerning its capabilities and limitations. The following chapters are designed to provide such a background. This background will enable persons completing the book not only to participate but to make a contribution in design of computer applications for their organization.

Chapter Examination

1. Define the following terms:

(a) Computer system. _____

_____

(b) Hardware. _____

_____

(c) Software. _____

_____

(d) System. _____

_____

2. Distinguish between a scientific and a business application of the computer.

_____

_____

_____

3. Is the computer essential for a management information system?

_____ Explain:

_____

_____

_____

4. How could identical computer systems produce different results?

_____

_____

_____

5. Can any system be computerized? _____ Explain:

_____

_____

6. What are the three objectives of a computer-based management information system?

(a) _____

_____

(b) _____

_____

(c) _____

_____

7. The key phrase in objective 1 is _____ _____

_____. Think of an illustration other than the one provided in the book. Use the college president's system to illustrate the key phrase in objective 1:

_____

_____

8. The key phrase in objective 2 is: _____ _____

_____ _____ _____. Use the college president's system to illustrate this one, too:

_____

_____

_____

9. The key phrase in objective 3 is: _____ _____

_____ _____. Use the college president's
system to illustrate this one, too:

_____

_____

_____

_____

10. Are the terms "business" application and "management" application interchangeable? _____ Explain:

_____

_____

_____

11. What is the management-by-exception principle?

_____

_____

_____

12. Complete the following to illustrate the horizontal/vertical applications for a college CBMIS, using Figure 2–6 as a guide:

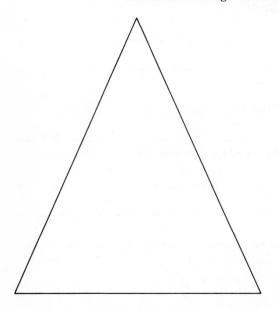

13. Which of the four levels of human needs are threatened by a computer-aided counseling system?

_____

_____

_____

_____

14. Explain how such a system could be designed and implemented to change the perception that the student's needs are threatened by the system.

_____

_____

_____

_____

15. Which of the four levels of human needs are threatened by a computer-processed faculty evaluation system?

_____

_____

_____

_____

16. What knowledge is needed to enable a person to contribute to the design of a system that will affect his/her job?

_____

_____

_____

_____

17. Prepare a schematic drawing of the major systems and subsystems of a college CBMIS; use Figure 2–3 as a guideline.

_____

_____

_____

_____

31 / CHAPTER EXAMINATION

Chapter 3

INTRODUCTION TO COMPUTERS

Overview

A general knowledge of computers is necessary for anyone who wishes to understand business information systems. The computer specialist — systems analyst, programmer, or data processing manager — certainly must be thoroughly familiar with the computer and its operation. However, the functional manager or specialist (for example, marketing manager) must also have a familiarity with computer principles and terminology, to communicate effectively with the data processing specialist. A basic introduction to computers is provided in this chapter; the chapters that follow examine these concepts in greater detail.

The term computer is generally used to refer to a stored-program general-purpose electronic digital computer. This is the basic type of computer used in business information systems. Electronic analog computers (and hybrid digital-analog computers) are used primarily in engineering and scientific applications. The characteristics of electronic digital computers that distinguish them from other computing devices are speed, internal storage, and automatic execution of a stored program.

All digital computers have functional units for input, storage, processing, control and output. From the point of view of the user, the most important of these functions are input (of data and inquiries), processing (retrieval, updating, and reporting), and output. Depending on the required response times, these functions may be performed either in a batch mode or in an on-line mode. A time-sharing system is an example of an on-line system in which many users simultaneously share a remote central computer.

Types of Computers

The word computer is derived from the Latin *computare*, meaning "to compute." Therefore any device that helps one compute — such as a slide rule, an adding machine, or a pocket electronic calculator — might tech-

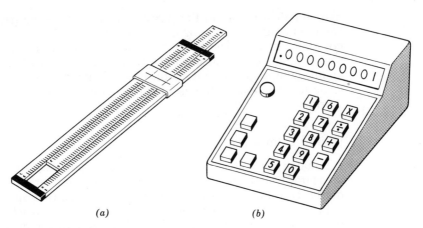

Figure 3–1. *Example of analog and digital computing devices. (a) Slide rule. (b) Electronic calculator.*

nically be called a computer. However, the term "computer" has generally come to mean a specific device: a stored program, electronic digital computer.

The characteristics that distinguish an electronic computer from other computing devices are speed, internal memory, and automatic execution of a stored program. The speed of an electronic computer is due to the use of electronic circuitry. Other devices such as calculators depend on electrical and mechanical components, which severely limit their speed of operation.

The internal memory of an electronic computer is used to store both data and instructions. A sequence of instructions (such as an entire payroll calculation) is carried out automatically, without human intervention. In contrast, a device such as a desk calculator requires human direction (by means of a keyboard) at each step in a computational routine.

There are two basic types of computers: *analog* computers and *digital* computers. A slide rule is a familiar example of an analog computing device, while an abacus or a pocket electronic calculator is a simple digital computing device (see Figure 3–1).

QUESTION: Which device in Figure 3–1 is a computer (according to the most common definition)? _____ .

ANSWER: Neither (the electronic calculator shown has electronic circuitry, but does not accommodate a stored program).

Analog Computers

The slide rule is an analog computing device because an analogy is constructed between length on the slide rule and the logarithm of a number. By adding two such lengths, the analog of the product of two such numbers is obtained.

In a similar manner, an electronic analog computer uses electrical components and circuits to represent a real physical system (usually a dynamic system such as a moving body or a chemical process). First, a mathematical model of the physical process is developed by an analyst. Next, an equivalent analog circuit is set up on the analog computer. The computer is then used to analyze the physical problem, by manipulating the variables on the electronic circuit. The advantage of modeling on an analog computer is that it enables us to find simple and inexpensive solutions to dynamic problems in the laboratory before going into the real world.

Digital Computers

An analog computer operates on data that varies continuously (or can be measured) such as voltage, pressure, and temperature. In contrast, a digital computer is basically a counting device that operates on discrete data or numbers. Since most business data is in discrete form (either numerical or alphabetical), the digital computer is readily adaptable to business data processing applications.

QUESTION: _____ computers operate on discrete or numerical data, while _____ computers operate on continuous or measurable data.

ANSWER: digital, analog.

A *hybrid* computer is a combination analog and digital computer. Hybrid computers are used in research and in some applications such as process control.

A further classification of digital computers is between general-purpose and special-purpose computers. *Special-purpose* computers are designed to perform specific tasks, such as air traffic control, satellite guidance and control, or highway toll collection. In contrast, *general-purpose* computers are designed to solve a wide range of problems. Special-purpose computers lack the versatility of general-purpose computers, but provide maximum efficiency and economy because they are engineered for a specific purpose or application.

QUESTION: A computer specifically designed for controlling a machine tool is an example of a _____-purpose computer, while a business or scientific application would be accomplished on a _____ _____-purpose computer.

ANSWER: special, general

This book is dedicated to the application of general purpose digital computers to business information systems.

Generations of Computers

Modern electronic computers were first developed during the 1940s. The earliest models were essentially "one-of-a-kind" machines that, although experimental in nature, were used for practical applications. The more important of these early computers were the following:

MARK 1 Developed by Howard Aiken at Harvard. Very large electromechanical calculator that automatically performed a sequence of numerical calculations.

ENIAC Developed by Eckert and Mauchly at the University of Pennsylvania. First all-electronic automatic calculator; however, did not have an internally stored program.

EDVAC, EDSAC First true electronic computers with internally stored programs. EDVAC developed in the United States, EDSAC in England.

UNIVAC The UNIVAC (for Universal Automatic Computer) was the first commercially available computer.

A number of computers became commercially available in the early 1950s following installation of two UNIVAC I computers in 1951. These computers are often referred to as first generation computers. Subsequent improvements led to second and third generations of computers.

First generation computers used vacuum tubes as the principal electronic components. The most important first generation computers were UNIVAC I, and IBM 650 and IBM 701. These computers were relatively slow and required extensive air conditioning because of the heat generated by the vacuum tubes.

Second generation computers (introduced in 1959 to 1960) replaced vacuum tubes with transistors. These computers were smaller, faster, and less expensive than first generation computers, and generated less heat. The most widely used second generation computers were the IBM 7094 (scientific) and IBM 1401 (commercial) computers.

Third generation computers were introduced beginning in 1965. In these computers miniaturized circuits are used, resulting in smaller, faster, and more reliable components. Third generation computers are also characterized by improved software and operating systems, and by an orientation to data communications. These features are discussed in subsequent chapters.

Computer Functions and Organization

Computers used in data processing range from small business systems renting for less than one thousand dollars per month, to large-scale systems renting for more than 100 times that amount. Despite the wide variety of sizes and configurations, all computer systems have components that perform certain basic processing functions. The functional units common to all computers are the following.

1. *Input* devices receive data and translate it into the internal code used by the computer.
2. *Storage* (or memory) devices store data to be operated on and instructions to be performed.
3. *Control* devices regulate and control all elements of the entire computer system.
4. *Arithmetic/logic* unit performs arithmetic operations and logical comparisons.
5. *Output* devices print, transmit or display the results of computer processing.

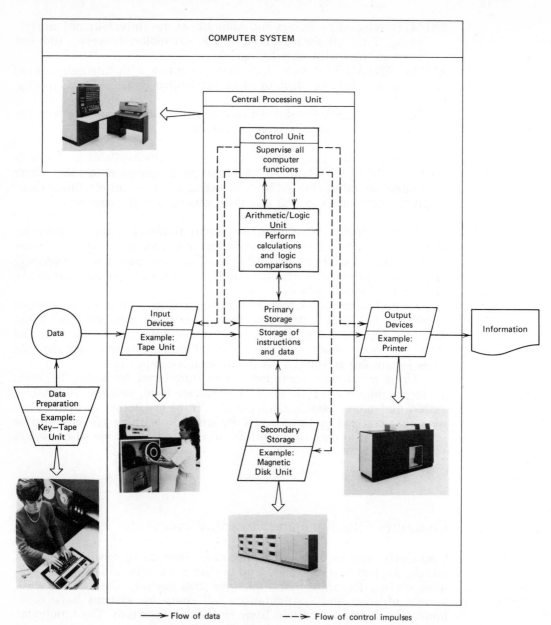

COMPUTER SYSTEM

Central Processing Unit

Control Unit
Supervise all computer functions

Arithmetic/Logic Unit
Perform calculations and logic comparisons

Primary Storage
Storage of instructions and data

Secondary Storage
Example: Magnetic Disk Unit

Data

Data Preparation
Example: Key–Tape Unit

Input Devices
Example: Tape Unit

Output Devices
Example: Printer

Information

→ Flow of data   ---→ Flow of control impulses

Figure 3–2. *Major functional units in a computer system.*

The relationships between these various functional units of a computer system are shown in Figure 3–2. The figure shows the flow of data and control impulses between the various units, and also provides typical examples of each major type of device.

In many applications it is necessary to prepare data in machine-readable form before it may be entered into the computer system. Devices commonly used for this purpose include key punches, key-tape units, and key-disk systems. A key-tape unit is shown in Figure 3–2. This and other data entry devices are described in Chapter 7.

36 / INTRODUCTION TO COMPUTERS

Exercise 3-1

Refer to Figure 3-2 in answering each of the following questions.

1. List the three functional units contained in the central processing unit, and describe the function of each:

(a) _____

(b) _____

(c) _____

2. Match each type of device with the example shown in the figure:

_____ input device   (a) printer
_____ output device   (b) magnetic disk unit
_____ secondary storage device   (c) magnetic tape unit

Central Processing Unit

The central portion of a digital computer is known as the central processing unit, or CPU. This unit processes data, supervises and coordinates the various functional units of the computer system, and provides primary storage capacity. To perform these functions the CPU consists of three major components: a control unit, an arithmetic/logic unit, and a storage unit (which may be located in a separate cabinet).

The control unit directs the activities of the computer by interpreting a set of instructions, called a program. Since the program is contained in the main storage unit, it is referred to as a *stored program*. The control unit causes data (also contained in main storage) to be transferred to the arithmetic/logic unit, and computational results to be transferred back to storage. Other instructions may cause data to be read into the computer or transferred to an output unit.

QUESTION: The set of instructions that a computer is to follow is called a _____ _____. These instructions are interpreted by the _____ unit that is a part of the _____.
ANSWER: stored program, control, CPU

Arithmetic/Logic Unit. The arithmetic/logic unit of the CPU operates on data stored in the computer, under the direction of the control unit. It performs all arithmetic operations—addition, subtraction, multiplication, and division. Also, it performs logical operations by examining numbers for relationships such as, "is the first number algebraically greater than the second number?" The results of these examinations or *tests* are sent to the control unit where they are used to govern subsequent actions of

37 / COMPUTER FUNCTIONS AND ORGANIZATION

the computer. Thus the control unit and arithmetic/logic unit, acting in harmony, may cause the computer to *branch*, or to take one of two different control paths at any given point. Alternative courses of action are therefore provided to the computer, and a decision is made by the computer as to which course of action to follow. The decision-making capacity of a digital computer, which is really nothing more than a testing and branching capability, is one of the major factors contributing to its usefulness.

QUESTIONS: Testing the relative magnitude of two numbers is an example of a _____ operation carried out by the arithmetic/logic unit. The result of the test may cause the computer to _____, or to take any one of several control paths.

ANSWER: control, branch

Computer Storage. There are two types of storage in most computer systems: primary (or main) storage, and secondary (or peripheral) storage. As is shown in Figure 3–2, primary storage may be considered a part of the central processing unit (although it is often physically located in one or more separate cabinets). Secondary storage is external to the CPU.

Primary storage contains both the computer program (or programs) and the data to be processed by the program. The computer can operate directly on data only if it is contained within main memory. Thus if data is stored outside the computer, such as on punched cards or magnetic tape, it must first be transferred or "read" into main storage before internal processing can occur.

QUESTION: Two types of computer storage are _____ (part of the CPU) and _____ storage. Main storage contains both _____ and _____.

ANSWER: primary (or main), secondary (or peripheral), program, data

At present, primary storage consists either of core storage, which is a large collection of tiny magnetic cores, or of monolithic integrated circuits which are essentially large collections of transistors. Core memories are rapidly being displaced by monolithic circuitry for two reasons: monolithic circuits permit faster execution speeds, and are rapidly becoming less expensive than core memories.

Since primary storage is relatively expensive, it must be restricted in size. Therefore, *secondary* (or peripheral) storage is generally used to increase total memory capacity. Peripheral storage devices include magnetic disk units, magnetic drums, and magnetic tapes. These storage media are sometimes called *mass storage* devices, since they generally have the capability to store vast amounts of information. They are characterized by slower speed of operation and correspondingly lower cost than that afforded by the devices used for main storage. Data stored in a mass storage device (e.g., magnetic disk) must be read into primary storage before it can be processed by the CPU.

The characteristics of primary and secondary storage are discussed in greater detail in Chapter 5.

Input-Output Devices

In most data processing applications, large quantities of data that originate from day-to-day activities of the organization must be input into the computer. Results of processing must be stored for further processing, and printed or displayed for users. Input-output (or I/O) devices are used to transfer external data into the computer, and to transfer the results of processing to external media.

Many types of input-output devices are used in data processing. The more frequently used input devices include keyboards, punched card readers, magnetic ink and optical character readers. Output devices include line printers, microfilm, visual displays, and audio response units. Some devices such as magnetic tape drives and magnetic disk units are used for input, storage, and output of data.

A complete description of input-output concepts and devices is given in Chapter 7.

Types of Processing Systems

From the point of view of the user, the major functions performed by a computer system are input, processing, and output. As is shown in Figure 3–3, there are two basic types of input: data to be processed, and inquiries concerning the status of some entity (such as inventory level). Input data is used to update historical and descriptive data contained in files (often part of secondary storage). In response to inquiries, data is retrieved from files and answers are prepared and displayed in some form. Reports and other documents are prepared and are output, often on a line printer.

QUESTION: From Figure 3–3, the major types of input are _____ *and* _____, while the basic types of processing are _____ , _____ , and _____ .

ANSWER: data, inquiries, retrieval, updating, reporting

Processing systems may be classified as *batch* systems or *on-line* systems, depending on the way these functions are performed. The distinction between a batch system and an on-line system is largely in terms of *response time*, which is the elapsed time between the submission of input data or inquiries, and the presentation of corresponding outputs.

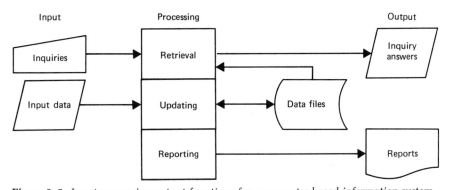

Figure 3–3. *Input-processing-output functions for a computer-based information system.*

(From Computer Based Information Systems in Organizations by Henry C. Lucas, Jr. © 1973, Science Research Associates, Inc. Reprinted by permission of the publisher.)

Batch Systems

In a batch processing system, input data is generally collected over a period of time before it is processed. As a result, data files are not updated immediately but at specified intervals. The user must be prepared to wait for answers to inquiries.

In batch processing, jobs are either processed in the order in which they occur, or according to some priority scheme. However, users are given no assurance as to response time. Batch processing systems are used extensively in applications with high input volume, where there is no great need for fast response times.

On-line Systems

For an on-line processing system, input data and inquiries may be processed as they occur. The user may access files from direct entry devices such as display units and may obtain near-instantaneous reports or inquiry responses, if he desires.

An example of an on-line processing system is the computer-based reservation system used by many large hotel chains. From a central computer file, an agent in a remote location can determine the availability of a room at a hotel in another location on a particular date. He can then book a reservation, with the entire transaction requiring not more than a minute or two. Airlines, rental car agencies, and other organizations depend on similar on-line systems.

There is actually a wide variety of on-line systems in use. The most common are on-line inquiry, on-line updating, and time-sharing systems.
On-line Inquiry. In this type of system the on-line user can enter inquiries and receive answers but cannot update or change data files. For example, the user might be able to display the stock level of a particular item, but he could not alter the record for the item. In this type of system the data files are often updated by using a batch processing procedure.
On-line Updating. In this type of system the on-line user may enter inquiries and update data files. For example, an airline ticketing agent may both determine the status of a particular flight and may book a reservation on that flight, thereby updating its corresponding data record.
Time-Sharing System. A time-sharing system is an on-line system in which many users with different processing needs share a remote central computer. Each user accesses a terminal connected by a communications link to the computer. The computer allocates its resources to each of its current users, so that it appears to each user that the computer is dedicated to his program alone. For example, many colleges and universities have time-sharing systems in which it is possible for several dozen users to access the computer at one time.

QUESTION: Two major types of processing systems are _____ systems and _____ systems. An example of the latter, in which it is possible for many users to share the use of a remote computer is called a _____ system.
ANSWER: batch, on-line, time-sharing

Figure 3–4. *The Hewlett-Packard Model 2100 minicomputer.*

Sizes of Computer Systems

Computers for data processing range from minicomputers costing a few thousand dollars, to very large-scale systems costing several million dollars. The tendency in third generation systems is to use a modular design approach, so that a given computer model can be expanded in terms of storage capacity, number of input-output units, or other features. As a result, there is no sharp distinction between "small" computers, "medium" computers, and so on. Nevertheless, these terms are useful in describing the range of computer systems in use.

41 / TYPES OF PROCESSING SYSTEMS

Figure 3–5. *The Burroughs B700 Small Direct-Entry system.*

Minicomputers

A minicomputer is a desk-top size computer which typically weighs less than 50 pounds and can be purchased at prices ranging from $2,000 to $20,000. These units generally have a relatively small internal memory, and can accept peripherals such as disk storage, magnetic tape units, and line printers.

A typical minicomputer is the Hewlett-Packard 2100, shown in Figure 3–4. The minicomputer processing unit is in the upper right corner. Peripheral devices shown in the picture include a Teletype-writer unit, magnetic disk, and magnetic tape.

Minicomputers have been used largely for special purposes such as communications processors, industrial controllers, and so on. Until recently they have lacked the peripheral units (input-output and secondary storage) and software (or computer programs) to be widely used in data processing applications. However, minicomputer-based small business systems have been introduced and are being marketed by an increasing number of firms. Such systems (described below) will play an increasingly important role in future business applications.

Memory technology is continually advancing, permitting ever smaller, faster and more reliable processing units. This has made possible the introduction of *microcomputers*—small but powerful computers mounted on a single semiconductor chip or printed circuit board. Such miniature computers can be easily mounted inside cabinets and can be used to control peripheral units such as terminals, printers and other devices.

Small Business Systems

Small business computers use a minicomputer central processing unit, with peripherals and software especially designed for data processing applications. Systems of this kind may sell at prices ranging from under

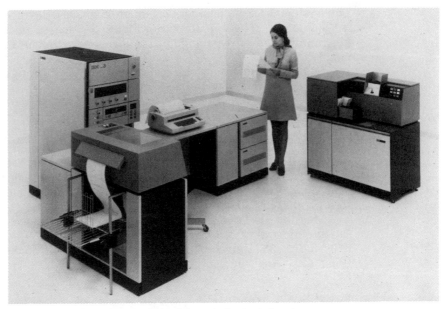

Figure 3–6. *The IBM System/3 Model 10 card-oriented system.*

$20,000 to nearly $100,000, or lease for under $2,500 per month. Main storage capacity may range from 4,000 to 32,000 positions or more.[1]

Small business systems permit the small business firm (under $10 million sales per year) to realize the benefits of computer-based information systems. Larger businesses also employ small computer systems for specialized applications.

Direct-entry Systems. A number of small-business systems are oriented to direct entry of data from a keyboard. Such systems typically include a disk storage unit for mass storage of data files. Output may be by means of line printer and/or visual display. Where input volume is low, direct-entry disk systems permit on-line inquiry and updating of integrated files for the small systems user. Typical applications include accounts receivable, invoicing, inventory, and accounts payable.

A typical example of a small direct-entry system is the Burroughs B700 system, shown in Figure 3–5. This system includes a work station for data entry and forms handling, disk storage capacity, line printer, and 32,000 bytes (or characters) of internal storage capacity. As with most small business systems, this computer is expandable to larger configurations.

Card and Tape Systems. When input volume increases, the small systems user may require media other than direct entry of data. Punched cards and/or magnetic tape are often used (perhaps in combination with direct entry) in such systems.

A popular card-oriented small business system is the IBM System/3 Model 10, shown in Figure 3–6. This unit contains a printer, disk storage capacity, and a multifunction card unit (combination card read/punch).

---

[1]The significance of storage capacity is discussed in Chapter 5.

The System/3 uses a business-oriented language called RPG II (discussed in Chapter 15). The unit shown in Figure 3–6 leases for less than $2,000 per month, and is expandable to much larger configurations (including magnetic tape).

Other computers in this category include Burroughs B1700, NCR Century 50, and Honeywell 58.

Medium-Scale Systems

Compared with small computers, a medium-scale computer system provides greater storage capacity (both primary and secondary) and a wider range of input-output devices. A typical system might provide from 32,000 to 128,000 positions (or more) of internal storage, and lease from $2,000 to $20,000 per month.

Most of the large computer manufacturers produce computers that satisfy this rather arbitrary definition. Typical examples are the IBM 370 Model 135, Univac 9400, Honeywell 2000, Burroughs 3700, and National Cash Register Century 251 (Fig. 3–7).

Large-Scale Systems

Large-scale computers are used primarily by large corporations and government organizations, and by computer service organizations such as service bureaus. These systems provide very large storage capacity— often more than one million positions of internal storage, and vast quantities of secondary storage. Also, large systems can accommodate a large number and variety of peripheral units—magnetic tape, optical readers, displays, and communications terminals.

Examples of large-scale computer systems are Burroughs 6700, Control Data 6400, UNIVAC 1108, Honeywell 6000, and IBM 370/165 (Figure 3–8).

Figure 3–7. *The NCR Century 251 medium-scale computer system.*

Figure 3–8. *The IBM System/370 Model 165 large-scale computer system.*

Exercise 3–2

1. Identify whether each of the following is a batch system or an on-line system.

(a) A business school has five typewriter terminals at which students can simultaneously work problems on a computer located across campus.

(b) A business school has a card reader and line printer connected to a computer across campus. Students submit their problems as punched card decks, which are run sequentially as they are submitted.

(c) A business has a small computer system in which data concerning orders, invoices, and payments are keyed directly into the computer by an operator, as the data is generated. The status of an order can be displayed on a visual display unit on request.

(d) A bank collects checks throughout the day and processes them in an evening run.

2. Explain each of the following.
   (a) How a very large company might use a minicomputer or small business system:

_____

_____

_____

   (b) How a very small firm might use a large-scale system:

_____

_____

_____

Summary

This chapter presents an overview of computers—the major types of computers, how they work, and how they are used. The major types of computers are analog (which are essentially measuring devices) and digital (which are basically counting devices). Only digital computers are of interest in business data processing.

The major functions performed by computers are input, storage, processing, control, and input. Of these, the user is directly concerned with input, processing, and output. Depending on the required response time, the computer may be used in either a batch or an on-line mode. Time-sharing is a form of on-line processing where several users simultaneously share the facilities of the computer.

Chapters 4 to 8 explain in greater detail hardware concepts introduced in this chapter.

Solutions to Exercises

Exercise 3–1

1. (a) Control unit—supervises all functions of the computer.
   (b) Arithmetic/logic unit—performs arithmetic operations and logical comparisons.
   (c) Primary storage—stores data and instructions.

Exercise 3–2

1. (a) On-line (time-sharing).
   (b) Batch.
   (c) On-line.
   (d) Batch.
2. (a) In specialized applications such as production control.
   (b) Purchasing time from a computer service company (i.e., time-sharing company or service bureau).

Chapter Examination

1. Match each of the following terms with the appropriate definition:

Terms	Definitions
_____ Minicomputer	(a) Performs arithmetic operations and comparisons
_____ Time-sharing	(b) Operation where computer selects one of two paths
_____ Analog computer	(c) Data input is processed as it occurs
_____ Digital computer	(d) Elapsed time between input and output
_____ Stored program	(e) Computer instructions contained in primary storage
_____ Control unit	(f) Computer which processes measurable data
_____ Arithmetic/logic unit	(g) Data input is collected and processed at intervals
_____ Branch	(h) Digital computer of desk-top size
_____ Batch	(i) Computer that processes numerical data
_____ On-line	(j) Several users share a central computer
_____ Response time	(k) Directs various functions of the computer

2. Briefly describe the five major functional units of a digital computer.

(a) _____

(b) _____

(c) _____

(d) _____

(e) _____

3. Explain the relationship between response time, cost and the selection between on-line and batch processing systems.

_____

_____

_____

4. Describe the three major functions of the central processing unit.

(a) _____

(b) _____

(c) _____

5. You are asked to comment on whether a computer can make decisions. How do you reply?

_____

_____

6. Fill out the following table, from information presented in the chapter.

Size of computer	Approximate range of: Primary storage capacity (positions)	Monthly rental cost ($)
Minicomputer	_____	_____
Small system	_____	_____
Medium-scale	_____	_____
Large-scale	_____	_____

7. At present, a firm uses a small business system with direct entry of data by keyboard. As the processing volume increases, how is this system likely to evolve?

_____

_____

_____

_____

8. Identify and briefly describe three types of on-line processing systems.

(a) _____

(b) _____

(c) _____

9. Give three examples of each of the following:

(a) Small business systems _____

(b) Medium-scale systems _____

(c) Large-scale systems _____

10. Identify the following statements as true or false.

_____ (a) Hybrid computers are widely used in business information systems.

_____ (b) The basic processing functions in a small digital computer are different from those in a large computer.

_____ (c) An airline reservation system is an example of an on-line updating system.

_____ (d) Small business systems are based on minicomputer central processing units.

_____ (e) If a pocket electronic calculator is designed to accept a small stored program, it might properly be termed a computer.

_____ (f) There are clear distinctions between small, medium, and large-scale computer systems.

_____ (g) Most business computers are special-purpose digital computers.

_____ (h) The term computer is generally used to refer to a general-purpose electronic digital computer.

Chapter 4

DATA REPRESENTATION AND ARITHMETIC

Overview

Communication in any written language is by means of symbols. We normally use about 75 symbols in written communication in the English language. These include the 10 digits 0 to 9, 52 letters (upper and lower case), and a number of special symbols such as the period, comma, dollar sign, and plus symbol.

Data input to the computer consists of the symbols used in written communication, plus a number of special characters used only when communicating with the computer. It is common for approximately 100 symbols to be used in computer applications, including computer programs. Reports and documents prepared as computer output also contain most of the same symbols. The entire set of characters is often referred to as alphanumeric characters.

Computer storage consists of a vast number of elementary devices, such as magnetic cores. Each device can be in one of two possible states, similar to a wall switch which is either "on" or "off." These states can be used to represent two symbols, commonly the digits 0 and 1.

How can a computer, which recognizes only two symbols, store and manipulate some 100 alphanumeric characters? This is done by an internal representation in terms of the digits 0 and 1, referred to as binary digits or bits. Each alphanumeric character is coded using a unique combination of binary digits. Arithmetic operations are also performed using the binary numbering system.

The conversion from alphanumeric symbols to internal representation is done automatically by the computer on input and output. As a result, an individual can use the computer without understanding computer data representation and arithmetic. Nevertheless, this understanding is important if the capabilities and limitations of a computer are to be fully appreciated. In particular, it is important in understanding the similarities and differences between computers.

Number Systems

The decimal number system we use originated in antiquity, and was perhaps derived from using the fingers in counting. The word decimal derives from the Latin *decem* meaning ten, which is the base of the decimal system.

Except for our familiarity with the decimal system, numbering systems using different bases are equally logical and, for the computer, more useful. Three such systems are particularly important in understanding computers: binary (base 2), octal (base 8), and hexadecimal (base 16). These systems are related and are discussed in this chapter.

The three concepts necessary to understanding a numbering system are base, absolute value, and positional value. An *absolute value* is an integer or whole number, represented by a symbol such as 5. The *base* (also called radix) of the number system indicates how many absolute values are used in the system. For example, in the decimal system there are 10 absolute values, represented by the digits 0 to 9.

QUESTION: The three concepts of a number system are _____, _____ value, and _____ value.

ANSWER: base (radix), absolute, positional

Positional values are found by raising the base of the number system to the power of the position. For example in the decimal system the zero (or units) position has positional value 10^0, or 1. The first (or tens) position has positional value 10^1, and so on. Some of the positional values in the decimal system are shown in Table 4–1.

QUESTION: Examine Table 4–1. What is the next higher positional value not shown in the table? _____ The next lower? _____.

ANSWER: 10^4 (Ten thousand), 1/1000 (Thousandths)

In any number system, the value of a number is determined by multiplying the absolute value of each digit by its positional value. For example, in the decimal system the number 328 means 3 hundreds, 2 tens, and 8 units or ones. Therefore, the number may be written as follows:

$$328 = 3 \times 10^2 + 2 \times 10^1 + 8 \times 10^0$$

TABLE 4–1
Some Positional Values in the Decimal System

				Decimal point		
Position number	3	2	1	0 .	−1	−2
Position value	10^3	10^2	10^1	10^0	10^{-1}	10^{-2}
Quantity represented by positional value	1000 (Thousands)	100 (Hundreds)	10 (Tens)	1 (Units)	1/1 (Tenths)	1/100 (Hundreths)

179408

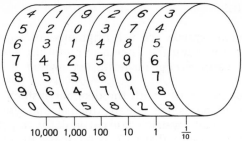

Figure 4–1. *The concept of state as illustrated by an electric calculator.*

Similarly, the octal number system has base 8. Therefore, there are eight absolute values, represented by the digits 0 to 7. The octal number 247 can be written as follows:

$$247 = 2 \times 8^2 + 4 \times 8^1 + 7 \times 8^0$$
$$= 2 \times 64 + 4 \times 8 + 7 \times 1$$
$$= 167 \text{ (decimal)}$$

In the above, the number is said to be written in extended form. This provides a convenient way to convert the octal number to decimal; the octal number 247 is equivalent to decimal 167. In the same manner a number in any other system may be converted to a decimal number.

QUESTION: Suppose a number system has radix (or base) 5. There are _____ absolute values, represented by the digits _____ to _____. The number 243 in this system may be written in extended form as follows:

243 = 2 × _____ + 4 × _____ + 3 × _____ = _____ (decimal)

ANSWER: 5, 0, 4; 5^2, 5^1, 5^0, 73

The Binary Number System

In an information processing machine such as a calculator or computer, numbers are represented by the states of mechanical or electronic devices. Each device can represent a number, provided that it has a different recognizable state corresponding to each absolute value in the number system.

As an example, an electric calculator uses the decimal number system. A series of adjacent wheels represent decimal numbers (see Figure 4–1). Each wheel corresponds to a position value; thus there is a wheel for the units position, tens position, and so on. Also, each wheel has 10 notches or spaces on the rim, containing the numerals 0 to 9. The wheels are connected so that when the units wheel turns past 9 it moves the tens wheel one position; when the tens wheel moves past 9, it moves the hundreds wheel one position, and so on.

QUESTION: In the electric calculator, each wheel has _____ recognizable states, each corresponding to an _____ value of the decimal number system.

ANSWER: 10, absolute

The storage elements in an electronic computer are two-state devices.

Of these, the most common at present are ferrite cores that are magnetized by applying an electric current. The polarity of the core is in one of two directions, depending on the direction of the magnetizing current. Thus the core is similar to a switch that is either in the "on" or "off" position.

Since each element has two recognizable states, the binary number system is used in computers. The binary system has base 2, so there are two absolute values, represented by the digits 0 and 1.

A binary number therefore consists of a string of 0's and 1's, for example 101011. The term *bit* is often used as an abbreviation for binary digit.

QUESTION: The number 10201 (could, could not) be a binary number.

ANSWER: could not, since only the binary digits (or bits) 0 and 1 are used in the binary number system.

Positional values in the binary system are powers of 2. Some of these values are shown in Table 4–2.

TABLE 4–2
Some Positional Values in the Binary System

						Binary point			
Position	4	3	2	1	0	.	−1	−2	−3
Position value	2^4	2^3	2^2	2^1	2^0		2^{-1}	2^{-2}	2^{-3}
Quantity represented by position value	16	8	4	2	1		½	¼	⅛

The decimal equivalent of a binary number is easily determined by writing the number in extended form. For example, to find the decimal equivalent of the binary number 1011:

$$1011 = 1 \times 2^3 + 0 \times 2^2 + 1 \times 2^1 + 1 \times 2^0$$
$$= 8 + 0 + 2 + 1$$
$$= 11 \text{ (decimal)}$$

QUESTION: The binary number 111.1 may be written as:

$$111.1 = 1 \times \underline{\qquad} + 1 \times \underline{\qquad} + 1 \times \underline{\qquad} + 1 \times \underline{\qquad}.$$

This number is equivalent to decimal _____.

ANSWER: 2^2, 2^1, 2^0, 2^{-1}; 7.5

A decimal number may be represented in the computer by using two-state devices (such as magnetic cores) to represent its binary equivalent. For example, the equivalent of the decimal number 37 is the binary number 100101. This number may be represented by six devices, corresponding to binary position values (see Figure 4–2).

Device	●	○	○	●	○	●	Code
Positional value	2^5 (32)	2^4 (16)	2^3 (8)	2^2 (4)	2^1 (2)	2^0 (1)	● device "on" (1 bit) ○ device "off" (0 bit)

Figure 4–2. *Representing the decimal number 37 (or binary 100101) with two-state devices.*

53 / THE BINARY NUMBER SYSTEM

LORETTE WILMOT LIBRARY
NAZARETH COLLEGE

QUESTION: What is the *largest* decimal number that may be represented by the six devices shown in Figure 4-2? _____.
ANSWER: 63 (all devices "on")

It is sometimes desired to convert a decimal number to its binary equivalent. For an integer (or whole) number this may be accomplished by successive divisions by 2, recording the remainder from each division. As is shown in Figure 4-3, applying this procedure to the decimal number 37 yields the binary equivalent 100101.

```
                    Remainder

2 | 37

2 | 18              1

2 | 9               0

2 | 4               1

2 | 2               0
                                Read binary number
2 | 1               0           from bottom to top.
                                Binary equivalent
    0               1   ←———    of 37 is 100101.
```

Figure 4-3. *Converting a decimal number to binary by successive division by 2.*

QUESTION: In the procedure shown in Figure 4-3, the decimal number 37 is successively divided by 2 which is the _____ or _____ of the binary number system.
ANSWER: base, radix

Binary Arithmetic

Arithmetic operations are carried out in the computer by using binary arithmetic. As with number conversion, the computer programmer or user does not usually need to perform binary arithmetic. However, a basic understanding of binary arithmetic is fundamental in understanding computers and computing concepts.

The rules and tables for binary arithmetic are much simpler than for decimal arithmetic, since only two symbols are available. Following are the rules for addition and subtraction.

Rules for Binary Addition

$$0 + 0 = 0$$
$$0 + 1 = 1$$
$$1 + 0 = 1$$
$$1 + 1 = 10 \text{ (zero with a carry to the next column)}$$

Examples

Binary	Decimal Equivalent	Binary	Decimal Equivalent
100101	37	10110.11	22.75
1011	11	1011.01	11.25
110000	48	100010.00	34.00

Rules for Binary Subtraction

$$0 - 0 = 0$$
$$1 - 0 = 1$$
$$0 - 1 = 1 \text{ (with a borrow from the next column)}$$
$$1 - 1 = 0$$

Examples

Binary	Decimal Equivalent	Binary	Decimal Equivalent
1001	9	1011.01	11.25
−110	−6	−110.10	−6.50
0011	3	0100.11	4.75

In subtraction, a borrow from the next column to the left reduces the bit in the minuend of that column by 1. If the bit in the next column is 1, it is changed to 0. If the bit is 0, it is changed to 1 and another borrow is made to the next column to the left. Borrowing is propagated until a 1 bit in the minuend can be changed to a 0.

To illustrate, the following are the steps in subtracting 0001 from 1000:

Problem	Step 1	Step 2	Step 3	Step 4
	1	11	011	011
1000	100̸0	10̸0̸0	1̸0̸0̸0	1̸0̸0̸0
−0001	−0001	−0001	−0001	−0001
	1	1	1	0111

To verify the above, add the result to the subtrahend, which gives the minuend:

$$
\begin{array}{r}
0111 \\
+0001 \\
\hline
1000 \text{ (minuend in problem)}
\end{array}
$$

The method of binary subtraction discussed above is generally not used in a computer. Instead, subtraction is usually performed by complementing the subtrahend (or number to be subtracted) and then adding the complement. This simplifies computer circuitry, since subtraction can make use of the addition circuitry, and the complementing process is itself very simple.

QUESTION: Subtraction in a computer is accomplished by _____ _____, which simplifies computer _____.

ANSWER: complementing, circuitry

Addition circuitry is also generally used in a computer for performing multiplication and division. Multiplication is basically a series of additions, and division is a series of subtractions. Also negative numbers are usually handled by complementing. Thus computer circuitry is greatly simplified by reducing all arithmetic to forms of addition.

55 / BINARY ARITHMETIC

Exercise 4–1

1. Convert each of the following binary numbers to decimal:

   (a) 11001 _____

   (b) 0101.11 _____

   (c) 1111 _____

2. Convert each of the following decimal numbers to binary:

   (a) 32 _____

   (b) 14.5 _____

   (c) 63.25 _____

3. Fill in the following table of positional values for the octal (base 8) number system:

Position		3	2	1	0	.	−1	−2
Position value					8^0			
Quantity represented by position value					1			

4. Perform the following binary arithmetic operations:

   (a) 11001   (b) 1011.01   (c) 1000.1
       +1111   −10.10   −1.0
       ─────   ──────   ─────

5. Suppose a base 4 number system is used:
   (a) What are the absolute values in the system?

   _____

   (b) What is the decimal equivalent of the number 323.12?

   _____

6. What binary number is represented by the following two-state devices?

   ○ ● ○ ● ●

   A shaded circle represents the 1 bit, an empty circle the 0 bit._____

Binary Based Notations

The preceding discussion shows how a number can be represented in the computer by a string of binary digits (or bits). By having a sufficiently large number of bit positions, a very large binary number can be stored. However the requirements of computer storage and circuitry are such that the number of bits used to represent a number must be specified in advance. There are two basic approaches used to accomplish this:

1. A fixed number of bits (called a *word*) is always used to represent a number. Any unused high-order bit positions in the word are set to zeros. Word sizes range from 16 to 60 bits, depending on the computer.
2. A variable number of small bit sets is used to represent a number. Each bit set is used to encode a digit, and may vary in size from 4 to 8 bits depending on the computer.

These two approaches, respectively, form the basis for fixed and variable word length computer design, discussed in Chapter 5.

QUESTION: Two approaches used to represent numbers in a computer are _____ length _____ and a _____ number of small bit _____.

ANSWER: fixed, words, variable, sets

When fixed length words are used there is potentially a problem in communicating with the computer. The computer operator may wish to read the contents of a word displayed on the console. Also, a programmer may wish to read the contents of storage locations as shown on a printout. In such cases it is difficult for a human to read and interpret a long string of binary digits (0's and 1's).

To illustrate, in the IBM System/370 a number is often represented as a 32-bit word. Thus the content of a storage location might appear as follows in binary:

00010110001101000110110101001101

If necessary, this number could be converted to decimal using the methods described in the previous section. However this procedure would clearly be cumbersome and conducive to error. To facilitate reading (and writing) binary numbers, a binary-based notation is normally used. This notation is generally either octal or hexadecimal, depending on the computer. By using this notation, the above binary number would appear as follows:

Octal	02615066515
Hexadecimal	16346D4D

It is quite clear that using either the octal or hexadecimal notation (such as in the above example) is more efficient and less conducive to error than the underlying binary notation. Computer console displays are generally marked off so that the operator can read off the contents of storage locations in octal or hexadecimal. Also, printouts of core storage (called "dumps") are generally in one of these notations.

QUESTION: The two binary based notations generally used in computer applications are _____ and _____.

ANSWER: octal, hexadecimal

Octal System

The octal number system has a base (or radix) of 8. The absolute values are the integers 0 to 7, and positional values are powers of 8. Table 4–3 shows the octal equivalents of the decimal numbers 1 to 20.

TABLE 4–3
Octal Numbers Corresponding to Decimal Numbers 1–20

Decimal	Octal	Decimal	Octal
1	1	11	13
2	2	12	14
3	3	13	15
4	4	14	16
5	5	15	17
6	6	16	20
7	7	17	21
8	10	18	22
9	11	19	23
10	12	20	24

QUESTION: Examine Table 4–3. In the octal number system, what is the result of 7 + 1? _____.

ANSWER: 10, which represents a 0 plus a carry of one to the next column. Recall that there is no "8" in the octal system.

Any decimal number may be converted to octal by dividing successively by 8 and saving the remainders. This procedure is the same as the successive division by 2 procedure for converting from decimal to binary discussed previously (see Figure 4–3). For example, to convert decimal 327 to octal:

```
                                    Remainder
    8 | 327
       8 | 40            7
          8 | 5          0
             8 | 0       5
                0
```

QUESTION: Decimal 327 is equivalent to octal _____.
ANSWER: 507. The remainder is read from bottom to top.

Conversion from binary to octal and octal to binary is easily performed. For a whole number, begin at the right (or low-order) position and block off groups of three binary digits. Replace each group of three bits with its decimal equivalent. The decimal equivalent of three binary digits will range from 0 to 7, and therefore may be represented as an octal number, as shown below:

Binary	Octal
000	0
001	1
010	2
011	3
100	4
101	5
110	6
111	7

The following are two examples of converting a binary number to octal.

Binary	011	101	110		1	000	111	110	100	101
Octal	3	5	6		1	0	7	6	4	5

QUESTION: A binary number is converted to octal by marking off groups of _____ bits starting at the binary point (or low-order position) and writing down the _____ equivalent of each group.

ANSWER: three, decimal

Converting an octal number to binary is accomplished by the reverse of the above process: replace each octal digit with the equivalent three binary digits. For example, the binary equivalent of octal 247 is 010100111.

Exercise 4–2

1. Convert the following decimal numbers to octal:

(a) 234 _____

(b) 863 _____

2. Convert the following octal numbers to decimal:

(a) 57 _____

(b) 234 _____

3. Convert the following binary numbers to octal notation:

(a) 110101 _____

(b) 10011001 _____

Hexadecimal System

In some computers it is more efficient to use a notation based on groups of four (rather than three) binary digits. This is due to the organization of computer storage, which will be discussed in the next chapter. The hexadecimal number system is used to represent groups of four bits, just as octal numbers represent groups of three bits.

The hexadecimal system has base 16, and uses characters representing the absolute values 0 to 15. These values correspond to groups of four binary digits, which range in value from 0000 (decimal equivalent 0) to 1111 (decimal equivalent 15). Positional values of the hexadecimal system are powers of 16.

QUESTION: The _____ system is a binary-based system for groups of four binary digits. It has a radix of _____ and positional values are powers of _____.
ANSWER: hexadecimal, 16, 16

Since only a single character may be used for each absolute value, the characters A to F are used to represent the values 10 to 15 in the hexadecimal system. Some equivalent decimal and hexadecimal numbers are shown in Table 4–4.

TABLE 4–4
Equivalent Decimal and Hexadecimal Numbers

Decimal	Hexadecimal	Decimal	Hexadecimal
0	0	16	10
1	1	17	11
2	2	18	12
3	3	19	13
4	4	20	14
5	5	21	15
6	6	22	16
7	7	23	17
8	8	24	18
9	9	25	19
10	A	26	1A
11	B	27	1B
12	C	28	1C
13	D	29	1D
14	E	30	1E
15	F	31	1F

QUESTION: Examine Table 4–4. What is the hexadecimal equivalent of decimal 32, as inferred from the table? _____.
ANSWER: 20

A hexadecimal number may be converted to decimal by writing it in extended form (powers of 16). For example, to convert hexadecimal 2C5, recall that C represents the value 12:

$$2C5 = 2 \times 16^2 + 12 \times 16^1 + 5 \times 16^0$$
$$= 709 \text{ (decimal)}$$

Conversion from decimal to hexadecimal is accomplished by successive division by 16, saving the remainders. Any remainder from 10 to 15 is replaced by the corresponding symbol A to F. For example, to convert decimal 687:

Remainder

```
16 | 687
   16 | 42              15
      16 | 2            10
          | 0            2
```

QUESTION: The hexadecimal equivalent of decimal 687 is _____.
ANSWER: 2AF. The value 10 is represented by A, 15 by F

A binary number is represented in hexadecimal by forming groups of 4 binary digits, starting at the low-order position. Following are two examples:

Binary	1011	1010	1011	0011	0111	0001	1111
Hexadecimal	B	A	B	3	7	1	F

Exercise 4–3

1. Convert 748 to hexadecimal.   _____

2. Convert hexadecimal B7C to decimal.   _____

3. Convert 1000110001111000 to
hexadecimal notation.   _____

Data Codes

Thus far the discussion has concerned representing numerical information in the computer. Two-state devices such as magnetic cores can represent binary digits, and combinations of binary digits in turn represent numbers in computer storage. The octal and hexadecimal number systems are convenient shorthand notations for these binary numbers.

In addition to numbers, computers must process and store letters and other nonnumeric symbols. In fact, in data processing applications much of the data consists of alphanumeric information—letters, special characters, and numeric data that is not used in arithmetic operations. To represent this information, various codes are used in the computer. Within each code, a particular combination of bits is used to represent each alphanumeric character. In one of these codes, for example, the combination 110001 represents the letter A. The more important codes used in data processing are discussed in this section.

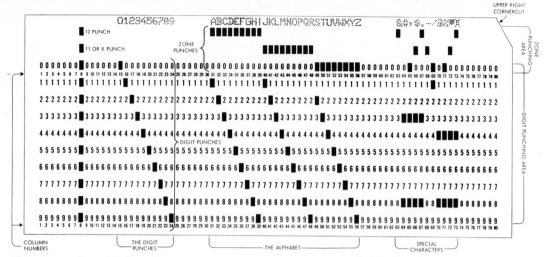

Figure 4–4. *The Hollerith code.*

Hollerith Code

Punched cards are among the most familiar type of input in computer applications. The most common type of punched card contains 12 horizontal rows and 80 vertical columns. A character is encoded in a card column by means of one or more punches. Theoretically there are 4,096 different punching combinations per column. However, only certain of these combinations are meaningful in a Hollerith coding system.

QUESTIONS: The most common type of punched card contains _____ rows and _____ columns. Data is encoded in cards using the _____ coding system.
ANSWER: 12, 80, Hollerith

A punched card containing many of the meaningful Hollerith punching combinations is shown in Figure 4–4. The Hollerith character represented by each combination is printed directly above each column at the top of the card.

QUESTION: Examine Figure 4–4. The Hollerith code characters shown include 10 digits, _____ alphabetic characters or letters, and _____ special characters or a total of _____ _____ characters.
ANSWER: 26, 11, 47 (if a blank is included, there is a total of 48 characters)

A punched card contains 10 rows numbered zero to nine, plus 2 rows at the top called zones. The top row is called the 12 zone; the next row is called the 11 zone. The zero row is used to punch the numeric zero, and also as a zone for some of the alphabetic and special characters.

In the Hollerith code, the digits 0 to 9 are each represented by a single punch in the corresponding row; the zones are not used. Letters and special characters are represented by a combination of zone and numeric punches.

QUESTION: Examine Figure 4–4 again. The letters A to I are represented by a _____ zone and a numeric punch; the letters J to R are represented by an _____ zone and a numeric punch; and the letters S to Z are represented by a _____ zone and a numeric punch.

ANSWER: 12, 11, 0

The holes in a punched card might be thought of as representing binary digits: a punch represents a 1-bit; no punch represents a 0-bit. The Hollerith code could theoretically be used in a computer, so that Hollerith characters on a punched card would be stored using the same bit combinations in the computer. However, to represent each character in computer storage by a 12-bit code would be wasteful of storage. Therefore, input data in Hollerith code is automatically converted to one of several internal codes before it is stored in the computer. These codes are all variations of the binary system. The most commonly used are binary coded decimal (or BCD), standard binary coded decimal interchange code (often called standard BCD), and extended binary coded decimal interchange code (EBCDIC).

Binary Coded Decimal

The BCD code is used to represent numeric information, and is one of the more commonly used codes. In this code, the first four binary positions (with position values of 1, 2, 4, and 8) are used to represent each decimal digit. For example, the digits 3 and 9 are represented in BCD as follows.

8	4	2	1	Decimal Digit
0	0	1	1	3
1	0	0	1	9

Position Value (above the 8 4 2 1 header)

Decimal numbers are represented in BCD code by using one 4-bit set for each digit in the number. To illustrate, the number 437 is represented in BCD as follows.

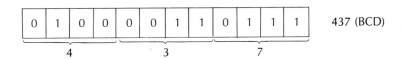

437 (BCD)

Since the BCD code is based on 4-bit sets, it can also be used to represent hexadecimal numbers. For example, the BCD representation of the hexadecimal number D5B is as follows.

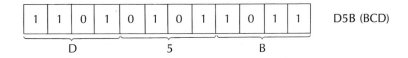

D5B (BCD)

Representing a decimal number in BCD code requires more binary positions than straight binary representation. Following is a comparison between BCD and binary representation for the number 437.

0	1	0	0	0	0	1	1	0	1	1	1

437 (BCD)

			1	1	0	1	1	0	1	0	1

437 (Binary)

QUESTION: Compare the efficiency of representing a number in BCD and in straight binary. In the above example the number 437 requires _____ bits in binary, while _____ bits are required in BCD.

ANSWER: 9, 12

Despite this comparison, representing numbers in straight binary generally does not conserve storage space. Binary numbers are stored in a fixed number of bit positions called a word. A given decimal number may require only a portion of a word, so that the remainder of the word is unused. In the above example, the decimal number 437 requires only 9 of the 12 available bit positions. On the other hand, the BCD code permits the use of only a required number of four-bit sets (called a variable word). The concept of fixed versus variable word structure is discussed in the next chapter.

Standard BCD

In the BCD code discussed above, it is possible to represent only 2^4 or 16 different characters. Thus it is not possible to encode alphanumeric characters using BCD representation. To accommodate alphabetic and special characters, the BCD code is often extended to six bit positions. This extended code is called the standard binary coded decimal interchange code, or simply standard BCD.

In standard binary coded decimal, all characters are represented by using six bit positions for data and one position for a check bit. The six positions consist of two zone bits and four numeric bits. The bit positions for the standard BCD code are shown in Figure 4–5.

Check Bit	Zone Bits		Numeric Bits			
C	B	A	8	4	2	1

Figure 4–5. *Bit positions for the standard BCD code.*

As shown, the four numeric bits represent decimal values 8, 4, 2, and 1. These are positional values in the binary number system. To represent a numerical value, the zone bits are set to zero. The numbers 0 to 9 are then represented by the appropriate numeric bit combinations, using binary notation. For example, the numbers 3 and 9 are represented in standard BCD as follows.

Bit Positions						
B	A	8	4	2	1	
0	0	0	0	1	1	3 (Standard BCD)
0	0	1	0	0	1	9 (Standard BCD)

Alphabetic and special characters are represented in standard BCD by combinations of zone and numeric bits. For example, the letters A and R and the special character $ are coded as shown in Figure 4–6.

Character	Standard BCD Code					
	B	A	8	4	2	1
A	1	1	0	0	0	1
R	1	0	1	0	0	1
$	1	0	1	0	1	1

Figure 4–6. *Examples of standard BCD codes.*

QUESTION: From Figure 4–6, can you guess the standard BCD code for the letter B? _____ .

ANSWER: 110010. The zone bits are the same as the letter A. The numeric 1-bit is moved from the one position to the two position

The C position in the standard BCD code (see Figure 4–5) is known as the check bit. It has no significance for encoding a character, but is used by the computer to check the validity of data. This is done automatically by internal computer circuitry through a system called *parity checking*.

Depending on the computer, the parity check may be for even or odd parity. Assume that the computer uses an odd parity check. When a character is stored in the computer in standard BCD code, the number of one bits in the first six-bit positions is counted. If this number is even, a one bit is stored in the C position; if it is odd, a zero bit is stored in this position. As a result, the seven bit positions of a standard BCD character always have an odd number of one bits (if an even parity check is used, the procedure is reversed).

To illustrate, following are the representations for the number 3 and the letter A, in a computer using odd parity checking:

BCD Position							Character
C	B	A	8	4	2	1	
1	0	0	0	0	1	1	3
0	1	1	0	0	0	1	A

QUESTION: How would the above codes change for a computer that uses an even parity check? _____

ANSWER: The check bit would be reversed; the C position would contain a 1 for the letter A, 0 for the digit 3.

Whenever data is transmitted from one storage location to another in the computer, the computer checks to determine if the necessary odd (or even) number of bits is present. If a bit has been lost or added during transmission, a parity error condition will occur and processing will be terminated. It is possible that offsetting errors will occur so that the parity check will fail to detect an error condition, but this condition is extremely unlikely.

QUESTION: Errors are detected in data transfer by means of a _____ check. Depending on the computer this check may be for _____ or _____ parity.

ANSWER: parity, odd, even

Extended Binary Coded Decimal Interchange Code (EBCDIC)

The number of characters that can be represented by a data code is a power of two. For example, the standard BCD code uses six bit positions to represent a character. The number of different characters that can be represented in standard BCD is therefore 2^6, or 64. Remember that in the four-bit BCD code only 16 characters (the hexadecimal digits) could be represented.

QUESTION: Examine Figure 4–4 again. Can all of the Hollerith characters shown in this figure be represented in a computer in standard BCD code? _____

ANSWER: Yes. There are 48 meaningful punching combinations, including the blank (no punches). The standard BCD code can accommodate 64 different characters.

In third generation computer systems additional characters are often needed. For this reason, the EBCDIC system has been devised and is used in many third generation computers. In the EBCDIC system, all characters are represented using eight bit positions, plus a check bit. The eight bit positions are divided into a zone portion (four bits) and a numeric portion (four bits), as is shown in Figure 4–7.

Check Bit	Zone Portion				Numeric Portion			
C	Z	Z	Z	Z	8	4	2	1

Figure 4–7. *Bit positions for the EBCDIC code.*

The extension from six to eight bit positions permits as many as 2^8 or 256 characters to be represented. EBCDIC permits the representation of both uppercase and lowercase letters, numeric digits, a wide range of special characters, and certain control characters used primarily to control input-output devices. However, at present less than one half the possible bit combinations are actually used; the remainder are available for future assignment, as needed.

QUESTION: To represent additional needed characters in third generation, the standard BCD system has been extended from six to _____ _____ bits. The extended system is termed _____.
This sytem can theoretically represent as many as _____
different characters.

ANSWER: eight, EBCDIC, 256

In EBCDIC, characters are represented by a combination of zone and numeric bits. For example, the upper- and lowercase letter d and the dollar sign ($) are represented as follows.

Zone				Numeric				
Z	Z	Z	Z	8	4	2	1	Character
1	1	0	0	0	1	0	0	D
1	0	0	0	0	1	0	0	d
0	1	0	1	1	0	1	1	$

In most computers using the EBCDIC code the eight bits are handled as a unit called a *byte*. A byte is equivalent to an 8 bit EBCDIC character and is usually the smallest addressable unit of information in such computers.

Decimal digits can be represented in EBCDIC in either of two formats: zoned decimal or packed decimal. In *zoned* decimal, each decimal digit is encoded as an eight-bit EBCDIC character. The zone bits represent the sign of the number. A bit pattern of 1111 in the zone portion represents an unsigned number, 1100 represents a positive number, and 1101 represents a negative number. Thus the numbers 9, +9, and −9 are represented in EBCDIC as follows.

Zone				Numeric				
Z	Z	Z	Z	8	4	2	1	Digit
1	1	1	1	1	0	0	1	9
1	1	0	0	1	0	0	1	+9
1	1	0	1	1	0	0	1	−9

A decimal number is represented by using consecutive eight-bit sets. The sign is stored in the zone portion of the rightmost character; all other zone positions are set equal to 1111. For example, the decimal number +437 appears as follows in zoned decimal.

67 / DATA CODES

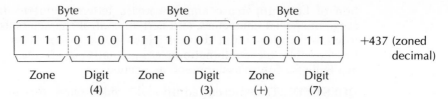

In *packed* decimal format the zone portions of numerical digits are removed and two digits are packed in each eight-bit set. The sign of the number is stored in the rightmost portion of the character string. For example, the number +437 appears as follows in packed decimal.

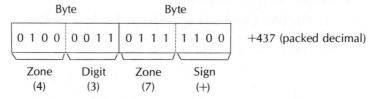

QUESTION: Compare the efficiency of representing decimal numbers in zoned versus packed decimal. From the above examples, the number +437 requires _____ bit positions in zoned decimal versus _____ positions in packed decimal.

ANSWER: 24, 16

When decimal numbers are read into the computer they are generally stored in zoned decimal format. If the numbers are merely to be printed or transmitted to another output device, they may be left in zoned decimal format. However, if arithmetic operations are to be performed, the numbers must first be converted to packed decimal format. After the calculations are performed, the results may then be converted back to zoned decimal for output. Figure 4–8 portrays the conversion of the number +437 from zoned to packed decimal format.

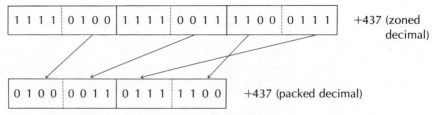

Figure 4–8. *Conversion from zoned to packed decimal.*

Since an EBCDIC character consists of eight bits, it may easily be represented by two hexadecimal numbers. For example, the EBCDIC code for the letter D is 11000100. By dividing this into two pairs of four digits each, the hexadecimal equivalent is shown to be C4.

QUESTION: In Figure 4–8 the number +437 is shown in both zoned decimal and packed decimal formats. Write the hexadecimal equivalent for each of these formats: zoned decimal _____ , packed decimal _____ .

ANSWER: F4F3C7, 437C

Exercise 4–4

1. State whether each of the following codes represents a character in BCD, standard BCD, or EBCDIC. If the code is standard BCD, express its octal equivalent. If BCD or EBCDIC, express its hexadecimal equivalent.
   (a) 111111   _____

   (b) 10100110   _____

   (c) 1011   _____

   (d) 011001   _____

   (e) 1010   _____

   (f) 11110111   _____

2. A data code used in some data processing equipment is called ASCII (American Standard Code for Information Interchange). In this code, all characters are encoded using seven bit positions. How many different characters can theoretically be represented using this code?

_____

Summary

This chapter describes the basic techniques for representing data in a computer. A knowledge of these techniques is important in using computers and in understanding the differences between computing systems.

In human communication we normally use the decimal number system and alphabetic characters and other symbols. In the computer all symbols are represented as combinations of binary digits or bits. Each binary digit is, in turn, represented by two-state devices such as magnetic core units.

Alphanumeric data is represented in the computer by using a coding system such as standard binary coded decimal (BCD) or extended binary coded decimal interchange code (EBCDIC). Combinations of binary digits are easily expressed using a shorthand notation, usually octal (base 8) or hexadecimal (base 16).

A variety of the codes that are discussed here are used in a typical computer system. Some of the more important uses of codes are shown in Figure 4–9.

The implementation of these techniques for data representation is discussed in the next chapter. This includes the characteristics of computer storage, types of storage devices, and storage concepts such as fixed versus variable word length.

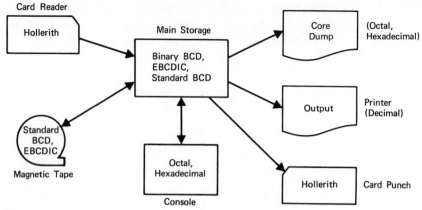

Figure 4-9. *Some uses of codes in a typical computer system.*

Solutions to Exercises

Exercise 4-1

1. (a) 25.   (b) 5.75.   (c) 15.
2. (a) 100000.   (b) 1110.1.   (c) 111111.01.
3. Position   3   2   1   0   −1   −2
    Value 8^3 8^2 8^1 8^0 8^{-1} 8^{-2}
    Quantity   512   64   8   1   1/8   1/64
4. (a)   11001   (b)   1011.01   (c)   1000.1
            +1111   −10.10   −1.0
            ‾‾‾‾‾‾   ‾‾‾‾‾‾   ‾‾‾‾‾
            101000   1000.11   0111.1
5. (a) 0, 1, 2, 3.
    (b) $323.12 = 3 \times 4^2 + 2 \times 4^1 + 3 \times 4^0 + 1 \times 4^{-1} + 2 \times 4^{-2}$
            $= 59.375.$
6. 01011.

Exercise 4-2

1. (a) 352.   (b) 1537.
2. (a) 47.   (b) 156.
3. (a) 65.   (b) 231.

Exercise 4-3

1. 2EC.
2. 2940.
3. 8C78.

Exercise 4–4

1. (a) Standard BCD, 77.   (d) Standard BCD, 31.
    (b) EBCDIC, A6.   (e) BCD, A.
    (c) BCD, B.   (f) EBCDIC, F7.

2. 2^7 or 128.

Chapter Examination

  1. Explain the differences between the following codes:

    (a) Hollerith _____

    (b) Standard BCD _____

    (c) EBCDIC _____

    (d) BCD _____

  2. Convert each of the following decimal numbers to binary:

    (a) 9 _____

    (b) 15 _____

    (c) 127 _____

  3. Convert each of the numbers in problem 2 to:

    (a) Octal _____

    (b) Hexadecimal _____

  4. Convert each of the following binary numbers to decimal:

    (a) 1101011 _____

    (b) 11110011 _____

  5. Convert each of the binary numbers in problem 4 to:

    (a) Octal _____

    (b) Hexadecimal _____

6. The duodecimal number system has base 12. Let A represent the value 10 and B the value 11.

(a) What are the absolute values in this system?

_____

(b) What are the first three positional values?

_____

(c) Convert the following decimal numbers to duodecimal:

8 _____

11 _____

12 _____

166 _____

(d) Convert the following duodecimal numbers to decimal:

15 _____

6B _____

AB _____

7. Perform the following binary arithmetic:

(a)   10110   (b)   10110.11   (c)   1100.10
      +111   +111.01   −101.01

      _____   _____   _____

8. How many characters can be represented in each of the following coding systems:

(a) BCD _____

(b) EBCDIC _____

(c) Hollerith _____

9. Show how to represent the decimal number −192 in:

(a) Zoned decimal _____

(b) Packed decimal _____

10. Following are the EBCDIC codes for several characters:

Character	EBCDIC Code	Check Bit
E	1100 0101	_____
R	1101 1001	_____
4	1111 0100	_____
+	0100 1110	_____
b (blank)	0100 0000	_____

Assuming that a computer uses an odd parity check, what binary digit would appear in the check bit position for each of these characters?

11. Use hexadecimal notation to represent each of the EBCDIC bit configurations in problem 10.

E _____

R _____

4 _____

+ _____

b _____

12. Identify the following statements as true or false:

_____ (a) There are eight absolute values in the octal numbering system.

_____ (b) The largest number that could be represented by three "on-off" devices is 7.

_____ (c) A decimal number may be converted to binary by successive divisions by 8, saving the remainder from each division.

_____ (d) Octal numbers are based on groups of three binary digits, while hexadecimal numbers are based on groups of four.

_____ (e) The EBCDIC code is limited to a representation of 128 distinct characters.

_____ (f) The zoned decimal format is used primarily for arithmetic calculations.

13. Match the following terms to the appropriate definitions:

_____ Positional value   (a) absolute values are integers 0 to 7

_____ Base   (b) coding system used for punched cards

_____ Bit   (c) obtained by raising the base to a power

_____ Parity   (d) code based on four binary positions

_____ Octal   (e) the number of absolute values in a numbering system.

73 / CHAPTER EXAMINATION

_____ BCD   (f) binary digit, represented by 0 or 1

_____ Hollerith   (g) code based on eight binary positions

_____ EBCDIC   (h) check for validity of data

_____ Byte   (i) 8-bit character

14. You observe a printout of computer memory (called a core dump).
    (a) The printout consists entirely of the digits 0 to 7. What notation

    is being used? _____
    (b) The printout consists entirely of the digits 0 to 9 and the letters

    A to F. What notation is being used? _____

15. Explain why it is convenient to represent EBCDIC characters using

    hexadecimal notation _____

    _____

    _____

16. Describe the difference between zoned decimal and packed decimal

    representation _____

    _____

    _____

17. What binary number is represented by each of the following two-
    state devices? A shaded circle represents the 1-bit, an empty circle
    the 0-bit.

    (a) ● ○ ○ ○ ○ ○   _____

    (b) ● ○ ○ ○ ○ ●   _____

    (c) ● ○ ● ○ ● ○   _____

    (d) ● ● ● ● ● ●   _____

Chapter 5

INFORMATION STORAGE AND RETRIEVAL

Overview

An important requirement of data processing systems is the ability to store and retrieve information. An organization uses information for a variety of purposes—operational, legal, and managerial decision making. The information storage requirements for these functions in a firm typically run into billions of characters. The information system must be able to rapidly locate, retrieve, and store the desired information for each application.

There are two main classifications of storage in a typical computer system—internal and external. Internal storage may in turn be divided into primary and secondary (also called mass or auxiliary) storage. External storage consists of media such as punched cards, magnetic tape, and documents encoded with optically readable characters.

Primary storage is integral to the central processing unit and consists of magnetic core, magnetic thin film memory, or large-scale integrated circuits. Each magnetic core (or other storage element) is a two-state device that can represent the binary digits 0 and 1. Combinations of these elements are then used to represent data, as is decribed in Chapter 4.

Data is located in storage devices by means of an addressing structure. The type and amount of data stored at an address depend on the method or organization of the particular computer. Variations include fixed word length, variable word length, and a fixed-variable combination.

Secondary storage devices include magnetic disk and drum and media such as magnetic cards and strips. New developments such as magnetic bubble memory and optical storage techniques may replace these devices and may soon eliminate the distinction between primary and secondary storage.

Classification of Computer Storage

Data is stored in a number of different forms and locations in a typical computer system. For example, in a payroll application, payroll transactions may be on punched cards, master records on magnetic tape, and the payroll program itself in magnetic core memory. The type of storage used depends on a number of factors including type and volume of data, required processing speed, and cost.

The major components of computer storage are shown in Figure 5–1. As shown, storage may be classified as primary, secondary and external storage. Primary and secondary storage may together be referred to as internal storage. *Internal* storage (also called on-line storage) is accessible to the computer program without human intervention. In contrast, *external* storage (or off-line storage) consists of media such as punched cards and magnetic tape which must be loaded into or mounted on some input-output device. Thus, a reel of magnetic tape on a storage shelf might be considered part of external storage; when the reel is mounted on a magnetic tape unit and is ready to be read, it might be considered part of secondary storage.

QUESTION: Two major types of computer storage are _____ and _____ storage. Internal storage consists of _____ and _____ storage.

ANSWER: Internal, external, primary, secondary

Primary storage (or main memory) is contained in the central processing unit. It stores the programs currently being executed by the computer, plus the data immediately being processed by the programs. After this data is processed, it is typically transferred to secondary storage and/or to an output device. New data is then entered from an input device and/or from secondary storage, and processing continues. Primary storage consists of magnetic core, thin film, and integrated circuits (or monolithic storage).

Secondary storage (also called auxiliary or mass storage) is used primarily to store data files used in the various data processing applications. Computer programs not currently being executed are also contained in mass storage; these programs are read into main memory when they

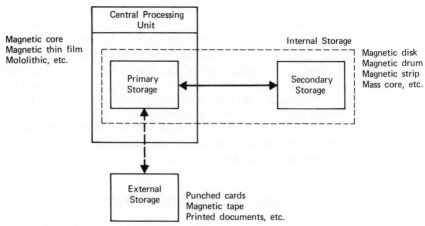

Figure 5–1. *Major types of computer storage.*

are needed. Secondary storage usually consists of magnetic disk or drum, and is typically of very large capacity. It may be regarded as an extension of primary storage.

External storage is used principally for storing data where high-speed access is not important. It consists largely of punched cards, magnetic tape, and documents encoded with magnetic ink characters (such as checks) or optical characters.

Exercise 5–1

1. Match each of the following types of storage to the most appropriate media or device:

(a) primary   _____ magnetic disk or drum

(b) secondary   _____ punched cards, magnetic tape

(c) external   _____ magnetic core

Primary Storage

The characteristics of primary (or main) storage are discussed in this section. This includes a description of storage devices and of the addressing structures most often used.

Magnetic Core Storage

The internal storage unit in many third generation computers consists of magnetic cores. A core is a tiny doughnut-shaped element about the size of a grain of salt. It is molded from a magnetic material like nickel-zinc ferrite or nickel-iron alloy. Cores are strung on intersecting wires to form a core plane, as is shown in Figure 5–2.

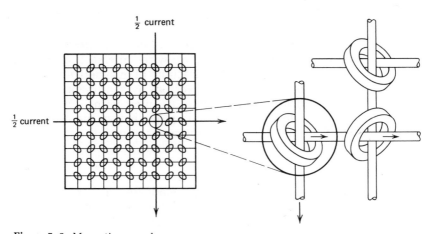

Figure 5–2. *Magnetic core plane.*

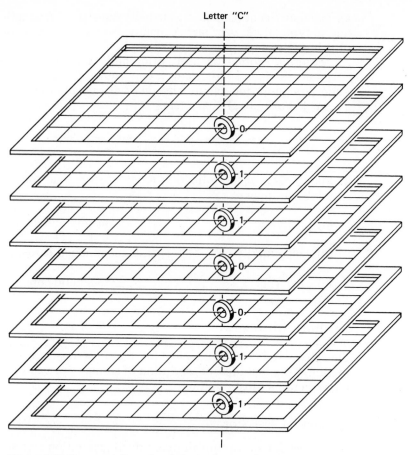

Figure 5–3. *Representation of a character in core storage.*

The important property of a magnetic core is its ability to be polarized in one of two directions, clockwise or counterclockwise. A core that is polarized in clockwise direction is said to be ON, while a core polarized in the counterclockwise direction is said to be OFF. Thus a core is a two-state element that can represent the binary digits 0 and 1, as described in Chapter 4.

A core can be polarized by sending one half of a given amount of current along each of the two wires intersecting at its center (see Figure 5–2). The polarity (or direction of magnetization) then remains fixed until it is "flipped" (or reversed) by sending a flow of current (or electrical pulse) through each of its intersecting wires in the opposite direction. The technique of sending one half of the necessary current through each of the two intersecting wires allows the polarity to be reversed for the desired core element without disturbing any other element in the core plane.

The above description concerns "writing" or storing information in cores. Provision must also be made for the computer to "read" or to sense the polarity of a core. This is generally accomplished by using two additional wires (called the sense and inhibit wires) through each core. Simply stated, these wires used in conjunction with logical circuitry permit the computer to sense the ON or OFF condition of each magnetic core element.

Magnetic core planes are stacked to form core stacks or units. Cores in the same location on adjacent planes are then used to form bit combinations to represent numbers and characters. For example in BCD notation the letter C is represented by the binary code 0110011. Representation of this character in core storage is shown in Figure 5–3.

QUESTION: A common form of internal storage in third generation computers consists of _____.
These elements are made of ferrite materials that can be _____ in one of two directions.

ANSWER: Magnetic cores, polarized.

Alternative Storage Techniques

Although magnetic cores have been the dominant form of internal storage, they are being replaced by new technology in recent computers. The most important of these are thin film memories and large-scale integrated circuits, or monolithic storage.

Thin film memory consists of tiny, very thin spots of a metallic alloy deposited on a ceramic plate. Each spot can be polarized in one of two directions similar to a magnetic core. Both "read" and "write" can be accomplished with only two wires which pass through each spot. Thin films require less space than magnetic cores and the magnetic properties of the film permit much faster switching times (therefore, faster internal speeds).

Monolithic Storage. The most recent advances in high-speed memory technology are in the area of large-scale integrated (LSI) circuitry. With this approach, miniature semiconductors (such as transistors) are used to form very small, compact memory arrays. Complex semiconductor circuits are etched in tiny chips of metal, plastic, or ceramic. An advanced chip of this type (called a Field Effect Transistor chip) is shown in Figure 5–4. This chip (about one-fourth inch square) is capable of storing 8,192 bits of information and dissipates only 22.5 milliwatts (0.0225 watt) of power. In contrast, 10,000 vacuum tubes similar to the one shown in the same figure would be required to create the equivalent circuitry. These tubes would generate enough heat to keep three average-sized homes warm during a Colorado winter!

Several chips of this type are mounted on a ceramic plate to form a memory module. Finally, the memory modules are mounted on a storage array card. For example, IBM uses large-scale integrated circuitry (also called monolithic storage) in the System/370 series of computers. More than 1,400 components (for instance transistors) are contained on a single chip less than one-fourth inch square—smaller than an aspirin tablet. The components are integrated to form 128 storage bits and their associated addressing, sensing, and decoding circuitry on each chip. Four of these chips are encased in a one-half inch square memory module with a capacity of 512 (4 × 128) bits. Twenty-four modules are in turn mounted on a storage array card as is shown in Figure 5–5. Each storage array card (approximately 6 in. × 8 in.) has a storage capacity of 12,288 bit positions.

QUESTION: Compare Figures 5–4 and 5–5 and, from the above discussion, answer the following:

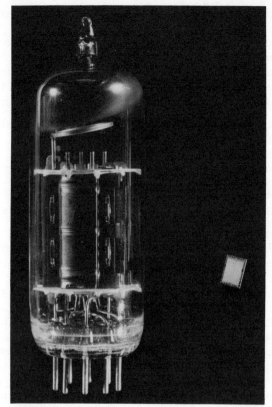

Figure 5–4. Field effect transistor chip (courtesy IBM).

Figure 5–5. An IBM System/370 storage array card (courtesy IBM).

Figure	Element	Size (inches)	Storage Capacity (bits)
5–4	Storage chip (advanced)	_____	_____
5–5	Storage array (present)	_____	_____

ANSWER: Chip ¼ in. × ¼ in., 8,192 bits
Array 6 in. × 8 in., 12,288 bits

Monolithic storage offers several important advantages over magnetic core or thin film memories:

1. Miniature components and shorter circuits permit much faster speeds. Typical cycle times at present are 500 nanoseconds for magnetic core, between 150 and 500 nanoseconds for thin film, and from 100 to 150 nanoseconds for large-scale integrated circuits.

QUESTION: Monolithic storage is approximately _____ to _____ times as fast as magnetic core storage at present.
ANSWER: three, five

2. Miniaturization and dense packaging reduce space requirements for a given memory capacity.

3. Although manufacturing costs are remaining about the same for magnetic core and thin film, they are decreasing for monolithic storage. In the near future the unit cost is expected to be lower for integrated circuits.

4. Monolithic storage is also considered to be more reliable and less sensitive to environmental changes than thin film or magnetic core.

For these reasons, large scale integrated circuit technology is rapidly displacing other forms of internal storage.

Addressing Structure

As mentioned previously, internal storage is used to store instructions and data currently being used by the computer. However, the computer must be able to locate data before it can be stored or retrieved. To achieve this, storage is divided into small areas called *locations*. Each location represents a certain number of bit positions, depending on the computer and the type of instructions used. An *address* is associated with each storage location which permits the computer to directly reference that location.

A storage address serves much the same function as a mailbox number in a post office. To store mail in a particular box, a person locates the desired box number (the computer goes directly to the desired location, whereas a human searches adjoining box numbers). To retrieve mail, he again identifies the location by the box number. In the same way, each storage location has an address or "box number" (see Figure 5–6).

An important difference exists between the mailbox and the storage location in the manner of storing and retrieving information. When the contents of the mailbox are removed, the box is emptied. However, when

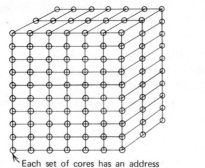
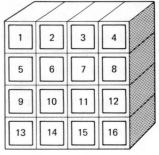

Each set of cores has an address   Each mailbox has an address

Figure 5–6. *A comparison of addresses for mailboxes and computer storage.*

the contents of a storage location are read by the computer, the contents remain in the location. In other words, the computer reads rather than removes the contents. For this reason the read operation is said to be *nondestructive*. On the other hand, when a new letter is inserted into a mailbox, the previous contents remain undisturbed. However, when the computer stores (or writes) new information in a location, the previous contents are completely replaced.

QUESTION: Suppose the computer storage location with address 405 contains the number 12345. What are the contents of address 405 after each of the following:

(a) The computer reads the contents of address 405;   _____
(b) The computer writes the number 678 at address 405? _____
ANSWER: (a) 12345, (b) 678.

As is shown in Figure 5–6, a storage location is a set of adjacent cores in a core stack. The number of core elements referenced by a storage address varies from one computer to the next, and in some computers may be specified by the instructions used to store and retrieve information. The number may range from a few bit positions (four to eight bits required to encode a single character) to a large number of bit positions. These variations depend on the word structure of the computer, as discussed in the next section.

QUESTION: Data is stored and retrieved in a computer by means of an _____ which references a certain number of bit positions called a storage _____. The number of positions referenced depends on the _____ _____ of the machine.
ANSWER: address, location, word structure

Storage Organization

Computers are sometimes classified as either fixed word length or variable word length machines. For a fixed word length machine a storage address always references a fixed number of bit positions called a *word*.

In a variable word length machine a storage address generally references a *character*—usually six- or eight-bit positions depending on whether the computer uses the Standard BCD or EBCDIC code. For this reason a fixed word length machine is said to be *word-addressable*, while a variable word length machine is termed *character-addressable*.

QUESTION: In a fixed word length machine a storage location is called a _____; while in a variable word length machine a storage location contains sufficient bit positions to store a _____.

ANSWER: word, character

Fixed and variable word length techniques each have advantages and disadvantages. The variable word length affords more efficient use of storage capacity, while the fixed word length approach results in significantly faster computational speeds. As a result, large scientific machines generally use the fixed word length approach, but small or medium-size business oriented machines often are variable word length. To obtain the advantages of both approaches, some third generation computers use a combination fixed and variable approach that permits the machine to be operated either way.

Fixed Word Length. In a fixed word length organization every storage location identified by an address consists of a fixed number of cores or bit positions. The size of a fixed word depends on the computer and may range from 16 bits in a small-scale computer to 60 bits in a larger computer. Some typical examples are as follows.

Computer	Type	Word Size (Bits)
H-P 3000	Minicomputer	16
IBM 370	Medium-large General Purpose	32
UNIVAC 1108	Large General Purpose	36
CDC 6400	Large General Purpose	60

In a fixed word length computer alphanumeric characters are stored in coded form within a fixed word. For example, in the CDC 6400 a 6-bit (or BCD) code is used, so that up to 10 alphanumeric characters may be stored in each word. In the IBM 370 an 8-bit (or EBCDIC) code is used, permitting up to 4 characters for each 32-bit word. Numeric data to be used in computations may be stored either in straight binary or in coded form.

QUESTION: How many alphanumeric characters may be stored in a UNIVAC 1108 word? A 6-bit representation is used. _____

ANSWER: Six alphanumeric characters in a 36-bit 1108 word.

The principal advantage of the fixed word length organization is speed of arithmetic calculations. In a fixed word length machine these operations are performed in parallel—that is, all the bits in a computer word are transferred and operated on simultaneously. This is accomplished largely through the use of addressable registers.

A *register* is a set of storage devices (e.g., magnetic cores) that acts as a temporary storage for data or instructions. The main storage of a computer is passive, merely storing data and instructions. To decode an instruction or operate on data, the computer must transfer the instruction or data to a register that is an active element. For example, to add two numbers the steps might be as follows.

1. Move the first number to the accumulator register.
2. Add the second number to the number in the accumulator.
3. Store the result from the accumulator to memory.

An *addressable* register is one that may be referenced by the programmer to load it with an operand or store its contents in a storage location. Ordinarily the length of an addressable register is the same as a computer word. Third generation computers have several addressable registers; for example, the IBM System/370 has 16 general-purpose registers for fixed word length operations. The use of registers in coding and executing instructions is discussed in greater detail in Chapter 6.

QUESTION: The principal advantage of _____ word length computers is computational speed. This is accomplished by _____ operations in conjunction with _____ registers.

ANSWER: fixed, parallel, addressable

Variable Word Length. In a variable word length computer each addressable storage location is a set of bits that encodes one character. The bit set (generally consisting of 6 or 8 bits) is often termed a *byte,* and the computer is said to be character or *byte-addressable.* For example, in the IBM System/370 each addressable byte consists of eight-bit positions.

Suppose the number 2468 is to be stored in a variable word length organization. Each numeral is stored (or represented) in an addressable location, so that the number occupies four storage locations. To retrieve this number it might seem that four separate references would be required. However, this is not necessary. The variable word length instructions permit accessing all of the characters in a group by specifying only the address of the *starting* character, plus the number of characters in the group (or word).[1] For example, Figure 5–7 shows the number 2468

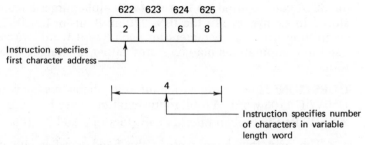

Figure 5–7. *Variable word length instructions specifies starting address and number of characters.*

[1]Another technique that is sometimes used is a special character called a word mark to indicate the end of a word.

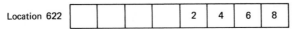

Location 622 | | | | 2 | 4 | 6 | 8 |

Figure 5–8. *Storage of the number 2468 in a fixed word length computer.*

stored in locations 622 through 625. An instruction to retrieve this number would reference the first location (622) and the number of locations in the word (4).

QUESTION: Suppose the word AUGUST is stored at addresses 207 through 212. To retrieve the data, what information must a variable word length instruction specify? _____

ANSWER: the starting address (207) and the number of characters (6)

A major advantage of the variable word length organization is that it conserves storage; only the required character positions are used. In a fixed word length computer the high-order positions of a word are often unused. For example, suppose the number 2468 is to be stored in a computer with a fixed word length of 48 bits. If a Standard BCD notation is used, the four digits are represented in only 4 × 6 or 24 bit positions. Figure 5–8 shows the number stored at storage location 622 for the fixed word length computer.

QUESTION: Compare Figures 5–7 and 5–8. Assuming both computers use a Standard BCD (6-bit) character representation, how many bit positions are required to store the number 2468 in the variable word length computer? _____ Fixed word length? _____ .

ANSWER: 24, 48.

A fixed word length computer uses addressable registers that are designed to hold a specified number of bits. This approach is not possible in a variable word length computer, since the size of a word varies from one operation to the next. Instead, variable word length instructions use a storage-to-storage approach in which a single character (or byte) is read from storage into a nonaddressable register, operated upon, and the result stored back into a character location. Operations are said to proceed *serially* – that is, one character at a time.

Since serial operations are slower than parallel operations, computational speeds are slower in a variable than in a fixed word length machine.
Fixed-Variable Combination. To provide the advantages of both approaches, several third generation computers can be operated either as fixed or variable length machines. The instruction set allows the programmer to use either or both modes in a given program. An example of such a computer is the IBM System/370. Each addressable storage location is an 8-bit byte. Four such bytes make up a 32-bit binary word. When operated as a fixed word length computer, an address references four bytes (32-bit word). A variable word length instruction references the first byte of a group, as well as the length of the word. This method of addressing is often termed byte-addressable.

The IBM System/370 also has fixed word length instructions that reference a half-word (2 bytes or 16 bits) or a double-word (8 bytes or 64 bits). This increases the storage efficiency of fixed word length organization. The word organization of the IBM System/370 is shown in Figure 5–9.

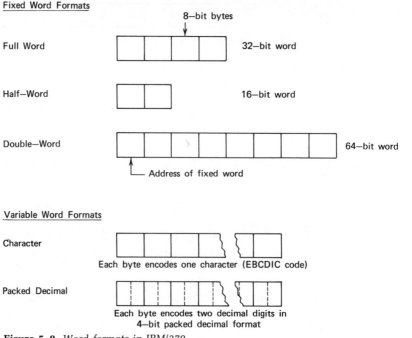

Fixed Word Formats

Full Word — 32—bit word

Half—Word — 16—bit word

Double—Word — 64—bit word

8—bit bytes

Address of fixed word

Variable Word Formats

Character

Each byte encodes one character (EBCDIC code)

Packed Decimal

Each byte encodes two decimal digits in 4—bit packed decimal format

Figure 5–9. *Word formats in IBM/370.*

QUESTION: Which word format in Figure 5–9 would the programmer select under each of these conditions:
(a) The data was primarily alphanumeric, with storage efficiency of prime importance. _____
(b) The data is primarily numeric, with extensive calculations required. _____

ANSWER: (a) Variable word length. (b) Fixed word length.

Signed Numbers. Numbers may be stored in a computer in either signed or unsigned form. A signed number is one that is preceded by either a plus (+) or a minus (−) sign. Different approaches are used in fixed versus variable length computers to designate a signed number.

In a fixed word length computer the sign position is the left-most (or highest order) bit position of a word. A plus sign is represented by the 0-bit, a negative sign by the 1-bit. For example, the decimal number +9 is represented in a 16-bit word as follows:

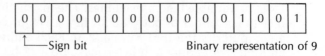

| 0 | 0 | 0 | 0 | 0 | 0 | 0 | 0 | 0 | 0 | 0 | 1 | 0 | 0 | 1 |

Sign bit   Binary representation of 9

The largest signed number that can be represented in the above word consists of a 0 in the sign position, followed by a string of 15 one-bits. This number is equivalent to the positive decimal number $2^{15} - 1$, or +32,767.

QUESTION: What is the largest positive number that can be represented in a fixed word of eight bits? _____

ANSWER: $2^7 - 1$, or +127.

In a variable word length computer signed numbers are generally stored in packed decimal (4-bit code) format, as is discussed in Chapter 4. Recall that the sign of a string of numeric characters is stored to the right-most numeric character. For example, the number +248 might be stored as follows.

0 0 1 0	0 1 0 0	1 0 0 0 1 1 0 0
2	4	8 +

The bit string 1100 in the above format is the EBCDIC code for plus (+). A bit pattern of 1101 would be used for minus (−).

Exercise 5–2

1. Fill in the following table which summarizes the characteristics of fixed and variable word length computers. Select your answers from the terms that follow the table.

	Fixed Word Length	Variable Word Length
(a) Length of word	_____	_____
(b) Type of operations	_____	_____
(c) Use of registers	_____	_____
(d) Computational speed	_____	_____
(e) Storage efficiency	_____	_____
(f) Content of storage location	_____	_____

    (a) variable, fixed or both
    (b) parallel, mixed or serial
    (c) nonaddressable, addressable or modular
    (d) relatively slow or relatively fast
    (e) relatively high or relatively low
    (f) word, byte or packed decimal

2. Describe the three major divisions of computer storage and their use.

(a) _____

(b) _____

(c) _____

3. Suppose a computer uses a fixed word length of six bits. What is the largest signed decimal number that can be represented in a word?

---

4. The number +37 is to be stored in a computer. Show how this signed number would be represented:
(a) In a computer with a fixed word length of eight bits;

(b) In a variable word length computer using packed decimal format

(EBCDIC code). _____

Secondary Storage

The internal storage capacity of a computer may be greatly extended by means of mass data files, called secondary or auxiliary storage. Secondary storage devices often have the capacity to store several million or even several hundred million characters of data. These devices are on-line to the computer and may be accessed by a program with little or no operator intervention. However, the access to data in mass storage is slower than for data in main memory, depending on the nature of the device used.

As mentioned at the beginning of the chapter, magnetic tape may be considered as part of auxiliary storage; however, it is more generally used as external (or off-line) storage. Magnetic tape and other input-output media are discussed in Chapter 7. The most commonly used auxiliary storage devices are magnetic disks, magnetic drums, mass core, and magnetic strip and cards. Mass memory based on laser technology is also under development.

An important distinction exists between direct access and sequential storage devices. Magnetic tape is an example of a *sequential access* medium. Records on magnetic tape must be accessed sequentially – that is, to locate a desired record, the tape must be searched from the beginning until the desired record is located. Storage locations on magnetic tape are not addressable.

In contrast, storage locations on a *direct access* device are addressable so that a particular record can be located without searching. This is important in applications when transactions must be processed immediately as they occur to update the status of a system, or where frequent inquiries are made to individual records. All of the secondary storage devices discussed in the following sections are examples of direct access devices.

QUESTION: Magnetic tape is an example of a _____ access medium, while magnetic disk is one type of _____ access device.
ANSWER: sequential, direct

Magnetic Disk

Perhaps the most common form of secondary storage at present is magnetic disk. A magnetic disk unit (or file) consists of a set of metal disks rotating at high speed on a common axis. Each disk is similar in appearance to a phonograph record, and may range from about 14 inches to over 2 feet in diameter. The disks are coated on both sides with a ferrous oxide, and data are recorded as a series of magnetized spots.

Basic Features. Each magnetic disk has an access arm that positions read-write heads over the desired locations of the disk. Both the top and bottom disk surfaces are used. Some units use the *moving head* principle—the access arm moves in and out to locate the read-write heads at the correct position. Other units use a *fixed head* or *head-per-track* principle—there is a read or write head over each recording position (or track) on the disk.

A magnetic disk unit with fixed heads (IBM 2305 Fixed Head Facility) is shown in Figure 5–10. Since there is no mechanical head movement, very low access times can be achieved. This type of unit is often used in systems with virtual storage (described later in this chapter) where rapid access to secondary storage is required.

In disk units used primarily for program storage (such as the one in Figure 5–10), the disks are fixed in position. In disk units used primarily for mass data storage, the disks are usually in a removable disk pack or module. The latter approach allows a pack containing one data file or set of computer programs to be replaced by another within the same physical storage unit. The capacity of a replaceable disk pack may range from approximately 2 to 100 million characters. Figure 5–11 shows a typical storage unit with removable disk pack. The disk pack in this unit has six disks and has a storage capacity of more than 7 million characters.

QUESTION: In summary, the major distinctions in disk unit design con-

Figure 5–10. *Fixed-head disk storage (courtesy IBM).*

Disk unit

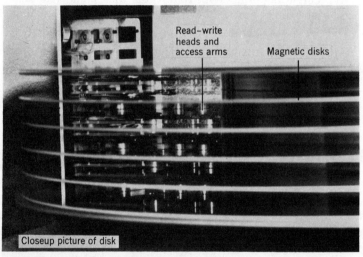

Read–write heads and access arms

Magnetic disks

Closeup picture of disk

Figure 5–11. *Disk storage unit (courtesy IBM).*

cern the access method and the ability to remove disk modules. The two major types of access methods are _____ _____ and _____-per-_____. Disks are either _____ or contained in removable _____ _____.

ANSWER: moving head, head-per-track, fixed, disk packs

In large systems, several disk files or units may be combined in a single large storage facility. Such a system (the IBM 3330 Disk Storage Facility) is shown in Figure 5–12. This facility (containing up to four

Figure 5–12. *Disk storage facility (courtesy IBM).*

units) has a maximum storage capacity of 800 million characters. This system is also available in a double density version that provides for storing up to 1.6 billion characters in each facility.

Addressing a Disk. For addressing purposes a disk surface (or face) is divided into tracks and sectors, as is shown in Figure 5–13. A *track* is a circular section on the disk face. A *sector* is a pie-shaped section of a track. A disk storage address specifies the disk face, track number, and sector number. Generally an entire sector is read or written in response to a read or write command. The sector may be of fixed or variable length, and may contain one record or a block of records.

The access arm (if a moving head) for each disk contains two read-write heads, one for the top and one for the bottom of the disk. The arms for each disk in a unit generally move in and out together, so that at any given time a *cylinder* of tracks extending vertically through the file is accessible (see Figure 5–14).

QUESTION: Suppose that a number of related records are to be stored on a disk file. If the number of records exceeds the capacity of a track, would it be better to store the overflow records on another track on the same disk face, or on another track in the same cylinder? _____

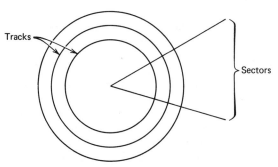

Figure 5–13. *Organization of disk storage.*

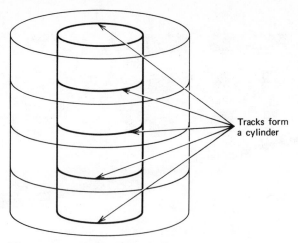

Figure 5–14. *Concept of a cylinder in a disk file.*

ANSWER: Another track on the same cylinder. This would permit accessing the records without moving the read-write heads.

Accessing a Disk. There are two sources of delay in accessing a disk, as shown in Figure 5–15. First, the access arm must move in or out to the correct track location. Second, the disk must rotate until the desired sector (or record) is positioned at the read-write head. These times are referred to, respectively, as the access motion time and the rotational delay time (also called latency). Typical average times are 75 milliseconds for the access motion and 12.5 milliseconds for the rotational delay (assuming a rotational speed of 1800 revolutions per minute). The access motion time is eliminated in head-per-track units; however, these units are more costly and are used primarily in large computer systems with virtual storage.

QUESTION: Two types of delay in using magnetic disk are _____
_____ time and _____ _____ time.
ANSWER: access motion, rotational delay.

Magnetic Drum

Magnetic drum storage is similar in concept to magnetic disk, except that data is stored on the surface of a drum rotating at high speed. Data is written and sensed by a set of read-write heads positioned close to the surface of the drum. Since the heads are fixed, there is no access motion time. However, there is a rotational delay while the drum turns to a desired sector.

Magnetic drum storage has a lower access time and transfers data faster than magnetic disk. However, it is also more expensive than disk storage. As a result, magnetic drum storage is used primarily where fast access to secondary storage is required. For example, segments of programs that will not fit in primary storage, may be temporarily stored on magnetic drum.

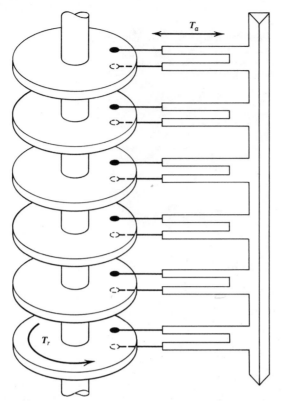

T_a: access motion time

T_r: rotational delay time (latency)

Figure 5–15. *Sources of delay in accessing a disk.*

Other Types of Secondary Storage

Mass Core Storage. Since there is no mechanical movement, magnetic core storage is faster and less subject to maintenance problems than disk or drum storage. On the other hand, magnetic core is significantly more expensive than these forms of storage. As a result, its use has been restricted to primary storage. At present, these units are confined to large systems where very fast access rates are required.

Magnetic Strip Storage. Magnetic strip storage consists of a number of small oxide-coated plastic strips or cards mounted on a cartridge holder. Each strip (or card) is addressable, and when referenced, the strip drops out of the holder, moves under a read-write head for storage or retrieval, and then is replaced in the holder. The cartridge holder may be removed and replaced by another holder. Typical units are the CRAM (Card Random Access Memory) system developed by NCR, and the IBM Data Cell. The Data Cell is shown in Figure 5–16.

Magnetic strip storage is less expensive than disk storage and provides very large capacity—for example, each cartridge in the IBM Data Cell provides for 400 million bytes. However access times are long and the units are less reliable than disk or drum storage, because of the mechanical movement. For these reasons, magnetic strip and card storage have not been widely used.

Figure 5–16. *IBM 2321 Data Cell Drive (courtesy IBM).*

Advanced Memory Systems

Research is continually underway to develop faster and cheaper storage devices. Present mass storage devices such as magnetic disk and drum and magnetic strip or card are shackled with the same limitations associated with all electromechanical devices: limited speed, limited reliability, and relatively high cost. Memory techniques are now under development which during the late 1970s are likely to replace these devices and provide fast, high density, low cost mass storage capacity. The two most promising techniques under development at present are magnetic bubble memories and optical memory techniques.

Optical Memory Techniques

In optical memory systems, an electron or laser beam is used to record bits of information on a photographic medium such as film chips or photographic plates. The recorded information is read by means of photosensitive scanners.

Photodigital Storage. In this method, an electron beam is used to record binary data on small film chips. The data is permanently recorded, so that the chips cannot be reused. The film is read by a flying spot scanner.

The use of laser beams for recording data on film is also under development. One such approach uses film chips, while a second uses magnetic-coated mylar tape wrapped about a drum. Exceedingly high recording densities (up to 13 million bits per square inch) are possible with laser techniques. This density is about 1,000 times greater than magnetic tape densities now in use.

A mass storage system using laser technology has recently been de-

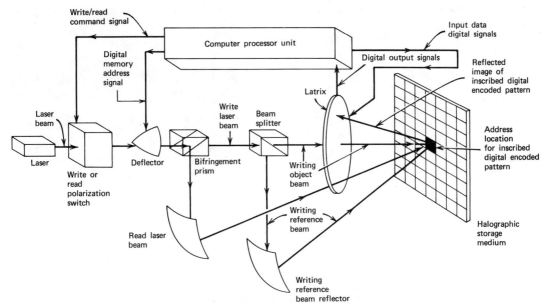

Figure 5–17. *The RCA optical memory system. (Reprinted with permission of Infosystems ®, copyright 1972, by Hitchcock Publishing Company, Wheaton, Ill. 60187.)*

veloped for the ILLIAC IV computer. Called the UNICON Laser Mass Memory System, this system provides the capability for permanently recording and retrieving on-line up to one trillion bits of digital data. Data is recorded on a photographic strip. A number of such strips are contained in a strip file or pack. When a strip is selected it is moved from the file to the surface of a rotating drum. A modulated laser beam is used to record data by vaporizing spots on the strip, corresponding to 1-bits. Each strip in the UNICON system can store the equivalent of 25 reels of magnetic tape, yet this costs about the same as one reel of tape. The entire strip file can hold about 25 of these strips, or the equivalent of 625 reels of tape. A disadvantage of the laser technique is that the recording is permanent, so the recording strip cannot be reused as with magnetic tape.

Halographic Memory. RCA has developed an experimental optical memory system that uses a halographic storage medium. This is a high-resolution photographic plate embedded in a heat sensitive plastic. When this plate is exposed to varying intensity laser light energy, a negative image of the varying light pattern called a "halogram" is etched on the plate. When the halogram negative is later exposed to a less intense laser light at a specified angle, the light energy reflected by the negative image is picked up by specially designed photosensors. The intensity variations are converted to digital signals which permits reading the recorded data. An important advantage of the halographic technique is that the halogram can be erased and the plate reused.

A conceptual diagram of the RCA halographic memory systems is shown in Figure 5–17. It is estimated that this system will be 1,000 times faster than modern disk systems.

95 / ADVANCED MEMORY SYSTEMS

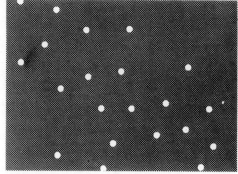

Figure 5–18. *Magnetic bubble memory technology (courtesy IBM).*

Magnetic Bubble Techniques

The second promising type of advanced high-speed memory uses magnetic bubble technology. "Magnetic bubbles" are simple microscopic spots or regions on a thin film that are magnetized in the opposite direction to that of the surrounding film (see Figure 5–18). Without an external magnetic field, areas of opposite magnetization in the film are approximately equal (left). When an increasing magnetic field is applied, the areas of opposite magnetization in the film shrink and form bubbles with a circular cross section of microscopic size (right).

In a bubble memory, the pressure of a bubble represents a binary "1" bit, while the absence of a bubble represents a "0" bit. Bubbles are created and erased by a conditioning magnetic field. Recording densities of from 10 million to one billion bits per square inch are predicted using this technique.

The feasibility of a bubble memory was demonstrated by Bell Labs in 1969. Bell Labs is continuing its development efforts using crystalline materials, while IBM is concentrating on noncrystalline (or amorphous) substances.

Evaluation of Secondary Storage Devices

A number of devices and media for auxiliary computer storage are discussed in this chapter. Selection of storage media for a given installation requires a careful evaluation of cost and performance factors. The more important of these factors are: (1) type of access, (2) access time, (3) capacity, and (4) cost.

Type of Access. All of the devices for secondary storage discussed in this chapter are direct access devices. Thus to locate a particular record, all that is needed is the address of the record; searching is not required. However in selecting storage media, sequential storage media such as punched cards and magnetic tape (considered external storage) must also be considered. The considerations in selecting direct access versus sequential storage are discussed in Chapter 10. In most installations, a combination of direct access devices (e.g., magnetic disk) and sequential access devices (e.g., magnetic tape) are used. This provides the flexibility needed for a typical mix of applications.

Access Time. Access time is defined as the time interval between a request for the transfer of data to or from a storage device and the completion of this operation. It is the sum of waiting time (if any) and transfer time:

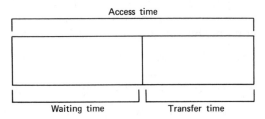

In devices with mechanical movement—magnetic tape, disk, drum, and strip storage—there is normally a delay or waiting time before data transfer may begin. For magnetic tape, the delay is the time required to accelerate the tape before reading or writing. Similarly, for magnetic strip storage there is a handling time in moving the magnetic strip under a read-write head.

In magnetic drum storage the drum must revolve until the desired storage location comes under the read-write head. The time required depends on the drum location when the read or write command is given, and so varies from one access to the next. For a magnetic disk unit, there are two sources of delay. If the moving-head principle is used, the access arm must first be moved in or out to the correct lateral position on the disk. The disk must then rotate until the desired location comes under the positioned read-write head. With the head-per-track approach the first source of delay is eliminated.

Transfer time is the time required for movement of data, once movement begins. Since the number of characters to be transferred varies, it is more meaningful to discuss transfer rates (characters per second). For devices with mechanical movement, transfer rate depends on recording density (characters per inch) and mechanical speed (inches per second for tape and revolutions per second for disk and drum).

QUESTION: Access time is the sum of _____ time (or delay) and _____ time. For devices with mechanical movement, transfer rate depends on mechanical _____ and recording _____.

ANSWER: waiting, transfer, speed, density

Magnetic core has negligible delay and very high transfer rates, and so is widely used for primary storage where very low access times are required. In terms of transfer rates, devices used for peripheral storage range from mass core (several million characters per second) to magnetic strip (less than 100,000 characters per second). Intermediate devices (in order of increasing transfer rates) are magnetic tape, disk, and drum.

Storage Capacity. Storage capacity is a primary consideration in selecting a computer system, and is very often the limiting factor when the data processing load exceeds the capacity of a system. In most third generation computers, both primary and secondary storage may be extended through the addition of storage modules. Keen competition in the computer industry is continually improving the performance and cost of storage devices and media.

Primary Storage. Capacity of primary storage is expressed in terms of the number of addressable storage locations. This capacity is often a multiple of 4096, which represents a 64×64 core array or module. Capacity is often expressed in terms of rounded thousands of positions, using the letter K to represent thousands. For example, 4,096 storage locations is referred to as a 4K memory, while a 65K memory most likely contains 65,536 (or $16 \times 4,096$) positions.

QUESTION: How many storage positions are contained in a 32K memory? _____.

ANSWER: there are $8 \times 4,096$ or 32,768.

Storage capacity is expressed as the number of addressable locations in primary storage. This capacity may range from 8K or 16K positions in a small computer to several million positions in a large-scale system.

The apparent capacity of primary storage is extremely large in some computers that use a concept called *virtual storage*. In virtual storage, the programmer is not limited to storage addresses corresponding to the range of actual storage capacity of main memory. For example, he may write a program requiring 100K storage positions and may execute this program in a virtual storage computer with only 32K actual positions of main memory. This is done by a combination of software and hardware in which the computer automatically segments the program into modules called *pages*. At any one time, only those pages that are actually being used are contained in primary storage; the remaining pages are stored on disk or other secondary storage. The computer swaps pages as they are required.

QUESTION: The apparent capacity of primary storage is greatly extended in a _____ _____ environment. In this technique, programs are segmented into _____.

ANSWER: Virtual storage, pages

Comparison of primary storage capacities for different computers may be somewhat complicated if different storage organizations or data representations are used. For example, an addressable storage location may range from a byte (8 bits) in a byte-addressable computer to a full word (up to 60 bits) in a fixed word length computer. When such differences exist, a comparison of memory sizes must be based on the effective number of characters that can be stored in the respective systems.

QUESTION: Suppose that an IBM System/370 and a CDC 6400 both have 65K (or 65,536 position) memories. Based on the previous discussion in this chapter, how many alphanumeric characters may be stored in each system? _____

ANSWER: IBM 370 stores 65,536 characters (one per byte). CDC 6400 stores a *maximum* of $10 \times 65,536$ characters (10 characters per 60-bit word). However, recall that in a fixed word length machine the *effective* storage capacity is less than the maximum due to unused bit positions within a word.

Most business-oriented computers use a variable word length or byte-addressable organization. In such computers, the effective storage capacity often depends on the type of data being stored. For example, in a byte-addressable computer alphanumeric data is stored one character per byte, while numeric data may be stored two characters per byte in packed-decimal format. In other computers, both numeric and alphanumeric data are stored in the same binary coded decimal format.

Secondary Storage. Capacity of secondary storage is most often expressed in terms of bytes (or characters). A wide range of storage capacities is generally available for a given computer through the addition of storage modules. A comparative indication of storage capacity for different devices is as follows.

Storage Device	Unit of Capacity (Bytes)
Mass core storage	Hundreds of thousands
Magnetic disk, drum	Millions
Magnetic strip, card	Hundreds of millions
Laser mass storage	Hundreds of billions

For devices with removable packs (such as magnetic disk or magnetic strip) the total storage capacity is virtually unlimited. However, only the packs that are on-line to the computer at a given time are considered part of secondary storage; the remainder by definition are part of external storage.

Cost. Technological advances and industry competition continue to result in improved performance and lower costs for storage media. Nevertheless, the selection of storage devices requires a trade-off between storage capacity, desired performance, and cost.

The cost of storage increases as capacity increases, and as access time is reduced. Thus the highest cost devices are those such as mass core storage, with very small access times. The lowest cost devices (per unit of capacity) are magnetic strip, card, or tape storage. Magnetic disk and drum are intermediate in cost and performance.

New memory systems such as magnetic bubble and optical storage are expected to have a dramatic impact on mass storage costs. The predicted unit cost (cents per bit) for disk systems and for bubble and optical memories is shown in Figure 5–19.

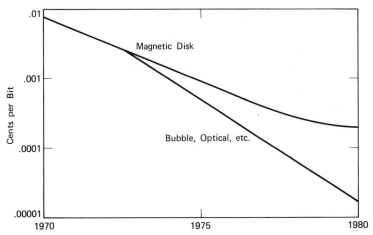

Figure 5–19. *A comparison of mass storage costs (reprinted with permission of Datamation ®, copyright 1972 by Technical Publishing Company, Greenwich, Connecticut 06830).*

99 / EVALUATION OF SECONDARY STORAGE DEVICES

Summary of Storage Devices

A summary of the characteristics of the most important storage devices is presented in Figure 5–20. Figure 5–20a shows the access time versus capacity (in bytes), while Figure 5–20b shows the cost (dollars per byte) versus capacity. A range of values is shown for each type of device. The term "mass storage systems" refers to new storage technology such as laser, optical, and magnetic bubble memories.

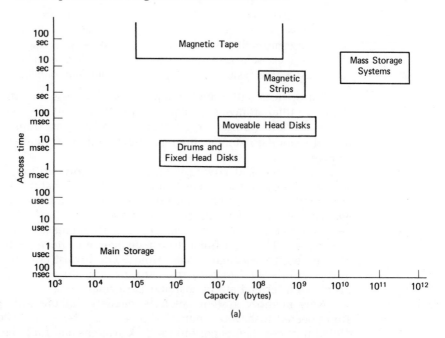

(a)

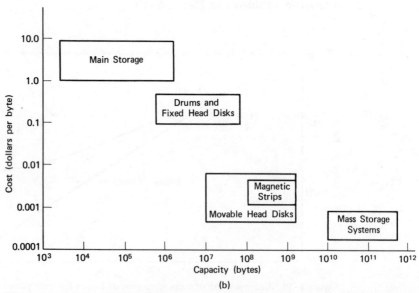

(b)

Figure 5–20. *A comparison of storage systems (reprinted with permission of* Datamation ®, *copyright 1973 by Technical Publishing Company, Greenwich, Connecticut 06830).*

Exercise 5-3

The following questions refer to Figure 5–20.

1. Rank the devices shown in the figure according to storage capacity (smallest to largest).

   (a) _____

   (b) _____

   (c) _____

   (d) _____

   (e) _____

   (f) _____

2. Rank the devices shown in the figure according to access time (smallest to largest).

   (a) _____

   (b) _____

   (c) _____

   (d) _____

   (e) _____

   (f) _____

3. Rank the devices shown in the figure according to cost, smallest to largest (notice the cost of magnetic tape is not shown in Figure 5–20, since it varies greatly between installations).

   (a) _____

   (b) _____

   (c) _____

   (d) _____

   (e) _____

Summary

The important concepts of information storage and retrieval have been discussed in this chapter. Computer storage may be classified as primary, secondary (or auxiliary), and external storage. Primary and secondary storage are on-line to the computer. Data is stored in primary storage either in fixed words or as variable length words. Many third generation computers store data either way.

Figure 5–21 summarizes the organization of primary and secondary storage, showing the devices most frequently used.

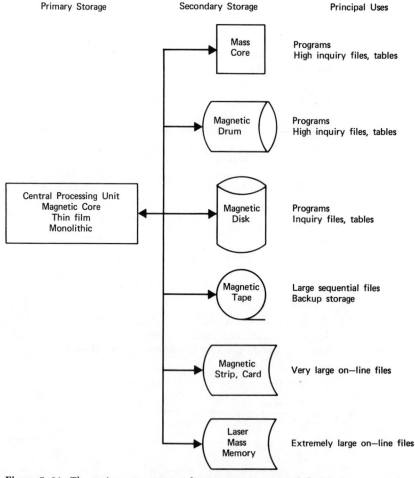

Figure 5–21. *The major components of computer storage and their uses.*

Solutions to Exercises

Exercise 5-1

1. (b) Magnetic disk or drum.
  (c) Punched cards, magnetic tape.
  (a) Magnetic core.

Exercise 5-2

1.

	Fixed Word Length	Variable Word Length
(a) Length of word	fixed	variable (or both)
(b) Type of operations	parallel	serial
(c) Use of registers	addressable	nonaddressable
(d) Computational speed	relatively fast	relatively slow
(e) Storage efficiency	relatively low	relatively high
(f) Content of storage location	word	byte

2. (a) Primary—used for storing programs currently being executed by the computer, plus data immediately being processed.
  (b) Secondary—used to store mass data files, plus programs not currently being executed.
  (c) External—storage of mass data with low-speed access requirements.

3. $2^5 - 1$, or $+31$.

4. (a) 00100101.
  (b) 001101111100.

Exercise 5-3

1. (a) Main storage.
  (b) Drums and fixed head disks.
  (c) Magnetic tape.
  (d) Moveable head disks.
  (e) Magnetic strips.
  (f) Mass storage systems.

2. (a) Main storage.
  (b) Drums and fixed head disks.
  (c) Moveable head disks.
  (d) Magnetic strips.
  (e) Mass storage systems.
  (f) Magnetic tape.

3. (a) Mass storage systems.
   (b) Moveable head disks.
   (c) Magnetic strips.
   (d) Drums and fixed head disks.
   (e) Main storage.

Chapter Examination

1. Distinguish between the following types of storage, giving the purpose of each and the major types of devices or media used:

   (a) Primary _____

   (b) Secondary _____

   (c) External _____

2. Match the following terms to the most appropriate definitions:

   ____ Monolithic storage   (a) consists of waiting time plus transfer time

   ____ Register   (b) mass storage for programs and data files

   ____ Byte-addressable   (c) unit of storage capacity on magnetic disk

   ____ Access time   (d) each character bit-set is addressable

   ____ Sector   (e) an addressable set of bit positions in storage

   ____ Storage location   (f) set of tracks under read-write heads at any time

   ____ Auxiliary storage   (g) integrated semiconductor circuits

   ____ Cylinder   (h) device for temporary storage of data or instructions

3. Show how the signed decimal number +37 would be represented:

   (a) In a 16-bit computer word: _____

   (b) In packed decimal (variable word); _____

4. What type of auxiliary storage device (or medium) would be most appropriate in each of the following situations?
   (a) An inventory file containing 10 million bytes of data, with on-line processing and inquiry required. _____

   (b) Storage for program segments to be transferred to and from primary storage. Up to 300 thousand positions, very high access rates required. _____

(c) An inventory file containing 500 million bytes of data, to be processed on-line. Each inventory item is referenced infrequently, so that fast access rates are not important. _____

_____

(d) A very large sequential inventory file, to be processed once each day. _____

(e) A very large file of names and addresses, to be used for preparing mailing labels. Up to five billion characters of on-line data are required. _____

5. Rank the following devices in terms of (1) access waiting time, (2) transfer rate, (3) storage capacity.

	Waiting Time	Transfer Rate	Storage Capacity
(a) Magnetic disk	_____	_____	_____
(b) Mass core	_____	_____	_____
(c) Magnetic drum	_____	_____	_____
(d) Magnetic strip or card	_____	_____	_____

6. Briefly describe two major approaches in advanced memory system design.

(a) _____

_____

(b) _____

_____

7. Identify the following statements as true or false:

____ (a) Monolithic storage (large scale integrated circuitry) is widely used for secondary storage.
____ (b) Programs currently being executed and data being processed are contained in primary storage.
____ (c) Large-scale integrated memories are faster, cheaper, and more compact than magnetic core memories.
____ (d) Primary storage is divided into small addressable areas called sectors.
____ (e) A storage address references a character (or byte) in a variable word length computer while in a fixed word length computer each address references a full word.

105 / CHAPTER EXAMINATION

_____ (f) A cylinder refers to a circular section on a magnetic drum unit.

_____ (g) Magnetic strip storage provides low cost, high capacity storage with relatively high access times.

_____ (h) The time interval between a request for transfer of data and completion of the transfer is referred to as waiting time.

_____ (i) Mass storage devices in the future are likely to be based on magnetic bubble and optical techniques.

_____ (j) Mass core storage is the most common form of secondary storage at the present time.

8. Give four advantages of large-scale integrated circuits over magnetic core storage:

(a) _____

(b) _____

(c) _____

(d) _____

9. Describe the main advantage of each of the following:

(a) Fixed word length organization _____

(b) Variable word length organization _____

_____

10. Define each of the following terms:

(a) Sequential access _____

_____

(b) Direct access _____

_____

(c) Head-per-track _____

_____

(d) Moving head _____

_____

(e) Sector _____

_____

(f) Cylinder _____

11. List the principal advantages of each of the following types of secondary storage:

(a) Magnetic disk _____

(b) Magnetic drum _____

(c) Mass core _____

(d) Magnetic strip _____

12. Explain briefly the principle used in each of the following advanced memory systems:

(a) Photodigital storage _____

(b) Halographic memory _____

(c) Magnetic bubble memory _____

13. Explain the concept of virtual storage _____

14. Minicomputers often use a fixed word length organization with 16 bits per word. What is the largest signed number that can be represented in such a machine? _____

_____

15. Describe the differences between and principal uses of each of the following magnetic disk systems:

(a) Fixed head, fixed disks _____

_____

_____

(b) Moving head, removable disk packs _____

_____

_____

Chapter 6

INSTRUCTING THE COMPUTER

Overview

The preceding chapters describe the basic organization and hardware concepts of a computer system. Before the computer can be used for a specific application, a set of instructions called a program must be prepared. A program is an explicit set of steps or instructions that directs the computer and coordinates the operation of the various hardware components. The concept of a stored program is fundamental in data processing. Once processing has begun, no human intervention is required unless an exceptional condition is encountered.

Preparation of a computer program is actually the last step in a problem-solving procedure that includes system analysis and design and program planning. These steps are described in later chapters. Actual preparation of the computer instructions is called programming or coding. After the program is coded it must be tested and "debugged" to remove all errors.

A program is stored in a computer in a binary representation called machine language. Each computer has a repertoire of machine language instructions based on its circuitry and design. The instructions of one computer will therefore not work on a different computer, although the basic formats are similar.

Computer instructions consist of an operation code that specifies the operation to be performed, plus one or more operand addresses. Fixed word length computers generally have a one-address instruction format that is used in conjunction with addressable registers. Variable word length computers follow a two-address format that permits storage to storage operations. Many third generation computers permit both types of instructions to be used.

Computer Instructions

A computer is controlled primarily by instructions stored in the machine. Each instruction causes a specific operation to be performed and, in total, execution of the program will produce a desired result. The instructions are prepared (or coded) by a programmer who enters them on a coding sheet. When the program is completed, the instructions are generally punched into cards, and are loaded into the computer prior to execution.

A computer instruction consists of two basic parts. The first part is an operation code (or "op code") which tells the computer *what* operation to perform. Typical operations include add, multiply, compare, and read. The second part of an instruction is the operand, which tells the computer *where* to find or store the data to be processed, or the location of the next instruction. An operand is actually the address of a storage location where the desired data or instruction is found. Some instructions may have more than one operand, depending on the computer.

QUESTION: The two basic parts of a computer instruction are an _____ _____ and one or more _____.

ANSWER: operation code, operands

Most third generation computers have a number of addressable registers that may be referenced by the programmer. For example, the IBM System/370 has 16 general purpose registers that may be used in a variety of ways. A typical instruction might contain two operands, one of which addresses a register while the second addresses a storage location. Thus the format would appear as follows.

Operation Code	Operand 1 (register)	Operand 2 (storage address)

The use of computer instructions may be illustrated by a simple example. Suppose that an inventory balance is stored at computer address 632. A quantity representing issues against the balance is stored at address 438. It is desired to write a set of computer instructions to subtract issues from the present balance and to store the result (the new balance) at address 9A7 (the addresses 632, 438, and 9A7 are hexadecimal). The result of the subtraction will be developed in general register 2, which functions as an accumulator for this calculation.

A set of computer instructions for this calculation (based on the IBM 370 instruction code) is shown in Figure 6–1. The first two digits of the operation code in each instruction specify the operation, while the third digit specifies the register number and is actually the first operand. For example, in the subtract instruction 5B2 438, 5B is the operation code, 2 the first operand, and 438 the second operand.

Instruction		
Op Code	Operand	Explanation
582	632	Load the contents of location 632 into the accumulator.
5B2	438	Subtract the contents of location 438 from the accumulator.
502	9A7	Store the results at location 9A7.

Figure 6–1. *Computer instructions for inventory calculation.*

QUESTION: Suppose a quantity representing inventory receipts (to be added to beginning inventory) is stored at location C81. If the operation code for "add" is 5A, what instruction should be included in Figure 6–1 to complete the calculation of the inventory balance? _____

ANSWER: 5A2 C81. If this instruction is inserted after the "load" instruction, it will cause receipts to be added to the old inventory balance.

The effect of executing the instructions in Figure 6–1 is as follows. Suppose at the beginning of the calculations, the inventory balance is 864 and the quantity issued is 138. Then the initial contents of storage positions 632 and 438 (shown in decimal rather than the actual binary representation) are as follows:

632	864	438	138

After the first instruction is executed, the inventory balance is loaded into register 2 (R2):

632	864	438	138	R2	864

The second instruction subtracts issues (location 438) from the contents of register 2, with 726 the resulting balance:

632	864	438	138	R2	726

The last instruction stores the new balance from register 2 into location 9A7:

632	864	438	138	R2	726	9A7	726

QUESTION: What is the function of register 2 (R2) in the above sequence of instructions? What are its contents after storing the result in location 9A7?

_____

_____

_____

ANSWER: Register 2 serves as an accumulator, to hold the result of the subtraction. Its contents (726) are unchanged by the store operation.

Each computer has a repertoire of machine language instructions based on its circuitry and design. Instructions are stored as binary digits (series of 0's and 1's) in computer storage. Generally the instructions are placed in sequential storage locations. Instructions are executed in sequential order unless the sequence is altered by a *branch* instruction that transfers control to another location.

Data to be processed by the stored program is also stored in memory as binary digits. The only distinction between instructions and data words is in the way they are used by the computer. If through program error a data word is retrieved from memory when an instruction word was intended, the computer will attempt to decode and execute the word as an instruction. Conversely, an instruction word may be treated as data and may be altered by other processing instructions. The ability of a program to modify itself through instructions written by the programmer is called program modification.

QUESTION: Deliberate modification of a computer instruction by other instructions in the program is called_____.
ANSWER: program modification.

Instruction Formats

A computer instruction may contain one or more operands, depending on the computer design. In the simple inventory calculation of Figure 6–1, each instruction contains two operands: a register number, and a storage address. These instructions are referred to as single-address (or one-address) formats, since only one storage location is referenced for each instruction. To perform a basic arithmetic operation such as add, three instructions are required: load, add, and store.

Some computers use two-address and even three-address formats. With these formats, fewer instructions are required to perform a given processing step. For example, Figure 6–2 shows the inventory calculation in single- (or one-) address, two-address, and three-address formats.

QUESTION: Examine Figure 6–2. Recall that storage location 632 contains the old inventory balance. What can be said about the contents of location 632 after executing the instructions in Figure 62A, 6–2B, and 6–2C.
ANSWER: The contents of 632 (old inventory balance) are unchanged after executing the single and three-address instructions, but are lost after executing the two-address instruction of Figure 6-2B.

A. Single-Address Format

Function	Op Code	Operand	Explanation
Load	582	632	Three steps are required to perform an arithmetic
Subtract	5B2	438	operation. The contents of 438 are subtracted
Store	502	9A7	from 632 and the result is stored at 9A7 (see Figure 6–1).

B. Two-Address Format

Function	Op Code	First Operand	Second Operand	Explanation
Subtract	5B0	632	438	The contents of 438 are subtracted from 632. The result is stored in location 632 (previous contents are lost).

C. Three-Address Format

Function	Op Code	First Operand	Second Operand	Third Operand	Explanation
Subtract	5B0	632	438	9A7	The contents of 438 are subtracted from 632. Result is stored in 9A7.

Figure 6–2. A comparison of single-, two-, and three-address instruction formats.

If the contents of the first operand in a two-address arithmetic instruction (such as Figure 6–2B) are to be saved, they must be moved to another location before the arithmetic instruction is executed. For example, the old inventory balance (contents of location 632) could be moved to location F3C before the subtract instruction is executed. After execution the new balance is stored in location 632, while the old balance appears at address F3C.

The single-address format is generally used in fixed word length computers. Although only one storage address is specified, these instructions often have provision for specifying one or more addressable registers to be used in the operation. For example in Figure 6–2A in each of the instructions, the third digit of the operation code specifies general register 2 to be used as an accumulator register.

Two-address (and sometimes three-address) formats are often used in variable word length computers. Although fewer instructions are required for a given processing step, the execution time is also longer than for single-address instructions.

QUESTION: Fixed word length computers generally use_____-address instructions while variable word length computers often employ _____-address instructions.

ANSWER: single, two (or three)

The instruction repertoire of large, general purpose computers such as the IBM/370 often employ several different instruction formats. For example, it is possible to reference one, two or even three addressable registers in addition to a storage location in some instructions. The various instructions may provide for a variety of operations such as register-to-register, register-to-storage with and without indexing, storage-to-storage, and others. The more important types of processing instructions are discussed later in this chapter.

Coding the Instructions

As is described above, instructions are stored in the computer as binary digits. For example, in Figure 6–1 the subtract instruction 5B2 438 is used. This instruction is in hexadecimal notation. If the instruction is stored in a 32-bit computer word, it will appear as follows in the computer:

Op Code (5B2)	Unused	Operand (438)

```
0 1 0 1 1 0 1 1 0 0 1 0 0 0 0 0 0 0 0 0 0 1 0 0 0 0 1 1 1 0 0 0
```

Bit Positions 0   4   8   12   16   20   24   28 31

In the above instruction, each hexadecimal digit is stored as its four-bit binary equivalent. For example, hexadecimal B is equivalent to binary 1011 (the hexadecimal number system was described in Chapter 4). The unused bit positions are reserved for referencing addressable registers in other instructions.

QUESTION: Show how the store instruction 502 9A7 would appear in the computer:

Bit   0   4   8   12   16   20   24   28   31
Positions

ANSWER: 01010000001000000000100110100111

It would be possible (but not very practical) for the programmer to code his instructions as binary digits, exactly as they are to appear in the computer. Instead, the machine language programmer uses the equivalent hexadecimal notation, such as the instructions in Figures 6–1 and 6–2. (In some computers, octal notation is used.)

Coding instructions in the language of the computer (using binary-based notation) is referred to as machine language programming. There are a number of disadvantages to machine language programming — it is slow, tedious, and conducive to error. As a result, this method is seldom used. Instead, programs are generally coded in a language more meaningful to humans and then are translated into machine language by the computer itself. These languages may be classified as symbolic (or assembly) languages and "higher-order" languages. To illustrate the advantage of these languages, Figure 6–3 shows the inventory problem of Figure 6–1 in machine language, assembly language, and in COBOL (a high-order language described in Chapter 14).

QUESTION: Study Figure 6–3 and answer the following:
1. Compare the number of machine and assembly language instructions.

---

2. Compare the machine and assembly language operation codes.

---

3. Compare the machine and assembly language operands.

---

4. Which language in Figure 6–3 is easiest for a programmer to code and read? _____

ANSWER: 1. The same. There is one assembly language instruction for each machine language instruction. 2. Machine language operation codes are hexadecimal, assembly language are indicative letters (called mnemonics). 3. Machine language operands are storage addresses, assembly language are data names (also called symbolic addresses). 4. COBOL.

Machine Language	Assembly Language	Explanation
582 632	L 2, OLDBAL	Load balance into accumulator (general register 2)
5B2 438	S 2, ISSUES	Subtract issues giving new balance
502 9A7	ST2, NEWBAL	Store new balance
COBOL: SUBTRACT ISSUES FROM OLD-BALANCE GIVING NEW-BALANCE		

Figure 6–3. *A comparison of instructions for inventory calculation.*

Exercise 6–1

1. For an accounts receivable calculation, data is stored in the computer as follows:

Data Item	Location
Old balance	C69
Payments	5F4
Charges	12A

The new balance is to be computed by subtracting payments and adding charges to the old balance. The new balance is to be stored at location 4E8. Register 3 is to be used as the accumulator.

Using instructions described above, write computer instructions to perform the accounts receivable calculation in (a) machine language, and (b) assembly language (the instruction code for "add" is 5A in machine language, and A in assembly language).

2. Show how the computer instruction 5B2 5F4 is stored in a 32-bit word:

Bit   0   4   8   12   16   20   24   28   31
Positions

3. Describe the advantages of assembly language over absolute machine language. _____

Executing the Instructions

In the preceding sections a simple inventory problem was described, in which a new balance was developed in an accumulator register. Several important hardware components are used by the computer in executing instructions: (1) registers, (2) adder, and (3) instruction counter.

Registers. A register is a storage device capable of receiving, storing, and transmitting data. Registers are often used as temporary storage devices,

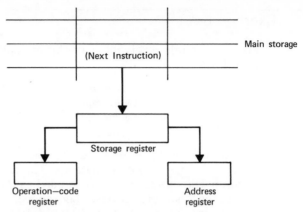

Figure 6–4. *The use of registers in executing instructions.*

holding information during the execution of a single instruction. Registers may be classified as general purpose and special purpose. General-purpose registers are usually addressable (may be referenced by the programmer), while special-purpose registers are not addressable.

QUESTION: Two types of registers are ——————————— purpose which are ——————————— and ——————————— purpose which are not ———————————.

ANSWER: general, addressable, special, addressable

The more important special-purpose registers in a typical computer are: (1) storage register, (2) address register, (3) operation-code register, and (4) accumulator.

A *storage register* is used to hold temporarily either a data word or an instruction word that is being transferred to or from main storage. An *operation-code register* holds the operation code of the instruction code currently being executed, while an *address register* holds the address of the current operand. These three registers are used together during the execution of an instruction, as is shown in Figure 6–4. The next instruction is fetched from main storage, and is transferred to the storage register. The operation code is then routed to the operation-code register and the operand (address portion) to the address register, as is shown in Figure 6–4.

QUESTION: Examine Figure 6–4. One of the instructions in the inventory calculation was the subtract instruction 5B2 438. Show the content of the storage, operation-code, and address registers as this instruction is being executed. ——————————————————————————

ANSWER: Storage register 5B2 438; operation-code 5B2; address register 438

An *accumulator* is a register that is used to accumulate the results of arithmetic operations. In some computers the accumulator is a special-purpose register whose use is implied in the operation code of an instruction. In other computers, several addressable general-purpose registers may be used as accumulators. For example, in the subtract instruction

5B2 438 the digit 2 in the operation code specifies general register 2 as the accumulator.

General-purpose (or general) registers may be used to perform a variety of functions in a program. The programmer specifies a register number as part of an instruction and the function the register is to perform depends on the type of instruction. Some uses of general registers will be discussed in subsequent sections.

Adder. An adder is a set of logical circuitry that receives data from two sources, performs addition, and stores the result. In a single-address computer, one operand is generally in an accumulator, while the second operand is in main storage. The result of the addition is then stored in the accumulator, replacing the first operand.

In Chapter 4 it was stated that subtraction is accomplished in a computer by complementing the subtrahend and then adding. Also, multiplication and division operations are accomplished as a series of additions and subtractions. Therefore, the adder is used for all arithmetic operations in the computer.

Instruction Counter. The instruction counter is a special-purpose register that contains the address of the next instruction to be executed. At the beginning of the program it is loaded with the storage address of the first program instruction. As each instruction is executed, the instruction counter is automatically set to the address of the next instruction to be executed. This may be the next sequential location or, if a branch instruction occurs, some other program location.

QUESTION: The address of the next instruction is contained in the

_____ .

ANSWER: instruction counter

Machine Cycles. The length of time required to execute an instruction depends on the computer and the type of instruction. For each computer there is a fundamental unit of time called the machine cycle (or cycle time). A machine cycle is the length of time required to perform a specific function, such as retrieving and interpreting an instruction.

Computational speeds have increased dramatically in modern computers. The best measure of computational speed is the machine cycle. In early (first generation) computers, cycle times were expressed in milliseconds (thousands of a second). In second generation computers the cycle time was reduced by a factor of about one thousand, and cycle times were expressed in microseconds (millionths of a second). In modern (third generation) computers, these times have again been reduced by a factor of nearly one thousand to nanoseconds (billions of a second).

QUESTION: The fundamental unit of operational time in a computer is called a _____ _____ . In third generation computers this time is expressed in _____ seconds.

ANSWER: machine cycle, nano

The number of machine cycles required to execute an instruction depends on the type of instruction. For example, a "multiply" takes longer to execute than an "add" instruction. To execute an instruction, the computer must complete two operational phases, called *instruction time* and *execution time*. During instruction time (or I-time) the computer

IBM System/360 Assembler Coding Form

PROGRAM *INVENTORY CALCULATION*								PUNCHING INSTRUCTIONS	GRAPHIC							PAGE
PROGRAMMER *FRM*					DATE *1 - 16*					PUNCH							CARD EL
STATEMENT																	

Name		Operation			Operand									Comments			
1	8	10	14	16	20	25	30	35	40	45	50	55	60	65	71		
* COMPUTE	NEW	INVENTORY BALANCE GIVEN OLD BALANCE AND ISSUES															
	L	2,OLDBAL			LOAD OLDBAL INTO REGISTER 2												
	S	2,ISSUES			SUBTRACT ISSUES FROM REGISTER 2												
	ST	2,NEWBAL			STORE NEWBAL												

Figure 6–5. *The IBM assembler coding form.*

moves the instruction from main memory to the storage register. The operation code is routed to the operation-code register, and the address portion is routed to the address register (as is shown above in Figure 6–4). Decoding circuitry interprets the operation code and sets up circuit paths to perform the instruction. The I-time generally requires one machine cycle.

During execution time (or E-time) the computer actually executes the instruction, under direction of the operation code. For example, an operand may be moved from storage to an accumulator, two operands may be added together, and so on. Several machine cycles are often required for execution time, depending on the instruction.

QUESTION: The two phases in executing an instruction are called _____ time and _____ time.
ANSWER: instruction, execution

Microprogram. A machine-language instruction (such as "add") causes a single functional step to be performed. Each such instruction is actually a composite of a number of still more elementary steps, called microinstructions. Each microinstruction is coded as several bits, one bit for each functional unit or data path in the computer hardware. The program that transforms each machine-language instruction into a series of microinstructions is called a microprogram.

Most present generation computers (including minicomputers) use use some form of microprogramming. In some computers, the microprogram is fixed and is not accessible to the user. In other computers the microprograms can be altered through special input operations; this permits greater programming flexibility and speed of operation.

Types of Instructions

In the remainder of this chapter, the major types of computer instructions used in data processing are described. Since it is widely used, IBM System/370 assembly language is employed to illustrate the various instructions. However, other languages have similar features and are similar in format. Both fixed and variable word length instructions are illustrated.

The programmer enters assembly language instructions on an assembler coding form. The IBM assembler coding form is shown in Figure 6–5. This form provides space for entering the operation code, operands, and comments that are helpful in explaining program steps (comments have no effect on the program). The coding form also provides a name field (columns 1–8) where names (or labels) can be inserted. These names identify instructions or data, and are explained in subsequent sections.

The assembly language instructions for the inventory problem (from Figure 6–3) are entered on the coding form. The first entry on the form is a comment statement. Such a comment statement is identified by an asterisk in column 1, and may be used at any point in a program to improve documentation.

Move Instructions

It is frequently necessary in data processing to move or transfer data from one location in storage to another storage location. For example, when data is read into the computer, it is stored in an input area. If the data is to be retained, it must be moved to another area (such as working storage) or the data will be destroyed by subsequent read operations. Similarly, data to be transmitted to an output device must generally be moved to an output area. Move instructions are sometimes used in conjunction with arithmetic operations, either to load operands into registers or to store results.

In a move instruction, the contents of one location (called the sending location) are copied into a second location (called the receiving location). After the move the contents of the sending location replace the contents of the receiving location, while the contents of the sending location remain unchanged. The following example illustrates the move operation:

	Sending Location	Receiving Location
Before move instruction	687593	2103059
After move instruction	687593	687593

QUESTION: In a move instruction, do the contents of the receiving location before the instruction affect the contents after the instruction?

_____.

ANSWER: No. The previous contents are erased

In fixed word length operations, move instructions use addressable registers. To move a data word from one storage location to another, two instructions are required. The first instruction loads the contents of the sending location into a register; the second stores the register contents into the receiving location. Thus the register is used as an intermediate storage device, as is shown:

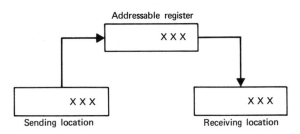

To illustrate, suppose that a quantity representing the unit price of an item is stored at a word location called PRICE in an input area. The following instructions will move the contents of the location PRICE to an output word location called PRICEOUT, using general register 4.

Name	Operation	Operand	Comments
	L	4,PRICE	
	ST	4,PRICEOUT	

QUESTION: Suppose the contents of PRICE, PRICEOUT, and register 4 before the above instructions are executed are as follows:

	PRICE	Register 4	PRICEOUT
Before execution:	1570	10038	68931

Show in the space provided the contents of these locations after the instructions are executed.

After execution: [ ] [ ] [ ]

ANSWER: 1570 in all three locations.

In variable word length operations, storage-to-storage move instructions are generally used. Such instructions specify as operands the sending and receiving storage locations, and (optionally) the number of characters to be moved. For example, suppose that data representing employee name is stored in a location called NAME. It is desired to move this data (which is 20 characters long) to a second location called NAMEOUT. This can be accomplished with a single machine instruction called move characters (MVC) as follows:

PROGRAM				PUNCHING INSTRUCTIONS	GRAPHIC				
PROGRAMMER			DATE		PUNCH				

STATEMENT

Name	Operation	Operand	Comments
	MVC	NAMEOUT(20),NAME	

In this instruction, the data in the location specified by the first operand (NAMEOUT) is replaced by the contents of the location specified by the second operand (NAME). The number of characters actually moved is specified in parentheses following the first operand (20 in this example). If the second operand were actually longer (say 25 characters), only the first 20 characters would be moved. If it were shorter (say 15 characters), five additional characters from adjacent memory positions would be moved into the field NAMEOUT. Thus it is important to specify the correct number of characters to be moved in a variable word length instruction.

Exercise 6–2

1. Write assembly language fixed word instructions to move a quantity called SALES to a location named TOTAL. Use general register 7.

2. Write an assembly language instruction to move the contents of an operand called PARTNUM to a location called ID. The field called ID is six characters long.

3. Consecutive storage positions (bytes) are reserved for two quantities, as follows:

Name	Number of Positions	*(hexadecimal)* Addresses
PARTNUMB	6	100–105
PARTNAME	8	106–10D

The current contents of these areas are as follows:

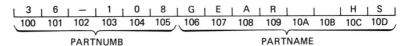

Describe the contents of a location called ID after each of the following instructions:

(a) MVC ID(6), PARTNUMB _____

(b) MVC ID(8), PARTNUMB _____

(c) MVC ID(4), PARTNUMB _____

Arithmetic Instructions

Most computer programs require a combination of addition, subtraction, multiplication, and division. As we stated previously in this chapter, all of these arithmetic operations are performed as additions by the computer, using a logical unit called the adder. However, nearly every computer has separate instructions for each of the four operations.

In some computers, arithmetic operations are performed using fixed word length instructions, in conjunction with addressable registers. One operand is loaded in a register, while the second operand is in a storage location. The result is developed in the addressable register, and then may be stored in memory. For example, the inventory calculations in Figure 6–1 were performed by using fixed word length instructions.

In business data processing it is frequently more convenient (where possible) to perform calculations using variable word length instructions.

PROGRAM										PUNCHING	GRAPHIC						PAGE	
PROGRAMMER						DATE				INSTRUCTIONS	PUNCH						CARD EL	

STATEMENT

Name		Operation				Operand								Comments				
		A P		B A L A N C E (3) , P U R C H A S E S (3)				A D D P U R C H A S E S T O B A L A N C E										
		S P		B A L A N C E (3) , P A Y M E N T S (3)				S U B T R A C T P A Y M E N T S F R O M B A L A N C E										

Figure 6–6. *Instructions for accounts payable calculation.*

There are two principal reasons for this. First, input data may be of various lengths; therefore, it is desirable to operate on variable length data rather than fixed words. Second, numerical data input into the computer is generally stored in coded decimal form, as is discussed in Chapter 4. Fixed word length arithmetic requires that the data be converted from decimal to binary before the arithmetic is performed. Since variable word length instructions use decimal data, this conversion is not necessary.

QUESTION: In business data processing, _____ word length arithmetic (using data in _____ format) is often preferable to _____ word length arithmetic.

ANSWER: Variable, decimal, fixed

In variable word length arithmetic, decimal digits are operated on serially (one digit at a time). Such operations are slower than fixed word length arithmetic. However, coding is simplified, since conversion operations are unnecessary. Since there are relatively few complex calculations in business data processing, it is generally preferable to sacrifice computational speed to eliminate data conversion. An exception might be detailed statistical calculations or management science applications, where fixed word length operations might be preferred.

Add Decimal (AP) and Subtract Decimal (SP) are variable word length arithmetic instructions. The "P" stands for packed—recall that for arithmetic operations, numeric data must be in packed decimal form. These instructions cause the contents of the second operand location to be added to (or subtracted from) the contents of the first operand location. The previous contents of the first operand location are lost, unless they are first moved to another location. The length of each operand (in bytes) may be specified in the instruction. Since the data is in packed decimal, each byte contains two decimal digits (or one digit and a sign).

To illustrate, suppose that an accounts payable balance is stored in a field called BALANCE. A quantity representing recent purchases (to be added to the accounts payable balance) is stored in a field called PURCHASES, and a second quantity representing payments (to be subtracted from accounts payable balance) is stored in a field called PAYMENTS. Each of the fields is three bytes in length. Figure 6–6 shows the assembly language instructions for this calculation.

QUESTION: Before the above calculations are performed suppose that the contents of the storage locations designated by the operands are as follows:

Location Name	Contents Before	Contents After
BALANCE	14387+	_____
PURCHASES	2168+	_____
PAYMENTS	10000+	_____

In the space provided, show the contents after the calculations are completed.

ANSWER: BALANCE 6555+, PURCHASES 2168+, PAYMENTS 10000+ (*Note:* In packed decimal, the sign of the number appears in the rightmost position. A plus sign is actually represented as hexadecimal C in the computer).

The length of each operand (three bytes) is specified in each of the arithmetic instructions in Figure 6–6. When two quantities (such as BALANCE and PURCHASES) are added, the result may be one digit longer than either of the two quantities because of a carry into the high-order position. Since the sum is contained in the first operand location of an AP instruction, the programmer should define this operand to be at least one byte longer than any quantity he expects to be stored in either operand location.

To illustrate, both BALANCE and PURCHASES have been defined to be three bytes long in Figure 6–6. Before the instructions are executed, the contents of these locations might be as follows:

BALANCE	98347+	(3 bytes)
PURCHASES	04216+	(3 bytes)
SUM	102563+	(3½ bytes)

When the instruction AP BALANCE(3), PURCHASES(3) is executed the resulting sum (102563+) is too long for the defined length of BALANCE (three bytes). This results in an error condition called an *arithmetic overflow*. When this condition occurs, core is generally dumped (contents printed), and processing is terminated.

To avoid an overflow condition in the above example, the operand BALANCE should be specified as four bytes long. Assuming the quantities stored at BALANCE and PURCHASES will never exceed three bytes, this will prevent an overflow condition when the quantities are added.

Multiply Decimal (MP) and Divide Decimal (DP) are also IBM 370 variable word length instructions. The MP instruction causes the quantity identified by the first operand to be multiplied by the quantity identified by the second operand. The result (product) is stored in the first operand field. For example, the following assembly language instruction multiplies QUANTITY by RATE:

PROGRAM						PUNCHING INSTRUCTIONS	GRAPHIC			
PROGRAMMER			DATE				PUNCH			

STATEMENT

Name		Operation			Operand							Comments	
1	8	10	14	16	20	25	30	35	40	45	50	55	60
		MP		QUANTITY(8), RATE(4)									

The number of bytes is specified with each operand. The length of the product field (QUANTITY in this example) must equal or exceed the *sum* of the lengths of the two operands. If this operand is not long enough to contain the result, an arithmetic overflow will occur.

Similarly, the Divide Decimal (DP) instruction divides the first operand quantity by the second operand quantity. The result (quotient) *and* remainder are both stored at the location specified by the first operand. For example, the following assembly language instruction divides COST by DAYS:

PROGRAM								PUNCHING	GRAPHIC				
PROGRAMMER					DATE			INSTRUCTIONS	PUNCH				

STATEMENT

Name	Operation	Operand					Comments
	DP	COST (10) , DAYS (2)					

In this example, the quotient and remainder are stored in the location labeled COST. In both the MP and DP instructions, the original contents of the first operand are lost unless they are first moved to another location.

Exercise 6–3

1. Write assembly language decimal instructions for each of the following:
   (a) Add a quantity called GROSS to a quantity called YTD. The quantity YTD requires four bytes, while GROSS requires three bytes. (Be careful to avoid overflow!)

   (b) Multiply a quantity called HOURS (two bytes) by a quantity called RATE (three bytes).

   (c) Subtract a quantity called DEDUCT (two bytes) from a quantity called GROSS (three bytes).

2. Suppose the following locations contain the quantities shown:

Location Name	Contents
YTD	98735+
GROSS	14324+
HOURS	032+
RATE	004+

Specify the contents of the first operand in each of the following instructions after the instruction is executed:

(a) AP YTD(4), GROSS(3) _____

(b) AP YTD(3), GROSS(3) _____

(c) MP HOURS(2), RATE(2) _____

(d) MP HOURS(4), RATE(2) _____

Defining Constants

Thus far it has been assumed that numbers to be manipulated were already present in computer memory. There are two ways to place numbers in memory: read them in from input devices, or define them as constants in the program. Techniques for reading data will be discussed in the next chapter.

Define Constant (DC) is an assembly language statement that assigns a symbolic name to a storage location and places a constant at that location. Following is an example:

PROGRAM								PUNCHING	GRAPHIC				
PROGRAMMER					DATE			INSTRUCTIONS	PUNCH				

STATEMENT

Name		Operation			Operand							Comments	
MAX		DC		F'2468'									

The above assembly language instruction defines a constant called MAX, which will occupy a full word (designated F). The value 2468 (enclosed within apostrophes) is inserted into this storage location. At any point in the program, the programmer may use MAX as an operand to refer to this constant.

QUESTION: Suppose that the following instruction is now executed:

L 4, MAX

What are the resulting contents of register 4? _____
ANSWER: The contents are 2468 (in binary notation).

When the F designator is used, constants are stored as binary numbers in full words. Variable length decimal constants may also be defined with the DC statement. Such constants may be in either zoned (Z) or packed (P) decimal form. Following are examples:

PROGRAM							PUNCHING	GRAPHIC		
PROGRAMMER					DATE		INSTRUCTIONS	PUNCH		

STATEMENT

Name		Operation			Operand					
VALUE		DC		Z'10'		ZONED DECIMAL				
ONE		DC		P'1'		PACKED DECIMAL				
COUNT		DC		Z'0'		ZONED DECIMAL				
QUANT		DC		P'-145'		PACKED DECIMAL				

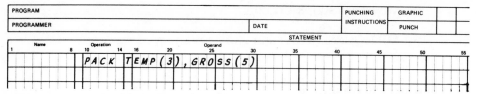

1	Name	8	Operation 10	14	16	20	Operand 25	30	35	40	45	50	55
			PACK		TEMP(3), GROSS(5)								

Figure 6–7. *Example of the PACK instruction.*

Data Conversion

When numeric data is read into the computer it is generally stored in zoned decimal form (one digit per eight-bit byte). Before decimal arithmetic operations can be performed, the data must be converted to packed decimal form. This is done by means of a PACK instruction. When the result has been obtained in packed decimal, it is converted back to zoned decimal by means of an UNPK (for unpack) instruction.

The use of the PACK instruction is illustrated in Figure 6–7. A quantity called GROSS is stored in five bytes in zoned decimal format. The PACK instruction converts the quantity to packed decimal and places it in a field called TEMP. The field TEMP requires only three bytes to contain the packed data.

QUESTION: Suppose in Figure 6–7 it were desired to reconvert the field TEMP (packed decimal) to GROSS (zoned decimal). What instruction would be used? _____
ANSWER: UNPK GROSS(5), TEMP(3)

If numeric data is to be manipulated in binary form, it must be converted from packed decimal to binary. This is accomplished by means of a Convert to Binary (CVB) instruction. Thus there is a two-step procedure in converting input data to binary: first, it is converted to packed decimal by means of a PACK instruction; second, it is converted to binary with the CVB instruction. A Convert to Decimal (CVD) instruction similarly converts binary data to packed decimal.

Exercise 6–4

1. Write Define Constant statements for each of the following:

(a) Define a full word constant called FACTOR, with value −36.

(b) Define a zoned decimal constant called COUNT, with value 0.

(c) Define a packed decimal constant called COUNT, with value 1.

---

2. Figure 4–8 (Chapter 4) shows an example of converting zoned decimal data to packed decimal. Write a PACK instruction for this example, assuming the zoned decimal field is called ZDATA and the packed decimal field is called PDATA.

Branching Instructions

A computer will execute instructions in the order they are stored in memory, unless it is instructed to diverge from this sequence. A program that could only execute a single sequence of instructions would be severely limited. Instead, most programs allow a number of alternative sequences or paths to be taken, depending on conditions encountered during execution. This ability to choose alternative paths (called branching) gives a digital computer much of its power and flexibility.

Branching may be illustrated as follows. Suppose there are five instructions in memory. Instruction 1, 3, 4, and 5 are processing instructions, while instruction 2 is a branch to instruction 5. The instructions, appear as follows:

```
1    Instruction
2    Branch to 5
3    Instruction
4    Instruction
5    Instruction
```

QUESTION: In the above sequence, what processing instructions are executed?

ANSWER: 1 and 5 (3 and 4 are skipped)

Branches may be conditional or unconditional. A conditional branch is taken only if a condition specified in the instruction has occurred in the program. If the condition has not occurred, the computer performs the next instruction in sequence. An unconditional branch (such as illustrated above) is always taken.

Unconditional Branching. An unconditional branch (B) causes the computer to branch to another location in the program—either a higher address or a lower address. Figure 6–8 shows an example of the use of this instruction. After three processing instructions are performed, the program branches to an instruction labeled "NEXT." The sequence of instructions at that location is then executed.

```
         Instruction
         Instruction
         Instruction
         B    NEXT
         Instruction
         Instruction
NEXT     Instruction
```

Figure 6–8. An illustration of unconditional branch instruction.

Conditional Branching. Conditional branching instructions are fundamental to most data processing programs. They permit altering the actions taken by the program, depending on the data being processed and
the resulting conditions encountered in the program.

Conditional branching instructions test the setting of an entity called
a condition code. A condition code is assigned a particular value depending on the results of certain other processing instructions. The most
important types of conditions that can be tested are the results of arithmetic operations and the results of comparing two numbers.

QUESTION: Conditional branching instructions test the setting of a
_____ _____. The value of this code depends on the result
of _____ operations or _____ two
numbers.

ANSWER: condition code, arithmetic, comparing

When an arithmetic instruction is executed, the result may be zero,
minus, positive, or an overflow may have occurred. The following instructions test these conditions and branch if the stated condition has
occurred:

Instruction Operation Code	Explanation
BZ	Branch if result is zero
BM	Branch if result is minus
BP	Branch if result is positive
BO	Branch if overflow has occurred

If the condition has not occurred, there is no branch and the computer "falls through" to the next instruction in sequence.

In Figure 6–6 instructions are shown for calculating a new accounts
payable balance (BALANCE). Recent purchases (PURCHASES) were
added to the balance, and recent payments (PAYMENTS) were subtracted
from the balance. If through error the payment was too large, the resulting balance would be negative. In Figure 6–9 a Branch on Minus (BM)
instruction is used to test for this condition.

PROGRAM							PUNCHING		GRAPHIC				
PROGRAMMER					DATE		INSTRUCTIONS		PUNCH				

Name		Operation			Operand						Comments	
		AP		BALANCE(3),PURCHASES(3)								
		SP		BALANCE(3),PAYMENTS(3)								
		BM		NEGBAL								
NEXT		(Instruction)										
		...										
NEGBAL		(Instruction)										

Figure 6–9. *An illustration of conditional branch instruction.*

QUESTION: Examine Figure 6–9. What instruction will be executed next if the computed value of BALANCE is (a) positive _____, (b) zero _____, (c) negative _____?

ANSWER: (a) NEXT, (b) NEXT, (c) NEGBAL

Compare instructions are used to compare the magnitude of two numbers. Two assembly language instructions used for this purpose are Compare (C) and Compare Decimal (CP). The former compares the contents of an addressable register with the contents of a storage location, while the latter compares two packed decimal numbers in storage. The two operands in a C or CP instruction are the locations of the numbers to be compared.

There are three possible results when two numbers are compared: the first number is either greater than, equal to, or less than the second number. Depending on the result, a condition code is set that may then be tested by a conditional branching instruction. The following assembly language instructions are used for this purpose:

Instruction Operation Code	Explanation
BH	Branch if first operand *higher* than second operand.
BL	Branch if first operand *lower* than second operand.
BE	Branch if two operands are *equal.*
BNE	Branch if two operands are *not equal.*
BNH	Branch if first operand *not higher,* (that is, lower than or equal to) second operand.
BNL	Branch if first operand *not lower* (that is, higher than or equal to) second operand.

In Figure 6–3 assembly language instructions were shown for computing a new inventory balance. If may be desirable to determine whether the new balance has fallen below an established minimum, called the reorder point. If so, an additional quantity should be ordered. This may be illustrated as follows:

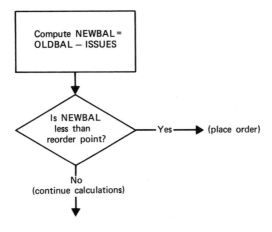

PROGRAM
PROGRAMMER
DATE
PUNCHING INSTRUCTIONS
GRAPHIC
PUNCH
PAGE
CARD EL
STATEMENT

Name	Operation	Operand	Comments
* INVENTORY CALCULATION WITH COMPARISON AGAINST REORDER POINT = 10			
RP	DC	F'10'	DEFINE REORDER POINT
	L	2, OLDBAL	LOAD OLDBAL
	S	2, ISSUES	SUBTRACT ISSUES
	ST	2, NEWBAL	STORE RESULT
	C	2, RP	COMPARE BALANCE, REORDER POINT
	BL	ORDER	BRANCH ON LOW TO ORDER
NEXT	(Instruction)		
	. . .		
ORDER	(Instruction)		

Figure 6–10. *An illustration of compare and conditional branch instructions.*

The modified set of instructions for the inventory calculation is shown in Figure 6–10. It is assumed that the reorder point is 10; this value is defined as a full word constant called RP. After NEWBAL is calculated and stored, the contents of register 2 (which still represent NEWBAL) are compared with the contents of RP. If NEWBAL is less than RP, the program goes to an instruction called ORDER; otherwise it goes to NEXT.

QUESTION: Examine Figure 6–10 and answer the following questions: (a) To what location does the program branch if NEWBAL is 7 _____, 15 _____, 10 _____? (b) Three of the instructions have entries in the name field, explain the purpose of each of these names:

ANSWER: (a) ORDER, NEXT, NEXT. (b) NEXT and ORDER are instruction labels; RP is the symbolic address of a constant.

The Compare Decimal (CP) instruction is used to compare two packed decimal numbers. The length of each operand (in bytes) may be specified in the instruction. To illustrate, a field called CHARGE may be compared with a second field called LIMIT with the following instruction:

PROGRAM
PROGRAMMER
DATE
PUNCHING INSTRUCTIONS
GRAPHIC
PUNCH
STATEMENT

Name	Operation	Operand	
	CP	CHARGE (3), LIMIT (3)	

In the above instruction each operand is assumed to be three bytes long. When the compare is executed, a condition code is set, and a conditional branch instruction may be used to test the resulting condition.

Programming Loops

In data processing it is often desired to repeat a sequence of instructions. For example, in a payroll program a set of payroll cards would be processed using the same basic set of instructions for each employee. This procedure, called looping, is illustrated in Figure 6–11.

There are many ways to program loops. However, all of them involve the following three steps:

1. *Initializing* a counter to a starting value.
2. *Incrementing* (or decrementing) the counter each time the computations are performed.
3. *Testing* to determine whether the counter has reached a limit. If not, looping is continued; otherwise the program proceeds beyond the loop.

QUESTION: The three steps in looping are _____, _____, and _____.

ANSWER: initializing (a counter), incrementing, testing

Program steps for the payroll calculations are shown in Figure 6–12. The first step is initializing a counter (COUNT); it is assumed that the calculations are to be performed for 1,000 employees. The next two DC statements define the increment (1) and the counter limit (0). The contents

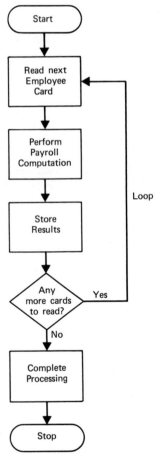

Figure 6–11. *An illustration of a loop for payroll calculations.*

131 / PROGRAMMING LOOPS

```
PROGRAM                                          PUNCHING       GRAPHIC           PAGE
PROGRAMMER                        DATE           INSTRUCTIONS   PUNCH             CARD EL
                                     STATEMENT
Name      Operation  Operand                  Comments
COUNT     DC         F'1000'                  INITIALIZE COUNTER
INC       DC         F'1'                     DEFINE INCREMENT
LIMIT     DC         F'0'                     DEFINE LIMIT
          L          3,COUNT                  LOAD COUNT IN ACCUMULATOR
COMP      (payroll calculations)              READ CARD, PERFORM CALCULATIONS
          S          3,INC                    DECREMENT COUNT
          C          3,LIMIT                  COMPARE COUNT, LIMIT
          BH         COMP                     BRANCH TO CONTINUE PAYROLL
NEXT      (remainder of program)
```

Figure 6–12. *An illustration of looping instructions.*

of COUNT (1000) are then loaded into register 3. The payroll calculations are then performed, and the increment 1 is then subtracted from the number of times the calculation is yet to be performed. The resulting value is then compared with the counter limit; if more employee cards remain, the program will branch (BH) to repeat the computations. When the limit is reached, the program "falls through" to the instruction NEXT.

QUESTION: Examine Figure 6–12. What program step would be changed if the loop were to be executed 2,000 times?

ANSWER: COUNT DC F'2000'

Looping is of such importance that most computers have special instructions for this purpose. For example, the IBM System/370 has an instruction called Branch on Count (BCT) that both increments and tests the loop counter. If the count has not reached zero, it causes looping to continue. Figure 6–13 shows the payroll program (from Figure 6–12) with this instruction.

QUESTION: Examine Figures 6–12 and 6–13. How many instructions are replaced by the special BCT loop instruction? ____________________.

ANSWER: Four

```
PROGRAM                                          PUNCHING       GRAPHIC           PAGE
PROGRAMMER                        DATE           INSTRUCTIONS   PUNCH             CARD EL
                                     STATEMENT
Name      Operation  Operand                  Comments
COUNT     DC         F'1000'                  INITIALIZE COUNTER
          L          3,COUNT                  LOAD COUNT INTO ACCUMULATOR
COMP      (payroll calculations)              READ CARD, PERFORM CALCULATIONS
          BCT        3,COMP                   DECREMENT COUNT, TEST, BRANCH
NEXT      (remainder of program)
```

Figure 6–13. Looping using BCT instruction.

Exercise 6–5

1. Suppose the following instructions are executed:

> AP QTY(3), AMT(2)
> BO ERR
> BP ONE
> BZ TWO
> THREE (instruction)

To what instruction will the program branch if the result of the addition (first instruction) is:

(a) An overflow condition? _____

(b) Minus? _____

(c) Positive? _____

(d) Zero? _____

2. The contents of two operand locations QTY and AMT are as follows: QTY 279+, AMT 143–. What will be the next instruction executed after the conditional branch instruction in each of the following:

(a)   CP QTY(2), AMT(2)
         BE FIRST
   ONE (instruction) _____

(b)   CP QTY(2), AMT(2)
         BNL FIRST
   ONE (instruction) _____

(c)   CP QTY(2), AMT(2)
         BNE FIRST
   ONE (instruction) _____

3. Write looping instructions to perform the following program instruction 100 times:

> CALC (instructions)

(a) Without the BCT instruction _____

_____

_____

_____

_____

_____

_____

_____

(b) With the BCT instruction _____

_____

_____

_____

_____

_____

_____

_____

_____

Summary

This chapter presents the basic concepts of instructing a computer to perform data processing operations. Although a variety of instruction formats are used, all instructions contain an operation code and one or more operands. Operands may be storage addresses or references to addressable registers. A basic distinction exists between fixed word length instructions, which often use addressable registers, and variable word length instructions, which use a storage-to-storage concept. Many third generation computers use both types of instructions.

The basic types of instruction in a computer include those for data conversion, data movement, arithmetic, defining constants, and branching. Conditional branching instructions are particularly important in testing conditions that have developed in the program and in controlling looping operations. Although the more important instructions have been discussed, these instructions comprise only a small portion of the repertoire of a large-scale computer—such a computer may employ some 100 different instructions.

Important processing instructions that have not been discussed in this chapter are those for input and output of data. Concepts of input/output devices and instructions are described in the next chapter.

Solutions to Exercises

Exercise 6–1

1. (a) 583 C69   (b) L   3, OLDBAL
      5B3 5F4   S   3, PAYMENTS
      5A3 12A   A   3, CHARGES
      503 4E8   ST   3, NEWBAL

134 / INSTRUCTING THE COMPUTER

2. 0101101100100000000010111110100

3. Three principal advantages:
    (a) Symbolic rather than absolute (numeric) data addresses.
    (b) Mnemonic rather than absolute operation codes.
    (c) Instruction names (or labels) where needed, rather than absolute
        storage locations.

Exercise 6–2

1. L   7, SALES
   ST 7, TOTAL

2. MVC ID(6), PARTNUM

3. (a) 36–108   (b) 36–108GE   (c) 36–1

Exercise 6–3

1. (a) AP YTD(5), GROSS(3)
   (b) MP HOURS(5), RATE(3)
   (c) SP GROSS(3), DEDUCT(2)

2. (a) 113059+   (b) overflow
   (c) 128+   (d) 0000128+

Exercise 6–4

1. (a) FACTOR DC F'–36'
   (b) COUNT DC Z'0'
   (c) COUNT DC P'1'

2. PACK   PDATA(2), ZDATA(3)

Exercise 6–5

1. (a) ERR   (b) None (program will "fall through" to THREE)
   (c) ONE   (d) TWO

2. (a) ONE   (b) FIRST   (c) FIRST

3. (a) COUNT DC F'100'   (b) COUNT DC F'100'
       INC   DC F'1'   L 1, COUNT
       LIMIT   DC F'0'   CALC   (instructions)
                L 1, COUNT   BCT 1, CALC
       CALC   (instructions)   NEXT   (instruction)
                S 1, INC
                C 1, LIMIT
                BH CALC
     NEXT   (instruction)
(*Note:* register 1 is used arbitrarily above.)

135 / SOLUTIONS TO EXERCISES

1. How are instructions and data words distinguished in storage? _____ .

_____

_____

2. How many instructions are required to perform a basic arithmetic operation (including storing the result) when using single-address instructions? _____

_____

Three-address? _____

3. Name three advantages of assembly language programming over machine language: _____

(a) _____

(b) _____

(c) _____

4. Match the following terms with their appropriate definitions:

_____ Register	(a) register that holds results of arithmetic operations
_____ Storage register	(b) device that performs addition
_____ Address register	(c) contains address of next instruction
_____ Accumulator	(d) device that receives, transmits, and store data
_____ Adder	(e) temporary storage for data or instruction
_____ Instruction counter	(f) one millionth of a second
_____ Machine cycle	(g) basic unit of time in computer operations
_____ Millisecond	(h) one billionth of a second
_____ Nanosecond	(i) contains address of current operand
_____ Microsecond	(j) one thousandth of a second

5. Explain why decimal arithmetic instructions are often used in data processing. _____

6. Explain the purpose of each of the following instructions:

(a) MVC _____

(b) SP _____

(c) DC _____

(d) BP _____

(e) PACK _____

(f) BCT _____

7. Two quantities called FIELDA and FIELDB are stored in zoned decimal format, each four bytes long. Write assembly language instructions to perform the following:

(a) Define a packed decimal constant called CONST with value

365+. _____

(b) Convert FIELDA and FIELDB to packed decimal format. Call the packed decimal fields QUANT and NUMB, respectively.

_____

(c) Obtain the sum of NUMB and QUANT.

_____

(d) Test to determine whether the sum in part (c) is less than or equal to the contents of CONST. If so, branch to a location called FINISH. If not, perform the next step below.

_____

(e) Subtract the contents of CONST from the sum from part (c).

_____

(f) Convert the result from part (e) to zoned decimal in a field called RESULT.

_____

137 / CHAPTER EXAMINATION

8. In Figure 6-10 fixed word length instructions are shown for an inventory calculation with a test for reorder point. Rewrite this program using variable word length instructions. Assume that data is stored in zoned decimal format in the computer. The maximum length of the inventory balance field is five digits, while issues requires a maximum of four digits.

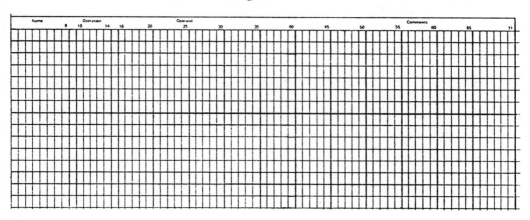

9. Add instructions to those in Figure 6-10 to perform the inventory calculation 500 times.

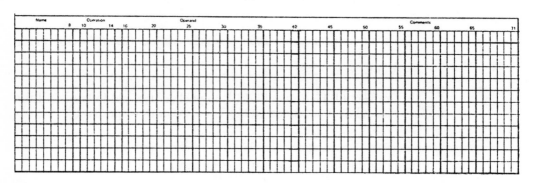

10. Identify the following statements as true or false:

_____ (a) A computer instruction consists of two basic parts, an operation code and one or more operands.

_____ (b) A computer instruction may be deliberately modified by other program instructions.

_____ (c) The single-address format is generally used in variable word length computers.

_____ (d) Computer programs are generally coded in machine language.

_____ (e) The instruction counter is a special purpose register that contains the address of the next instruction to be executed.

_____ (f) Cycle times in third generation computers are often expressed in nanoseconds.

_____ (g) The execution time for two-address instructions is generally shorter than for single-address instructions.

11. Name and briefly describe the three basic steps required in programming a loop.

(a) _____

(b) _____

(c) _____

12. In a payroll calculation, the contents of two operands are as follows:

GROSS	849.75
DEDUCT	257.35

Suppose that the following assembly-language instructions are executed:

L	3, GROSS
S	3, DEDUCT
ST	3, NET

Show the contents of each of the following after execution:

GROSS _____

DEDUCT _____

NET _____

Register 3 _____

13. Nine consecutive storage positions (bytes) are reserved for a field called MONTH. The current contents of this field is DECEMBERb (the characters DECEMBER followed by a blank). Show the contents of a field called CURMONTH after each of the following instructions is executed:

MVC CURMONTH (9), MONTH _____

MVC CURMONTH (3), MONTH _____

14. Suppose that the following statements are executed:

AP	SALARY (4), BONUS (3)
SP	SALARY (4), DEDUCT (3)

If the contents of the storage locations before execution are as shown below, indicate the contents after execution:

Location	Contents Before	Contents After
SALARY	18000+	_____
BONUS	3500+	_____
DEDUCT	800+	_____

15. Explain the meaning of an arithmetic overflow condition.

_____

_____

16. The current content of register 3 is 150, and the current content of the operand BALANCE is 139. Indicate the next instruction that will be executed after each of the following comparisons and conditional branching instructions. Assume that the next instruction in sequence after each conditional branching instruction is called NEXT.

(a) C   3, BALANCE
     BH   REPEAT   _____

(b) C   3, BALANCE
     BL   REPEAT   _____

(c) C   3, BALANCE
     BE   REPEAT   _____

(d) C   3, BALANCE
     BNE   REPEAT   _____

(e) C   3, BALANCE
     BNH   REPEAT   _____

(f) C   3, BALANCE
     BNL   REPEAT   _____

17. Repeat problem 16, assuming that the number 150 is stored in both register 3 and the location BALANCE.

(a) _____

(b) _____

(c) _____

(d) _____

(e) _____

(f) _____

Chapter 7

INPUT/OUTPUT CONCEPTS AND DEVICES

Overview

Most data processing applications require the preparation and input of substantial amounts of data resulting from the daily transactions of the organization. This data must be converted to machine-processable form before it can be input into the computer. As a result, costs of input data preparation may represent from 25 to 50 percent of the total operating budget of a typical installation. Also, throughput (number of jobs processed per unit of time) is often limited by input-output operations, rather than by internal computer processing speeds.

For installations with large input volumes, data preparation costs have led to replacing the familiar keypunch machine with more efficient devices. The most important of these are key-tape and key-disk systems for converting data to machine-processable form. Also, optical character recognition equipment which reads printed data directly (thus eliminating manual preparation) is used by an increasing number of organizations.

A large number of devices and media are used for input and output of data. These may be categorized according to the type of medium used. When input and output volumes are low, devices using paper media (punched cards, punched paper tape, and printed output) may be used. For on-line data entry and display, keyboard printers and video display terminals are often used. Magnetic media (magnetic tape, disk, and diskette) provide very high speed input and output, and are used in high volume applications. Optical media are comparable in speed to punched cards, but data is read directly without transcription.

Some of the more important input/output devices and their uses are summarized in Figure 7–1.

Input/Output Concepts

The major steps in the input/output cycle are (1) identifying data sources, (2) converting data to machine processable form, (3) input of data into the computer, and (4) output of information (following internal processing).

Device	Purpose	Typical Applications
Key-tape or key-disk system	Recording source data on magnetic media-tape, disk or diskette	Data entry for high-volume applications such as sales order processing, and inventory.
Card read-punch	Input and output of data on 80-column or 96-column punched cards	Low-volume batch processing applications—small business systems, and turnaround documents.
Magnetic tape unit	Storage and high-speed input-output of large sequential files	High-volume batch processing applications—sales order processing, inventory, etc.
Line printer	Recording relatively low volumes of output information on paper	All applications requiring printed output for operating documents, management reports, etc.
Video display	Keyboard entry of data and inquiries; video display of alphanumeric and graphical output	On-line inquiries and updating such as time-sharing and reservations systems.
Optical character reader	Source data automation—reading printed data directly from documents without keyboard entry	High-volume input where data is in standard printed form—processing airline tickets, invoices, etc.
Point-of-sale recorders	Input of sales data at point of sale, using optical or magnetic reading techniques.	Sales data entry and credit checking in retail stores, banks, and supermarkets.

Figure 7–1. *The principal input/output devices.*

Identifying Data Sources

The data to be processed by a computer system may originate from a number of different sources, depending on the nature of the organization. Much of the data typically results from transactions with customers and suppliers—for example, customer orders, payments on accounts, and receipts of goods. Other data results from activities within the organization—for example, employee hours worked, and usage of materials and supplies.

The variety of data sources in different organizations can be illustrated by several examples:

1. In a hospital, various supplies and services—medicines, X-rays, surgical facilities—are used in patient care. Data concerning the supplies and services used for each patient must be recorded for billing the patient and, perhaps, for updating inventory records. Relevant data include the patient name, and quantity and unit cost of each supply or service used.
2. In a manufacturing facility, jobs are performed at work centers. When an employee completes a job, he reports the actual time he spent on that job. The data reported includes work station number, job number, employee number, and elapsed time.
3. In a bank, checks are presented for payment. Relevant data include bank identification number, customer account number, and amount of check.
4. In a mail order firm selling stationery, customer orders arrive by mail on a preprinted order form. An example of such a form is shown in Figure 7–2.

QUESTION: Examine Figure 7–2. What are the relevant data for processing the customer order? _____

_____

ANSWER: Customer name and address, order code, quantity and price for each item ordered, total items, total amount, total enclosed, and amount charged

Converting to Machine Processable Form

Before data can be processed by a computer it must be in machine-readable form. This step (often referred to as data preparation or entry) may be accomplished in one of three basic ways:

1. Data may be converted from manual form to machine-readable form. A common method is punching the data into cards.
2. Data may be prerecorded in machine-readable form, such as magnetic ink or optically readable characters.
3. Data may be directly entered into the computer system, as from a terminal keyboard.

The method of capturing or converting data to machine-readable form depends on several factors such as the source and nature of the data, the volume of data, time and accuracy requirements, and cost constraints. Data entry devices (including key-tape and key-disk systems) are described later in this chapter.

Two basic principles should be applied in converting data to machine-processable form:

1. Data should be captured in machine-processable form at the earliest opportunity. Ideally, the data is recorded in machine-readable form when it is originated. Often this is not possible, especially when data originates from outside the organization. In such instances, the data should be converted to machine-processable form as soon as practicable after it enters the organization.

Order Blank

PLEASE PRINT

Please Use One Name
For All Orders In
Your Household

(Please Do Not Write In This Space)

CH						
A/RP		ORG	
SVC			

TODAY'S DATE _3-1-74_

YOUR NAME _Mrs. J. Bishnow_

ADDRESS _2635 Bitters Rd_

CITY _San Antonio_ STATE _Texas_ ZIP _78217_

PRICE SCHEDULE

On orders of 1 to 5 items (any assortment): Retail Price
On orders of 6 or more items (any assortment): Fund Raiser Price
Please add 30¢ Handling Charge on orders under $6.60.

ORDER CODE	HOW MANY ITEMS?	NAME OF ARTICLE	RETAIL PRICE	FUND RAISER PRICE	TOTAL AMOUNT
38	3	Just-A-Note (Butterfly Designs)	$1.00 ea.	$ .55 ea.	1.65
75	1	Farmyard Friends	1.00 ea.	.55 ea.	.55
123		Recipe Cards (Garden Harvest)	1.25 ea.	.70 ea.	
158	5	North American Birds (Ecology Cards)	1.00 ea.	.55 ea.	2.75
159		American Country Cards	1.00 ea.	.55 ea.	
301		Wildwood Stationery (Blue)	2.00 ea.	1.10 ea.	
302		Wildwood Stationery (Yellow)	2.00 ea.	1.10 ea.	
309		Post-A-Notes (Mini Merchants)	1.00 ea.	.55 ea.	
310	2	Pantry Post Cards	1.50 ea.	.85 ea.	1.70

TOTAL ITEMS _11_

TOTAL AMOUNT

Total From Above $ _6.65_

30¢ Handling Charge
On Orders Under
$6.60 $_____

Total Amount $ _6.65_

IMPORTANT
Please Do Not Send Stamps or Cash.
We Welcome Your Comments
or Suggestions at Any Time.

Please Charge My Order
Add Postage to My Bill

MY TELEPHONE IS:
(To Expedite Your Order)

AMOUNT CHARGED

Area Code_____

$_____ Number_____

Check or Money Order Enclosed
Current Pays the Postage

TOTAL ENCLOSED

$ _6.65_

Effective through August 31, 1974

CURRENT, INC., THE CURRENT BLDG., COLORADO SPRINGS, COLO. 80941

Figure 7–2. Order form for mail-order firm.

Capturing data in machine-processable form at an early stage reduces manual operations, with the advantages of greater processing speed and reduced error rates.

2. Constant data should be prerecorded in machine-processable form or should be entered automatically into the system. For example, in the banking industry it is common practice to prerecord the bank identification number and customer number in magnetic ink characters on the check by machine before they are sold or issued to a bank customer. When the customer writes a check, only the amount of the check is encoded by the bank before processing. The use of magnetic ink characters on checks is illustrated later in this chapter.

Entering constant information as prerecorded machine-processable data significantly reduces manual conversion of data and the attendant chances for error. In the above example, entering the bank and customer number on each check before it is processed would be an extremely inefficient procedure, resulting in a prohibitive amount of manual data encoding and a resultant high error rate.

QUESTION: Two basic principles of data entry are to capture the data in _____-_____ form at the earliest possible stage and to enter _____ data in _____ form.

ANSWER: machine-processable, constant, prerecorded

Exercise 7–1

1. A hospital records the type, amount, and cost of each type of supply and service issued to a patient. At present this data is recorded manually on a work sheet. Suggest a way to capture this data, using punched cards, that recognizes the basic principles discussed in the previous section.

2. Figure 7–2 showed a customer order form for a mail order firm. Suppose data is to be keypunched for entry into the order processing system. What information from the order form would be keypunched? Is it necessary to keypunch all of the data shown on the form? Explain your reasoning.

Input of Data into the Computer

The data to be used by a computer program must first be encoded on a machine-readable medium such as punched cards, magnetic tape, or documents encoded with magnetic ink. The data may then be read into the computer through an input (or input/output) device. An input/output device consists basically of (1) a transport mechanism that holds and moves the cards, tape, or other medium, and (2) a read-write mechanism that reads from or writes data on the medium. The basic input-output devices used in most systems are card readers, card punches, magnetic tape units, line printers, and typewriters. Disk storage units and other secondary storage devices are also used for input and output of data; these devices are discussed in Chapter 5.

QUESTION: The basic elements of an input/output unit are a _____ mechanism that moves the medium and a _____-_____ mechanism.

ANSWER: transport, read-write

The Input-Output Cycle. When data is to be read into the computer, the following sequence of events occurs:

1. A computer "read" instruction is executed, which specifies the address of the device from which the data is to be obtained, and the address of the area in computer memory into which the data is to be read.
2. An electrical signal is sent to the device control unit, which activates the transport mechanism for the device. If the device is busy or inoperable, a signal is returned by the control unit to the central processor.
3. The input device reads the contents of the record from the input medium and encodes the data into electrical signals.
4. The control unit converts the data input code (such as Hollerith) into the internal code for the computer (such as EBCDIC) and transmits the data to main memory via a data channel to be discussed below.
5. When the input operation is completed, a signal is transmitted to the central processor which may be used to interrupt the sequence of program instructions.

The sequence of events for the output of data is similar to the input cycle.

Overlapped versus Nonoverlapped Processing. Compared with internal operating speeds, input and output of data are very slow operations. For example, a high-speed card reader might operate at 1,200 cards per minute. At this rate, the time required to read a card is 50,000 microseconds. In this same time a third generation computer would be able to execute 10,000 or more internal processing instructions.

QUESTION: In this example, a single read instruction would take _____ times as long as a processing instruction (such as addition).

ANSWER: 10,000

In data processing the typical cycle of events is to read an input record, process the data, and write an output record. If these operations were performed serially (in sequence), processing would be suspended during most of the cycle while the computer waited for an input/output operation to be completed. This type of operation is termed nonoverlapped processing and is shown schematically in Figure 7–3.

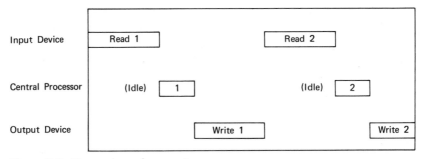

Figure 7–3. *Nonoverlapped processing.*

QUESTION: Examine Figure 7–3. Suppose that a read operation requires 50,000 microseconds, a write operation 100,000 microseconds, and the average processing time per record is 10,000 microseconds.
(a) What is the total time per cycle? _____ microseconds.
(b) How many records are processed per second? _____.
(c) What percent of the time is the central processing unit idle? _____.
ANSWER: (a) 160,000   (b) 6¼   (c) 150/160 or 94 percent

In many data processing applications, the central processor would be idle more than 99 percent of the time with nonoverlapped processing. To overcome this, most systems provide for overlapped processing. In this mode, reading, processing, and output occur simultaneously. This method of operation is depicted in Figure 7–4.

QUESTION: Assume that in Figure 7–4 (as in the previous example) a read operation requires 50,000 microseconds, a write operation 100,000 microseconds, and the average processing time per record is 10,000 microseconds.
(a) What is the total time per cycle? _____ micro-
seconds.
(b) How many records are processed per second? _____.
(c) What percentage of the time is the CPU idle? _____.
ANSWER: (a) 100,000   (b) 10   (c) 90/100 or 90 percent

In present generation computers, the use of overlapped processing provides much more efficient use of the central processor than would

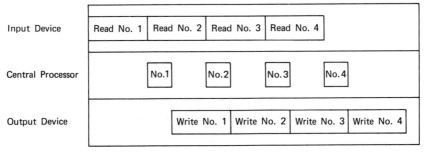

Figure 7–4. *Overlapped processing.*

147 / IDENTIFYING DATA SOURCES

seem to be indicated by the above example. This is accomplished by the simultaneous operation of several input/output devices, under the control of one or more computer programs.

Data Channels. Overlapped processing is accomplished by means of data channels. A *channel* is essentially a minicomputer that is either contained in the CPU or is located in a separate cabinet near the CPU. A channel permits input/output operations to be controlled independently of the central processing unit.

The configuration for a simplified computer input/output system is shown in Figure 7–5. A channel is generally connected to a control unit, which in turn is connected to one or more input/output devices. The connection between the channel and control unit is termed the interface.

QUESTION: Input and output operations are controlled by a _____, which is part of the CPU. This unit is connected to a _____ unit across an _____.

ANSWER: channel, control, interface

A data channel functions as an independent processing unit. The channel is activated by an input or output instruction written by the programmer. After it activates the channel, the CPU is free to continue with other processing instructions. In older computers, input/output was controlled by the CPU. This precluded or, at least, limited the capacity for overlapped processing.

The channel controls the transfer of information to and from the computer by executing channel programs and by transmitting signals to and from the control unit. The channel also provides a *buffer*, or temporary storage capacity, for data being transferred. When transfer is completed, the channel interrupts the CPU; it will also interrupt the CPU if an error condition is encountered in transfer.

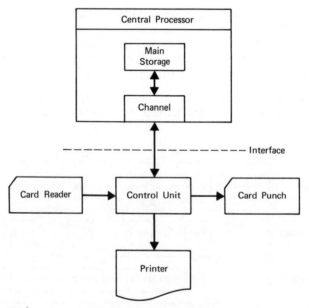

Figure 7–5. *A simple input-output configuration.*

There are two basic types of channels: selector channels and multi-plexor channels. At any one time a selector channel is used with a single high-speed input or output device such as a magnetic tape or disk. This high-speed transfer is often referred to as "burst" mode. A multiplexor channel has several subchannels and may be simultaneously shared by several input/output devices.

Most third generation computers have a number of channels, which can be operated simultaneously. The number and capacity of channels supplied are important considerations in selecting a computer. The number of channels determines the number of devices that can be operated simultaneously, and the capacity limits the rate of data transfer.

Input/Output Instructions. Programming input/output operations is quite complex if the instructions are written in machine language. Fortunately, almost all input/output instructions referencing secondary storage are programmed using either assembly language or a higher-level language. In a higher-level language (discussed in Chapter 10) the programmer writes a simple description of the files and records used by the program. He then codes a simple READ or WRITE instruction to transmit data to or from the computer.

Information Output

The last stage in the processing cycle is the output of information. Information may be stored on a machine-readable medium such as magnetic tape or disk for further processing, or it may be printed or otherwise displayed for humans. In most programs both types of output are produced.

Figure 7–2 showed a customer order form for a mail order firm. As a result of processing this data, the following types of output information are produced:

1. An updated inventory record for each item, reflecting the amount sold. This information is output on magnetic tape.
2. A shipping notice, used by a clerk to select and pack the order. An example is shown in Figure 7–6. This notice is also used as a customer invoice if the order is not prepaid.

Exercise 7–2
1. List five steps in the cycle for output of information:

(a) _____

(b) _____

(c) _____

(d) _____

(e) _____

2. In a particular program a read operation and a write operation each require 20,000 microseconds, and the average processing time per

CURRENT, INC.
CURRENT BUILDING
COLORADO SPRINGS
COLORADO 80941

SHIPPING NOTICE

MRS. J. BISHNOW   DATE 03/04/74   UL5
2635 BITTERS RD
SAN ANTONIO   TX 78217   PAGE 01   0306101983

ORDER NUMBER			AMOUNT RECEIVED	
78217BSH042635J			$	6.65

ARTICLE NUMBER	NO. OF ITEMS	NAME OF ARTICLE	AMOUNT	
X 38	3	JAN BUTTERFLY	$	1.65
X 75	1	FARMYARD FRIENDS	$	.55
X 158	5	NORTH AM BIRDS	$	2.75
X 310	2	PANTRY POST-CARDS	$	1.70

TOTAL BOXES →	11		AMOUNT DUE →	$	.00

PLEASE USE ENCLOSED ORDER BLANK OR REVERSE SIDE
WHEN REORDERING

Figure 7–6. *Customer shipping notice for mail-order firm.*

record is 10,000 microseconds. Calculate the total time per cycle, number of records processed per second, and percent idle time for the CPU for (a) nonoverlapped, and (b) overlapped processing.

(a) _____

(b) _____

3. A computer has two data channels, one a selector channel and the other, a multiplexor channel. The selector channel is connected to a disk or tape control unit with four tape units. The multiplexor channel is connected to an I/O control unit with card reader, card punch, and line printer. Draw a configuration diagram (similar to Figure 7–5).

Data Entry Systems

In the majority of data processing applications, source data is in printed or handwritten form and must be converted to machine-processable form before input into the computer. The conventional method for doing this is to keypunch the data into cards (either 80-column or 96-column). In many data processing installations, anywhere from 25 to 50 percent of the total operating budget is devoted to data preparation—mostly keypunching. The problems of rapidly increasing amounts of data and skyrocketing keypunching costs have led to improved data entry techniques—principally key-to-tape (or key-tape) and key-disk systems.

Key-Tape System

In a key-tape system, data is entered on a keyboard similar to that of a typewriter or keypunch machine. The data is recorded directly on magnetic tape, rather than in cards. Generally, the data being keyed is stored in a buffer (or small memory) and is displayed on a video display, so that the operator can see what is being recorded. In the event of an error, the operator merely backspaces and retypes the data. When the record is completed, it is released and recorded onto the magnetic tape. Key-tape devices use either one-half inch computer tape, cartridges, or cassettes.

Key-tape systems (like the one shown in Figure 7–7) offer a number of significant advantages over keypunch machines:

1. A key-tape machine is faster since recording is electronic instead of mechanical (rates from 25 to 35 percent faster are common).
2. Key-tape machines permit record sizes of up to several hundred characters, compared to the 80-column card. This increases entry speed and eliminates arbitrary record design.
3. Error recovery is much easier. Rather than having to repunch an entire card, the operator merely backspaces to the error and rekeys the correct character.
4. The cost of ordering, handling, and storing cards is eliminated. Unlike cards, magnetic tape can be reused.

151 / DATA ENTRY SYSTEMS

Figure 7-7. *Key-tape data entry system (courtesy Honeywell).*

Key-Disk System

When a number of key-tape systems are being used to record data for an application, records from each of the tapes must be pooled on a single tape for entry into the computer. Some systems use a key-to-central-tape concept, where records keyed at each of several input stations are recorded on a single tape under control of a controller unit.

A more recent concept is that of an integrated data entry system under control of a minicomputer. In that system, data is entered through keyboard stations (or terminals), is processed by the system's shared minicomputer, and is stored on magnetic disk. A record that is stored on magnetic disk may be verified by displaying the data on a video display and comparing it with the original record. The computer may be programmed to perform a number of editing and validation functions normally performed by the central computer.After these operations, the data may be input directly to the central computer or may be batched on a single magnetic tape for later processing.

A data entry system of this type (sometimes referred to as a key-disk system) can handle a large number of individual keystations. Since editing and validation are performed by the minicomputer, the central processor is freed from these tasks so that the overall throughput of jobs is increased. However, these systems are relatively expensive and can generally be justified only by the larger user. Key-disk systems increase data preparation rates by 25 to 75 percent, depending on the application.

One versatile type of key-disk system uses a removable disk called a *diskette* as the recording medium. A diskette (also called a "floppy" disk) is a small magnetic disk that resembles a 45-rpm record, is sealed in a plastic jacket about 8 inches square, and weighs less than 2 ounces. The diskette is reusable, can easily be corrected or updated, and can be used to record nearly 2,000 records up to 128 characters in length. This is equivalent to an entire day's output from a typical key station, or a complete tray of punched cards. An IBM 3740 Data Entry System employing this diskette is shown in Figure 7–8.

This type of system can be used in a variety of ways. Data can be entered and recorded on the diskettes in remote locations such as branch sales offices, then can be mailed or carried to a central location for computer processing. Alternatively, the data may be read from the diskettes and transmitted by telephone lines directly to the central computer.

QUESTION: In high volume applications, key punch machines may be replaced by data entry devices that record data on magnetic _____, _____, or _____.

ANSWER: tape, disk, diskette

Input/output devices may be categorized according to the type of recording medium used: paper, mechanical (keyed devices), magnetic, and optical. The principal devices using each of these types of media are discussed in the following sections (some of the devices use more than one type of medium).

Devices Using Paper Media

Paper is widely used for computer input and output in the form of punched cards, punched paper tape, and printed output. It is relatively

Figure 7–8. *IBM 3740 Data Entry System (courtesy IBM).*

inexpensive (at least in small quantities) and is readily handled and interpreted by humans. On the other hand, paper has low recording density and cannot be reused. Also, since electromechanical devices are used, input and output of data using paper media is comparatively slow. As a result, paper media are used in applications where the volume of data to be input or output is relatively low, and where high speed is not important.

Punched Cards

Punched cards were the most common form of input medium in early computer systems. In today's systems, emphasis has switched to magnetic media such as magnetic tape, disk, and diskette. However, punched cards are still in widespread use, especially in smaller computer systems. Also punched cards are widely used as "turnaround" documents in billing and similar applications. For example, utilities often send monthly bills in the form of cards with prepunched customer number, name and address, month, amount billed, and other information. When the card is returned, the amount paid is punched into the card, and it is used to update the customer's account.

The 80-column Hollerith card is discussed in Chapter 4 (see Figure 4-4). This is the most commonly used punched card. However, several small business systems such as the IBM System/3 have introduced the small 96-column card, shown in Figure 7-9. Data is punched on the lower area of this card and is printed in the upper area. The punch area is divided into three parts called tiers. Each tier has 32 positions or columns where data characters can be punched.

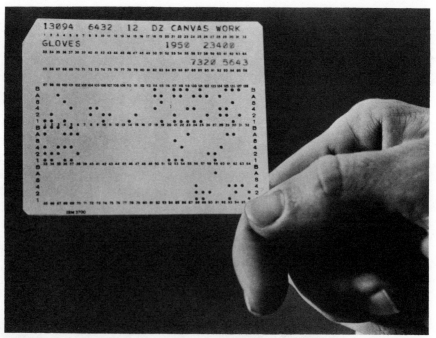

Figure 7-9. *A 96-column punched card (courtesy IBM).*

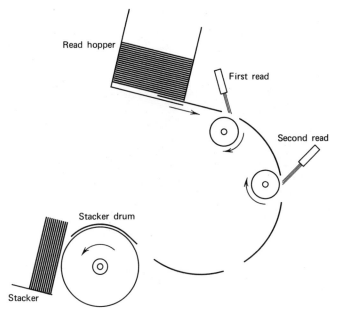

Read hopper

First read

Second read

Stacker drum

Stacker

Figure 7–10. *A card reader mechanism.*

Characters are represented on the 96-column card by means of punched holes (See Figure 7–9). Each card column has six positions in which punches can be placed, similar to the standard binary coded decimal code. As a result, up to 64 different characters can be represented by different punching combinations. The main advantages of the 96-column card are its compact size (about one third the size of a Hollerith card) and greater capacity (96 versus 80 characters).

QUESTION: The 96-column cards uses _____ tiers with _____ columns per tier. Each column permits _____ punching combinations, or up to _____ different characters.
ANSWER: 3, 32, 6, 64

Cards are read by a card read unit and are punched by a punch unit. In a read unit, the file of cards is placed in a read hopper. In response to a read command a card is moved past two sensing stations, as is shown in Figure 7–10. The sensing stations use either wire brushes or photoelectric cells to sense the presence of card punches. The reason for two stations is to compare the results of the two read operations, to detect possible errors in reading. After the cards are read, they are placed in one or more output stackers.

A card punch may punch only blank cards or, in some units, may be programmed to punch additional data in the same cards. Card punching is generally only one fourth to one third as fast as reading, because of the mechanical action of punching the cards.

In third generation systems, the card reader and punch are often combined into a single unit. One such unit, the IBM 2540 Card Read-Punch, is shown in Figure 7–11. This unit, used with the IBM Systems /360 and 370, reads 80-column cards at 1,000 cards per minute and punches at 300

Figure 7-11. *A combination card read-punch unit (courtesy IBM).*

cards per minute. The input stacker (or file feed) holds more than 3,000 cards, and there are five stackers for punched output.

Another combined unit is the Multi-Function Card Unit, used with the IBM System /3. This unit reads 96-column cards at a rate of 500 per minute and punches at a rate of 120 per minute. It can read cards from two separate files, can punch cards, and can perform most card-related operations such as collating, interpreting, reproducing, and summary and gang punching.

Punched Paper Tape

Paper tape is used instead of (or in addition to) punched cards in many smaller computer installations, because of its low cost and versatility. Characters are represented by holes punched on a continuous tape, using

Figure 7-12. *A paper tape punch (courtesy IBM).*

either a five-channel or eight-channel code. The recording density is 10 characters per inch. Reading rates range from about 100 characters per second using mechanical readers to as many as 2,000 characters per second with photoelectric readers. Data is punched on paper by a tape punch at a rate of about 300 characters per second (see Figure 7–12).

Paper tape is often created as a by-product of typing or keying data into a teletype machine. The principal advantages of tape are its low cost and the fact that data is not limited to 80 columns, as with punched cards. However, paper tape is more difficult to correct and cannot be sorted or manipulated like punched cards.

Printed Output

The most familiar form of computer output is that produced on printers. Management reports, journals, invoices, and bank statements are typical examples of printed output.

There are two basic types of printers—character printers, and line printers. A *character* printer prints serially (one character at a time) and, as a result, is generally limited to speeds of from 10 to 120 characters per second. Character printers are often used in on-line applications such as time-sharing where the volume of printed output is relatively small.

A *line* printer prints an entire line (typically up to 132 characters) at a time. The line printer shown in Figure 7–13 prints alphanumeric data (such as that shown in the figure) at a rate of 1,500 lines per minute.

The speed at which either a character or line printer produces output depends on the printing technique used. There are two basic methods—impact printing and nonimpact printing. In *impact* printers, print hammers press the paper and ribbon against selected type characters as they pass in front of the paper. In such printers, type characters are generally mounted on a moving chain or are engraved on the face of a rotating drum. *Nonimpact* printers produce an image by transferring electrical charges to the paper.

Impact printers produce output at a rate of from about 500 to 2,000 lines per minute. Some nonimpact printers can print more than 5,000 lines per minute. However, multiple copies can be produced on an impact printer, but the nonimpact printer produces only a single copy.

QUESTION: two types of printers are _____ (or serial) and _____ printers. The fastest printers use a _____ printing technique.

ANSWER: character, line, nonimpact

Graph Plotter

It is often easier for humans to visualize statistical data after it has been plotted rather than in numerical form. Examples are comparisons of actual versus forecasted sales over time, or results of quality control tests. A graph plotter is a device for plotting graphs, either as direct computer output or from magnetic tape. A graph plotter and typical output are shown in Figure 7–14.

```
┌─────────────────────────────────────────────────────────────────────────────┐
│ O ┆                              INCOME STATEMENT                          ┆ O │
│ O ┆                               MARCH 31, 197-                           ┆ O │
│   ┆                                                                        ┆   │
│ O ┆                    MONTH TO DATE                  YEAR TO DATE          ┆ O │
│   ┆  ACCOUNT       ACCT.                                                   ┆   │
│ O ┆                 NO.      ACTUAL       %        ACTUAL        %         ┆ O │
│   ┆  INCOME                                                                ┆   │
│ O ┆     SALES  1    510    20,149.99    37.03      55,169.89    35.67      ┆ O │
│   ┆           2    511    34,273.43    62.97      99,509.22    64.33      ┆   │
│ O ┆           3                                                            ┆ O │
│   ┆     TOTALS            54,423.42   100.00     154,697.11   100.00      ┆   │
│ O ┆  COST OF SALES 610    20,542.80    37.75      56,098.79    36.27      ┆ O │
│   ┆  GROSS PROFIT        33,880.62    62.25      98,580.32    63.73      ┆   │
│ O ┆  OFFICE SALARIES 810   2,478.50     4.55       5,723.50     3.70      ┆ O │
│   ┆  TELEPHONE     811       466.66      .86       1,431.21      .93      ┆   │
│                                                                              │
│ O ┆  EXPENSES            14,980.99    27.53      48,423.51    31.31      ┆ O │
│   ┆  NET PROFIT         18,899.63    34.73      50,156.81    32.43      ┆   │
│ O ┆                                                                        ┆ O │
└─────────────────────────────────────────────────────────────────────────────┘
```

```
┌─────────────────────────────────────────────────────────────────────────────┐
│ O ┆                                 ABC CO.                                ┆ O │
│ O ┆                              BALANCE SHEET                             ┆ O │
│   ┆                              MARCH 31, 197-                            ┆   │
│ O ┆                                                                        ┆ O │
│   ┆  ACCOUNT                  ACCT.                                        ┆   │
│ O ┆                            NO.    INCREASE/DECREASE      BALANCE        ┆ O │
│   ┆  CURRENT ASSETS                                                        ┆   │
│ O ┆                                                                        ┆ O │
│   ┆  CASH ON HAND              100          460.19        20,406.91        ┆   │
│ O ┆  CASH IN BANK              101        1,190.00        42,770.00        ┆ O │
│   ┆  INVENTORY                 200        3,329.99        17,329.99        ┆   │
│ O ┆  ACCOUNT RECEIVABLE        210        4,732.00        22,721.00        ┆ O │
│   ┆     LESS - ALLOW BAD DEBTS              500.00CR       2,980.00CR       ┆   │
│ O ┆                                                                        ┆ O │
│   ┆     TOTAL CURRENT ASSETS              9,212.18        99,947.90        ┆   │
│ O ┆  FIXED ASSETS                                                          ┆ O │
└─────────────────────────────────────────────────────────────────────────────┘
```

Figure 7–13. *A line printer and typical output (courtesy IBM).*

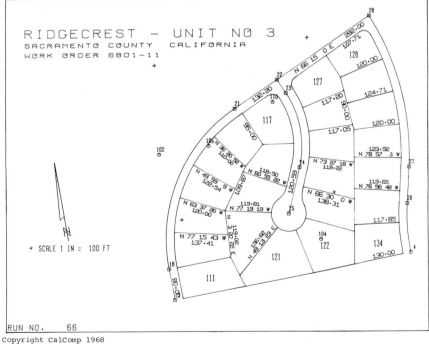

Copyright CalComp 1968

Figure 7–14. (a) Graph plotter. (b) Typical output. (Courtesy California Computer Products, Inc.)

Figure 7–15. *A Teletype automatic send-receive unit (courtesy Teletype Corporation).*

Keyed Devices

Keyboard terminals and similar devices are used in many computer systems for on-line entry of data or inquiries. These are generally combination input/output devices, with keyed input and printed or video display output. Keyboard devices are often used in locations remote to the computer, and are limited to low-input volumes, since input occurs at typewriter speeds. The uses of terminal devices in data communications systems are described in Chapter 8.

Keyboard Printers

The most familiar type of keyboard devices are Teletype terminals (see Figure 7–15). These devices provide a versatile means of transmitting messages and data between a remote user and the computer. Data is entered on a typewriter keyboard and is printed on a low-speed character printer (10 to 30 characters per second).

Some Teletype machines (and similar keyboard terminals) are equipped to transmit data recorded on punched paper tape or magnetic tape cassette, or to record data on these media. Keyboard printers are widely used for interactive computing (or time-sharing) an for transmitting business data—for example, sales orders, invoices, payroll checks, and sales reports—when volume is low.

Data Collection Devices

A wide variety of specialized terminal devices are used to enter data at its point of origin. For example, the terminal shown in Figure 7–16 (IBM Data Entry Unit) is designed to be used in manufacturing plants. As jobs are completed, the operator inserts a punched card containing his employee number and other identifying information. Variable information such as the number of units completed is entered by setting the dials and depressing the keys on the unit. This data is then trans-

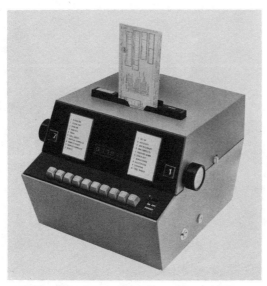

Figure 7–16. *A data entry unit (courtesy IBM).*

mitted to a central computer and is used for production scheduling, inventory control, and other applications.

QUESTION: The data collection device shown in Figure 7–16 employs two types of media: _____ (punched cards) and _____ (keys and dials).

ANSWER: paper, mechanical

Video Display Terminals

In many on-line applications, rapid response to inquiries is required. For example, in an airline reservation system, the operator must be able to display quickly the status of a particular flight. Although a keyboard printer (such as a Teletype machine) may be used for this type of application, printing speeds are slow, and it may take several minutes to print out an entire message.

Video display terminals (see Figure 7–17) use a cathode-ray tube (or CRT), similar to a home television tube, for output. With a video display an entire message (generally up to about 2,000 characters) can be displayed in seconds. The displayed output is normally large, distinct, and easier to read than printed output. The only disadvantage is that (unlike printed copy) the message is lost when it is displaced by another message. Input data and messages are entered on a keyboard similar to a typewriter keyboard.

A rapidly growing area in the use of visual displays is called *graphics*. From data stored in the computer, graphical images of three-dimensional objects are displayed on a screen. Some units use a light pen or other device that permits an operator to input data, by touching the screen.

Display units are widely used in on-line computing systems such as time-sharing and airline reservations. As was discussed previously, CRT displays are also used in key-tape and key-disk data entry systems to check the accuracy of data before it is transmitted to the computer.

Figure 7–17. *IBM 3270 Display Unit (courtesy IBM).*

QUESTION: In on-line applications, a _____ _____
terminal provides much faster output than a keyboard printer. However,
_____ of data is limited to typing speed.
ANSWER: video display, input

Computer Console

Every computer has a console with a control panel, used by the operator
to monitor and control the activities of the computer. The console may
be mounted on the cabinet containing the central processing unit, or
it may be a separate unit. The console for the IBM System/370 Model
155 is shown in Figure 7–18.

The console control panel contains lights that display the contents
of the various registers. These displays are generally read in a binary-
based notation such as hexadecimal or octal. During program execution
these lights change far too rapidly to be read by an operator. However,
when the computer halts, the displayed register contents may be a valuable aid in determining what has happened.

The console also contains lights to indicate the status of programs
or system components. For example, there is generally an overflow indicator, parity-error indicator, power on/off light, and lights to indicate
error conditions in peripheral equipment. The console also contains
switches and buttons for manual entry of instructions or control commands to the computer.

The computer console generally has a low-volume input/output
device such as a typewriter or cathode-ray tube (CRT). This device is

Figure 7–18. *Console for IBM/370 Model 155 (courtesy IBM).*

used by the computer program to send messages to the operator, and for the operator to respond or input data manually. For example, a message may be displayed on the typewriter (or CRT) when a program is completed. Also the operator may use the typewriter or CRT keyboard to inquire concerning the status of programs in the current stack of jobs to be run.

QUESTION: Communication between the operator and the computer is largely by means of the _____ _____ or _____ unit.

ANSWER: console typewriter, CRT

Devices Using Magnetic Media

Both keyed devices and devices using paper media have relatively low input and output speeds. Where large volumes of data must be input into or read from the computer, the data is often converted to a magnetic medium. The principal magnetic media are magnetic tape and magnetic disk and diskette. Other types of magnetic media include magnetic ledger cards, inscribed magnetic characters, and audio response units.

The principal advantage of the magnetic media is high recording density, resulting in compact storage and high input/output speeds. Also magnetic media can be repeatedly erased and reused.

Magnetic disk units are described in Chapter 5; hence, their description will not be repeated here. Also diskettes are discussed earlier in this chapter under key-disk systems.

Magnetic Tape

Magnetic tape is used very extensively in data processing, primarily for storage of large sequential data files. It offers a number of significant advantages over punched cards, and consequently has replaced cards in many applications. Although the use of magnetic tape is often associated with larger systems, many small computers are available with either standard magnetic tape or small tape cassettes similar to the ones used in home or automobile cassette units.

Recording on Tape. Magnetic tape is made of a plastic base coated with a metal oxide film that is magnetized in the presence of an electric field. Data is recorded on tape in much the same way as a home tape recording. A reel of tape is mounted on a tape drive which moves the tape past read-write heads for reading or recording. Writing on tape destroys the previous contents. However, reading from the tape is nondestructive so that the contents may be read repeatedly. Some magnetic tape units will read only when the tape is moving in the forward direction, while other units will read in both the forward and reverse directions. Standard magnetic tape is one-half inch wide. However, tape widths may range from about one-fourth inch for cassettes to one inch for high capacity tape. A standard reel of tape is 2,400 feet long, but smaller and larger sizes are also common.

Tapes written on a particular drive may be incompatible with a different model drive, because of differences in tape size, recording density, or code used. This may be a important consideration, especially in large decentralized systems where tapes are to be exchanged. Special tape-to-tape converters are available to perform this function, but these units increase total system costs.

The physical beginning and end of a reel of magnetic tape are identified by reflective spots that are sensed by photoelectric cells. When the tape reel is mounted, the tape drive positions the reel at the reflective spot at the front, called the load point. The reflective spot at the end indicates that no more information may be written on the tape.

Tape Drive. A tape drive has two reels—a supply reel and a take-up reel.

Figure 7–19. *IBM 3420 Magnetic Tape Unit (courtesy IBM).*

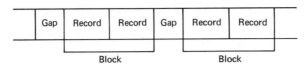

Gap	Record	Record	Gap	Record	Record

Block   Block

Figure 7–20. *Blocking of records with two rec-ords per block.*

Tape is driven by magnetic read-write heads, commonly by means of a vacuum mechanism. The read-write head generally has separate sections (called gaps) for reading and writing. Data that has been written on tape by the write gaps is immediately read by the read gap, and the two are compared to check on the accuracy of recording. A typical tape drive is shown in Figure 7–19.

Tape Records. Data is stored on magnetic tape in the form of blocks. A *block* consists of one or more records in a data processing application. A *record*, in turn, is a set of data pertaining to a particular item. For example, typical records in data processing applications are inventory records and personnel records. The concepts of records and other data structures are discussed in detail in Chapter 12.

Blocks on magnetic tape are separated by gaps, called interblock (or interrecord) gaps. A typical gap is three-fourths inches in length. When a read instruction is given, an entire block is read into memory. The interblock gap allows the tape to accelerate to reading speed before reading to detect the end of block and to decelerate after reading. Figure 7-20 shows a tape organization with two records per block, and with interblock gaps.

QUESTION: Starting and stopping a magnetic tape requires a relatively large amount of time. What is the advantage of blocking records like those shown in Figure 7–20? _____

ANSWER: The effective transmission rate is increased by reading or writing a large amount of data each time the tape is moved

Data is recorded on magnetic tape in binary coded decimal format—generally either standard BCD (six bit) or EBCDIC (eight bit). For the BCD format the tape width is divided into seven channels, as is shown in Figure 7–21. These channels consist of two zone bits, four numeric bits, and a parity or check bit. For the EBCDIC format the tape width is similarly divided into nine channels—four zone, four numeric, and check bit. A character is recorded across the tape in a row, often called a frame. Figure 7–21 illustrates the recording of the number 5 and the letter A on seven-channel tape, with the check bit set for even parity.

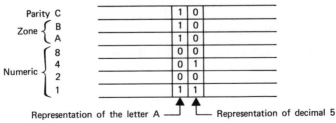

Figure 7–21. *A method of recording data on magnetic tape.*

QUESTION: Data is encoded across the tape in seven _____, one character per row or _____ .
ANSWER: channels, frame

Two important characteristics of magnetic tape are recording density and tape speed. Both tape capacity and transmission rate depend on recording density, measured in frames (or characters) per inch. Typical tape densities are 200 (low), 556 (medium), 800 (high), and 1,600 (very high) frames per inch. Some typical tape speeds are 36 (low), 75 (medium), 112.5 (high), and 200 (very high) inches per second. The transmission rate is the rate (characters per second) of reading or writing on magnetic tape, and it is equal to tape density times tape speed. For example, with a tape density of 200 characters per inch and a speed of 75 inches per second, the transmission rate is 200×75 or 15,000 characters per second.

QUESTION: What is the transmission rate for the highest tape density and speed mentioned in the above paragraph? _____ .
ANSWER: $1,600 \times 200$ or 320,000 characters per second

The first record on a magnetic tape file is generally a header label that contains identifying information about the file. When the tape is mounted, the header record is read and checked to make sure the correct file is being used. Also the last record in a file is often a trailer label containing control information such as block and record count and control totals.

Evaluation of Magnetic Tape. Magnetic tape offers the following important advantages over punched cards.

1. *Speed.* The transfer of data to and from internal memory is performed at rates from 100 to 1,000 times faster with magnetic tape than with cards.
2. *Capacity.* A single tape can hold 10 million or more characters. This is equivalent to 125,000 eighty-column cards punched full with data — or a deck about 73 feet in length.
3. *Convenience.* Tape is much more compact and easy to handle and store than cards. Cards are subject to dropping, getting out of sequence, and damage. Also tape records are not limited to 80 or 96 character lengths.
4. *Cost.* A reel of magnetic tape costs less than $25. Punched cards cost about $1 per 1,000 cards, so that 100,000 cards (with less storage capacity than a reel of tape) would cost $100. Furthermore, the tape can be erased and used over and over again.

QUESTION: To summarize, magnetic tape permits transfer rates from _____ to _____ times faster than cards and costs less than one-_____ as much as the cards it can replace.
ANSWER: 100, 1,000, fourth.

On the other hand, punched cards have certain advantages over magnetic tape:

1. Cards can be read by humans (when interpreted at the top of the cards).
2. A punched card record may be more easily corrected, by removing it from the file and by replacing it with a corrected card.

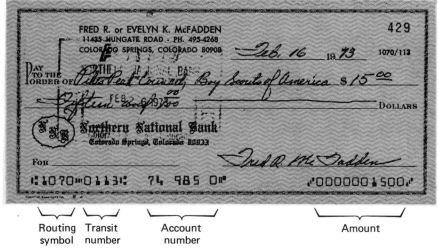

Figure 7–22. *A check inscribed with magnetic ink characters.*

3. When files are small, only a portion of a magnetic tape is utilized. Thus when written on magnetic tape, a file of 100 punched cards requires the same tape reel as does a file of 100,000 punched cards.

In comparison with direct access devices such as magnetic disk, both punched cards and magnetic tape have the disadvantage that individual records are not addressable.

Magnetic Ink Character Recognition

In 1952, approximately 8 billion checks were written and processed in the United States. By 1960, this figure had grown to 13 billion, and at present over 25 billion checks are processed annually. Faced with this burgeoning paperwork, the American banking industry pioneered the development of magnetic ink character recognition, or MICR. Today almost all checks, deposit slips, and related documents are encoded with magnetic ink characters and are processed with MICR equipment.

With MICR, characters are inscribed on documents with magnetic ink containing particles of iron oxide. The document reader senses the magnetic pattern formed by the characters. Only 14 characters are used in MICR—the 10 digits 0 to 9, plus four special characters. These characters are standard throughout the banking industry.

Constant information is recorded on the check in magnetic characters before it is issued to the bank customer. This includes the check routing symbol, transit number, and customer account number (see Figure 7–22). After the check is cashed, the amount is inscribed in the lower right-hand corner.

QUESTION: Examine Figure 7–22. The check routing symbol and transit number are preprinted in the upper right-hand corner of the check, and are inscribed in the lower left-hand corner. The check amount is inscribed in the lower right-hand corner. Identify these three quantities for the check shown: (a) routing symbol _____ , (b) transit number _____ , and (c) amount _____ .

ANSWER: (a) 1070   (b) 113   (c) 1500 (interpreted as 15.00)

167 / DEVICES USING MAGNETIC MEDIA

Figure 7-23. *IBM 3890 Doceument Processor (courtesy IBM).*

Checks are processed by document processors at speeds comparable to punched cards. A typical processor is shown in Figure 7–23.

Point-of-Sale Terminals

The retail merchandise industry is rapidly introducing computer technology to process transactions and to capture sales data at the point of sale. A typical store system includes a number of point-of-sale terminals on the sales floor, linked through a store controller to a remote central computer.

A typical point-of-sale terminal (serving as both a modified cash register and a computer terminal) is shown in Figure 7–24. In a cash transaction, the salesperson passes a hand-held "wand" (shown in the picture) over a thin magnetic stripe on the price tag, without removing the tag from the merchandise (some systems use an optical rather than a magnetic medium). The terminal reads the price and identifying information from the tag, records and prints this information, and displays the price on a lighted panel. It also computes the amount due including taxes, calculates and returns change, and prints a cash receipt. The terminal then forwards this data to the central computer where it is used for inventory control and sales analysis.

In a credit transaction the "wand" can be used to read a customer's credit card and initiate a credit check. The terminal also contains a keyboard for entry of data or messages. For example, the salesperson can enter a request to locate and reserve a "big ticket" item such as a refrigerator of a certain model and color.

QUESTION: From the point of view of the customer, describe two advantages of the terminal shown in Figure 7–24 over a conventional cash register.

(1) _____.

(2) _____.

ANSWER: (1) Speedier sale (less waiting)   (2) Fewer errors

Magnetic Ledger Cards

Magnetic ledger cards are used in accounting applications in some small business computer systems. Data is recorded on magnetic stripes on the

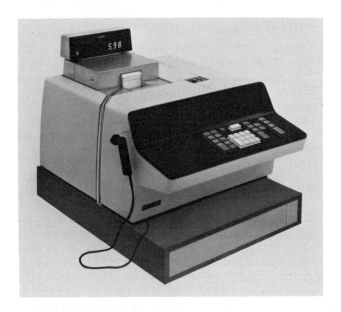

Figure 7–24. *IBM 3653 Point-of-Sale Terminal (courtesy IBM).*

side or back of a ledger card. The cards are read by a ledger card reader, and the results are printed on the card and also are recorded on the magnetic stripe. These readers can read ledger cards at a rate of about 50 cards per minute, so that they are confined to low-volume applications. The principal advantages of ledger cards are the low cost and the fact that individual records are easily interpreted by humans without computer processing.

Audio Response

The ultimate in man-machine communication is a voice response unit. In such a unit, an inquiry is made to the computer by means of a keyboard. The computer transmits the response to an audio response unit which contains a magnetic drum. The unit selects words and phrases from a prerecorded vocabulary stored on the drum, and forms a spoken reply. Only a relatively small number of standardized replies are possible. Audio response units are used in applications such as credit inquiries, stock quotations, and order status.

Devices Using Optical Media

Improved data preparation devices such as key-tape and key-disk systems provide more efficient means for conversion of source data to machine-processable form. However, with all of the media discussed thus far — paper, mechanical, magnetic — preparation rates are still limited by the manual manipulation of a keyboard. With optical character recognition, data is read directly from a printed or marked document. Since manual transcription is eliminated, the use of optical media is sometimes referred to as *source data automation*. The advantages to the user are the reduction of costs and errors associated with keyed data entry.

Data can be read optically only if it has been recorded in some prescribed format. The degree of difficulty and the resulting reading speeds and error rates depend on the type and quality of the recorded data. At present, there are four types of data (in increasing order of difficulty) that can be read optically:

1. Optical marks or special codes.
2. Data recorded in a special printing font.
3. Data recorded in standard type, or in multiple printing fonts.
4. Hand-printed data.

Devices that use optical media include optical mark readers, optical character readers, special terminals (such as point-of-sale recorders), and computer output microfilm devices.

Optical Mark Readers

An optical mark reader reads data recorded by an ordinary pencil in the form of marks (such as "X" or "/") on cards or other documents. The data that is read may be transmitted directly to a computer for processing, or may be automatically recorded on another medium such as punched cards or magnetic tape.

An example of an optical mark reader (Bell & Howell MDR Optical Mark Reader) is shown in Figure 7–25. This illustration also shows some typical documents that can be read by this device. The reader will read punched holes and computer-generated marks, as well as marks from an ordinary pencil. The reading rate is up to 200 cards per minute.

An optical mark reader detects the presence or absence of a mark in a specified location. Therefore, it is useful in reading two basic types of data:

1. Numerical data, such as customer number or quantity ordered.
2. Simple indicative information, such as "defective" or "nondefective."

QUESTION: Examine Figure 7–25. From the sample documents, give two additional examples of each of the following:
(1) Numerical data: _____ , _____ .
(2) Indicative data: _____ , _____ .
ANSWER: Following are some examples:
(1) commodity number, on hand, on order, date, min. bal., max. bal., item number, production quantity
(2) absent, tardy

Optical Character Recognition (OCR)

Unlike an optical mark reader, an optical character reader must be able to read and to identify individual characters. The key elements of an optical character reader are a transport mechanism, a scanner unit, and a recognition unit. After a document is moved into position by the transport mechanism, characters to be read are scanned by a photoelectric device that converts the characters to an electrical signal. The signals are then matched against internally stored reference patterns in the recognition unit. Patterns that cannot be read cause the document to be rejected. Data that is accepted is either read directly into the computer or is recorded on punched cards, magnetic tape, or other media. A typical optical character reader is shown in Figure 7–26.

QUESTION: The major elements of an optical character reader are a _____ mechanism, a photoelectric _____ unit and a _____ unit.
ANSWER: transport, scanner, recognition

Special Fonts. Reading optical characters is facilitated if the documents are printed with a special font. Unfortunately there is a large number of such fonts, either proposed or in use. However, the most commonly used today is the American National Standard font, shown in Figure 7–27. The The use of a single font such as the one shown increases reading rates and minimizes rejection rates. However, the user must have a high degree of control over his source data, to ensure that all data is recorded in this font.
Multiple Fonts. Some optical character readers are equipped to handle multiple fonts, as well as standard typewriter characters. This type of device can read data produced by typewriter, adding machine, card interpreter, and high-speed printer—either individually, or mixed together. This permits much greater flexibility to the OCR user. However, reading rates are typically slower than when a single font (such as in Figure 7–27) is used.
Handprinted Data. A universal document reader would be capable of optically reading handwritten or cursive characters, as well as printed characters. Although much research is being performed, it is not yet possible to read most handwriting with machines. The technical problems are great because of wide variations in handwriting style. However, some document readers will read handprinted characters, where the characters are carefully formed block letters and numbers. For exam-

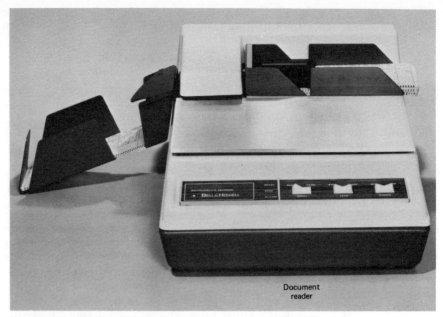

Document
reader

Figure 7–25. *MDR Optical Mark Reader (courtesy Bell & Howell).*

ple, the following message could likely be read without error with this type of device:

APRIL 22 1973

Evaluation of OCR. Optical character recognition is an important and rapidly growing method of source data automation. Reading speeds vary over a wide range—depending on type and size of documents, character fonts, and type of equipment used. At present, OCR readers are capable of reading from about 100 to 1,500 documents per minute. Character reading rates may vary from 100 to several thousand characters per second. Thus reading rates are comparable to those for punched cards.

Reliability is an important consideration in selecting an OCR application. Two measures of reliability are the reject rate and the error rate. The *reject* rate is the percentage of documents that cannot be read by the reader. Depending on the application, this currently ranges from 1 to 10 percent. The error rate is the percentage of documents read on which one or more characters is incorrectly identified; at present, the error rate is less than 1 percent.

QUESTION: Two measures of reliability in OCR are the _____ rate and the _____ rate.

ANSWER: reject, error

The principal deterrent to using optical character recognition is its cost. It has been estimated that an installation must have a volume of

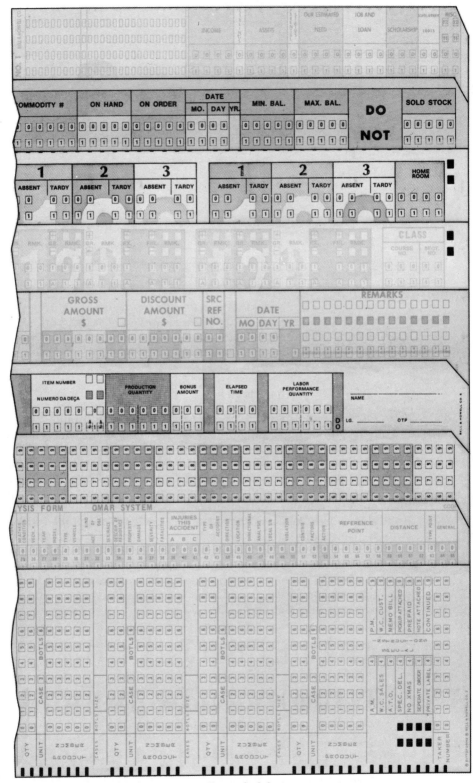

Figure 7-25 *(continued). Typical optically-marked documents.*

173 / DEVICES USING OPTICAL MEDIA

Figure 7–26. An optical character reader (courtesy IBM).

about 10,000 documents per day or more (equivalent to about 10 keypunch operators) to justify OCR. However, cost and performance of OCR equipment are improving, and it appears that use of OCR equipment will continue to increase at a rapid rate in the future.

Optical Terminal Devices

Optical scanning devices are used in many additional ways for source data entry and automation. For example, some supermarkets are now using a computerized checkout system consisting of optical scanner devices, modified cash registers, and an in-store minicomputer or remote central computer (see Figure 7–28). Each grocery package or item is imprinted on the bottom with a special product code adopted by the grocery industry. As each grocery item is checked it passes over a reading slot, where the scanner mechanism optically reads the product code and transmits the information to the computer. On recognizing the code, the computer looks up the current price for the item and prints or displays the information on the cash register. When checkout is completed, the cash register computes the total and prints out a customer receipt. At the computer, data is collected to maintain inventory and provide management information.

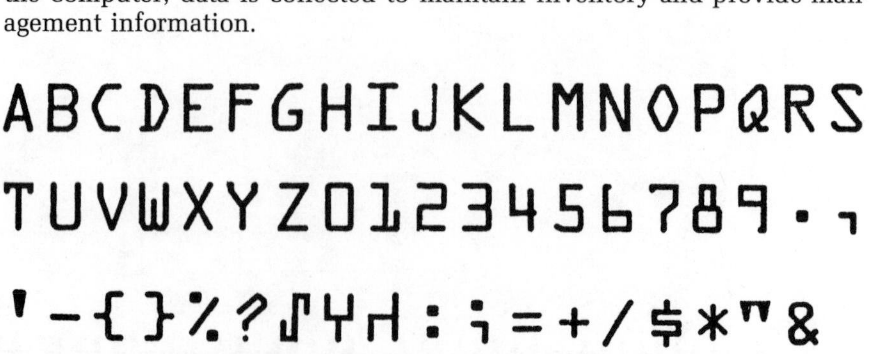

ABCDEFGHIJKLMNOPQRS

TUVWXYZ0123456789.

'-{}%?♪ЧН:;=+/$*"&

Figure 7–27. American National Standard character font.

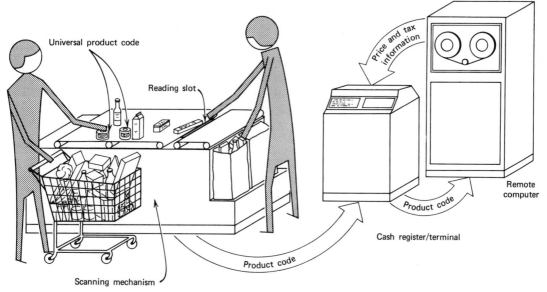

Figure 7-28. *A computerized grocery checkout system.*

QUESTION: Examine Figure 7–28. The principal elements of the computer checkout system are an optical _____, a modified _____ _____, and a _____ processor.

ANSWER: scanner, cash register, computer

An example of a terminal device for this type of system (IBM 3663 Supermarket Terminal) is shown in Figure 7–29. A computerized checkout system speeds customer service, reduces costs, and provides timely information for sales analysis and inventory management.

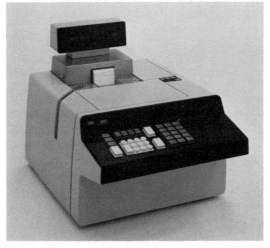

Figure 7-29. *A supermarket terminal (courtesy IBM).*

175 / DEVICES USING OPTICAL MEDIA

Computer Output Microfilm

In many computer applications, printed output is used or retained for reference purposes. For example, in processing customer sales orders, information concerning orders shipped—items, quantities, dates, and amounts—must be accessible to answer customer inquiries. Similarly, extensive parts and catalogs are maintained by parts suppliers. Printed output for such purposes is bulky and is slow and costly to access. An alternative is to use computer output microfilm (COM).

A COM device displays data on a CRT screen, and the data is exposed to microfilm. The device may display data on-line from the computer, or off-line from magnetic tape. Output is a microfilm copy of the data, either in roll or microfiche form. The computer then produces an index to locate the proper roll and frame for a given output.

Computer output microfilm equipment is relatively expensive. However, it offers the following advantages over printed output:

☐ Recording on COM is much faster than printing (from 25 to 50 times faster).
☐ The cost of microfilm is less than that for an equivalent amount of paper.
☐ Microfilm is much more compact; vast quantities of data can be stored in a small space.
☐ Microfilm is much easier to access. In some systems, desk-top inquiry stations can be used to retrieve and display microfilm data in seconds.

Exercise 7–3

1. Explain the difference between key-tape and key-disk systems. Under what conditions would they be used to replace keypunch machines?

2. Give two reasons why optical character recognition is not more widely used for data entry applications.

(a) _____

(b) _____

3. Give four advantages of magnetic tape over punched cards.

(a) _____

(b) _____

(c) _____

(d) _____

4. Why are records blocked on magnetic tape?

_____

_____

Summary

A wide variety of devices is available for preparation, input, and output of information. These devices may be loosely classified according to the media used — paper, keys and dials, magnetic, and optical. Another method of classification is according to input and output rates. As a general rule of thumb, devices that depend on human manipulation of a keyboard — key punches, key-tape and key-disk systems, and keyboard terminals — can be operated (at best) at a few hundred characters per minute. Devices that manipulate paper documents — card readers, line printers, optical mark and character readers, and magnetic ink document processors — can process data at from one thousand to several thousand characters per second. Devices that process magnetic media (tape or disks) can read or output data up to several hundred thousand characters per second.

Input/output and secondary storage devices represent the means by which data is input, stored, retrieved, and output from the computer. Taken together, these devices are often referred to as computer peripherals. In the past few years, peripherals have been among the fastest growing areas of the computer industry. Intense competition has improved performance, reduced cost, and has led to "mixed" systems in which a central processing unit of a major manufacturer is surrounded by peripherals produced by several smaller manufacturers. This type of competition has undoubtedly been healthy for the industry, as well as beneficial to the user.

In many computer applications, input and output devices are remotely located with respect to the computer. Communications channels and devices are used to link the computer with these remote devices. Concepts and devices for data communications are discussed in the next chapter.

Solutions to Exercises

Exercise 7–1

1. Each department could be issued prepunched cards for the various services or supplies that it dispenses. Each card would contain a stock number (if applicable), description of the supply or service, and unit cost. For example, the X-ray department could have cards for each major type of X-ray. As various services are performed and supplies are issued, cards would be assembled for the patient. A tabulation of the cards would then provide patient billing.

2. It is only necessary to keypunch customer name and address, and for each item the order code and quantity ordered. The name and price of each article are constants that can be stored in the computer system (for example, on magnetic tape or disk). The computer multiplies unit price by quantity to obtain the total for each item and computes the total amount for the order.

Exercise 7–2

1. (a) A "write" instruction is executed.
   (b) An electrical signal is sent to the output device control unit.
   (c) The control unit converts the internal code into a code suitable for the output device.
   (d) The output device writes the contents of the record onto the output medium.
   (e) When the output operation is completed, a signal is transmitted to the central processor.

2.

	Cycle Time	Records per Second	Percent Idle
(a) Nonoverlapped	50,000	20	80
(b) Overlapped	20,000	50	50

3.

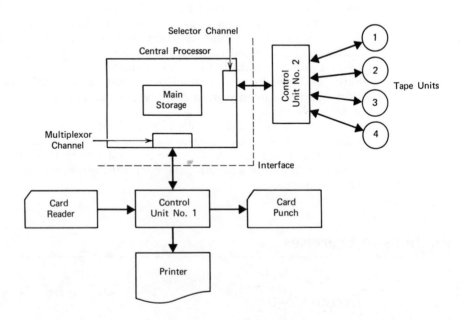

4. GET, PUT, OPEN, CLOSE.

Exercise 7–3

1. In a key-tape system, data is input on a keyboard and is recorded on magnetic tape. A key-disk system is an integrated data entry system with a minicomputer control unit. As data is keyed in, it is stored on magnetic disk. The computer may be programmed to perform edit and validation functions.

   Both key-tape and key-disk systems would be used where input volume is sufficiently high to justify their additional cost.
2. (a) OCR equipment is expensive, although costs have been declining.
   (b) OCR requires a special font or, in the case of handprinted characters, very close control over character format.
3. (a) Magnetic tape is much faster.
   (b) Tape has much greater capacity and requires less storage space.
   (c) Tape is more compact, convenient, and easier to handle.
   (d) Tape is much less costly for a given storage capacity.
4. Blocking permits reading or writing a large amount of data each time the tape is moved, thus increasing the effective transmission rate.

Chapter Examination

1. Define each of the following abbreviations:

   (a) MICR _____

   (b) COM _____

   (c) OCR _____

   (d) CRT _____

2. Match the applications shown in the first column with the most appropriate device shown in the second column:

   _____ Processing large sequential files   (a) video display unit (CRT)

   _____ Processing checks   (b) optical character recognition

   _____ Capture of sales data in a retail store   (c) computer output microfilm

   _____ Large-volume data preparation   (d) line printer

   _____ Low-volume input of data in a small business system   (e) magnetic tape

   _____ Storing large-volume output for ease of visual retrieval   (f) point of sale recorder

   _____ Direct input of large volumes of data recorded in a special printing font   (g) computer console typewriter

   _____ On-line display of inventory status   (h) magnetic ink character recognition

_____ Manual entry of control
instructions to the computer
_____ Output of a 1,000-item stock
status report

(i) punched cards

(j) key-tape or key-disk

3. Define each of these terms:

(a) Graphics _____

(b) Interface _____

(c) Channel _____

(d) Buffer _____

(e) Multiplexor channel _____

4. Inventory records are stored on a 2,400-foot reel of magnetic tape. Each record is 80 characters in length. Each record is stored as a single block and the interblock gap is ¾ inches. Fill in the following table:

Density (Char/In)	Speed (In/Sec)	Transfer rate (Char/Sec)	Records per Reel
200	75	_____	_____
556	75	_____	_____
800	112.5	_____	_____
1600	200	_____	_____

5. Assume that the cost of punched cards is $1 per thousand, and the cost of a 2,400-foot reel of magnetic tape is $25. Compare the cost of storing the inventory records (from problem 4) on magnetic tape and punched cards. Assume a density of 800 characters per inch on

magnetic tape. _____

_____

6. Compute the same table as for problem 4, but assume that the inventory records are blocked on tape, five records per block.

Density (Char/In)	Speed (In/Sec)	Transfer rate (Char/Sec)	Records per Reel
200	75	_____	_____
556	75	_____	_____
800	112.5	_____	_____
1600	200	_____	_____

7. Identify the following statements as true or false:

_____ (a) Data preparation generally accounts for less than 10 percent of the data processing budget.

_____ (b) Ideally, data is recorded in machine-processable form when it is originated.

_____ (c) Data channels make possible the overlapping of input/output and processing.

_____ (d) Constant information (routing symbol, transit number, and account number) are inscribed on checks after they are cashed.

_____ (e) For high input/output rates (say 100 thousand characters per second), magnetic media must be used.

_____ (f) Reading rates for optical character devices are significantly higher than for punched cards.

_____ (g) Compared with printers, video display units offer the advantages of faster output rates and the ability to display graphical information.

_____ (h) Although computer output microfilm provides very compact information storage, it has the disadvantages of slower output than with printed output.

_____ (i) Key-disk systems provide editing and format controls that increase the throughput of the central computer.

_____ (j) Present-day optical character readers can read handwritten data.

8. List three applications of minicomputers as applied to input/output devices or operations, as described in this chapter.

(a) _____

(b) _____

(c) _____

9. Calculate the data rates (characters per second) for each of the following:

(a) Punched card reader that reads 1,000 cards per minute (80 characters per card) _____

(b) Optical character reader that reads 500 documents per minute (average 200 characters per document) _____

(c) Magnetic ink document reader that processes 600 checks per minute (average 35 characters per check) _____

181 / CHAPTER EXAMINATION

(d) Line printer that prints 1,200 lines per minute (132 characters

per line) _____

(e) Magnetic tape unit that reads or writes data with a density of 800

characters per inch and speed of 112.5 inches per second _____

_____

10. What is the principal difference between an optical mark reader and

an optical character reader? _____

_____

_____

11. List three examples of each of the following:

(a) Devices using paper media _____

_____

(b) Devices using magnetic media _____

_____

(c) Devices using optical media _____

_____

(d) Devices using mechanical media _____

_____

12. List four types of data that can be read with optical techniques.

(a) _____

(b) _____

(c) _____

(d) _____

13. Give four advantages of computer output microfilm over printed
output.

(a) _____

(b) _____

(c) —————————————————————————————————

(d) —————————————————————————————————

14. Describe the meaning of each of the following:

(a) Reject rate ——————————————————————

——

(b) Error rate ————————————————————————

——

15. Describe the function of a data channel.

——

——

——

——

Chapter 8

DATA COMMUNICATIONS SYSTEMS

Overview

In many (if not most) organizations, data originates at one location, is processed at a second location, and the results are transmitted to a third location. In such instances, it is necessary to design a balanced system for the collection, transmission, processing, storage, and retrieval of data. For example, it probably makes little sense to mail sales orders from a branch office in Atlanta to a central office in Los Angeles, and then process the orders on a third generation computer. Faster response may dictate the use of a data communications system linking sales offices and warehouses to a central computer.

A data communications system is a system of terminals, communications equipment and channels, and software that links together the various elements of a data processing system. It may range from a single terminal in an executive's office connected to a computer in another part of the building, to a nationwide network of interconnected computers and terminals. Among other advantages, properly designed data communications systems permit faster response, better service, reduced errors, and improved utilization of data processing facilities.

The use of data communications in data processing systems is growing very rapidly. According to a recent survey, there were 185,000 data terminals in use in 1970. This number was predicted to increase to 800,000 by 1975 and to 2.5 million by 1980 — an annual growth rate of about 30 percent. This growth will occur through the increased use of terminals in banks, retail stores, hospitals, plants, sales offices, and many other establishments.

Systems combining computers and communications systems are often referred to as teleprocessing or telecommunications systems. The major concepts and devices used in these systems are described in this chapter.

Applications of Data Communications

Teleprocessing systems may be used in a variety of ways. To illustrate, suppose that a wholesale distributing company consists of four branch offices, a home office, and a warehouse — all located in different cities. At present, the company uses a system in which orders received at the branch sales offices are accumulated in batches and mailed to the home office where they are keypunched and processed. After the shipping orders are printed by the home-office computer, they are mailed to the warehouse for filling and shipment.

With this system, there is an average delay of nearly one week (primarily because of mailing) between the time a customer order is received and shipped. A data communication system could be used to reduce this time to one day—or minutes, if necessary. Following are some of the ways such a system could be used.

Off-line Batch System

In an off-line communications system data is recorded on a machine-readable medium, instead of being transmitted directly to or from the computer. An off-line system for the distributing company is shown in Figure 8–1. Here, transaction cards are keypunched from customer sales orders in each branch office. When a batch of cards has accumulated, the cards are read by a card reader terminal and transmitted over communications lines to the home office. The receiving device is a card punch terminal which punches cards identical to those that were transmitted. The cards from the various branches are then processed by the computer, perhaps at the end of each day's activity.

The principal advantage of such an off-line data communication system is that it reduces delays in sending data between two geographical points. In the above example, orders would be delivered at the home office the same day (or several times each day, if desired)—rather than one or two days after receipt. If a similar system were used to connect the home office and warehouse, the distributing company could reduce the time to fill orders from one week to about one day.

In addition to punched cards, other devices and media such as punched paper tape, magnetic tape and line printers can be used in off-line data communications systems. For example, if a sales report is to be printed for branch office management, data can be read from punched cards or magnetic tape at the home office and printed on a line printer at each branch sales office.

On-line Batch System

On-line means that data is transmitted directly to the computer for processing. An on-line batch system for the wholesale distributor is

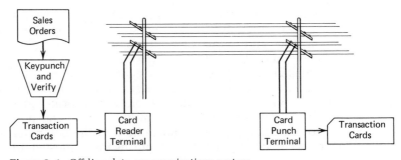

Figure 8–1. *Off-line data communications system.*

185 / APPLICATIONS OF DATA COMMUNICATIONS

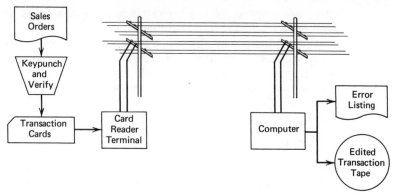

Figure 8–2. *On-line batch-processing system.*

shown in Figure 8–2. As in the off-line system, customer orders are key-punched at each branch office. After a batch of cards has been accumu-lated, the cards are transmitted to the computer where they are used as input for an editing run. The computer writes the edited transactions on magnetic tape, and prints an error listing. After the transactions from all the branches are edited and written, the tapes are merged and processed to produce shipping orders.

QUESTION: Compare Figures 8–1 and 8–2. In the off-line system (Figure 8–1) transmitted data is recorded on _____ _____ while in the on-line system data is input into the _____.
ANSWER: punched cards, computer

If the computer were connected on-line to the warehouse, data would be transmitted and shipping orders would be printed on a terminal in the warehouse. The principal advantage of an on-line system is that data is immediately available for processing by the computer when it is trans-mitted. With such a system, the distributor could fill orders the same day they are sent from the branch sales office.

On-line Real-time System

An on-line real-time system provides near-instantaneous responses to inquiries from a terminal. These responses can be used to answer a cus-tomer's questions or to trigger an activity such as shipment of an order.

A real-time order processing system for the wholesaler is shown in Figure 8–3. A teletypewriter (or similar terminal) is located in each branch office and in the warehouse. An on-line printer is also located in the warehouse. The computer has on-line access to inventory files and other files used in the order processing application.

When a customer requests information concerning a certain item, a clerk can type an inquiry on the teletypewriter keyboard. This informa-tion might concern price, availability of the item, possible substitutes, and so on. This inquiry is transmitted to the computer which searches an on-line inventory record and returns the requested information, which

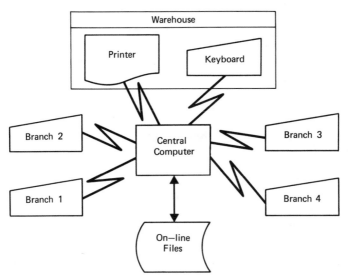

Figure 8–3. *Real-time order processing system.*

is printed on the teletypewriter (alternatively, it could be displayed on a CRT device). This information is provided in seconds—while the customer is still on the phone.

This same on-line system can be used for filling orders. An order for an item is keyed into the typewriter terminal and transmitted to the computer which updates the inventory record and prints the shipping order at the warehouse. The computer prepares an invoicing file which, at the end of each day, is used to print customer invoices. The warehouse keyboard terminal can be used for entering transactions such as receipt of orders. With this system, the distributor could fill customer orders within minutes.

On-line real-time systems are comparatively expensive to develop and to maintain, and are justified only when very rapid response times are justified. They are widely used by airline companies, hotel chains, and large distributing firms. For example, Westinghouse Corporation uses a real-time system that links more than 350 factories, offices, and warehouses. Several thousand orders are received and processed daily. For most of these orders, shipping instructions are printed on a terminal in the warehouse nearest the customer within seconds after they are received.

Data Communications Elements

A data communications system is a system of computers, terminals, communications equipment and channels, and software that links together the various elements of a data processing system. It may range from a single terminal in an executive's office connected to a computer in another part of the building, to a nationwide network of interconnected computers and terminals.

Despite the wide range of possible configurations, there are five basic elements or building blocks in a data communications system. These

187 / DATA COMMUNICATIONS ELEMENTS

Figure 8-4. *Elements of a teleprocessing system.*

elements (whose interrelationship is shown in Figure 8–4) are the following:

1. Computer (or "host processor").
2. Communications control unit (CCU).
3. Data set (or modem).
4. Communications link (or network).
5. Terminal.

QUESTION: Examine Figure 8–4. In sending a message from a remote terminal to the computer, the message passes through the following elements (in order):

(a) _____ .

(b) _____ .

(c) _____ .

(d) _____ .

ANSWER: (a) Data set   (b) Communications link   (c) Data set
(d) Control unit

Computer and Control Unit

There may be one or several computers in a data communications system. If there are several computers, some may be assigned specialized functions such as message switching and local processing. In these systems, there is generally a large central computer that performs the major data-processing tasks. This computer is often referred to as the "host processor."

As is described in the previous chapter, the computer central processing unit communicates with input/output devices by means of control units. These units are connected to the CPU by means of data channels, which coordinate the flow of information into and out of the computer. In the same way, in teleprocessing systems the CPU communicates with data sets by means of a communications control unit (CCU). This device is connected to a data channel by means of a multiplexor channel (described in Chapter 7). An IBM 3705 Communications Control Unit is shown in Figure 8–5.

Data Set

Digital data from a computer or terminal is represented in the form of direct current (dc) signals. Most present-day communications systems

Figure 8–5. *IBM 3705 Communications Control Unit (courtesy IBM).*

(such as ordinary telephone networks) are not capable of transmitting dc signals directly. Instead, these systems use a carrier or set of tones that "carries" the dc signal. The process of converting a dc signal to tones for transmission is called *modulation,* while converting from tones back to a dc signal is called *demodulation.*

This process of signal conversion (necessary in most systems) is performed by a *data set.* This unit is often referred to as a modem, which is derived from the words modulation and demodulation. Data sets are obtainable both from common carriers (such as the Bell System) and from independent equipment manufacturers. A typical data set is shown in Figure 8–6.

QUESTION: In transmitting from a remote terminal to a computer, the signals are first _____ by the data set connected to the terminal and then are _____ by the data set connected to the computer.

ANSWER: modulated, demodulated

Data Transmission

Data is transmitted between remote terminals and the computer by means of a communications link or network. A company may install its own private communications facilities if it so desires. However, most firms cannot justify the cost of installing and maintaining a private network. Instead, these firms use facilities provided by common carriers like the telephone system.

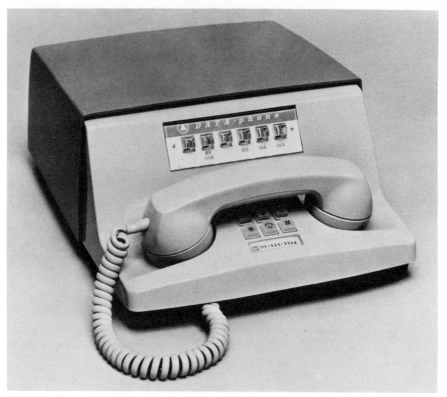

Figure 8–6. *DATA-PHONE data set (courtesy American Telephone & Telegraph Co).*

Common carrier services are offered for public hire in intrastate, interstate, and foreign traffic. All interstate traffic is regulated by the Federal Communications Commission (FCC), which approves the rates and services offered. Intrastate traffic is regulated by state utility boards. The largest common carrier in the United States is the Bell System, which consists of a large number of subsidiaries of the American Telephone and Telegraph Company. In addition, there are many independent operating companies such as Western Union Telegraph Company and General Telephone and Electronics Company.

Data is transmitted either by wire (such as a telephone line) or by microwave. Microwave channels utilize a network of relay stations spaced about 50 miles apart (actual distance depends on the terrain). Space satellites are sometimes used as microwave relay stations for long distance transmission.

Classes of Service

The services offered by common carriers may be classified according to bandwidth as follows: narrowband, voiceband, and broadband (or wideband). *Bandwidth* refers to the frequency range that can be accommodated by the transmission line, which in turn determines the rate at which data can be transmitted.

The three classes of service are defined as follows:

1. *Narrowband.* Data may be transmitted at rates from 45 to 300 bits per second. Narrowband services are limited to applications with low data volumes.
2. *Voiceband.* Voiceband circuits are used in ordinary telephone conversations. Data rates up to 2,400 bits per second are possible using common carrier data sets. Rates up to 9,600 bits per second are achieved with some noncommon carrier data sets.
3. *Broadband.* Very high data rates (up to several million bits per second) can be achieved with broadband facilities, which generally use coaxial cable or microwave transmission.

QUESTION: The rate at which data can be transmitted depends on _____. Three categories of service are _____, _____, _____.

ANSWER: bandwidth, narrowband, voiceband, broadband

Data is transmitted as a series of bits. In the above discussion, transmission rates were specified in terms of bits per second. The term *baud* is often used in describing data rates.

In narrowband transmission, bits are transmitted serially (one at a time). However, in wideband transmission, bits are transmitted in sets — that is, several (or many) bits in parallel. In narrowband transmission, a *baud* is equivalent to one bit per second. However, in broadband transmission, a baud is equivalent to a "bit set" per second. Therefore, if a set consists of eight bits, one baud is equivalent to eight bits per second.

QUESTION: In narrowband transmission a baud equals _____ bit per second; in broadband transmission, a baud is _____ than one bit per second.

ANSWER: one, greater

Leased Versus Dialed Service

Communications facilities may be used in one of two basic ways. First, the user may lease a line from a common carrier on a full-time basis. The leased (private or dedicated) line is available 24 hours a day for the exclusive use of the user. A flat rate is charged for the service, depending on distance. For example, for a typical voiceband facility a good rule of thumb is about $1 per mile per month mileage charge.

The second type of arrangement is dialed (or switched) service. When a message is to be transmitted, the user dials the destination number (either computer or remote terminal), just as for a telephone call. The user must compete with other users for an available line, and may encounter a busy signal at any given time. The user is charged only for the time used, with rates depending on the time of day, day of the week, and distance involved.

The basic mechanical difference between leased and dialed service occurs in establishing a connection. With leased lines, all terminals are physically connected by transmission lines to the central processor all of the time. A "polling discipline" is generally used — the processor sends each terminal that is not busy a special character at short intervals, asking if it has anything to send. If it has a message, the processor allows it to send; if not, the processor may check if it has a message to send to the terminal.

With a dialed (or switched) service, the processor is not connected to terminals except when a message is being transmitted. For this reason, polling is impossible. To send a message to the processor, the terminal user must first dial the processor and establish a connection. The call request causes an interrupt at the processor, which returns a ready signal to the terminal—thus allowing transmission to begin. When the computer has a message for a terminal, it can dial the terminal through an Automatic Calling Unit.

QUESTION: The two basic types of service are ＿＿＿＿＿＿＿ lines (which are based on flat rates) and ＿＿＿＿＿＿＿ lines (rates are based on usage). The former generally operate under a ＿＿＿＿＿＿ discipline.

ANSWER: leased (or private), dialed (or switched), polling

Evaluation of Alternatives. The choice between leased and dialed lines is based on an analysis of costs, message volume, and service requirements. As a general rule, low-message volume favors dialed facilities, while heavy volume favors leased facilities. The situation might be portrayed as follows:

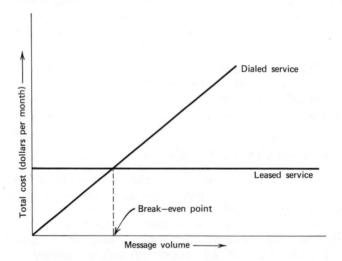

QUESTION: At message volumes below the break-even point, ＿＿＿＿＿ service is less expensive. Beyond this point, ＿＿＿＿＿＿＿ service is less expensive (since it incurs a fixed monthly rate).

ANSWER: dialed, leased

In addition to the cost-volume trade-off, a number of factors related to quality of service should be considered. Compared with dial-up systems, private lines tend to offer these advantages:

1. *Faster response time.* Establishing a dialed connection may require a minute, assuming a line is available. If there is a busy signal, the call

will take longer. For a dedicated line the overhead for processor polling and terminal response is only seconds.

2. *Better quality transmission.* Dialed lines are more subject to transmission errors, because of "poor connections." Private lines are often *conditioned* (electronically upgraded) to reduce error rates.
3. *Privacy.* In a dialed network, any outsider (who knows the correct dial digits and passwords) can access the data communications system. With private lines, access is limited to terminals in the network.
4. *Flexibility.* Private lines provide more user options than dialed systems. Examples are supervisory control (a single terminal in the network monitors and controls all other terminals, through the computer) and multipointing (several remote terminals share a single communications line).

On the other hand, dialed lines provide greater access to the "outside world." For example, if a terminal is part of the telephone network, it can call any other terminal attached to that network.

Transmission Modes

There are three modes of transmission in a data communications system — simplex, half duplex, and full duplex. These modes are shown in Figure 8–7, and described below.

1. *Simplex.* Transmission in one direction only. This mode would be used, for example, in a simple data collection system.
2. *Half duplex.* Transmission in both directions, but only one direction at a time.
3. *Full duplex.* Transmission in both directions at the same time.

Most data communications systems use either a half duplex or full duplex mode. The obvious advantage of full duplex operation is that data transmission can occur in both directions at the same time. For example, a remote card reader can transmit data to a computer and the computer can simultaneously transmit data for printing at the remote location.

Another advantage of full duplex operation is in error control when using an interactive terminal. When an operator strikes a key on the typewriter terminal, it is transmitted to the computer where it is received and

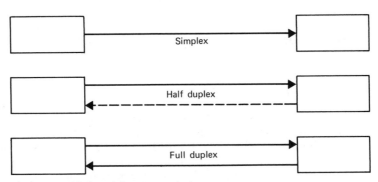

Figure 8–7. *Modes of data transmission.*

checked. The character is then transmitted back to the terminal and printed. If the character that is printed is the same as the key that was struck, the operator is assured that the message has been properly received by the computer. This type of checking is referred to as *echo-checking* or *loop checking*.

QUESTION: Most data communications systems use either a_____ duplex or _____ duplex mode. Full duplex facilitates the use of _____ checking.

ANSWER: half, full, loop (or echo)

Transmission Codes

Just as several different internal codes are used in computers, so are several different codes used in data transmission. It is important in designing a data communications system to consider code compatibility (or methods to overcome incompatibility) between terminals and other system elements. Hardware or software to convert from one code to another is often costly and inefficient.

Recall from Chapter 4 that if a code uses n bits to represent a character, then 2^n characters can be represented in that code. For example, a six-bit BCD code can represent 2^6 or 64 different characters.

Transmission codes generally use from five to eight bits (or levels) to represent a character. Of these, the most important are the following.

1. Baudot (five-level) code.
2. American Standard Code for Information Interchange (ASCII) seven-level code.
3. EBCDIC (eight-level) code.

The Baudot code was devised late in the nineteenth century by Jean Baudot, an engineer in the French telegraph service. Since five levels are used, only 32 code characters are possible. However, the terminal devices used have provision for shifting modes—say, from numeric to alphabetic. By using a shift character, alphabetic and numeric characters can be represented with the same code set. As a result, a total of 62 code combinations can be represented in this code.

The ASCII code represents an attempt to standardize communications codes, and it is widely used in newer equipment. Eight bits are used—seven for coding data, plus a parity bit. This permits a total of 128 characters.

The EBCDIC (Extended Binary Coded Interchange Code) is widely used in IBM computers and terminal devices. This code is described in Chapter 4.

Synchronization

Data is transmitted as a series of coded pulses representing zero and one-bits. How can the receiving terminal properly sense the beginning or end of a character? This is accomplished by means of synchronization (or timing) between the sending and receiving terminals. Two techniques are used: synchronous and asynchronous transmission.

In *asynchronous* transmission, additional bits are included with each character to indicate the beginning and end of the character. For example in the ASCII code, 7 bits are used for coding the character, 1 bit is used for parity, and 3 additional bits are used for synchronization (for a total of 11 bits per character). These added bits include a start bit at the beginning of a character and 2 stop bits at the end of the character.

In *synchronous* transmission, the sending and receiving terminals are kept in constant synchronization by the data sets. Synchronizing information is transmitted in the modulated signal, and special timing circuitry is used in the receiving station.

The advantage of asynchronous transmission is that each character can be transmitted immediately, so that a buffer (temporary storage for the message) is not required. This is important in low-cost terminals such as teletypewriters. On the other hand, synchronous transmission is more efficient, since the added synchronization bits are not required for each character.

QUESTION: From the above discussion, a remote high-speed card reader would transmit data by _____ transmission, while an interactive teletypewriter terminal would likely use _____ transmission.

ANSWER: synchronous, asynchronous

Error Control

Communications links (such as telephone lines) inherently have higher error rates than computers and other electronic devices. Therefore, in a data communications system, it is important to use effective error detection and correction procedures, or otherwise system performance will be degraded.

Sources of Error. The principal sources of transmission error are noise, fading, and distortion.

Noise refers to random signals that interfere with the transmitted signal. There are two basic types of noise: background noise (such as one might experience in a telephone call) and impulse noise. Impulse noise, which is the greater source of error, is caused by electrical storms (or other disturbances) which cause a burst of short-duration pulses.

Fading (temporary loss of signal) occurs primarily in microwave transmission and may be caused by atmospheric conditions, severe rainstorms, or even a bird flying between towers. Distortion is a form of interference within or between transmitted signals, and also sometimes occurs in microwave transmission.

Error Rates. Two types of error rates are of concern in a data communications system: nominal rate, and effective rate.

The *nominal* error rate is the rate that is inherent in the transmission link used. In common carrier voiceband (telephone) lines, for example, the nominal error rate at present is about 1 bit in error out of 10^5 bits transmitted. This rate depends on a number of factors such as type of equipment, distance, transmission speed, and weather.

Most communications systems incorporate techniques for detecting and correcting errors. The *effective* error rate is the rate at which undetected errors occur in transmission.

QUESTION: From the discussion on dialed versus private lines, dialed lines tend to have higher _____ error rates than do private lines.

ANSWER: nominal

Effective error rates depend on the nominal error rates (quality of lines used), and on the sophistication of the error detection and correction techniques used. Following are some examples.

1. Using simple error detection and correction equipment, the effective error rate of a telephone line may be reduced to one error in 10^7 bits transmitted (approximately a 100-fold reduction from the nominal rate of 1 in 10^5).
2. A large time-sharing company uses block error detection techniques (discussed in the next section) and automatic alternate routing—that is, if a noisy connection is encountered, the computer automatically selects an alternate route. By using telephone lines, the effective error rate has been reduced to 1 in 4×10^{13} bits.
3. A large computer network (the ARPA network) connects 25 computing centers throughout the United States. The network uses common carrier facilities with nominal error rates of about 1 in 10^5 bits. Using sophisticated error detection and correction, and automatic alternate routing, users claim they have never detected a single erroneous message that the data communication system passed as correct.

Error Detection and Correction. Three techniques are commonly used for detecting errors in transmission:

1. *Simple parity check.* A bit is added to each character to make the total number of one bits in each character transmitted either odd or even. Each character is then checked for correct parity at the receiving end. This simple parity check (also discussed in Chapter 5) will not detect errors involving an even number of bits, and does not permit error correction.
2. *Block parity check.* In addition to parity bits, one or more check characters are added to each message. These characters are derived from the data bits in the message by the transmitting circuitry. On receiving the message, the receiving circuitry uses the same process to derive the same set of check characters. If these characters match the ones transmitted, the message is assumed correct; otherwise, an error is noted.
3. *Loop checking.* This is described in the discussion of the full duplex transmission mode.

QUESTION: In a particular system, one additional character is added to each message transmitted. The character added depends on the content of the message. This is an example of _____ parity checking.

ANSWER: block

When a transmission error is detected (by one of the methods described above), provision must be made for correcting the error. At present, there are two primary techniques that are used:

1. *Retransmission of the message.* This is the method most generally used today.
2. *Automatic error correction.* A sophisticated way to correct errors is to build enough redundancy into the code so that the receiving end not only can detect errors (block parity check) but also can correct most errors that occur without retransmission.

Redundancy refers to parity bits and check characters that are added to the message, and such codes are called *error correcting codes.* Adding redundancy to the code reduces errors, but it also reduces transmission efficiency (since the redundant characters are not part of the message).

QUESTION: Two techniques of error correction are simple _____ of the message, and use of an _____ _____ code with redundant characters.
ANSWER: retransmission, error correcting

Exercise 8–1

1. Specify whether private or dialed service would be more appropriate for each of the following applications:

   (a) An airline has remote terminals throughout the country for on-line reservations, linked to a central computer. _____
   (b) A small engineering company has two time-sharing terminals. Time is purchased from a nationwide time-sharing company to solve engineering problems that arise from time to time. _____
   (c) A business school has six time-sharing terminals that are connected to a computer across campus. Usage is heavy throughout the day and early evening. _____
   (d) A real estate broker subscribes to a listing service. Calls are placed at irregular intervals throughout the day. _____

2. Contrast each of the following:

   (a) Loop checking versus block parity checking

   (b) Half duplex versus full duplex

   (c) Synchronous versus asynchronous transmission

(d) Nominal versus effective error rates

3. Describe three sources of error in data transmission.

(a) _____

(b) _____

(c) _____

Common Carrier Services

The basic concepts of data transmission are described in the previous section. Services offered by the common carriers — present and proposed — are described in this section.

Narrowband Services

Narrowband services provide transmission rates from 45 to 300 bits per second. This type of service is frequently used when there are many transmission locations, with a low volume of data at each location. Data may be entered by keyboard or punched paper tape.

The most commonly used narrowband services are teletypewriter and telegraph.

1. *Teletypewriter Exchange Service (TWX).* This is a dial-up service offered by Western Union. This service offers transmission at either 60 words per minute (45 bits per second) or 100 words per minute (110 bits per second).
2. *Telex.* This is a teletypewriter service offered by Western Union, comparable to TWX. Switched service is at 66 words per minute (50 bits per second).
3. *Telegraph.* This is a low-grade leased service (about 10 characters per second).

Voiceband Services

Voiceband services use ordinary telephone lines. Transmission rates vary from 300 to 4,800 bits per second or more. Both leased and dialed services are available.

1. *Direct distance dialing (DDD).* This is the familiar dialed telephone service. Rates are based on distance and length of call. Data rates up to 4,800 bits per second or more are possible with some data sets.
2. *Foreign exchange service.* This is a dialed service in which the user pays a fixed monthly charge and has access to foreign (nonlocal) exchanges. For example, a user in Denver can dial San Francisco through a local number.

198 / DATA COMMUNICATIONS SYSTEMS

3. *Wide Area Telephone Service (WATS).* This is a dialed service offered by the Bell System. The user pays a monthly charge that is based on the size of the service area, not on the number or length of calls placed. Under the WATS plan, the United States is divided into six zones of increasing size. The user is charged a flat rate on either a full-time basis or a measured-time basis, depending on the zone to be called (the entire United States, if desired). This service is widely used by customers with a large volume of widespread one-way traffic.

4. *Leased line.* A variety of leased voiceband services are available in addition to the above dialed services.

Wideband Services

Wideband services provide data rates from several thousand to several million bits per second. These services are limited to high-volume applications.

1. *Telpak.* This is a leased service offered by the Bell System. This service consists of groupings or packages of voice channels. For example, groupings of 60 and 240 voice channels are available. This service is used primarily for on-line communication between computers and high speed input/output devices — for example, computer-to-computer, or magnetic tape-to-computer.

2. *Switched broadband service.* Both Western Union and the Bell System offer switched broadband services. An example is the Bell System Dataphone-50 service, which permits the user to handle peak loads without the expense of leasing a wideband data channel.

Future Developments

At present, the bulk of data communications traffic is handled by the telephone companies, using voiceband channels. This service has proved adequate for a large majority of applications. Increasing competition and demand for improved services will inevitably lead to new communications techniques and facilities. Some of these emerging developments are the following.

1. *Digital data service.* To transmit data on voice channels, data sets must be used to modulate and demodulate the signals. The Bell System has proposed to develop a system exclusively for data transmission, which will eliminate the need for signal modulation. This system will be a private (leased) service with transmission rates of from 2,400 to 56,000 bits per second. It would eventually connect 100 or more large cities in the United States.

2. *Special service common carriers.* A number of independent companies (outside of the telephone system) have announced plans and have received approval from the FCC to build data communications systems. Among these are Data Transmission Company (Datran), Microwave Communications, Inc. (MCI), and Western Tele-Communications, Inc. (WTCI). These companies plan to offer private-line services in the voiceband and wideband ranges. Competition between carriers will likely lead to improved service and lower cost.

3. *Domestic satellite.* Satellites have been successfully employed in international communications since 1965. It has been proposed by various agencies to develop a satellite program for domestic communications — voice, video, and data. Major questions have been raised concerning who would operate the system, how it would be financed, and how existing common carriers would be affected. It has been estimated by one source that domestic satellites should be competitive with terrestrial channels at distances over 600 miles. At this time, the FCC has given authority to Western Union and to a consortium of three companies (Lockheed, MCI, and Comsat) to proceed with domestic satellite programs.

Exercise 8–2

1. Fill in the following table:

Name of Service	Bandwidth (Narrow, Voice, Wide)	Dialed or Private
Telegraph	_____	_____
TWX	_____	_____
Telex	_____	_____
DDD	_____	_____
WATS	_____	_____
Telpak	_____	_____
Dataphone-50	_____	_____

2. What is the prospective advantage of:

(a) Digital data service _____

_____

(b) Growth of special service common carriers _____

_____

(c) Domestic satellite program _____

_____

_____

_____

Data Communications Terminals

The functional units of a typical data terminal are shown in Figure 8–8. They are the following.

1. Input and/or output device, such as card reader, printer, magnetic tape unit, and so on.
2. Input or output control unit. The input control unit of a transmitting terminal accepts data from the input device and temporarily stores the data in a buffer unit (low-speed terminals often do not have a buffer). The output control unit accepts data from the communications link, stores it temporarily, and transfers it to an output device.
3. Error control units detect (and possibly correct) errors that occur during transmission.
4. The data set (described earlier) modulates and demodulates transmitted signals.
5. Synchronization units provide proper timing between transmitting and receiving stations.

QUESTION: Examine Figure 8–8. Is the data set considered to be part of the terminal? _____ How about the input or output device? _____

ANSWER: Yes—both are shown as part of the terminal. However the various functional units may be in the same physical cabinet, or in separate cabinets (in Figure 8–4, the data set was shown as a separate unit to emphasize its function).

Input/output devices are discussed in the previous chapter. Most of these devices may be used as data terminals. For example, the input device of a transmitting terminal may be a keyboard, paper tape reader, card reader, magnetic tape unit, OCR device, or computer. The output device at a receiving terminal may be a tape or card punch, magnetic tape unit, printer, display device, or computer.

Following are the major types of terminal devices used in data communications.

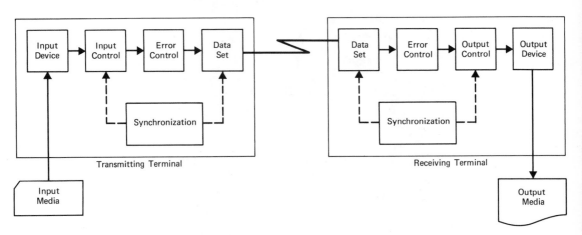

Figure 8–8. *Functional units of a data terminal.*

201 / DATA COMMUNICATIONS TERMINALS

Keyboard-Only Devices. The simplest and lowest cost data entry devices are touch-tone telephones, like the one shown in Figure 8–9. Calls are placed by depressing buttons on the key pad, which generates tone signals. Once the call is placed, the same buttons are then depressed to enter data. As is shown in the figure, the device also permits automatic dialing or entry of data by inserting a punched plastic card the size of a standard credit card.

Following are typical applications of a touch-tone system.

1. *Credit verification.* To verify a customer's credit, a department store clerk can dial a central computer number and enter the customer credit card number and amount to be charged. Within seconds, a voice response will approve or disapprove the charge. The same audio response unit (discussed in Chapter 7) can provide a warning in the event of a lost or stolen credit card.
2. *Ordering merchandise.* A retailer may order items from a wholesaler by dialing the wholesaler's number and inserting a prepunched identity card into the reading device. He then inserts a prepunched card describing the first item he wishes to order. On receiving a signal that the contents of the card have been transmitted, he keys in the quantity to be ordered on the telephone keyboard. He repeats this procedure for each item to be ordered. At the receiving end an automatic key punch produces a set of cards completely describing the order. This procedure eliminates the written purchase order, thus providing faster response and eliminating a large keypunch operation for the whole-saler.

QUESTION: Assuming a computerized file of house listings, how could a real estate broker use a touch-tone telephone? _____

_____

_____

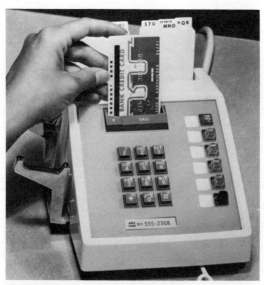

Figure 8–9. *A touch-tone telephone (courtesy American Telephone & Telegraph Co).*

ANSWER: Enter coded information describing desired location, size of house, and price range. Audio response unit would describe listings satisfying these specifications.

Keyboard Printers. Keyboard printers as input/output devices were described in Chapter 7. These units are widely used in data communications systems, especially for time-sharing applications. The most commonly used device is the teletype terminal (see Figure 7–15).

A wide variety of keyboard printer terminals is available. Many of these devices employ a nonimpact printing technique, such as thermal printing, and as a result they are essentially noise-free. These units are often faster, more compact, and (as a result) more expensive than teletype units. For example, the unit shown in Figure 8–10 uses thermal printing and transmits or receives up to 30 characters per second.

Special Function Terminals. A wide variety of terminals used in data communications are oriented to special functions or applications. Several of these devices are discussed in Chapter 7:

☐ Point of sale recorders (Figure 7–24).
☐ Data collection units (Figure 7–16).
☐ Supermarket systems (Figure 7–29).

Special purpose terminals are widely used in the financial community. A terminal used in stock brokerage is shown in Figure 8–11. This unit includes a keyboard for making inquiries and entering transactions, and a display for displaying stock prices or other information.

QUESTION: Most readers have seen the special function terminals used by banks to do passbook accounting. Describe the operation of such a terminal. _____

_____

_____

Figure 8–10. *A thermal printing terminal (courtesy Texas Instruments).*

Figure 8–11. *Brokerage terminal (courtesy IBM).*

ANSWER: The passbook (with encoded customer number) is inserted into a special slot on the terminal. The operator keys in transaction data, including transaction code and amount. The remote computer updates the customer's account, and relevant information (including new balance) is printed in the passbook.

Display Units. In many applications, a printing terminal (such as a teletype machine) is too slow to display the desired information. For example in an on-line inquiry system it may be desired to frequently display an entire page of information. At 10 characters per second, the user simply could not wait for a full page to be printed.

In such applications, a video display unit is often used. Such a unit consists of a keyboard for data entry, and a CRT screen on which a full page of information can be displayed almost instantaneously. CRT displays are discussed in Chapter 7 (see Figure 7–17).

A miniature display unit (Plantronics ComSet Visual Display Terminal) is shown in Figure 8–12. This unit can be connected to any standard push-button telephone to access and display checking account balances (as is shown in the figure) or other computer-based information.

Combination Display/Printer Terminals. Video display terminals provide the advantages of greater input accuracy (data is displayed on the screen before transmission) and high-speed, high-resolution display of output information. On the other hand, a printer terminal provides the advantage of a printed (or hard copy) output, which can be saved for reference purposes. All of these advantages can be achieved with a data terminal that combines a printer with a video display unit.

An integrated display/printer terminal is shown in Figure 8–13. This unit (Teletype Model 40 Data Terminal) includes an operator keyboard,

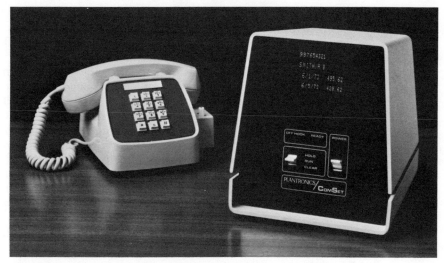

Figure 8–12. *ComSet Visual Display terminal (courtesy Plantronics, Inc).*

display, line printer, and controller. Up to 1,920 characters of information can be displayed on the screen. Printing speed is 220 lines per minute (80 characters per line) so that the information displayed on a full screen can be printed in about 6 seconds. The impact printer can print single or multiple copies of data stored in the display memory, or of data received from the communication line.

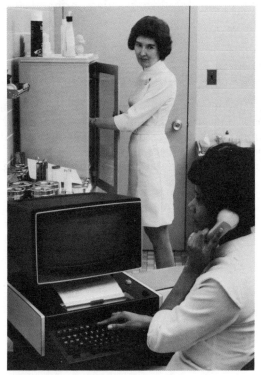

Figure 8–13. *Teletype Model 40 Data terminal (courtesy Teletype Corporation).*

Batch Terminals. All of the above terminals are oriented to low-volume, on-line applications. When large volumes of data are to be transmitted from remote locations to a central data processing center, batch terminals are generally used. Data is accumulated (or batched) at each location — generally on punched cards or magnetic tape — before transmission.

A batch terminal often includes high-speed card readers, line printers, and magnetic tape units (these devices are described in Chapter 7). These units are buffered to provide maximum overlap between record handling and data transmission. Wideband communications facilities are often required for high-speed transmission when batch terminals are used.

Intelligent Terminals. A recent trend in data terminals is toward programmable devices for data entry and transmission. An "intelligent terminal" is essentially a minicomputer with an input keyboard and (often) a CRT display. Other terminal devices (such as card readers) can generally be connected to the intelligent terminal.

An intelligent terminal can perform the following important functions.

1. Checking, editing, and formatting of input data.
2. Error control, including retransmission of messages that are found to be in error.
3. Message routing and switching.
4. "Stand alone" computing — performing small-scale processing tasks at the remote location, thus reducing the load on the central computer and data communications system.

An example of an intelligent video terminal (GTE Information System IS/7800 Series Intelligent Video Terminal) is shown in Figure 8–14.

Calculating Data Throughput

In designing a telecommunications system, it is important to achieve a balance between data transmission rates, and terminal input/output rates. Throughput is the rate (in messages per minute) at which data is transmitted from source to destination.

Throughput can be calculated by using the following formula:

$$T = \frac{60,000}{\dfrac{N}{r} + t_L + t_D + t_P + t_A}$$

where

T = throughput (messages per minute)
N = total number of bits in each message
r = transmission rate (bits per millisecond)
t_L = line turnaround delay (milliseconds)
t_D = transmission delay (milliseconds)
t_P = peripheral delay (milliseconds)
$t_A = \dfrac{N_A}{r}$ $\left(\text{i.e., is calculated from } \dfrac{N_A}{r}\right)$

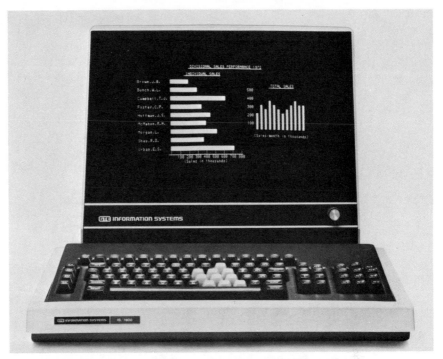

Figure 8–14. An intelligent video terminal (courtesy GTE Information Systems).

where

$$N_A = \text{total bits in acknowledgement}$$

To illustrate the use of this formula, suppose that a terminal with a card reader is capable of reading 100 cards (80 columns) per minute. Transmission is over a voiceband line at 2,400 bits per second, using the ANSCII (8-bit) code. The card reader has only one buffer, so that, when a card is read into the buffer, the reader must wait until the record is successfully transmitted and an acknowledgement is returned before the next card can be read. Assume a half duplex transmission facility with a 200-millisecond line turnaround time. Assume 5 characters are added to each message for error detection and correction, for a total message length of 85 characters. Assume the acknowledgement consists of 6 characters. Finally, assume that transmission is over a short distance so that the transmission delay is negligible.

The calculations are as follows:

$$
\begin{aligned}
N &= 85 \text{ characters per message} \times 8 \text{ bits per character} \\
&= 680 \text{ bits per message} \\
r &= 2{,}400 \text{ bits per second} \div 1{,}000 \text{ milliseconds per second} \\
&= 2.4 \text{ bits per millisecond} \\
t_L &= 2 \times 200 \text{ milliseconds each direction} \\
&= 400 \text{ milliseconds (including return acknowledgement)} \\
t_D &= 0
\end{aligned}
$$

$$t_p = 60,000 \text{ milliseconds per minute} \div 100 \text{ cards per minute}$$
$$= 600 \text{ milliseconds per card}$$
$$N_A = 6 \text{ characters} \times 8 \text{ bits per character}$$
$$= 48 \text{ bits}$$
$$t_A = \frac{N_A}{r} = \frac{48}{2.4}$$
$$= 20 \text{ milliseconds}$$

The throughput is calculated as follows:

$$T = \frac{60,000}{\dfrac{680}{2.4} + 400 + 0 + 600 + 20}$$

$$= \frac{60,000}{1303}$$

$$= 46 \text{ messages per minute}$$

Thus although the card reader is *capable* of reading 100 cards per minute, the *actual* rate of reading and transmission is only 46 cards per minute—less than one half of capacity. A faster card reader would not improve this throughput rate.

Exercise 8–3

A number of techniques can be used to improve throughput rate. Assume in the above example that two changes are made:

(a) Two buffers are used on the card reader instead of one. While one message is being transmitted, the next card can be read into the second buffer. Since the total transmission time in this example exceeds the time to read a card, the effective peripheral delay time is zero—that is, $t_p = 0$.

(b) A full duplex line is used (rather than half duplex), so that the line turnaround time is zero—that is, $t_L = 0$.

Assuming that all other factors remain the same, calculate the new throughput rate for this system.

$$T = \frac{60,000}{\rule{3cm}{0.4pt}}$$

$$= \rule{3cm}{0.4pt} \text{ messages per minute}$$

Distributed Versus Centralized Processing

In our discussion to this point we have assumed that the telecommunications system consists of a central computer facility interconnected to a system of remote data terminals. All data is transmitted to the central computer, which maintains and updates the data base. Results of processing data and inquiries are transmitted to the remote locations.

As the processing requirements in such a centralized system grow, it is necessary to expand the size of the central computer facility. Also the volume of message transmission increases. This raises important questions concerning economics of scale, organizational flexibility, and other issues.

An important alternative to centralized processing—one that is being successfully used by a number of large organizations—is distributed (or decentralized) processing. In *distributed processing*, the processing workload is spread out through the teleprocessing network. This offers a number of important advantages, including greater flexibility and growth potential.

There are several important features of distributed processing. Two are discussed briefly here: (1) the use of front-end processors, and (2) the use of decentralized computers (or intelligent terminals).

Front-End Processors

Recall from the discussion earlier in this chapter that the computer communicates with remote terminals by means of a communications control unit, or CCU (see Figure 8–5). This unit is a hardware device that contains logic peculiar to the transmission lines, terminals, and CPU being used. The CCU performs functions such as assembling and disassembling characters, recognizing special control characters (such as end of message), and monitoring the line to "time out" inactive terminals.

When a CCU is used, most of the actual communications control functions are performed by the computer (or host processor). The user program assembles a message for transmission, and then accesses a special communications control program. This program typically performs the following functions.

1. Code conversion—translating the internal computer code to the code used by the terminal.
2. Queueing—stacking messages for transmission.
3. Polling—sending out queries to remote terminals.
4. Error recovery—performing a defined procedure when a transmission error is detected.

These communications control functions consume both processing time and main storage capacity in the central computer. One solution to this problem which is used in distributed systems is to replace the communications control unit with a *communications processor*. A communications processor is itself a computer, typically a minicomputer, although larger computers are used in some systems. Since the processor is connected to the "front end" of the host computer, it is often referred to as a *front-end processor*, or simply *front end*. The configuration of a simple system with front-end processor is shown in Figure 8–15.

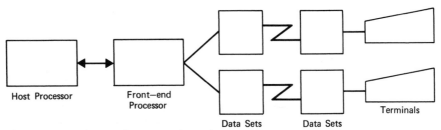

Host Processor   Front—end Processor   Data Sets   Data Sets   Terminals

Figure 8–15. *A front-end processor in a teleprocessing system.*

With a front-end processor, all communications control functions are removed from the central processor to the front end. The communications control program (formerly resident in the host processor) is now resident in the front end. There are two important advantages of using a front-end processor:

1. Throughput and capacity are increased, often at a fraction of the cost to increase the capacity of the central processor.
2. The front end can serve as a message switching unit for a large telecommunications network—receiving incoming messages and routing them to the computer or to other destinations in the network.

QUESTION: The capacity of the central processor can be effectively increased by replacing the ＿＿＿＿＿＿ ＿＿＿＿＿＿ ＿＿＿＿＿＿ with a ＿＿＿＿＿＿ ＿＿＿＿＿＿ ＿＿＿＿＿＿.

ANSWER: communications control unit, front-end processor

Decentralized Computers

A second important feature of distributed processing is the location of smaller computers (or intelligent terminals) in remote locations. These computers perform local processing tasks as well as transmitting messages to the central computer for updating central files or processing inquiries. Large-scale configurations of this nature are referred to as *computer networks*.

An example of a distributed system is one that is used by an increasing number of large national retail merchandising firms (see Figure 8–16). Each store has many point-of-sale (POS) terminals, which are them-

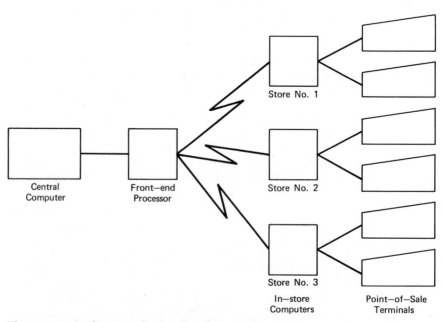

Figure 8–16. *Configuration for distributed processing systems.*

selves small minicomputers. The POS terminal computes the amount of each sale (including tax), and records the details of the sale. Each terminal is connected to a small in-store computer for credit verification and for pooling of information concerning sales and other transactions.

The in-store computers in this system are linked by a communications system to a large central computer at the firm's national headquarters. At periodic intervals (say once or twice a day) this computer polls the local computers and accepts the accumulated sales information. This data is used for centralized inventory control, analysis of sales trends, and other central functions.

QUESTION: Examine Figure 8–16. What are the two elements of a distributed processing system that are present?

1. _____

2. _____

ANSWER: Front-end processor. Decentralized computers.

Summary

The important concepts of data communications systems are discussed in this chapter. Such a system (also called a teleprocessing or telecommunications system) consists of one or more computers and remote terminals, linked together by transmission lines or channels. A properly designed teleprocessing system reduces errors and delays, improves customer service and, in some instances, permits the routine performance of services that would not otherwise be feasible or possible. Examples are the on-line reservations system maintained by many airlines, hotel chains, and car rental agencies.

Solutions to Exercises

Exercise 8–1

1. (a) Private.   (c) Private.
   (b) Dialed.   (d) Dialed.

2. (a) In loop checking, the transmitted message is returned to the sending terminal; in block parity checking, additional check characters are added to the message.
   (b) Half duplex—transmission in two directions, but only one direction at a time. Full duplex—simultaneous transmission in two directions.
   (c) In asynchronous transmission, synchronizing characters are included in the message; in synchronous transmission, synchronization is maintained by the transmitted signal and circuitry.

(d) Nominal-error rate inherent in the circuit; effective-rate of undetected errors.

3. Noise, fading, distortion.

Exercise 8–2

1. Name	Bandwidth	Dialed or Private
Telegraph	Narrow	Private
TWX	Narrow	Dialed
Telex	Narrow	Dialed
DDD	Voice	Dialed
WATS	Voice	Dialed
Telpak	Wide	Private
Dataphone-50	Wide	Dialed

2. (a) Improved quality of service with elimination of signal modulation
and demodulation.
(b) Customized service, benefits of increased competition.
(c) Economical long-distance transmission.

Exercise 8–3

$$T = \frac{60,000}{\frac{680}{2.4} + 20}$$

$$= \frac{60,000}{304} = 195 \text{ messages per minute}$$

The system has a *potential* throughput of 195 messages per minute.
However, since the card reader can read at only 100 cards per minute,
the *actual* throughput is 100 messages per minute (the card reader
speed is now the limiting factor).

Chapter Examination

1. Define each of the following abbreviations:

(a) Modem _____

(b) CCU _____

(c) FCC _____

(d) ASCII _____

(e) WATS _____

2. Match each of the following terms with the most appropriate definition:

_____ Front-end processor (a) simultaneous transmission in two directions

_____ Host processor (b) private or leased line

           (c) timing data included in message

_____ Data set (d) bandwidth greater than voice-band

_____ Full duplex (e) error correction characters included

_____ Echo checking (f) device for modulating and demodulating

_____ Asynchronous (g) master computer in a network

           (h) message returned to sender for verification

_____ Distributed (i) computer for communications control

_____ Narrowband

           (j) processing capacity is decentralized

_____ Redundancy

           (k) transmitting by telegraph and teletypewriter

_____ Dedicated

_____ Wideband

3. Describe the following:
   (a) Three common methods of error detection.

   (i) _____

   (ii) _____

   (iii) _____
   (b) Two common techniques of error correction.

   (i) _____

   (ii) _____

4. Describe the five functional units of a data terminal.

   (a) _____

   (b) _____

   (c) _____

   (d) _____

   (e) _____

5. Describe six typical types of data terminals, and a typical application of each type.

(a) _____

(b) _____

(c) _____

(d) _____

(e) _____

(f) _____

6. In the beginning of this chapter, a wholesale distributing company is described and various data communications systems are illustrated (see Figures 8–1 to 8–3). Explain and illustrate (similar to Figure 8–16) how such a firm might use a distributed processing system.

_____

_____

_____

_____

_____

7. Briefly describe each of these types of systems:

(a) Off-line batch _____

_____

(b) On-line batch _____

_____

(c) On-line real-time _____

_____

8. Describe the function of each of the following:

(a) Communications control unit (CCU) _____

_____

_____

(b) Data set (modem) _____

_____

(c) Front-end processor _____

_____

_____

9. What type of terminal would be most appropriate in each of the following situations?
   (a) Device on which a bank customer can inquire concerning his current balance from his own home, with audio response.

_____

(b) Terminals for the use of students that permit transmitting data

and receiving printed output. _____

(c) Data entry terminal that edits and formats data before transmis-

sion to the computer. _____

(d) Device to be used in an airline terminal for the rapid display of

flight information. _____
(e) Device for entering production data from employee badges,

punched cards, and dial settings. _____

10. List four functions performed by an intelligent terminal.

   (a) _____

   (b) _____

   (c) _____

   (d) _____

11. Identify the following questions as true or false:
   _____ (a) Most data transmission is by narrowband service.
   _____ (b) The principal advantage of an on-line real-time system is that it provides near-instantaneous response to user inquiries.
   _____ (c) Data sets are required only when using leased lines.
   _____ (d) WATS is a dialed service for which the user is charged a flat monthly rate.
   _____ (e) The main sources of transmissions error are noise, fading and distortion.
   _____ (f) Low message volume tend to favor leased transmission service.
   _____ (g) The most common method of correcting errors is to re-transmit the message.

215 / CHAPTER EXAMINATION

12. What type of service (leased or dialed) would be used by each of the following:

(a) Small engineering firm doing occasional calculations using a terminal connected to a remote computer _____.

(b) Large multi-plant firm transmitting sales orders to a central computer _____.

13. What is the difference between nominal and effective error rates?

_____

_____

14. What is the advantage of visual displays (CRT's) over printing terminals?

_____

_____

15. What is distributed processing and what are its advantages?

_____

_____

_____

16. What are the advantages and disadvantages in moving from a simple off-line communications system (Figure 18–1) to an on-line real-time system (Figure 18–3)?

(a) Advantages _____

_____

_____

(b) Disadvantages _____

_____

_____

17. What are the prospective advantages of:

(a) Direct digital service _____

_____

(b) Growth of special purpose common carriers _____

_____

(c) Domestic satellite program _____

_____

18. Briefly describe three sources of error in data transmission:

(a) ————————————————————————————————————

(b) ————————————————————————————————————

(c) ————————————————————————————————————

Chapter 9

CONCEPTS OF DATA PROCESSING

Overview

Throughout this book, the term information system (or data processing system) is used instead of more restrictive terms such as computer or computer system. An information system consists of an integrated system of hardware and software, together with the organization and support functions required to operate, maintain, and improve the system.

This chapter provides an introduction to the concepts of data processing. These concepts derive from the very nature of business operations and from the way information is stored, retrieved, and processed. They have a major influence on the type of software systems that have evolved and will evolve in the future.

First, the various forms of data (termed data structures) are described. These include files, tables, arrays, lists, and data bases. Of these, the most important structure to date has been the file; in the future, it will be the data base.

Next, the most important types of file organizations are discussed. Emphasis is placed on sequential and random forms of organization. More advanced concepts of file and data base design are considered in later chapters.

Following the discussion of file organization, the various forms of data manipulation performed on data structures are described. These include classifying, merging, sorting, and computing.

In essence, this chapter explores the basic "building blocks" of data processing. An understanding of these concepts is fundamental to acquiring a knowledge of data processing and is important in understanding the remaining chapters on software principles.

Data Structures

If data is to be useful, it must be organized in a systematic way. For example, an individual assembles records in a file during the course of a year to support his personal income tax calculations. A physician normally maintains two files for his patients, one containing medical records and the other containing his business accounts.

Methods of organizing (or visualizing) data are referred to as data structures. The more important structures used in data processing are discussed in this section. These include vertical hierarchy, tables, arrays, lists, and data bases.

Hierarchy of Data

The first important concept is that of a vertical hierarchy of data: files, records, and fields (also called data items). A *file* is a set of related records. Each *record* in the file in turn is made up of a number of related fields, which contain the information required by the application.

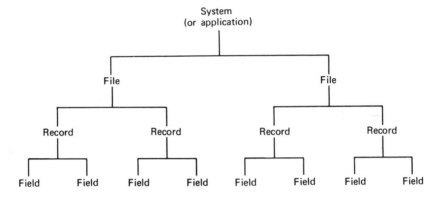

Here are several examples of this data hierarchy:

1. A physician's medical file contains a folder (or record) for each patient. Each record has fields like the following:
   (a) General information—name, age, sex, address, and telephone number.
   (b) Medical history—date of visit, diagnosis, treatment.
2. A parts distributor has an inventory file, in which there is one record for each type of part. This example is discussed in greater detail below.
3. A personnel department maintains a file of employee records. Each record contains employee number, position code, present salary, department number, and data concerning previous assignments with the company.

QUESTION: A college records office maintains a student record file. Name five fields that would appear in the record for each student:

——————————— , ——————————— , ——————————— ,

——————————— , ——————————— .

ANSWER: The fields might be selected from the following list: name, address, date of birth, sex, class, major, grade point average, units remaining

To further illustrate the file-record-field data structure, consider the inventory file maintained by a parts distributor. There is one record in the file for each part in his inventory. A typical record might be as follows.

Stock No.	Part Description	Qty. on Hand	Qty. on Order	Reorder Point	Reorder Qty.
3284	Switch Toggle	1200	1000	1500	1000

↑
└─Key

The last two fields are used as follows: whenever the sum of quantity on hand plus quantity on order falls below the reorder point, a new order is placed. The quantity ordered is equal to the reorder quantity.

Each record in a file is identified by a data item, usually called an *identifier* or *key*. This field is used for arranging the records in sequence in a file and for locating records. The identifier may be numeric, such as the stock number in the above record, or it may be alphabetic, such as a name. A record may contain two or more keys. For example, invoices might be sequenced by customer number, and by invoice number within customer number:

Customer Number	Invoice Number	Name
3184	10892	Smith, Robert M.
3184	10934	Smith, Robert M.
3187	10963	Bell, Marilyn A.
3187	11014	Bell, Marilyn A.
3187	11020	Bell, Marilyn A.

Types of Files. A number of different files are used in data processing applications. The most important are the following.

Type	Purpose	Examples
Master file	Set of relatively permanent records containing identifying, statistical, and historical information, used as a source of reference for an application	Inventory file Student file
Transaction file	Set of records resulting from transactions that affect the status of items in the master file. Used to update the master file	Stock requisitions Registration file

Type	Purpose	Examples
History file	An obsolete master or transaction file, retained for historical use or reference	Material receipts Grade transcripts
Report file	Set of records extracted from data in master files, used to prepare reports	Inventory status file Enrollment report file

QUESTION: The set of personnel records for the employees of an organization constitutes a _____ file. Records of employee transfers or changes in the number of dependents would appear in a _____ file. Data extracted from the personnel file to prepare a monthly personnel summary might appear in a _____ file.

ANSWER: master, transaction, report

Physical and logical files and records. It is often important to distinguish between physical and logical files and records. A physical file is a physical unit such as a reel of magnetic tape. A logical file is a complete set of records for a specific area or purpose that may occupy a fraction or all of a physical file, or that may require more than one physical file. For example, an inventory master file is a logical file containing a record for each item in inventory; it may require one or more reels of magnetic tape.

Similarly, a logical record consists of those fields or data items chosen to describe some entity. A logical record may extend over part or all of a physical record such as a punched card, or may require two or more physical records.

Data Item Design. A data item or field may be comprised of two or more lower-level items. For example, the data item DATE may be formed from three items: MONTH, DAY, and YEAR. The structure is as follows:

When the item DATE is specified, the entire date is obtained. When YEAR, MONTH, or DAY is specified, only the specified portions are obtained. These three fields are referred to as *elementary items*, because they are not subdivided.

A data item may vary in length from one record to another. For example, an item called EMPLOYEE-NAME could be expected to vary from one employee to the next. This leads to two possibilities in the design of items—fixed item size and variable item size. In a fixed length field, the field must be long enough to accommodate the largest item anticipated.

For a variable length field, the length of the item must be specified. This is done in one of two ways: (1) a subfield containing the length of the item is placed at the beginning of the item, or (2) a special symbol is placed at the end of the item. This may be shown as follows:

Length of field ——| Variable length field ——|

Variable length field ——| Terminating symbol

Record Design. The number of fields in each record within a file may also vary. For example, a personnel record file contains a record for each employee. Among other data items, the record contains a field for each previous position held by the employee within the company. Some employees will have many such entries, while others will have only one.

This situation leads to the possibility of fixed or variable length records. If the record size is fixed, there must be sufficient fields to accommodate all anticipated employee records. Data items not used are filled with blanks or some other fill character. If the record size is variable, there is normally a data item identifying the number of items present.

Following is an example of using the variable length record approach for two records from a personnel file. The first employee (Jones) had one previous position with the company, the second (White) had two.

Name	Position Code	Department Number	Salary	Length	Previous Position	
Jones, Robert S.	318	34	975	10	264	

Name	Position Code	Department Number	Salary	Length	Previous Position	
White, James E.	154	27	1135	20	87	304

In the above example, the field *Previous position* has been allocated 10 characters for each item. The field *length* identifies the variable number of characters to follow.

QUESTION: In the example, the item design is _____ length, and the record design is _____ length.
ANSWER: fixed, variable

The approach using fixed item and record size is simpler to program and requires less execution time. However, it also tends to require more storage. Thus variable item and record size are used only when the saving in storage requirement more than offsets the other disadvantages.

For third generation computing systems, an approach called hierarchial organization is often used instead of variable length records. In this technique, records are segmented into master and subordinate sections. The hierarchial method of organization is discussed in Chapter 19.

Tables

Another important data structure is the table. Suppose an individual is preparing his federal income tax forms and has computed his adjusted gross income. His next step is to determine his tax. He does this by finding the appropriate tax table, searching down until he finds an amount corresponding to his adjusted gross income, and then reading across to an appropriate column to find the tax amount.

A simple table may be defined as a set of paired entries. The first entry in each pair is called the *argument*, while the second entry is referred to as the *function* of the argument. The table is searched until the desired argument is located; the value read out of the table is its function.

For example, consider the following partial federal tax table (1971) for an individual claiming three exemptions:

Adjusted Gross Income	Tax (head of household)
5100 to 5149	309
5150 to 5199	318
5200 to 5249	327
5250 to 5299	336
5300 to 5349	345

Suppose an individual has an adjusted gross income of $5231. From the above table, his federal income tax is $327.

QUESTION: In the tax table, adjusted gross income is referred to as the _____; the corresponding tax is called the _____.

ANSWER: argument, function

Tables are frequently used in data processing applications. In particular, tables stored in computer memory are often used as an index to locate records in a direct-access file. Suppose, for example, that a company has personnel records for 200 employees stored on seven tracks of a magnetic disk. An internally stored table could be used to locate records, as follows:

Track Number	Employee Number
1	1 to 30
2	31 to 60
3	61 to 90
4	91 to 120
5	121 to 150
6	151 to 180
7	181 to 200

QUESTION: If the record for employee number 124 is desired, a search of the table would disclose that the record was located on track _____. In this case, the table argument is _____ _____, while the function is _____ _____.

ANSWER: five, employee number, track number

Arrays. A special form of table is one in which the argument is simply the position of the data in the table. For example, following is a table showing the gross sales for a sporting goods store during a particular week:

Day	Gross Sales
1	$ 48.75
2	223.47
3	241.19
4	169.32
5	472.18
6	369.93

Tables in which data are stored by position in this manner are called arrays. Thus an array is an ordered set of data, for which the argument is one of the integers: one, two, three, and so on.

An important property of arrays is that it is not necessary to store the array argument in computer memory. Instead, the computer need store only the data itself, plus the location of the first data element. The location of any other element may then be determined by addition. For example, if sales for day one is stored at computer address 1001, then sales for day four is normally stored at address 1001 plus 3, or 1004.

In the above example, gross sales appeared as a single column of data. An array may also appear as a two-way table, with both rows and columns. For example, the students in a particular course might be categorized by class and major, as follows:

Major	Class			
	1	2	3	4
1	10	4	4	3
2	2	6	3	1
3	0	5	7	2

In this table, class refers to freshman (1), sophomore (2), junior (3), and senior (4). Each entry in the table represents the number of students in the course who are in a particular class and major. For example, there are six students who are sophomores and in major two.

Three items are needed to describe and use arrays: coordinate, dimension, and subscript.

Coordinate refers to the way the data are visualized as being spread out. If data are spread over a single row or column (such as the above example of sporting goods sales), they have one coordinate. If data are spread over both rows and columns (such as the student example), they have two coordinates. A third coordinate would be created if the students were further classified as male or female.

The *dimension* of an array is the number of elements that comprise each coordinate. For the sales example, the array is of dimension six. The array of students has three rows and four columns, and so is of dimension (3, 4).

QUESTION: If the students were further classified as male or female, the array would be of dimension _____.

ANSWER: (3, 4, 2)

Subscripts are coordinate positions used to reference individual elements within an array. They are normally placed in parentheses after a name that has been assigned to the array. For example, suppose that the student array has been given the name STUDENT. Then the element in the second row and third column is referenced as STUDENT (2, 3). In the example shown above, STUDENT (2, 3) has the value 3.

A special case of an array is a single element of data, usually a number. Such an element is called a *scalar*. Examples of scalars are the numbers 1975 and 3.1416.

Lists

Another form of data structure that is of central importance in modern data base design is the list. In a list organization, logical records are connected by means of pointers (or links). A *pointer* is a field in a record which gives the address of another record that is logically related to the first.

To illustrate a simple list structure, suppose that a company maintains a customer file on magnetic disk (or other direct-access device). Each customer record contains the customer number (which is the key or identifier), customer name and address, credit information, and other related data.

At any given time, there may be one or more outstanding invoices for a given customer. A record of each invoice is maintained in a second disk file, called the invoice file. When an order is billed to the customer, a new invoice is added to this file; when the customer pays an invoice amount, the invoice is deleted from the file.

It is necessary for the system to be structured so that the company can determine at any time the outstanding invoices for a particular customer. To do this, a list organization as is shown in Figure 9–1 would be used. Each customer record contains a pointer (or address) that "points to" the location of the first invoice for that customer in the

Address	Customer No.	Customer Information	Pointer
100	1		*
101	2		252
102	3		
103	4		

CUSTOMER FILE

Address	Invoice No.	Invoice Information	Pointer
250	100		
251			
252	103		255
253	127		
254	116		
255	109		*
256	114		

INVOICE FILE

Figure 9–1. *An illustration of list organization.*

225 / DATA STRUCTURES

invoice file. If there is no invoice for a customer, a special symbol is contained in the pointer field. The first invoice, in turn, contains a pointer that "points to" the location of the second invoice for that customer, and so on. Again, the last invoice for the customer contains a special symbol in the pointer field.

QUESTION: Examine Figure 9–1 and answer the following questions.
(a) What invoice numbers are now outstanding for:
   Customer number one? _____
   Customer number two? _____ , _____ .
(b) Suppose a new invoice (number 130) is added to the invoice file for customer number two, at address 251. What will the pointer be for:
   Invoice number 109? _____
   Invoice number 130? _____
(c) Instead of (b), suppose that customer number two pays the amount for invoice number 103. List two changes that will occur in Figure 9–1:

   (i) _____

   (ii) _____

ANSWER: (a) none; 103, 109 (b) 251; * (special symbol). (c) (i) Invoice number 103 is deleted from the invoice file; (ii) The pointer for customer two is changed to 255.

An important type of list organization is referred to as a *ring*. A ring is a list (or chain) in which the last record "points back" to the first. This may be illustrated as follows:

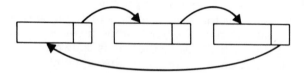

The advantage of this type of organization is that all records in the ring can be easily located, regardless of the starting point.

QUESTION: Refer to Figure 9–1 again. If the pointer for invoice number 109 is changed to the number _____ , a ring will be formed.
ANSWER: 101

Database

Historically, the approach to data processing has been rather fragmented. The total data processing requirements for an organization have normally been split into a series of applications, with a separate file or files for each application. This has proved to be a satisfactory approach for each application but has led to a proliferation of files, some with similar data. For example, a payroll file and a personnel file contain much common data for each employee. If they are maintained as separate files, they may contain conflicting information because of delays in updating one file or the other when changes occur. Also it is often very difficult for management to obtain an answer to an inquiry that crosses both applications.

To overcome these difficulties, managers and system designers have become aware of the need to develop more integrated approaches to data processing. This has led to the concept of a computer-based management information system, which is introduced in Chapter 2.

In terms of data structures, the management information system approach leads to the concept of a database. A *database* is an integrated set of files, tables, arrays, and other data structures. Separate files may exist in a database, but they are linked together (using list organizations) to facilitate providing the information needed by a whole segment of an organization or, ultimately, the organization as a whole. For example, many banks maintain central information files that link together all information concerning an individual's relationships with the bank— checking account, savings account, loans, trust account, and the like.

Databases require large storage capacities, and the trend in file design in large systems is toward the use of a hierarchy of storage devices. Databases also require sophisticated software systems which are currently available in many third generation computer systems. Such systems, termed data management systems, are discussed in the next chapter.

Exercise 9–1

1. A vertical hierarchy of data consists of _____,

_____, and _____ _____ or

_____.

2. Match the following definitions to the appropriate terms:
   (a) Set of associated or linked elements   file

   (b) Integrated set of data structures   table

   (c) Set of related records   array

   (d) Set of ordered data   list

   (e) Set of paired entries   database

3. Describe two methods for identifying the length of a variable length field.

   (a) _____

   (b) _____

4. Following is an array showing the sales (in thousands of units) for a company, by period and product number.

Period	Product Number		
	1	2	3
1	27	43	34
2	13	9	17
3	24	36	48

(a) How many coordinates does the array have? _____ .

(b) Suppose the array is called SALES. Then the dimension of the array may be expressed as SALES (_____ , _____).

(c) What is the value of SALES (1, 3)? _____ .

5. A record in a file is located by means of an _____

   or _____ .

6. Two important methods of item and record design are _____ and _____ length.

7. The four most common types of files encountered in data processing applications are _____ , _____ ,

   _____ , _____ .

File Organization

As with manual files, there are several methods for organizing computer-based data files. The choice of method depends on the objectives of the system designer, and involves important trade-offs in terms of cost, processing speed, and accessibility of information. The basic objectives of a file organization are:

1. To facilitate file creation and maintenance.
2. To provide an efficient means for storing and retrieving records in the file.

To achieve these objectives, the system designer should use to advantage the characteristics of the data, the equipment (including storage), and available software systems.

The basic methods of file organization are sequential access, direct access, and index sequential. These methods are discussed in this chapter. More advanced methods are covered in Chapter 19.

Sequential Organization

In a sequential file, records are arranged in ascending or descending order according to a key that may be numeric (such as stock number) or alphabetic (such as customer name). To locate a specific record it is necessary to start at a given reference point (often the beginning of the file) and to examine each record in sequence until the desired record is located. There are often gaps in the numbering of records: for example, record number 78 may be followed by number 86, and so forth.

Figure 9–2 shows a portion of a punched card inventory file. Each record is contained on a separate card, with the record key (stock number) punched in columns one to six.

QUESTION: To locate the record for item number 134, it is first necessary to read and examine the cards for stock numbers _____, _____, and _____.

ANSWER: 56, 79, 129

Sequential files are generally maintained on magnetic tape (punched cards are sometimes used in smaller systems). In many applications, batching transactions and processing them sequentially at periodic intervals is the most efficient approach. For this reason, and because magnetic tape is an inexpensive file medium, the sequential file organization is widely used.

Direct access devices such as magnetic disk may be also used for sequential storage and processing. When disk storage is used, sequential processing is sometimes referred to as SAM for sequential access method.

Sequential File Updating. With a sequential file organization, transactions to be processed against the master file are accumulated in batches. For example, inventory transactions might be accumulated throughout the

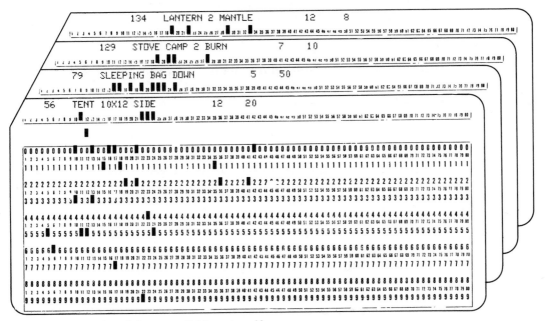

Figure 9–2. *A portion of the sequential inventory file.*

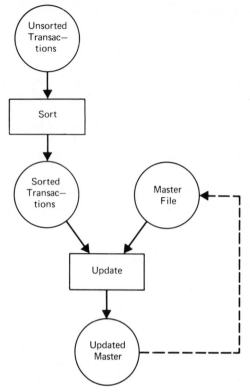

Figure 9–3. *Sequential file updating.*

day. Next, the transactions are sorted into the same sequence as the master file. Finally, the master file is updated using the sorted transaction file. This process is referred to as *sequential file updating* and is illustrated in Figure 9–3.

QUESTION: In sequential file updating, two separate processing runs are required.

(a) _____.

(b) _____.

ANSWER: (a) Sort transactions (b) Update master file

As each transaction record is read, the master file is searched to locate the matching master file record. If a match is found, the record is updated. Master file records that have no activity are merely copied from the old master to the updated master. The entire master file must be passed through the computer, even if there are only a few transactions to be processed.

QUESTION: A master file contains 1,000 records. During an update run there are 80 transaction records to be processed against the file (so the activity rate is 80/1000 or 8%).

(a) How many master records are updated in this run? _____.

(b) How many master records are simply copied from the old master and written on the updated master file?_____.

ANSWER: (a) 80   (b) 920

Processing Inquiries. Sequential file organization is impractical or inefficient for on-line systems, where it is necessary to determine (or update) the status of a particular record. For example, in an airline reservation system an agent at a remote terminal must frequently determine the available seating capacity for a particular flight, and must post transactions such as reservations or cancellations. In a sequential file it would be necessary to search the entire file each time it was desired to locate a specific record. A direct access organization is required for these applications.

Evaluation of Sequential File Design. The advantages and disadvantages of sequential file organization are summarized below:

Advantages	Disadvantages
☐ Low cost file media (magnetic tape)	☐ Transactions must be sorted before processing
☐ Very efficient processing when transactions can be batched and activity rate is relatively high	☐ Entire file must be processed, no matter how low the activity rate
	☐ Cannot handle on-line inquiries or on-line updating of records

Direct Access Organization

The second important method of file organization is termed direct access. In contrast to sequential access files, each reference on a direct access file must be to a specific address in the file. For this reason, transactions need not be sorted before updating direct access files. Processing transactions in the order in which they occur (without sorting) is termed *random* processing. Random processing is frequently used in on-line systems, where rapid response and updating are important. An important example is the on-line airline reservation system discussed above.

A direct access file is maintained on storage devices such as magnetic disk, drum, magnetic strip, or mass core. The important feature of such direct access storage devices is that individual records can be stored and retrieved, without searching the file. The important characteristics of these devices are discussed in Chapter 5.

QUESTION: A direct access file (could, could not) be maintained on magnetic tape? _____

ANSWER: Could not (since tape is not addressable).

Disk files. Magnetic disk units are the most commonly used direct access devices at present. As explained in Chapter 5, data is recorded on numerous tracks on the surface of each disk. In some systems, each track in turn is divided into a number of sectors. When data is read from or written on a magnetic disk, it is transferred a sector at a time. The size of a sector depends on the particular device used, and may range from one word (5 or 6 characters) to several hundred characters or bytes.

The sector size of a direct access device is an important consideration in laying out master file records. If the record length is the same as a sector, one record is stored per sector. If the record is considerably shorter, then it may be possible to store two or more records per sector. Conversely if the record exceeds a sector length, then two or more sectors will be required per record. This may complicate the problem of addressing a record and may also result in less efficient usage of storage space.

Each sector on a magnetic disk has a unique address. For example, the number 12345 might refer to a specific sector.[1] To obtain a record stored in this sector, the computer references the given address.

To locate a specific record on a direct access file, the record key or identifier is used. There are several different methods to obtain the address of a record, each with certain advantages and disadvantages. These techniques are discussed in Chapter 19.

Evaluation of Direct Access Organization. The direct access technique is the fastest available for locating specific records within a file. However, since records cannot be referenced sequentially, this method of file organization is inefficient if a transaction file must be processed against the master file. This follows from the fact that a comparatively large access time is necessary to locate and transmit each master record. Also, direct access files often do not utilize storage as efficiently as do sequential files.

In processing a transaction against a direct access file, the record to be altered is copied from direct access storage, updated, and then written back in the same location. This destroys the previous contents of the location. If there was an error in updating, the record prior to updating is no longer available. This is in contrast to sequential file updating, where the old master file is intact after the file updating run.

Since the direct access file is exposed to the risk of error in updating, special precautions must be taken to safeguard the file. These include careful editing by the computer of all input transactions, the retention of transaction data for some time, and other security provisions.

The advantages and disadvantages of direct access file organization are summarized as follows.

Advantages	*Disadvantages*
☐ Transactions need not be sorted	☐ File devices (such as magnetic disk) are relatively expensive
☐ On-line inquiries and updating are easily handled	☐ Processing is slower, less efficient than batch-sequential processing for high activity rates
☐ Several files can be processed or updated concurrently	☐ Special precautions needed to safeguard the direct access files

Index Sequential

A file organization which combines the advantages of sequential and direct access techniques is termed *index sequential*. In this method, records are stored sequentially on a magnetic disk (or other direct access device). For sequential processing (such as periodic file updating), records are read sequentially as on magnetic tape.

For direct access operation, tables stored on the disk file are used to locate the addresses of individual records. In this approach, at least two references are required to locate a record. First, the record key is used to

[1]The number actually identfies the unit, position, head (or track), and sector. However, in this section it is sufficient to associate a number with a sector.

look up a sector address in one (or more) tables. Next, the sector address is used to reference the desired record.

Exercise 9–2

1. The physical arrangement of records within a storage medium or device is called _____ _____ .

2. A file in which it is not possible to reference a specific record without first examining the preceding records is called a _____ _____ file.

3. The operation in which a master file is updated with a transaction file is called _____ _____ .

4. A magnetic disk surface is divided into _____ and _____ .

5. The _____ _____ technique is the fastest method for locating specific records within a file.

6. _____ _____ is a technique which combines the features of sequential and direct access files.

7. Sequential access files are normally maintained on _____ _____ , while direct access files are normally maintained on _____ _____ .

8. Processing transactions in the order in which they occur (without sorting) is referred to as _____ processing.

Data Manipulation

Data processing consists largely of processing transactions, updating master files, and preparing detailed output and/or management summaries. This process may be broken down into five general phases, called the *data processing cycle*: (1) data origination, (2) data input, (3) data manipulation, (4) information output, and (5) data storage.

Structures for storing data are described in the previous sections. Input and output of data are described in Chapter 7. The remaining phase of the data processing cycle, data manipulation, is discussed in this section.

Unclassified		Classified	
Name	Major	Major	Name
Anderson, James	Business	Business	Anderson, James
Douglas, Karen	Business		Douglas, Karen
Gregory, Robert	Computer Science		Olson, Ann
Louis, Charles	Engineering	Computer Science	Gregory, Robert
Olson, Ann	Business		Stevens, John
Stevens, John	Computer Science	Engineering	Louis, Charles

Figure 9–4. *An example of grouping data.*

Data manipulation is at the core of most data processing operations. It exists in manual as well as computer-based information systems. Balancing checking accounts, computing income taxes, posting general ledgers, and sorting mail are familiar examples of data manipulation.

Data manipulation consists of any combination of the following operations: (1) classifying, (2) merging, (3) sorting, (4) computing, and (5) moving and editing.

Classifying is the grouping of data into categories or classes. For example, Figure 9–4 shows a list of students taking a course in management information systems. The list is arranged alphabetically, and shows each student's major. In the same figure the students' names have been grouped according to major.

QUESTION: Classifying data (does, does not) imply that the data entries in each category are sorted into a given sequence.

ANSWER: Does not. In Figure 9–4 the names in each major are in alphabetical order, as in the original list. However, sorting is not a necessary part of the classifying operation

Another example of classifying is the arranging of data into frequency distributions. A *frequency distribution* is a table that shows the number of data elements in each of several categories. To illustrate, a city maintains records over a 30-day period of the number of automobile accidents involving bodily injury. This data is then arranged into a frequency distribution, as follows.

Number of Accidents on a Given Day	Number of Days Observed
0	8
1	12
2	6
3	3
4	1
Total	30

Merging is the combining of two or more files into a single file in the same sequence. For example, a company has two sales branches. At branch

Branch 1	Branch 2	Merged
138	92	92
235	144	138
761	473	144
	820	235
		473
		761
		820

Figure 9–5. *An example of merging two files into a single file.*

1, the company has three large industrial accounts, while there are four such accounts at branch 2. The customer numbers for each branch (in increasing sequence) are shown in Figure 9–5. The result of merging the customer numbers is also shown in the same figure.

Merging is often used to consolidate two or more transaction files into a single file, in preparation for file updating. It is also used in the sorting operation, as will be shown in the next section.

Sorting is the arranging of a list (or file) of data into a desired sequence. For example, consider the following lists of stock numbers, where the first is in random order and the second is in ascending sequence.

Random	Sorted
79	56
134	79
56	129
129	134

Sorting is basic to the sequential processing method, since transaction files are sorted into the same sequence as master files before file updating is performed. In most applications, an ascending numerical sequence is used. Examples would include stock numbers, employee numbers, and customer account numbers. In some applications, an ascending alphabetic sequence is used — employee names, for example.

Sorting is normally accomplished on a digital computer by manipulating magnetic tape or disk files. If transaction records are on punched cards or other media, they are first converted to magnetic tape. Sort routines furnished by the manufacturer are almost always used, so that it is not necessary for individual users to write sort programs. The packaged sort routine is used by specifying the record key on which the file is to be sorted, the record length, and other file characteristics.

There are two phases in sorting a magnetic tape file. First, records are sorted into initial strings. Second, the strings are progressively merged into longer strings until the entire file is sequenced. A *string* is a group of records that have been sorted.

The first phase is often referred to as an *internal sort*. Groups of unsorted transactions are read into memory; the size of a group depends on record size, available memory capacity, and other factors. The group is then sorted into a string and written on an output tape. This process is

Step	1	2	3	4	5	6	Final
Record Keys	79	79	56	56	56	56	56
	134	134	134	134	79	79	79
	56	56	79	79	134	134	129
	129	129	129	129	129	129	134
	No exchange	Exchange	No exchange	Exchange	No exchange	Exchange	

Figure 9–6. *An example of exchange sorting.*

repeated until the input file is exhausted, with consecutive strings ordinarily being alternated between two (or more) output tapes.

The internal sort may be accomplished by several methods. One of the simplest is referred to as exchange sorting. Figure 9–6 shows the use of exchange sorting for a group of four records.

Starting with the first record in the group, the record key is compared, one at a time, with those following. If any following record has a smaller key (for an ascending sort), the records exchange places (see steps 2 and 3, Figure 9–6.) The new record key (in the first record) is now used to continue comparing to the end of the list. When the end of the list is reached, the first record is known to have the smallest key.

The second record is now compared with the third and those below, and again exchanges are made until the second record has the second smallest key. This process continues as is shown in Figure 9–6 until the string is sorted.

QUESTION: Suppose it happens that the four records in Figure 9–6 are in the correct sequence (56, 79, 129, 134) when read into the computer. How many steps are necessary in the exchange sorting method to generate the output string? _____.

ANSWER: Six. The comparisons are exactly the same as in Figure 9–6

In the second phase, strings are read into the computer and are merged into longer strings. For example, Figure 9–7 shows two input files, each with two strings of length four. In output file 1, the first strings from the

	Input File			*Output File*	
	1	*2*		*1*	*2*
	26	09		09	19
String 1	39	23		23	25
	44	32		26	37
	52	38	String 1	32	49 String 2
				38	57
	37	19		39	61
String 2	49	25		44	67
	61	57		52	73
	67	73			

Figure 9–7. *An example of merging.*

input files have been merged to produce a single string of length eight. Similarly, output file 2 results from the merging of the second strings from the input file, merged into a single string of length eight.

QUESTION: On the next pass, the output files would become _____ files and the strings would be merged into a single string of length _____ .

ANSWER: input, 16

The number of passes required to sequence the entire file depends on the length of the initial strings. To illustrate, suppose there is a total of 4,096 records to be merged. The initial strings are of length four, so that there are 512 strings on each of two input tapes. The number of passes, string length, and number of strings are as follows:

Pass Number	String Length at End of Pass	Number of Strings on Each Output Tape
1	8	256
2	16	128
3	32	64
4	64	32
5	128	16
6	256	8
7	512	4
8	1024	2
9	2048	1
10	4096	1 (on one tape)

QUESTION: If the initial string length was 16 in the above example, the number of passes required would be reduced to _____ .
ANSWER: eight

The use of two input and two output tapes is referred to as a two-way merge. The efficiency of the sort can be improved by using more tapes, if available.

Computing consists of arithmetic operations performed on data and logical operations necessary for program control. Arithmetic operations include addition, subtraction, multiplication, division, extracting square roots, and exponentiation. Logical operations include conditional and unconditional branching.

As might be expected, computing is central to most processes of data manipulation.

Moving and editing are used primarily to structure data into desired output formats. For example, data items are moved from input or working storage areas to output areas, in the process of assembling output records. Editing operations include the suppression of leading zeros and the insertion of editing symbols such as commas, dollar signs, and decimal points.

Exercise 9–3

1. Data manipulation consists of any combination of the following operations:

_____ , _____ , _____ ,

and _____ and _____ .

2. Match the following definitions to the appropriate terms:
   - (a) Combining two or more files into a single file in the same sequence
   - (b) Grouping of data into categories or classes
   - (c) Table that shows the number of data elements in each of several categories
   - (d) Arithmetic operations performed on data and logical operations necessary for program control
   - (e) Arranging a file of data into a desired output sequence
   - (f) Used to structure data into desired output formats

   moving and editing

   frequency distribution

   merging

   sorting

   computing

   classifying

3. Sorting a magnetic tape file is normally divided into two phases: the

   first is called an _____ sort which develops initial

   _____ , while the second is a series of _____
   operations.

Summary

The basic concepts of data processing are described in this chapter. More advanced concepts such as indexed sequential files and hierarchial organization are only briefly introduced, and are discussed in greater detail in Chapter 19.

It is apparent that the system designer has a number of alternatives available in planning for a particular system. There is a fundamental choice between sequential and random processing of transactions. A number of alternatives exist in designing files and records. Also numerous methods for data manipulation are available. The various techniques for systems analysis and design are discussed in Chapters 16 to 21.

In the following chapters, various languages for data manipulation are considered. In large part, the choice of language depends on the data structures and other concepts discussed in this chapter.

Solutions to Exercises

Exercise 9–1

1. Files, records, data items, fields.
2. (a) List.
   (b) Database.
   (c) File.
   (d) Array.
   (e) Table.
3. (a) Subfield describing length of record.
   (b) Special (terminating) symbol.
4. (a) Two.
   (b) 3, 3.
   (c) 34.
5. Identifier, key.
6. Fixed length, variable length.
7. Master, transaction, report, and history.

Exercise 9–2

1. File organization.
2. Sequential access.
3. File updating.
4. Tracks, sectors.
5. Direct access.
6. Index sequential.
7. Magnetic tape, magnetic disk.
8. Random.

Exercise 9–3

1. Classifying, merging, sorting, computing, moving, editing.
2. (a) Merging.
   (b) Classifying.
   (c) Frequency distribution.
   (d) Computing.
   (e) Sorting.
   (f) Moving and editing.
3. Internal, strings, merging.

Chapter Examination

1. Define the following terms:

   (a) Master file _____

(b) Transaction file _____

_____

(c) Record _____

_____

(d) Data item _____

_____

(e) Elementary item _____

_____

(f) Identifier _____

_____

2. Distinguish the following:

(a) Physical versus logical file _____

_____

(b) Physical versus logical record _____

_____

3. Explain the advantages and disadvantages of fixed and variable length records in terms of:

(a) Computer storage _____

_____

(b) Processing requirements _____

_____

4. Give an example of each of the following data structures (other than those mentioned in the text):

(a) File _____

(b) Table _____

(c) Array _____

(d) List _____

5. Define and give an example of each of the following:

(a) Sequential access file _____

_____

(b) Direct access file _____

_____

6. For the following list, perform an exchange sort for groups of four, then, do a merge sort to obtain a sorted list. Show the strings at each stage.

388	021
116	580
741	912
129	643
057	191
443	363
237	040
812	776

7. Explain the logic of sequential file updating. Why is the transaction file sorted before the update run?

_____

_____

_____

8. For each of the following situations, state whether sequential processing or random processing is more appropriate. Give reasons.
(a) A customer accounts receivable file must be updated weekly,

with exception reports prepared each run _____.

(b) A rental car agency has a central data processing system for car reservations, which processes inquiries from many remote locations throughout the country _____.

241 / CHAPTER EXAMINATION

(c) A student record file is updated three times each semester — after registration, at mid-semester, and after final grades. Occasional inquiries must be made of student records on other occasions

_____ .

(d) A data processing system is used for job control in a large manufacturing facility. Job status must be updated frequently, and management desires up-to-the-minute information on the status

of each job in the shop. _____ .

9. Identify the following statements as true or false:

_____ (a) A common data structure is a vertical hierarchy consisting of files, records, and fields.

_____ (b) A history file is a set of records used to update a master file.

_____ (c) A table consists of a set of paired entries called the argument and its function.

_____ (d) An array used to store sales amount by salesman, product, and territory would be a two-coordinate array.

_____ (e) In a list, logical records are connected by means of identifiers.

_____ (f) The advantage of a sequential file is that it is possible to locate a specific record without examining previous records.

_____ (g) Random processing is possible with direct access files.

_____ (h) Index sequential combines the advantages of sequential and direct access file organizations.

10. Briefly define each of the following:

(a) Classifying _____

_____

(b) Merging _____

_____

(c) Sorting _____

_____

(d) Computing _____

_____

(e) Moving and editing _____

_____

11. Describe two ways of specifying the length of a variable length field.

(a) _____

(b) _____

12. Define the concept of a database. _____

_____

_____

13. Describe two techniques used to safeguard direct access files against updating errors.

(a) _____

(b) _____

14. Explain how an index sequential file organization is used for:

(a) Sequential processing _____

_____

(b) Direct access processing _____

_____

15. State the advantages of each of the following:

(a) Fixed item and record size _____

_____

(b) Variable item and record size _____

_____

243 / CHAPTER EXAMINATION

16. Following is a list organization for customer orders.

Address	Customer No.	Customer Information	Pointer
200	1		375
201	2		*
202	3		*
203	4		377

Address	Order No.		Pointer
375	1093		379
376	1140		*
377	1062		380
378			
379	1128		376
380	1157		*

(a) What orders are now outstanding for:

Customer number 1? _____, _____, _____.

Customer number 2? _____.

Customer number 4? _____, _____.

(b) Suppose a new order (number 1174) is added to the order file for customer number 4, at address 378. What will the pointer be for:

Order number 1157 (address 380)? _____

Order number 1174 (address 378)? _____

(c) Suppose that order number 1093 is shipped and removed from the file. Specify the resulting pointer at each of the following addresses:

Address	Pointer
200	_____
375	_____
376	_____
379	_____

17. State three advantages of direct access file organization:

(a) _____

(b) _____

(c) _____

18. State three disadvantages of direct access file organization:

(a) _____

(b) _____

(c) _____

Chapter 10

INTRODUCTION TO SOFTWARE SYSTEM

Overview

Before a user's problems can be solved on a computer, the problems must be stated in the form of a program, or a concise set of instructions to the computer. When computers were first introduced, it was necessary for a user to state his problem in machine language. However, this was very difficult and tedious, and the number of successful applications was quite limited.

To overcome these problems, a body of techniques and computer programs called software has been developed. *Software* consists generally of computer programs and related techniques that bridge the gap between a user's problems on the one hand and strictly hardware functions and requirements (including machine language) on the other. Software includes programming languages and translators, operating systems, and applications programs.

Software systems greatly improve the efficiency with which people use computers. They facilitate man-computer interaction and reduce programming time and cost. They reduce the dependence of the computer on human action and judgment, thereby increasing productivity. To a large extent, the rapid increase in data processing applications in recent years can be attributed to improved software systems.

This chapter presents an introduction to the major languages and computer programs used in most data processing systems. First, computer programming languages are discussed. Programming languages may be categorized as low-order languages and high-order languages. Next, programs for translating user-written programs into machine language are described. Finally, operating systems, the concept of multiprogramming, and data management systems are considered.

Computer Languages

The concept of a stored program and the basic types of computer instructions are discussed in Chapter 6. Recall that a computer instruction consists of an operation code that specifies the operation to be performed, plus one or more operand addresses. The instruction may also reference one or more addressable registers, such as accumulator or index register. Generally, the instructions are placed in sequential storage locations. The computer circuitry is designed to execute these instructions in sequential order. However, the programmer can alter the order of execution by means of a branch instruction, which causes the computer to seek its next instruction at an alternate location.

The most direct way for a programmer to communicate with the computer is to code his instructions in machine language – the language of the computer. The instructions may then be loaded into the computer without translation. However, machine language is foreign to human beings, and the process of coding in machine language tends to be slow, tedious, and conducive to error. As a result, from the earliest days computer programmers have sought to design languages and software systems to facilitate communicating with the computer. Generally, these languages are oriented to the language of human beings and to the problems they wish to solve by using computers. Instructions coded using these languages must first be translated into machine language before they can be used to instruct the computer. Fortunately, the computer itself is used to translate programmer-oriented instructions to machine language.

Programming languages may be divided into two categories: low-order and high-order languages. *Low-order languages* are those that most closely resemble machine language. Generally, each instruction is equivalent to one machine instruction. In contrast, *high-order languages* are more powerful. Each instruction may represent a logical procedure and is often equivalent to a sequence of machine language instructions. Figure 10–1 (based on an example in Chapter 6) is a comparison of languages for an inventory calculation.

QUESTION: In the above example, the high-order language instruction (in COBOL) is equivalent to _____ low-order instructions.
ANSWER: three

Low-order Languages

There are a number of disadvantages in using machine languages:

1. Numerical operation codes (such as 5B2 in Figure 10–1) are difficult to remember and interpret. A third generation computer like the IBM

Machine Language	Assembly Language	Explanation
582 632	L 2, OLDBAL	Load balance into accumulator (General register 2)
5B2 438	S 2, ISSUES	Subtract issues giving new balance
502 9A7	ST2, NEWBAL	Store new balance
COBOL: SUBTRACT ISSUES FROM OLD-BALANCE GIVING NEW-BALANCE		

Figure 10–1. *A comparison of languages for inventory calculation.*

System/370 may have in excess of 100 commands in its instruction set, many with optional usages.

2. The programmer must supply and keep track of each storage address where instructions and data items are located. This is a very tedious procedure, especially in a large program.
3. It is difficult to read and interpret a machine language program and to locate errors.
4. It is difficult to modify a machine language program and to correct errors. For example, suppose it is necessary to insert a new instruction between two existing instructions. With the insertion, the address portion of an instruction that references displaced instructions must be changed. This procedure is tedious and conducive to error.

For these reasons, computer programs for data processing are seldom written in machine language. Instead, the program is coded in symbolic language, if a low-order language is to be used. A *symbolic language* enables the programmer to use symbols or mnemonics rather than binary or hexadecimal notation. For example, an operation code such as ADD might be used to specify adding a quantity to the contents of the accumulator.

Assembly Language. The most frequently used low-order symbolic language is termed assembly. It is called assembly language because a machine language program is "assembled" when this program is translated to machine language. The features of an assembly language, which overcome many of the disadvantages of machine language, are the following:

1. Operation codes are understandable mnemonics, rather than alphanumerical. In the IBM System/370 assembly language, for example, the operation "add" is specified by the symbol A, rather than the hexadecimal number 5A. Symbolic codes are much easier to read and interpret.
2. The programmer need not specify the storage address where data is stored. Instead, he assigns a label (or "symbolic address") to each data item and uses the label when referring to the item. For example, he can use RATE for hourly wage or BALANCE for an inventory balance. A program in which meaningful labels are used is much easier to read and understand than one in which absolute storage addresses are used.
3. The programmer need not assign instructions to particular storage locations. Instead, he merely specifies the beginning address of the main storage area to be used for his program. If he wishes to refer to a particular instruction in the program, he simply labels that instruction and refers to it by using that label.

QUESTION: Examine Figure 10–1. For the operation "store new balance," the assembly language operation code for "store" is _____, while the symbolic address for "new balance" is _____.
ANSWER: ST, NEWBAL

Although assembly language notation varies from one computer to another, there are basic similarities between systems. A number of assembly language instructions for the IBM System/370 are described and illustrated in Chapter 6.

Macroinstructions. In many situations, the same sequence of assembly language instructions appears at several locations in a program. Common examples are various input-output operations and certain arithmetic calculations. Ideally the programmer wants to instruct the assembler how to construct the desired sequence of instructions, without tediously repeating the sequence each time it is needed.

Many assembly systems have facilities for generating sequences of instructions under control of the programmer. An instruction that causes other instructions to be generated is called a *macroinstruction*, or more briefly, a *macro*. When a macro is encountered in an assembly language program, the translating program simply inserts the desired sequence of instructions. The sequence of instructions inserted in response to a macroinstruction is referred to as a *subroutine*. The concept of subroutines is of great importance in computing, and is further discussed in Chapter 12.

QUESTION: A single instruction written by the programmer that causes several machine language instructions to be generated is called a _____ instruction. The sequence of instructions is called a _____.
ANSWER: Macro, subroutine

There are two types of macroinstructions in many assemblers: those provided by the system, and those written by the programmer-user. *System* macros provide instructions for standard functions such as input and output of data, whereas *user-written* macros permit the programmer to define other functions that are to be used repeatedly in a program. After the macro has been defined, the user merely writes one macroinstruction when the corresponding function is required.

Of particular importance are the system macros that control input-output operations. Data processing systems typically include a number of input-output devices such as card readers, magnetic tape and disk units, and printers. Coordinating the flow of information between these devices and the computer is a complex programming task. For example, in reading data from an input device, some of the tasks that must be performed are the following: specifying the device from which the data is to be obtained and the address of the area into which it is to be read; testing to see whether the device is ready; reading the data; and checking to see whether errors have occurred while reading.

If the programmer had to write all the input-output coding in detail, each program would be an enormous task indeed. In fact, it is likely that up to 50 percent of his programming time would be spent in coding only input-output operations. Also many programmers would not be able to write efficient input-output codes.

Fortunately, most computer manufacturers provide the instructions necessary for input and output of data. These instructions are in the form of subroutines that take care of the many "housekeeping functions" or details associated with transmitting data between the computer and input-output devices.

The programmer communicates with these subroutines by means of input-output macros. Many assembly languages provide the following system macros for this purpose:

Macroinstruction	Function
OPEN	Causes specified files to be made available for reading or writing and checks "header labels" to insure correct file is being used.
GET	Causes a record to be read from a specified input file. The record is read into an area specified by a Define the File (DTF) macroinstruction.
PUT	Causes a record to be written on a specified output file. The record is written from an area specified by a DTF macroinstruction.
CLOSE	Causes specified files to be made unavailable to the stored program.

Input-output Control System. The macros OPEN, GET, PUT, and CLOSE are called *imperative* macroinstructions because they specify particular I/O operations that are to be performed. These macroinstructions, together with file definition macros and the I/O subroutines referenced by the macros, are referred to as an input-output control system, or IOCS. Thus an IOCS is an integrated software system that greatly facilitates the programming of I/O operations. It is provided by most manufacturers as part of the assembly language.

The file definition macros in an IOCS are called *declarative* macros, since they are used to define files rather than to identify specific I/O operations. In some assembly languages (such as IBM Basic Assembly Language) these are called Define and File (or DTF) macros. For example, the DTFCD macro is used to define a card file, while a printer file is defined by the macro DTFPR.

Advantages of Macros. There are a number of advantages in using macroinstructions when coding in assembly language. Some of the more important ones are:

1. Programming time and effort are saved.
2. The chance of committing programming errors is reduced, since the sequence of instructions in a macro is a pretested routine that does what it is supposed to.
3. The skill of one programmer can be made available to many. Thus a complex programming task can be programmed and tested by a skilled programmer and stored in a subroutine library, where it can be easily called by other programmers by simply writing a macroinstruction.

Exercise 10–1

1. Programming languages may be divided into two categories:

_____-_____ and _____-

_____ languages.

2. In machine language, instructions are normally coded using

_____ or _____ notation.

3. When coding in (machine, assembly) language, the programmer must keep track of each storage address where instructions and data items are located.

4. In assembly language, operation codes are _____ rather than alphanumeric. Also operands are specified by _____ addresses.

5. (True or False) Each assembly language instruction is generally equivalent to several machine language instructions.

6. An instruction that causes several computer instructions to be generated is called a _____-_____ or simply, _____.

7. The most important macros are those that control _____-_____ operations. Four typical macros for this purpose are _____, _____, _____, and _____.

8. An integrated software system for I/O that is included in many assemblers is termed an _____-_____ _____, or _____.

9. The sequence of instructions inserted into a program in response to a macro is referred to as a _____.

10. Two types of macros are _____ and _____ macros.

High-order Languages

The preceding material discusses how the use of a symbolic or assembly language facilitates the process of writing computer programs. However, the assembly language is oriented to the computer instead of to the problem to be solved. Except when macroinstructions are used, each assembly language statement is generally equivalent to only one machine language instruction. Therefore, the programmer is limited in the rate at which he can code assembly language programs.

To further improve the efficiency of writing computer programs, a number of higher-order languages have been developed. These languages are sometimes classified as *problem-oriented* or *procedure-oriented* languages. It is estimated that more than 100 such languages have been developed during the past 20 years. About 10 of these languages are in widespread use today. The remainder are no longer used or are used only for specialized applications or equipment.

High-order languages permit the programmer to write computer instructions in procedural form or in the language of the problem to be solved. Generally, each statement in the language is equivalent to several machine or assembly language instructions—perhaps as many as 10 or 20. This greatly increases the productivity of the programmer and also facilitates reading and interpreting the program.

Equally important is the fact that some of these languages are "universal" languages; that is, they may be processed with only slight modifications on any of the computers of the major manufacturers. Machine and assembly languages are not universal; they can be used only on one manufacturer's equipment. For example, programs written in CDC assembly language cannot be processed by Honeywell computers. In fact, the machine and assembly languages for one line of equipment are generally not transferable to a second line of the same manufacturer.

These advantages of higher-order languages can be illustrated with some examples. First, consider the simple problem of adding two numbers, A and B, to obtain the result C. Typical assembly language instructions, and the statements in two of the more popular higher-order languages, FORTRAN and COBOL, are:

Assembly Language	FORTRAN	COBOL
L 2, A	C = A + B	ADD A, B GIVING C
A 2, B		
ST2, C		

It is obvious that the FORTRAN and COBOL statements are more "natural" than assembly language, as well as more concise and easier to read.

Higher-order languages may be classified as mathematical and scientific languages, business-oriented languages, time-sharing languages, list-processing languages, and simulation languages. Many of the more important languages are discussed in the following sections; more complete descriptions of some of these languages are presented in later chapters.

Scientific Programming Languages. Most of the early applications of computers were for mathematical computations in science and engineering. Thus the programming languages that were developed were designed to express mathematical notation and procedures. Although a number of scientific languages are widely used, the most important ones to date have been FORTRAN and ALGOL.

In 1954, IBM began work on FORTRAN, which stands for FORmula TRANslation. The goal of this effort was to develop a language that would enable the programmer to solve problems using a concise notation, similar to mathematics. For example, the formula to compute the compound amount after N years at interest rate R, and the corresponding FORTRAN statement, are shown below:

Formula $\qquad A = S \times (1 + R)^N$

FORTRAN statement $\qquad A = S * (1. + R) **N$

FORTRAN reportedly took 18 man-years to develop. The language has gained wide acceptance by the scientific data-processing community, and today nearly all manufacturers of scientific computers provide for the use of FORTRAN on their computer systems. The language is also widely used for quantitative and statistical applications in business data processing. A more complete description of FORTRAN is presented in Chapter 13.

In 1958, a scientific language called ALGOL (ALGOrithmic Language) was introduced. ALGOL was developed by an international committee of representatives from a large number of professional organizations. In some respects, ALGOL resembles FORTRAN. It has gained wider acceptance in some foreign countries than in the United States.

Business-Oriented Languages. Although the initial applications were in scientific disciplines, it was also apparent that the computer had enormous potential for business data processing. The early data processing programs were written in machine or assembly language. However, the process was slow and cumbersome, and it was soon recognized that there was a need for a high-level business-oriented language.

In 1959, a meeting was called by the Department of Defense that included representatives of a small group of computer manufacturers and users. The original committee meeting was called the Conference on Data Systems Languages, or CODASYL. The purpose of the meeting was to initiate the development of a common language for data processing applications.

The result of this effort was COBOL, an acronym for Common Business-Oriented Language. The specifications for COBOL were first released in 1960; since that time, a number of revisions and additions have been made. Today, COBOL is the most widely used language for business data processing applications. The CODASYL committee remains intact and is continually reviewing and updating the language.

COBOL is an English-like language. For example, a COBOL statement to add receipts to a current balance might appear as follows:

ADD RECEIPTS, BALANCE GIVING TOTAL.

COBOL has a number of advantages, including increased readability, which simplifies program documentation. The language is discussed more fully in Chapter 14.

Another language that is designed for business applications is RPG (Report Program Generator). RPG is designed for relatively simple applications in which there is need for generating routine business reports. It has gained wide acceptance among users of third generation computers, particularly small systems such as the IBM System/3. However, it is also available on larger IBM systems such as the System/370 and is sometimes used on these systems in addition to COBOL. Other manufacturers also provide for RPG processing.

RPG programs are recorded on a series of specification forms. The programmer merely records a series of entries on the specification forms that describe the files to be used, the program input, the calculations to be performed, and the program output. RPG is described more fully in Chapter 15.

A third important business-oriented language is termed PL/1 (Programming Language One). PL/1 was developed starting in 1963 by a language-development committee sponsored by IBM.

Actually, PL/1 is a general purpose language that is suitable for both scientific and business applications. The impetus for the development of this language was twofold. First, unlike earlier computers, third generation computing systems are truly general purpose. They are designed to encompass both scientific and business applications. Second, the needs of business and scientific users have changed during the 1960s and 1970s. Scientific users require more sophisticated data management techniques. Also, with the introduction of management science techniques, business users require greater computational capabilities. Although most applications could be programmed in either FORTRAN or COBOL, these special purpose languages could not fully exploit the computational capabilities of third generation computers.

Although PL/1 combines many of the features of FORTRAN and COBOL, it is not simply an extension of these languages. The main advantage of the language is its versatility and range of application. It has two disadvantages: (1) its complexity, which makes the language comparatively difficult to learn and use, and (2) the fact that it is not yet a universal language (one that is available on most computers).

Time-sharing Languages. One of the fastest growing segments of the computer industry is time-sharing (discussed in Chapter 3). In this approach, several users share the resources of a large computing system through remote terminals.

Several higher-order languages are available to users of time-sharing systems. A time-sharing version of FORTRAN is widely used. Two languages that are used almost exclusively for time-sharing applications are BASIC and APL.

BASIC (Basic All-purpose Symbolic Instruction Code) was developed at Dartmouth College as an instructional tool for the teaching of fundamental programming concepts. It has since gained wide acceptance as a time-sharing language. BASIC is considered to be perhaps the easiest programming language to learn. A person with little or no programming experience can often write simple programs after only a few hours of self-instruction.

Arithmetic statements in BASIC are similar to those in FORTRAN. The language has considerable power, although its input-output capabilities are quite limited. As a result, BASIC is not widely used for data processing applications. It is quite widely used as an instructional language in schools. BASIC is available for almost all time-sharing computers.

APL (A Programming Language) was developed by Kenneth Iverson of IBM. It is most often used with time-sharing systems. APL is a mathematically oriented language of enormous power, especially when the programmer must deal with more complex data structures such as arrays. The language has a relatively complex notation and set of rules and is, therefore, somewhat difficult to learn. Also, the input-output capability of APL is limited, so that it is not widely used for data processing applications. However, it seems likely that APL will gain increasing use for management science applications within business systems. It is available for some non-IBM computers but is not yet a universal language.

List-processing Languages. In some applications, it is necessary to manipulate alphabetical data and words rather than numbers and algebraic symbols. Examples are language translation, information retrieval, and text editing. Several high-order languages have been developed for this purpose. Two of the most important are LISP and SNOBOL. These languages are essentially symbol manipulation languages and are usually termed list-processing languages.

Simulation Languages. Simulation is a technique for representing and experimenting with the essential elements of a large system on a computer. For example, a mass transit system or a production system can be described as a mathematical model that is then programmed for a computer to study the system in question.

Simulation is a powerful tool for designing and improving real-world systems. Unfortunately, simulation programs often are complex and costly to program. To facilitate this process, several high-order simulation languages have been developed. Two of the most widely used are SIMSCRIPT and GPSS (General Purpose Simulation System). These languages provide a wide range of commands (similar to macroinstructions) that greatly reduce the required programming effort.

Exercise 10–2

1. Generally, a single statement in a high-order programming language is equivalent to (one, many) machine language instructions.

2. Match the following categories of high-order languages to the examples in the second column.

   _____ Business-oriented languages   (a) LISP, SNOBOL

   _____ Scientific languages   (b) PL/1

   _____ List-processing languages   (c) SIMSCRIPT, GPSS

   _____ Time-sharing languages   (d) FORTRAN, ALGOL

   _____ General purpose languages   (e) COBOL, RPG

   _____ Simulation languages   (f) APL, BASIC

3. Identify the following statements as true or false:

   (a) _____ COBOL is an English-like language for common scientific-oriented problems.
   (b) _____ BASIC and APL are widely used for data-processing applications.
   (c) _____ RPG is most widely used for large-scale computers.

(d)_____ Third generation computers are separated into two basic categories: scientific and business oriented.

(e) _____ Simulation programs are easier to write in FORTRAN or COBOL than in SIMSCRIPT or GPSS.

Language Translation

As mentioned previously, the computer can execute instructions only in machine language form. Therefore, a program written in a symbolic form (assembly language or high-order language) must first be translated into machine language form prior to program execution.

The process of translation is itself performed by a computer. The computer performing the translation is referred to as the *source computer*; the computer that is to execute the translated instructions is called the *object computer*. In most instances, the source and object computer are one.

When assembly languages are used, the translator is commonly called an *assembler*. In high-level languages such as FORTRAN and COBOL, the process of translating programs is referred to as *compiling*, and the translating program is called the *compiler*. Compilers and assemblers are normally provided by the computer manufacturer.

QUESTION: Of the two types of translators — assemblers and compilers — which is likely to be the more complex? _____ Why?

_____

_____

ANSWER: Compilers, since they must be able to translate a single statement written in a high-level program language into several (or many) machine language instructions

The basic steps in language translation (shown in Figure 10–2) are the following.

1. The assembler or compiler program is read into computer memory. On a large-scale system, the translating program is likely to be stored on magnetic disk and is loaded, as needed, into central memory.
2. The set of instructions written by the programmer is then read into the memory unit. This set of instructions is called the *source program*.
3. The translator then translates the source program into machine language instructions. This step may require one or more phases or computer passes. The resulting machine language instructions are referred to as the *object program*. The object program may be punched on cards to form an *object deck*, or it may be loaded directly into the memory unit for processing.
4. The object deck (if any) and data cards are then read into memory and program execution begins.

Compilers and assemblers provide a number of auxiliary functions that assist the programmer in correcting and documenting his program. For example, in the translation process common errors in use of the lan-

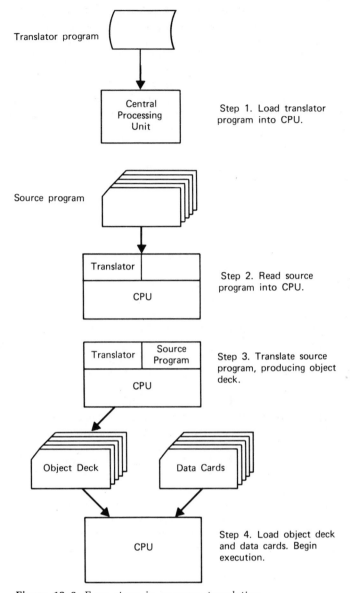

Figure 10–2. *Four steps in program translation.*

Translator program

Step 1. Load translator program into CPU.

Central Processing Unit

Source program

Step 2. Read source program into CPU.

Translator

CPU

Step 3. Translate source program, producing object deck.

Translator | Source Program

CPU

Object Deck

Data Cards

Step 4. Load object deck and data cards. Begin execution.

CPU

guage are detected and indications are printed. Since the computer is "diagnosing" errors, these indications are called *diagnostics*. Diagnostics are very useful in correcting errors in a source program. The process of correcting errors, referred to as *debugging* the program, is further discussed in Chapter 12.

Operating Systems

A typical third generation computer is a complex, costly system with enormous processing capacity. Such a system will provide an acceptable return on its investment only if its capacity is fully utilized. For efficient use, there must be as little manual operation or intervention as possible. The speed of the computer is such that even a short delay for operator intervention might exceed the time to process several jobs.

Instead of manual control, modern computers use advanced software systems called operating systems to coordinate and control the flow of work. An *operating system* is an integrated set of programs and subroutines that controls the execution of programs and provides services such as language translation, input-output control, and job scheduling.

QUESTION: In third generation systems, the flow of work is automatically controlled by software called the _____ _____.
ANSWER: Operating system

Stacked Job Processing

During the course of a day a computer system processes a stream of programs, or jobs. For example, a payroll program might be followed by a tape sort of inventory transactions, then an inventory update run. To minimize manual intervention, the jobs awaiting processing are stacked to form a single input deck. These jobs are then loaded and executed by the computer under control of the operating system.

Before stacked job processing was developed, the computer system typically executed one program and then stopped while the operator removed the program output and readied the input-output units for the next job. He then loaded the next program for execution. This manual intervention was wasteful of computer time.

Even with stacked job processing there is some operator intervention. The operating system only loads the programs—the operator must still mount tapes, change forms on the line printer, and so on. However with proper sequencing of jobs, stacked job processing significantly increases the productive running time for the computer.

Job Deck. In stacked job processing, the programs to be executed are generally stored on a peripheral storage device such as magnetic tape or magnetic disk. For example, a company's payroll program, inventory update program, and accounts receivable program might be located on a magnetic disk unit. The unit containing such programs is often referred to as a *system residence device*. This unit is most often a direct-access device such as magnetic disk. Programs are loaded from the system residence device into the CPU for execution as needed.

At the start of each day's operations, the computer operator loads a supervisor program (which is part of the operating system) into the computer. Under control of the supervisor, the programs to be executed are loaded into memory from the system residence device. To tell the supervisor which programs are to be executed, the operator places a stack of *job control cards* into the card reader. These cards provide the names of the programs to be executed, together with information such as which tape units to mount on which tape drives. There are usually several job control cards for each program to be executed. Also, if a program requires punched card input, the data deck follows the job control cards for that program. The stack of job control cards is referred to as the *job deck*.

The use of a job deck in stacked job processing is illustrated in Figure 10–3.

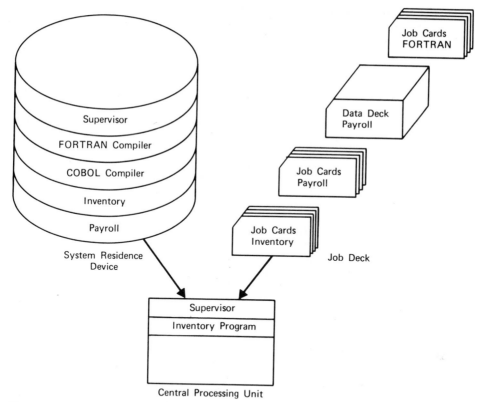

Figure 10–3. *Job control cards and stacked job processing.*

QUESTION: Examine Figure 10–3 and answer the following:
(a) How many jobs are in the job deck? _____.
(b) What program is currently being executed? _____.
(c) What program will be executed next? _____.
(d) What program includes a data deck? _____.
ANSWER: (a) 3 (b) Inventory (c) Payroll (d) Payroll

Job Control Language. The content of the job control cards depends on the operating system being used. Each computer manufacturer typically supplies one or more operating systems with each of its computer systems. For example, following are the most commonly used operating systems for the IBM System/370 computers:

System	Explanation
Disk Operating System (DOS)	Used with smaller 370s
Disk Operating System, Virtual Storage (DOS/VS)	Used with smaller 370s with Virtual Storage (see Chapter 5)
Operating System (OS)	Used with large scale 370s
Operating System, Virtual Storage (OS/VS)	Used with large scale 370s with Virtual Storage

Each of these operating systems requires different job control cards, and is therefore said to have its own *job control language*. For example, job control cards used under DOS could not be used for OS.

The job control cards for a given program depend on a number of factors such as options desired and type of files used. For example, the minimum job control cards required to compile and to execute a program written in COBOL under DOS are shown in Figure 10–4. They are the following:

1. / /Job (Job Card) — assigns a name to the source program (in this case, STUDENT).
2. / /EXEC FCOBOL — causes the COBOL compiler to be loaded from the system residence device and executed. FCOBOL is the name given to the COBOL compiler stored in the library of the system residence device for this system.
3. Source deck — the program written in COBOL language, which is to be compiled and executed.
4. End of file (/*) — indicates end of source deck.
5. End of job (/ E) — indicates that the job is completed.

QUESTION: The contents of the above cards are an example of the _____ _____ language for a particular operating system.
ANSWER: job control

Supervisor Program

An operating system consists of two basic types of programs: (1) control programs; and (2) processing and service programs.

The principal control program in an operating system is referred to as the *supervisor* or *monitor*. The supervisor controls and coordinates all operations in the computer system. Specifically, following are four of the major functions performed by most supervisor programs.

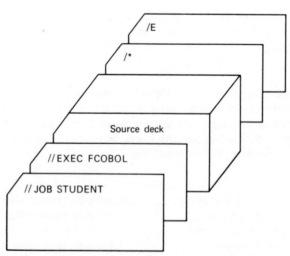

Figure 10–4. *Job control cards for a COBOL program.*

1. Loads processing programs into computer storage from the system library or from an input device.
2. Schedules and controls input-output operations for maximum efficiency. This includes loading IOCS subroutines and causing them to be executed.
3. Handles interrupts, or signals to the CPU that an exceptional condition exists in the system. An example is a signal that a previously busy input-output device is now available for use.
4. Opens and closes files and handles error situations encountered during input-output operations.

In addition to the above functions, in a multiprogramming system the supervisor schedules the sequence of jobs to be run. To accomplish this, the supervisor typically reads the entire job deck and records information about each run. The supervisor then determines the most efficient sequence of jobs, taking into consideration job priority, input-output devices to be used, and so on. After determining the most efficient schedule, the supervisor prints messages on the console typewriter indicating which actions the computer operator should take.

Some of the supervisor functions are required by every program executed by the computer and consequently they reside permanently in main storage throughout the processing of a stream of jobs. Examples are program load and interrupt-handling subroutines. Other portions of the supervisor are stored in a system library and are loaded into main memory only when needed. When no longer needed, another program or subroutine can be loaded into the same area, thereby conserving storage.

Processing and Service Programs

The second basic type of program in an operating system consists of processing and service programs. These programs (nearly always provided by the manufacturer) include language translators, utility programs, sort/merge programs, and library-maintenance programs.

Language Translators. Language translators were discussed earlier in the chapter, and include assemblers and compilers. The specific translators that are included depend on the operating system used.

Utility Programs. In many computer applications, data is converted from one input or output form to another — for example, printing the contents of a magnetic tape file, or converting punched card records to magnetic tape. The operating system includes standard utility programs for this purpose, in which the user need only specify the characteristics of the files involved on the job cards. Most systems provide routine programs for card-to-tape, card-to-printer, tape-to-printer, card-to-disk, and many similar functions.

Sort/Merge Programs. The process of sorting and merging records is one of the most common data processing functions. Recall from Chapter 9 that in sequential processing applications, transaction records must be sorted into sequential order before they are processed against a master file. Also transaction records from a number of different locations (such as sales offices) are often merged to form a single input file.

Most operating systems provide one or more generalized sort/merge programs for applications of this kind. The user merely provides coded specifications describing record length, blocking factor, length and location of the key on which the file is to be sequenced, and input-output devices to be used. The sort/merge programs are designed to perform these operations as efficiently as possible, within the constraints of the computer system being used.

Library-Maintenance Programs. Many operating systems provide for user-written programs or subroutines to be stored in *libraries* on a system residence device and to be called (or used) as needed. For example, a programmer might write a general program for regression analysis. A library-maintenance program is used to add new routines to the library, and to delete old routines. Such a program can also print the names of all routines stored in a library, or can provide a listing of the programs themselves.

Exercise 10–3

1. A processor that translates an assembler-language program into machine language is called an _____, but a processor that translates a higher-order language is called a _____.

2. The set of instructions written by a programmer is referred to as a _____ program, but the translated instructions are referred to as the _____ program.

3. The errors detected by a compiler are called _____.

4. The process of correcting errors in a program is called _____ the program.

5. An integrated set of software that controls the execution of programs is called the _____ _____.

6. Two major types of programs contained in an operating system are _____ programs and _____ and _____ programs.

7. Name four types of processing and service programs:

   (a) _____.

   (b) _____.

   (c) _____.

   (d) _____.

8. The set of control programs in an operating system is called the

_____ or _____ .

9. The operating system is directed by user-prepared _____-

_____ cards.

Multiprogramming

To provide more effective utilization of data processing systems, a technique called multiprogramming is often used. *Multiprogramming* is the concurrent execution of two or more programs simultaneously resident in the main storage.

Since the CPU can execute only one instruction at a time, it cannot simultaneously execute instructions from two or more programs. However, it can execute instructions from one program, then from a second program, and then from the first program again, and so on. This type of processing is referred to as *concurrent* execution.

Concurrent execution of programs is desirable because input-output operations are much slower than internal data-processing and computation. If only one program is being processed, the CPU is often idle, waiting for an input-output operation to be completed. In a multiprogramming environment the CPU can execute one program while a second program is waiting for I/O operations. In the IBM System/370, for example, as many as 15 programs can be executed simultaneously.

QUESTION: In multiprogramming, the CPU simultaneously executes instructions from two or more programs (True or False) _____ .
ANSWER: false

In multiprogramming, areas of main storage are allocated for each program to be executed concurrently. These areas are referred to as *partitions*. Partitions provide two major functions: *storage protection* and *priority*. The storage protection feature is required so that a program in one partition cannot write over (and thus destroy) instructions in another partition. To accomplish this function, each program is assigned a range of memory locations; the program cannot modify storage locations outside of this range.

Priority in multiprogramming is established by loading the programs in specific partitions. High priority partitions are called *foreground partitions;* programs loaded in these areas are called *foregound programs.* Low priority partitions are called *background partitions;* programs loaded into this area are called *background programs.*

Programs that have high input and output requirements but relatively low processing requirements are normally located in the foreground (high priority) partition. Conversely, programs that have comparatively large processing requirements are treated as background programs. The reason for this arrangement is that when a foreground program is waiting for input-output operations, the CPU will execute background programs that have relatively high processing requirements.

QUESTION: Programs such as file-to-file conversion (card-to-tape, tape-to-printer, etc.) and remote terminal or inquiry programs would reside in

_____ partitions, but inventory and payroll programs would likely reside in _____ partitions.

ANSWER: foreground, background

The allocation of main storage in a multiprogramming environment is illustrated as follows:

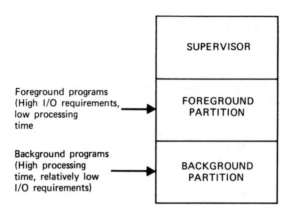

Data Management Systems

Data processing has always been characterized by the frequent manipulation of data files and the emphasis on input-output operations. Relatively sophisticated programs have been necessary to perform these operations while maximizing the overall efficiency of the computer system. As a result, most manufacturers have provided software systems for many of the input-output functions—for example, the sort routines described in the preceding section.

Current trends in data processing are toward more complex data structures and file organizations. Integrated data bases and direct-access storage devices permitting on-line inquiry and updating are quite common. These trends signal the need for more comprehensive software systems for data management.

A *data management system* is a comprehensive software system to store, retrieve, and update data. It provides for the definition and creation of files or databases or both, the maintenance of indexes, and for file security. Data management systems are a necessity for more complex structures such as index sequential.

In using a data management system, the user simply writes macro-commands that specify the data management operation to be performed; the software system takes care of the details of execution. The data management system often does not stand alone, but is associated with a "host" language such as COBOL. In this case the data management macros are imbedded in the user's COBOL program.

A number of data management systems are currently in use or are under development. Considerable differences exist between these systems, which has led the data processing community to move toward a standardization of data management procedures. Of particular significance is the work of the Database Task Group of CODASYL. This group has proposed a set of specifications for common data management languages. The languages consist of two parts: a Data Description Language (or DDL) for describing a database, and a Data Manipulation Language (or DML) which, when associated with a host language, allow the manipulation of databases described by the DDL. The languages are especially compatible with COBOL, but could also be used with other host languages.

Summary

Software is sometimes referred to as the application phase of data processing. It bridges the gap between computer hardware and data processing applications. Enormous advances have been made in software systems in recent years. Business-oriented languages such as COBOL and RPG have greatly facilitated the use of computers in data processing applications. Also, database management systems have facilitated the creation, maintenance, and interrogation of files and databases, especially for on-line applications. Further improvements in software systems may be expected in the future.

A number of different programming languages are available to the data processing user. Further descriptions of business-oriented languages are given in chapters that follow. In the next chapter, techniques for flow-charting solution logic to data processing problems are discussed.

Solutions to Exercises

Exercise 10–1

1. High-order, low-order.
2. Octal, hexadecimal.
3. Machine.
4. Mnemonics, symbolic.
5. False.
6. Macroinstruction, macro.
7. Input-output, OPEN, GET, PUT, CLOSE.
8. Input-output control system, IOCS.
9. Subroutine.
10. Declarative, imperative.

Exercise 10–2

1. Many
2. (e) Business-oriented languages.
   (d) Scientific languages.
   (a) List-processing languages.
   (f) Time-sharing languages.
   (b) General purpose languages.
   (c) Simulation languages.
3. All are false.

Exercise 10-3

1. Assembler, compiler.
2. Source, object.
3. Diagnostics.
4. Debugging.
5. Operating system.
6. Control, processing and service.
7. Language translators, utility programs, sort/merge programs, library maintenance programs.
8. Supervisor, monitor.
9. Job control.

Chapter Examination

1. Match the following terms to the most appropriate definition:

———————Compiler	(a) several programs executed concurrently
———————Subroutine	(b) translator for low-order languages
———————Supervisor	(c) Instruction that generates several instructions
———————Job Control language	(d) software that controls flow of work
———————Multiprogramming	(e) translator for high-order languages
———————Assembler	(f) program segment inserted by a macro
———————Macroinstruction	(g) used to instruct the operating system
———————Operating system	(h) control programs in an operating system

2. Describe three advantages of assembly language over machine language programming.

(a) ——————————————————————————

(b) ——————————————————————————

(c) ——————————————————————————

3. Describe three advantages of using macroinstructions when coding in assembly language.

(a) ——————————————————————————

(b) ——————————————————————————

(c) ——————————————————————————

4. What programming language would be most appropriate for each of the following applications?

(a) Inventory processing and updating _____ .

(b) Engineering stress analysis _____ .

(c) Business application combining data processing and complex mathematical calculations _____ .

(d) Generating simple financial reports on a small computer, including balance sheet and sources and applications of funds

_____ .

(e) Simulation of a production-inventory system _____ .

(f) Introducing beginning students to time-sharing _____ .

(g) Text editing _____ .

5. Define multiprogramming. What are its advantages? _____

_____

_____

_____

6. Describe the four major functions performed by the supervisor program in a large computer system.

(a) _____

(b) _____

(c) _____

(d) _____

7. The job control cards (together with source deck) for a COBOL program called STUDENT are shown in Figure 10–4. Referring to Figure 10–2, what are the four steps in translating this program?

(a) _____

(b) _____

(c) _____

(d) _____

8. Name and briefly describe four processing and service programs in an operating system.

(a) _____

(b) _____

(c) _____

(d) _____

9. In a multiprogramming environment, would each of the following jobs more likely be in a foreground partition or background partition?

(a) Simulation program with extensive calculations _____ .

(b) Communications control program that handles on-line inquiries

_____ .

(c) Disk dump (magnetic disk to magnetic tape) _____ .

10. What is stacked job processing and what is its principal advantage?

_____

_____

_____

_____

11. The data management languages proposed by the COBOL Database Task Group consist of two separate languages:

(a) _____

(b) _____

12. Identify the following statements as true or false:

_____(a) A single low-order language instruction is generally equivalent to one machine language instruction.

_____(b) A machine language program is easier to read and interpret than one written in a high-order language.

_____(c) Symbolic language is a low-order language in which mnemonic symbols are used rather than binary-based notation.

_____(d) Use of a macroinstruction in an assembly language program results in a sequence of instructions called a subroutine to be inserted into the user program.

_____(e) COBOL and RPG are high-order languages designed primarily for scientific applications.

_____(f) Under multiprogramming, instructions from two or more programs are executed simultaneously.

13. Briefly describe the function performed by each of the following input-output macros.

(a) OPEN _____

(b) GET _____

(c) PUT _____

(d) CLOSE _____

14. Give two examples of each of the following:

(a) Business-oriented languages _____ , _____ .

(b) Scientific and engineering languages _____ , _____ .

(c) Time-sharing languages _____ , _____ .

(d) List-processing languages _____ , _____ .

(e) Simulation languages _____ , _____ .

15. Briefly describe four steps in translating a program.

(a) _____

(b) _____

(c) _____

(d) _____

16. Briefly describe the function of each of the following.

(a) Job card _____

_____

(b) End of file card _____

_____

(c) End of job card _____

_____

17. Briefly describe two functions of partitions in multiprogramming.

(a) _____

_____

(b) _____

_____

18. What is the function of a data management system? _____

_____

_____

Chapter 11

FLOWCHARTING SOLUTION LOGIC

Overview

In Chapter 4 computer programming is defined as the process of preparing the instructions required to solve a problem by means of a computer. Computer programming is accomplished in three steps:

1. Developing the logic to solve the problem.
2. Coding the solution in a language acceptable to the computer.
3. Testing or debugging the program to insure its validity.

Deriving the logic to solve a problem, step number one, can be facilitated through preparation of a flowchart. A flowchart is a schematic or graphic presentation of the logic required to solve a problem.

In Figure 11-1, logic is flowcharted for solution of a compound interest problem. Only three symbols were required to depict the logic of the desired solution. Examine the flowchart and indicate the function of each symbol:

QUESTION:

The flat oval represents a terminating or starting activity, either _____

or _____.

The rectangle represents an _____

_____.

The parallelogram represents _____

or _____.

ANSWER: start or stop, operation or process, input or output

It is apparent that a flowchart was not necessary to visualize the logic required to solve the elementary problem shown in Figure 11–1. Nor does this problem require the use of all the symbols in the flowcharting repertoire. However, most problems to be computer processed are complex enough to require flowcharting.

Analyze the following flowchart. The program causes the computer to read, process, and write *one* record.

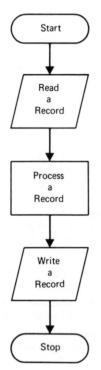

If the flowchart included a means for returning to the Read function, *any* quantity of records could be processed. The process of cycling back through a set of functions is referred to as *looping*.

QUESTION: The verb "loop" is synonymous with the terms "cycle" or "iterate." An iteration is one _____ through a set of logical steps.

ANSWER: loop or cycle

Use of the looping process is key to the efficiency of solving a problem via a computer. By cycling back through the same set of instructions, that set of logic can be used for an almost infinite set of data. For example, the logic in the above flowchart can be used to process thousands of records if an additional line is added to branch from the Write block to the Read block.

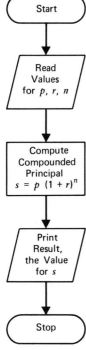

Figure 11–1. *Logic for compounding principal.*

Decision Logic

In both of the previous flowcharts, each step was performed in sequence. Use of the decision function permits alternative actions. Computer processing will branch to one of several alternatives, depending on the outcome of the decision depicted in the block as shown below.

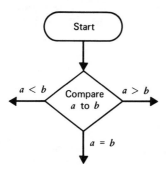

To illustrate the use of the decision symbol, the logic for maintaining inventory will be flowcharted. The procedure is as follows: in processing an inventory record, reorder when the quantity of electric toasters in inventory falls below 75.

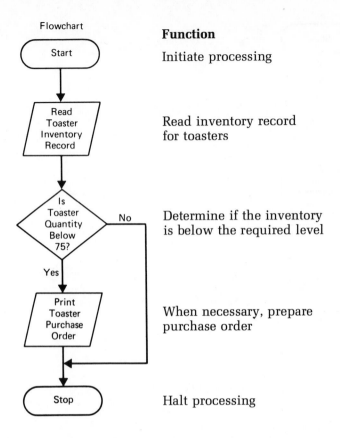

Flowchart	Function
	Function
Start	Initiate processing
Read Toaster Inventory Record	Read inventory record for toasters
Is Toaster Quantity Below 75? No	Determine if the inventory is below the required level
Yes	
Print Toaster Purchase Order	When necessary, prepare purchase order
Stop	Halt processing

QUESTION: Is the following terminology equally acceptable for the decision block? Quantity ≥ 75? If not, change it to produce the same results as that shown above. _____

ANSWER: The terminology is correct. However, the "Yes" and "No" terms must be reversed. If "Quantity > 75?" was used, an order would be prepared when a quantity of 75 remained in inventory.

Generalized Flowcharts

The preceding inventory flowchart was a *special-purpose* flowchart, designed specifically for maintaining an inventory level for toasters. A *general-purpose* flowchart permits the same logic to be used to maintain inventory for all products.

QUESTION: Revise the wording in the blocks to make the flowchart general purpose, appropriate for maintaining specified levels for *any* item in inventory, not just toasters.

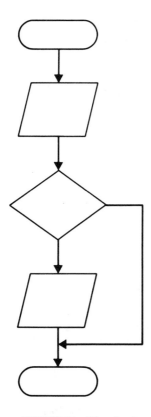

ANSWER: The logic would be identical to that shown previously, with the removal of the word "toaster" from the I/O blocks and the rewording of the decision block "Quantity below the reorder point?"

The preceding paragraph indicates the primary purpose of flowcharting: to develop a generalized set of logic that will represent all the conditions of the problem.

Flowcharting Multiple Alternatives

When more than three alternatives are possible, several decision blocks are used in conjunction. Decision criteria in a real-life admission procedure are used below to illustrate this point. Procedure: "Persons scoring over 550 on the ATGSB (admissions test for graduate schools of business) will be automatically accepted. Persons scoring in the range of 475 to 550 will be admitted with an undergraduate GPA (grade point average) of 3.0 or better. Persons scoring below 475 will be rejected." (See Figure 11–2.)

QUESTION: Check the logic in the above illustration. What happens when the test score is:

(a) 474 _____.   (b) 475 _____.

(c) 551 _____.

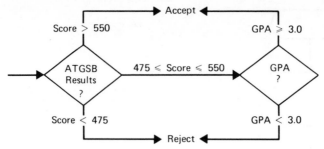

Figure 11-2. *Logic for admission procedure.*

ANSWER: (a) Reject (b) Check GPA (c) Accept

Connectors

The circle symbol provides a way to connect segments of a flowchart. Few solutions can be shown on a single page. Connectors may also be used on a single page, to avoid intersecting lines that might confuse the understanding of the logic.

To illustrate the function of a connector, assume the inventory procedure for reordering varies according to the price of the item. Not all of the solution logic can be provided on one sheet. Figure 11–3 shows the continuation of the flowchart on another page and how connector circles are used to keep track of the flow of logic.

QUESTION: Circle the letter designating the appropriate connector for the two pages of logic in Figure 11–3:

(a) Reenter original loop to read another record.   Connector A or B?
(b) When reorder is necessary, use a procedure
     determined by the price of the item.   Connector A or B?

ANSWER: B, A

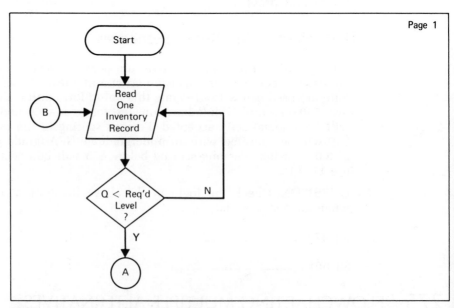

Figure 11-3a. *Page 1 of two pages of logic.*

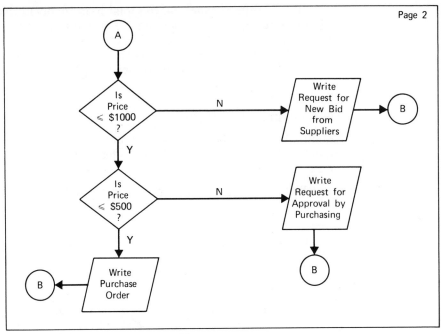

Figure 11–3b. *Page 2 of two pages of logic.*

Exercise 11–1

Review the logic in Figure 11–3 and answer the following questions.

1. What action is taken when the inventory quantity is less than the required level? _____

2. What action is taken when the quantity in inventory is exactly equal to the required level? _____

_____

3. What action is taken when the price of the inventory item is $1,500?

_____

_____

4. What action is taken when the price of the inventory item is $999?

_____

_____

5. What action is taken when the price of the inventory item is $1?

_____

In the inventory example, the total loop involved the processing of each inventory item. The processing consisted of an inner loop, returning from the decision block to read another record when the inventory level was satisfactory. The total loop accomplished the reorder process when inventory fell below the required level, then returned to read another record.

Testing End of Processing

Examine Figure 11–3a and note that an endless loop exists. To avoid this situation, the programmer could add a test at the end of the loop. The test would determine if all inventory records had been processed.

QUESTION: Fill in the decision block description to show the logic of such a test:

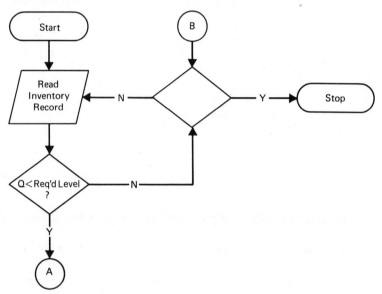

ANSWER: The description should say something like the following: "Have all records been read?"

The programmer may have placed his test at the start of the loop instead of the end. In doing this, the following logic is incorporated: "Test to determine if all inventory records have been read."

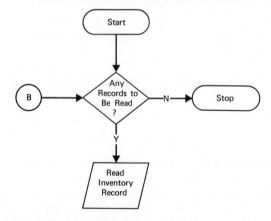

As an example of use of such logic, assume that we have an "activity file" containing a daily record of activity in inventory such as additions or withdrawals from inventory. The file is processed each evening to update the inventory file. It would be appropriate to test for activity to avoid processing the inventory file when no changes occurred.

Logic for Terminating Loops

Loops are terminated according to conditions provided in the programmer's solution logic. In the inventory problem it would be logical to establish the terminating condition as follows: "When all records have been read, halt processing."

The following flowchart illustrates logic for terminating processing. A storage location is established for the value used to control the number of cycles. This location functions as a "counter," that is, it keeps track

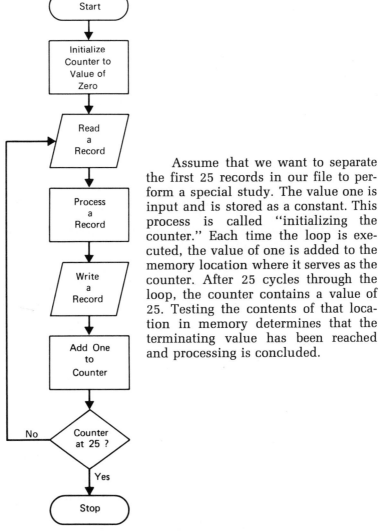

Assume that we want to separate the first 25 records in our file to perform a special study. The value one is input and is stored as a constant. This process is called "initializing the counter." Each time the loop is executed, the value of one is added to the memory location where it serves as counter. After 25 cycles through the loop, the counter contains a value of 25. Testing the contents of that location in memory determines that the terminating value has been reached and processing is concluded.

Figure 11–4. *An illustration of counter concept.*

of the number of cycles. After the specified number of cycles is complete, processing is terminated.

QUESTION: Often, instead of the above approach, a programmer includes logic to *decrement*, rather than *increment* the counter. Reword the logic in the selected blocks to represent *decrementing* instead of *incrementing* the counter for 25 cycles.

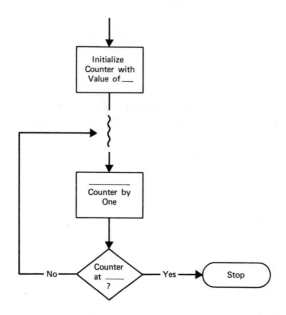

ANSWER: 25, decrement, Zero.

The flowchart in Figure 11–4 is special purpose. Only a few changes are required to make it a generalized flowchart, for terminating processing after *any* specified number of cycles. A function is added at the start, to read in a value to be used for terminating processing after *n* cycles (illustrated in Figure 11–5).

QUESTION: For conversion to a generalized format, the flowchart required only one other change. Compare the two charts. What was the second change? _____

_____

ANSWER: The initialization block is changed from a specific value, 25, to a variable value, *n*.

Value in Flowcharting

The preceding descriptions demonstrate the value of a flowchart in developing and evaluating the logic of a solution to a problem. Coding a program from a flowchart decreases programming time and effort. An error in logic would be difficult to trace without a flowchart. Most computer installations require flowcharts for this reason.

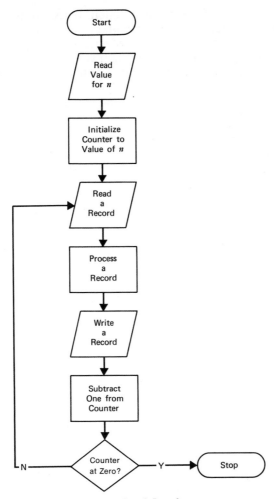

Figure 11-5. *A generalized flowchart.*

The old adage, "a picture is worth a thousand words," can be accurately paraphrased for the task of programming. "One flowchart can save 1000 minutes in debugging a complex program."

The authors have seen this adage proved again and again by students who bypass the flowcharting phase to rush into the coding of a problem.

Exercise 11-2

The flowchart in Figure 11-6 was prepared by a student of the authors. It incorrectly portrays the logic in the following procedure. In the space next to the flowchart, draw a flowchart that correctly portrays the logic of the procedure below.

PROCEDURE: An organization has a "talent bank" system that contains key information for determining promotable employees: birthdate, sex, address, social security number, years of education, experience in a maximum of three jobs (e.g. three years summer work as a chauffeur, two years as a bank teller and four years as a computer programmer). Develop a flowchart to sort the file and print the record for a female employee with one year of college and a minimum of one year of secretarial experience.

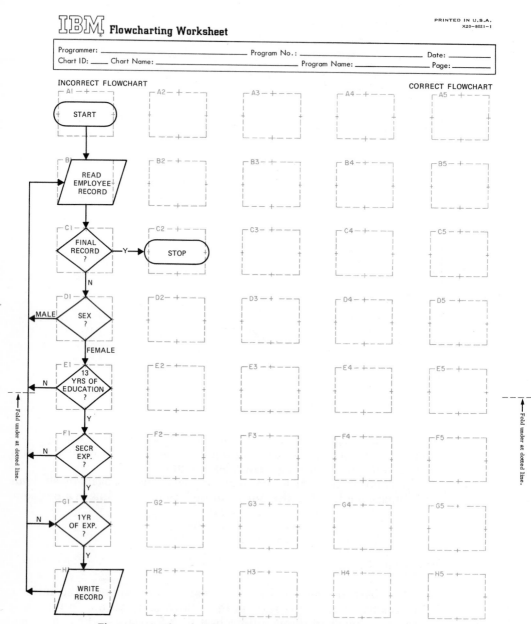

Figure 11–6. *Flowchart for talent bank procedure.*

Program Documentation

Flowcharts are valuable for another reason. They serve as documentation of a program, facilitating revision of the program when procedures change. Documentation is particularly important in organizations where personnel turnover is high. Analyzing another person's computer program is quite difficult if one must work solely with the code. Reviewing the logic of the program, displayed in the flowchart form, greatly facilitates incorporation of changes.

QUESTION: The package of flowcharts and instructions is referred to as

_____.

ANSWER: documentation

Terminology in a Flowchart

The decision functions are the key ones in most programs. The programmer has considerable flexibility in recording decision logic. Review the variations in Figure 11–7 in displaying identical logic for comparing the experience of a prospective employee to the specified amount of experience in the job requirement.

QUESTION: If you were discussing the logic in your flowchart with the personnel manager, the preferred representation would be (circle one):

right-most   center   left-most

ANSWER: left-most. See explanation below.

The left-most example in Figure 11-7 is best for person to person communication. The logic is expressed from a qualitative standpoint, in terms easily understood. The right-most example is better from a computer processing standpoint. It permits a quantitative comparison. The numerical value for the requirement is subtracted from the numerical value reflecting experience; computer processing then follows the branch according to the *algebraic sign* of the resultant numerical value.

QUESTION: Although people can make qualitative comparisons, programs for computers must provide for _____ comparisons.

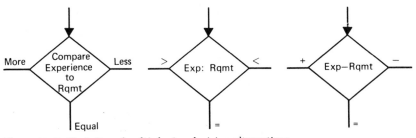

Figure 11–7. *Variations for displaying decision alternatives.*

ANSWER: quantitative

Types of Flowcharts

The typical computer department uses two types of flowcharting. One type is *problem-oriented;* the flowchart is expressed in terms commonly used in the activity to be computerized. For example, using problem-oriented terminology we might find a description in a decision block as follows: "Have all payroll deductions been made?"

Up to this point in the chapter, most of the flowcharts have been *programmer-oriented.* The symbols and terms used have been commonly required by a programmer in developing a computer application. For example, the functions of reading a record or writing a record are pro-grammer-oriented, not problem-oriented.

The expression "update the inventory" is problem-oriented. The expressions, "read, process, and write an inventory record" are programmer oriented.

QUESTION: Refer again to Figure 11–2. Is this flowchart segment problem-oriented or programmer-oriented? _____ .

ANSWER: Problem-oriented; it uses the terminology of the problem

For problem oriented flowcharts, one must take the viewpoint of the user of the computer application; that is, the viewpoint of persons for whom the program was designed. If a flowchart is problem oriented it must meet this test: "Can the user interpret the logic without prior computer background?"

QUESTION: Is the flowchart in Figure 11-4 problem oriented? _____

Why? _____

_____

ANSWER: No. Terms like "initialize the counter" have significance only to people who are using the flowchart to prepare a computer program

Problem-oriented flowcharts are sometimes referred to as *user-oriented* flowcharts. Another common description of these charts is *machine-independent* flowcharts. Figure 11–4 depicts *machine-dependent* logic rather than a machine-independent logic. The concept of a counter is a computer-oriented concept, not a user-oriented concept.

Why is it important to have problem-oriented flowcharts in addition to programmer-oriented flowcharts? The programmer is rarely as knowledgeable about the activity being computerized as is the user—the person for whom the application is designed. Therefore, the logic of the application needs to be verified by the user. Preparation initially of summary-level, user-oriented flowcharts permits verification of logic by the user. Once the logic is validated, the programmer can prepare detailed level flowcharts.

User-oriented flowcharts are useful for reasons other than verification of design logic. Once validated, user-oriented flow-charts may be used in training personnel in the user organization. Visual representation of a procedure is considerably more effective as a training device than are printed procedures.

QUESTION: User and problem-oriented flowcharts are the same. What is their purpose? _____

_____

ANSWER: They depict the system logic in the user's terminology. They are used for communication between user and data processing personnel

Responsibility for Preparing Flowcharts

In practice, computer application development is separated into two major tasks: (1) design, and (2) programming. In many organizations personnel specialize in one or the other of these tasks. The systems designer works with the user to define system requirements. The logic of the design is recorded in problem-oriented flowcharts. After these charts are reviewed by the user, they are provided to the programmer.

The programmer develops programmer oriented flowcharts from the problem-oriented flowcharts. Since more than one programmer may be assigned to the task of computerizing an activity, programmer oriented flowcharts are invaluable in delineating the relationships between the program modules. In some organizations, senior programmers develop programmer-oriented flowcharts, and junior programmers write the code to accomplish the logic in these flowcharts.

QUESTION: Programmer oriented flowcharts are useful for communication when several _____ are involved in computerizing a task.

ANSWER: programmers

Standard Flowchart Symbols

The key symbols in portraying solution logic have now been described. However, the professional programmer uses additional, specialized symbols to provide for the specific circumstances of his computer environment. He may be using a system limited to magnetic tape for input. He may be in a disk-only environment. Or, he may have a tape and disk environment. He may output results on paper or on a cathode-ray tube (CRT).

The standards association provides for all possibilities in its array of logic symbols. Figure 11–8 provides the American National Standards Institute set of symbols. Use of the standard symbols facilitates sharing of programs. For example, the University of Colorado uses programs developed at Dartmouth, Stanford, Texas, and many other schools. Availability of standardized flowcharts for programs facilitates sharing of programs. The flowcharts also permit students to follow the logic embedded in these programs before using them. Some of the additional flowcharting symbols shown in Figure 11–8 are used in the advanced chapters on flowcharting.

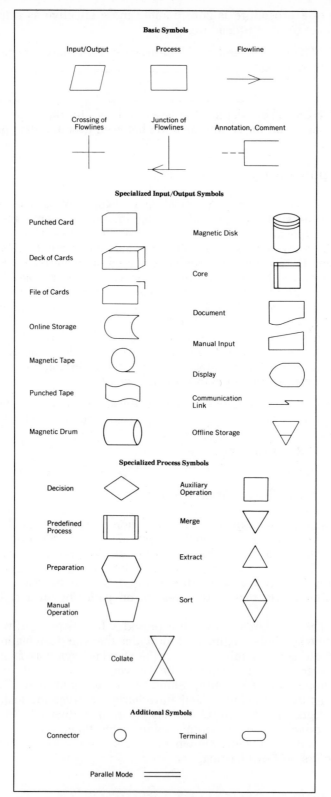

Figure 11–8. *American National Standards Institute (ANSI) flowchart symbols.*

QUESTION: Use of ANSI symbols facilitates_____

ANSWER: understanding of another person's program and sharing of programs

Guidelines for Development of Flowcharts

In addition to standards for flowchart symbols, a standard exists for preparing flowcharts. Figure 11–9 provides the Guidelines for Flowchart Development.

Adherence to these guidelines facilitates the review of logic in a flowchart. A person may need to revise a program several months after original development. Use of the guidelines makes it easy to reorient before incorporating those changes. Also, when several programmers are preparing modules to be integrated, use of the guidelines is mandatory to insure compatibility. Finally, when organizations share programs, use of nationally recognized guidelines facilitates communication and understanding of the program logic.

---

1. **Use standard flowcharting symbols.**

2. **Develop machine-independent flowcharts and evaluate logic before reducing to machine-dependent flowcharts.**

3. **Try to keep flow of logic from top to bottom and from left to right.**

4. **Avoid intersection of lines used to depict flow of logic.**

5. **Use connectors to reduce the number of flow lines.**

Figure 11–9. *Guidelines for flowchart development.*

Exercise 11–3

1. Three reasons for use of flowcharts are:

(a) _____

(b) _____

(c) _____

2. Why is it important to use ANSI flowcharting symbols?

_____

_____

_____

3. Problem-oriented flowcharts are useful for _____

_____

_____

4. Programmer-oriented flowcharts are more appropriate for_____

_____

_____

5. Item three (Figure 11–9) indicates that the flow of logic should be "southeasterly" on a sheet. In your opinion, what is the reason for this rule? _____

_____

_____

Summary

Flowcharting is an important part of the programming task. The logic of the solution of the problem (system) is first flowcharted using the terminology of the user of the system. For example, the system designer develops problem-oriented flowcharts with the supervisor of the payroll department. They use these charts to reach agreement on the procedure for processing payroll.

Then, the problem-oriented charts are converted to programmer-oriented flowcharts, which require much more detail. Programmer-oriented flowcharts use the terminology of the programmer, depicting solution logic quantitatively. The programmer codes directly from these flowcharts.

Try to be especially thorough in completing the chapter examination. If a proficiency in flowcharting is gained at this point in the course, the computer programming part of the course will be much easier—and more enjoyable.

Solutions to Exercises

Exercise 11–1

1. Program branches to further decision functions to determine various actions based on the price of the item.
2. No action taken. The next inventory record is read and analyzed.
3. Program branches to output function, printing a request for a new bid from the suppliers.
4. Program branches to another decision function, with a price of $500 as the determinant for further action.
5. Program branches to output function, printing a purchase order to procure the reorder quantity.

Exercise 11–2

The flowchart has the following errors: (see corrected flowchart on next page).
1. The procedure did not call for a person with 13 years of education but for a person with one year of college. A girl may have had a year of preschool or a year of airline hostess training beyond the normal 12 years and still meet the logic of this flowchart.
2. The procedure asked for a girl with a *minimum* of one year of secretarial experience. The flowchart excludes persons with less than one year and persons with more than one year of experience.
3. The arrow on the next to the last symbol is pointing the wrong direction. The "No" branch should go back to the Read step.

Exercise 11–3

1. (a) As an aid in developing and evaluating solution logic.
   (b) To reduce coding and debugging time.
   (c) To provide documentation for subsequent revision.
2. Use of standard symbols simplifies revision of programs when a change in the application occurs. It also facilitates sharing of programs between organizations (or passing on programs to next year's students!).
3. Problem-oriented flowcharts are useful for user evaluation and review of program logic, before approving the system.
4. Programmer-oriented flowcharts are useful for communicating between programmers who are preparing modules of a major system. Also, a programmer can more easily validate the logic of his program if flowcharts were prepared. Finally, debugging is simplified.
5. Why record the flow of logic southeasterly on a sheet? This simplifies interpretation of a flowchart by another person.

Corrected flowchart for Exercise 11–2.

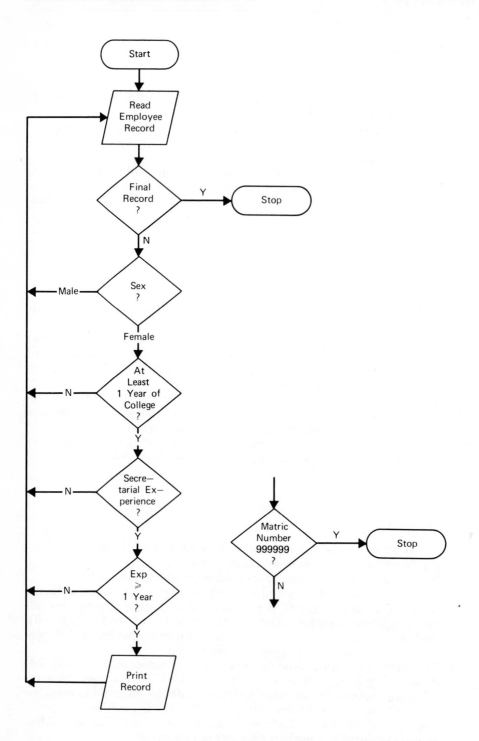

Chapter Examination

1. What are the three steps in computer programming?

   (a) ―――――――――――――――――――――――――

   (b) ―――――――――――――――――――――――――

   (c) ―――――――――――――――――――――――――

2. What are the three principal symbols used to depict logic to solve a problem (explain the use of each)?

―――――――――――――――――――――――――――――――――――

―――――――――――――――――――――――――――――――――――

―――――――――――――――――――――――――――――――――――

―――――――――――――――――――――――――――――――――――

―――――――――――――――――――――――――――――――――――

―――――――――――――――――――――――――――――――――――

3. Another, less important symbol is the small circle, used to ―――――

―――――――――――――――――――――――――――――――――――

4. A loop is a key programming technique. Define and explain a loop.

―――――――――――――――――――――――――――――――――――

―――――――――――――――――――――――――――――――――――

5. Counters are also important in solution logic. Explain the concept

   of a counter. ―――――――――――――――――――――――

―――――――――――――――――――――――――――――――――――

―――――――――――――――――――――――――――――――――――

6. What have flowcharts to do with documentation?―――――――――

―――――――――――――――――――――――――――――――――――

―――――――――――――――――――――――――――――――――――

―――――――――――――――――――――――――――――――――――

7. Describe the differences between problem-oriented flowcharts (that is, user-oriented flowcharts) and programmer-oriented (computer-oriented) flowcharts. _____

_____

_____

_____

_____

_____

8. Why all the fuss about standardizing flowchart symbols?_____

_____

_____

9. Match the terms to the appropriate definitions:

_____ Loop

_____ Counter

_____ Initialize

_____ Decision function

_____ Documentation

_____ Design logic

_____ Problem oriented

_____ Flowcharts

_____ Programmer-oriented

_____ Flowcharts

_____ Systems analyst/ designer

(a) user-oriented flowcharts
(b) computer-oriented flowcharts
(c) the set of logic used in developing an improved system
(d) establish an initial value for a counter
(e) a series of instructions used repeatedly
(f) A physical location in the CPU which keeps track of the number of cycles of processing
(g) flowcharts and computer programs for a computerized activity
(h) the process of evaluating criteria and selecting alternatives
(i) person who develops problem-oriented flowcharts

10. Develop a problem-oriented flowchart for the following situation, making sure you adhere to the ANSI standards listed in Figure 11–8 (use one of the forms at the end of the chapter examination).

The Accounts Receivable Department receives payments, pulls ledger cards for each customer, records amount and date of payment, determines balance, and attaches a red tab to the card if the account is not paid in full. Checks and cash are sent to the cashier. Once a month another clerk pulls all cards with red tabs and types invoices for amount owed. Amount and date of most recent payment are also entered on the invoice.

11. Develop a programmer-oriented flowchart to depict the logic in solving the problem in question 9 above via computer. (Use a form at the end of the chapter examination.)

12. Develop a programmer-oriented flowchart to revise the logic in Figure 11-6 to the following (use a form at the end of the chapter examination).

   The talent bank is revised to include data on promotion potential of employees. The supervisor's evaluation is entered on the file every six months. The ratings are numerical, from 1 (lowest rating) to 10 (highest rating). Once per year all employees with ratings averaging 7.5 or better on the last three evaluations are sorted out for consideration of promotion. The output is sorted in three ways: (1) one listing by job experience category, (2) one listing by rank in supervisory evaluations, and (3) a listing by years of education.

13. Prepare a programmer-oriented flowchart to depict the logic in computer processing of the PERT network procedure (explained on pages 604 and 605; however, you will need to review pages 600 to 604 if you are not familiar with the PERT technique). Record your logic on one of the forms at the end of the chapter examination.

14. Add logic to the flowchart from problem 12 to cover calculation of probability of project completion for the PERT network (explained on pages 606 to 609).

15. Add to the logic prepared for questions 12 and 13 to calculate slack for the PERT network (explained on pages 610 and 611).

16. Prepare a programmer-oriented flowchart to depict the logic for computer solution for determining Return-On-Investment (explained on pages 573 and 574).

17. Prepare a programmer-oriented flowchart to depict the logic for computer solution for determining cash flow (explained on pages 571 to 573).

18. Prepare a programmer-oriented flowchart to depict the logic for computer solution for calculating payback (explained on pages 570 and 571).

19. Prepare programmer-oriented flowcharts for questions 8, 9, 10 of the chapter examination for Chapter 13.

20. Prepare a user-oriented flowchart for the final question in the chapter examination of Chapter 14.

21. Prepare a programmer-oriented flowchart for the final problem in the chapter examination of Chapter 14.

22. Prepare a user-oriented flowchart for the following problem: develop the logic for end-of-the-semester processing of the student record file. Student records are set up as follows:

Field 1   Name – last name, first name, middle name
Field 2   Class – freshman, sophomore, junior, senior, graduate
Field 3   Course record – course number, semester hours and grade
Field 4   Grade Point Average – total grade points divided by total semester hours (A = 4, B = 3, C = 2, D = 1, F = 0)
Field 5   Remaining Requirements – courses completed this term deducted from degree program

The end of semester processing should accomplish the following:
(a) Update each student record.
(b) Prepare following reports:
  (1) A class report arranged alphabetically within each class. The report should list total hours, total points, and GPA.
  (2) A Dean's List arranged according to GPA. (Only students with GPA higher than 3.0 are eligible.)
  (3) A Course Report listing all students by course, arranged in GPA order.
(c) Include logic to accomplish the following:
  (1) Compute GPA for entire class on the Class Report.
  (2) Print the number of students in each class at the end of the Class Report.
  (3) Print the number of students in each course at the end of the Course Report.

23. Prepare a programmer-oriented flowchart for the problem in question 22 above.

IBM Flowcharting Worksheet

PRINTED IN U.S.A.
X20-8021-1

Programmer: _____ Program No.: _____ Date: _____

Chart ID: _____ Chart Name: _____ Program Name: _____ Page: _____

A1 A2 A3 A4 A5

B1 B2 B3 B4 B5

C1 C2 C3 C4 C5

D1 D2 D3 D4 D5

E1 E2 E3 E4 E5

F1 F2 F3 F4 F5

G1 G2 G3 G4 G5

H1 H2 H3 H4 H5

J1 J2 J3 J4 J5

K1 K2 K3 K4 K5

Fold under at dotted line.

Fold under at dotted line.

295 / CHAPTER EXAMINATION

IBM **Flowcharting Worksheet**

PRINTED IN U.S.A.
X20-8021-1

Programmer: _____ Program No.: _____ Date: _____

Chart ID: ____ Chart Name: _____ Program Name: _____ Page: _____

| A1 | A2 | A3 | A4 | A5 |

| B1 | B2 | B3 | B4 | B5 |

| C1 | C2 | C3 | C4 | C5 |

| D1 | D2 | D3 | D4 | D5 |

| E1 | E2 | E3 | E4 | E5 |

Fold under at dotted line.

| F1 | F2 | F3 | F4 | F5 |

Fold under at dotted line.

| G1 | G2 | G3 | G4 | G5 |

| H1 | H2 | H3 | H4 | H5 |

| J1 | J2 | J3 | J4 | J5 |

| K1 | K2 | K3 | K4 | K5 |

296 / FLOWCHARTING SOLUTION LOGIC

PRINTED IN U.S.A.
X20-8021-1

IBM Flowcharting Worksheet

Programmer: _____ Program No.: _____ Date: _____

Chart ID: ____ Chart Name: _____ Program Name: _____ Page: _____

A1	A2	A3	A4	A5
B1	B2	B3	B4	B5
C1	C2	C3	C4	C5
D1	D2	D3	D4	D5
E1	E2	E3	E4	E5
F1	F2	F3	F4	F5
G1	G2	G3	G4	G5
H1	H2	H3	H4	H5
J1	J2	J3	J4	J5
K1	K2	K3	K4	K5

Fold under at dotted line.

Fold under at dotted line.

297 / CHAPTER EXAMINATION

PRINTED IN U.S.A.
X20—8021—1

IBM Flowcharting Worksheet

Programmer: _____ Program No.: _____ Date: _____

Chart ID: _____ Chart Name: _____ Program Name: _____ Page: _____

A1 A2 A3 A4 A5

B1 B2 B3 B4 B5

C1 C2 C3 C4 C5

D1 D2 D3 D4 D5

E1 E2 E3 E4 E5

F1 F2 F3 F4 F5

G1 G2 G3 G4 G5

H1 H2 H3 H4 H5

J1 J2 J3 J4 J5

K1 K2 K3 K4 K5

Fold under at dotted line.

Fold under at dotted line.

298 / FLOWCHARTING SOLUTION LOGIC

Chapter 12

THE PROGRAMMING TASK

Overview

Developing instructions in the code of a particular programming language is only part of the programming task. As we discuss in the preceding chapter, the programmer must first develop programmer-oriented flowcharts depicting the logic of the system. After coding comes debugging and testing. The total task is an exacting one.

Special techniques have been developed to facilitate the job of programming. *First*, the system designer documents system specifications in a format to expedite programming. System documentation consists of narrative description, user-oriented flowcharts, file descriptions, input/output layouts, system controls, test and conversion plan, and program specifications. *Second*, the task of program design is facilitated by use of modular programming concepts. *Third*, the task of coding and debugging are facilitated by use of a high-level language where syntax errors (errors in use of the language) are identified by the system during compilation. Other special software, for example, trace routines, enable the programmer to isolate errors in coding.

This chapter explains these programmer-aids in context of the preparation of the complete programming package (documentation): problem description, program abstract, program description, operating instructions, program controls, and test plan.

Planning the Program

The documentation prepared by the systems designer (problem definition, flow charts, layout forms, etc.) provides a general set of specifications for a computer program. Before the program is coded, the programmer must plan the program in detail and must prepare detailed processing logic. The following steps are generally required.

1. Prepare a narrative problem description. This insures that the programmer understands the problem to be solved by the program.

2. Design the program. This often includes dividing the overall program into a series of logical subunits or moduies.
3. Decide on the use of library functions, subroutines, subprograms, and other programming aids.
4. Develop program flowcharts showing the processing logic. In some programs the programmer may prepare several levels of flowcharts — macro flowcharts showing the overall logic, and micro flowcharts showing the detailed logic of each program module. Flowcharting techniques are described in Chapter 11.
5. Plan for testing the program. This includes deciding on the test data and procedures to be used. There should be a test plan for each program module, as well as a system test for the entire program.

Program Documentation. This documentation is prepared by the programmer, and provides a complete description of each program. The complete documentation of the program used in a run is often referred to as the *run manual*. These sections are generally included in program documentation:

Section	Description
Problem description	A description of the problem to be solved by the program
Program abstract	A brief description of the various tasks a program performs, the files used, and other miscellaneous information
Program description	Detailed description of the program, including logical flowcharts, decision tables (if used), and program listing. The listing should include a *data dictionary* showing the meaning of each variable (or data name) used in the program
Operating instructions	Instructions to the computer operator on running the program
Program controls	Summary of error controls built into the program
Test plan	Documentation of the test plan and data used to test the program, record of changes made, and record of approvals

Modular Programming Concepts. An important concept in program design is called modular programming. In this approach, a large program is divided into a number of small, self-contained modules. Each module is designed to accomplish a single, well-defined task, for example, edit data from an input record, or format an error message.

The modules in a program are written as small subprograms or subroutines. A main routine in the program uses or "calls" each module as it is required. After a program module has been executed, it may either call another module or return to the main program. The modules may be written by the programmer who codes the program, or may be called from a library of precoded programs.

There are several important advantages to modular programming:

1. A modular program is inherently less complex and easier to understand, since it contains fewer branching instructions.
2. Several programmers can concurrently code the modules, thus reducing overall coding time.
3. Program testing is simplified, since the small modules are tested individually as they are completed. The modules are then tested together for system performance.
4. A modular program is easily modified, since it is necessary to revise only those modules that are affected by the change.
5. Modular programs are less constrained by memory, since modules can be stored in secondary storage and brought into primary storage as needed.
6. Perhaps the greatest advantage is that a generally used function can be programmed once as a module and then can be used by all programs needing this function.

An example of a modular design for a payroll program is shown in Figure 12-1. The total program is broken down into 14 modules. The modular design for this program follows a hierarchical structure, with the more encompassing modules at the top and the simpler modules at the bottom. For example, module 1 (process payroll file) processes the master records for each individual, module 2 (process employees) processes the pay data for each individual, and module 12 (calculate taxes) performs a simple tax calculation.

QUESTION: Examine Figure 12–1. Module 11 (calculate gross pay) calls three modules that perform tasks related to gross pay calculation. These modules are:

1. _____

2. _____

3. _____

ANSWER: calculate taxes, calculate dues, calculate insurance

Assignment of Responsibilities. For a large program such as the payroll program, a team of programmers headed by a lead programmer will often be assigned to the project. The lead programmer will design the program, deciding on the program modules to be used and the relationship between modules. The lead programmer then creates program specifications for the individual modules. Each module specification must be self-contained, describing fully the data to be used, the processing to be done, and the calls to be made by the module. The quality of work done at this planning and design stage will determine whether or not the system is going to be effective.

After the program planning is completed, the lead programmer assigns the program modules to individual programmers for coding. He assists the programmers with any specification inconsistencies, and provides technical support. The modular approach facilitates project scheduling and control. Figure 12–2 shows a simple schedule chart for the payroll program.

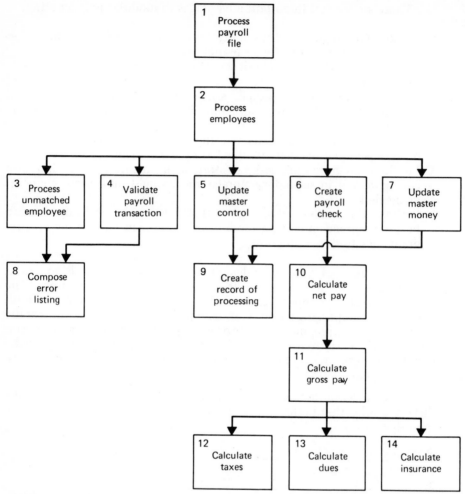

Figure 12-1. *A modular design of a payroll program (reprinted from* Computer Decisions, July 1972, page 25, copyright 1972, Hayden Publishing Company).

QUESTION: Examine Figure 12-2 and answer the following questions:
(a) Who is responsible for testing individual program modules?

_____

(b) Who is responsible for testing the complete program?

_____

(c) How many weeks are scheduled for the entire payroll program?

_____

ANSWER: (a) programmer who coded the module
(b) lead programmer   (c) fifteen weeks

302 / THE PROGRAMMING TASK

Figure 12-2. A schedule chart for a modular payroll program (reprinted from Computer Decisions, July 1972, page 27, copyright 1972, Hayden Publishing Company.)

		Programmer supervision			Program testing
Lead programmer	Design payroll program	Code module 1 / Test module 1	Code module 2 / Test module 2		Program testing
Programmer A		Code module 3	Code module 4 / Test module 3	Code module 8 / Test module 4	Code module 14 / Test module 8	Test module 14
Programmer B		Code module 5	Code module 6 / Test module 5	Code module 7 / Test module 6	Code module 9 / Test module 7	Test module 9
Programmer C		Code module 10	Code module 11 / Test module 10	Code module 12 / Test module 11	Code module 13 / Test module 12	Test module 13
Week 0	6	7	8	9	15

Exercise 12-1

1. List five steps in planning a computer program:

(a) _____

(b) _____

(c) _____

(d) _____

(e) _____

2. List six advantages to modular programming:

(a) _____

(b) _____

(c) _____

(d) _____

303 / PLANNING THE PROGRAM

(e) _____

(f) _____

3. An accounts payable program consists of 17 modules, as follows:

Module Number	Module Name	Modules Called by This Module
1	System executive	2, 3, 4, 5, 6
2	Initial housekeeping	none
3	Input control	7, 8
4	Process control	12, 13, 14, 15, 16
5	Report control	9, 10
6	Final housekeeping	none
7	Read input data	none
8	Edit input data	17
9	Format report data	none
10	Write reports	17
11	Process errors	17
12	Validate invoices	17
13	Cash forecast	17
14	Select payment	17
15	Cost distribution	17
16	Check reconciliation	17
17	Manage file/core transfer	none

Develop a diagram (similar to Figure 12–1) showing the modular design of this program.

Coding the Program

After program planning has been completed, the computer program is ready to be coded. *Coding* is the process of writing a sequence of computer instructions to accomplish a desired task. As is described in Chapter 10, coding may be accomplished in a low-level language (machine or assembly language) or in a higher-level language. Most business applications are programmed in a higher-level language such as COBOL, RPG, or PL/I.

Instructions are generally entered on preprinted coding paper, which assists the programmer in following the correct format for the language being used. For example, Figure 12–3 shows a program coded on a FORTRAN coding sheet. This program, which locates and prints out the largest of five numbers, will be used to illustrate several points in the remainder of this chapter.

Improving Program Documentation. When the program coding is completed, the program is translated (assembled or compiled) into machine language instructions. The computer translator produces a listing of the program coded by the programmer. This program listing is one of the best (and most frequently used) sources of program documentation.

Higher-level languages produce better documentation than low-level languages. This is because the language is problem or procedure oriented,

```
      DIMENSION M(5)
      READ (5,10) M
   10 FORMAT (5I2)
      LARGE = M(1)
      DO 20 J = 2,5
      IF (M(J).LE.LARGE) GO TO 20
      LARGE = M(J)
   20 CONTINUE
      WRITE (6,30) M
   30 FORMAT (1HO,'THE NUMBERS ARE ',5I3)
      WRITE (6,40) LARGE
      FORMAT (1HO,'THE LARGEST NUMBER IS ',I3)
      STOP
      END
```

Figure 12–3. A FORTRAN coding sheet.

rather than computer oriented. COBOL programs are particularly easy to read, since COBOL is an English-oriented language.

The programmer can improve program documentation by following good coding practice. For example, most programming languages permit the insertion of notes or comments at any point in a program to explain the purpose of a given segment of coding. These comments are a valuable aid when the programmer (or someone else) must read the program several weeks or months after it has been coded.

The use of comments in a program is illustrated in Figure 12–4. This FORTRAN program (introduced in Figure 12–3) computes and prints out

```
        PROGRAM LARGEST(INPUT,OUTPUT,TAPE5=INPUT,TAPE6=OUTPUT)
        C*************************************************************************
        C***THIS ROUTINE READS FIVE NUMBERS FROM A CARD
        C***THE FIRST NUMBER IS IN COLUMNS 1 AND 2. THE SECOND IN COLUMNS 3 AND
        C***4,AND SO ON.
        C***IT THEN COMPUTES AND PRINTS OUT THE LARGEST OF THE FIVE NUMBERS.
        C*************************************************************************
        C***VARIABLE NAMES ARE THE FOLLOWING
        C*****M--ARRAY IN WHICH THE FIVE NUMBERS ARE STORED
        C*****LARGE--LARGEST VALUE ENCOUNTERED IN THE ARRAY M
        C*************************************************************************
        C***DIMENSION THE ARRAY M
000003        DIMENSION M(5)
        C***READ THE NUMBERS INTO M
000003        READ (5,10) M
000011     10 FORMAT (5I2)
        C***SET LARGE EQUAL TO THE FIRST NUMBER. THEN EXAMINE THE REMAINING
        C***NUMBERS, SETTING LARGE EQUAL TO ANY NUMBER WHICH IS GREATER THAN
        C***THE CURRENT VALUE.
000011        LARGE = M(1)
000013        DO 20 J = 2,5
000014            IF (M(J).LE.LARGE) GO TO 20
000017            LARGE = M(J)
000020     20 CONTINUE
        C***PRINT OUT THE FIVE NUMBERS.
000022        WRITE (6,30) M
000030     30 FORMAT (1H0,*THE NUMBERS ARE *,5I3)
        C***PRINT OUT THE LARGEST NUMBER, THEN TERMINATE THE PROGRAM.
000030        WRITE (6,40) LARGE
000036     40 FORMAT (1H0,*THE LARGEST NUMBER IS *,I3)
000036        STOP
000040        END

THE NUMBERS ARE   8  5  1  9  3

THE LARGEST NUMBER IS   9
```

Figure 12–4. A FORTRAN program with comments.

the largest of five numbers. Even the reader who is not familiar with FORTRAN can follow the logic of the program, aided by the comment statements (which begin with the letter "C" in the first column).

QUESTION: Examine Figure 12–4 and answer the following questions:

(a) Briefly state the purpose of the program _____

_____

(b) Complete the data dictionary

　　M – _____

　　LARGE – _____

(c) Look at the output. Did the program identify the largest number?

_____

ANSWERS:
(a) Compares numbers and prints largest
(b) M – the array in which the numbers are stored
　　LARGE – the largest number in the array
(c) Yes, it identified the number nine

Using Library Routines. Programming may be considerably simplified by the use of precoded library routines. Many programming language systems include these library routines for solving common computational problems, such as inverting a matrix or obtaining the square root of a number. Some of these routines are included in the manufacturer-supplied software systems, while others are coded by the user and stored in the program library for common usage.

Two types of library routines are commonly used: open subroutines, and closed subroutines. An *open subroutine* is spliced into the main program whenever it is referenced by the programmer. For example, if the programmer references a particular subroutine at three different points in a program, the same section of coding is inserted in the program at three different locations. The open subroutine format is generally used for relatively short sections of coding.

In contrast, a *closed subroutine* is stored once as a separate program in computer memory. Each time the programmer references a closed subroutine, information is "passed" to the subroutine for computation, and results are "passed" back to the main program. This is accomplished by means of *linkages* between the two programs. Closed subroutines are used for more extensive computations, and are extremely important in programming.

The distinction between open and closed subroutines is illustrated in Figure 12–5.

QUESTION: Examine Figure 12–5. After a closed subroutine is executed, control is returned to what instruction in the calling program?

_____

ANSWER: The instruction immediately following the subroutine call

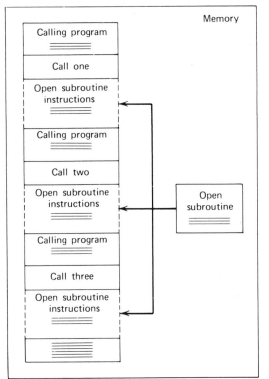
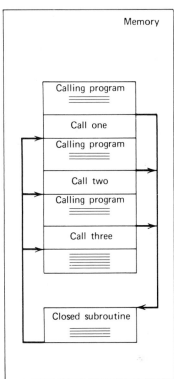

Figure 12–5. *A comparison of open and closed subroutines.*

Exercise 12–2

1. Explain whether each of the following is an open or closed subroutine:
   (a) The FORTRAN function subprogram SQRT (for square root), which is inserted into a FORTRAN program each time it is referenced by a programmer.

   (b) A programmer-coded FORTRAN subroutine subprogram called MATINV (for matrix inversion), which is stored in memory as a separate program.

---

2. Examine Figure 12–4 again. From the comments included in the program, explain the function of each of these statements:

   (a) READ (5, 10) M _____

   (b) LARGE = M(1) _____

   (c) IF (M(J).LE.LARGE) GO TO 20 _____

   (d) LARGE = M(J) _____

Testing and Debugging the Program

Programming is an exacting task. Even the smallest error in coding a program will usually cause the program not to run at all, or to produce incorrect results. Careful planning and coding will reduce errors; however, a program rarely runs perfectly the first time it is tried. The program must be tested and errors (bugs) removed. The process of removing errors is called *debugging*. The trials and tribulations associated with testing and debugging a program are summarized in Figure 12–6.

There are two principal types of errors that occur in coding computer programs:

1. *Syntax errors*. Errors in usage of the programming language.
2. *Logical errors*. Errors in programming logic.

Syntax Errors. Every programming language has a set of rules concerning format, spelling, punctuation naming of variables, and other conventions that must be observed by the programmer. An error in usage of the language (similar to a spelling or punctuation error) is often referred to as a syntax error.

DEFINITION	A "working" program is one that has only unobserved bugs.
LAW	Every nontrivial program has at least one bug.
COROLLARY I	A sufficient condition for program triviality is that it has no bugs.
COROLLARY II	At least one bug will be observed after the author leaves the organization.
LAW II	The subtlest bugs cause the greatest damage or problems.
COROLLARY I	A subtle bug will modify storage, thereby masquerading as some other problem.
LAW III	Bugs will appear in one part of a working program when another "unrelated" part is modified.
LAW IV	*Lulled into Security Law*. A "debugged" program that crashed will wipe out source files on storage devices when there is the least available backup.
LAW V	A hardware failure will cause system software to crash, and the CE (computer company's customer engineer) will blame the programmers.
LAW VI	A system software crash will cause hardware to act strangely, and the programmers will blame the CE.
LAW VII	The documented interfaces between standard software modules will have undocumented quirks.
LAW VIII	The probability of a hardware failure disappearing is inversely proportional to the distance between the computer and the CE.
LAW IX	Murphy designed the computer in your organization.
LAW X	(O'Shea's law) Murphy was an optimist.

(*Note*. For those who may be in doubt, Murphy's law states that if anything can go wrong, it will, and always at the most inconvenient time.)

Figure 12–6. The "Laws" of programming (source unknown).

```
         PROGRAM LARGEST(INPUT,OUTPUT,TAPE5=INPUT,TAPE6=OUTPUT)
C******************************************************************
C***THIS ROUTINE READS FIVE NUMBERS FROM A CARD
C***THE FIRST NUMBER IS IN COLUMNS 1 AND 2, THE SECOND IN COLUMNS 3 AND
C***4,AND SO ON.
C***IT THEN COMPUTES AND PRINTS OUT THE LARGEST OF THE FIVE NUMBERS.
C******************************************************************
C***VARIABLE NAMES ARE THE FOLLOWING
C*****M--ARRAY IN WHICH THE FIVE NUMBERS ARE STORED
C*****LARGE--LARGEST VALUE ENCOUNTERED IN THE ARRAY M
C******************************************************************
C***DIMENSION THE ARRAY M
000003         DIMENSION M(5)
         C***READ THE NUMBERS INTO M
000003         READ (5,10) M
000011      10 FORMAT (5I2)
         C***SET LARGE EQUAL TO THE FIRST NUMBER. THEN EXAMINE THE REMAINING
         C***NUMBERS, SETTING LARGE EQUAL TO ANY NUMBER WHICH IS GREATER THAN
         C***THE CURRENT VALUE.
000011         LARGE = M(1)
000013         DO 20 J = 2,5
000014         IF (M(J) LE LARGE) GO TO 20
***LXF**********
000015            LARGE = M(J)
000017      20 CONTINUE
         C***PRINT OUT THE FIVE NUMBERS.
000021         WRITE (6,30) M
000026      30 FORMAT (1H0,*THE NUMBERS ARE *,5I3)
         C***PRINT OUT THE LARGEST NUMBER, THEN TERMINATE THE PROGRAM.
000026         WRITE (6,40) LARGE
000034      40 FORMAT (1H0,*THE LARGEST NUMBER IS *,I3)
000034         STOP
000036         END

LX********IMPROPER LOGICAL EXP. WITHIN LOGICAL IF STMT
     000014
```

Figure 12-7. *A FORTRAN program with syntax error.*

An example of a syntax error in a computer program is shown in Figure 12–7. This program is identical to the one shown in Figure 12–4, except for a syntax error in the statement at line number 000014.

QUESTION: Compare Figures 12–4 and 12–7, and identify the syntax error in the statement at line number 000014.

Incorrect statement: _____

Correct statement: _____
ANSWER: Incorrect IF (M(J) LE LARGE) GO TO 20
Correct IF (M(J).LE.LARGE) GO TO 20

Errors in usage such as this are normally detected during translation by the assembler or compiler. The program will generally not be run but, instead, an error message called a *diagnostic* will be printed for each error that is detected. The diagnostic will indicate the nature of the error and the location (line number) in the program where it was detected.

QUESTION: Examine Figure 12–7 again. The FORTRAN diagnostic that was printed is the following:

Diagnostic: _____

Line number: _____
ANSWER: IMPROPER LOGICAL EXP. WITHIN LOGICAL IF STMT (line number 000014)

309 / TESTING AND DEBUGGING THE PROGRAM

Logical Errors. Although the compiler (or assembler) will detect syntax errors, it will *not* detect errors in programming logic. Thus a program with an error-free listing may still contain logical errors that produce incorrect results, or cause the program to be aborted during execution.

An example of a logical program error is shown in Figure 12–8. This is the same program (to compute and print out the largest of five numbers) that was illustrated in Figures 12–4 and 12–7. However, the logical IF statement at line number 000014 has been reversed:

Correct Statement	*Statement in Figure 12–8*
IF (M(J).LE.LARGE) GO TO 20	IF (LARGE.LE.M(J)) GO TO 20

As a result of this logical error, the program computes and prints out the *smallest* of the five numbers instead of the largest, as intended. Notice that the program listing contains no diagnostic message to warn the programmer of this error, and that the program runs and produces output. Only by careful testing (using methods to be discussed in the next section) can this type of error be detected.

A logical program error will lead to one of two results:

1. The program will produce incorrect results but terminate normally, as in the above program.
2. An unusual condition will be encountered which will lead to early termination of the program, for example:
   (a) The program may contain an endless loop, in which case the operating system should terminate the program after a certain time has elapsed.

```
          PROGRAM LARGEST(INPUT,OUTPUT,TAPE5=INPUT,TAPE6=OUTPUT)
        C*********************************************************************
        C***THIS ROUTINE READS FIVE NUMBERS FROM A CARD
        C***THE FIRST NUMBER IS IN COLUMNS 1 AND 2. THE SECOND IN COLUMNS 3 AND
        C***4,AND SO ON.
        C***IT THEN COMPUTES AND PRINTS OUT THE LARGEST OF THE FIVE NUMBERS.
        C*********************************************************************
        C***VARIABLE NAMES ARE THE FOLLOWING
        C*****M--ARRAY IN WHICH THE FIVE NUMBERS ARE STORED
        C*****LARGE--LARGEST VALUE ENCOUNTERED IN THE ARRAY M
        C*********************************************************************
        C***DIMENSION THE ARRAY M
000003         DIMENSION M(5)
        C***READ THE NUMBERS INTO M
000003         READ (5,10) M
000011    10 FORMAT (5I2)
        C***SET LARGE EQUAL TO THE FIRST NUMBER. THEN EXAMINE THE REMAINING
        C***NUMBERS, SETTING LARGE EQUAL TO ANY NUMBER WHICH IS GREATER THAN
        C***THE CURRENT VALUE.
000011         LARGE = M(1)
000013         DO 20 J = 2,5
000014         IF (LARGE.LE.M(J)) GO TO 20
000017         LARGE = M(J)
000020    20 CONTINUE
        C***PRINT OUT THE FIVE NUMBERS.
000022         WRITE (6,30) M
000030    30 FORMAT (1H0,*THE NUMBERS ARE *,5I3)
        C***PRINT OUT THE LARGEST NUMBER, THEN TERMINATE THE PROGRAM.
000030         WRITE (6,40) LARGE
000036    40 FORMAT (1H0,*THE LARGEST NUMBER IS *,I3)
000036         STOP
000040         END

THE NUMBERS ARE   8  5  1  9  3

THE LARGEST NUMBER IS   1
```

Figure 12–8. *A FORTRAN program with logic error.*

(b) The program (and data used by the program) may lead to an impossible or unacceptable operation, such as division by zero. In such cases, the operating system generally prints out an error message and terminates the program. Messages of this kind are termed *execution-time* (or run-time) error messages, in contrast to the diagnostics printed out by the compiler during *compile time*.

Program Testing

Several stages in testing a program are as follows.

1. Desk checking.
2. Compiler or assembler system checking.
3. Program run with hypothetical data.
4. Diagnostic procedures, if needed.
5. Full-scale test with actual data.

Desk Checking. The programmer should carefully check each step in coding a program. When the program is completed, the programmer should manually step through the program using sample data, to insure that the logic is correct. The program should also be reviewed by another programmer or by the programming supervisor, before it is released for keypunching.

Careful desk checking is an often neglected aspect of program testing. Too often the programmer follows the maxim "let the compiler do the checking." Unfortunately, the compiler is unable to detect logical errors, and such errors may be missed in subsequent testing stages.

QUESTION: Manual checking of a program before it is keypunched is called _____ _____ .
ANSWER: desk checking

Compiler Checking. After the program has been desk checked, it is keypunched and submitted for compilation (or assembly, if an assembly language has been used). As indicated previously syntax errors are detected during this stage and are indicated by diagnostics. The programmer corrects these errors and resubmits the program, until an error-free listing is obtained.

Run With Hypothetical Data. When the above steps are completed, the programmer should conduct several trial runs of the program by using hypothetical data. The results to be expected from each set of test data should be known. For example, in the program of Figure 12–4 the test data consisted of the numbers 8, 5, 1, 9, 3; it was known in advance that the correct output would be 9, the largest of these numbers.

The test data should include all important variations in input data, including data with errors. This will test the handling of error conditions by the program. Also all of the various paths in the processing logic should be tested. There are examples of "checked-out" programs that have produced correct output for months or even years, only to produce erroneous output when a previously unused condition or path is encountered.

QUESTION: Is the input data used in the program of Figure 12–4 adequate for a comprehensive test of this program? State your reason why or why not. _____ .

ANSWER: No, the data does not test all possible conditions. For example, what happens if one of the numbers is zero or negative?

Diagnostic Procedures. Sometimes a program does not run correctly, but the logical errors in the program are difficult to find. This often happens in complex programs. In such circumstances various diagnostic procedures may be used, depending on the programming language and compiler being used.

A common diagnostic procedure makes use of a program called a *trace routine*. Such a routine prints out the results of key processing steps in the program being tested, such as the value of selected variables and the indication of various paths taken in the program. If a trace routine is not available, the programmer may insert temporary instructions in the program to print out results at critical points.

It is good programming practice where possible to print out information read into a program, to insure that the program is reading data as intended. More errors occur on data input than any other processing phase. In the program shown in Figure 12–4, the numbers read into the computer are printed out as part of the output, even though only the largest of these numbers is required.

Test with Actual Data. Programs for data processing are typically run in parallel with the existing system for a short time, to insure acceptable system performance. This test is made using actual input data, for example, payroll data. The parallel test is part of the implementation phase of the system development cycle, and is discussed in greater detail in Chapter 21.

Exercise 12–3

1. In desk checking a program, the programmer manually "steps through" his program using sample data. Refer to Figure 12–4. Assume the following data has been correctly read into the array M:

Position (I)	Value M(I)
1	8
2	5
3	1
4	9
5	3

Step through the program in Figure 12–4 and complete the following:

(a) LARGE = M(1) = _____
      J = 2

(b) Is M(J) less than or equal to LARGE?_____

(c) GO TO _____
     J = 3

(d) Is M(J) less than or equal to LARGE? _____

(e) GO TO _____
     J = 4

(f) Is M(J) less than or equal to LARGE? _____

(g) LARGE = M(_____) = _____
     J = 5

(h) Is M(J) less than or equal to LARGE? _____

(i) GO TO _____

Print out results and terminate the program.

2. Run the program of Figure 12–4 to determine whether it will produce correct results when one of the numbers is negative. To do this, keypunch the program (to simplify the keypunching, all comment cards may be omitted). You will need a set of control cards to precede your FORTRAN program. Ask your instructor about job cards for your school's computer system. Use the following input test data: 8, −5, 1, 9, 3.

Does the program produce the correct output for this data? _____

Summary

Program preparation is the second major phase in the system development cycle that includes systems analysis and design, programming, and implementation. System documentation provides the specifications for each computer program. The major steps in program preparation are program planning, coding, testing and debugging, and documentation. The overall flow of events in program preparation is shown in Figure 12–9.

Solutions to Exercises

Exercise 12–1

1. (a) Prepare narrative problem description.
   (b) Design the program (decide on modules).
   (c) Decide on the use of library routines.
   (d) Develop program flowcharts.
   (e) Develop a plan for program testing.

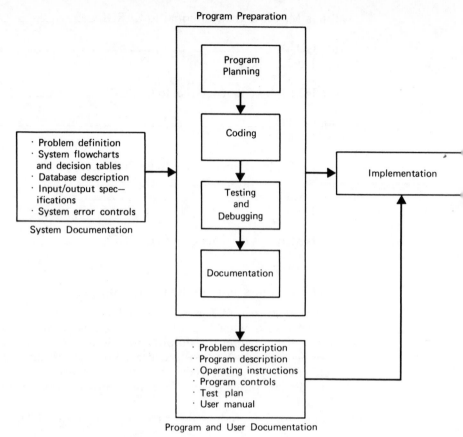

System Documentation

· Problem definition
· System flowcharts and decision tables
· Database description
· Input/output spec—ifications
· System error controls

Program Preparation

Program Planning

Coding

Testing and Debugging

Documentation

Implementation

Program and User Documentation

· Problem description
· Program description
· Operating instructions
· Program controls
· Test plan
· User manual

Figure 12–9. *Steps in program preparation.*

2. (a) Less complexity.
   (b) Reduced coding time.
   (c) Simplifies program testing.
   (d) Simplifies modification.
   (e) Eases memory constraints.
   (f) Common functions programmed once.
3. See diagram on next page.

Exercise 12–2

1. (a) Open.
   (b) Closed.
2. (a) Read five numbers into the array M.
   (b) Set the variable LARGE equal to the first number stored in the array M.
   (c) If the number stored in position J of the array M is less than or equal to the number stored in LARGE, go to statement number 20.
   (d) Set LARGE equal to M(J).

314 / THE PROGRAMMING TASK

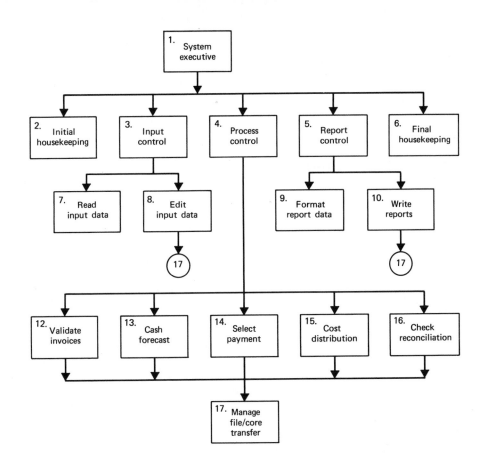

```
          PROGRAM LARGEST(INPUT,OUTPUT,TAPE5=INPUT,TAPE6=OUTPUT)
C**********************************************************************
C***THIS ROUTINE READS FIVE NUMBERS FROM A CARD
C***THE FIRST NUMBER IS IN COLUMNS 1 AND 2, THE SECOND IN COLUMNS 3 AND
C***4,AND SO ON.
C***IT THEN COMPUTES AND PRINTS OUT THE LARGEST OF THE FIVE NUMBERS.
C**********************************************************************
C***VARIABLE NAMES ARE THE FOLLOWING
C*****M--ARRAY IN WHICH THE FIVE NUMBERS ARE STORED
C*****LARGE--LARGEST VALUE ENCOUNTERED IN THE ARRAY M
C**********************************************************************
          C***DIMENSION THE ARRAY M
000003        DIMENSION M(5)
          C***READ THE NUMBERS INTO M
000003        READ (5,10) M
000011    10 FORMAT (5I2)
          C***SET LARGE EQUAL TO THE FIRST NUMBER. THEN EXAMINE THE REMAINING
          C***NUMBERS, SETTING LARGE EQUAL TO ANY NUMBER WHICH IS GREATER THAN
          C***THE CURRENT VALUE.
000011        LARGE = M(1)
000013        DO 20 J = 2,5
000014        IF (M(J).LE.LARGE) GO TO 20
000017        LARGE = M(J)
000020    20 CONTINUE
          C***PRINT OUT THE FIVE NUMBERS.
000022        WRITE (6,30) M
000030    30 FORMAT (1H0,*THE NUMBERS ARE *,5I3)
          C***PRINT OUT THE LARGEST NUMBER, THEN TERMINATE THE PROGRAM.
000030        WRITE (6,40) LARGE
000036    40 FORMAT (1H0,*THE LARGEST NUMBER IS *,I3)
000036        STOP
000040        END

THE NUMBERS ARE   8 -5 -1  9  3

THE LARGEST NUMBER IS   9
```

1. (a) 8   (d) Yes.   (g) M(4), 9
   (b) Yes.   (e) 20   (h) Yes.
   (c) 20   (f) No.   (i) 20

2. Yes. The program is shown on the previous page.

Chapter Examination

1. Match the following terms to the most appropriate definition:

_____ Program abstract

_____ Data dictionary

_____ Run manual

_____ Open subroutine

_____ Closed subroutine

_____ Syntax error

_____ Debugging

_____ Logical error

_____ Diagnostic

_____ Trace routine

(a) removing program errors

(b) used for diagnosing errors

(c) compiled as a separate program

(d) brief description of program

(e) program produces incorrect results

(f) error message during compilation

(g) description of variables used

(h) inserted in program whenever referenced

(i) error in usage of language

(j) complete program description

2. What is modular programming?

_____

_____

_____

3. What is the difference between open and closed subroutines?

_____

_____

_____

_____

4. Describe five components of programmer documentation.

(a) _____

(b) _____

(c) _____

(d) _____

(e) _____

5. Suppose that a FORTRAN program has been keypunched and is ready for compilation and trial run with test data. Indicate whether the following program errors are most likely to result in (1) compiler diagnostic, (2) abnormal termination with run-time error message, or (3) normal termination with incorrect results produced.

(a) _____ Programmer uses variable name GROSS-PROFIT, which exceeds the allowable length for a FORTRAN variable name.

(b) _____ Program attempts to divide by zero.

(c) _____ Program computes the area of a rectangle by adding length to width, instead of multiplying.

(d) _____ Programmer fails to include a program check to determine whether the amount of a payroll check is reasonable, in case erroneous payroll data is read into the computer.

(e) _____ Multiplication leads to a number that exceeds the computer word size.

(f) _____ Programmer omits a right parentheses in a FORMAT statement.

6. Explain why a modular program (compared to a nonmodular program) does the following:

(a) Generally reduces coding time _____

_____

(b) Is easier to test and debug _____

_____

(c) Is less complex _____

_____

(d) Is easier to maintain and modify _____

_____

7. Why is good program documentation so important?

_____

_____

_____

_____

_____

_____

8. Identify the following statements as true or false.

_____ (a) Documentation is generally prepared after programming has been completed.

_____ (b) Modular programming involves dividing large programs into a number of small self-contained units, or modules.

_____ (c) Although modular programming tends to reduce errors and to simplify testing, it generally requires more time than conventional programming.

_____ (d) Liberal use of comment statements can improve program documentation.

_____ (e) Closed subroutines are spliced into the main program each time they are called in the program.

_____ (f) The process of removing program errors is called tracing.

_____ (g) The compiler will generally detect logical program errors during translation.

_____ (h) A program with a logical error may terminate normally.

9. Indicate whether each of the following would be found in (a) system documentation, (b) run manual, or (c) user's manual.

_____ (a) Overall processing logic.

_____ (b) Detailed program description.

_____ (c) Instructions on filling out forms and requests.

_____ (d) File descriptions.

_____ (e) Instructions on restarting a program.

_____ (f) Instructions on operating a terminal.

10. List four major steps in preparing a computer program.

(a) _____

(b) _____

(c) _____

(d) _____

11. List five steps in testing a program.

(a) _____

(b) _____

(c) _____

(d) _____

(e) _____

12. Describe two possible results when a logical program error is encountered.

(a) _____

_____

(b) _____

_____

Chapter 13

INTRODUCTION TO FORTRAN AND BASIC

Overview

FORTRAN is a high-level language oriented to the description of mathematical and procedural problems for computer solution. FORTRAN (acronym for FORmula TRANslator) is largely machine independent and is the most widely used, scientifically oriented programming language. In a recent survey of United States business schools, approximately two thirds of those schools that require a programming language require a knowledge of FORTRAN.

FORTRAN was originally developed by IBM in the mid-1950s. The United States of America Standards Institute (USASI) has set uniform standards for the FORTRAN language. Today most manufacturers of third generation computers provide FORTRAN compilers as part of their software systems. This chapter describes the basic features of FORTRAN IV, which is the version in most general use today.

FORTRAN Coding Form

A FORTRAN program is a series of statements designed to solve a specific problem. The program may also include comments, or explanatory information, inserted to make the program easier to read.

FORTRAN statements and comments must be key punched in program cards in a specific format. In preparation for key punching, the program is first written on a coding form that has the same format as the program card.

A sample FORTRAN coding form is shown in Figure 13–1. The form contains a sample program based on a compound amount calculation.

QUESTION: Examine Figure 13–1. The program will compute and print out the amount in $N =$ _____ years for a principal of $P =$ _____ dollars at an interest rate of $R =$ _____ percent compounded annually.

FORTRAN Coding Form

PROGRAM COMPOUND AMOUNT

PROGRAMMER FRM

DATE 7/24

PUNCHING INSTRUCTIONS

GRAPHIC

PUNCH

FORTRAN STATEMENT

```
C ØMMENT P IS PRINCIPAL, R IS INTEREST, N IS YEARS, S IS AMOUNT

    P = 1000.
    R = .10
    N = 10
    S = P * (1.+R) **N
    WRITE (6,10) S
10  FØRMAT (1H0,'CØMPØUND AMØUNT IS',F8.2)
    STØP
    END
```

Figure 13–1. A sample FORTRAN program.

ANSWER: 10, 1000, 10

Statement Field. FORTRAN statements are entered in the statement field, which extends from columns 7 to 72. A statement need not start in column 7, but must be confined to this field. If a statement cannot be completed at column 72, it must be continued on the following card in the statement field. No more than one statement may be written in the field.

Statement Number Field. Some statements in a FORTRAN program must be numbered, since they are referenced by other statements in the same program. Statement numbers are entered (right justified) in columns 1 to 5. Any integer not exceeding the field width may be used as a statement number. All numbers must be unique; that is, two or more statements may not be assigned the same number.

In Figure 13–1, only one statement is numbered—a "format" statement, which is arbitrarily assigned the number 10. This statement must be numbered, since it is referenced by the "write" statement that immediately precedes it. This combination of statements will be explained in subsequent sections.

Continuation Field. The first card of a FORTRAN statement must contain a blank (or zero) in column 6. If the statement extends beyond column 72, it must be continued on a following card. In this case, the following statement is referred to as a continuation statement, and must have a continuation character punched in column 6. A continuation character is any valid FORTRAN character other than zero or blank. Continuation statements are illustrated later in the chapter.

Identification Field. Columns 73 to 80 may be left blank or used for sequence numbers or other identifying information. This field is ignored by the FORTRAN compiler.

Comments. FORTRAN permits the insertion of comments at any point, to improve readability of the program. Comments are printed in the program listing, but do not affect the program. Column 1 is punched with the letter C to indicate that a card contains a comment, rather than a program statement. Notice that the first line of coding in Figure 13–1 is a comment.

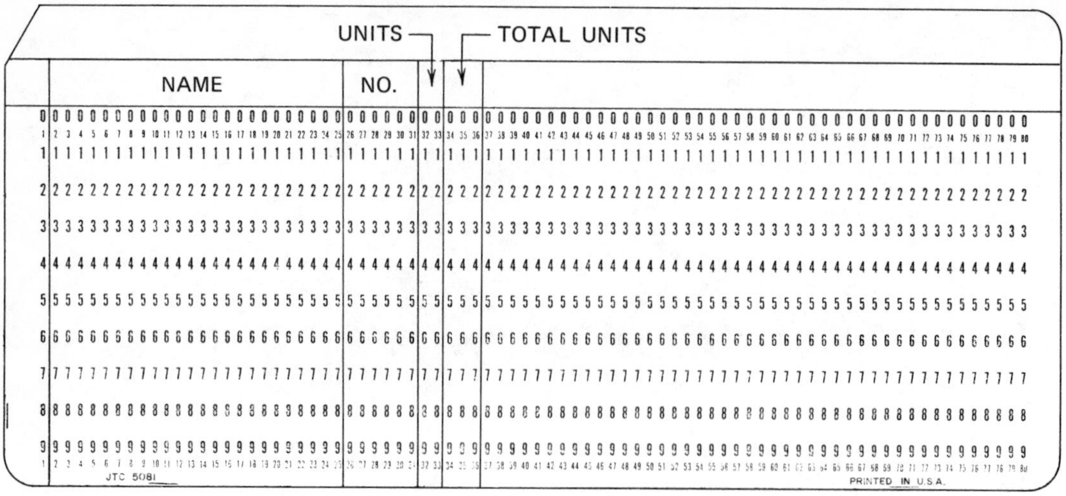

Figure 13-2. *Input student record for Example 1.*

To illustrate the basic concepts of FORTRAN programming, three example problems will be introduced in the remainder of the chapter. These examples are all based on processing a student record file.

Example 1: Basic Input-Output Operations

A student file is maintained on punched cards, one card per student. The format of the record is shown in Figure 13-2. Each card contains student name (columns 2-25), number (26-31), units taken this semester (32-33), and total units prior to this semester (34-36). Column 1 and columns 37 to 80 are not used.

The last card in the data deck is a trailer card, with the number 999999 punched in columns 26 to 31.

An output listing is to be prepared from the cards. Each card field is to be printed, with blank spaces between fields. A printer spacing chart of the desired output format is shown in Figure 13-3.

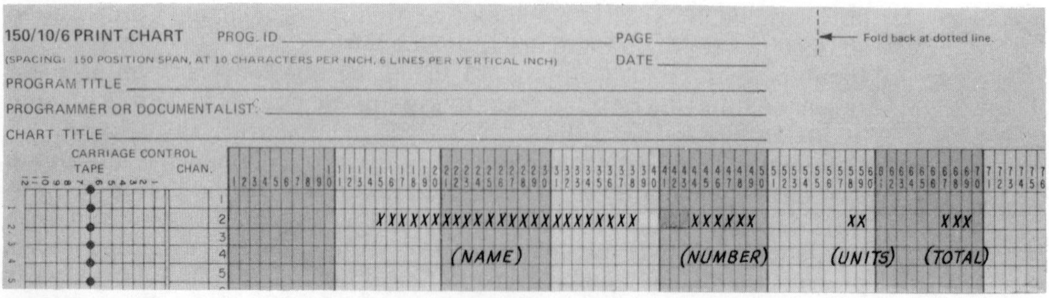

Figure 13-3. *Printer spacing chart for Example 1.*

322 / INTRODUCTION TO FORTRAN AND BASIC

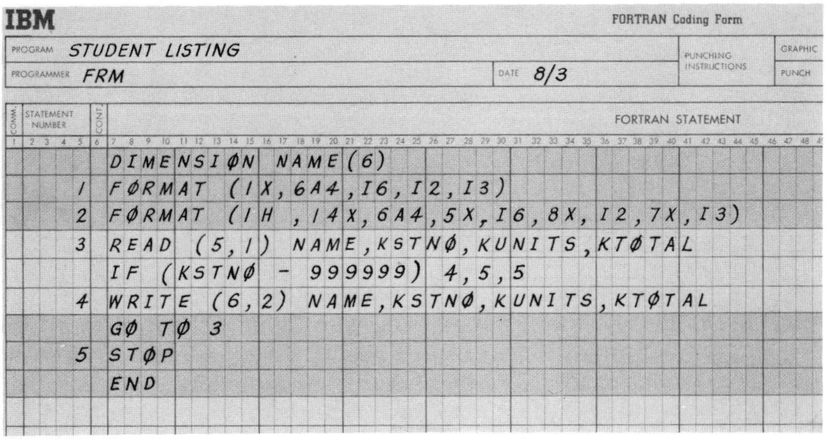

Figure 13-4. *FORTRAN program for Example 1.*

Program

The FORTRAN program to prepare the printed report is shown in Figure 13-4.

Data Items. Two types of data items appear on the input card for Example 1: alphanumeric and integer data. Integer data consists of whole numbers, or numbers that do not contain decimal points. Student number, units, and total units are all integer data items. The student name field is an example of an alphanumeric data item.

In FORTRAN, each input data item is assigned a symbolic name, which is referred to as a variable name, or more simply, as a variable. A variable name may consist of from one to six characters (in many systems), the first of which must be a letter. The *type* of field is designated by the letter at the beginning of the name. For integer and alphanumeric data items, the first letter must be I, J, K, L, M, or N. For decimal fields, the first letter must be any of the letters A to H or O to Z.

QUESTION: Examine the FORTRAN "read" statement in Figure 13-4 (statement number 3 appears in column 5). What symbolic names are used for the input data items? Why is the letter K used as the first character for each of the last three names?

ANSWER: NAME, KSTNO, KUNITS, KTOTAL. The last three items are integer, therefore, they must begin with one of the letters I to N. The name STNO (for student number) for example, is unacceptable. The prefix K was added to each name to satisfy this condition. Notice that NAME is acceptable without change

Dimension Statement. The first statement in the FORTRAN program is a dimension statement, as shown in Figure 13-5.

In Chapter 4 it is explained that alphanumeric data is stored in the computer in coded form—generally either 6 or 8 bits per character. If

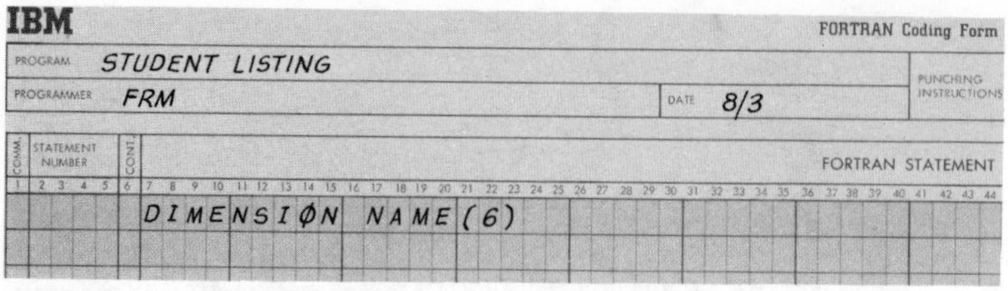
IBM FORTRAN Coding Form
PROGRAM STUDENT LISTING
PROGRAMMER FRM DATE 8/3
PUNCHING INSTRUCTIONS
STATEMENT NUMBER | CONT. | FORTRAN STATEMENT
DIMENSIØN NAME(6)

Figure 13-5. *FORTRAN dimension statement for Example 1.*

the computer uses a fixed word length, the number of characters that can be stored depends on the word length and the type of code used. For example, the CDC 6400 stores 10 alphanumeric characters in each 60-bit word.

The student name field in Example 1 (called NAME) is 24 characters long. It is assumed that this data is stored four characters per word, so that 24 ÷ 4 or 6 words are required. To illustrate, the name JOHNSTON, STANLEY R. would appear as follows:

Word 1 |J|O|H|N|

Word 2 |S|T|O|N|

Word 3 |,| |S|T|

Word 4 |A|N|L|E|

Word 5 |Y| |R|.|

Word 6 | | | | |

In FORTRAN, a table like the one above is termed an *array*. Each array used in a program must be identified by a DIMENSION statement that reserves the necessary memory positions. In Figure 13–5 the statement DIMENSION NAME (6) indicates that the variable NAME will require six positions. DIMENSION statements must appear at the beginning of a program.

QUESTION: Suppose that the FORTRAN program for Example 1 were to be run on a computer that could store only two alphanumeric characters per word. How would the DIMENSION statement be changed in Figure 13–5, if at all? ______________________________

______________________________.

ANSWER: DIMENSION NAME (12). Since 2 characters are stored per word, the 24-word character name field requires 12 words

In addition to storing alphanumeric data, arrays are widely used in FORTRAN for storing tables of numbers. For example, a table showing number of students by class and major could be represented as a two-dimensional array in FORTRAN.[1]

Input FORMAT Statement. Every command to read or print information in FORTRAN must be accompanied by a FORMAT statement. This state-

[1]Arrays and other data structures are discussed in Chapter 9.

PROGRAM	STUDENT LISTING				PUNCHING INSTRUCTIONS	GRAPHIC
PROGRAMMER	FRM		DATE	8/3		PUNCH

```
       DIMENSIØN NAME(6)
    I  FØRMAT (IX,6A4,I6,I2,I3)
```

Figure 13–6. *Input format statement for Example 1.*

ment describes each data field as to type, size, and location. The input FORMAT statement for Example 1 is shown in Figure 13–6.

Each FORMAT statement must be numbered, since it is referenced by a READ or WRITE statement. The input FORMAT statement in Figure 13–6 is identified by a 1 in the statement number field. The word FORMAT then identifies the statement as a FORMAT statement.

The entries in parentheses describe the data fields in the input cards. Entries are separated by commas, and appear in the same order as the data item on the punched card input. Three types of format codes appear in the example:

X   Designates spaces or unused card columns

A   Designates alphanumeric data

I   Designates integer data

The number *preceding* the X code designates the number of spaces or unused card columns. In Example 1, card column 1 is unused (see Figure 13–2); therefore 1X is the correct specification.

The number *following* an A or I code indicates the number of card columns for an alphanumeric or integer field. In Figure 13–6, A4 means a four-position alphanumeric field, while I6 means a six-position integer field.

The number *preceding* an A or I code is a repeat specification, indicating the number of times the particular format is repeated. In Figure 13–6, the entry 6A4 is used. This indicates the format A4 (repeated four times) is required for the name field. Recall that the student name is to be stored in an array of six words, each four characters long.

QUESTION: To summarize the input format specifications, the first column on the input card is a _____. The first data item (student name) is to be read as six, _____-position alphanumeric items. The last three items (student number, units, total units) are, respectively, _____-position, _____-position, and _____-position integers.

ANSWER: space, four, six, two, three

Output FORMAT Statement. Similar to the input FORMAT statement, the output FORMAT statement describes the data items to appear in the printed report. The output FORMAT statement for Example 1 is shown in Figure 13–7.

When output is for the line printer, the first entry in an output

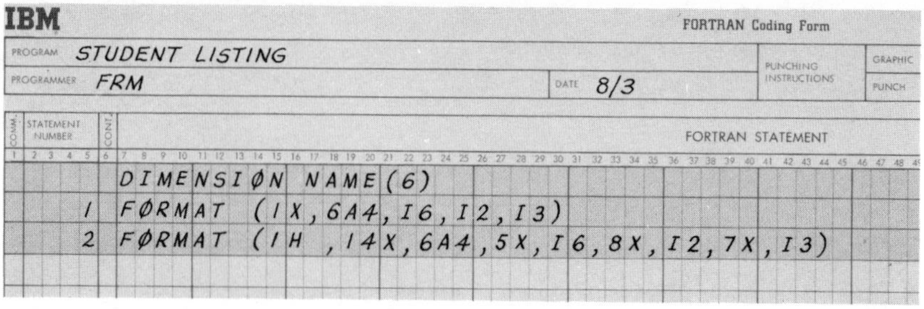

Figure 13-7. *Output format statement for Example 1.*

FORMAT statement is for carriage control. The acceptable entries in FORTRAN are as follows:

1H	Designates single spacing before printing
1H0	Designates double spacing before printing
1H1	Designates advance to top of next page before printing

That is, a blank, zero, or one following the entry 1H specifies (respectively) single spacing, double spacing, and skip to top of next page. In the example, the entry 1H (blank) is used for a single-spaced report.

The remaining entries in the output FORMAT statement conform to the desired format shown in the printer spacing chart (Figure 13-3). For example, the second entry in parentheses in the FORMAT statement is 14X; this causes the printer to space 14 columns and start printing student name in column 15, as desired. The entries for each of the four data items to be printed are the same as in the input FORMAT statement.

READ Statement. The FORTRAN READ statement causes an input record to be read into storage. The READ statement for Example 1 is shown in Figure 13-8.

The statement is numbered 3, since it is referenced by another statement in the program (discussed later). The entry after READ is (5,1). As is shown in Figure 13-8, the "5" is a device number that indicates to the computer the input device to be used. In many installations the number 5 designates the card reader; however, the FORTRAN user should check with his installation to determine the correct number.

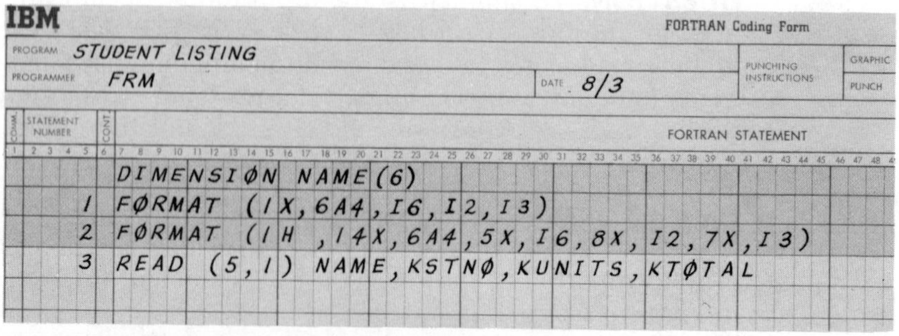

Figure 13-8. *READ statement for Example 1.*

The "1" in the entry (5,1) references the FORMAT statement for input. The effect of this entry is to cause a card to be read according to the format specified in the FORMAT statement (statement number 1).

The last entries in the READ statement are the symbolic names assigned to the input data items. The names appear in the same order as the data items on punched cards, and also in the same order as the format codes in the corresponding FORMAT statement. Blank card columns or unused fields are not assigned symbolic names in the READ statement.

QUESTION: Examine the READ statement (Figure 13–8). What symbolic name is assigned to the second input data item, student number? _____. What is the format specification code for this item? _____.

ANSWER: KSTNO, 16

IF Statement. A convenient method to detect the end of data cards to be processed in a FORTRAN program is to place a trailer card at the end of the data deck. The trailer card normally contains some distinguishing value in a data field, such as blanks or all nines. In the program logic, a test is made when each card is read. If the card contains the distinguishing value, it branches to an end of file routine; otherwise normal processing takes place.

In Example 1, the last card contains the number 999999 in the student number field (it is assumed no actual student is assigned a number this large). The program tests each card to determine if a card with this number has been read. The test is made using the FORTRAN IF statement shown in Figure 13–9.

When the IF statement is executed, the arithmetic expression in parentheses is evaluated. In the example, 999999 is subtracted from the variable called KSTNO, which represents student number. As a result of this subtraction, the program branches to one of the statement numbers following the parentheses. If the result is less than zero, the program branches to statement number 4. If the result is equal to zero (indicating the last card has been read), the program branches to statement number 5.

If the result of the operation is greater than zero, the program branches to the last statement number. In the example, no student number will exceed 999999, so that a "greater than" condition will never be encountered. However, FORTRAN requires that three statement numbers appear after the parentheses. In Figure 13–9, statement number 5 is used to satisfy this requirement.

```
IBM                                              FORTRAN Coding Form

PROGRAM   STUDENT LISTING                         PUNCHING
PROGRAMMER   FRM                      DATE  8/3   INSTRUCTIONS

STATEMENT                                         FORTRAN STATEMENT
NUMBER

    DIMENSION NAME(6)
 1  FORMAT (1X,6A4,I6,I2,I3)
 2  FORMAT (1H ,14X,6A4,5X,I6,8X,I2,7X,I3)
 3  READ (5,1) NAME,KSTNO,KUNITS,KTOTAL
    IF (KSTNO - 999999) 4,5,5
```

Figure 13–9. FORTRAN IF statement for Example 1.

FORTRAN Coding Form

IBM

PROGRAM STUDENT LISTING
PROGRAMMER FRM
DATE 8/3

FORTRAN STATEMENT

```
    DIMENSIØN NAME(6)
  1 FØRMAT (1X,6A4,I6,I2,I3)
  2 FØRMAT (1H ,14X,6A4,5X,I6,8X,I2,7X,I3)
  3 READ (5,1) NAME,KSTNØ,KUNITS,KTØTAL
    IF (KSTNØ - 999999) 4,5,5
  4 WRITE (6,2) NAME,KSTNØ,KUNITS,KTØTAL
```

Figure 13–10. WRITE statement for Example 1.

```
2   FØRMAT   (1H , 14X,  6A4,  5X,  I6,  8X,  I2,  7X,  I3)

4   WRITE (6, 2)   NAME,  KSTNØ,  KUNITS,  KTØTAL
```

Figure 13–11. Correspondence between variable names and format specifications for Example 1.

FORTRAN STATEMENT

```
    DIMENSIØN [NAME(6)
  1 FØRMAT (1X,6A4,I6,I2,I3)
  2 FØRMAT (1H ,14X,6A4,5X,I6,8X,I2,7X,I3)
  3 READ (5,1) NAME,KSTNØ,KUNITS,KTØTAL
    IF (KSTNØ - 999999) 4,5,5
  4 WRITE (6,2) NAME,KSTNØ,KUNITS,KTØTAL
    GØ TØ 3
  5 STØP
    END
```

Figure 13–12. FORTRAN GO TO, STOP and END statements for Example 1.

328 / INTRODUCTION TO FORTRAN AND BASIC

QUESTION: David Jones has student number 10355. When the computer processes his record, to what statement number will the program branch when the IF statement is executed? _____.

ANSWER: The number 4 (since the result of the subtraction is less than zero)

WRITE Statement. The WRITE statement causes a record to be transmitted to an output device. In the example, the output device is the line printer. The WRITE statement for the example is shown in Figure 13-10.

The WRITE statement is assigned statement number 4. Recall that if a valid student number is read, the preceding IF statement causes the program to branch to statement number 4. Thus the processing continues and the student record is listed on the line printer.

The entry (6,2) in the write statement specifies the device number "6," and the output FORMAT statement "2." In many installations the device number 6 is used to specify the line printer.

The symbolic names following the parentheses specify the variables to be printed. The names are associated with format specifications in the output FORMAT statement (statement number 2) as is shown in Figure 13-11.

GO TO Statement. A FORTRAN GO TO statement causes the program to branch to the statement number following the GO TO. In the example, after a line is printed, control must be transferred to the READ statement to read another record. The effect of the GO TO statement shown in Figure 13-12 is to transfer control to statement number 3, which reads the next student record.

STOP Statement. The STOP instruction in a FORTRAN program terminates execution of the object program. In the example, when the trailer card is read, the IF statement transfers control to statement number 5 to terminate the program.

END Statement. The END statement is always the last statement in a FORTRAN program. The statement defines the end of the source program for the FORTRAN compiler.

This completes the description of the FORTRAN program for Example 1. A listing of the program, together with a sample output is shown in Figure 13-13.

```
  DIMENSION NAME(6)
1 FORMAT(1X,6A4,I6,I2,I3)
2 FORMAT(1H ,14X,6A4,5X,I6,8X,I2,7X,I3)
3 READ(5,1)NAME,KSTNO,KUNITS,KTOTAL
  IF(KSTNO-999999)4,5,5
4 WRITE(6,2)NAME,KSTNO,KUNITS,KTOTAL
  GO TO 3
5 STOP
  END
  ADAMS, PETER R.                  13978        9      104
  GOODMAN, HAROLD R.               20875       16        0
  JOHNSON, SHARON C.               24432       15       74
  LARSON, JAMES L.                 47739        6       48
  LEWIS,BARBARA C.                  1339       18      107
  ROTHSCHILD, CHARLES K.           80336       10      100
  THOMPSON, LAURA W.               59325        7       88
```

Figure 13-13. *FORTRAN program and output for Example 1.*

329 / BASIC INPUT-OUTPUT OPERATIONS

Exercise 13-1

1. Indicate whether the following variable names specify integer or decimal data values:

SUM _____   MEAN _____

GROSS _____   AVE _____

COUNT _____   CODE _____

KOUNT _____   STNO _____

J _____   KSTNO _____

X _____   LARGE _____

2. An address field contains 20 alphanumeric characters. The item is to be stored in a computer that contains four bytes per word. Write a dimension statement to define an array called KADDR for storing the

data item. _____

3. Write an input format statement to define punched card input as follows:

Card Columns	Content
1–2	Unused
3–10	Integer
11–14	Unused
15–19	Integer
20–25	Integer
26–80	Unused

4. Write a FORTRAN IF statement for the following flowchart segment:

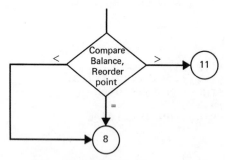

Use the variable names BAL for balance and RP for reorder point. The numbers in circles are statement numbers.

Example 2: Simple Calculations

This example introduces simple FORTRAN calculations. The card record for each student is to be read, and "units taken this semester" is to be

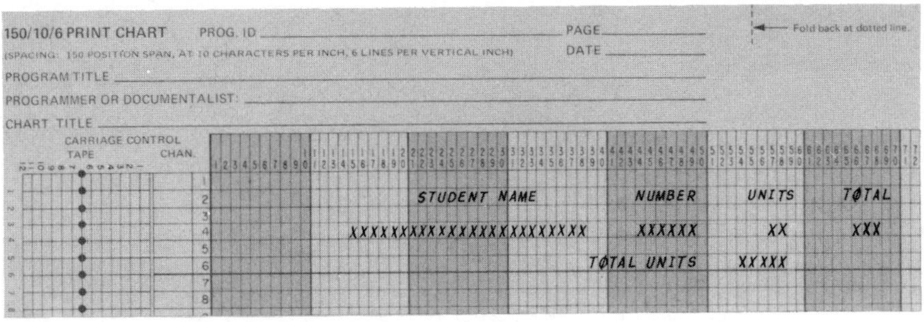

Figure 13–14. *Printer spacing chart for Example 2.*

added to "total units to date" to obtain an updated total. The record is then to be printed, with the updated total replacing the previous total.

In addition to updating each record, the units taken this semester is to be totaled for all students and printed at the end of the listing. Header information is also to be printed at the top of the listing.

The input format for Example 2 is the same as for Example 1 (see Figure 13–2). The output format is shown on the printer spacing chart, Figure 13–14.

DIMENSION Statement. As in Example 1, the student name field is stored as an array. The statement DIMENSION NAME(6) is used to define this field.

FORMAT Statements. The FORMAT statements for Example 2 are shown in Figure 13–15.

The first two FORMAT statements (numbered 1 and 2) define the input and output layouts, and are the same as those in Example 1. Statement number 3 provides the header information to appear at the top of the output listing, while statement number 4 provides the total information to appear at the end of the listing.

Statements 3 and 4 both include *literals*, or strings of characters to be printed as they appear in the FORMAT statement. A literal is specified by enclosing the string within single quotes.[2]

QUESTION: Examine statement number 4 in Figure 13–15. Describe the output format as specified by the entries within parentheses. __________

____

____.

ANSWER: The symbol 1H specifies single spacing before printing. The printer will indent 38 columns, then print the literal TOTAL UNITS.

```
      DIMENSIØN NAME(6)
    1 FØRMAT (1X,6A4,I6,I2,I3)
    2 FØRMAT (1H ,14X,6A4,5X,I6,8X,I2,7X,I3)
    3 FØRMAT (1H1,21X,'STUDENT NAME       NUMBER        UNITS        TØTAL'
     1)
    4 FØRMAT (1H ,38X,'TØTAL UNITS',5X,I5)
```

Figure 13–15. *FORMAT statements for Example 2.*

[2]In some compilers, the asterisk (*) is used instead of the single quote.

```
  STATEMENT                                              FORTRAN STATEMENT
   NUMBER
       WRITE  (6,3)
       KCUM  =  0
  5    READ  (5,1)  NAME,KSTNØ,KUNITS,KTØTAL
       IF (KSTNØ  -  999999)6,7,7
  6    KTØTAL  =  KTØTAL + KUNITS
       KCUM  =  KCUM + KUNITS
       WRITE  (6,2)  NAME,KSTNØ,KUNITS,KTØTAL
       GØ TØ 5
  7    WRITE  (6,4)  KCUM
       STØP
       END
```

Figure 13–16. *Computational steps for Example 2.*

Five columns are skipped, and a five-position integer (representing total units) is then printed

In statement 3, the header to be printed is defined as a literal. The spaces between entries correspond to the format on the printer spacing chart (Figure 13–14). Notice that the literal extends to column 72. Since a FORTRAN statement cannot continue beyond this column, the closing right parenthesis must be continued on the following line. The number 1 is used as a continuation character (in column 6) to indicate the continuation of the previous line.

QUESTION: Examine statement number 3. Where will the header information be printed on the output report? _____

_____.

ANSWER: At the top of a page, since the space control symbol 1H1 is used

Program Logic. The computational steps for Example 2 are shown in Figure 13–16.

First, the program executes a WRITE statement to print the header defined in statement number 3. The cumulative units taken (called KCUM) is then initialized by setting the variable equal to zero. These two steps are only performed once by the program.

In statement 5, the next student record is read. An IF statement is then used to test whether the last (or trailer) card has been read. If not, the total units taken by the student is updated by addition, as is the cumulative units taken by all students. The program then prints the record and returns to statement number 5 to read the next card.

When the last card has been encountered, the program branches to statement number 7 to print the cumulative total and then terminates execution.

A listing of the program for Example 2, together with a sample output is shown in Figure 13–17.

Arithmetic Statements

The main purpose of most computer programs is to perform computa-

```
       DIMENSION NAME(6)
     1 FORMAT(1X,6A4,I6,I2,I3)
     2 FORMAT(1H ,14X,6A4,5X,I6,8X,I2,7X,I3)
     3 FORMAT(1H1,21X,*STUDENT NAME          NUMBER      UNITS       TOTAL*
       1)
     4 FORMAT(1H ,38X,*TOTAL UNITS*,5X,I5)
       WRITE(6,3)
       KCUM = 0
     5 READ(5,1)NAME,KSTNO,KUNITS,KTOTAL
       IF(KSTNO-999999)6,7,7
     6 KTOTAL = KTOTAL + KUNITS
       KCUM = KCUM + KUNITS
       WRITE(6,2)NAME,KSTNO,KUNITS,KTOTAL
       GO TO 5
     7 WRITE(6,4)KCUM
       STOP
       END
```

STUDENT NAME	NUMBER	UNITS	TOTAL
ADAMS, PETER R.	13978	9	113
GOODMAN, HAROLD R.	20875	16	16
JOHNSON, SHARON C.	24432	15	89
LARSON, JAMES L.	47739	6	54
LEWIS,BARBARA C.	1339	18	125
ROTHSCHILD, CHARLES K.	80336	10	110
THOMPSON, LAURA W.	59325	7	95
TOTAL UNITS		81	

Figure 13-17. *FORTRAN program and output for Example 2.*

tions and manipulate data for a desired result. These functions are accomplished in FORTRAN largely by arithmetic statements.

An arithmetic statement assigns a specific value to a FORTRAN variable. In Example 2, total units taken was updated by the following statement:

$$\text{KTOTAL} = \text{KTOTAL} + \text{KUNITS}$$

This statement causes the variable KUNITS to be added to the variable KTOTAL; the sum is then assigned to KTOTAL. The value of KUNITS is unchanged as a result of the addition.

The general form of an arithmetic statement is:

$$\text{variable name} = \text{arithmetic expression}$$

A single variable name must appear to the left of the equals sign. There are five arithmetic operations in FORTRAN. They are:

**	exponentiate	A**B means A raised to the B power
*	multiply	A*B means A times B
/	divide	A/B means A divided by B
+	add	A+B means A plus B
−	subtract	A−B means A minus B

Parentheses may (and often must) be used in arithmetic expressions to group constants and/or variables so that operations will be performed in the correct order. For example, to multiply the sum A plus B by 8.5, the correct expression is 8.5* (A + B).

Rules for Writing Expressions. The following rules must be followed in writing arithmetic expressions which contain two or more constants and variable names.

1. Each constant and/or variable name must be separated by an arithmetic operator. Arithmetic operators are never implied in FORTRAN. For example, in algebra, the expression XY is often used to indicate "X times Y." In FORTRAN, XY would be interpreted as a variable name. Similarly to indicate four times the quantity J plus K, the correct FORTRAN expression is 4 ∗ (J + K) not 4(J + K).
2. Two or more arithmetic operators must not appear in sequence in an arithmetic expression. For example, in FORTRAN the quantity "X times minus 4.2" cannot be written X ∗ − 4.2. However, it is permissable to use parentheses to separate arithmetic operators, so that the above expression may be written X ∗ (−4.2).

QUESTION: Two of the following three expressions are incorrect FORTRAN expressions. Which are incorrect, and for what reason?

1. WAGES = (40 + OTIME) RATE_____.

2. SALARY = 1.2 ∗ BASE + COMISH _____.

3. SALARY = BASE ∗ + 1.2 + COMISH _____.
ANSWER: 1. Multiplication symbol omitted   3. Two operators in sequence

Evaluating Arithmetic Expressions. The order of computation in a FORTRAN expression is very similar to that in algebra. There is a hierarchy of operations, as follows:

FIRST: Quantities within parentheses are computed. If there are parentheses within parentheses (nested parentheses) the innermost pair is evaluated first.
SECOND. Exponentiation operations are performed.
THIRD. Multiplication and division operations are done. Neither takes precedence over the other.
FOURTH. Addition and subtraction operations are done. Neither takes precedence over the other.
FIFTH. If two or more operations of the same precedence occur in the same expression, they are generally performed from left to right.

The use of the above rules in evaluating a FORTRAN expression can be illustrated with this example:

$$A ∗ (B + C) − D / E ** 2 ∗ G$$

The computer would first scan from left to right and would evaluate the parenthetical expression B + C. If the result of this calculation is called "S," the expression now appears as follows

$$A ∗ S − D / E ** 2 ∗ G$$

The computer next scans from left to right looking for exponentiation operations, and evaluates E ** 2. Calling this result "T," the expression now becomes

$$A ∗ S − D / T ∗ G$$

The computer now performs all multiplications and divisions from left to right. Let "X" stand for the result A ⋆ S and let "Y" stand for the result D / T ⋆ G, the result becomes X − Y.

Finally, the computer subtracts Y from X to complete the evaluation of the expression.

In the above sequence, Y represents the result D / T ⋆ G. A word of caution is in order in writing such expressions. Since evaluation proceeds from left to right, D / T is performed first; the result is then multiplied by G. Thus, the result corresponds to the algebraic expression $(D \cdot G)/T$, and not $D/(T \cdot G)$. If the latter result is desired, it may be expressed in FORTRAN as

$$D / (T \star G) \text{ or as } D / T / G$$

QUESTION: Five FORTRAN variables have been assigned the following values:

$$A = 2, B = 5, C = 3, D = 18, E = 3, F = 4$$

Using the rules for evaluating FORTRAN expressions, what is the resulting value of Y in the statement Y = A ⋆ (B − C) + D/E⋆⋆2⋆F?

ANSWER: The value is 12

Blanks separating constants, variable names, and arithmetic operators are ignored by the compiler. Thus these two statements would be interpreted as being the same:

$$Y = A \star X \star\star 2 + B$$

$$Y = A \star X \star\star 2 + B$$

Mixed Mode Expressions. Recall that two types of numbers are defined in FORTRAN: integer, and decimal. Decimal numbers are often termed real numbers. Variable names beginning with the letters I through N always represent integer numbers; names beginning with any other letter represent decimal or real numbers.

If all of the constants and variable names in an arithmetic expression are real numbers, the expression is said to be in the real mode. Similarly, an expression is in the integer mode if all constants and variable names are integer. If an expression contains a combination of integer and real constants and/or variable names, it is called mixed mode.

Following are examples of expressions in each of the three modes:

Real	Integer	Mixed
X / Y	M / N	X / N
6. ⋆ UNITS	6 ⋆ NUNITS	6 ⋆ UNITS
XJ ⋆ XK + XL/3.	J + K + L/3	XJ + K + ZL/3.

An exception to the above definition of a mixed mode expression is that an integer exponent may be used in a real expression. For example, the expression X**2 and Y**K are real, not mixed mode. In fact if a number is to be raised to a whole number power, it is computationally faster to express the exponent as an integer constant or variable.

QUESTION: Except for the case of an integer exponent, when an expression contains a combination of integer and real constants and/or variable names, it is said to be in _____ mode.

ANSWER: mixed

Integer Mode Division. When division is performed in an integer mode expression in FORTRAN, the result is in integer mode. Thus any fractional part of the quotient is lost. Following are several examples:

J	K	J ÷ K
1	2	0
2	2	1
3	2	1
4	2	2
5	2	2

If the fractional part of a division operation is to be retained, the division must be performed in real mode.

QUESTION: Last semester Stephen Billiard took 15 units and earned 55 total points. If 55 is divided by 15 in integer mode, what is his grade point average? _____

_____ .

ANSWER: 3. The whole number result is 3.67, but the fractional part is lost in integer mode division

Mixed Mode Statements. A mixed mode statement is one in which the variable name to the left of the equal sign and the arithmetic expression to the right are not in the same mode. For example,

$$NET = GROSS - DEDUCT$$

In this example, the variable NET is integer while the expression GROSS − DEDUCT is real.

In a mixed mode statement, the result of evaluating the arithmetic expression will be stored as integer or real, depending on whether the variable name to the left of the equal sign is integer or real. If the expression is real and the variable name is integer, any fractional part of the result is truncated (dropped without rounding) and lost. For example, if the statement M = 10.35 is executed, the value stored at the symbolic address M is 10.

Use of an integer variable name can lead to undesired results, if truncation is not wanted. For example, consider this sequence of statements in a payroll program:

$$GROSS = 135.40$$
$$DEDUCT = 29.75$$
$$NET = GROSS - DEDUCT$$

When deductions are subtracted from gross pay, the result is 105.65. However, since the variable name NET is integer mode, the result will be stored as 105. The fractional part may be retained simply by assigning the variable NET a real name, such as ZNET.

Exercise 13–2

1. Write an output format statement to print a header line. The header should appear at the top of a new page. The output format is as follows:

Print Positions	Content
1–10	unused
11–23	EMPLOYEE NAME (literal)
24–29	unused
30–36	ADDRESS (literal)

2. Write an output format statement to print a total line. The printer should double space before printing this line. The output format is as follows:

Print Positions	Content
1–35	unused
36–40	TOTAL (literal)
41–44	unused
45–50	six-position integer

337 / ARITHMETIC STATEMENTS

3. Which of the following arithmetic statements are invalid in FOR-TRAN? Explain why.

(a) Y = AX² + BX + C _____

(b) AREA = PI ★ R ★★ 2 _____

(c) X + 3.2 = 10.4★Y _____

(d) NET = GROSS − DEDUCT _____

(e) AVE = SUM ÷ NUMB _____

(f) YTD = YTD + AMT _____

4. Evaluate each of the following FORTRAN expressions. Assume the following values: A = 9.0, B = 2.0, C = 10.0, D = 5.0

(a) Y = A / B _____

(b) N = A / B _____

(c) X = A ★ B ★★ 2 _____

(d) X = A ★ B ★★ 2 + C − D _____

(e) X = C / D ★ B _____

(f) X = C / (D ★ B) _____

Example 3: Simple Logical Operations

This example introduces additional FORTRAN logical operations. The student record cards are to be read, and tuition is to be computed according to this formula:

> If units is less than 12, tuition is units times $35
> If units is 12 or more, tuition is $420

Total student fees consist of tuition plus an incidental fee of $12.50. This total is to be printed along with student name, number, and hours taken. Also, total fees for all students is to be computed and printed at the end of the listing.

The input format for Example 3 is the same as for Examples 1 and 2 (see Figure 13–2). The desired output format is shown in Figure 13–18.

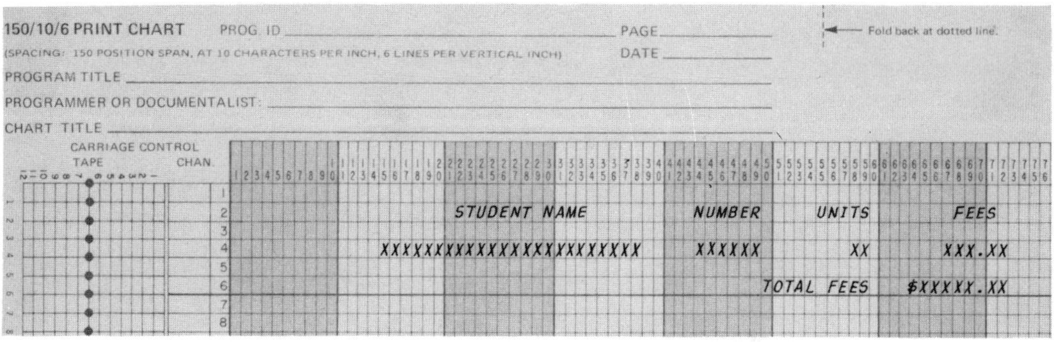

Figure 13–18. *Printer spacing chart for Example 3.*

Program

The FORTRAN program for Example 3 is shown in Figure 13–19.

The data items to be printed for each student are name, number, units, and fees. The last data item (fees) is a real number, representing dollars and cents. From the printer spacing chart, the format for this item is XXX.XX.

The FORMAT statement number 2 specifies the format for output student records. In Figure 13–19, the format specification for the student fee item is F6.2. The letter F in a format specification designates a real (or decimal) number. The numbers following F designate the total number of positions (including decimal point) and the number of positions to

```
      DIMENSION NAME(6)
    1 FORMAT (1X,6A4,I6,I2)
    2 FORMAT (1H ,14X,6A4,5X,I6,8X,I2,7X,F6.2)
    3 FORMAT (1H1,21X,'STUDENT NAME          NUMBER        UNITS              FEE
     1S')
    4 FORMAT (1H ,49X,'TOTAL FEES       $',F8.2)
      WRITE (6,3)
      CFEES = 0
    5 READ (5,1) NAME,KSTNO,KUNITS
      IF(KSTNO - 999999)6,7,7
    6 IF(KUNITS.GE.12) GO TO 8
   10 TUIT = KUNITS * 35.00
      GO TO 9
    8 TUIT = 420.00
    9 FEES = TUIT + 12.50
      CFEES = CFEES + FEES
      WRITE (6,2) NAME,KSTNO,KUNITS,FEES
      GO TO 5
    7 WRITE (6,4) CFEES
      STOP
      END
```

Figure 13–19. *FORTRAN program for Example 3.*

```
   5  READ  (5,1)  NAME,KSTNØ,KUNITS
      IF(KSTNØ -  999999)6,7,7
   6  IF(KUNITS.GE.12)  6Ø TØ 8
  10  TUIT = KUNITS * 35.00
      GØ TØ 9
   8  TUIT = 420.00
   9  FEES = TUIT + 12.50
      CFEES = CFEES + FEES
      WRITE (6,2)  NAME,KSTNØ,KUNITS,FEES
      GØ TØ 5
   7  WRITE (6,4)  CFEES
      STØP
      END
```

Figure 13–20. *Computations steps for Example 3.*

the right of the decimal point. Thus, F6.2 specifies a real number with six positions, and two positions to the right of the decimal.

QUESTION: Examine FORMAT statement number 4. What is the meaning of the format specification for total fees? _____

_____.

ANSWER: F8.2, which means an eight-position field with two decimal positions. This is equivalent to the format XXXXX.XX

After the header is printed, the program initializes the variable CFEES, representing total student fees. The program then reads a student record, and tests for all nines in the student number field. If the last card has not been read, the program branches to statement number 6 to continue processing the record.

Logical IF Statement. The sequence of steps for processing a student record is shown in Figure 13–20.

Statement number 6 is a logical IF statement, used in this example to determine student tuition. The entry within parentheses (KUNITS.GE.12) tests whether units (called KUNITS) is greater than or equal to (GE) 13. If the condition is true, the program branches to statement number 8 where tuition is set equal to $420.00. If the condition is not true, the program goes to the next instruction where tuition is computed by multiplying units times $35.00.

QUESTION: An arithmetic IF statement could have been used at statement 6, instead of the logical IF. Write an arithmetic IF statement that will give the same result.

ANSWER IF (KUNITS – 12)10,8,8

After tuition is computed, the incidental fee of $12.50 is added to obtain total fees. Cumulative fees for all students are then updated, the student record is printed, and the program branches to read another record.

The output listing for Example 3 is shown in Figure 13–21.

```
      DIMENSION NAME(6)
    1 FORMAT(1X,6A4,I6,I2)
    2 FORMAT(1H ,14X,6A4,5X,I6,8X,I2,7X,F6.2)
    3 FORMAT(1H1,21X,*STUDENT NAME          NUMBER      UNITS           FEE
      1S*)
    4 FORMAT(1H ,49X,*TOTAL FEES    $*,F8.2)
      WRITE(6,3)
      CFEES = 0
    5 READ(5,1)NAME,KSTNO,KUNITS
      IF(KSTNO-999999)6,7,7
    6 IF(KUNITS.GE.12) GO TO 8
   10 TUIT = KUNITS * 35.00
      GO TO 9
    8 TUIT = 420.00
    9 FEES = TUIT + 12.50
      CFEES = CFEES + FEES
      WRITE(6,2)NAME,KSTNO,KUNITS,FEES
      GO TO 5
    7 WRITE(6,4)CFEES
      STOP
      END


             STUDENT NAME            NUMBER      UNITS          FEES
      ADAMS, PETER R.                 13978         9         327.50
      GOODMAN, HAROLD R.              20875        16         432.50
      JOHNSON, SHARON C.              24432        15         432.50
      LARSON, JAMES L.                47739         6         222.50
      LEWIS,BARBARA C.                 1339        18         432.50
      ROTHSCHILD, CHARLES K.          80336        10         362.50
      THOMPSON, LAURA W.              59325         7         257.50
                                   TOTAL FEES    $ 2467.50
```

Figure 13–21. *FORTRAN program and output for Example 3.*

The DO Statement

One of the most powerful features of the FORTRAN language is the DO statement. This statement makes it possible to loop or to perform a section of a program repeatedly, while incrementing the value of an integer variable at each repetition. Suppose that it is desired to execute the following program segment 10 times and then exit from the loop and continue further processing:

$$\text{READ } (5, 1)X$$
$$\text{SUM} = \text{SUM} + X$$

This segment (repeated 10 times) would read and form the sum of 10 numbers. A loop could be set up by intializing a counter, incrementing the counter each time a card is read, and testing the counter value with an IF statement. The instructions would appear as follows:

```
        K = 0
   4    READ (5, 1) X
        K = K + 1
        SUM = SUM + X
        IF (K − 10)4,5,5
   5    (next instruction)
```

The loop can be controlled with a DO statement, as follows:

```
        DO 4 I = 1, 10, 1
        READ (5, 1) X
4       SUM = SUM + X
5       (next instruction)
```

In the DO statement, the first number indicates the loop range—in this case, all statements up to and including number 4 are to be executed each cycle. The counter is given the integer variable name I. The three numbers after the equal sign are, respectively, the initial counter value, the test value, and the value used to increment the counter each cycle.

The counter is initially set to 1. Since this is less than 10, the segment is executed. The counter is now incremented by 1; since its value ($I = 2$) is still less than 10, the cycle is repeated, and so on. When the counter has been incremented to $I = 11$, it exceeds the test value; the cycle is terminated, and the program proceeds to the statement following the last one in the range of the DO statement (in this instance, statement number 5).

The counter in a DO statement must have an integer variable name. The three numbers following the equal sign may be either constants and/or integer variable names.

The value used to increment the counter in a DO statement need not be 1. In fact, when this number is 1, it may be omitted. Thus the following two statements are equivalent:

```
        DO 25 I = 1, 10, 1
        DO 25 I = 1, 10
```

QUESTION: Explain the meaning of the following statement:

```
        DO 10 J = 1, 11, 2
```

ANSWER: Execute all statements through statement number 10 for $J = 1, 3, 5, 7, 9, 11$ (the program segment is executed six times)

FORTRAN Subprograms

The concept—and importance—of subroutines is discussed in Chapter 12. Recall that a subroutine is a precoded program segment designed to accomplish a specific computational task. When the programmer requires a particular subroutine, he writes a macroinstruction (or subroutine "call") that causes the subroutine to be inserted into his program. There are two basic types of subroutines: open subroutines (spliced into the users program each time they are called), and closed subroutines (inserted only one time, regardless of the number of calls).

FORTRAN provides considerable flexibility in the use of subroutines (or subprograms). There are two basic types of FORTRAN subprograms:

1. Library (or built-in) functions, stored in the FORTRAN library.
2. User-written subprograms (these may be added to the library, if they are to be used by several different programs).

Library Functions

A number of functions are so commonly used that they are included in most FORTRAN IV system libraries. These include functions to compute square roots, find the minimum or maximum of a set of numbers, and so on. When the programmer needs a particular function, he simply inserts the function name and its arguments in his program.

A few of the most commonly used library functions are illustrated in Figure 13–22.

QUESTION: Suppose four variables currently have the following values:

$$A = 23.4, B = 38.2, C = -15.7, D = 0.0$$

1. If the following instruction is executed, what is the resulting value of Y? _____
   Y = AMAX1(A,B,C,D)

2. If the following instruction is executed, what is the resulting value of Y? _____
   Y = AMIN1(A,B,C,D)

ANSWER: (1) 38.2   (2) −15.7

Most FORTRAN libraries contain approximately 30 or 40 functions similar to those shown in Figure 13–22. Users add new functions to the library as needed.

User-written Subprograms

The FORTRAN programmer often requires subprograms that are not part of the present FORTRAN library. In such instances he may write his own subprograms and either include them in his own program or add them to the system library.

Function name	Explanation	Example of use
SQRT	Computes the square root of the argument	Y = SQRT(X)
ABS	Computes the absolute value of the argument	Y = ABS(X)
AMAX0	Computes the maximum of a set of integer arguments	S = AMAX0(J,K,L)
AMAX1	Computes the maximum of a set of real arguments	S = AMAX1(X,Y,Z)
AMIN0	Computes the minimum of a set of integer arguments	S = AMIN0(J,K,L)
AMIN1	Computes the minimum of a set of real arguments	S = AMIN1(X,Y,Z)

Figure 13–22. *Common FORTRAN library functions.*

There are three basic types of user-written subprograms: statement functions, function subprograms, and subroutine subprograms. The differences between these types are the following.

1. Statement functions may consist of only a single FORTRAN statement.
2. Function subprograms may consist of a large number of FORTRAN statements, but may "output" only a single value.
3. Subroutine subprograms may consist of a large number of FORTRAN statements, and may "output" a number of values.

User-supplied FORTRAN subprograms are illustrated by a simple function subprogram. Suppose a programmer wishes to write a subprogram to compute the compound amount at a given interest rate (a FORTRAN program for this calculation is shown in Figure 13–1). The formula for compound amount is

$$S = P(1 + R)^N$$

where P is the principal, R the interest rate per period, N the number of periods, and S the compound amount.

The following FORTRAN function (called AMOUNT) will perform this calculation.

```
FUNCTION AMOUNT (P,R,N)
AMOUNT = P★ (1.+R) ★★N
RETURN
END
```

This subprogram is very simple; however, it has the essential features of any function subprogram:

1. The word FUNCTION, which identifies the type of subprogram.
2. The function name (in this case, AMOUNT) followed by the argument list in parentheses.
3. The program steps defining the calculation (here, there is only one step). In a function subprogram, at least one instruction must contain the function name on the left-hand side of an assignment statement.
4. A RETURN statement, which returns control to the main program.
5. An END statement, identifying the end of the subprogram.

A subprogram is used by referencing its name in the main program, together with the actual arguments to be used in the calculation. For example, the function AMOUNT might be used in a program (similar to the one in Figure 13–1) as follows:

```
     S = AMOUNT (1000., .10,10)
     WRITE (6,10) S
 10  FORMAT (1H0, 'COMPOUND AMOUNT IS', F8.2)
     STOP
     END
```

The first statement in this program "calls" the function AMOUNT. The quantities in parentheses are assigned to the arguments in the same order that they appear in the function definition. Therefore, the values used are the following: P = 1000., R = .10, N = 10.

It is not necessary to use constants in the argument list (within parentheses) when calling the function. Instead, other variable names (or even simple expressions) may be used. In the above program, for example, the following statement could be used:

$$S = AMOUNT(PRIN,X,10)$$

With this statement the function would compute the compound amount using as principal the current value of PRIN, as interest the current value of X, and 10 as the number of periods.

BASIC Programming

BASIC is a high-level language developed for use with time-sharing systems. BASIC is an acronym for Beginner's All-purpose Symbolic Instruction Code, developed by Professors John Kemeny and Thomas Kurtz at Dartmouth College in 1963.

The language was intended for interactive use with on-line devices, such as the teletype terminals. The characters of the language are the same as those on a teletype device. The use of BASIC facilitates the storage of programs during development, the correction of errors in debugging, and the revision of programs.

BASIC is not yet a universal language. Not all computer manufacturers have developed BASIC compilers. However, the language is available for the majority of computers and should become a universal language in the near future.

To permit the reader to compare BASIC with the other languages described in this book, a BASIC program is illustrated in Figure 13–23. This same problem has been programmed in FORTRAN (Figure 13–21), COBOL (Figure 14–15), and PL/1 (Figure 14–16).

At first glance, BASIC appears to be quite different from FORTRAN. However, only a brief description of the BASIC commands will reveal much similarity in the two languages. Examine the program for Example 3 in Figure 13–23 and note the following comparison of the two languages.

1. REM denotes REMARK. It is a nonexecutable statement, like COMMENT in FORTRAN.
2. DIM the same function as the DIMENSION statement in FORTRAN.
3. BASIC variable names are limited to a single letter or a single letter followed by a single digit. The equivalent variables in the two programs are

BASIC	FORTRAN
N	NAME
K1	KSTNO
K2	KUNITS

4. Variables are defined with the command LET.
5. In READ or PRINT statements, a dollar sign following a variable identifies alphabetic information associated with that variable (i.e., N$ allows for a student name to be read or printed).
6. Data is inserted between the program and the END statement.

```
005 REM PROGRAM STUDENT
010 DIM N(6)
015 LET C=0
020 READ N$,K1,K2
025 IF K1=999999 THEN 100
030 IF K2>=12 THEN 80
035 T=K2*35.00
040 GOTO 85
080 LET T=420.00
085 LET F=T+12.50
090 LET C=C+F
095 PRINT "STUDENT NAME",N$,"NUMBER",K1,"UNITS",K2,"FEE IS",F
098 GOTO 020
100 PRINT "TOTAL FEES ARE $",C
200 DATA "ADAMS, PETER R.",13978,9
201 DATA "GOODMAN, HAROLD R.",20875,16
202 DATA "JOHNSON, SHARON C.",24432,15
203 DATA "LARSON, JAMES L.",47739,6
204 DATA "LEWIS,BARBARA C.",1339,18
205 DATA "ROTHSCHILD,CHARLES K.",80336,10
206 DATA "THOMPSON, LAURA W.",59325,7
207 DATA " ",999999,0
999 END
READY.
RUN

  74/10/24.  11.41.02.
PROGRAM    FRED

STUDENT NAME   ADAMS, PETER R.NUMBER          13978          UNITS
9              FEE IS          327.5
STUDENT NAME   GOODMAN, HAROLD R.             NUMBER         20875
UNITS          16            FEE IS           432.5
STUDENT NAME   JOHNSON, SHARON C.             NUMBER         24432
UNITS          15            FEE IS           432.5
STUDENT NAME   LARSON, JAMES L.               NUMBER         47739
UNITS          6             FEE IS           222.5
STUDENT NAME   LEWIS,BARBARA C.               NUMBER         1339
UNITS          18            FEE IS           432.5
STUDENT NAME   ROTHSCHILD,CHARLES K.          NUMBER         80336
UNITS          10            FEE IS           362.5
STUDENT NAME   THOMPSON, LAURA W.             NUMBER         59325
UNITS          7             FEE IS           257.5
TOTAL FEES ARE $                2467.5


CP        0.078 SECS.
RUN COMPLETE.
BYE
```

Figure 13–23. *BASIC program for Example 3.*

One of the advantages of BASIC is its ability to input an entire matrix with two commands. For example, the following statements instruct the computer to read and store a 5 by 8 matrix:

10 DIM A (5, 8)
15 MAT READ A

The first statement defines precisely the dimensions of the matrix and the second statement causes the storage of that 5 by 8 matrix.

QUESTION: BASIC is a FORTRAN-like language which was designed to facilitate _____ computer use.

ANSWER: on-line or interactive

346 / INTRODUCTION TO FORTRAN AND BASIC

Summary

FORTRAN is designed primarily for mathematical and scientific applications. It has several shortcomings that limit its usefulness in a business data processing environment. First, the language is not designed to describe and to manipulate complex file structures and databases. Second, the ability to edit output data is limited in FORTRAN. Finally, the language is not easily read or understood by the manager who is not a trained programmer.

FORTRAN does have application in management science and quantitive business analysis. Also FORTRAN is widely used in business schools to introduce the student to basic programming techniques.

Solutions to Exercises

Exercise 13–1

1. Integer:KOUNT, J, MEAN, KSTNO, LARGE
   Decimal: SUM, GROSS, COUNT, X, AVE, CODE, STNO
2. DIMENSION KADDR (5)
3. FORMAT (2X, I8, 4X, I5, I6, 55X)
4. IF (BAL − RP) 8, 8, 11

Exercise 13–2

1.

```
FØRMAT (1HI, 10X,'EMPLØYEE NAME',6X,'ADDRESS')
```

2.

```
FØRMAT (1H0,35X,'TØTAL',4X,I6)
```

3. (a) Arithmetic operators for multiplication (*) and exponentiation (**) are missing.
   (c) Only a single variable (not an arithmetic expression) may appear to the left of equals sign.
   (d) This statement is valid but may give an undesired result.
   (e) Divide operator is not ÷.

4. (a) 4.5   (d) 41.
   (b) 4   (e) 4.
   (c) 36.   (f) 1.

Chapter Examination

1. Assign valid FORTRAN variable names to each of the following quantities:

   (a) Principal (real) _____

   (b) Temperature (real) _____

   (c) Student number (integer) _____

   (d) Zip code (integer) _____

   (e) Acceleration (real) _____

2. Compute and record the results of each of the following statements, given these variables and their values: $A = -5, B = 1, C = 8, I = 3, K = 4$.

   (a) $Y = I / K$ _____

   (b) $Z = K / I$ _____

   (c) $N = A + C - B$ _____

   (d) $M = C \ast A - B$ _____

   (e) $Y = B \ast C - I / K$ _____

3. Three FORTRAN variables have the following current values: COST = 10.98, PRICE = 14.95, NUMBER = 50.
   Specify the output, giving the exact spacing, for each of the following WRITE statements:

   (a)   WRITE (6, 5) COST, PRICE, NUMBER
       5   FORMAT (1H0, 2F6.2, 3X, I3)

   (b)   WRITE (6, 5) COST, PRICE, NUMBER
       5   FORMAT (1H0, 'COST', F6.2, 2X, 'PRICE', F6.2, 2X, 'NUMBER', I3)

4. Cards are punched with data as follows:

Columns	Contents
1–5	unused
6–11	COST (XXX.XXX)
12–15	unused
16–21	PRICE (XXX.XXX)
22–25	unused
26–28	NUMBER (XXX)

Write FORTRAN READ and FORMAT statements to read data from the cards.

_____

_____

_____

5. In a FORTRAN program, the variable PAY is to be compared with $4200. If PAY is less than $4200., the program is to go to statement number 15; if PAY is equal to or greater than $4200., it is to go to statement number 20.

(a) Write a FORTRAN arithmetic IF statement for this logical operation. _____

_____

(b) Write a FORTRAN logical IF statement for this logical operation.

_____

_____

6. What is the resulting value of the variable J after executing the following FORTRAN segment? _____

```
J = 1
DO 10 I = 1,5
10 J = J* I
```

349 / CHAPTER EXAMINATION

7. Find the errors in each of these pairs of statements:

	STATEMENT NUMBER		
(a)	10	WRITE (6,10) I,J,K FORMAT (1H ,2I4,F8.2)	
(b)		WRITE (6,11) A,B FORMAT (1H0,F4.2,F6.2)	
(c)	12	WRITE (6,12) A,T FORMAT (2F6.2)	
(d)	13	READ (6,13) M,X,Y FORMAT (4X,I3,5X,F7.2)	

(a) _____

(b) _____

(c) _____

(d) _____

8. List the rules for evaluating FORTRAN expressions.

(a) First: _____

_____

(b) Second: _____

_____

(c) Third: _____

_____

(d) Fourth: _____

_____

9. Write a FORTRAN function subprogram called KFACT that for any
   integer K will calculate K! (K factorial). (*Hint:* see problem 6.)

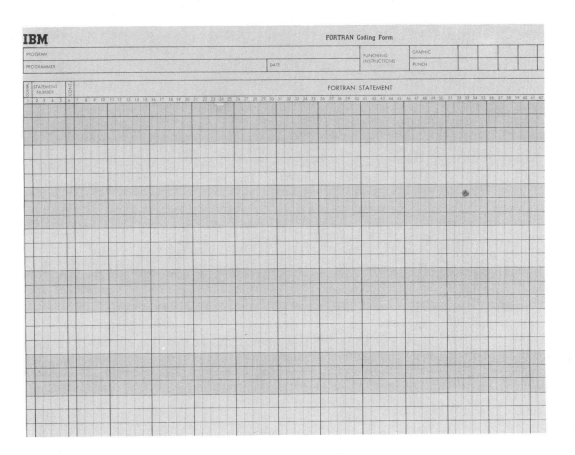

10. Fifty students took an examination. The grade for each student is
    punched on a card in columns 2 to 4 (grades range from 0 to 100).
    Write a FORTRAN program to do the following:
    (a) Compute and print out the average grade for the 50 students.
    (b) Determine and print out the number of students who received a
        grade higher than the average. [*Hint:* read and store the data as
        an array called GRADE. For example, GRADE(6) is the grade
        received by the sixth student].

| PROGRAM | | | | PUNCHING INSTRUCTIONS | GRAPHIC | | | | |
| PROGRAMMER | | | DATE | | PUNCH | | | | |

STATEMENT NUMBER   CONT   FORTRAN STATEMENT

11. The 1960 United States Census shows that five central cities (CC) had populations of more than one million. The following table shows the populations and areas in square miles of the five central cities and their standard metropolitan statistical areas (SMSA), which includes the central cities:

	Population		Area (square miles)	
	CC	SMSA	CC	SMSA
New York	7,781,984	10,694,633	315	2,149
Chicago	3,550,404	6,220,913	224	3,714
Philadelphia	3,002,512	4,342,897	127	3,549
Detroit	1,670,144	3,762,360	140	1,965
San Francisco	1,104,035	2,783,359	98	3,313

Write a program to read the above data and compute and print out the following:

(a) Population density (population per square mile) for each CC, SMSA, and SMSA ring (SMSA excluding the CC).
(b) Area of each CC as a percentage of the area of the SMSA.

12. Write a program to condense some statistics on the students in a class. One data card is punched for each student, as follows:

Item	Columns	
Age	1 and 2	
Sex	5	(1 = male, 2 = female)
Class standing	7	(1 = freshman, 2 = sophomore, 3 = junior, 4 = senior)

The required output is the following:
(a) Average age of the students
(b) Percent males, percent females
(c) Percent freshmen, sophomores, juniors, seniors.
Use the following data:

20	1	2
18	2	1
26	2	4
21	1	3
23	1	2
19	2	1
21	1	4
20	2	2
23	1	4
17	2	1

The cards are not counted; therefore, use a blank card to indicate the end of the data deck.

13. Write a FORTRAN program to compute the mean, variance, and standard deviation of a sample. Use the following formulas:

$$\text{Mean} = \overline{X} = \frac{\sum\limits_{i=1}^{N} X_i}{N}$$

$$\text{Variance} = S^2 = \frac{\sum\limits_{i=1}^{N} X_i^2 - \left(\sum\limits_{i=1}^{N} X_i\right)^2 \Big/ N}{(N-1)}$$

$$\text{Standard deviation} = S = \sqrt{S^2}$$

The sample size, N, is contained in columns 1 to 3 of the first card in the data deck. Values of X_i are punched one per card in the form XXX.X, beginning in column 1 of the data card.

Print as output the value of N and the sample mean, variance, and the standard deviation.

Use the following values to test your program.

$N = 10$

i	X_i
1	134.7
2	68.9
3	761.0
4	54.2
5	165.5
6	512.8
7	48.9
8	326.0
9	261.3
10	420.7

14. Write a FORTRAN program to compute employee net pay. This program should do the following:
    (a) Read employee cards with the following information:

    Clock number, columns 1 to 5 (integer)
    Gross pay, columns 6 to 15, format XXXXXXX.XX

    (b) Use the following table to compute the tax and find the net pay, where net pay is equal to gross pay less tax.

Gross Pay	Tax
Less than $2000	0
$2000 or more, but less than $5000	5% of excess over $2000
$5000 or more	$150, plus 10% of excess over $5000

    (c) Print the clock number, gross pay, tax and net pay for each employee.
    (d) Terminate when the employee's clock number is zero.
    Test your program with the following data:

Employee Clock Number	Gross Pay
01000	1420.68
01001	2000.00
01002	2538.49
01003	5000.00
01004	25389.50
00000	

15. The sales slips on merchandise sold in a department contain the amount of the sale and the salesperson's ID number. At the end of the day these are punched onto cards with the salesperson's ID number in columns 1 to 3 and the amount of the sale in F format in columns 4 to 13. The cards are neither counted nor ordered in any particular way.

    Prepare a FORTRAN program to (1) calculate the total sales of each salesperson, (2) calculate the percentage of total sales represented by each salesperson total, and (3) calculate his or her commission for the day (3% of the sales above $50). The program output should be columns containing ID number, total sales for the day, percentage of the total, and his or her commission. Make up data cards to test the program.

16. Write a FORTRAN program to locate and print out the largest number in an array of numbers. The program should print out both the largest number, and its location in the array. In case there are two or more such numbers, arbitrarily print out the location of the first one. Test your program with the data of problem 13.

17. What are the principal differences between FORTRAN and BASIC?

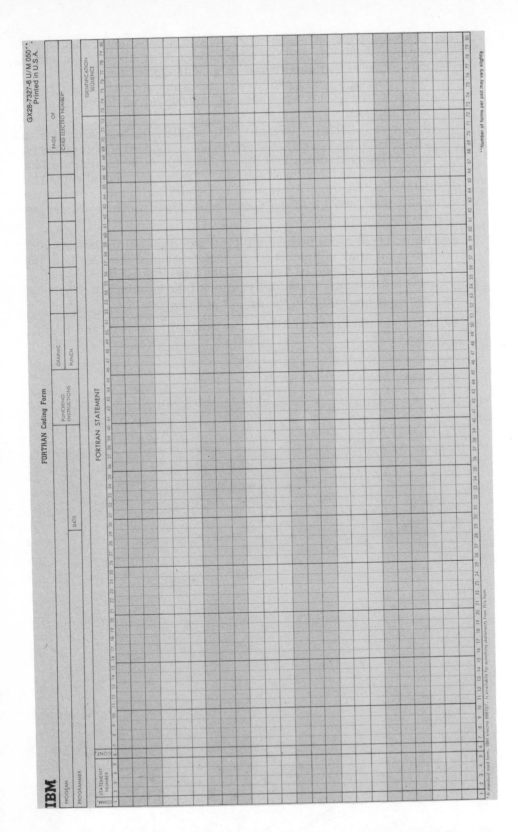

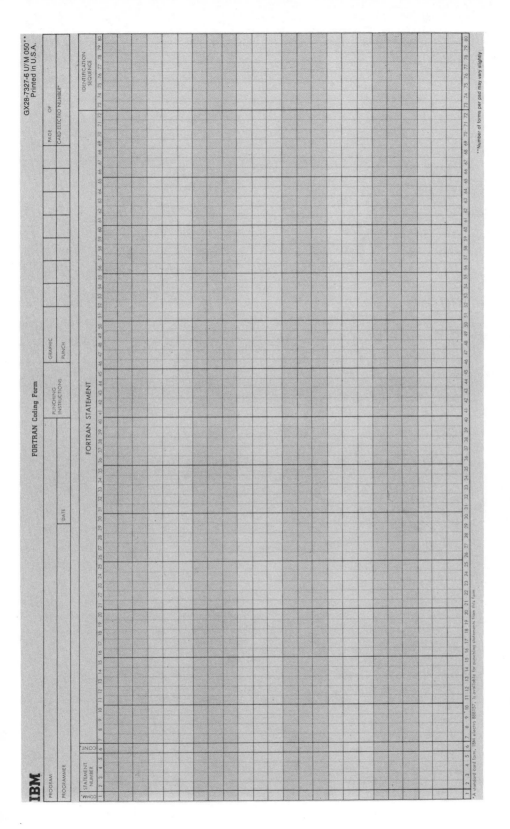

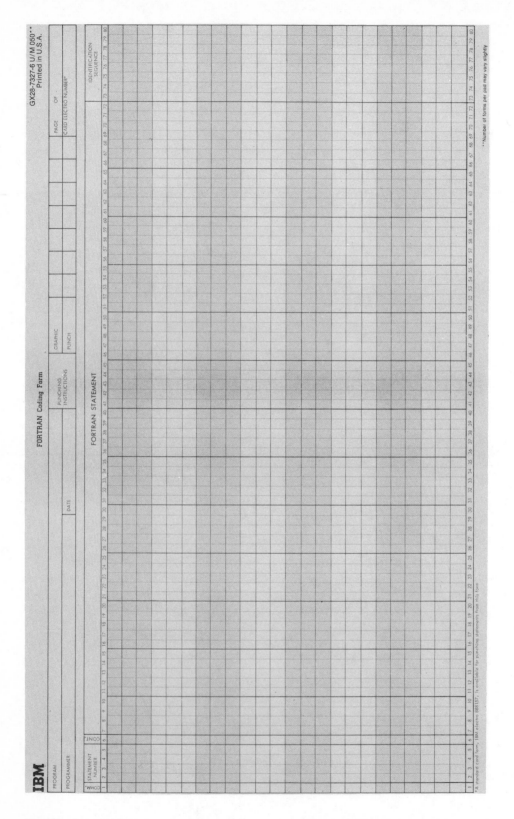

Chapter 14

INTRODUCTION TO COBOL AND PL/1

Overview

In the preceding chapter a powerful language for coding mathematical and logical procedures is presented. FORTRAN is widely used for scientific applications, and is also very useful for quantitative business applications, including statistical analysis and management science.

Most business data processing applications do not require extensive computation or the use of complicated mathematical formulas. Instead, they usually involve processing large files of data, with a relatively small amount of calculation needed for each record or transaction. For example, a typical application involves processing inventory transactions—sales, receipts, and adjustments—against an inventory master file.

A scientifically oriented language such as FORTRAN may be (sometimes is) used for data processing applications. However, it was not designed for this purpose and as a result is not ideally suited to it.

There are two principal reasons why FORTRAN is not more widely used for data processing applications:

1. It is not well suited to describe and manipulate large data files.
2. Its elements and syntax are not readily understood by the user who is not a trained programmer.

To overcome these disadvantages, the federal government sponsored a major effort in the late 1950s to develop a new, data processing-oriented language. Representatives of several large users and computer manufacturers formed a committee called the Conference on Data Systems Languages, or CODASYL. This effort resulted in COBOL, an abbreviation of Common Business-Oriented Language.

The first version of COBOL appeared in 1960. A maintenance committee of CODASYL was formed to initiate and to review recommended changes to keep the language up to date. Subsequent versions of the language have appeared in 1961, 1964, and 1965. The most recent version of COBOL was approved by the American National Standards Institute in 1974.

COBOL is an English-like language. Most instructions are coded using English names instead of symbols or more restricted names. For example, instead of the symbol *, the word MULTIPLY is most often used. Descriptive names such as AMOUNT-OF-SALES and CUSTOMER-FILE (illegal in FORTRAN) may also be used. This feature makes COBOL easier to write for the programmer and easier to read for anyone else. The manager who knows little about computers can check the logic of a program written in COBOL much more easily than the same program written in any other language.

Like FORTRAN, COBOL is largely machine-independent. Only a brief environment section is required in each program to describe the particular hardware configuration being used. Also, most computer manufacturers have developed COBOL compilers. These features make it relatively easy for a user to convert a program from one computer model to a more advanced one, or to that of another manufacturer.

The impetus for COBOL in the early stages of its development came from the federal government, which required that COBOL compilers be available for all large computers used by the government. Acceptance by the business community came more slowly. Early COBOL compilers had long compile times and tended to develop inefficient object coding. However, compilers for third generation computers are much improved. As a result, COBOL is the most widely used programming language in use today for data processing applications. It has been estimated that more than three fourths of all installations having COBOL capability now use COBOL as the major language for these applications.

Exercise 14–1

1. A manager would find it much easier to understand a program written

in (FORTRAN or COBOL) _____.

2. The word COBOL is an abbreviation for _____

_____.

3. Instructions for describing and manipulating large files are more easily

written in _____.

4. COBOL was developed under the direction of a steering committee

known as CODASYL, which stands for _____.

5. COBOL (is, is not) suited for scientific applications.

6. Like FORTRAN, COBOL is largely _____-_____.

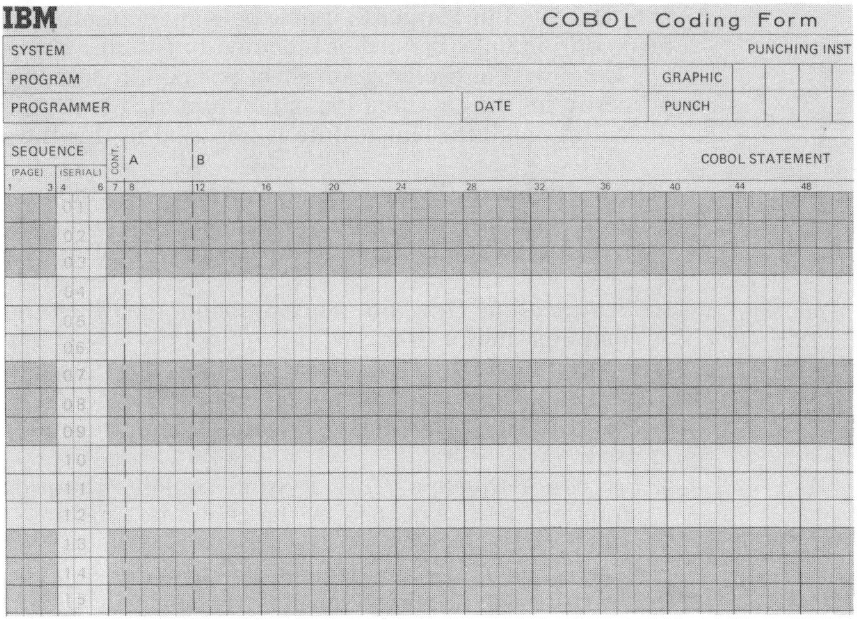

Figure 14–1. *COBOL coding form.*

COBOL Program Organization

COBOL programs are arranged in a standard format which facilitates their writing and interpretation. The programs are coded on a standard COBOL coding form which is shown in Figure 14–1.

Columns 1 to 6 are used for page and serial number, which are optional in a COBOL program. Page number appears in columns 1 to 3. Thus the first page is numbered 001, the second 002, and so on.

Serial Number (columns 4–6) refers to line number. The first line is generally given serial number 010, the second 020, and so on. Lines are numbered by tens so that insertions may easily be made. Using this numbering system, 001080 refers to page 1, line 8; 002040 to page 2, line 4, and so on.

Identification Characters (columns 73–80) are also optional in a COBOL program. They are often useful to identify a program further.

QUESTION: On the COBOL coding form, page and serial numbers and identification characters are (required, optional)? _____

ANSWER: Optional. However, they are recommended to improve documentation

All COBOL program entries must be entered in the statement section, which extends from columns 8 to 72. Referring to Figure 14–1, this section is divided into Margin A (columns 8–11) and Margin B (columns 12–72). Some entries must be coded in Margin A; all such entries must begin in column 8. Many other entries are coded in Margin B. If an entry is to be coded in Margin B, it may begin in column 12 or, at the programmer's option, may be further indented to column 13, 14, and so on.

Column 7 of the program sheet is a continuation position. It is used primarily for the continuation of nonnumeric literals that cannot be completed on one line. This feature is not used in this introductory chapter.

COBOL Divisions. Every COBOL program is divided into four divisions. Each division provides a unique and essential portion of the information required by the COBOL compiler. The four COBOL divisions are as follows.

1. *Identification Division.* This division identifies the program to the computer and/or user.
2. *Environment Division.* This specifies the computer equipment (or hardware) to be used by the program.
3. *Data Division.* This defines the files, record layouts, and storage areas used.
4. *Procedure Division.* This division contains the program logic or instructions to be executed by the computer.

Each COBOL division is identified by a division header, for example, DATA DIVISION. Division headers are coded in Margin A.

QUESTION: To summarize, every COBOL program must contain four division headers. These headers must appear in the following order: _____ DIVISION, _____ DIVISION, _____ DIVISION, _____ DIVISION. Each division header starts in column _____ .

ANSWER: IDENTIFICATION, ENVIRONMENT, DATA, PROCEDURE, 8

Coding a COBOL program consists of writing entries for the four divisions. The divisions are, in turn, comprised of sections, paragraphs, and entries. To illustrate the basic concepts of COBOL programming, three examples are introduced in the remainder of this chapter. These example problems are all based on processing a student record file.

Example 1: Basic Input-Output Operations

A student file is maintained on punched cards, one card record per student. The format of the records is shown in Figure 14–2. Each card contains student name (columns 2–26), number (27–31), units taken this semester (32–33), and total units prior to this semester (34–36).

An output listing is to be prepared from the cards. Each card field is to be printed, with blank spaces between fields. Leading zeros (if any) are to be suppressed for numeric fields. A printer spacing chart of the output format is shown in Figure 14–3.

Identification Division

The Identification Division supplies the name of the program, together with several optional entries to improve program documentation. The Identification Division for Example 1 is shown in Figure 14–4.

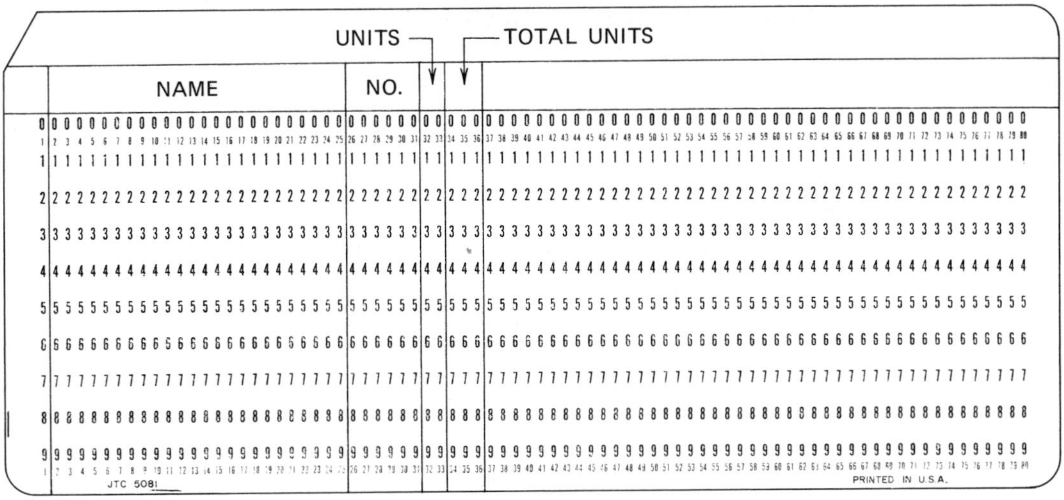

Figure 14–2. Input student record card.

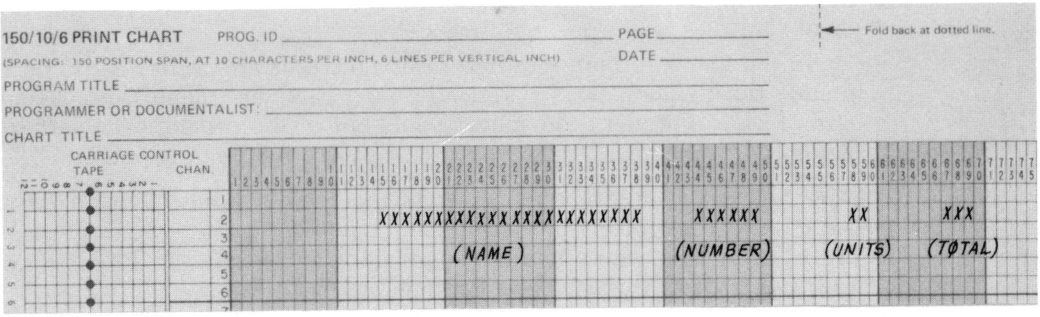

Figure 14–3. Printer spacing chart for Example 1.

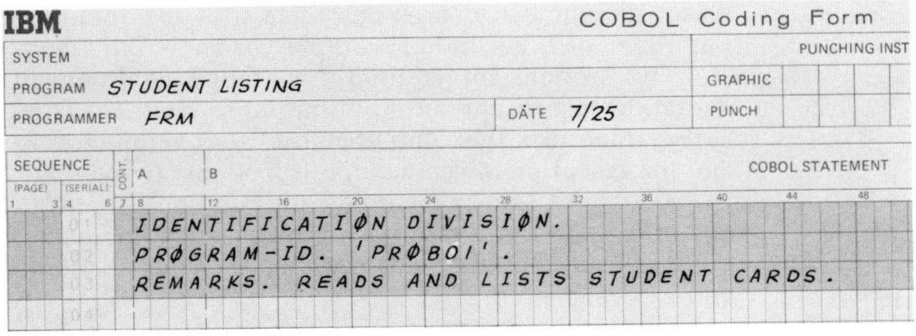

Figure 14–4. Identification Division for Example 1.

363 / IDENTIFICATION DIVISION

Every COBOL program must have a PROGRAM-ID entry. For some compilers, the program name must not exceed eight characters. The first character must be a letter, and the remaining characters may be letters or digits, but not special characters. The name must be enclosed in single quotes, as in Figure 14–4.

QUESTION: The program name 'PROB-01' (would, would not) be acceptable. _____ .

ANSWER: would not (the hyphen is a special character)

The REMARKS entry in Example 1 is optional. A number of other optional entries may be made in the Identification Division, to improve documentation. The general format of the Identification Division is as follows:

> IDENTIFICATION DIVISION
> PROGRAM-ID. 'program name'.
> [AUTHOR. entry]
> [INSTALLATION. entry]
> [DATE-WRITTEN. entry]
> [DATE-COMPILED. entry]
> [SECURITY. entry]
> [REMARKS. entry]

In the above format, required reserved words are underlined. These include the division header and following paragraph names. Bracketed terms [ ] are optional, and may be left out of the program. Lowercase words indicate names or entries to be supplied by the programmer.

QUESTION: The minimum entries in the Identification Division for a COBOL program consist of the division header, _____ _____ , and the paragraph entry _____ .

ANSWER: IDENTIFICATION DIVISION, PROGRAM-ID

Environment Division

The second division of a COBOL program is the Environment Division. It specifies the computers to be used in compiling and processing the object program. It also assigns data files to input-output devices. The Environment Division for Example 1 is shown in Figure 14–5.

Two sections are required in a COBOL environment division: a configuration section and an input-output section. The configuration section simply identifies the computer used for compilation (source computer) and for execution (object computer). Normally these are the same.

Example 1 is to be compiled and run on a CDC 6400. For some manufacturers, both the computer name and model number are required. The COBOL user should check with his own installation to determine the correct designation.

```
ENVIRØNMENT DIVISIØN.
CØNFIGURATIØN SECTIØN.
SØURCE-CØMPUTER. 6400.
ØBJECT-CØMPUTER. 6400.
INPUT-ØUTPUT SECTIØN.
FILE CØNTRØL.
     SELECT STUDENT-FILE ASSIGN TØ INPUT.
     SELECT PRINT-FILE ASSIGN TØ ØUTPUT.
```

Figure 14-5. *Environment Division for Example 1.*

QUESTION: The configuration section consists of two entries:

_____ _____ and _____

_____.

ANSWER: SOURCE COMPUTER, OBJECT COMPUTER

The input-output section identifies input and output files used in the program. The only required paragraph in this section is called file control. This paragraph associates each file used in the program with an input or output device.

The actual assignment of files to devices is accomplished with a Select statement, as follows:

SELECT (file name) ASSIGN TO (device)

In Example 1, the input file is given the name STUDENT-FILE; the device is the card reader that has the symbolic device name INPUT.

QUESTION: Examine Figure 14–5. What are the names given to the output file and device for Example 1? _____, _____.
ANSWER: PRINT-FILE, OUTPUT

File names (such as STUDENT-FILE and PRINT-FILE) are specified by the programmer, and there are a number of such *programmer-defined words* in a COBOL program. The programmer has considerable flexibility in defining words, but must follow these rules:

1. A programmer-defined word must not exceed 30 characters.
2. A programmer-defined word may contain alphabetic and numeric characters, and embedded hyphens. However, it may not contain any other special characters, including spaces.
3. COBOL reserved words may not be used. COBOL *reserved words* are those that have special significance to the compiler. Examples are SELECT, ASSIGN, FILE, ADD, REPORT. These words must be used without alteration in meaning or definition. There are well over 200 COBOL reserved words, with some variation between compiling systems.

```
     DATA DIVISION.
     FILE SECTION.
     FD   STUDENT-FILE LABEL RECORDS ARE OMITTED
          DATA RECORD IS STUDENT-REC.
     01   STUDENT-REC.
          02 FILLER                    PICTURE X.
          02 STUD-NAME                 PICTURE X(24).
          02 STUD-NUMB                 PICTURE 9(6).
          02 UNITS                     PICTURE 9(2).
          02 TOTAL-UNITS               PICTURE 9(3).
          02 FILLER                    PICTURE X(44).
     FD   PRINT-FILE LABEL RECORDS ARE OMITTED
          DATA RECORD IS PRINT-LINE.
     01   PRINT-LINE.
          02 FILLER                    PICTURE X(15).
          02 NAME-OUT                  PICTURE X(24).
          02 FILLER                    PICTURE X(5).
          02 NUMB-OUT                  PICTURE ZZZZZ9.
          02 FILLER                    PICTURE X(8).
          02 UNITS-OUT                 PICTURE Z9.
          02 FILLER                    PICTURE X(7).
          02 TOTAL-OUT                 PICTURE ZZ9.
          02 FILLER                    PICTURE X(63).
```

Figure 14–6. *Data Division for Example 1.*

QUESTION: Two types of COBOL words are _____-
_____ words and _____ words.

ANSWER: Programmer-defined, reserved

Data Division

The data division in a COBOL program describes:

1. Input and output files and records.
2. Data items in computer storage.

The data division for Example 1 is shown in Figure 14–6.

The *file section* is the only section required in the data division for this example. The reason for this is that data is read into an input area, moved to an output area, and then listed. Thus no intermediate computer storage is required.

File description. In Example 1, there are two files: Student-file (input) and Print-file (output). These files were named and assigned to devices in the Environment Division (see Figure 14–5). In the File Section there is a File Description (identified by the header FD) for each of these files. The entry following the header FD for the input file is as follows:

```
FD   STUDENT-FILE LABEL RECORDS ARE OMITTED
     DATA RECORD IS STUDENT-REC.
```

In this entry, the file name (STUDENT-FILE) is given first. A clause concerning label records is then presented. Label records are used in many processing applications, to ensure that the correct file is being accessed. In the examples in this chapter, label records are not used. The above clause must be used to indicate this condition.

The last clause in the entry identifies the data record within the file. The Student-File contains only one type record, which has been given the programmer-assigned name, STUDENT-REC.

QUESTION: Examine the FD for the output file in Figure 14–6. What can be said regarding (a) label records, (b) record name?

(a) _____ . (b) _____ .

ANSWER: (a) Label records are omitted   (b) Record name is Print-line

Record Description. After a given data file has been described, each different record contained in the file must be described. This description consists of a record header, followed by entries that describe each data item in the record.

In the example (Figure 14–6), the input file contains only one record, which has been named Student-rec. The description header is as follows:

01   STUDENT-REC

The number 01 is called a COBOL *level number*. Level number 01 is always used to introduce a record, which is the highest level of data structure contained in a file.

Item Description. A separate entry is made under the record header for each data item (or field) contained in the record. This entry specifies the level number, data name (or the reserved word FILLER), and a clause indicating the length and type of field.[1]

Refer again to Figure 14–2, which shows the format for the input student record cards. Each card contains a blank (column 1), student name (columns 2–25), student number (columns 26–31), units taken (columns 32–33), and total units (columns 34–36). Now refer to the item descriptions (Figure 14–6), which describe these same fields.

Each item in STUDENT-REC is coded at the 02 level. This indicates that the items are subordinate to the 01 level entry (the record itself), but are independent of each other—that is, they are separate fields, to be treated equally.

In many instances, a data field may be further subdivided into dependent fields. For example, the field EMPLOYEE-NAME might be subdivided as follows:

EMPLOYEE – NAME		
LAST	FIRST	MI
1 10	11 19	20

[1]The item description may also contain a USAGE or VALUE clause.

In this instance, the level structure might be coded as follows:

02	EMPLOYEE–NAME		
	03	LAST	(entry)
	03	FIRST	(entry)
	03	MI	(entry)

An item that is further subdivided (such as EMPLOYEE-NAME above) is referred to as a *group* item, but an item that is not further subdivided is called an *elementary* item.

QUESTION: A field called Date might be subdivided into Month, Day, Year. In this case, Date is called a _____ item, while Month, Day, and Year are called _____ items.
ANSWER: Group, elementary

The word FILLER is used to designate unused portions of the record. In Example 1, the first column and the last 44 columns are unused, and so are designated FILLER.

The final entry in each item description is a *picture* clause, which indicates the length and type of data field. The *type* of data field is designated by one of three characters, as follows.

Character	Type of Field
9	Numeric
A	Alphabetic
X	Alphanumeric

The length of field is indicated by repeating the above characters, or by enclosing the length in parentheses after the type character. For example, a four-position numeric field may be indicated by 9999 or by 9(4).

QUESTION: Examine the picture clause for student number (called STUDENT-NUMB) in Figure 14–6. What is the length and type of field? Based on the input student cards, is this designation correct?

ANSWER: Six position numeric; yes. Student number is contained in card columns 26 to 31

The item descriptions for the output record (Print-Line) are also shown in Figure 14–6. Entries include FILLERS to separate the fields on the output listing, as is specified on the printer spacing chart (Figure 14–3).

A feature of COBOL is the ability to edit data on output, to improve the readability of listings. This is accomplished by means of COBOL editing symbols. One such symbol is the letter Z, indicating zero suppresion. In the example problem, the picture clauses for output fields Numb-out (for student number), Units-out and Total-out contain the zero suppression symbol.

As an example, the student number field in the output area is called NUMB-OUT, and has PICTURE ZZZZZ9. Leading zeros will be suppressed for any quantity moved to the field NUMB-OUT. Following are some examples:

STUD-NUMB		NUMB-OUT	
Picture	Value	Picture	Value
9 (6)	123456	ZZZZZ9	123456
9 (6)	023456	ZZZZZ9	23456
9 (6)	003456	ZZZZZ9	3456
9 (6)	000456	ZZZZZ9	456
9 (6)	000056	ZZZZZ9	56
9 (6)	000006	ZZZZZ9	6
9 (6)	000000	ZZZZZ9	0

In each of the above examples, if the Picture clause for NUMB-OUT were 9(6), the printout would contain leading zeros as in the second column. Suppressing leading zeros improves the readability of the listing. Further use of COBOL editing symbols will be discussed in subsequent sections.

The card reader and line printer are fixed record length devices. A card reader normally reads 80 characters of information. In many computing systems, the line printer can print up to 132 characters of information. In addition, an initial character (not accessible to the programmer) is used for printer carriage control.

In the Data Division, the number of characters specified for each input and output record should correspond to the above record lengths. The input card record should specify 80 characters. The output printer record should specify 133 characters, including an initial character which is left blank.

QUESTION: Examine the picture clauses in Figure 14–6. The input record (STUDENT-RECORD) specifies a total of 80 characters. Analyze the output record (PRINT-LINE) to determine the number of characters specified (be sure to count editing characters such as "Z" for zero suppression). Is the correct number of characters specified?_____

ANSWER: Yes, 133 characters are specified (see below).

Data Item	Picture	Number of Characters
FILLER	X	1 (carriage control)
FILLER	X(14)	14
NAME-OUT	X(24)	24
FILLER	X(5)	5
NUMB-OUT	ZZZZZ9	6
FILLER	X(8)	8
UNITS-OUT	Z9	2
FILLER	X(7)	7
TOTAL-OUT	ZZ9	3
FILLER	63	63
Total		133

SEQUENCE			A	B	COBOL STATEMENT
(PAGE)	(SERIAL)	CONT			

```
PROCEDURE DIVISION.
START.
        OPEN INPUT STUDENT-FILE.
        OPEN OUTPUT PRINT-FILE.
NEXT-CARD.
        READ STUDENT-FILE RECORD AT END GO TO EOJ.
        MOVE SPACES TO PRINT LINE.
        MOVE STUD-NAME TO NAME-OUT.
        MOVE STUD-NUMB TO NUMB-OUT.
        MOVE UNITS TO UNITS-OUT.
        MOVE TOTAL-UNITS TO TOTAL-OUT.
        WRITE PRINT-LINE.
        GO TO NEXT-CARD.
EOJ.
        CLOSE STUDENT-FILE, PRINT FILE.
        STOP RUN.
```

Figure 14–7. *Procedure Division for Example 1.*

Procedure Division. The Procedure Division of a COBOL program defines the processing steps necessary to solve a given problem. The Procedure Division for Example 1 is shown in Figure 14–7.

The English-like nature of a COBOL program is particularly apparent in the Procedure Division. Briefly, the program performs the following steps in Figure 14–7:

1. Input and output files are opened. This step is necessary to make the files available to the program.
2. A record is read from Student-file. If the file has been exhausted, the program goes to an End-of-Job routine (called EOJ).
3. Spaces are moved into the output record area. This step is necessary to clear the output area before each line is printed.
4. Each input field is moved to the corresponding output field in the print record. If editing symbols have been used, data is edited during this operation.
5. The output line is printed on the report.
6. The program returns to process the next record.
7. When an end-of-file condition is encountered, the program closes the files and terminates the program.

QUESTION: A number of words in the Procedure Division have been previously defined by the programmer in the Environment Division (Figure 14–5) or in the Data Division (Figure 14–6). List the programmer-defined words in Figure 14–7 according to where they were first defined:

(a) Environment Division _____.

(b) Data Division _____.

_____.

(c) Procedure Division _____.

ANSWER: (a) Environment Division: STUDENT-FILE, PRINT-FILE
(b) Data Division: PRINT-LINE, STUD-NAME, NAME-OUT, STUD-NUMB, NUMB-OUT, UNITS, UNITS-OUT, TOTAL-UNITS, TOTAL-OUT
(c) Procedure Division: NEXT-CARD, EOJ (paragraph names)

Input-Output. Input-output statements process data into and out of the computer. The statements most often used are OPEN, CLOSE, READ, and WRITE. All of these statements are used in Example 1.

The open statement performs two basic functions: (1) it indicates which files are used for input and which will serve as output; and (2) it makes files available for processing by accessing specific devices, checking labels (input files), and writing label records (output files).

The general format of an OPEN statement is as follows:

$$\text{OPEN} \begin{bmatrix} \text{INPUT} \\ \text{or} \\ \text{OUTPUT} \end{bmatrix} \text{(file name)}$$

QUESTION: In Example 1, what file is used for input? _____.

For output? _____.
ANSWER: STUDENT-FILE, PRINT-FILE

A READ statement transmits data from an input device to an input storage area defined in the file section of the Data Division. In sequential files, it provides for branching on an end-of-file condition. The general form of the READ statement is as follows:

READ (file name) AT END (statement)

A WRITE statement transmits data from an output area (defined in the file section of the Data Division) to an output device. The general format of a WRITE statement is

WRITE (record name) AFTER ADVANCING [N] LINES

The number of lines advanced, called N, must be an integer such as 1, 2, or 3. This provides single, double, or triple spacing between lines of printed output.

QUESTION: Compare the formats for READ and WRITE statements. The verb READ is followed by a _____ name, while WRITE must be followed by a _____ name.
ANSWER: file, record

When processing has terminated, all files used in the program must be closed. The general form of the CLOSE statement is

CLOSE (file name(s))

Data Movement. An important operation in data processing is moving data from one storage location to another. For example, an output record is often assembled by moving data from input and working storage areas to the output area. The editing of data is often an important part of this operation.

Movement of data is accomplished by the MOVE statement. The general format is

MOVE (data-name-1) TO (data-name-2)

Data-name-1 is the sending field, data-name-2 is the receiving field. Both fields must be defined by a picture clause in the Data Division.

Following are two important rules in the use of the MOVE statement.

1. An alphabetic item must not be moved to a numeric item (as defined in the picture clause), or vice versa.
2. Data transferred from a numeric sending area to a numeric receiving area are positioned according to the decimal point in the receiving area, with excess characters truncated. If no decimal point is specified, data received will be right-justified.

The following examples illustrate the use of the MOVE statement.

Sending Field		Receiving Field		Comment
Picture	Contents	Picture	Contents (after MOVE)	
999	328	999	328	Whole number 328 moved
99V99	41.25	99V99	41.25	Implied decimal point after first 2 digits
A(5)	JONES	9(5)		Illegal (alphabetic to numeric)
99V99	41.25	99V9	41.2	Excess digit truncated

The MOVE statement has a second format that permits transmitting literals:

MOVE (literal) TO (data-name)

The following are examples:

Statement	Comment
MOVE 175 TO WEIGHT-LIMIT.	175 moved to receiving field
MOVE 'AUG 1, 1975' TO DATE.	Aug. 1, 1975 moved to receiving field
MOVE ZEROS TO GROSS PAY.	Receiving field filled with zeros
MOVE SPACES TO PRINT-LINE.	Receiving field filled with spaces

QUESTION: Examine the Procedure Division (Figure 14–7). Which statement causes a literal to be transmitted to a receiving field?

ANSWER: MOVE SPACES TO PRINT-LINE. In this case, the receiving field is the entire record called PRINT-LINE.

This completes the description of the COBOL program for Example 1. The complete program for this example is shown in Figure 14–8.

```
IDENTIFICATION DIVISION.
PROGRAM-ID. #PROB01#.
REMARKS. READS AND LISTS STUDENT RECORD CARDS.
ENVIRONMENT DIVISION.
CONFIGURATION SECTION.
SOURCE-COMPUTER. 6400.
OBJECT-COMPUTER. 6400.
INPUT-OUTPUT SECTION.
FILE-CONTROL.
     SELECT STUDENT-FILE ASSIGN TO INPUT.
     SELECT PRINT-FILE ASSIGN TO OUTPUT.
DATA DIVISION.
FILE SECTION.
FD   STUDENT-FILE LABEL RECORDS ARE OMITTED
     DATA RECORD IS STUDENT-REC.
01   STUDENT-REC.
     02 FILLER         PICTURE X.
     02 STUD-NAME      PICTURE X(24).
     02 STUD-NUMB      PICTURE 9(6).
     02 UNITS          PICTURE 9(2).
     02 TOTAL-UNITS    PICTURE 9(3).
     02 FILLER         PICTURE X(44).
FD   PRINT-FILE LABEL RECORDS ARE OMITTED
     DATA RECORD IS PRINT-LINE.
01   PRINT-LINE.
     02 FILLER         PICTURE X(15).
     02 NAME-OUT       PICTURE X(24).
     02 FILLER         PICTURE X(5).
     02 NUMB-OUT       PICTURE ZZZZZ9.
     02 FILLER         PICTURE X(8).
     02 UNITS-OUT      PICTURE Z9.
     02 FILLER         PICTURE X(7).
     02 TOTAL-OUT      PICTURE ZZ9.
     02 FILLER         PICTURE X(63).
PROCEDURE DIVISION.
START.
     OPEN INPUT STUDENT-FILE.
     OPEN OUTPUT PRINT-FILE.
NEXT-CARD.
     READ STUDENT-FILE RECORD AT END GO TO EOJ.
     MOVE SPACES TO PRINT-LINE.
     MOVE STUD-NAME TO NAME-OUT.
     MOVE STUD-NUMB TO NUMB-OUT.
     MOVE UNITS TO UNITS-OUT.
     MOVE TOTAL-UNITS TO TOTAL-OUT.
     WRITE PRINT-LINE.
     GO TO NEXT-CARD.
EOJ.
     CLOSE STUDENT-FILE, PRINT-FILE.
     STOP RUN.
ADAMS, PETER R.              13978          9      104
GOODMAN, HAROLD R.           20875         16        0
JOHNSON, SHARON C.           24432         15       74
LARSON, JAMES L.             47739          6       48
LEWIS,BARBARA C.              1339         18      107
ROTHSCHILD, CHARLES K.       80336         10      100
THOMPSON, LAURA W.           59325          7       88
```

Figure 14–8. *COBOL program for Example 1.*

Exercise 14-2

1. All COBOL programs are composed of four divisions. The names of these divisions, in the order that they appear in a program, are

   _____ , _____ , _____ , and _____ .

2. Which of the following program names are not valid?

'RECEIVABLES'	'2RUN'
'PAY-ROLL'	'SORT'
'INVENTORY'	'RUN2'

   _____ , _____ , _____ , _____ , _____ .

3. If a COBOL program is to run on a different computer, the only division that would change significantly is the _____ division.

4. The first time a file name appears in a COBOL program is in a

   _____ clause of the _____ division.

5. The file section of the data division consists of a hierarchy of entries for each file. First, there is a _____ description, next

   a _____ description and, finally, an _____
   description.

6. The length and type of data field is defined by a _____
   clause.

7. An item that is further subdivided is referred to as a _____

   item, while an item that is not further subdivided is called an

   _____ item.

8. State the result of each of the following MOVE operations:

	Sending field		Receiving field
Picture	Contents	Picture	Contents (after MOVE)
99V99	94.67	99V99	
99V99	94.67	99V9	
99V99	94.67	9V99	
A(4)	JOHN	A(4)	
	SPACES	A(8)	

9. The Environment Division contains two sections, the _____

   section and the _____-_____ section.

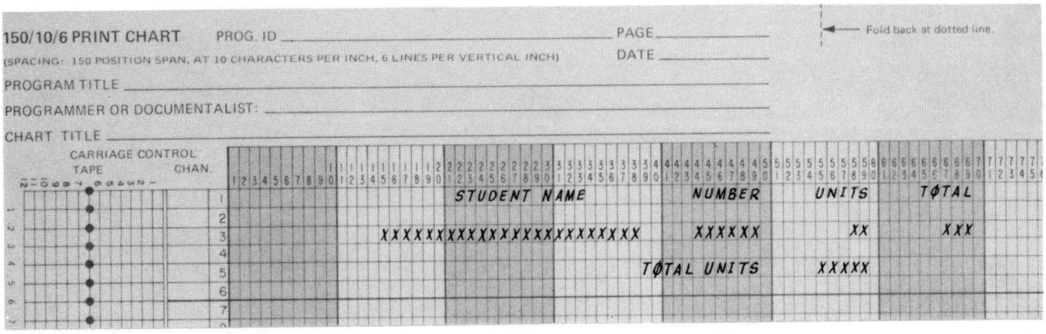

Figure 14-9. *Printer spacing chart for Example 2.*

10. In most COBOL programs the Data Division contains a _____

section and a _____-_____ section.

11. Division, section, and paragraph names are coded in margin _____.

Most other COBOL entries are coded in margin _____.

Example 2: Simple Calculations

This example introduces the use of calculations in a COBOL program. The card for each student is to be read, and "units taken this semester" is to be added to "total units to date" to obtain an updated total. The record is then to be printed, with the updated total replacing the previous total.

In addition to updating each record, the units taken this semester is to be totaled for all students and printed at the end of the listing. Header information is also to be printed at the top of the listing.

The input format for Example 2 is the same as for Example 1 (see Figure 14-2). Figure 14-9 shows the output format on a printer spacing chart.

Data Division

The principal changes in Example 2 are in the Data and Procedure divisions. The Data Division for this example is shown in Figure 14-10.

Example 2 introduces the use of the COBOL working storage section. *Working storage* contains a description of all constants, intermediate totals, and work areas that are not part of input or output. In the example, working storage is used to store header and trailer information, plus the quantity FTOTAL which is the running total of units taken by students this semester. There are two types of items in working storage: *group* items that are further subdivided, and *independent* data items that are not subdivided. Group items are coded at the 01 level, while independent data items are coded at the 77 level.

QUESTION: Examine the working storage section (Figure 14-10). Identify the group items and the independent data items: _____

_____.

375 / DATA DIVISION

```
DATA DIVISION.
FILE SECTION.
FD  STUDENT-FILE LABEL RECORDS ARE OMITTED
    DATA RECORD IS STUDENT-REC.
01  STUDENT-REC.
    02 FILLER           PICTURE X.
    02 STUD-NAME        PICTURE X(24).
    02 STUD-NUMB        PICTURE 9(6).
    02 UNITS            PICTURE 9(2).
    02 TOTAL-UNITS      PICTURE 9(3).
    02 FILLER           PICTURE X(44).
FD  PRINT-FILE LABEL RECORDS ARE OMITTED
    DATA RECORD IS DUMMY.
01  DUMMY.
    02 FILLER PICTURE X(133).
WORKING-STORAGE SECTION.
77  FTOTAL              PICTURE 9(5) VALUE ZERO.
01  PRINT-LINE.
    02  FILLER          PICTURE X(15).
    02  NAME-OUT        PICTURE X(24).
    02  FILLER          PICTURE X(5).
    02  NUMB-OUT        PICTURE ZZZZZ9.
    02  FILLER          PICTURE X(8).
    02  UNITS-OUT       PICTURE Z9.
    02  FILLER          PICTURE X(7).
    02  TOTAL-OUT       PICTURE ZZ9.
    02  FILLER          PICTURE X(63).
01  HEADER
    02 FILLER      PICTURE X(22).
    02 NAME-HDR    PICTURE A(12) VALUE 'STUDENT NAME'.
    02 FILLER      PICTURE X(11).
    02 NUMB-HDR    PICTURE A(6) VALUE 'NUMBER'.
    02 FILLER      PICTURE X(5).
    02 HRS-HDR     PICTURE A(5) VALUE 'UNITS'.
    02 FILLER      PICTURE X(5).
    02 TOT-HDR     PICTURE A(5) VALUE 'TOTAL'.
    02 FILLER      PICTURE X(22).
01  TRAILER
    02 FILLER      PICTURE X(38).
    02 TRLR        PICTURE A(11) VALUE 'TOTAL UNITS'.
    02 FILLER      PICTURE X(5).
    02 TOT-OUT     PICTURE ZZZZ9.
    02 FILLER      PICTURE X(74).
```

Figure 14-10. *Data Division for Example 2.*

ANSWER: Group items are PRINT-LINE, HEADER, and TRAILER; an independent item is FTOTAL

PRINT-LINE is used to assemble the output data for each student. HEADER and TRAILER are used to set up the print lines to appear at the beginning and at the end of the listing. Each of these three group items is moved to an output area called DUMMY before printing occurs.

Initial values are assigned to items in working storage by means of *value* clauses. The value clause contains either a literal or a figurative constant such as ZERO or SPACES. In Figure 14–10, for example, the entry STUDENT-NAME is stored in the field NAME-HDR, while the independent item FTOTAL is initialized with the value zero.

The literal in a value clause for an item should agree in size and type with the Picture clause for that item. In Figure 14–10, for example, the group item TRAILER contains a data item called TRLR, with Picture clause PICTURE A(11). The value to be stored in TRLR is TOTAL UNITS which is an alphabetic field with 11 positions (including space).

Procedure Division

The Procedure Division for Example 2 is shown in Figure 14–11. The example includes statements to add "units" to "total units" to obtain an updated total, and to accumulate units taken for all students.

In Figure 14–11, the following steps are performed.

1. Input and output files are opened.
2. The header line is moved from working storage to the output area and printed.

```
PROCEDURE DIVISION.
START.
    OPEN INPUT STUDENT-FILE OUTPUT PRINT-FILE.
    MOVE HEADER TO DUMMY.
    WRITE DUMMY AFTER ADVANCING 3 LINES.
NEXT-CARD.
    READ STUDENT-FILE AT END GO TO EOJ.
    ADD UNITS TO TOTAL-UNITS.
    ADD UNITS TO FTOTAL.
    MOVE SPACES TO DUMMY.
    MOVE STUD-NAME TO NAME-OUT.
    MOVE STUD-NUMB TO NUMB-OUT.
    MOVE UNITS TO UNITS-OUT.
    MOVE TOTAL-UNITS TO TOTAL-OUT.
    MOVE PRINT-LINE TO DUMMY.
    WRITE DUMMY AFTER ADVANCING 1 LINES.
    GO TO NEXT-CARD.
EOJ.
    MOVE FTOTAL TO TOT-OUT.
    MOVE TRAILER TO DUMMY.
    WRITE DUMMY AFTER ADVANCING 2 LINES.
    CLOSE STUDENT-FILE, PRINT-FILE.
    STOP RUN.
```

Figure 14–11. *Procedure Division for Example 2.*

3. A student card is read.
4. Units are added to total units and the cumulative sum (FTOTAL) is updated.
5. The record is processed and listed.
6. At end of file, the sum FTOTAL is moved into the record TRAILER, which is, in turn, moved to the output area and printed. Files are closed and the run is terminated.

This completes the description of the Data and Procedure divisions for Example 2. The complete COBOL program for this example is shown in Figure 14-12.

Arithmetic Statements

Arithmetic statements are at the core of many programs. Only the simple Add statement is used in Example 2. This section discusses the COBOL statements Add, Subtract, Multiply, Divide, and Compute.

Add. A simple Add statement has two possible formats:

Format 1   ADD $\begin{bmatrix} \text{data-name-1} \\ \text{(or)} \\ \text{literal} \end{bmatrix}$ TO (data-name-2)

Examples:

ADD A TO B
ADD 40 TO HOURS

In each example, the sum is stored in the second field, while the first field remains unchanged.

Format 2   ADD $\begin{bmatrix} \text{data-name-1} \\ \text{(or)} \\ \text{literal-1} \end{bmatrix}$ $\begin{bmatrix} \text{data-name-2} \\ \text{(or)} \\ \text{literal-2} \end{bmatrix}$ GIVING (data-name-3)

Examples:

ADD A, B GIVING C.
ADD A, 39.40 GIVING C.

In each example, the sum is stored in the third field (field C). The other fields remain unchanged.

The choice of format for the ADD statement depends on the result desired. If the contents of all operands are to be retained, format 2 (the GIVING format) should be used. Otherwise, the TO format may be used.

```
IDENTIFICATION DIVISION.
PROGRAM-ID. #PROB02#.
ENVIRONMENT DIVISION.
CONFIGURATION SECTION.
SOURCE-COMPUTER. 6400.
OBJECT-COMPUTER. 6400.
INPUT-OUTPUT SECTION.
FILE-CONTROL.
    SELECT STUDENT-FILE ASSIGN TO INPUT.
    SELECT PRINT-FILE ASSIGN TO OUTPUT.
DATA DIVISION.
FILE SECTION.
FD  STUDENT-FILE LABEL RECORDS ARE OMITTED
    DATA RECORD IS STUDENT-REC.
01  STUDENT-REC.
    02 FILLER        PICTURE X.
    02 STUD-NAME     PICTURE X(24).
    02 STUD-NUMB     PICTURE 9(6).
    02 UNITS         PICTURE 9(2).
    02 TOTAL-UNITS   PICTURE 9(3).
    02 FILLER        PICTURE X(44).
FD  PRINT-FILE LABEL RECORDS ARE OMITTED
    DATA RECORD IS DUMMY.
01  DUMMY.
    02 FILLER        PICTURE X(133).
WORKING-STORAGE SECTION.
77  FTOTAL           PICTURE 9(5) VALUE IS ZERO.
01  PRINT-LINE.
    02 FILLER        PICTURE X(15) VALUE IS SPACES.
    02 NAME-OUT      PICTURE X(24).
    02 FILLER        PICTURE X(5) VALUE IS SPACES.
    02 NUMB-OUT      PICTURE ZZZZZ9.
    02 FILLER        PICTURE X(8) VALUE IS SPACES.
    02 UNITS-OUT     PICTURE Z9.
    02 FILLER        PICTURE X(7) VALUE IS SPACES.
    02 TOTAL-OUT     PICTURE ZZ9.
    02 FILLER        PICTURE X(63) VALUE IS SPACES.
01  HEADER.
    02 FILLER        PICTURE X(22) VALUE IS SPACES.
    02 NAME-HDR      PICTURE A(12) VALUE IS #STUDENT NAME#.
    02 FILLER        PICTURE X(11) VALUE IS SPACES.
    02 NUMB-HDR      PICTURE A(6) VALUE IS #NUMBER#.
    02 FILLER        PICTURE X(5) VALUE IS SPACES.
    02 HRS-HDR       PICTURE A(5) VALUE IS #UNITS#.
    02 FILLER        PICTURE X(5) VALUE IS SPACES.
    02 TOT-HDR       PICTURE A(5) VALUE IS #TOTAL#.
    02 FILLER        PICTURE X(62) VALUE IS SPACES.
01  TRAILER.
    02 FILLER        PICTURE X(38) VALUE IS SPACES.
    02 TRLR          PICTURE A(11) VALUE IS #TOTAL UNITS#.
    02 FILLER        PICTURE X(6) VALUE IS SPACES.
    02 TOT-OUT       PICTURE ZZZZ9.
    02 FILLER        PICTURE X(73) VALUE IS SPACES.

PROCEDURE DIVISION.
START.
    OPEN INPUT STUDENT-FILE OUTPUT PRINT-FILE.
    MOVE HEADER TO DUMMY.
    WRITE DUMMY AFTER ADVANCING 3 LINES.
NEXT-CARD.
    READ STUDENT-FILE AT END GO TO EOJ.
    ADD UNITS TO TOTAL-UNITS.
    ADD UNITS TO FTOTAL.
    MOVE SPACES TO PRINT-LINE.
    MOVE STUD-NAME TO NAME-OUT.
    MOVE STUD-NUMB TO NUMB-OUT.
    MOVE UNITS TO UNITS-OUT.
    MOVE TOTAL-UNITS TO TOTAL-OUT.
    MOVE PRINT-LINE TO DUMMY.
    WRITE DUMMY AFTER ADVANCING 1 LINES.
    GO TO NEXT-CARD.
EOJ.
    MOVE FTOTAL TO TOT-OUT.
    MOVE TRAILER TO DUMMY.
    WRITE DUMMY AFTER ADVANCING 2 LINES.
    CLOSE STUDENT-FILE. PRINT-FILE.
    STOP RUN.
```

STUDENT NAME	NUMBER	UNITS	TOTAL
ADAMS, PETER R.	13978	9	113
GOODMAN, HAROLD R.	20875	16	16
JOHNSON, SHARON C.	24432	15	89
LARSON, JAMES L.	47739	6	54
LEWIS, BARBARA C.	1339	18	125
ROTHSCHILD, CHARLES K.	80336	10	110
THOMPSON, LAURA W.	59325	7	95
TOTAL UNITS		81	

Figure 14–12. *COBOL program and output for Example 2.*

379 / ARITHMETIC STATEMENTS

QUESTION: Suppose the three fields A, B, C contain the following numbers: A = 5, B = 7, C = 6. Indicate the contents of each of the fields after the following operations:

(a) ADD A TO B: A____, B____, C____

(b) ADD A, B GIVING C: A____, B____, C____.
ANSWER: (a) A_5_, B_12_, C_6_ ; (b) A_5_, B_7_, C_12_

Care must be taken to use arithmetic statement formats without alteration. For example, the following statement is *invalid:*

ADD A TO B GIVING C

It is illegal to use TO with the GIVING option. Instead, the expression ADD A,B GIVING C should be used.

Both formats may be expanded to include an arbitrary number of operands. For example, the following statements are valid:

ADD A, B, C, 109 TO D.
ADD INSURANCE, TAX, RETIREMENT GIVING DEDUCTIONS.

Subtract. The Subtract statement also has two formats. Some examples illustrate its usage.

SUBTRACT A FROM B.
SUBTRACT A FROM B GIVING C.
SUBTRACT A, B, 25 FROM D GIVING E.

QUESTION: Suppose the three fields A, B, C contain the following numbers: A = 5, B = 7, C = 6. Indicate the contents of each of the fields after the following operations:

(a) SUBTRACT A FROM B: A____, B____, C____.
(b) SUBTRACT A FROM B GIVING C: A____, B____, C____.
ANSWER: (a) A_5_, B_2_, C_6_ ; (b) A_5_, B_7_, C_2_

Multiply. The Multiply statement multiplies two quantities and stores the result in the second item, or if desired, in a third field. The following examples illustrate its usage.

MULTIPLY A BY B. (product in B)
MULTIPLY A BY B GIVING C. (product in C)
MULTIPLY HOURLY-RATE BY HOURS GIVING GROSS-PAY.

QUESTION: Suppose the three fields A, B, C contain the following numbers: A = 5, B = 7, C = 6. Indicate the contents of each of the fields after the following operations.
(a) MULTIPLY A BY B: A____, B____, C____.

(b) MULTIPLY A BY B GIVING C: A____, B____, C____.
ANSWER: (a) A_5_, B_35_, C_6_ ; (b) A_5_, B_7_, C_35_

Divide. The Divide statement also permits storing the quotient of two numbers in the second field or, by using a GIVING clause, in a third field. Examples are:

```
DIVIDE A INTO B. (quotient in B)
DIVIDE A INTO B GIVING C. (quotient in C)
DIVIDE 12 INTO SALES GIVING MONTHLY-SALES.
```

Compute. Although COBOL is not used for scientific applications, it is sometimes necessary to evaluate more complicated algebraic expressions. Such expressions could be evaluated by using several simple COBOL arithmetic statements. However, it is often easier to use the COMPUTE statement, which also permits exponentiation to be performed.

The general form of this statement is

$$\text{COMPUTE (data name)} = \text{(expression)}$$

In the expression after the equals sign, arithmetic symbols are used rather than COBOL reserved words such as ADD and MULTIPLY.

As an example, the compound amount in an interest calculation is computed using the formula AMOUNT = PRINCIPAL $\star$ (1+RATE) $\star\star$ PERIODS where $\star\star$ means exponentiation. This would be expressed in COBOL as follows:

$$\text{COMPUTE AMOUNT} = \text{PRINCIPAL} \star (1 + \text{RATE}) \star\star \text{PERIODS}.$$

Exercise 14–3

1. Descriptions of constants, intermediate totals and work areas used in

   a COBOL program are entered in the _____-_____

   section of the _____._____ division.

2. Two types of items contained in working storage are _____

   items and _____ _____ items.

3. Initial values may be assigned to items in working storage·by means

   of _____ clauses.

4. Indicate the content of FLDA in each of the following examples:

   (a) FLDA PICTURE 9(4) VALUE 329 _____

   (b) FLDA PICTURE 99V99 VALUE 3.29 _____

   (c) FLDA PICTURE 99V99 VALUE 623.294 _____

   (d) FLDA PICTURE A(10) VALUE 'LOIS MOREY' _____

   (e) FLDA PICTURE X(5) VALUE SPACES _____

5. Three fields, FLDA, FLDB, FLDC are defined as follows:

	FLDA	FLDB	FLDC
Picture	99V99	99V99	99V99
Present contents	4.50	17.75	56.25

Indicate the contents of each of the three fields after the following operations:

(a) ADD FLDA TO FLDB
(b) ADD FLDA, FLDB TO FLDC
(c) ADD FLDA, FLDB GIVING FLDC
(d) ADD FLDA TO FLDB GIVING FLDC
(e) SUBTRACT FLDA FROM FLDB
(f) SUBTRACT FLDA FROM FLDB GIVING FLDC
(g) SUBTRACT FLDA, FLDB FROM FLDC

	FLDA	FLDB	FLDC
(a)	____	____	____
(b)	____	____	____
(c)	____	____	____
(d)	____	____	____
(e)	____	____	____
(f)	____	____	____
(g)	____	____	____

6. Three fields, FLDA, FLDB, FLDC are defined as follows:

	FLDA	FLDB	FLDC
Picture	9	9V99	99V99
Present contents	4	9.60	20V37

Indicate the contents of each of the three fields after the following operations:

(a) MULTIPLY FLDA BY FLDB
(b) DIVIDE FLDA INTO FLDB
(c) DIVIDE FLDA INTO FLDB GIVING FLDC
(d) MULTIPLY FLDA BY FLDB GIVING FLDC

	FLDA	FLDB	FLDC
(a)	____	____	____
(b)	____	____	____
(c)	____	____	____
(d)	____	____	____

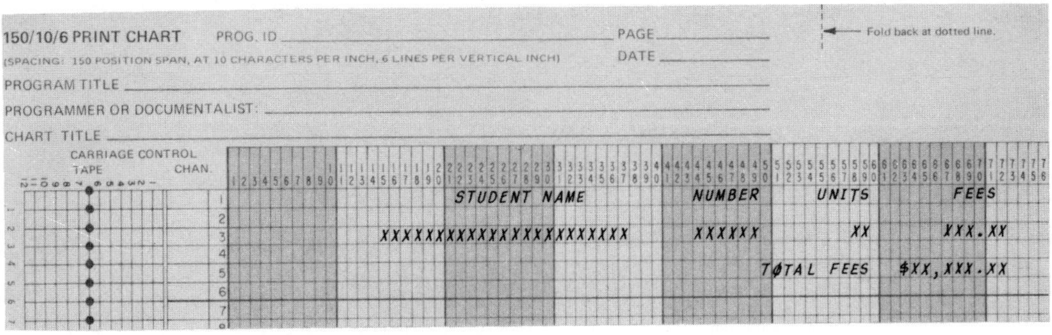

Figure 14–13. *Printer spacing chart for Example 3.*

> **7.** Write COBOL compute statements for each of the following expressions:
>
> (a) $Y = AX^2 + BX + C$
>
> (b) $HOURS = 1.5 (HOURS\text{-}WORKED - 40) + 40$
>
> (a) _____
>
> (b) _____

Example 3: Simple Logical Operations

This example introduces the use of simple comparisons or logical operations in COBOL. The student record is to be read, and tuition is to be computed according to the following formula:

> If Units is less than 12, tuition is UNITS times $35
> If Units is 12 or more, tuition is $420

Total student fees consist of tuition plus an incidental fee of $12.50. This total is to be printed along with student name, number, and units taken. Also total fees for all students is to be computed and printed at the end of the listing.

The input format for Example 3 is the same as for Examples 1 and 2 (see Figure 14–2). The desired output format is shown in Figure 14–13.

Procedure Division

The Identification, Environment, and Data divisions for Example 3 are substantially the same as for Example 2. Therefore, only the Procedure Division (shown in Figure 14–14) will be described in detail.

383 / PROCEDURE DIVISION

```
       PROCEDURE DIVISION.
       START.
           OPEN INPUT STUDENT-FILE OUTPUT PRINT-FILE.
           MOVE HEADER TO DUMMY.
           WRITE DUMMY AFTER ADVANCING 3 LINES.
       NEXT-CARD.
           READ STUDENT FILE AT END GO TO EOJ.
           IF UNITS IS LESS THAN 12 MULTIPLY UNITS BY
           35.00 GIVING TUITION ELSE MOVE 420.00 TO
           TUITION.
           ADD 12.50, TUITION GIVING FEES.
           ADD FEES TO TFEES. MOVE SPACES TO DUMMY.
           MOVE STUD-NAME TO NAME-OUT.
           MOVE STUD-NUMB TO NUMB-OUT.
           MOVE UNITS TO UNITS-OUT.
           MOVE FEES TO FEES-OUT.
           MOVE PRINT-LINE TO DUMMY.
           WRITE DUMMY AFTER ADVANCING 1 LINES.
           GO TO NEXT-CARD.
       EOJ. MOVE TFEES TO TOT-OUT.
           MOVE TRAILER TO DUMMY.
           WRITE DUMMY AFTER ADVANCING 2 LINES.
           CLOSE STUDENT-FILE, PRINT-FILE.
           STOP RUN.
```

Figure 14–14. *Procedure Division for Example 3.*

The main feature of this example is the conditional statement used as follows:

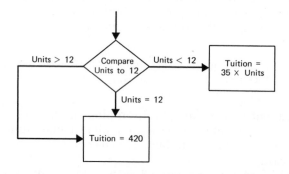

The comparison and resulting computation of tuition is expressed by this COBOL statement:

IF UNITS IS LESS THAN 12 MULTIPLY UNITS BY 35.00
GIVING TUITION ELSE MOVE 420.00 TO TUITION.

After tuition is computed, the $12.50 incidental fee is added to it to determine the total student fee, called FEES in Figure 14–14. FEES is then added to TFEES, which is the cumulative sum of fees for all students. At the end of the program, TFEES is printed in a total or trailer line.

384 / INTRODUCTION TO COBOL AND PL/1

The complete COBOL program for Example 3 is shown in Figure 14–15.

```
IDENTIFICATION DIVISION.
PROGRAM-ID. #PROB03#.
ENVIRONMENT DIVISION.
CONFIGURATION SECTION.
SOURCE-COMPUTER. 6400.
OBJECT-COMPUTER. 6400.
INPUT-OUTPUT SECTION.
FILE-CONTROL.
     SELECT STUDENT-FILE ASSIGN TO INPUT.
     SELECT PRINT-FILE ASSIGN TO OUTPUT.
DATA DIVISION.
FILE SECTION.
FD  STUDENT-FILE LABEL RECORDS ARE OMITTED
     DATA RECORD IS STUDENT-REC.
01  STUDENT-REC.
     02 FILLER        PICTURE X.
     02 STUD-NAME     PICTURE X(24).
     02 STUD-NUMB     PICTURE 9(6).
     02 UNITS         PICTURE 9(2).
     02 TOTAL-UNITS   PICTURE 9(3).
     02 FILLER        PICTURE X(44).
FD  PRINT-FILE LABEL RECORDS ARE OMITTED
     DATA RECORD IS DUMMY.
01  DUMMY.
     02 FILLER        PICTURE X(133).
WORKING-STORAGE SECTION.
77  TUITION          PICTURE 999V99.
77  TFEES            PICTURE 999999V99.
77  FEES             PICTURE 999V99.
01  PRINT-LINE.
     02 FILLER        PICTURE X(14).
     02 NAME-OUT      PICTURE X(23).
     02 FILLER        PICTURE X(6).
     02 NUMB-OUT      PICTURE 9(6).
     02 FILLER        PICTURE X(8).
     02 UNITS-OUT     PICTURE 9(2).
     02 FILLER        PICTURE X(7).
     02 FEES-OUT      PICTURE ZZ9.99.
     02 FILLER        PICTURE X(61).
01  HEADER.
     02 FILLER        PICTURE X(22) VALUE IS SPACES.
     02 NAME-HDR      PICTURE X(12) VALUE IS #STUDENT NAME#.
     02 FILLER        PICTURE X(9) VALUE IS SPACES.
     02 NUMB-HDR      PICTURE X(16) VALUE IS #NUMBER      UNITS#.
     02 FILLER        PICTURE X(7) VALUE IS SPACES.
     02 FEES-HDR      PICTURE X(4) VALUE IS #FEES#.
     02 FILLER        PICTURE X(63) VALUE IS SPACES.
01  TRAILER.
     02 FILLER        PICTURE X(50) VALUE IS SPACES.
     02 TRLR          PICTURE X(10) VALUE IS #TOTAL FEES#.
     02 FILLER        PICTURE X(2) VALUE IS SPACES.
     02 TOT-OUT       PICTURE $$$,$$9.99.
     02 FILLER        PICTURE X(61) VALUE IS SPACES.
PROCEDURE DIVISION.
START.
     OPEN INPUT STUDENT-FILE OUTPUT PRINT-FILE.
     MOVE HEADER TO DUMMY.
     WRITE DUMMY AFTER ADVANCING 3 LINES.
NEXT-CARD.
     READ STUDENT-FILE AT END GO TO EOJ.
     IF UNITS IS LESS THAN 12 MULTIPLY UNITS
     BY 35.00 GIVING TUITION ELSE MOVE 420.00 TO TUITION.
     ADD 12.50, TUITION GIVING FEES.
     ADD FEES TO TFEES.
     MOVE SPACES TO PRINT-LINE.
     MOVE STUD-NAME TO NAME-OUT.
     MOVE STUD-NUMB TO NUMB-OUT.
     MOVE UNITS TO UNITS-OUT.
     MOVE FEES TO FEES-OUT.
     MOVE PRINT-LINE TO DUMMY.
     WRITE DUMMY AFTER ADVANCING 1 LINE.
     GO TO NEXT-CARD.
EOJ.
     MOVE TFEES TO TOT-OUT.
     MOVE TRAILER TO DUMMY.
     WRITE DUMMY AFTER ADVANCING 2 LINES.
     CLOSE STUDENT-FILE, PRINT-FILE.
     STOP RUN.
```

STUDENT NAME	NUMBER	UNITS	FEES
ADAMS, PETER R.	013978	09	327.50
GOODMAN, HAROLD R.	020875	16	432.50
JOHNSON, SHARON C.	024432	15	432.50
LARSON, JAMES L.	047739	06	222.50
LEWIS, BARBARA C.	001339	18	432.50
ROTHSCHILD, CHARLES K.	080336	10	362.50
THOMPSON, LAURA W.	059325	07	257.50
		TOTAL FEES	$2,447.69

Figure 14–15. *COBOL program for Example 3.*

Sequence Control. Program statements in the procedure division are executed sequentially unless some type of branching instruction is encountered. This section discusses the major types of statements used to control the flow of a COBOL program. These include the GO TO statement, IF statement, PERFORM statement, and STOP statement.

Go to Statement. Frequently in a program it is desired to transfer control from one part of the program to another. This is accomplished with the GO TO statement, which may be written in unconditional or conditional form.

The form of the *unconditional* GO TO statement is as follows:

GO TO (paragraph name).

In all three examples discussed in this chapter the following statement is used to return to read another student card:

GO TO NEXT-CARD

The form of the *conditional* GO TO statement is

GO TO (paragraph-name-1), paragraph-name-2, . . . paragraph-name-n)
DEPENDING ON (data-name).

An example is the following:

GO TO SALES, PAYMENTS, RETURNS DEPENDING ON CODE.

In this statement, the program will branch to the paragraph SALES if the current value of CODE is 1; if CODE equals 2, it will branch to PAYMENTS; and if CODE equals 3, it will branch to RETURNS. If CODE is not equal to an integer value of 1, 2, or 3, the conditional GO TO statement is ignored, and the program goes to the next sequential instruction.

QUESTION: Examine the following COBOL statement:

GO TO (FRESH, SOPH, JR, SR) DEPENDING ON CLASS.

To what paragraph will the program branch if CLASS is equal to 2?

_____ 4? _____ 7? _____ .

ANSWER: SOPH, SR, next sequential instruction

IF Statement. The path to be taken in a program often depends on the result of comparing two quantities. In Example 3, the calculation of student tuition depended on the number of units taken. The testing of a condition and branching depending on the result is accomplished with a COBOL If statement. In Example 3, the statement is as follows:

IF UNITS IS LESS THAN 12 MULTIPLY UNITS BY 35.00
GIVING TUITION ELSE MOVE 420.00 TO TUITION.

The general form of the IF statement is

IF (test condition) (statement-1) ELSE (statement-2).

The *test condition* generally specifies a relation between two quantities. The general form is:

$$\begin{bmatrix} \text{data-name-1} \\ \text{(or)} \\ \text{literal} \end{bmatrix} \quad \text{(relational operator)} \quad \begin{bmatrix} \text{data-name-2} \\ \text{(or)} \\ \text{literal} \end{bmatrix}$$

The *relational operator* specifies the type of comparison. It may be any one of the following:

IS EQUAL TO (or =)
IS GREATER THAN (or >)
IS LESS THAN (or <)
IS NOT EQUAL TO
IS NOT GREATER THAN
IS NOT LESS THAN

Following are several examples of the use of the If statement.

Example	*Comment*
IF A IS GREATER THAN B GO TO START	If A is less than or equal to B, the program goes to the next sequential instruction.
IF A IS GREATER THAN B GO TO NEXT ELSE GO TO START	The program branches to either NEXT or START, depending on the relation between A and B.
IF PAYMENT IS GREATER THAN BALANCE GO TO ADJUST ELSE SUBTRACT PAYMENT FROM BALANCE	If PAYMENT is less than or equal to BALANCE, it is subtracted from BALANCE and the program goes to the next sequential instruction.
IF A < B ADD C TO D GO TO FIRST ELSE MULTIPLY A BY C GIVING E GO TO START	Several COBOL statements may be executed for each test condition.

QUESTION: Suppose six fields contain the following data: FLDA 12, FLDB 7, A 14, B 3, C 6, D 9. What are the contents of each field after executing the following instruction:

IF FLDA IS NOT EQUAL TO FLDB ADD A TO B
ELSE SUBTRACT C FROM D.

FLDA____, FLDB____, A____, B____, C____, D____.

ANSWER: A 14, B 17, C 6, D 9, FLDA 12, FLDB 7.

Perform. Much like a subroutine call, a Perform statement permits execution of a specified routine from several points in a program. The format is as follows:

PERFORM (paragraph name).

The Perform statement will execute all statements in the named paragraph, and will transfer control to the next sequential step following the Perform statement.

Following is an example:

> PERFORM PRINT-OUT.
> GO TO START.
> .
> .
> .
> PRINT-OUT.
> WRITE PRINT-LINE.

The Perform statement will cause the record PRINT-LINE to be written, and then will transfer control to the following statement, which results in a branch to START.

There are several options to the Perform statement that increase its power and flexibility. The following forms may be used:

> PERFORM (paragraph-name-1) THRU (paragraph-name-n).
> PERFORM (paragraph-name-1) THRU (paragraph-name-n)

$$\begin{bmatrix} \text{integer} \\ \text{(or)} \\ \text{data-name} \end{bmatrix} \quad \text{TIMES.}$$

> PERFORM (paragraph-name-1) THRU (paragraph-name-n)
>   UNTIL (condition).
> PERFORM (paragraph-name-1) THRU (paragraph-name-n)
>   VARYING (data-name-1) FROM (data-name-2)
>   BY (data-name-3) UNTIL (condition).

The last form resembles a FORTRAN DO statement.

Stop. The Stop statement causes either a temporary or permanent halt in program execution.

The following statement will cause a permanent halt:

> STOP RUN

A temporary halt will result if a literal is used in place of RUN:

> STOP (literal)

An example of this option is:

> STOP 'ERROR'.

The computer will stop and print the literal on the console typewriter. When the start button is pushed, continuation of the run begins with the next sequential statement.

Exercise 14–4

1. Write a COBOL IF statement corresponding to the following test condition:

Order and Next item are paragraph names.

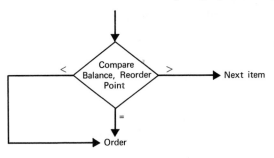

2. Write a COBOL GO TO statement corresponding to the following test condition:

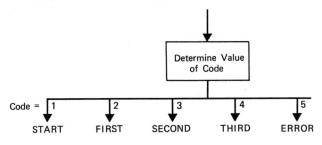

PL/1 Programming

Programming Language/One (or PL/1) is a high-level language that was developed jointly by IBM and major users of IBM computers. It combines the major features of COBOL and FORTRAN (as well as certain other languages) into a language of great power and versatility. Although PL/1 is a general purpose language, it is not a universal language, since it is not available on many non-IBM computers. As a result, COBOL is more widely used in business applications, and FORTRAN is more widely used in scientific applications. Nevertheless PL/1 is an important language that could ultimately become standard for large computer applications.

The use of PL/1 for Example 3 is shown in Figure 14–16. This same example has been programmed in COBOL (Figure 14–15), FORTRAN (Figure 13–21), and BASIC (Figure 13–23) to enable the reader to compare the four major languages.

The main features of the PL/1 program for this example are the following.

1. PROCEDURE OPTIONS statement which identifies the main program and assigns it the name STUDENT. This statement (except for the name) is standard for all PL/1 programs.
2. DECLARE statements which identify the variables used in the program and their type. For example, the last DECLARE statement identifies a floating point variable called CUMFEES and assigns it the initial value zero.
3. GET and PUT statements for input and output of data. GET EDIT statements cause data to be read according to the end of the statement. Similarly, PUT SKIP EDIT statements cause data to be edited and printed out. The format statements resemble those in FORTRAN, although COBOL-like picture clauses may be used (as in the last PUT statement).
4. Procedure statements (for computing student fees and total fees) are very similar to the corresponding COBOL statements (see Figure 14–16).

QUESTION: PL/1 procedure statements closely resemble those of _____, while editing symbols for input and output resemble those of _____.

ANSWER: COBOL, FORTRAN

```
PL/1 Coding & Keypunch Form

Program Name/No.                    Date          Prepared By           Page      Of      Pages

/* PL/1 PROGRAM FOR EXAMPLE 3 */
STUDENT:      PROCEDURE OPTIONS(MAIN);
              DECLARE NAME CHARACTER (24);
              DECLARE (NUMBER, UNITS, TUITION, FEES) FLOAT;
              DECLARE CUMFEES FLOAT INITIAL (0);
              PUT SKIP EDIT (X(21),'STUDENT NAME',X(10),'NUMBER',X(5),
              'UNITS',X(8),'FEES');
              ON ENDFILE (SYSIN) GO TO JOBEND;
NEXT CARD:    GET EDIT (NAME, NUMBER, UNITS) (X(1), A(24), F(6,0), F(2,0));
              IF UNITS < 12 THEN TUITION = 35 * UNITS
              ELSE TUITION = 420;
              FEES = TUITION + 12.50; *
              CUMFEES = CUMFEES + FEES;
JOBEND:       PUT SKIP EDIT (NAME, NUMBER, UNITS, FEES) (X(14), A(24),
              X(5), F(6,0), X (8), F(2,0), X(7), F(6,2));
              P'$$,$$9V.99');
              END STUDENT;
```

Figure 14–16. PL/1 program for Example 3.

Solutions to Exercises

Exercise 14–1

1. COBOL.
2. Common Business Oriented Language.
3. COBOL.
4. Conference on Data Systems Languages.
5. Is not.
6. Machine-independent.

Exercise 14–2

1. Identification, Environment, Data, Procedure.
2. In many compilers, the following are invalid:

    RECEIVABLES (exceeds 8 characters)
    PAY-ROLL (special character)
    INVENTORY (exceeds 8 characters)
    2RUN (first character not a letter)

3. Environment.
4. Select, Environment.
5. File, record, item.
6. Picture.
7. Group, elementary.

8.

Sending Field		Receiving Field	
Picture	Contents	Picture	Contents
99V99	9467	99V99	9467
99V99	9467	99V9	946
99V99	9467	9V99	467
A(4)	JOHN	A(4)	JOHN
	SPACES	A(8)	bbbbbbbb

9. Configuration, input-output.

10. File, working-storage.

11. A, B.

Exercise 14–3

1. Working-storage, data.

2. Group, independent data.

3. Value.

4. (a) 0329,   (b) 0329,   (c) 2329,   (d) LOIS MOREY,   (e) bbbbb.

5.

	FLDA	FLDB	FLDC
(a)	450	2225	5625
(b)	450	1775	7850
(c)	450	1775	2225
(d)	Illegal		
(e)	450	1325	5625
(f)	450	1775	1325
(g)	450	1775	3400

6.

	FLDA	FLDB	FLDC
(a)	4	840	2037
(b)	4	240	2037
(c)	4	960	0240
(d)	4	960	3840

7. (a) COMPUTE Y = A ∗ X ∗∗ 2 + B ∗ X + C
    (b) COMPUTE HOURS = 1.5 ∗ (HOURS-WORKED − 40) + 40

Exercise 14–4

1.   IF BALANCE IS GREATER THAN REORDER-POINT GO TO NEXT-ITEM ELSE GO TO ORDER.

2.   GO TO (START, FIRST, SECOND, THIRD, ERROR) DEPENDING ON CODE.

Chapter Examination

1. Each of the following statements contains one error. Identify each error.

    (a) ADD A, B TO C GIVING D _____

    (b) DIVIDE A BY G GIVING C _____

    (c) MULTIPLY X TIMES Y _____

    (d) MOVE A INTO B _____

    (e) DIVIDE A INTO 20 _____

2. Fill in the "after" line in each of the following statements:

		A	B	
(a) MOVE A TO B	Before	139	620	
	After	___	___	

		A	B	C
(b) ADD A, B TO C.	Before	9	5	18
	After	___	___	___

		A	D	F
(c) SUBTRACT A FROM D GIVING F.	Before	9	42	91
	After	___	___	___

		A	B	S
(d) MULTIPLY A BY B GIVING S.	Before	11	4	50
	After	___	___	___

		A	B	
(e) DIVIDE A INTO B	Before	4	20	
	After	___	___	

3. Write COBOL statements for each of the following:

(a) There are two data items called QUANTITY and AMOUNT in storage. Write a statement to make the value of AMOUNT the same as the value of QUANTITY, leaving the latter unchanged.

_____

(b) Write a statement to make the value of QUANTITY equal to zero.

_____

(c) Move the literal JOHN DOE to a field called NAME.

_____

(d) Determine whether the value of BALANCE is greater than 50; if so, transfer to a paragraph called NEXT; if not, subract AMOUNT

from BALANCE. _____

4. A salesman's commission is calculated based on the type of product, as follows:

PRODUCT-CODE	COMMISSION
1	(0.15) x (SALES-PRICE)
2	(0.30) x (SALES-PRICE)
3	$50 + (.10) x (SALES-PRICE)
4	$100

Given values for PRODUCT-CODE and SALES-PRICE, write COBOL statements to compute COMMISSION.

_____

_____

_____

_____

_____

5. Identify the errors in each of the following:

(a) WORKING STORAGE SECTION _____

(b) 02 BALANCE PICTURE 9(5) VALUE '50' _____

(c) FILE-SECTION _____

(d) 02 BALANCE PICTURE 9(5). VALUE ZERO _____

(e) 03 NAME PICTURE X(6) VALUE 'HOSTETTLER' _____

6. Following is a student record layout:

STUDENT-REC					
NAME	MATRIC-DATE			NUMBER	ADDRESS	GP-AVE
	MONTH	DAY	YEAR			

Each item is as follows:

NAME	20 letters
MONTH	2 digits
DAY	2 digits
YEAR	2 digits
NUMBER	6 digits
ADDRESS	20 alphanumeric
GP-AVE	3 digits, 2 decimal places

Write a complete COBOL record description:

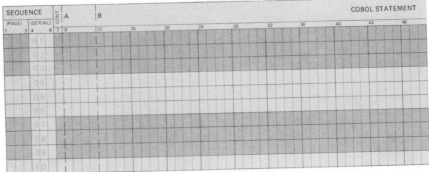

7. Fill in the "edited result" column in each of the following:

Source Area		Receiving Area	
Picture	Sample Data	Picture	Edited Result
9(5)	00345	ZZZ,999	
999V99	02345	Z,ZZ9.99	
999V99	02345	$,$$9.99	
9(5)	00003	ZZ,999	

8. Write a COBOL program for problem 11 of Chapter 13 (coding sheets are provided at the end of the Chapter Examination).
9. Write a COBOL program for problem 12 of Chapter 13 (coding sheets are provided at the end of the Chapter Examination).
10. Write a COBOL program for problem 14 of Chapter 13 (coding sheets are provided at the end of the Chapter Examination).
11. Write a COBOL program for problem 15 of Chapter 13 (coding sheets are provided at the end of the Chapter Examination).
12. What are the principal differences between PL/1 and COBOL?

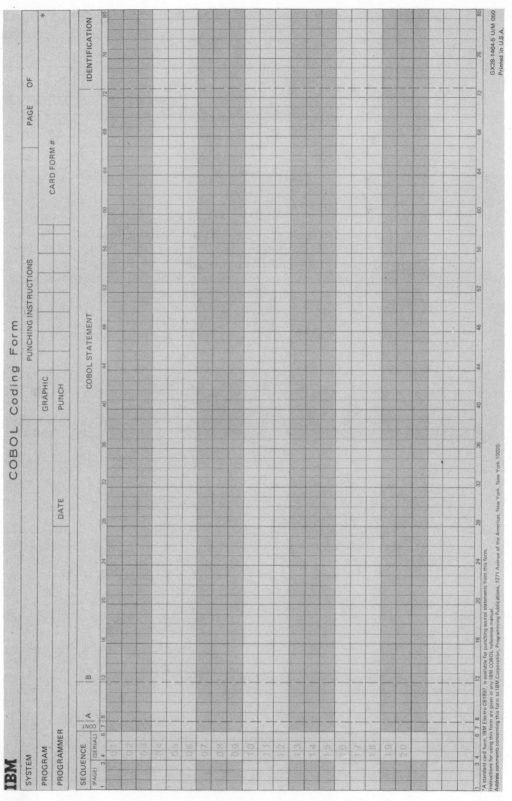

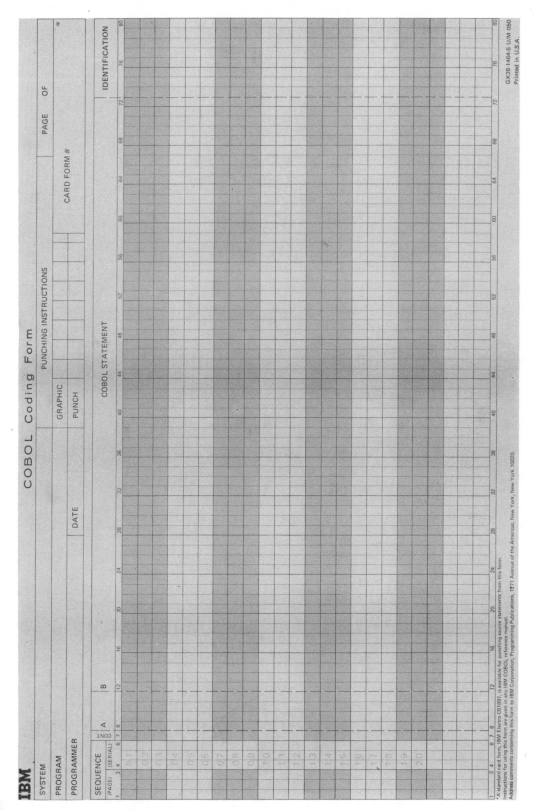

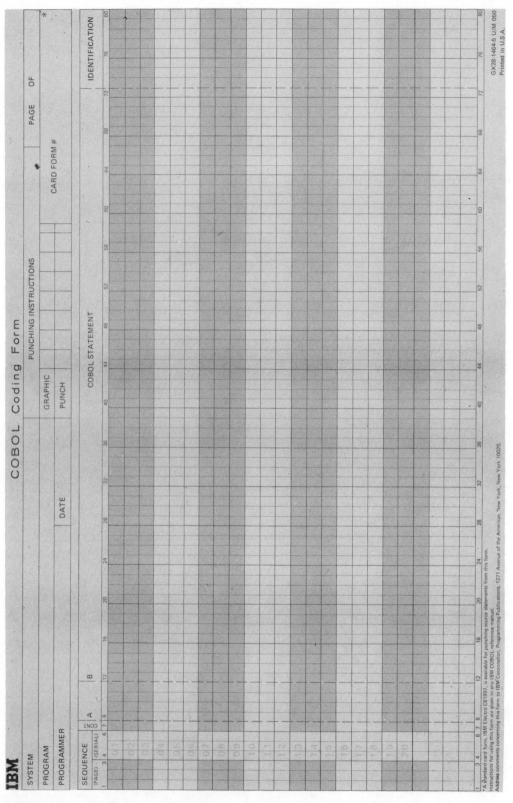

COBOL Coding Form

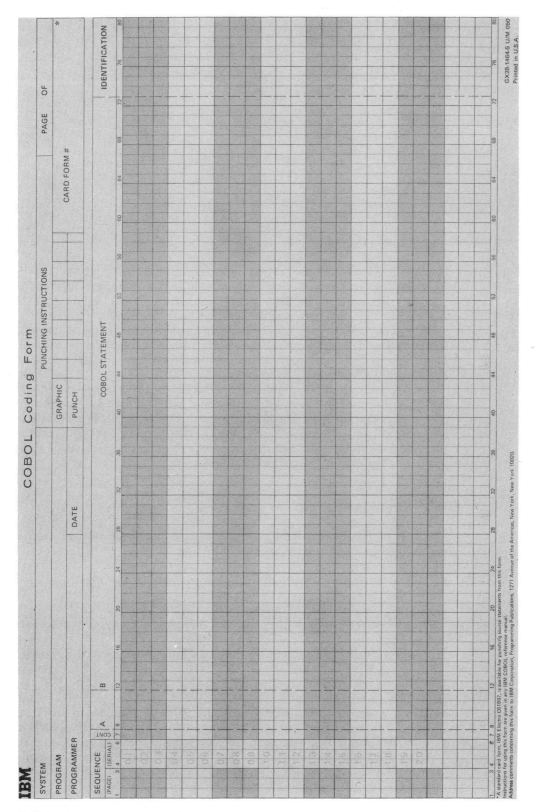

COBOL Coding Form

Chapter 15

INTRODUCTION TO RPG II

Overview

Report Program Generator, or RPG, provides an efficient method for writing computer instructions for many simple data processing jobs. RPG is particularly useful for the generation of routine business reports in situations where file structures and computational procedures are relatively simple. The language is widely used in many small business systems, for example, IBM System/3, and is also gaining wide acceptance in medium and large-scale computer installations where it is often used in addition to COBOL or other languages.

RPG is a high-order, problem-oriented language. The user starts with a desired format for a listing or report and writes a set of specifications for the report and the input file to be used. The language is particularly easy to learn and use, and does not require knowledge of machine instructions or lengthy training and experience. The current version of RPG, termed RPG II, is described in this chapter.

RPG Specification Forms

RPG programs are recorded on a series of specification forms. The forms required for most programs are the following.

(a) **File Description Specifications.** Entries describe the files to be used by the program.
(b) **Input Specifications.** Entries describe input records.
(c) **Calculation Specifications.** Entries describe calculation and data manipulation.
(d) **Output-Format Specifications.** Entries describe output record formats.

Some programs require the use of tables, such as tax tables or frequency distributions. For such programs, the format and size of the tables are described on an additional form, termed the *File Extension Specifications*. This form will not be used in this chapter.

The RPG Specification forms (except File Extension) are shown in Figure 15–1. After the forms have been completed for a given program, they are ready to be keypunched to obtain the source deck.

IBM

International Business Machines Corporation
GX21-9094-1 U/M 050*
Printed in U.S.A.

RPG INPUT SPECIFICATIONS

Date _____
Program _____
Programmer _____

Punching Instruction | Graphic | | Punch |

Page 1 2

Program Identification 75 76 77 78 79 80

Record Identification Codes
1 2 3

Field Location

Field Indicators

IBM

International Business Machines Corporation
GX21-9093-1 U/M 050*
Printed in U.S.A.
*No. of forms per pad may vary slightly

RPG CALCULATION SPECIFICATIONS

Date _____
Program _____
Programmer _____

Punching Instruction | Graphic | | Punch |

Page 1 2

Program Identification 75 76 77 78 79 80

Indicators

| Line | Type | | And | And | Factor 1 | Operation | Factor 2 | Result Field | Field Length | | | Resulting Indicators Arithmetic | | | | Comments |

Plus | Minus | Zero
Compare
High | Low | Equal
1 > 2 | 1 < 2 | 1 = 2

IBM

International Business Machines Corporation
GX21-9092-2 UM/050*
Printed in U.S.A.

RPG CONTROL CARD AND FILE DESCRIPTION SPECIFICATIONS

Date _____
Program _____
Programmer _____

Punching Instruction | Graphic | | Punch |

Page 1 2

Program Identification 75 76 77 78 79 80

Control Card Specifications

Sterling | Model 20 | Model 20 | Dump Conversion

IBM

International Business Machines Corporation
GX21-9090-1 U/M 050*
Printed in U.S.A.

RPG OUTPUT - FORMAT SPECIFICATIONS

Date _____
Program _____
Programmer _____

Punching Instruction | Graphic | | Punch |

Page 1 2

Program Identification 75 76 77 78 79 80

| | | | Space | Skip | Output Indicators | | | | | | Edit Codes | | | | | | |

| Line | Form Type | Type (H/D/T/E) | Stacker Select/Fetch Overflow (F) | Before | After | Before | After | Not | And | Not | And | Not | Field Name | Edit Codes | Blank After (B) | End Position in Output Record | Packed/B = Binary | | | | | | | Sterling Sign Position |

Commas	Zero Balances to Print	No Sign	CR	-	X = Remove Plus Sign
Yes	Yes	1	A	J	Y = Date Field Edit
Yes	No	2	B	K	Z = Zero Suppress
No	Yes	3	C	L	
No	No	4	D	M	

Constant or Edit Word

3 4 5 | 6 | 7 8 9 10 11 12 13 14 | 15 | 16 | 17 18 | 19 20 | 21 22 | 23 | 24 | 25 | 26 | 27 | 28 | 29 30 | 31 | 32 33 34 35 36 37 | 38 | 39 | 40 41 42 43 | 44 | 45 46 47 48 49 50 51 52 53 54 55 56 57 58 59 60 61 62 63 64 65 66 67 68 69 70 | 71 72 73 74

0 1 0

Figure 15-1. *RPG Specification forms.*

QUESTION: What specification forms are required for most RPG programs? _____

_____.

ANSWER: File Description, Input, Calculation, Output-Format

At the top of each specification form, space is provided for general information about the program. Entries include program name, programmer, date, and punching instructions. These entries are not punched on the RPG program cards.

401 / RPG SPECIFICATION FORMS

Program specifications are recorded in positions 1 to 80 of the RPG Specification Forms. There are four basic entries that are common to all of the forms. These are: Page Number, Line Number, Form Type, and Program Identification.

Page Number (positions 1–2) The pages of each specification form may be numbered for reference. The pages are numbered beginning with the File Description Specification, in ascending order as follows:

> File Description page(s)
> Input Specification page(s)
> Calculation Specification page(s)
> Output-Format page(s)

Line Number (positions 3–5). Each specification line is normally identified by a line number. The first two digits are preprinted on the specification form and Position 5 is normally left blank, so that lines are numbered 010, 020, 030, and so on. Then if it is necessary to add an entry between two lines, the entry may be given a subnumber such as 015, 026, and so on.

Form Type (position 6). Each specification form has a type code preprinted in column 6. This code must be punched into the specification cards. These codes are as follows:

> F   File Description Specifications
> I   Input Specifications
> C   Calculation Specifications
> O   Output-Format Specifications

Program Identification (positions 75–80). An entry identifying the program may be placed in positions 75 to 80. Entries in these positions are not punched into the source deck, but into columns 75 to 80 of a control card that precedes the source deck. The Program Identification entry appears on the program listing, but does not affect the object program.

QUESTION: What are the four entries common to all of the RPG specification forms? _____

_____

Which of the entries are *required* to be punched into the source deck?

_____

_____.

ANSWER: Page number, Line number, Form type, and Program identification. Of these, only Form type is required. However, the others are recommended

In addition to the above entries, comment lines may be inserted on any of the RPG specification forms to improve documentation. An asterisk (★) in position 7 specifies that a comment follows. Comments appear on the program listing, but do not affect the program.

To illustrate the basic concepts of RPG programming, three example problems will be introduced in the remainder of the chapter. These examples are all based on processing a student record file.

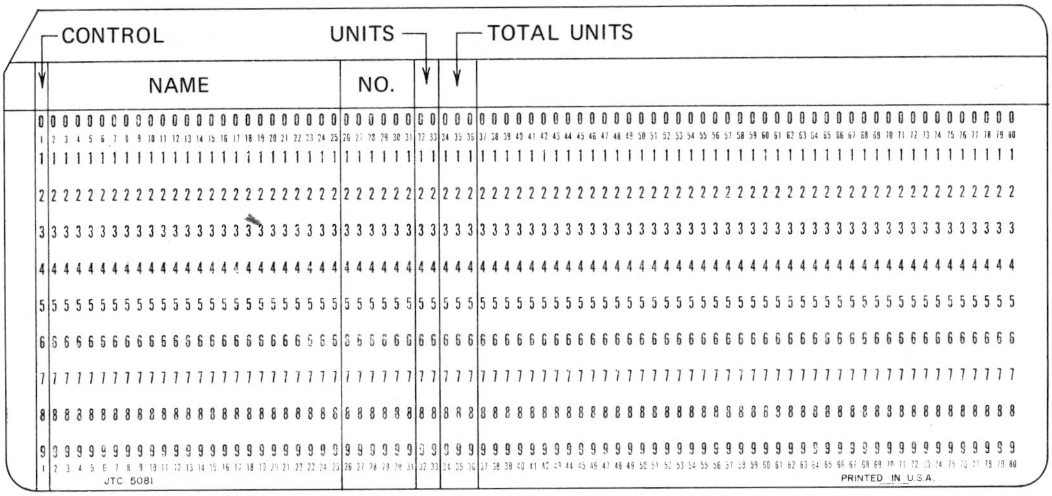

Figure 15-2. *Input student record card.*

Example 1: Basic Input-Output Operations

A student file is maintained on punched cards, one card record per student. The format of the records is shown in Figure 15-2. Each card contains student name (columns 2-25), number (26-31), units taken this semester (32-33), and total units prior to this semester (34-36). In addition, column 1 contains an "S" control punch.

An output listing is to be prepared from the cards. Each card field is to be printed, with blank spaces between fields. Leading zeros (if any) are to be suppressed for numeric fields. A printer spacing chart of the output format is shown in Figure 15-3.

File Description Specifications

The first step in writing an RPG program for this example is to describe the input and output files. This information is recorded on the File Description Specifications form. The entries for the example are shown in Figure 15-4.

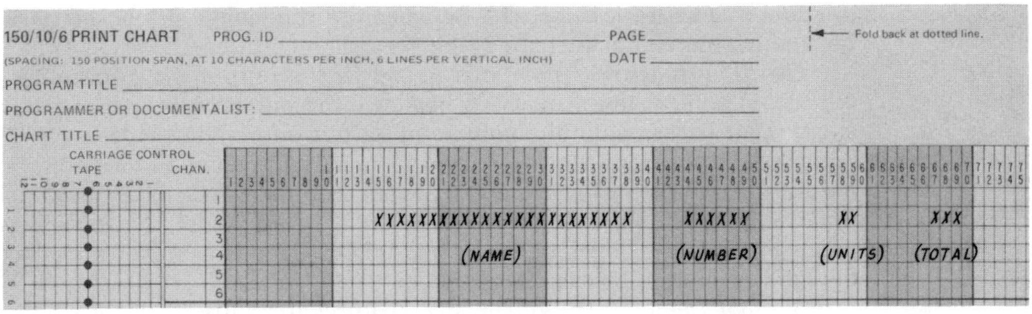

Figure 15-3. *Printer spacing chart for Example 1.*

403 / FILE DESCRIPTION SPECIFICATION

IBM

International Business Machines Corporation

RPG   CONTROL CARD AND FILE DESCRIPTION SPECIFICATION

Date __7/19__

Program __STUDENT LIST__

Programmer __FRM__

Punching Instruction — Graphic: Ø O — Punch: Zero II-6

Line	Filename	Form Type	File Type	File Designation	End of File	Sequence	File Format	Block Length	Record Length	Mode of Processing	Length of Key Field or of Record Address Field	Record Address Type	Type of File Organization or Additional Area	Overflow Indicator	Key Field Starting Location	Extension Code E/L	Device	Symbolic Device	Labels S/N/E/M	Name Label
0 2	Ø F STUDFL		I	P			F	8Ø	8Ø								READ4Ø	SYSRDR		
0 3	Ø F PRINTFL		O				F	132	132					ØF			PRINTER	SYSLST		
0 4	F																			

Figure 15–4. *File Description Specifications for Example 1.*

File Name (positions 7–14) is used to assign symbolic names to input and output files. In the example, the input file was called STUDFL; the output file was called PRINTFL. File names must start with a letter, may be up to seven characters long, and are left justified in the field. File names are referenced by the programmer at other points in the RPG program.

QUESTION: The names STUDFL and PRINTFL are mnemonics. What terms do they stand for? _____

_____

ANSWER: Student File, Print File

File Type (position 15) is used to designate whether the file is input (I), output (O), or some other type. In Figure 15–4, STUDFL is designated I, PRINTFL is designated O.

File Format (position 19) specifies whether the input records are fixed length (F) or variable length (V). In the example both files are designated F.

Record Length (positions 24–27) specifies the length of input and output records. For STUDFL the record length is 80 (corresponding to card columns); for PRINTFL the record length is 132 (corresponding to print positions).

Block Length (positions 20–23) specifies the length of blocked data. For the example, block length is the same as record length.

Overflow Indicator (positions 33–34 in the output file description) is used to control the printing of header information on the second and subsequent pages, when the volume of output information is large.

Device (positions 40–46) is used to specify the name of the input or output unit. The appropriate entry depends on the device being used. In the example, cards are read from an IBM 2501 card reader, whose device name is READ40. The output unit is an IBM 2203 printer, which has device designation PRINTER.

Symbol Device (positions 47–52) requires the entry SYSRDR for the 2501 card reader and SYSLST for the 2203 printer.

QUESTION: Of the above entries on the File Description Specifications, which are at the programmers option? _____

_____

ANSWER: Only File Name (STUDFL and PRINTFL). The remaining entries are determined by file characteristics and devices used

Input Specifications

Now that the files to be used have been described, the next step is to complete the input format specifications. The entries in Figure 15–5 provide the specifications for Example 1.

File Name (positions 7–14) repeats the symbolic name of the input file, in this case STUDFL. Each input file named on the File Specifications form must be described on Input Specifications.

Sequence (position 15) allows for checking the sequence of records within a control group. This feature is not used in Example 1. When sequence checking is not used, RPG requires the entry of any two alphabetic characters. In Figure 15–5, the letters AA are used arbitrarily to meet this requirement.

Resulting Indicator (positions 19–20) represents an important feature of the RPG language. With RPG every input card must contain a control punch. If the control punch is present when the card is read, a "record identifying indicator" is turned on and the card is processed. If the control punch is not present, the card is not processed, and the next card is read.

The "record identifying indicator" is referenced by a two-digit number from 01 to 99. In the example, the Resulting Indicator is arbitrarily assigned the number 01.

IBM

International Business Machines Corporation

RPG   INPUT SPECIFICATIONS

Date _7/19_

Program _STUDENT LIST_

Programmer _FRM_

| Punching Instruction | Graphic | 0 Ø | | | | Page |
| | Punch | 1/-6 Zero | | | | |

Line	Form Type	Filename	Sequence	Number (1-N) Option (O)	Record Identifying Indicator or **	Position 1	Not (N)	C/Z/D	Character	Position 2	Not (N)	C/Z/D	Character	Position 3	Not (N)	C/Z/D	Character	Stacker Select	P = Packed/B = Binary	From	To	Decimal Positions	Field Name
0 1	Ø I	STUDFL		AA	Ø1	Ø1		C S														
0 2	Ø I																		2	26		NAME
0 3	Ø I																		27	31	Ø	STNO
0 4	Ø I																		32	33	Ø	UNITS
0 5	Ø I																		34	36	Ø	TOTAL
0 6	I																					

Figure 15–5. *Input Specifications for Example 1.*

Position (columns 21–24) indicates the card column that contains the control punch. In Example 1, the control punch is contained in column 1 of the student cards.

C/Z/D (position 26) indicates the *type* of control punch used; the punch may be a character (letter), designated by C; a zone punch (Z), or a digit (D). In this example, a letter (S) is used, so the appropriate entry is C.

Character (position 27) indicates the actual control code character used. In this example, the letter S is entered in position 27.

QUESTION: To summarize, the above entries will cause the program to check for the character _____ in card column _____ of each student record. If the character is present, record identifying indicator _____ is turned on and the card is _____.

ANSWER: S; 1; 01; processed

Field Name (positions 53–58) is used to assign a symbolic name to fields (or data items) contained in the file whose name appears in positions 7 to 14. All fields to be processed must be described. Field name must begin with a letter and may contain up to six characters.

QUESTION: In Example 1 (Figure 15–5) the field names are _____, _____, _____, and _____.

ANSWER: NAME, STNO, UNITS, TOTAL

Field Location (positions 44–51) specifies the card columns containing the fields named above. *From (positions 44–47)* indicates the beginning card column of each field, and *To (position 53–58)* the ending card columns. For example, STNO begins in column 27 and ends in column 31.

Decimal Positions (position 52) indicate the number of decimal positions in a numeric field. Whenever a numeric field is to be zero suppressed or edited on output, or involved in a calculation, an entry must appear in Decimal Position. Since the fields STNO, UNITS, and TOTAL are to be zero suppressed when listed, an entry is required in position 52. Since the fields are integer numbers, the entry Ø (zero) is recorded for each field.

Output-Format Specifications

The RPG Output-Format Specifications form is used to describe output records, and is similar to the Input Specification form. The Output-Format Specifications for Example 1 is shown in Figure 15–6.

File Name (positions 7–14) is used to record the name of the output file, in this case, PRINTFL.

Type (position 15) indicates when the output is to occur. An output may be a header (H), detail (D), or Total (T). The listing of Example 1 is to occur at detail time (D).

Output Indicators (positions 24–25) controls the printing of output. On the Input Specifications the indicator 01 was designated to be turned on when a valid student record was read. The effect of entering indicator number 01 in positions 24 to 25 is to cause a line to be printed only when this same indicator is on, as desired.

International Business Machines Corporation

RPG   OUTPUT - FORMAT SPECIFICATIONS

Date __7/19__

Program __STUDENT LIST__

Programmer __FRM__

Punching	Graphic	O	Ø			
Instruction	Punch	II-6 Zero				

Line	Form Type	Filename	Type (H/D/T/E)	Stacker Select/Fetch Overflow (F)	Space Before	Space After	Skip Before	Skip After	Output Indicators Not	And Not	And Not	Field Name	Edit Codes	Blank After (B)	End Position in Output Record	P = Packed/B = Binary	Commas	Zer
																	Yes	Yes
																	Yes	
																	No	
																	No	
0 1	O	PRINTFL	D		1				Ø 1									
0 2	O											NAME			39			
0 3	O											STNO	Z		49			
0 4	O											UNITS	Z		59			
0 5	O											TOTAL	Z		69			
0 6	O																	

Figure 15–6. *Output Format Specifications for Example 1.*

Field Name (positions 32–37) is used to record the symbolic name of data items to be listed. These are the same names as were recorded on the Input Specifications.

Zero Suppression (position 38) is used to indicate numerical fields that are to be zero suppressed when printed. In Figure 15–6, the symbol Z is recorded in this position for STNO, UNITS, and TOTAL.

End Position (positions 40–43) records the last position of each printed field, as specified on the printer spacing chart (Figure 15–3).

This completes the RPG program specifications for Example 1. Since no calculations are required, the Calculation Specifications form is omitted. The completed specification forms for this problem, together with sample output, are shown in Figure 15–7.

```
FSTUDFL   IP  F   80   80                READ40 SYSRDR
FPRINTFL  O   F  132  132       OF       PRINTERSYSLST
ISTUDFL   AA   01   01  CS
I                                             2    26 NAME
I                                            27    31OSTNO
I                                            32    33OUNITS
I                                            34    36OTOTAL
OPRINTFL D 1            01
O                                NAME        39
O                                STNO   Z    49
O                                UNITS  Z    59
O                                TOTAL  Z    69


END  OF  SOURCE

     ADAMS,  PETER R.           0     13978         9        104
     GOODMAN,  HAROLD R.        0     20875        16
     JOHNSON,  SHARON C.        0     24432        15         74
     LARSON,  JAMES L.          0     47739         6         48
     LEWIS,BARBARA C.           0      1339        18        107
     ROTHSCHILD,  CHARLES K.    0     80336        10        100
     THOMPSON,  LAURA W.        0     59325         7         88
```

Figure 15–7. *RPG program for Example 1.*

Exercise 15–1

1. What forms are required for most RPG programs? List the forms in the order in which they are used in a program.

   (a) _____

   (b) _____

   (c) _____

   (d) _____

2. In Example 1, suppose that the student record cards contained the control code 2 in column 79. What changes would be required in the Input Specifications form (Figure 15–5)?

   (a) _____

   (b) _____

   (c) _____

3. What entries in the completed program (Figure 15–7) would likely have to be changed if the program were to be run on a different com-

   puter? _____

   _____

   _____

   _____

   _____

4. Explain the significance of the zero entries in position 52 of the Input Specifications (Figure 15–5) for Example 1. How are entries related to the Z entry of the Output-Format Specifications (Figure 15–6)?

   _____

   _____

   _____

   _____

Example 2: Simple Calculations

This example introduces the use of the Calculation Specifications form. The card record for each student is to be read, and "units taken this semester" is to be added to "total units to date" to obtain an updated

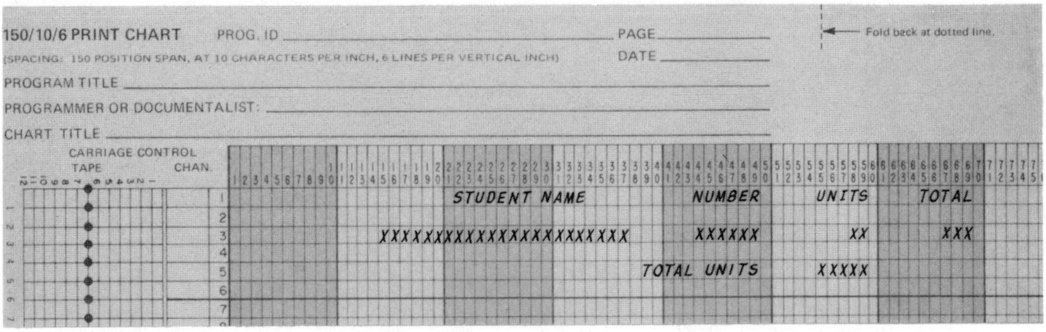

Figure 15–8. *Printer spacing chart for Example 2.*

total. The record is then to be printed, with the updated total replacing the previous total.

In addition to updating each record, the units taken this semester is to be totaled for all students and printed at the end of the listing. Header information is also to be printed at the top of the listing.

The input format for Problem 2 is the same as for Problem 1 (see Figure 15–2). The output format is shown on the printer spacing chart, Figure 15–8.

File Specifications

The File Specifications for Example 2 are identical to Example 1 (see Figure 15–4).

Input Specifications

The Input Specifications for Example 2 are also the same as for Example 1. However, the Record Identifying Indicator (position 19–20) has arbitrarily been assigned the number 05. Thus when a card with control punch S in column 1 is read, indicator number 05 is turned on. The Input Specifications for Example 2 are shown in Figure 15–9.

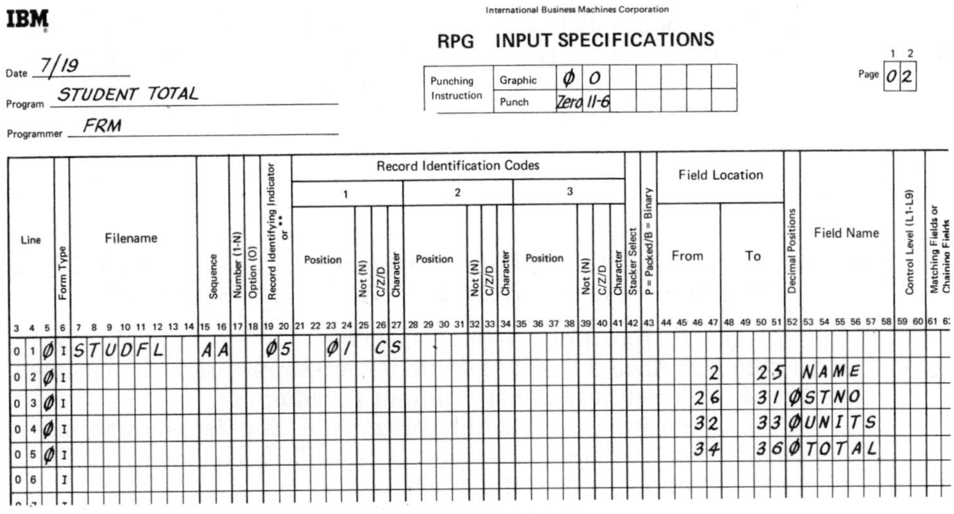

Figure 15–9. *Input Specifications for Example 2.*

409 / SIMPLE CALCULATIONS

IBM

International Business Machines Corporation

RPG   CALCULATION SPECIFICATIONS

Date _7/19_

Program_STUDENT TOTAL_

Programmer _FRM_

| Punching | Graphic | $\emptyset$ | 0 | | | |
| Instruction | Punch | Zero ll-6 | | | | |

Figure 15–10. *Calculation Specifications for Example 2.*

Calculation Specifications

In most programs, calculations and logical operations are required. These operations are described on the RPG Calculation Specifications form. The specifications for Example 2 are shown in Figure 15–1.

Indicator (positions 10–11) permits the desired calculations to occur when a valid control punch is present. In Example 2, indicator 05 is used.

In RPG, calculations are specified by four entries: Factor 1, Factor 2, Operation, and Result Field. Also, the Field Length of Result Field is specified.

In Example 2, the first operation is to add UNITS to TOTAL for each student. The result field is the updated total, also called TOTAL. Next, UNITS is added to a field called FTOTAL, resulting in FTOTAL. FTOTAL is a running total of the number of units taken this semester by students.

QUESTION: Suppose that a student has taken 15 units this semester and had a total of 74 units at the beginning of the semester. When the student's record is read, the running total of units for all students is 1680. What are the values for each of the fields shown in Figure 10? _____

_____

_____.

ANSWER: UNITS = 15, TOTAL = 74 (Factor 2), TOTAL = 89 (Result Field), FTOTAL = 1680 (Factor 2), FTOTAL = 1695 (Result Field)

Field Length (positions 49–51) specifies the length of the Result Field. Since TOTAL and FTOTAL are to be zero suppressed when printed, the entry $\emptyset$ is placed in Decimal Positions (position 52).

Although addition is the only arithmetic calculation required in Example 2, other operations may also be specified. The format for basic arithmetic operations is the following:

Factor 1	Operation	Factor 2	Comment
A	ADD	B	Add A to B, sum in Result Field
A	SUB	B	Subtract B from A, difference in Result Field
A	MULT	B	Multiply B by A, product in Result Field
A	DIV	B	Divide A by B, quotient in Result Field

Output-Format Specifications

The output format must be expanded for Example 2 to provide header information as well as the final total of student hours. The Output-Format Specifications for this example are shown in Figure 15–11.

The entry "H" in position 15 (type) specifies that header information is to follow. The entry "01" in skip before causes the printer to be positioned at the first printing line when the header is printed. The entry "2" in SPACE AFTER causes the printer to double space after the header is printed.

There are two Output Indicators that will cause a header to be printed. These are 1P (for first page) and OF (for overflow). These indicators are coupled with the entry OR in positions 14 to 15. The effect of these entries is that a header will be printed on the first page or at the top of succeeding pages.

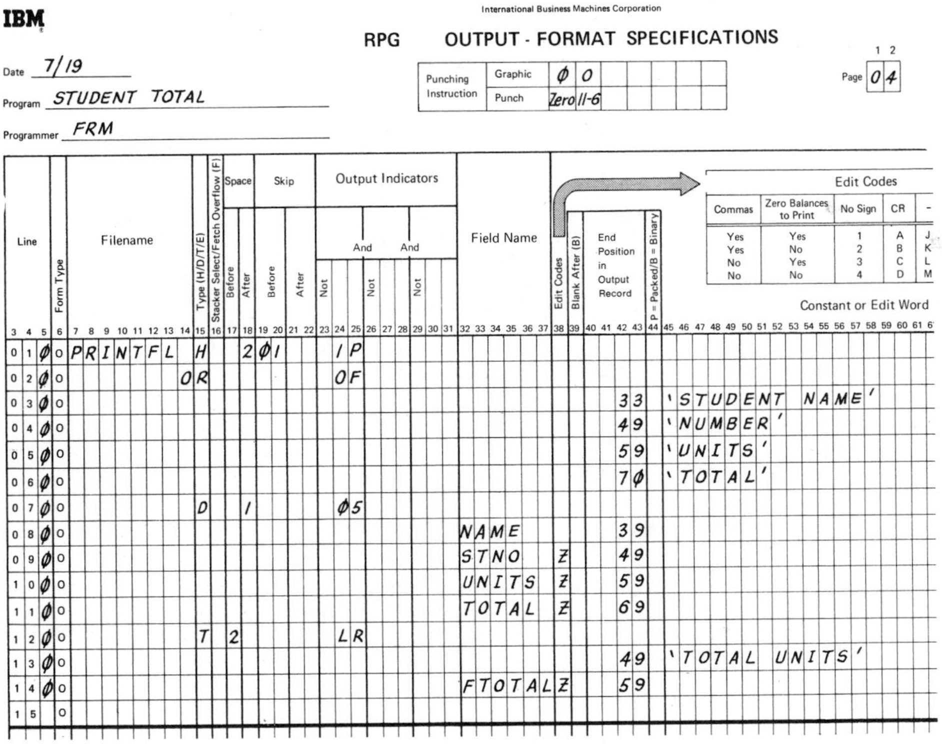

Figure 15–11. *Output-Format Specifications for Example 2.*

The header data to be printed is recorded under Constant or Edit Word. In the example, the headings "STUDENT NAME," "NUMBER," "UNITS," and "TOTAL" are to be printed. Constants or literals must be enclosed in single quotes. The printed location of each heading is specified under end position (positions 40–43).

The entries for the student records are the same as for Example 1. The entry D under Type indicates "detail."

The last entries on the Output-Format Specifications specify the printing of total hours. The entry T indicates "total." After the last record has been processed, the indicator LR (for "last record") is turned on. This indicator permits the total information to be printed.

QUESTION: From Figure 15–11, what entries will appear at the end of the listing? _____ .

ANSWER: The notation TOTAL UNITS, followed by the cumulative total, whose symbolic name is FTOTAL

This completes the RPG program specifications for Example 2. The complete program together with sample output, is shown in Figure 15–12.

```
FSTUDFL   IP  F   80  80              READ40 SYSRDR
FPRINTFL  O   F  132 132      OF      PRINTERSYSLST
ISTUDFL   AA  05  01 CS
I                                              2   25 NAME
I                                             26   31OSTNO
I                                             32   33OUNITS
I                                             34   36OTOTAL
C    05         UNITS      ADD  TOTAL    TOTAL
C    05         UNITS      ADD  FTOTAL   FTOTAL  50
OPRINTFL  H     201    1P
O         OR           OF
O                                         33 'STUDENT NAME'
O                                         49 'NUMBER'
O                                         59 'UNITS'
O                                         70 'TOTAL'
O         D   1        05
O                             NAME        39
O                             STNO   Z    49
O                             UNITS  Z    59
O                             TOTAL  Z    69
O         T 2          LR
O                                         49 'TOTAL UNITS'
O                             FTOTALZ    59
```


STUDENT NAME	NUMBER	UNITS	TOTAL
ADAMS, PETER R.	13978	9	113
GOODMAN, HAROLD R.	20875	16	16
JOHNSON, SHARON C.	24432	15	89
LARSON, JAMES L.	47739	6	54
LEWIS, BARBARA C.	1339	18	125
ROTHSCHILD, CHARLES K.	80336	10	110
THOMPSON, LAURA W.	59325	7	95
TOTAL UNITS		81	

Figure 15–12. *Output listing for Example 2.*

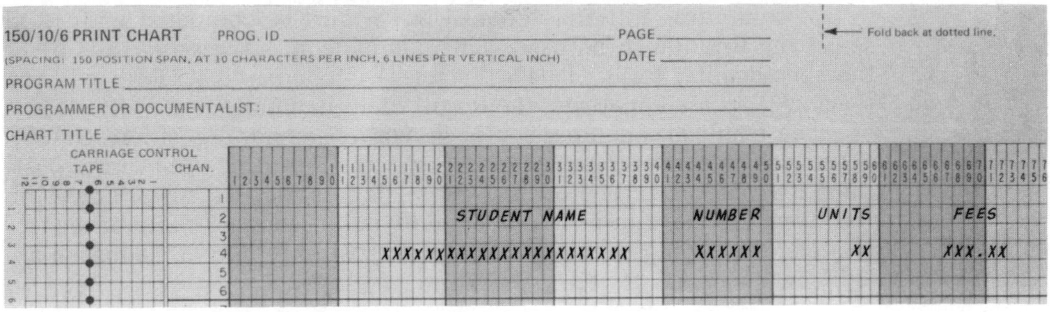

Figure 15–13. *Printer spacing chart for Example 3.*

Example 3: Simple Logical Operations

The use of simple comparisons in RPG is shown in this example. The student record cards are to be read, and tuition is to be computed according to the following formula:

If UNITS is less than 12, tuition is UNITS times $35

If UNITS is 12 or more, tuition is $420.00

Total student fees consist of tuition plus an incidental fee of $12.50. This total is to be printed along with student name, number, and units taken. Also, total fees for all students is to be computed and printed at the end of the listing.

The input format for Example 3 is the same as for Examples 1 and 2 (see Figure 15–2). The desired output format is shown in Figure 15–13.

Calculation Specifications

The main feature of this example is the introduction of the comparison operation. In RPG, comparisons are specified on the CALCULATION SPECIFICATIONS form. The specifications for Example 3 are shown in Figure 15–14.

IBM International Business Machines Corporation

RPG CALCULATION SPECIFICATIONS

Date 7/19
Program STUDENT FEES
Programmer FRM

Punching Instruction: Graphic Ø O; Punch Zero 11-6

Page 03

Line	Form Type	Control Level	Indicators	Factor 1	Operation	Factor 2	Result Field	Field Length	Decimal Positions	Half Adjust	High (1>2)	Low (1<2)	Equal (1=2)
01Ø	C		Ø1	UNITS	COMP	12					Ø2	Ø3	Ø2
02Ø	C		Ø2		MOVE	42Ø.ØØ	FEES	5	2				
03Ø	C		Ø3	UNITS	MULT	35	FEES	5	2				
04Ø	C		Ø1	FEES	ADD	12.5Ø	FEES	5	2				
05Ø	C		Ø1	FEES	ADD	TFEES	TFEES	7	2				
06	C												

Figure 15–14. *Calculation Specifications for Example 3.*

In computing tuition, student UNITS must be compared with 12 to select the formula to be used. This comparison is shown on line 01 of the specification form. UNITS (Factor 1) is compared (COMP) with 12 (Factor 2). In a comparison, the Result Field is not used.

The result of a comparison is shown in *Compare* (positions 54–59). If Factor 1 is greater than Factor 2 (High), the Resulting Indicator in positions 54 to 55 is turned on. If Factor 1 is less than Factor 2 (Low), the Resulting Indicator in positions 58 to 59 is turned on. Finally, if the factors are equal, the Resulting Indicator in positions 56 to 57 is turned on.

QUESTION: In Figure 15–14, what Resulting Indicator will be turned on for a student who has taken 9 units, 15 units, 12 units? _____ , _____ , _____ .

ANSWER: 03, 02, 02

After the comparison is made, the calculations performed by the computer depend on the indicators that have been turned on. If indicator 03 is on (indicating UNITS is less than 12), UNITS is multiplied by 35, giving the Result Field called FEES. If indicator 02 is turned on, the constant 420.00 is moved to FEES. Since either indicator 02 or 03 (but not both) is on, only one of the above operations is performed.

Indicator 01 is used in Example 3 as the Resulting Indicator for the card control punch. After tuition is computed, the result (called FEES) is added to the incidental fee of $12.50, yielding total fees (also called FEES). This quantity is then added to the running total of student fees, called TFEES. Each of these quantities has two decimal positions positions, as is indicated on position 52.

QUESTION: A student has taken 10 units during the previous semester. The running total of student fees (before his card is processed) is $8439.00. What should be the values of each of the variables in Figure 15–14 as the student's card is processed? _____ .

ANSWER: UNITS = 10; FEES = 350.00 (tuition); FEES = 362.50 (with incidental fee); TFEES = 8801.50

The MOVE entry in Figure 15–14 causes Factor 2 to be moved to the Result Field. Factor 2 may be a literal (as in this example) or a field name. It may be a numeric or alphanumeric quantity. The move is from the rightmost positions of Factor 2 to the rightmost positions of the Result Field, with the shorter field terminating the move.

The use of the MOVE operation in RPG may be illustrated by three examples:

Example No.	Operation	Factor 2	Result Field	Field Length
1	MOVE	DATA	RSLT	6
2	MOVE	'DATA'	RSLT	6
3	MOVE	25	RSLT	6

IBM

International Business Machines Corporation

RPG   OUTPUT - FORMAT SPECIFICATIONS

Date **7/19**

Program **STUDENT FEES**

Programmer **FRM**

| Punching Instruction | Graphic | Ø | O | | | | |
| | Punch | Zero II-6 | | | | | |

Page

Figure table (Output-Format Specifications form):

Line	Form Type	Filename	Type (H/D/T/E)	Stacker Select/Fetch Overflow (F)	Space Before	Space After	Skip Before	Skip After	Output Indicators Not	And Not	And Not	Field Name	Edit Codes	Blank After (B)	End Position in Output Record	Packed/B = Binary	Commas	Zero Balances to Print	No Sign	CR	–	Constant or Edit Word
0 1	O	PRINTFL	H		2	Ø	1		1 P													
0 2	O			OR					O F													
0 3	O														3 3		'STUDENT NAME'					
0 4	O														4 9		'NUMBER'					
0 5	O														5 9		'UNITS'					
0 6	O														7 1		'FEES'					
0 7	O			D	1				Ø 1													
0 8	O											NAME			3 9							
0 9	O											STNO	Z		4 9							
1 0	O											UNITS	Z		5 9							
1 1	O											FEES			7 2		' Ø.'					'
1 2	O			T	2				L R													
1 3	O														5 5		'TOTAL FEES'					
1 4	O											TFEES			7 2		'$, Ø.'					'
1 5	O																					

Figure 15–15. *Output-Format Specifications for Example 3.*

Assume that the field DATA contains the quantity 1234, and that RSLT contains ABCDEF. The result of the above MOVES is as follows:

Example No.	Contents of Result Field	Comment
1	AB1234	Content of DATA moved to RSLT
2	ABDATA	Literal DATA moved to RSLT
3	ABCD25	Literal 25 moved to RSLT

QUESTION: In example 2 above, suppose that the field RSLT had Field Length 3 and contained ABC. What is the result of the MOVE?

ANSWER: ATA. Since the field RSLT is only three positions, it cannot contain the entire literal "DATA." Since movement is from right to left, the "D" is truncated

Output-Format Specifications

The Output-Format Specifications for Example 3 are shown in Figure 15–15. The format provides for listings of header, detail, and total information, similar to Example 2.

The only feature in Figure 15–15 not previously discussed is the use of Edit Words (lines 11 and 14). Editing symbols (blanks, commas, decimals, dollar signs, etc.) are enclosed in single quotes, in the relative positions they are to appear in the output listing. A zero in an Edit Word indicates that zero suppression of a numeric field is to occur up to and including the zero symbol. When an Edit Word is used, position 38 of the Output-Format Specifications form should be left blank.

In Figure 15–15, the field FEES is to be zero suppressed, and a decimal point is to be inserted in the output field to indicate dollars and cents. The field TFEES is also to be zero suppressed, with a dollar sign, comma, and decimal point inserted in the indicated positions.

QUESTION: How will the quantity TFEES appear on the output listing if TFEES is $8640.50; $125.00? _____ , _____ .

ANSWER: $ 8,640.50; $ 125.00.

The complete RPG program for Example 3, together with sample output, is shown in Figure 15–16.

```
FSTUDFL   IP  F   80   80              READ40 SYSRDR
FPRINTFL  O   F  132  132      OF      PRINTERSYSLST
ISTUDFL   AA  01   01 CS
I                                           2   25 NAME
I                                          26   310STNO
I                                          32   330UNITS
C    01       UNITS      COMP 12                    020302
C    02                  MOVE 420.00    FEES      52
C    03       UNITS      MULT 35         FEES      52
C    01       FEES       ADD  12.50      FEES      52
C    01       FEES       ADD  TFEES      TFEES     72
OPRINTFL  H   201     1P
O          OR          OF
O                                          33 'STUDENT NAME'
O                                          49 'NUMBER'
O                                          59 'UNITS'
O                                          71 'FEES'
O          D   1       01
O                            NAME          39
O                            STNO  Z       49
O                            UNITS Z       59
O                            FEES          72 '   0.   '
O          T   2       LR
O                                          55 'TOTAL FEES'
O                            TFEES         72 '$  ,   0.   '
```

```
        STUDENT NAME                NUMBER    UNITS        FEES

ADAMS, PETER R.                     13978        9       327.50
GOODMAN, HAROLD R.                  20875       16       432.50
JOHNSON, SHARON C.                  24432       15       432.50
LARSON, JAMES L.                    47739        6       222.50
LEWIS,BARBARA C.                     1339       18       432.50
ROTHSCHILD, CHARLES K.              80336       10       362.50
THOMPSON, LAURA W.                  59325        7       257.50


                                TOTAL FEES        $ 2,467.50
```

Figure 15–16. RPG program for Example 3.

Exercise 15-2

1. FLDA contains the number 100, FLDB contains 25. The result field RSLT has Field Length 6, with zero decimal positions. Indicate the content of RSLT for each of the following arithmetic operations:

Factor 1	Operation	Factor 2	Contents of RSLT
(a) FLDA	SUB	FLDB	_____
(b) FLDA	ADD	FLDB	_____
(c) FLDA	MULT	FLDB	_____
(d) FLDA	DIV	FLDB	_____
(e) FLDA	DIV	100	_____

2. Explain the operations performed by the following segment of an RPG calculation.

	Indicator	Factor 1	Operation	Factor 2	Result Field	Compare High	Low	Equal
(a)	01	AMT	COMP	25		02	03	04
(b)	02	AMT	SUB	15	AMT			
(c)	03	AMT	SUB	5	AMT			
(d)	04	AMT	SUB	10	AMT			

(a) _____

_____

(b) _____

_____

(c) _____

_____

(d) _____

_____

417 / SIMPLE LOGICAL OPERATIONS

3. FLDC contains the quantity 1000, and RSLT contains 000185. RSLT has Field Length 6. Indicate the content of RSLT after each of the following operations:

Operation	Factor 2	Contents of RSLT
(a) MOVE	FLDC	_____
(b) MOVE	'FLDC'	_____
(c) MOVE	35	_____

4. The edit word for an output report appears as follows:

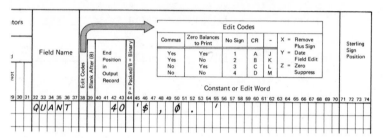

					Edit Codes						
tors						Commas	Zero Balances to Print	No Sign	CR	–	X = Remove Plus Sign	Sterling Sign Position
	Field Name		End Position in Output Record			Yes	Yes	1	A	J	Y = Date
						Yes	No	2	B	K	Field Edit
						No	Yes	3	C	L	Z = Zero
						No	No	4	D	M	Suppress
								Constant or Edit Word			

Field positions 29 30 31 32 33 34 35 36 37 38 39 40 41 42 43 44 45 46 47 48 49 50 51 52 53 54 55 56 57 58 59 60 61 62 63 64 65 66 67 68 69 70 71 72 73 74

`QUANT` `40` `'$ , 0 . '`

Indicate how QUANT will be printed out for each of the following values:

QUANT	Format
(a) 1,643.38	_____
(b) 519.31	_____
(c) 6.72	_____
(d) .47	_____

Summary

This chapter has provided an introduction to RPG II programming. The language contains many additional capabilities, including the ability to process magnetic tape and disk files. Also, a number of additional computational features are available.

The principal advantages of RPG are its simplicity and the ease of learning and using the language. Smaller installations that do not have skilled programmers can train their people in a relatively short time to use RPG. On the other hand the language is quite flexible, and a surprising number of data processing tasks can be successfully programmed in RPG.

The principal disadvantage of RPG is its limited ability to handle calculations and more complicated data structures. Also, since it is a general purpose language, RPG tends to be somewhat inefficient in terms of computational speed and use of storage. However, when used in applications for which it is suited, RPG often results in considerable savings in programming time and effort.

Solutions to Exercises

Exercise 15–1

1. (a) File Description Specifications.
   (b) Input Specifications.
   (c) Calculation Specifications.
   (d) Output-Format Specifications.

2. The Record Identification Codes would be changed as follows:
   (a) Position (columns 23–24) would contain the entry 79, which is the location of the control code.
   (b) Column 26 would contain the entry D, to indicate that the control code is a digit.
   (c) Column 27 would contain 2, the actual digit used.

3. The File Description Specifications, which are the first two lines of the program.

4. When a numeric field is to be edited or zero suppressed on output, an entry must appear in the Decimal Position field (column 52). Since the fields are integer, the entry "zero" is used to indicate zero decimal positions.

Exercise 15–2

1. (a)   75
   (b)   125
   (c) 2500
   (d)   4
   (e)   1

2. (a) Compare AMT with 25, and turn on an indicator as follows: If AMT is greater than 25, turn on indicator 02; if AMT is less than 25, turn on indicator 03; if AMT equals 25, turn on indicator 04.
   (b) If indicator 02 is on, subtract 15 from AMT and store the result in AMT.
   (c) If indicator 03 is on, subtract 5 from AMT and store the result in AMT.
   (d) If indicator 04 is on, subtract 10 from AMT and store the result in AMT.

3. (a) 001000
   (b) 00FLDC
   (c) 000135

4. (a) $1,643.38
   (b) $ 519.31
   (c) $ 6.72
   (d) $ 0.47

Chapter Examination

1. The following is a segment of an RPG calculation:

					Compare		
Indicator	Factor 1	Operation	Factor 2	Result Field	High	Low	Equal
01	QTY	COMP	38		03	07	05
03	QTY	SUB	38	AMT			
07	QTY	ADD	15	AMT			
05	QTY	DIV	2	AMT			

What is the content of the field AMT after the above instructions are executed if the present content of QTY is

(a) 38? _____

(b) 54? _____

(c) 7? _____

2. The field RSLT has field length 5, with current contents 00139. The field AMT contains the quantity 016. Indicate the contents of RSLT after each of the following operations:

Operation	Factor 2	Contents of RSLT
MOVE	AMT	
MOVE	6240	
MOVE	'AMT'	

3. The edit word for an output report appears as follows:

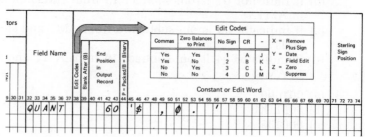

Indicate how QUANT will be printed out for each of the following values:

	QUANT	Format
(a)	13,238.65	_____
(b)	6,921.08	_____
(c)	846.29	_____
(d)	24.79	_____
(e)	6.12	_____
(f)	.98	_____

4. Write an RPGII program for problem 11 of Chapter 13.

5. Write an RPGII program for problem 12 of Chapter 13.

6. Write an RPGII program for problem 14 of Chapter 13.

7. Write an RPGII program for problem 15 of Chapter 13.

REPORT PROGRAM GENERATOR FILE DESCRIPTION SPECIFICATIONS

IBM System/360

Date _____

Program _____

Programmer _____

Punching Instruction

Graphic

Punch

Page | 1 | 2 |

Program Identification | 75 76 77 78 79 80 |

Card Electro Number _____

| Line | Form Type | Filename | File Type | File Designation | End of File | Sequence | File Format | Block Length | Record Length | Mode of Processing | Length of Record Address Field | Record Address Type | Type of File Organization | Overflow Indicator | Key Field Starting Location | Extension Code E/L | Device | Symbolic Device | Labels (S, N, or E) | Name of Label Exit | Extent Exit for DAM | Comments |

I/O/U/C — 15
P/S/C/R/T — 16 17 (E)
A/D — 18
F/V — 19
20 21 22 23 Block Length
24 25 26 27 Record Length
L/R — 28
29 30 K/I — 31
I/D/T — 32
33 34 Record Address Type
35 36 37 Type of File Organization
Overflow Indicator
Key Field Starting Location
38 Extension Code E/L — 39
40 41 42 43 44 45 46 Device
47 48 49 50 51 52 Symbolic Device
Labels (S, N, or E) — 53
54 55 56 57 58 59 Name of Label Exit
60 61 62 63 64 65 Extent Exit for DAM
66 67 68 69 70 71 72 73 74 Comments

Line 3 4 5 6 7 8 9 10 11 12 13 14

0 1
0 2
0 3
0 4
0 5
0 6
0 7
0 8
0 9
1 0
1 1
1 2
1 3
1 4
1 5

REPORT PROGRAM GENERATOR INPUT SPECIFICATIONS

IBM System/360

Date _____
Program _____
Programmer _____

Punching Instruction | Graphic | Punch

Page

Program Identification

Card Electro Number

Field Indicators
Sterling Sign Position
Zero or Blank
Plus Minus

Field-Record Relation
Matching Fields or Chaining Fields
Control Level (L1-L9)
Field Name
Decimal Positions

Field Location
To
From
Packed (P)
Stacker Select

Record Identification Codes
Position
Character
C/Z/D
Not (N)

Resulting Indicator
Option (O)
Number (1-N)
Sequence

Filename
Form Type
Line

IBM System/360

Punching Instruction

Graphic

Punch

Page

Program Identification

75 76 77 78 79 80

Card Electro Number

Constant or Edit Word

Sterling Sign Position

Field Name

End Position in Output Record

Packed Field (P)

Blank After (B)

Zero Suppress (Z)

Output Indicators

And

Nol

And

Nol

Nol

Skip

After

Before

Space

After

Before

Stacker Select

Type (H/D/T)

Filename

Form Type

Line

gram

 grammer

te

Chapter 16

THE SYSTEM SURVEY

Overview

There are seven phases in the business system development cycle: (1) documentation of the existing system, (2) analysis of the system in relation to its objectives, (3) design of an improved system, (4) programming and testing, (5) implementation, (6) operation, (7) maintenance and modification.

In the early days of computing, Phase I (documenting the existing system) was simple, relative to the other phases. In those days, the early 1950s, only subsystems were analyzed, such as the payroll system. Today, in the era of integrated systems, the scope of the system is many times enlarged. The payroll subsystem is only one part of the accounting system, which is only one part of the finance system.

The third generation approach to system analysis emphasizes the interrelationship of systems. First, the company is viewed as a system, consisting of major subsystems. However, the company is also a subsystem of the industry.

Designing a system to provide information for managerial decision making requires analysis of the environment in which those decisions are made. The environment includes areas external to the company as well as internal. The first and second generation systems approach concentrated on internal systems. The third generation system approach includes all areas of managerial information needs—external as well as internal.

This chapter discusses methodology for gathering information about the company and the environment in which it operates. This initial phase of the system development cycle is referred to as the System Survey.

The System Development Cycle

The seven phases in system development are depicted in Figure 16–1. Costs of system development are considerably higher today than in the 1950s.

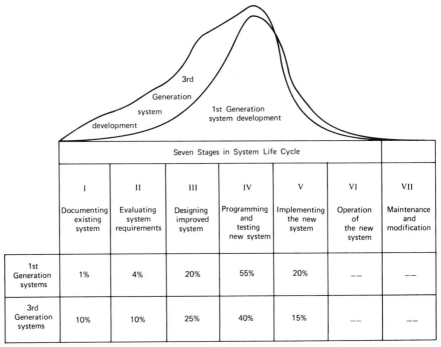

Seven Stages in System Life Cycle						
I	II	III	IV	V	VI	VII
Documenting existing system	Evaluating system requirements	Designing improved system	Programming and testing new system	Implementing the new system	Operation of the new system	Maintenance and modification
1st Generation systems 1%	4%	20%	55%	20%	--	--
3rd Generation systems 10%	10%	25%	40%	15%	--	--

Figure 16–1. *Comparative costs of first and third generation system development.*

QUESTION: Figure 16–1 shows that the first three phases consumed _____ percent of first generation costs compared to _____ percent for third generation systems.

ANSWER: 25, 45

This situation might appear surprising in light of the reduction in cost per calculation produced by the improvement in computers during three generations of hardware evolution.

The increase in development cost is due to the expanded scope and complexity of computer applications. Where the typical computer user was applying computer technology to relatively simple systems in the 1950s, he is today using the computer closer to true potential, in a broad range of applications. Today's systems are also more difficult to develop. In the 1950s *independent* subsystems were designed for *interdependent* activities. The most common business application at that time, payroll, was designed as an entity. In actuality, the payroll subsystem is a part of both the accounting system and the personnel system of the firm. When converted from an earlier computerized version, the payroll subsystems of today are redesigned to feed both these major systems.

QUESTION: Cost of development, therefore, is higher than it was for first generation applications, because _____

_____.

ANSWER: systems are now designed for integration.

Not only are development costs higher, operation costs are higher. Systems encompass more activities than their predecessors. For example, in a division of one of the major oil companies, 6,500 of 35,000 employees are involved in development and operation of computerized information systems. Even though computing activities now require one sixth of all employees, the division's total cost of operation has decreased — as a result of converting many operations to the computer.

QUESTION: Costs of computing are higher today, but only because _____ operations are computerized.
ANSWER: more.

Because of increases in scope and complexity of systems, it has been necessary to develop more sophisticated system analysis and design techniques. The remaining chapters cover these new system analysis and design techniques — those required for developing effective third generation systems.

This chapter concentrates on the methodology for Phase I of the system development cycle, documenting the existing system. In the 1950s, this phase was the least interesting.

Today it is one of the most interesting, because of the third generation emphasis on integrated systems. The documentation of the payroll subsystem alone would be rather mundane and could be assigned to a person with few system analysis skills. However, it is a challenging task to analyze the payroll system when considering its effect on other systems of the firm and how it relates to the objectives of the firm. No longer can a subsystem be considered as an entity. Each subsystem must be designed to fit into the set of integrated systems for the organization. The goal is a set of systems producing optimal results for the entire organization, instead of suboptimization for one function, as was done in previous years.

Third generation system design gives priority to computerization of *life-stream activities* of the firm; that is, those activities key to the life of the organization. Therefore, Phase I documentation provides data to assess the impact of new systems on the entire organization.

QUESTION: Phase I of the system development cycle is more challenging today because systems are not designed as _____ but as _____.
ANSWER: entities, integrated systems for the entire organization

QUESTION: The goal is optimization of the objectives of the _____ organization; not just one function.
ANSWER: entire

The Survey Team

Phase II of the system development cycle consists of analysis of the existing company system, to define the requirements for an improved system. To enable this analysis, a thorough job in Phase I is necessary. A team is typically involved, to gain the proper perspective of the organization and how subsystems interrelate. The team begins this analysis by gathering information on company history, environment, objectives, and policies. The information is obtained from a variety of sources, through use of published materials and through interviews.

QUESTION: Whereas one person might have performed Phase I for first generation systems, a team is typically used today, because _____

_____.

ANSWER: the systems are larger in scope, and a team is usually required to determine how subsystems interrelate

It is apparent by now that Phase I is no small undertaking. The System Survey team is gathering information that will be used in design of a large number of systems, not just one system. For example, the inventory and the production control systems are highly interrelated and information can be gathered for both systems in the same survey.

The team often is comprised of two specialties: system analysts and representatives from the organizations where the study is being conducted. The team approach is quite useful, since it is rare that either specialist knows enough about the other's operation to determine alone feasibility for computerization. The titles information analyst and system analyst are interchangeable. Appendix I describes qualifications for information analysts and system designers.

QUESTION: The minimal constituency of a System Survey team would be the following specialties: (1) _____ and (2)

_____.

ANSWER: (1) System Analyst (2) representative of the area of application, that is, the user.

The job of the system analyst, therefore, is to define the interfaces among systems and document those relationships so that the design phase of the system development cycle may be effectively accomplished. The task is an interesting *and* an exacting one.

Exercise 16–1

1. Refer to Figure 16–1. In which Phase of the System Development Cycle would you find the following activities?

   (a) Developing a computer-oriented flowchart _____

   (b) Developing a procedure-oriented flowchart _____

   (c) Checking out the program on test data _____

   (d) Checking out the program on actual data _____

   (e) Training users in operating the new system _____

   (f) Developing procedures for users _____

   (g) Developing procedures for data processing personnel _____

2. Why does Phase I require more resources for third generation systems?

_____

_____

3. What does the following statement mean to you? "In first generation approach, independent systems were designed for interdependent activities."

_____

_____

_____

4. True or False? In Phase I of the system development cycle, the analyst is determining the requirements for an improved system? Explain your answer.

_____

_____

Documenting Organizational Environment

Phase I of the system development cycle is documentation of the existing business system. This activity is often referred to as the _Systems Survey_ and organizes its findings in the following categories.

1. Company history.
2. External environment: industry background and government regulations.
3. Objectives and policies.
4. The Master Plan.

Phase I not only produces useful information for the system designers of each major system area, but also insures that all designers are working on common assumptions and common objectives.

Gathering Data on Company History

A summary of significant events in the organization's history is required for the System Survey. The objective of this activity is to provide a basis for projecting the future of the business.

For publicly-held firms, information of this type is usually available in the annual report. In other organizations it may be necessary to obtain the information through interviews. In general, the historical documentation stresses the reasons for starting the company and the reasons for change during the evolution of the company.

The information is organized from the perspective of management of the enterprise. In developing a computer-based management information system, emphasis is placed on providing the kinds of information needed by *each* level of management. The system analysts will later be interviewing management to determine its informational requirements. Documentation of the history enables analysts to have a better perspective of the management of the enterprise so as to understand managerial information needs. The historical section of the documentation package is normally limited to two or three pages.

QUESTION: The gathering of historical information on managerial decisions of the organization provides _____ necessary for developing information systems for decision making.

ANSWER: the managerial perspective

Included in the history are:

1. Growth statistics (personnel, sales, profit, plant capacity).
2. Evolution of products or services (types, quantities, product names).
3. Management pattern (organizational structure, decentralized/centralized decision making).
4. Expansion characteristics (mergers, spin-offs, acquisitions).

QUESTION: The four categories for documenting the firm's history are:

(1) _____ , (2) _____ ,

(3) _____ , (4) _____ .

ANSWER: Growth statistics, evolution of products or services, management pattern, expansion characteristics

As an example, an excerpt from a system survey conducted by one of the authors for a small mail-order firm is provided below.

History of Looart Press, Inc.

Looart Press, founded in 1947 and incorporated in the state of Colorado in 1950, maintains its offices and manufacturing facilities at 3525 North Stone, Colorado Springs. An operating company with one other wholly owned operating subsidiary, Looart designs and manufactures printed products, marketing them through direct mail and through retail stores.

Having begun modestly with two commercial lithographers cramped into an empty garage, Looart today employs over 600 people, occupies more than 160,000 square feet of space, has sales of $22 million. Sales increased by more than 2200 percent since 1965. Looart Press is recognized for quality, original design, and fine printing.

Looart's comprehensive product line includes greeting cards for all occasions, personalized and wedding stationery, and decorative wall posters. The firm's direct-mail marketing division annually mails four sales brochures to more than 15 million individuals. Assorted retail cards and stationery products are marketed through catalogs placed in department, stationery, and gift stores nationwide.

Direct mail marketing is conducted under the trade name Current, Inc., and contributes approximately 80% of the company's revenues. The products of the Current line consist of stationery items sold to groups and individuals who resell them for fund-raising, personal use and gift giving purposes. Sales come primarily from the mailing of approximately 15 million catalogs, full color space ads in McCalls, House Beautiful, Woman's Day, Family Circle and many other magazines and sales booths at conventions of women's organizations. The largest percentage of the Current product line sales is to previous purchasers, the "house list," numbering over 2 million people.

Retail sales are made under the name, Looart Press, Inc., with the principal products being Christmas cards, wedding invitations and decorative wall posters.

Christmas cards designed and manufactured by the company are displayed in albums placed at 6,000 department, stationery and gift stores throughout the nation. Approximately 7.5 million cards in 115 different designs are offered each year in two albums, "Looart" (new designs) and "The Holly Tree" (the most successful designs in recent prior years). The retail stores do not stock these cards but forward the customer's order to one of the company's three distribution points located in Colorado Springs; Brooklyn, New York; and Walnut Creek, California.

The New York and California distributors, operating as Looart branch offices and warehouses, are responsible for all but the actual production of the cards in their particular areas. For the service of order-taking, warehousing and imprinting they receive 27% of sales dollars in their territories.

For some years Looart has also been marketing Christmas cards packaged and priced for over the counter sales. The industry normally calls this solid pack sales.

A line of wedding invitations and social announcements is designed and produced under the name "White Lace by Looart." These invitations are sold in much the same manner as Christmas cards, that is, through albums displayed at bridal shops, stationery and department stores, and small printing companies. Orders are taken by these retailers and forwarded to the company for fulfillment. The marketing of the wedding line is now concentrated in the western states.

American Stationery Company, located in Peru, Indiana, is a wholly owned subsidiary acquired through capital stock purchase in April 1970, and is engaged in marketing personalized products by mail advertising. Its revenue amounts to 20% of the corporation revenue and comes principally from the sale of stationery products manufactured and imprinted at the American Stationery plant in Peru, with the remainder from items drop-shipped by other manufacturers from orders sent to American.

The company is family owned with a board of directors consisting of 40% membership outside the corporation. The executive committee is comprised of the president, executive vice-president of production, vice-president of marketing, and the controller.

1. Carefully examine the historical information on the mail-order firm. This firm will be used for illustration throughout this chapter. In the three principal categories of historical documentation, one finds the following information which reveals the managerial environment:

    (a) Growth statistics: From 1947 to 1964 sales grew from $_____

    to $_____; since 1965, sales grew _____%, from

    $_____ to $_____. (*Hint.* _____ × 2200% =
    $22 million)

    (b) Management pattern: the company is family owned, with execu-

    tive decisions made by how many persons? _____.

    (c) Expansion characteristics: Growth has been achieved primarily by which of the following:

    (1) New products _____

    (2) Merger _____

    (3) Acquisitions _____

2. The historical background on the mail-order firm provides the following managerial perspective, affecting the approach to design of a computer based information system for decision making:

    (a) Few decisions are made at the first line supervisory level; most

    decisions are made by _____

    (b) Marketing is a key activity for retail-oriented firms like this one. Marketing decisions are made at corporate headquarters.

    (True or False) _____ Explain your answer: _____

    (c) A managerial decision-making system for this company would, in

    all likelihood, have a centralized data base. (True or False) _____

    Why? _____

Gathering Data on the External Environment

The growth of a firm is constrained by the environment in which it operates. The firm may be competing in regional, national, or international markets. It may be a nonprofit organization or an agency in the local, state, or federal government. It may produce a product or may be a service organization.

Both industry and government regulations are considered in designing the management information system to meet the special characteristics of the organization.

As in the historical section of the System Survey, data on the external environment is recorded from the perspective of the management of the enterprise. Included are:

1. Industry background (total volume, constituency, share of market, demand curves, technological characteristics).
2. Industry regulations (trade agreements, labor practices).
3. Government regulations (monopoly and antitrust laws, labor laws, fair-employment laws).

QUESTION: The three categories of information in the documentation on external environment are: (1) _____,

(2) _____ and (3) _____.
ANSWER: (1) industry background, (2) industry regulations, and (3) government regulations.

An example of the external environment section of the System Survey Package is provided below, again using the mail-order firm.

External Environment — Looart Press, Inc.

The company has less than two percent of the total U.S. market in each of the three principal product areas: greeting cards, personalized and wedding stationery, and decorative wall posters. Foreign sales amount to less than 5 percent of total sales revenue in each product area.

Although there are trade associations for both the greeting card and stationery product areas, their effect on the market and producers is nominal. The primary effect of these associations is to sponsor trade shows for product display.

Companies are reluctant to share information in either marketing or design. The largest firm, Hallmark Cards, Inc., is not publicly held, so figures are not available as they are for firms which must publish an annual report to stockholders.

Looart has always maintained an open-door policy. Management's stated policy in this respect is that the firm can learn a great deal from its visitors — that each tour group provides market information as well as receiving company goodwill.

Special governmental regulations do not exist for the industry. General governmental regulations apply to Looart, such as interstate commerce and fair labor laws.

QUESTION: Would you say that the mail-order firm operates in a nonregulated or regulated industry? _____.
ANSWER: Nonregulated

There are very few legal or industry constraints on this firm that must be included in the system design. Banks, airlines, and utilities are organizations where government and industry regulations play an important role in design of information systems.

The discussion of regulations in the environment section of the report should answer three basic questions:[1]

1. Which government regulations help the company do business (for example, charters, tariffs, franchises, enabling acts, subsidies)?
2. Which restrict its business activities (for example, consent decrees, utility regulations, regulations on financial enterprises)?
3. Which affect its record-keeping activities?

Exercise 16–3

1. Referring to item one in the above list, give an example of how a government regulation, such as a charter, is beneficial to a company (e.g., telephone company is given sole rights to one geographic area).

_____

_____

_____

_____

_____

_____

2. Referring to item two in the list, give an example of how a government regulation restricts business activities (e.g., approval of the Federal Aviation Agency for an airline to add or to drop a feeder line to a small city).

_____

_____

_____

_____

_____

_____

[1]The list is taken from, Glans et al., _Management Systems_, Holt, Rinehart & Winston, New York, 1968, p. 54.

3. Referring to item three in the list, give an example of how a government regulation on record-keeping might affect a company (*Hint:* utilities must keep records on each customer for 50 years).

_____

_____

_____

Gathering Information on Company Objectives

Understanding of the historical perspective and the external environment enables the system team to have a better feel for the managerial task of the organization. Integration of systems is quite difficult without delineation of the objectives of the organization. In earlier years, when analysts were working solely on subsystems, relating subsystem objectives to the firm's objectives was rarely done.

In third generation systems approach, the company objectives are translated into system objectives. Subsystems are then designed to correlate with major system objectives.

QUESTION: In third generation systems approach, system objectives are developed within the framework of _____.
ANSWER: company objectives

An illustration of company objectives is provided for the mail-order firm, below.

Objectives for Looart Press, Inc.

1. *To achieve a strong, well balanced, well managed manufacturing and marketing enterprise, international in scope, and returning maximum benefits to customers, employees, shareholders, and the communities in which it operates.*

2. *To seek and develop opportunities for growth with particular emphasis in fields where the company might enjoy an advantageous position due to management or manufacturing skills.*

3. *To capitalize on change by entering new product areas or activities which may diversify, balance, and profitably strengthen the company's economic position. Diversification and growth may be accomplished both internally and through the acquisition of other companies, and shall be tempered with careful consideration of financial stability and in recognition of the danger of overextension.*

4. *To pursue our major business of designing and manufacturing both printed products for the consumer and related products which may be sold through direct mail and retail outlets.*

5. *To conduct systematic research and design programs that will assure leadership in bringing new and improved products to a constantly changing market.*

6. To build and maintain an organization to meet present and future needs by attracting personnel of competence and growth potential, maximizing this capability through carefully developed programs for on-the-job and personal growth.

7. To create a company environment of stable employment, fair pay, good working conditions, work satisfaction and good communications, toward realizing maximum contributions from employees at all levels.

QUESTION: After gathering and analyzing the list of objectives for the mail-order firm, the system analyst can deduce the following factors that affect approach to system design:

(a) _____ (True or False) The company plans to reduce its manufacturing activities.

(b) _____ (True or False) The company plans to concentrate on the domestic market.

(c) _____ (True or False) The company will continue to concentrate on printed and related products.

ANSWER: (a) False

Objective 2 states the opposite.

(b) False

Objective 1 states the objective to be "international in scope."

(c) True

Although management wants to diversify, it states in objective 4 that it will pursue its "major business of designing and manufacturing both printed products ... and related products ..."

Company objectives are translated to system design criteria for each of the major systems—for example, the marketing system has a subsystem (sales statistics) that is designed to provide information on performance against sales objectives. However, requirements for the design of that subsystem would also include the sales information needed as input to the financial reporting subsystem, which produces the income statement.

Figure 16–2 shows some of the interrelationships of systems and subsystems for Looart Press, Inc., using the third generation system approach. Whereas these subsystems were designed virtually independently in the 1960s, they are integrated today. The translation of company objectives to system and subsystem objectives is a major part of the system survey.

QUESTION: Examine Figure 16–2. The connecting lines show communication (sharing of information) between systems. For example, the market forecasting subsystem communications with the _____, _____, and _____ subsystems.

ANSWER: production planning, financial planning, and manpower planning

In addition to the overview chart shown in Figure 16–2, the System Survey would include subsystem interaction charts for each major area

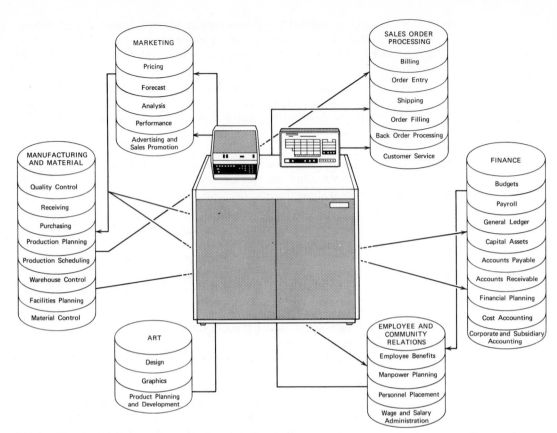

Figure 16-2. *Computer-based management information system for a mail-order firm. (Not all interrelationships are shown; if all lines of interaction were included, the illustration would appear to be a spiderweb.)*

of the firm. One for the Sales Order Processing system is shown in Figure 16-3. Two major inputs are the sales forecast and the customer order. Based on the sales forecast, production planning develops a production forecast and determines which items should be purchased and which should be manufactured. By the time the second major input, the customer order, is received, finished goods are available for order filling. The two levels of system integration charts, illustrated in Figures 16-2 and 16-3, are an essential part of the System Survey package. They show the systems presently used to implement company objectives.

QUESTION: Unfortunately, there are no standard symbols for depicting system/subsystem interrelationships. Typically an organization sets its own standard. In Figure 16-3, the eliptical symbol represents a function outside the company, in this case _____ and
_____.

ANSWER: customer and vendor (supplier)

QUESTION: Systems vary from company to company, or it would not be necessary to prepare the charts shown in Figures 16-2 and 16-3. For example, the Looart Press sales order processing system produces a "pick-

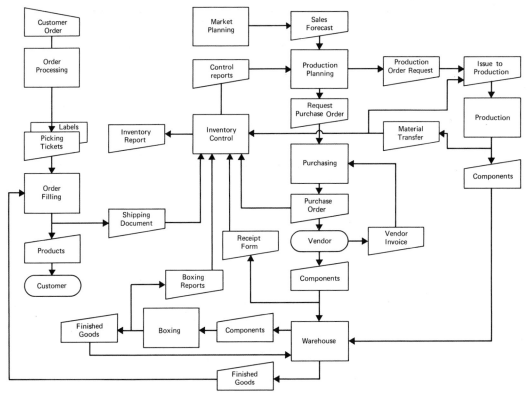

Figure 16–3. *Interrelationships of subsystems within the Sales Order Processing system, using mail-order firm as an illustration.*

ing ticket" to facilitate order filling. The customer order is not used to "pick" items but is transcribed on another form where the items are placed in the same sequence as the products in the order filling department. This information is important to the system designer because the task of sorting items and printing a picking ticket has good potential for

_____ processing.

ANSWER: computer

Gathering Information on Company Policies

Policies are guidelines for implementation of objectives. Policies are also statements of philosophy for management of the organization. By identification of policies during the System Survey, the CBMIS can be designed to support those policies. The following policies of the owners of the mail-order firm illustrate their philosophy of management.

Policies of Looart Press, Inc.

1. *People are the most important asset of the corporation. Their intelligence and ingenuity must not be wasted or neglected but allowed to grow in a creative and challenging environment.*

2. Customers are the lifeblood of the company and, within the bounds of prudent management, all available resources should be used to insure their satisfaction.

3. The company must be operated on a profitable basis. The corporation, as a legal and economic entity, is a risk-taking organization and profits are remuneration for risk taken.

4. The company must always operate within the confines of contemporary definition of taste and style.

Although policies 1, 2, and 3 may be similar to those of other organizations, policy 4 is unique. This means the company will not design cards or posters with a risque message. The policy greatly restrains the marketing activity of the firm. It also affects system design. Market research will determine what is "contemporary" style and taste. The marketing system must include techniques to sample statistically the market and to analyze the responses to maintain the standards for "taste and style."

Policy 1 states the emphasis on risk taking. Adherence to this policy without suffering losses necessitates a comprehensive accounting system and a responsive performance reporting system.

QUESTION: Using this same approach to analyzing the effect of policies on system design, examine policy 2. What must be designed into the marketing system to support the policy of customer satisfaction?

_____

_____

_____

_____ .

ANSWER: The system must provide for analysis of customer satisfaction. Waiting to see if customers reorder is the most expensive and risky approach to determining customer satisfaction. The sales order processing system could include a process for sampling of customers to obtain detailed information on customer opinions of the products as they use them. The samples could be designed for automatic computer processing and analysis to provide fast response to management

Exercise 16–4

1. What is the difference between an objective and a policy? _____

_____

_____

2. Why are objectives identified in the System Survey? _____

_____

_____

3. Why are policies included in the System Survey? _____

_____

The Master Plan

The objectives of the firm are usually quantified in its Master Plan. The Master Plan identifies the means by which the firm plans to achieve its objectives. The firm may seek to become much more capital intensive, thus drastically affecting the priority of development of subsystems. The financial subsystem would take priority over many of the labor-control subsystems for such an organization. An illustration of a Master Plan is provided in Figure 16–4. Although the items listed are appropriate for the mail-order firm, the figures are hypothetical, to protect the proprietary interests of Looart Press, Inc.

The organization's growth objective, for example, might be stated as follows: "to expand sales at a compounded rate of 10 percent annually" or "to maintain the existing share of the market." An approach to implement such objectives might be: "utilize the existing capability in the organization to expand the product line to be more competitive." A very different policy for meeting those objectives would be "to grow by acquisition of other companies in the same industry."

The difference in these two approaches has significant effect on the design of an information system.

Some data processing managers have found their CBMIS plan drastically affected by acquisitions and mergers. Mergers typically occur between companies of comparable size. On the other hand, a company typically "acquires" a smaller firm. Although it is rarely possible to anticipate the exact type of union, companies that list growth by merger or acquisition among their objectives need a more open-ended approach to CBMIS design. Companies that seek merger as the primary avenue to growth must also design their CBMIS to facilitate change.

As an illustration, we attended a presentation at a national meeting where system designers of a firm were complaining of changes necessitated by a merger. Yet the annual report of the firm clearly stated management's intention to seek mergers. Those designers were guilty of concentrating too much on the short-term system requirements instead of the needs reflected in the objectives of the firm.

QUESTION: A person who designs systems without regard to company objectives will likely find himself _____

_____.

ANSWER: changing the system soon after its implementation. (Perhaps you said "without a job, because the system didn't meet management's needs.")

Five-Year Master Plan (In 000's of Dollars)

	1976	1977	1978	1979	1980
SALES					
Current Products					
Fall Products	10,000	12,000	14,000	16,000	18,000
Spring Products	5,000	6,000	7,000	8,000	9,000
Christmas Products					
Personalized Cards	1,000	1,200	1,400	1,600	1,800
Solid Pack	300	350	400	450	500
Posters	650	700	750	800	850
Personalized Stationery	250	350	450	550	650
Wedding Announcements	580	1,000	1,500	2,000	2,500
Acquisition no. 2	2,000	2,200	2,400	2,600	2,800
Acquisition no. 3			2,000	2,200	2,400
Acquisition no. 4					2,000
TOTAL GROSS INCOME	19,600	23,800	29,900	34,200	40,500
EXPENSES					
Equipment Amortization	2,050	2,250	3,100	3,500	4,800
Equipment Purchase	1,280	2,600	3,000	4,000	3,450
Working Capital					
Accounts Receivable	2,750	3,070	4,000	4,400	5,220
Inventory	2,550	2,890	3,740	4,100	4,900
Other	370	415	540	590	700
Land Amortization	1,350	1,350	2,450	2,450	3,400
Land Down Payment	—	3,200	—	3,800	—
Acquisition Amortization	1,500	3,000	3,000	4,500	4,500
Acquisition Down Payment	5,000	—	5,000	—	5,000
Income Tax	1,400	1,735	1,870	2,060	2,830
TOTAL GROSS EXPENSES	18,250	20,500	26,700	29,400	34,800

Figure 16–4. *Specific objective as incorporated in a Master Plan, using mail-order firm as an illustration, with hypothetical figures.*

A company which plans growth by merger may be united with a firm that has its own computer and CBMIS. Special data processing needs arise from such situations, for example, the account number system problem. System designers who are aware of their company's merger objectives can design an account numbering system with great flexibility. Otherwise, they must design a translator, which converts the two accounting systems into some degree of compatibility for preparing financial reports.

A situation of that kind is considerably more complicated than one where a company plans growth by expansion of sales. For the latter, the accounting system is designed to handle new products—a less complex design than one which must correlate with another firm's accounting system.

QUESTION: The system analyst gathers information on the firm's objectives and the plan for implementing those objectives, because _____

ANSWER: the way those objectives are implemented affects the approach to system design

Referring to the Master Plan for the mail-order firm are provided in Figure 16–4. Note that the Master Plan identifies: (1) specific goals, (2) the resources required to attain those goals, and (3) a time-frame for use of resources.

QUESTION: What information is provided to the system analyst that was not available in prior documentation steps? _____

ANSWER: Time-frame information

Prior documentation included goals and resources, but did not put them into the perspective of specific product lines and levels of resource allocation by time period. Only the Master Plan provides that perspective.

How would the information in the Master Plan aid the system analyst? The Master Plan shows where the majority of resources are applied, as a potential for savings through computerization. It also shows which activities are constraints, in terms of the time available to perform them.

Exercise 16–5

1. The System Survey documents four major areas concerning the organization:

(a) _____

(b) _____

(c) _____

(d) _____

2. Why is the term "documentation" used for Phase I of the System Development Cycle?

_____

_____

_____

_____

_____

3. Is the main purpose for the system survey the gathering of data for determining feasibility? Explain your answer.

_____

_____

_____

_____

4. Another widely-used textbook does not identify the Master Plan as one of the documents to be included in the System Survey. Give two reasons for including the Master Plan.

(a) _____

_____

(b) _____

_____

Summary

The System Survey consolidates information about the company and the environment in which it operates. This phase of the system development process is more complex today than it was in the early days of computer use. The third generation system design approach concentrates on integration of the systems of the firm. The first generation design approach was suboptimal because it produced independent systems for interdependent activities.

Systems cannot produce optimal results unless the design undergirds the objectives of the organization. Therefore, the System Survey identifies the firm's objectives, in light of its environment. Company history is included because it provides perspective on present objectives and policies. Objectives and policies are identified as a basis for designing the computer-based management information system. The external, as well as the internal environment, is analyzed, to determine the inputs and outputs necessary to support the CBMIS. The Master Plan is the final part of the documentation phase of the System Survey – quantifying the organizational objectives.

The System Survey provides the data to determine how the set of company systems may be improved, the subject of the next chapter.

Solutions to Exercises

Exercise 16–1

1. (a) *Phase IV*. Programming – developed by programmer from procedure-oriented flowchart.
   (b) *Phase III*. Design – developed by system analyst for programmer.
   (c) *Phase IV*. Programming.
   (d) *Phase IV*. Programming.
   (e) *Phase V*. Implementation.
   (f) *Phase IV*. While programmers are preparing the program, system analysts are preparing user procedures.
   (g) *Phase IV*. Upon completion of the program, the programmer writes procedures on its use for the computer operators and data input personnel.

2. When designing systems for integration, that is, sharing information between systems, all the interfaces must be identified.

3. Systems were treated as entities when, in actuality, all areas of an organization are interrelated. A system should be designed to accept inputs compatible with other systems and to meet output requirements for all other systems that use information from that system.

4. False. In Phase I the analyst, in cooperation with representatives of the using organization, gather facts about the existing system. Requirements for an improved system are identified in Phase II, and the design of an improved system is Phase III.

Exercise 16–2

1. (a) From 1947 to 1964, $ zero to $1 million. Since 1965, sales grew 2200 percent, from $1 million to $22 million.
   (b) 4.
   (c) New products; the acquisition produces only 10% of the corporation's revenue.

2. (a) The executive committee.
   (b) True. The firm uses manufacturer's representatives instead of their own sales force. Marketing research and analysis is done by the corporate marketing group.
   (c) True. Except for the small subsidiary all managerial personnel are located at the corporate headquarters.

Exercise 16-3

1. Before another telephone company could operate in an area, it must have its charter approved by the Federal Communication Commission. This protects the existing telephone company because a long period of time is required to amortize its large investment in equipment and facilities.

2. Airlines and railroads cannot decide to add new routes or drop existing routes, based on the profit decision alone. Their applications for changes must be approved by the federal agencies.

3. Large resources might be required to store and maintain records. For example, a Texas based gas utility buries records to avoid building warehouses. Storage costs are low; however, access costs are rather high!

Exercise 16-4

1. Policies are guidelines for implementation of objectives.

2. The purpose of the CBMIS is to undergird managerial objectives; therefore, it is necessary to identify objectives in the System Survey. Objectives are translated into design criteria for each major system within the CBMIS.

3. Policies are statements of philosophy for management of the organization. By identification of policies the CBMIS can be designed to support those policies.

Exercise 16-5

1. (a) Company history.
   (b) External environment: industry background, government regulations.
   (c) Objectives and policies.
   (d) The Master Plan.

2. The system team gathers documents and information about the organization. It "documents" the system as it presently exists.

3. Yes. It also provides reasons for the way the company has evolved. It shows how the company met its environmental constraints and may shed light on the information needs of the future in meeting those as well as evolving environmental constraints.

4. (a) The Master Plan identifies the means by which a firm plans to achieve its objectives. The way those objectives are implemented affects the approach to system design.
   (b) The Master Plan identifies specific goals, resources required to attain those goals, and a time-frame for use of resources. Prior documentation included goals and resources but did not put them into the perspective of specific product lines.

Chapter Examination

1. Why is company history of value in designing a management information system for the future? Wouldn't it tend to force the system analyst to think in traditional ways?

_____

_____

_____

_____

2. What are the four categories of the documentation acquired in the System Survey?

(a) _____

(b) _____

(c) _____

(d) _____

3. What distinguishes Phase I from Phase II on the system development cycle?

_____

_____

_____

_____

4. (True or False). The System Survey and Phase I of the system development cycle are the same activity. _____

5. Describe the difference between policies and objectives.

_____

_____

_____

_____

6. The System Survey is a costly and time-consuming activity. Give three reasons for not bypassing it and going directly to Phase II of the system development cycle:

(a) _____

_____

(b) _____

_____

(c) _____

_____

7. Phase I consumes at least 9 percent more resources in third generation systems than Phase I activities for a first generation system. Give three reasons for this difference:

(a) _____

_____

(b) _____

_____

(c) _____

_____

8. What is meant by the expression "integration of systems?"

_____

_____

_____

_____

_____

9. What kinds of statistics are acquired for the portion of documentation on company history?

_____

_____

_____

10. How do such statistics affect the approach to system design?

_____

_____

_____

11. Give three reasons for gathering information on the environment in which an organization operates.

(a) _____

_____

(b) _____

_____

(c) _____

_____

12. Would the System Survey be required for developing systems for nonprofit organizations? Give your answer in consideration of the following organizations:

(a) A state college: _____

_____

_____

_____

(b) A state government agency, such as the motor vehicle department:

_____

_____

_____

_____

13. Would a System Survey be as valuable in a heavily regulated industry, such as the banking industry, as one with few regulations, such
as the mail-order business? Why?

_____

_____

_____

_____

14. How would a team be organized and what sources would be used in
collecting the data needed for the System Survey?

_____

_____

_____

_____

15. Examine the Five-Year Master Plan of the mail-order firm, shown in
Figure 16–4. What priorities in system development are suggested
in this firm's five-year projections?

_____

_____

_____

_____

16. Examine the documentation in the System Survey for the mail-order
firm.
(a) What would appear to be the most important contribution in its
rapid growth?

_____

_____

_____

_____

(b) What would appear to be the limiting factors in future growth?

_____

_____

_____

_____

(c) What effect, if any, on the data processing operation would be caused by the seasonal characteristics of this firm?

_____

_____

_____

_____

_____

17. Further examination of the documentation for the System Survey of the mail-order firm should reveal the areas that would have the greatest potential for computerization. What three areas appear to have that potential? Give your reasons. (Do a careful job on this question because this case will be expanded in subsequent chapters.)

System 1.

_____

_____

_____

_____

System 2.

_____

_____

_____

_____

System 3.

_____

_____

_____

_____

18. What effect on systems design would result from the following dif-
    ferences in objectives for an organization?
    (a) "The company plans a growth of 10 percent per year by improving
        quality and advertising on its one product line, lawnmowers."

    (b) "The company plans growth of 10 percent per year by expanding
        its line from lawnmowers to include related consumer products,
        including motorized hedge trimmers, lawn sprinkling systems,
        and fertilizers."

_____

_____

_____

_____

_____

19. On a separate sheet, demonstrate your understanding of the System
    Survey by preparing a schematic that records all of the documents
    gathered during the System Survey. Use Figure 21–11 as a model,
    showing the four major categories and the set of data supporting each
    category.

20. What skills should exist in the System Survey team, to insure the
    thoroughness and quality of the System Survey?

_____

_____

_____

Chapter 17

TECHNIQUES FOR ANALYSIS OF THE EXISTING SYSTEM

Overview

Phase I of the system development cycle consists of two parts: (1) The System Survey, and (2) Analysis of the System. The System Survey gathers information about the system and the environment in which it operates. System analysis is the delineation of resources required for proper operation of the system—personnel, equipment, materials, and facilities.

A system is defined as an activity consisting of input, processing, and output. A change must occur in the intermediate step—the processing—if the activity is to be classified as a system. For example, the activity of a secretary in receiving a letter from the mail carrier and passing it on to her boss does not comprise a system. This activity is just a step in the input phase of a system. Opening the envelope to enable the letter to be read is still a part of input. The reading of the letter is the process step. Taking action on the letter is the output step.

Analysis of complex systems is facilitated by use of special techniques for gathering and displaying information about the system. The System Survey provides information about the company and the environment in which it operates. It gives a managerial perspective to the system analyst, whose task is to identify sources and processes for producing the information needed for decision making.

However, System Survey documentation needs further breakdown to permit system analysis. This chapter discusses the techniques for organizing and studying the information obtained in the System Survey. The initial analysis is aimed at determining whether the existing manual system can be improved. However, the information is organized in such a manner that it can also be used to determine feasibility for conversion to computer processing.

Evolution of System Analysis Techniques

Although not as spectacular as the evolution of computer systems, there has been a refinement of systems analysis techniques over the years.

Although there is general agreement that three stages of computer hardware have evolved in the past two decades, the three stages of evolution in system analysis techniques are not as widely recognized. As a basis for better understanding of third generation techniques, the earlier generations are briefly described below.

Precomputer System Analysis Techniques

Process Flowchart. The process flowchart has been utilized since the early 1900s to portray physical flow of materials and products as shown in Figure 17–1a. Each symbol represents an activity or a delay in the flow: the circle represents an activity, the square an inspection, the arrow a transportation, the half circle a delay, and the triangle a temporary storage. When clerical operations began to expand, this technique was adapted to show the flow of paper. Figure 17–1b shows the revision of the process flowchart to handle clerical activities.

QUESTION: Examine Figure 17–1b. What delays occur in the operation of processing incoming mail and for how long? _____ .

ANSWER: Only one delay, step 14 – the mail is held until the messenger returns from his mail delivery route, an average delay of 30 minutes

Forms Flowchart. As paperwork processes began to be a problem, special key entry machines were introduced to automate other portions of the paperwork flow. Machines such as the Friden Flexowriter permitted capturing data on punched paper tape as a document was typed, to avoid rekeying this information at a later time.

For example, while typing a purchase order, the machine could simultaneously punch a paper tape with all the information that was common to every purchase order sent to that vendor, for example: name, address, terms, and shipping methods. The tape was rolled, rubber banded, and placed on a peg identified by vendor's name. The next time an order was placed, the tape was fed through the tape reader (attached to the typewriter) allowing the typist to enter only the variable data, such as, identification of the item, quantity, and unit cost. Figure 17–2 shows the forms flowchart used to depict those operations. It is easily recognizable as evolving from a physical product flowchart.

QUESTION: What is the primary difference in this variation of the process flowchart from the one shown in Figure 17–1b? _____

ANSWER: Organizations are identified for each activity performed. Another significant difference over the process chart is the emphasis on the flow of information (in forms) rather than the flow of materials

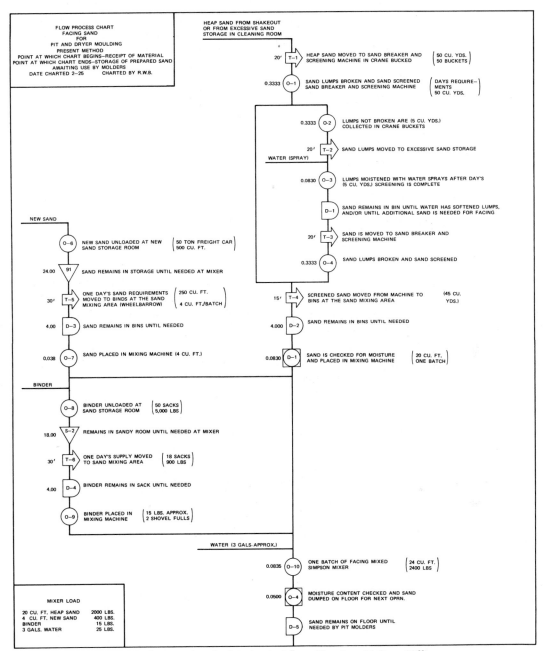

Figure 17–1a. *Process flowchart used to depict physical flow. (Courtesy McGraw-Hill).*

DETAILS OF (PRESENT/PROPOSED) METHOD	Step No.	Operation/Transport/Inspection/Delay/Storage	Distance in Feet	Time in Minutes	NOTES
		O⇨□D∇			
Messenger picks up mail from post office & places it at work table	1	O⇨□D∇	3B	25	Walks to post office (3 blocks away) with special cart
Clerk opens bag and dumps contents on table	2	●⇨□D∇			
Sorts mail into two categories	3	●⇨□D∇			
(1) General mail (company)		O⇨□D∇			
(2) Individually addressed mail		O⇨□D∇			
Time stamps envelope of individual mail	4	●⇨□D∇			Uses automatic date time stamp machine
Counts number of individual mail	5	●⇨□D∇			
Posts number in log book by date	6	●⇨□D∇			
Places individual mail in outgoing basket for sorting by department	7	●⇨□D∇			
Sorts general mail by size of envelope	8	●⇨□D∇			
Places in slicer for slicing edge	9	●⇨□D∇			Slicer on work table
Extracts contents, 1 envelope at a time, time stamps contents & staples to envelope	10	●⇨□D∇			If contents contains check, places aside for special handling
Rubber stamps routing stamp	11	●⇨□D∇			Use dept. routing stamp A
Reads contents & checks rating and places in outgoing basket	12	●⇨□D∇			
Delivers all "read" mail to department sorting	13	O●□D∇	20		
Holds mail until messenger returns from route	14	O⇨□D∇		30	Average time mail waits
Checks mail for time stamp (continued on next page)		O⇨■D∇			
		O⇨□D∇			
		O⇨□D∇			
		O⇨□D∇			

ACTIVITY CHARTED: PROCESSING INCOMING MAIL   CHARTED BY: JOHN SMITH   DATE: 1/16/67

ORGANIZATIONAL UNIT: MAIL DEPARTMENT   APPROVED BY: L J   DATE: 1/25/67

SUMMARY

ELIMINATE! COMBINE! SIMPLIFY! CHANGE SEQUENCE! IMPROVE!

	PRESENT		PROPOSED		DIFFERENCE	
	NO.	TIME	NO.	TIME	NO.	TIME
○ OPERATIONS						
⇨ TRANSPORTATIONS						
□ INSPECTIONS						
D DELAYS						
∇ STORAGES						
DISTANCE TRAVELED	FT.		FT.		FT.	

USE REVERSE SIDE FOR DRAWING IF REQUIRED.

PAGE 1 OF 2

Figure 17–1b. *Process flowchart used to depict clerical activity (courtesy McGraw-Hill).*

    Figure 17–2 illustrates the purchase order operation described above. In actuality, two punched paper tapes were automatically produced as the purchase order was typed. Follow the flow of the first tape, the "composite" tape. In the Receiving Department it is used to automatically prepare a Receiving Report. The second paper tape is called the "on order" tape. It goes to the data processing department and is used automatically to produce punched cards. Those cards eventually cause a report to be prepared.

QUESTION: What report? _____. What is the purpose of the report? _____.

ANSWER: The commitment and open order report, which show how much money is tied up (that is, committed) on purchase orders, and which of those orders have not been filled (that is, remain open)

Tabulating Operations Flowcharts. Widespread use of punched card machines occurred in the 1930s and the process flowchart was again modified to meet the special characteristics of punched card processing.

The left side of Figure 17–3 shows that, instead of one symbol to represent operations, several symbols were used:

Sorting, collating

Tabulating

Calculating

Punched card

Reproducing, gang punching

Output

In formal presentations to management, actual pictures of the machines were used, as is shown on the right side of Figure 17–3.

Punched card departments were called "tabulating" departments because the primary activity consisted of "tabulating" figures into reports. The printing machine was referred to as a tabulator. Today, punched card operations are more appropriately referred to as unit record operations, because the information concerning a single transaction is usually recorded in one card. Examine the left-hand side of Figure 17–3. The activity flowcharted is the payroll procedure. Notice that different machines were required for each step in the processing of payroll. Pick out the discrepancy in the following narrative description of the procedure, assuming that the flowchart depicts the correct procedure.

Payroll cards for each employee are sorted into employee number sequence and collated with the master payroll card for each employee. Descriptive data about the employee is reproduced from the master into the payroll card, which contains only the data concerning this pay period. The master cards are sorted out. Pay is calculated for each employee. A payroll report is then produced. The summary punch, attached to the accounting (tabulating) machine, simultaneously punches a summary card for each employee.

QUESTION: What is the discrepancy? _____

_____.

ANSWER: The summary card is for the entire payroll, not each employee. The data for each employee has been already punched and calculated in the steps prior to the accounting machine

Computer-Oriented System Analysis Techniques

Techniques for analysis of potential computer applications evolved from those used for key entry and tabulating operations. Once the study is made of the organization within its environmental context (the System Survey), the system analyst has the background to begin developing a set of requirements for the system, consistent with organization objectives. However, to develop the set of system requirements, the analyst needs techniques to analyze the System Survey data in more detail. Two levels of documentation are required, as is shown in Figure 17–4.

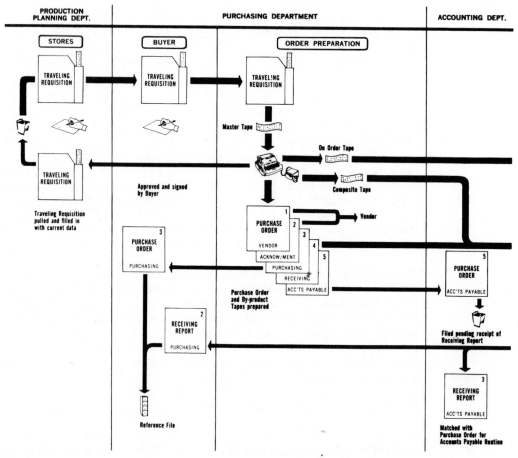

Figure 17-2. *Flowchart showing typical ADP Purchasing-Receiving system (courtesy Moore Business Forms, Inc).*

RECEIVING DEPARTMENT   MACHINE ACCOUNTING DEPARTMENT

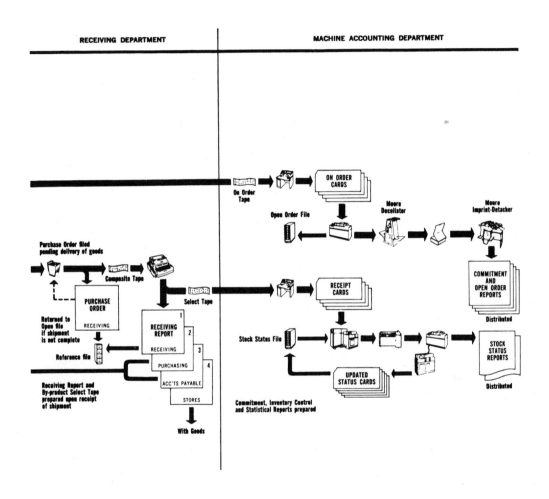

Job Accounting — Payroll Procedure

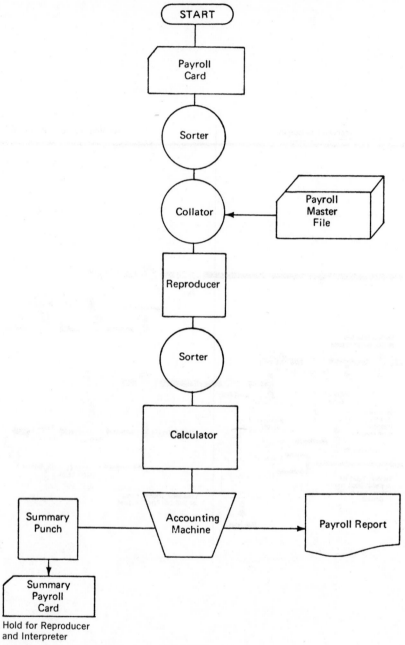

Figure 17–3. (a) Logical flow of operations.

ACTION UPON RELEASE OF SCHEDULE

When a schedule is released, a schedule card is punched for each type of model scheduled. This card is punched with model number and the quantity scheduled for each month. Step by step, the following procedure is used:

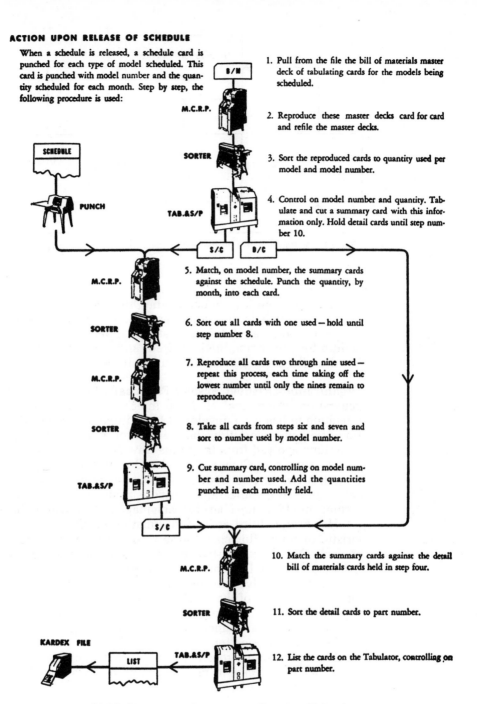

1. Pull from the file the bill of materials master deck of tabulating cards for the models being scheduled.

2. Reproduce these master decks card for card and refile the master decks.

3. Sort the reproduced cards to quantity used per model and model number.

4. Control on model number and quantity. Tabulate and cut a summary card with this information only. Hold detail cards until step number 10.

5. Match, on model number, the summary cards against the schedule. Punch the quantity, by month, into each card.

6. Sort out all cards with one used — hold until step number 8.

7. Reproduce all cards two through nine used — repeat this process, each time taking off the lowest number until only the nines remain to reproduce.

8. Take all cards from steps six and seven and sort to number used by model number.

9. Cut summary card, controlling on model number and number used. Add the quantities punched in each monthly field.

10. Match the summary cards against the detail bill of materials cards held in step four.

11. Sort the detail cards to part number.

12. List the cards on the Tabulator, controlling on part number.

(b) Machine processing sequence (courtesy Univac).

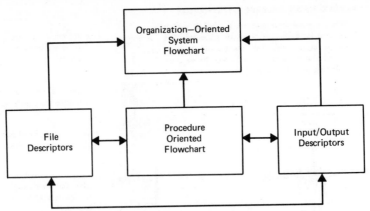

Figure 17-4. *Relationship of documents used for system analysis.*

The overview is provided by the Organization-Oriented System Flowchart. The detailed information required to analyze the system is provided in the second level of documentation: contents of input documents, procedure for processing, files utilized, and contents of output documents. We describe each of these documents in detail.

Organization-Oriented System Flowchart. Since the emphasis in third generation system analysis is on integration of systems within the firm, a technique has been developed to facilitate this analysis—the organization-oriented system flowchart. However, one easily recognizes that the technique evolved from the forms flowchart used in previous years.

As shown in Figure 17-5, the Organization-Oriented System flowchart has two characteristics in common with the forms flowchart: (1) delineation of organizational responsibility for each activity within the system, and (2) a flowchart for each major system within the organization.

However, a third area of information on this chart was not characteristic of forms flowcharts—the resource requirements. At the bottom of each O²S flowchart (we use this simplification for Organizational-Oriented System flowcharts) is shown the resources utilized in each organization involved in the system. The figures will not represent the total expenditures of that organization, but only that portion of expenditures involved in the system under study. Resources are identified in three categories: personnel, materials, and equipment.

With the information from such a chart, the analyst has a good basis for developing an improved system. He first analyzes the system to determine what improvements might be made, before any analysis to determine if the system will be computerized.

Factors to Examine in System Analysis

The analyst examines the O²S flowchart to isolate the following: (1) bottlenecks, or unnecessary delays in processing, (2) ways to reduce the amount of paperwork, (3) approaches to simplifying each activity, (4) high-cost activities, as high priority areas for further analysis.

The chapter examination contains four problems of this type, which require preparation of O²S flowcharts and analysis to develop an improved method. In preparation for that assignment, we will perform the same kind of analysis on the system depicted in Figure 17–5. This is the purchasing activity for the mail-order firm used as an illustration for the System Survey.

First, we must explain some additional flowcharting symbols that are required for organization-oriented flowcharts. The following symbols are added to the set established in Chapter 11.

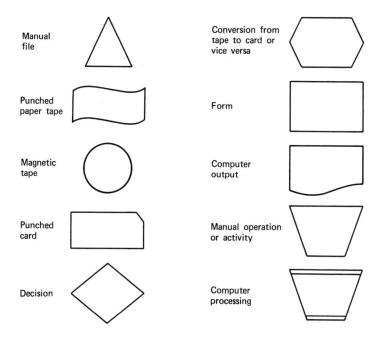

Now, examine the operations of the Receiving Department in Figure 17–5. Observe that copy 4 of the Purchase Order is filed there, awaiting receipt of the goods ordered. When the goods arrive, the Bill of Lading supplied by the Vendor is compared to the PO, to insure that all items ordered were delivered and in the correct quantities. A Receiving Report is prepared to notify all affected departments. The original is filed in the Receiving Department, along with Copy 4 of the Purchase Order.

However, Copy 2 of the Receiving Report is sent to the Buyer, where it is matched against Copy 3 of the PO filed there. Hence, we now have copies of the PO attached to copies of the Receiver, filed in two locations. The system analyst should question the need for duplicate files.

QUESTION: Which of the two files could be eliminated, in your opinion? _____. Explain: _____

_____.

ANSWER: Wouldn't the Buyer's file be sufficient? That is where most questions would be directed. Why not eliminate the file in the Receiving Department and have those personnel call the Buyer's secretary when any question arises concerning a completed order

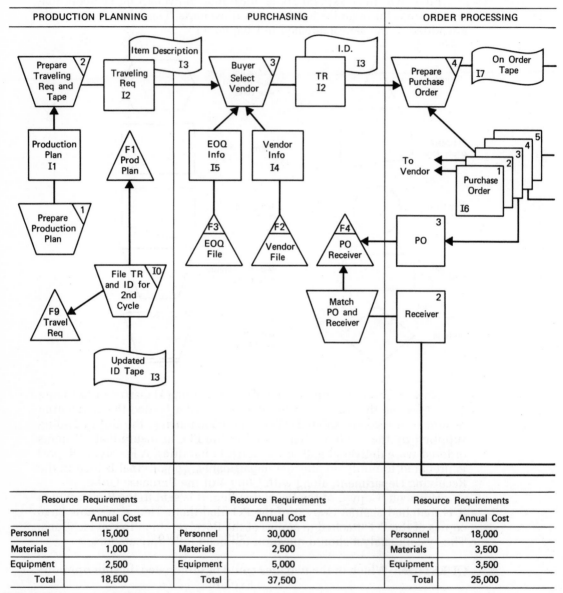

Figure 17–5. *System flowchart.*

SYSTEM

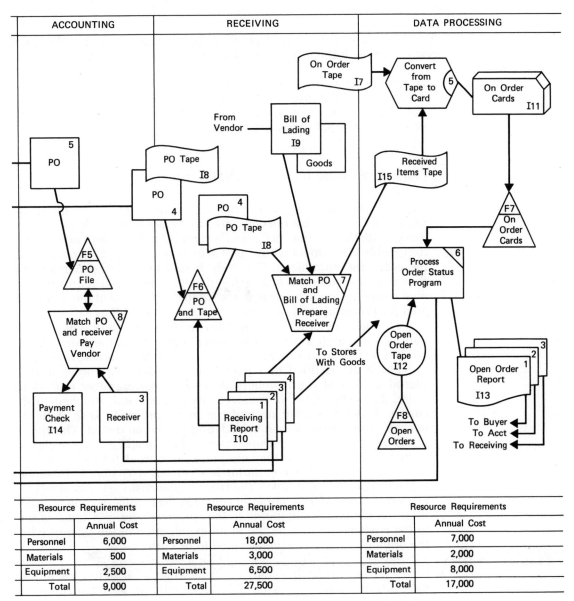

| ACCOUNTING | RECEIVING | DATA PROCESSING |

On Order Tape I7

Convert from Tape to Card 5

On Order Cards I11

From Vendor — Bill of Lading I9

Goods

Received Items Tape I15

5 PO

PO Tape I8

PO 4

PO 4

PO Tape I8

F7 On Order Cards

F5 PO File

F6 PO and Tape

Match PO and Bill of Lading Prepare Receiver 7

Process Order Status Program 6

Match PO and receiver Pay Vendor 8

To Stores With Goods

Open Order Tape I12

Open Order Report 1 2 3 I13

Payment Check I14

3 Receiver

Receiving Report I10 1 2 3 4

F8 Open Orders

To Buyer
To Acct
To Receiving

Resource Requirements			Resource Requirements			Resource Requirements	
	Annual Cost			Annual Cost			Annual Cost
Personnel	6,000		Personnel	18,000		Personnel	7,000
Materials	500		Materials	3,000		Materials	2,000
Equipment	2,500		Equipment	6,500		Equipment	8,000
Total	9,000		Total	27,500		Total	17,000

465 / FACTORS TO EXAMINE IN SYSTEM ANALYSIS

This example shows the advantages of the Organization-Oriented System flowchart in analyzing information flows. The following exercise will provide further experience in the use of this analytical device.

Exercise 17–1

The advantages of the Organization-Oriented System flowchart becomes apparent through the following exercise.

1. Develop an Organization-Oriented System flowchart from the narrative description of the procedure below. (Omit the resources section of the flowchart.) Compare your flowchart with the one at the end of the chapter, in the Solutions to Exercises.

Order Processing for a Mail-Order Firm

A clerk opens each envelope and dumps the contents on the work-table. Checks and cash are compared to the order, to see if the amount agrees with the customer's figure. Cash and checks are sent to Accounts Receivable. For orders whose payment is not received, two copies of the order are reproduced. One copy is sent to Customer Service and filed in case complaints arise. The other copy goes to Accounts Receivable where an invoice is typed and mailed. One copy of the invoice is filed for follow-up and another is sent to Customer Service.

The original order is forwarded to a second clerk who types a mailing label with a carbon and paper clips them to the order. Orders are batched in groups of 25 and forwarded to order processing.

The order is filled and packed in a carton. The order form is placed on top of the merchandise with a mailing label and blank order. The other label is removed, moistened, and attached to the carton. Paper is stuffed around the merchandise to keep it tightly packed. The carton is then sealed, and placed on a skid. The skid is transported to the Mail Department where packages are weighed, postage is attached, and they are placed in a truck for shipment.

When a customer complaint is received, it is sent to Customer Service. The company takes the word of the customer and sends the requested items. If the complaint concerns the invoice, a copy is pulled from the file and is compared to the customer's tally. A letter is sent to the customer with a refund or an explanation of the invoice when the original invoice was determined to be correct.

2. Now, review your flowchart to determine what activities appear unnecessary. You should be able to identify at least two unnecessary activities:

(a) ―――――――――――――――――――――――――

(b) _____

3. What activities might be reassigned to other organizations, to improve the system? At least one reassignment is feasible. Compare your ideas with the list provided in the Solutions to Exercises.

The Input/Output Descriptor. All information entering the system under study is identified on the Input/Output Descriptor. The same form is used to identify all information exiting from the system. Input is most often received on a form of some type. However, it may enter via some other media, such as the telephone or from an individual who comes by to provide some verbal input.

If the system is to be computerized, all input must be identified and described. Likewise, the information produced by an operation, whether verbal or written, must be quantified. The Input/Output Descriptor is the device used to record this information.

Another category of information exists. An activity may begin, not from an outside input, but according to a schedule. For example, in the system described for Exercise 17–1 invoices were filed. If they were filed by "due date," say 60 days from preparation date, unpaid invoices could be pulled from the file on the due date to send the follow-up invoice. We refer to such as activity as an *internally triggered* activity. An *externally triggered* activity is one where input is received from another organization.

An illustrative Input/Output Descriptor is shown in Figure 17–6. Notice that each source of input is identified, along with its frequency and volume. This information is essential in determining the cost to convert input media to computer media. Verbal messages are also identified with this form. While a verbal message can be readily received by a human, it must be converted to some physical medium for computer input.

Each item of input or output is tied to the O²S Flowchart by the I/O number. Look back at Figure 17–5 and locate input I6.

QUESTION: Input I6 is the _____ _____
prepared in _____ copies.
ANSWER: purchase order, 5

There was not enough space on the O²S Flowchart to list all the important descriptive material concerning I6. The I/O Descriptor, therefore, is the second documentation level. It provides the system analyst detailed information on each item of input or output.

Another category of information is required for the analyst to complete the analysis of input and output. Alphabetic information requires

467 / FACTORS TO EXAMINE IN SYSTEM ANALYSIS

computer representation that is different from straight numeric information. To determine costs of converting data to computer media, the analyst must know the precise characteristics of the data. Figure 17–6 shows that each field of information is identified according to its alpha and numeric characteristics.

QUESTION: Examine Figure 17–6. What additional information is provided which has not yet been discussed? _____

_____

_____

_____

ANSWER: The number of characters of information, which enables the analyst to determine message sizes for comparison of cost and speed of various input media to the computer

QUESTION: Referring to Chapter 7, what types of computer input media might be used: (1) _____ (2) _____
(3) _____ (4) _____ (5) _____
ANSWER: Punched cards, punched paper tape, magnetic tape, keyboard coupled to computer, magnetic disk, magnetic strip, and the like

QUESTION: In Figure 17–6, "Source" refers to the document or organization where the data originated. For example, information for the field "item address" came from the _____.
ANSWER: traveling requisition

Exercise 17–2

Examine the Input/Output Descriptor (Figure 17–6) and answer the following questions:

1. (a) In the section on "Method of Preparation," we learn which data is obtained from the previously prepared punched paper tape. In

general, that information is _____

_____

_____

(b) In the Order Processing Department additional information is keyed into a paper tape, as a by-product of typing the Purchase

Order. In general, that information is _____

_____

_____

	INPUT/OUTPUT DESCRIPTOR			

I/O Identifier		I/O No.	
	Purchase Order		16

Originator		Media		Frequency
	Order Processing Department	Preprinted Form		As Required

Description	Prepared from two sources: (1) traveling requisition, which contains the description of the items to be ordered, and (2) the vendor selection sheet, which contains the information on the vendor.
Method of Preparation	Item description is captured in punched paper tape, as a by-product of the production order. Tape is inserted in Flexowriter to prepare heading and item description. Vendor information is then input through the keyboard.
Disposition	Five copies are distributed: two to vendor, one each to Receiving and Accounting, and one copy is retained in the PO file.

CONTENTS

Data No.	Data Name	Frequency	No. of Characters	Type	Source
1	Purchase Order Number	1	6	N	Buyer
2	Purchase Order Date	1	6	N	Order Proc
3	Vendor Name	1	25 Max	A/N	Vendor Sheet
4	Vendor Address	1	50 Max	A/N	Vendor Sheet
5	Item Address	3	8	N	Travel Req
6	Item Name	3	25 Max	A/N	Travel Req
7	Specifications	3	100 Max	A/N	Travel Req
8	Quantity Ordered	3	6	N	Travel Req
9	Unit Price	3	10	N	Vendor Sheet
10	Requested Delivery Date	3	6	N	Travel Req
11	Total Order Price	1	15	N	Order Proc
	Total		567		

Date	Analyst	User Rep
4-1-74	K. Siler	J. Emery

Figure 17–6. *Input/Output Descriptor used to provide detailed information for each system input and output.*

2. The specific data on the input form are listed in the "Contents" section.
   (a) How many total characters of information are contained (maximum) on the typical Purchase Order? _____

(b) Since alphabetic characters require different handling in computer processing, determine how many characters are alphanumeric

(A/N) at the maximum? _____

3. The column headed "Source" enables the analyst to trace a data element back to its originator. From the standpoint of integration of a system, why is this information important? (Use data items 3 and 4 as a basis for your answer.) _____

_____

_____

_____

The File Descriptor. In the precomputer era, systems and procedures specialists concentrated on simplification of operations. They also sought to reduce the number of copies of documents, to cut down on filing space and equipment. Computer system analysts also seek to reduce file space. However, the need is much more imperative in the computer era, because of the high cost of storage media. Computer files are maintained on media that can communicate directly with a computer and are many times more expensive than filing cabinets.

The system analyst searches for ways to combine files. To facilitate this analysis, he prepares the File Descriptor, Figure 17–7. Again, each file is keyed to the Organizational-Oriented System flowchart for continuity in analysis. The first file identified in Figure 17–5 is the Production Plan, file F1.

QUESTION: Examine Figure 17–5 and circle all files. How many files in total? _____.

ANSWER: Nine. Three files are used to store copies of purchase orders: F4, F5, and F6

The design of a computerized purchase order system must provide means for these three departments to have access to the information previously contained on their copy of the purchase order. Or, the analyst may develop a logical design that computerizes one or more of the functions in these departments, eliminating the need for access to the purchase order file.

For example, the Receiving Department pulls its copy of the PO when an item is received on the dock to compare with the Bill of Lading. On completion of that inspection, the Receiving Report is prepared. It verifies that the vendor supplied all items, or it initiates action when there is a discrepancy between the PO and the Bill of Lading.

Assume an approach is devised to computerize the PO system. A terminal is placed at the dock. When an item arrives, the receiving clerk keys in a PO number to the computer and the PO is displayed on a CRT connected to the terminal. Also keyed are the results of comparing the CRT record to the Bill of Lading. The PO file is immediately updated without paper handling. Therefore it is not necessary to keep a copy of the PO filed in the Receiving Department.

Thus, the purpose of the File Descriptor is to provide in-depth infor-

FILE DESCRIPTOR				

File Identifier

Purchase Order/Receiver

File No.

F4

Location

Buying Department

Media

Preprinted Forms

Description

Copy of P.O. filed in open order file until receiver arrives. The two are then stapled, placed in a folder, and transferred to the inactive section of the same file.

Access Requirements

Within 1 minute when Buyer is called concerning status of order

Sequence

By Purchase Order Number

Retention Requirements

Until product is discontinued; then transferred to historical records file

Frequency of Updating

Within 2 hours of arrival of P.O. and Receiver in department

CONTENTS

Data No.	Data Name	Quantity in File	Characters Per Input	Characters per File	
				Average	Peak
	File contains copy of each P.O. and each Receiver. Refer to Input/Output Descriptors for identification of data on those forms (I6 and I10)				
12	Open Orders	230	760	175,000	250,000
13	Inactive Orders	6500	760	46,000,000	60,000,000

Date

5-12-74

Analyst

R. Sprague

User Rep

H. Morgan

Figure 17–7. *The File Descripter, used to provide detailed information for each file in the system, whether or not computerized.*

mation about the contents of each file, to facilitate combination of files through computerization.

To prove this point, perform some system analysis of your own through answering several questions. Examine Figure 17–5 and circle the four files that contain PO and Receiver copies. If this information can be placed on a computer file and can be accessed by terminals, in each department, the manual files can be eliminated.

QUESTION: What are the four files? _____

_____

_____.

ANSWER: PO/Receiver files are in Purchasing, Accounting, Receiving, and the Open Order card file in Data Processing

Although the space required for manual files is costly, the significant factor for cost reduction is paper handling. Another significant saving is the delay time in updating files. Notice in Figure 17–7 that each department has several hours of delay time in updating files. If the PO is entered to the computer by the Buyer's secretary, the system is up to date for *all* departments who have access through terminals.

Examine Figure 17–7. If information were transferred from the PO and Receiver to a card and only the card retained in the file, the Contents section would describe the data elements on that card. For example, the first entry in the Contents section would be the following.

CONTENTS					
				Characters in File	
Data No.	Data Name	Quantity in File	Characters per Input	Average	Peak
1	P.O. Number	850	6	4000	6000

QUESTION: Compare this entry with the one for the PO number on the I/O Descriptor (Figure 17–6). What additional information is provided in the File Descriptor?

_____

_____

ANSWER: The total volume of data involved in storing all purchase order numbers. Therefore, the File Descriptor identifies storage requirements for an entire file not just an individual form or document.

Exercise 17–3

The following questions refer to the File Descriptor (Figure 17–7)

1. The section on "Access Requirements" shows that the demand for access must be met in _____ minutes because the Buyer (or his secretary) must respond while the inquirer is on the phone. The O²S flowchart shows that questions concerning the delivery date do not require access to this file. Why? _____

_____

_____

2. Why is the "Retention Factor" of significance to the system analyst?

_____

_____

_____

3. The "Frequency of Updating" has what significance for computer processing of the file? _____

_____

_____

Procedure-Oriented Flowcharts

As defined earlier, a system exists if the following occur: input, processing, and output. The O²S flowcharts depict the major systems of the company. There may be a dozen or more of these charts to cover these systems. For example, a typical bank system would include the demand deposit accounting system, savings system, installment loan system, and commercial loan system.

To provide the complete set of information needed for a system analysis, the O²S flowcharts must be subdivided into Procedure-Oriented flowcharts (Figure 17–8). One can readily recognize that Procedure-Oriented flowcharts evolved from the Tabulating flowchart (Figure 17–3). However, the Procedure-Oriented flowchart also provides a narrative description of the procedure, so a user can examine and verify it. The

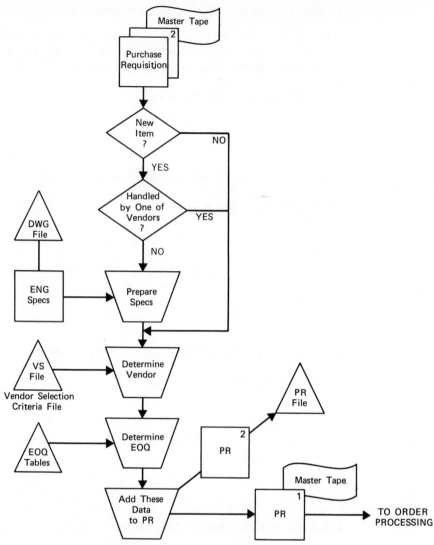

Figure 17–8. *Procedure-Oriented flowchart buyer operation.*

symbols used in the Procedure-Oriented flowchart differ from those in Figure 17–3. They now conform to the symbols of the American National Standards Institute (ANSI) to enable exchange of systems documentation between organizations.

In Chapter 11 two levels of flowcharting are covered. Procedure-Oriented flowcharts use the terminology of the task to be computerized.

In an inventory problem a procedure-oriented decision might be stated as follows:

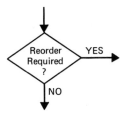

The logic must be more detailed for the task of programming. A Programmer-Oriented flowchart for the same application might be as follows:

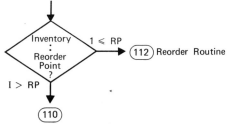

Evaluate Next Inventory Item

The second chart is program oriented because it identifies a quantitative comparison that the programmer can translate to decision criteria for computer processing; it is shown in FORTRAN as follows:

IF (INV.LE.ORDPT) GO TO 112

However, the system analyst must verify the logic of his system with the user of the system, in this instance, the buyer. A Procedure-Oriented flowchart is prepared, using the terminology of the buying procedure. Figure 17–8 depicts this procedure. It also contains a brief narrative description of the operation. Once the logic of the procedure is agreed on by the buyer and the system analyst, the chart can be detailed into Programmer-Oriented flowcharts, to facilitate coding.

QUESTION: In your opinion who should perform the task of preparing Programmer-Oriented flowcharts? _____ Why? _____

_____ .

ANSWER: In most organizations, the programmer prepares these charts. Sometimes a senior programmer prepares them, then breaks the system into modules and assigns them to several programmers. The system analyst must make certain that Procedure-Oriented flowcharts provide all the information necessary to develop Programmer-Oriented flowcharts

Exercise 17-4

Compare the O²S flowchart (Figure 17–5) with the Procedure-Oriented flowchart (Figure 17–8). To make certain you understand the relationship of these two charts, list the differences provided on each.

Comparison of Information Provided

Organization-Oriented Flowchart	Procedure-Oriented Flowchart
1. (e.g.) General flow of information through each organization	1. (e.g.) Detailed flow of information for one activity
2. _____	2. _____
3. _____	3. _____

Summary

While Chapter 16 covered the System Survey, this chapter describes the analysis of the system and the environment in which it operates. The System Survey concentrates on all major systems for the firm. In-depth analysis of each major system determines if the system can be improved. The analysis is computer-independent. That is, the analyst looks for ways to improve the system irrespective of whether the system is to be computerized. However, information about the system is portrayed in a manner to permit improvement analysis of all types: manual improvement, semiautomated improvement, and automated improvements.

Two levels of information portrayal are used:

Level I	Organization-Oriented Flowcharts
Level II	Input/Outout Descriptors
	File Descriptors
	Procedure-Oriented Flowcharts

All data pertinent to improving the flow of information through the major system are available on these charts. Analysis of system documentation provides the basis for the logical system design that is described in the next chapter.

Solutions to Exercises

Exercise 17–1

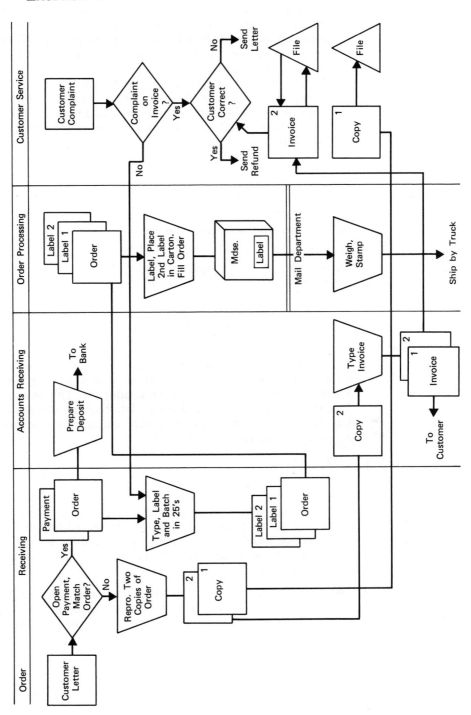

2. Unnecessary activities:
   (a) *Reproducing two copies of order.* Customer Service can use its copy only to verify quantity of items ordered against customer complaint. There is no assurance that order filling sent all the items or that the Post Office got the package to the customer.
   (b) *Sending customer complaints on invoices to Customer Service.* When a customer complaint concerns the invoice, it should be routed to Accounts Receivable where records of payment are maintained. Therefore, Customer Service does not need a copy of the invoice, eliminating one file.
   (c) *Typing two labels.* Although the second label comes at no cost except for materials, it must be handled in shipping. A study should be made to determine the percentage of these labels that are actually used by customers. Many will be discarded or lost, or addresses will be changed.

Exercise 17–2

1. (a) Description of each item to be ordered.
   (b) Information concerning the vendor.

2. (a) 567
   (b)

Data No.	*Characters*
3	25
4	50
6	$25 \times 3 = 75$
7	$100 \times 3 = 300$
	450

3. If the Vendor File were converted to computer media, the Vendor information on the PO would not require key entry. Data elements 3 and 4 could be pulled from the vendor file. This is more important from an accuracy standpoint than a labor-saving standpoint. By entering data at its source and thereafter using only that original entry, accuracy can be better controlled.

Exercise 17–3

1. (a) One minute.
   (b) An "open order" report is prepared by data processing and is sent to the Buyer. It lists all unfilled orders. Although O²S flowchart does not provide the contents of this report, we can assume that it contains, as a minimum, the PO number, need date and promised delivery date.

2. The retention factor is one factor determining file size. The file may be so huge as to be infeasible for conversion to on-line media, such as a disk file. It may require magnetic tape, an off-line medium, to economically contain the file.

3. The present file is updated within 2 hours of receipt of the PO or Receiver. Added to that delay is the flow time from the originating department. The analyst must determine what advantages might result from storing the file on computer media. If the Receiver were sent through Keypunch it could be processed in 2 hours, as under the manual system. However, there is no flow time for the PO since it is prepared in that department. Therefore, unless input of the PO is on-line, through a terminal in the Buyer's area, updating would be slower through a computer file.

Exercise 17–4

O^2S Flowcharts	Procedure-Oriented Flowcharts
1. General flow of information through each organization	1. Detailed flow of information for one activity
2. Cost by organization	2. Brief narrative description
3. Depicts interrelationship of all activities involved in a major company system	3. Delineation of steps as an operation or decision in a subsystem

Chapter Examination

1. What does the abbreviation O^2S represent? _____

2. Trace the evolution of the Organization-Oriented System flowchart.

It evolved directly from the _____ which evolved

from the _____.

3. What information is provided on the O^2S flowchart that is not available on the charts depicted in Figure 17–1?

(a) _____

(b) _____

(c) _____

4. What information does the O²S flowchart provide that is not provided in the System Survey? _____

_____

_____

5. Draw a diagram that shows the relationship of the documents in the System Survey and the documents required for detailed system analysis described in this chapter.

6. What information is provided in the Input/Output Descriptor that is not available on the O²S flowchart? _____

_____

_____

_____

7. What information is provided in the File Descriptor that is not available on the O²S flowchart? _____

_____

_____

_____

8. What is shown in the O²S flowchart that can not be seen in the I/O Descriptors and File Descriptors? _____

_____

_____

_____

9. What kinds of improvements is the system analyst seeking in the analysis of the O²S flowcharts?

(a) _____

(b) _____

(c) _____

(d) _____

10. How does the I/O Descriptor aid the analyst in deciding whether an operation should be computerized? _____

_____

_____

_____

_____

481 / CHAPTER EXAMINATION

11. How does the File Descriptor aid the analyst in deciding whether an

operation could be computerized? _____

_____

_____

_____

12. What are the four factors to isolate in examining systems for possible improvement?

(a) _____

(b) _____

(c) _____

(d) _____

13. Prepare an O²S flowchart for the following system, to analyze for improvements (like Exercise 17–1). Be thorough because you will be working with the same problem in the following chapter, developing the logical system design.

Student Records System

Applicant sends two copies of his transcript, along with his application, to the Admissions Office. There the high school or prior college grades are compared to the admission standard. The results of the College Board examinations are also analyzed against the admission standard. Rejected applicants are notified by letter, as are those accepted. One copy of each transcript and the application are retained in Admissions, the permanent student file. A second copy of each is forwarded to the department where the applicant plans to major. There a degree plan is prepared, showing credits earned toward degree requirements. One copy is sent to the student; one is retained in the permanent file for that department. A third copy is sent to the Student Adviser who sets an appointment with the student each semester to prepare class schedules. The adviser updates his copy of the degree plan each semester when grades are received. Faculty prepare grade slips in triplicate: (1) to Admissions, (2) to Department, and (3) to Adviser. The student learns his grade from a list posted on the doors of faculty offices. In his final semester the student completes an application for the degree. The application is sent to the Head of the Department who approves it and forwards it to his secretary. Copies go to Admissions, Department File, and the Adviser. Admissions prepares the degree when the final grade slips are received.

14. Prepare an O²S flowchart for the following system, to analyze for improvements (like Exercise 17–1). Be thorough because you will be working with the same problem in the following chapter, developing the logical system design.

Checking Account System

The customer applies for an account, is issued checks and an account number. Checks are forwarded to the bank by the payee. A Bookkeeping Department clerk posts the withdrawal to the customer account sheet. Deposits are entered on the same record. Once per month the account sheet is reproduced; one copy is sent to the customer unless it is a joint account when a copy is made for each party. Monthly summaries for all accounts are forwarded to the president who compares checking account totals to balances in other systems (e.g., personal loan, savings, and commercial loan). He requests funds from the Federal Reserve system as needed and is provided funds in proportion to his deposit level and reserves.

15. Prepare an O²S flowchart for the following system, to analyze for improvements (like Exercise 17–1). Be thorough because you will be working with the same problem in the following chapter, developing the logical system design.

Department Store Accounting System

The store accepts credit with customers who pass the Credit Bureau check. Purchases are made in cash, check, the store's credit card, or a Master Charge credit card. A sales slip is prepared for each charge sale with a copy going to Bookkeeping. Bookkeeping prepares listings and sends to Master Charge for reimbursement. Customer records are kept on an account ledger and monthly statements are typed and mailed. The store has a line of credit with the bank and draws on this each month as needed.

16. Prepare an O²S flowchart for the following system, to analyze for improvements (like Exercise 17–1). Be thorough because you will be working with the same problem in the following chapter, developing the logical system design.

Production Control System

Production planning prepares a list of materials required to produce the product, a kitchen blender. The Make-or-Buy department analyzes the list to determine which materials should be purchased. Two reports are produced—one is sent to Purchasing, the other to Production Control. In the Production Control department, the production package is prepared: schedule, raw materials requirement list, facilities loading plan. Cards are key punched for each of these documents. Material requirements cards are entered to update the inventory system. Facilities loading cards are input to allocate specific machines. Schedule cards are input to the computer system as a basis of production control. A duplicate set of schedule cards accompany the job through production. As each activity is completed, the pre-punched card for that activity is sent to the computer and entered to the system to identify progress. A daily report is provided to the Production Control department; copies go to the supervisors of each production department to enable them to determine their potential workload.

17. Convert Figure 17–2 to an O²S flowchart. Omit the Resource Requirements section, since that information is not provided.

18. Analyze the O²S flowchart prepared in question 13 and suggest improvements using the list of factors for investigation described in the chapter.

_____

_____

_____

19. Examine Figure 17–1b and determine potential improvements for the activity depicted there.

_____

_____

_____

20. Phase I of the System Development process consists of two steps: System Survey, and Analysis of the Existing System. List three activities performed in each of these steps.

System Survey	Analysis of the System
(a) _____	_____
(b) _____	_____
(c) _____	_____

Chapter 18

LOGICAL SYSTEM DESIGN

Overview

Phase I of the system development process concentrated on documenting and analyzing the existing systems of the organization. Phase II concentrates on development of improved systems, and is concerned with logical system design. Logical system design is essentially hardware independent. The system analyst works with the user, or his representative, to define precisely what the system is intended to perform. The result of logical system design is a set of specifications for physical system design.

The logical system design consists of four components: output specifications, processing specifications, decision logic, and input specifications.

Formal techniques have been developed for each of these four areas of specification. Programmer-oriented flowcharts, with supporting narrative descriptions, are used to record processing specifications. Decision logic tables are used to specify those decisions to be performed within the system. Input/Output Descriptor forms are used to specify input and output.

The procedures and techniques for preparing specifications are described and demonstrated in the pages that follow.

Logical versus Physical Design

Phase II of the system development cycle produces the logical design of the new system: the specification for input and output of the system along with the decision criteria and processing rules. Phase III, the physical design phase, determines the organization of files and the devices to be used.

Logical and physical design are distinct functions, although the same person may perform both tasks. Typically, the functions are performed by different persons because the scope and skill requirement in each function justifies specialization. However, as a reminder that some firms combine the two functions, the term analyst/designer will be used occasionally to indicate when the combined tasks are performed (e.g., the user representative, analyst/designer team develops data for feasibility analysis).

QUESTION: Would layout of a computer output (report) be the task of system analysis or of system design? Explain. _____

_____

_____

ANSWER: Specifying contents of the report would be accomplished by the analyst. Formatting the report would be accomplished by the designer, since a specific device is involved

Levels of Sophistication in Design

Often it is necessary to implement the system in several stages, not only for economic reasons but also because of organizational impact. People within the organization need to develop an attitude toward an understanding of the advantage of computer use. A revolutionary instead of an evolutionary change in the organization's system may have a detrimental rather than a positive effect on the employees. Their ability to blend effectively into a synergistic man/computer environment depends on their capacity for change. The behavioralists' studies have shown that such an environment is reached through meticulous training and careful planning for the system to meet the job satisfaction needs of the individual. The clash between human needs and an individual's perception are discussed in Chapter 2. Designing a system to be implemented in stages reduces the impact on the individual.

For explanation purposes, four levels of sophistication in system design will be considered.

Level 1   Basic Mechanization of Subsystems
Level 2   Combining Subsystems
Level 3   Utilization of the Management Science Techniques
Level 4   Integration and Optimization of Systems

A graphic illustration of developing a system in stages is provided in Figure 18–1. In this example one level of sophistication was achieved in each stage. In reality, several levels of sophistication might be designed into one stage. However, such an approach would lengthen the design process considerably or would require a large amount of resources. Also, as mentioned above, the impact on the organization would be significant. The firm may be in a competitive situation which requires the telescoping of levels of systems design sophistication. For example, an airline may find it imperative to combine all four levels of sophistication into one stage to meet the competition of other airlines that began computer use much earlier. Risk is associated with the telescoping of levels of sophistication. Considerable advantage accrues to the company that implements its system in stages. Its employees gain experience with each successive stage. They are able to contribute more to the design of each succeeding level of sophistication.

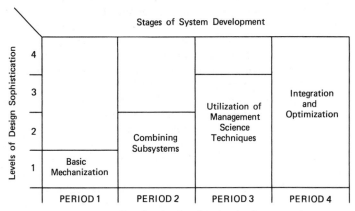

Figure 18–1. *Designing four levels of sophistication in successive stages of development.*

Table 18–1 provides a narrative description of levels of sophistication achieved in the design of an inventory system. Read that description and reinforce your understanding of this important design concept by the following exercise.

TABLE 18–1
Levels of Sophistication in System Design

LEVEL 1. A mechanized system is designed to replace the manual inventory system. Reports on inventory levels for each item are printed and distributed to each affected organization, resulting in elimination of a variety of inventory forms and records. The system standardizes the documents used for recording inventory transactions and automatically schedules cyclical physical inventory audits. Since the inventory file is maintained on punched cards, a variety of reports can be prepared, such as dollar commitment per inventory category or per vendor. Simplification of the manual system and use of a common system among all organizations permit personnel to initiate procurement actions more quickly and more accurately, resulting in reduced inventory levels and reduced costs.

LEVEL 2. The system is expanded to provide for keypunching of all requirements. Cards are also punched for the transactions involved in ordering, receiving, and maintaining inventory. These cards accompany the flow of inventory paperwork, and one is returned to data processing as each transaction is completed. The inventory, maintained on magnetic tape or magnetic disk file, is updated through periodic processing of the transaction cards. Reports are prepared for the material analysts to use in updating inventory ledger cards. Discrepancies between physical and financial inventories are printed, facilitating reconciliation of the two systems. Reports on the value of inventory and inventory item levels are automatically produced when they exceed specified levels. Expediting reports are prepared for materials behind schedule. Prepunched transaction cards are automatically prepared as a by-product of data processing, to be used for the next ordering cycle. An editing routine is incorporated in the program, to increase reliability. The net effect of increased scope and sophistication is a more reliable, more responsive system that permits further reduction of inventory costs and fewer delays in manufacturing.

LEVEL 3. The system is expanded to include the "A-B-C" approach to item classification, permitting variable levels of control corresponding to the value of the
item. An economic order quantity formula is incorporated to reduce the costs
of carrying inventory and costs of ordering. The program includes the capability
to alter the formula to handle the effects of quantity discounts, price changes,
production stoppages due to inventory shortages, lost sales due to shortages in
finished goods inventory, and rush orders or back orders. Lead times are developed and incorporated to calculate reorder points in conjunction with Economic
Order Quantity (EOQ) determination. The system is refined to print inventory
ledgers during the evening shift for delivery to material analysts each morning.
This eliminates manual transcribing from printed reports to the ledger cards and
permits faster reaction to changes in item usage. Since inventory levels are not
determined intuitively, but according to the techniques of the management
sciences, inventory costs are further reduced and items are procured closer to
the time of need.

LEVEL 4. The Requirements, Material, and Financial Inventory systems are
integrated. Requirements are punched once then are shared among the subsystems, eliminating separate input and justifying expanded editing. The flow
of inventory paperwork is replaced by remote data collection devices that permit electrical transmission of transactions to the computer. Probabilistic models
are incorporated to handle variations in demand, usage rates, delivery rates,
lead times, and prices. Purchase orders are printed automatically when the
need for procurement is determined by EOQ and reorder point analyses. Material analysts are no longer needed. A vendor evaluation subsystem is incorporated to permit automatic vendor selection. Reports are prepared on an
exception basis, since analyses previously performed manually are now performed by the computer. Remote inquiry units allow all affected personnel to
obtain inventory status as needed. Buyers, freed of paperwork, can concentrate
on the search for new materials, better vendors, and negotiation of improved
contracts. Supervisors, freed from the burden of paperwork, can spend more
time on planning and employee motivation. Integration of the three systems
eliminates the need for three separate organizations, reducing labor costs.
Concise and timely information is produced for each level of management for
optimum execution of its functional objectives.

Exercise 18-1

1. In Sophistication Level 1 the goals of the designers are _____,

   then _____ of the manual system to provide reports
   for improved control.

2. In Sophistication Level 2 the goals of the designers are the capturing

   of data for use in more than one subsystem, providing for _____

   of the system. The result is input that is more _____ and

   more _____, further reducing costs and delays.

3. In Sophistication Level 3 the goals of the designers are utilization of

the techniques of the ＿＿＿＿＿＿＿＿＿ ＿＿＿＿＿＿＿＿＿,
such as ABC inventory classification, economic order quantity deter-

mination, and linear programming. Also, manual ＿＿＿＿＿＿＿＿＿
are eliminated as the computer assumes the function of record-
keeping.

4. In Sophistication Level 4 the goal of the designers is integration of

major systems, in order to ＿＿＿＿＿＿＿＿＿ separate input and
to share data between modules of the integrated system. Instead of
merely providing information for action-taking, whenever possible
the computer performs those actions. This permits personnel to con-

centrate on ＿＿＿＿＿＿＿ and ＿＿＿＿＿＿＿ ＿＿＿＿＿＿＿.

Design Objective: The Computer-Based Management Information System

Circumstances of organizations vary and some may reach the fourth level
of sophistication in only three stages of refinement of systems, through
combining levels 1 and 2. In a few cases, the fourth level of sophistication
has been achieved in two stages, where levels 1 to 3 were combined into
the first stage.

However, it is a rare situation where an organization is able to design
the fourth level of sophistication in its initial implementation. Not only
are the behavioral aspects difficult, but the resource requirements are
prohibitive for most organizations. Developing several major systems
concurrently requires a large staff of designers, programmers, and user
representatives. Developing the systems in stages permits the system to
be implemented within the resource constraints of almost any organization.

Also, because of its complexity, the design of the fourth-level system
will take much longer, for example, two years. The firm would not be
realizing benefits until it is implemented. Utilizing the four-stage approach may require 4 to 5 years before the fourth level of sophistication
is achieved; however, benefits of computerization are occurring within
one year. Benefits increase as each sophistication level is implemented.

The progressive-stage approach permits an orderly growth in data
processing expenditures. National studies show that total data processing
costs represent less than 2 percent of gross annual sales for most firms.
Compressing the stages may cause a surge to 5 or 6 percent. Although
the benefits will pay for such an expenditure, they will not be realized
until the system is implemented. The firm may not be in a financial
position to afford the high level of expenditure. Therefore, the typical
approach is to develop systems in stages. However, as is shown in Figure
16–1 (which compared costs of first and third generation systems development), firms today achieve greater compression of the time period
between stages. This is possible because of (1) improvement in quality of

personnel (they are better trained), (2) improvement in the hardware and software supplied by the vendors and (3) less apprehension on the part of the employee (more adjusted to a computer-oriented world).

Also, where 10 years ago professionals speculated about the feasibility of integrated management information systems, such systems are commonplace today. The ingredients of a computer-based management information system, enumerated in Chapter 2, are all found in the fourth level of sophistication described in Table 18–1. Exercise 18–2 reinforces the concept of the CBMIS.

Exercise 18–2

Chapter 2 defines a computer-based management information system in terms of its objectives. That definition is repeated below:

The objective of a CBMIS is to:

1. Capture or generate all data pertinent to firm operations.
2. Process the data in the most efficient and economical manner, utilizing the management sciences to the fullest extent possible.
3. Produce concise and timely information as is required by each level of management for optimum execution of its functional objectives.

Refer to Table 18–1 once more. At which level is each of these objectives realized?

Objective 1: Level _____. Explain. _____

_____

_____

Objective 2: Level _____. Explain. _____

_____

_____

Objective 3: Level _____. Explain. _____

_____

_____

Overview of Logical System Design

As defined previously in this chapter, logical system design is concerned with specification of the requirements of the system: input requirements, output requirements, and processing rules and decision criteria. We present an overview of each of these tasks before describing each.

Output Specifications. Through in-depth discussions with users of the system, the system analyst identifies the output required of the system, both content and media.

In delineating the *content*, the analyst identifies precisely what the system should provide the user. For example, reports to various levels of management may differ in the degree of detail. The chief executive may be interested only in total value of inventory while the controller must know cost of the raw material, Work-In-Progress (WIP), and finished goods inventory to perform that control function properly. The supervisor of raw material must have reports separated by value and quantities, while the dock clerk who maintains raw material records needs to have detailed reports for each item in stock: receipts, results of incoming inspection, and issues.

In identifying *media*, the analyst determines the most appropriate form of output. For the chief executive, this may be a printed exception-report, providing information on activities not meeting the executive's criteria for performance. For example, a report will not be produced unless inventory levels exceed, or are forecast to exceed, an amount prescribed by the executive. For the controller, in addition to a printed report, a visual display may be the appropriate output medium. When the exception report reveals a discrepancy, the visual display unit may be used to trace the cause of the inventory overage. The dock clerk may need the visual display unit for both input and output. Receipts and issues could be entered to the system via the keyboard and visually verified on the display unit. Inquiries about specific stock items could be entered through the keyboard and status displayed on the screen. In contrast to output specifications, the media for processing are not specified. That is the task of physical system design. The analyst is responsible for specifying I/O media because they are user-oriented. The analyst is in the best position to determine what the user needs. The system designer is responsible for determining which media should be used in processing (e.g., tape, disk, cards, etc). So long as processing requirements are met, the analyst is not concerned with which processing media are used.

Processing Specifications. The analyst determines the appropriate procedures for processing data including: file processing specifications, file size (characters), frequency of update, peak and average message volume, access requirements, and retention requirements.

Decision Criteria. Each decision is identified, along with the conditions that necessitate the decision and the possible actions. An example can be derived from the inventory system explained above: the analyst would record the decision logic as specified by the chief executive for exception reports on inventory.

Input Specifications. When output requirements, processing rules and decision criteria have been specified, the analyst determines input requirements. As with output, both content and media are specified.

The *content* of input cannot be specified until output requirements have been established. To enable the controller to differentiate kinds of inventory, the analyst must designate the organization for initiating input. For the chief executive, work-in-process inventory may be calculated as the difference between starting and ending inventory. The controller often needs a further breakdown, such as WIP by product type or by physical location. The analyst must determine if WIP input is to be made by each manufacturing organization, or at points in production that facilitate measurement, or by random audits, or the like.

As a consequence, input *media* are also suggested by the analyst. However, determination of feasibility of media must wait until the physical design has been completed.

The analysis of input media is interdependent with that for output, as is illustrated previously by the dock clerk who used the same visual display terminal for input and output.

QUESTION: Logical design is a computer-independent task while physical design is computer-dependent. Why? _____

_____.

ANSWER: Logical design specifies what the system is to accomplish. Physical design specifies how the various units in the computer system are used to meet the logical specifications

QUESTION: The four kinds of specifications resulting from logical system design are: (1) _____ (2) _____
(3) _____ (4) _____.
ANSWER: input, output, decision logic, processing rules

User Coordination

Chapter 17 explains techniques for data gathering and portrayal. With this information the analyst has the basis for discussion of an improved system with the user.

Although the singular term "user" is referred to throughout this chapter, in reality there are multiple users of the system. That is why so many firms have established the function of system analyst to consolidate the requirements of all users of the proposed system. The analyst may report to the functional department where the system will be installed, to provide assurance that the system will effectively meet that department's needs. The system designer works for the data processing department, to insure that the system specifications are stated in a form to permit effective computerization. However, in small organizations, system analysis and design may be performed by the same person.

QUESTION: Although the function may be separated and performed by several persons, the task of identifying user needs is referred to as

_____.

ANSWER: system analysis. If you answered logical system design, you were a step ahead. Logical system design occurs after user needs are identified

Analyzing User Needs

The initial phase of preparing output specifications concentrates on content and ignores output media.

Using the Output Descriptors prepared in the data-gathering phase, the analyst can easily ascertain the output requirements of the system as it presently exists. Referencing this sheet, the analyst discusses with the user the possible changes in output that would enable the user's job to be performed more easily and more effectively.

INPUT/OUTPUT DESCRIPTOR				

I/O Identifier — Work Center Load Report   **I/O No.** 07

Originator — Computer Department   **Media** Preprinted Form   **Frequency** Weekly

Description

Provides capacity information and expected load: for each work center, the number of work stations, staff by shift, hours of capacity per week, accumulation of setup and run times for jobs that have an estimated arrival date within the report period, available capacity for the work center

Method of Preparation

Produced as standard output from weekly production control system processing

Disposition

A copy to each unit head, five to Production Control, one copy retained in Mfg. Report File

CONTENTS

Data No.	Data Name	Frequency	No. of Characters	Type	Source
250	Work Center Number	1	6	A/N	Mfg. File
137	Number of Work Stations	1	2	N	Mfg. File
251	Staff by Shift	1	6	N	Mfg. File
105	Hours per Week	1	3	N	Mfg. File
312	Capacity Adjustment	1	5	N	Mfg. File
313	Hours Capacity per Week	1	4	N	Mfg. File
05	Period Number	1	2	N	Mfg. File
314	Available Capacity (Hrs.)	1	4	N	Mfg. File

Date 4-1-75   **Analyst** K. Siler   **User Repr.** B. L. Trippett

Figure 18–2. *Output specification using I/O Descriptor form.*

The key to effective output analysis is understanding clearly the task of the user. The analyst tries to visualize himself performing that role to evaluate properly output possibilities. Since it is not possible to exchange roles, the analyst most often gains his knowledge on the needs of the system by step-by-step progression through existing reports, asking the user how the present information is used. The questioning technique common to all forms of analysis is utilized: the five "W's" and the "H": who, where, why, when, how, and with what.

493 / ANALYZING USER NEEDS

Exercise 18-3

Demonstrate the use of the five "W's" and the "H" on Output Descriptor (Figure 18-2). Write the set of questions you would ask in reviewing the Work Center Load Report with the user.

Who? _____

_____

_____

Where? _____

_____

_____

Why? _____

_____

_____

When? _____

_____

_____

_____

How? _____

_____

_____

With What? _____

_____

_____

Preparing Output Specifications

With the information gathered in discussing existing reports with the user, the analyst has the basis for determining an improved set of outputs.

Here is where management science techniques may be employed to increase the quality and reliability of information.

In some organizations the analyst has the education necessary to incorporate the appropriate management science techniques in the logical system design. In other organizations, development of optimization schemes is assigned to a management science group. In the latter case, the management scientist may accompany the system analyst in interviewing the user.

Output specifications are recorded in a manner to facilitate physical system design. The same form as the I/O Descriptor can be used for those specifications. A narrative would accompany the form, providing explicit definition of each data element, as is shown in Figure 18–3.

Field No.	Symbol	Field Name	Definition
1	WCEFC	Work Center Efficiency	Ratio of standard hours to actual hours.
5	WKCTR	Work Center	Department number or machine group number in which work is performed.

Figure 18–3. *Definition of data elements.*

QUESTION: Observe Figure 18–3 and answer the following question: Who would derive the data definitions? _____

_____

_____.

ANSWER: The analyst, in cooperation with the user responsible for generating the report

Figure 18–4 illustrates the set of output reports that might result from the above process.

QUESTION: What advantage would the Queue Time Analysis report provide: _____

_____.

ANSWER: The Work Center Load report indicates scheduled load but does not show the effect of varying arrivals of jobs, as does the Queue Time Analysis report

495 / PREPARING OUTPUT SPECIFICATIONS

Figure 18–4 illustrates output in hard-copy form. The medium to be used for output is determined after the analysis of output requirements.

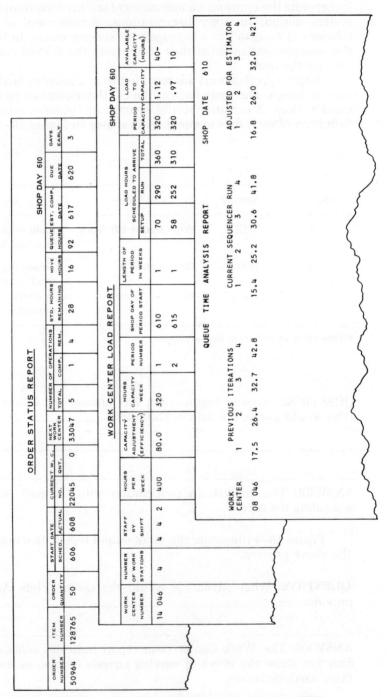

Figure 18–4. Examples of manufacturing reports (courtesy IBM).

User	Response Requirement	Maximum Data Requirement	Appropriate Medium
Executive	As Required	Product Group (40 Ch. Ea.)	Hard Copy
Controller	Weekly	Product Group by Inventory Category (5500 Ch. Ea.)	Hard Copy
Raw Materials Supervisor	Daily	Stock Category (80 Ch. Ea.)	Visual Display
Dock Clerk	Each Transaction	Stock Number Record (120 Ch. Ea.)	On-line Output, Visual or Hard Copy

Figure 18–5. *Output Media Analysis table.*

In general, the factors determining media are: response requirement, amount of information required, and cost. Recalling the inventory level situation, the response needs and information requirements might be as shown in Figure 18–5.

QUESTION: Observe Figure 18–5. Hard copy is specified for the controller because of the volume of output (5500 characters for each product group). Why do you suppose hard copy is specified for the executive?

ANSWER: He receives a report *only* when an exception occurs

Preparing Processing Specifications

The processing specifications consist of programmer-oriented flowcharts and narrative statements. The flowcharts are the skeletal framework and the narrative is the substance; together they provide the whole picture of the procedure required in processing the system.

Rarely is a system simple enough to bypass the flowcharting step. The complicated systems being computerized today require flowcharts to visualize the interdependent tasks of the system. On the other hand, flowcharts are, alone, insufficient to describe processing. The accompanying narrative explains actions that cannot be completely described in the limited space of a flowchart symbol.

To prepare processing specifications, the analyst works with the information gathered in the system survey, particularly the O²S flowcharts and procedure-oriented flowcharts. An example of processing specifications is provided in Figure 18–6. Although in this example the narrative is recorded on the same page as the flowchart, in more complicated systems the two are separated.

INVENTORY FILE UPDATE PROCEDURE

There are three categories of inventory entries. The three groups are (1) Update Entries, (2) Transaction Entries, and (3) Product Structure Entries.

1. *Update Entries.* This entry group is used to add a new item or items to the file, or to change one or more data fields of existing items. The fields changed include descriptions, codes, projections, which cannot be accessed by transaction entries.
2. *Transactions.* The normal day-to-day actions taken in manufacture and shipment of products to customers are receipts and adjustments to inventory.
3. *Product Structure Entries.* These entries provide the computer with the information necessary to record product/component relationships. For example, a particular finished goods item on file is made up of specific components and raw material items. The relationships recorded provide access to information such as where a component or raw material is used, how much of each component or raw material is required to meet a given sales projection, or what materials are required to meet existing projections.

The above information is stored in two computer files, the product master file and the product structure file. The product master file contains an item for each finished good, component, or raw material item. The product structure file contains an entry for each relationship. The product structure file data is an index by item-location in the product master file.

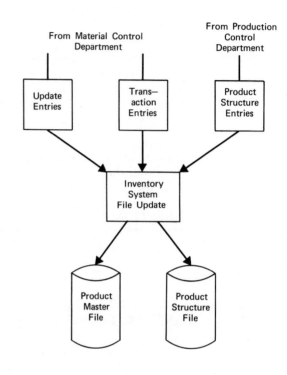

Figure 18–6. *Processing specifications: programmer-oriented flowchart and narrative procedure.*

QUESTION: Observe the input forms on the flowchart and the related narrative. What information is provided in the narrative that is difficult to depict in the flowchart?

_____

_____

ANSWER: The definition of each input

QUESTION: What information does the flowchart provide that is not immediately discernible from the narrative? _____

_____.

ANSWER: Relationship of inputs, system and files

Exercise 18–4

The registration process is familiar to every student (often, too familiar!). The user-oriented flowchart was prepared for a portion of the registration process for a typical college. Using your knowledge of registration procedure, change the flowchart segment to a processing specification (i.e., programmer-oriented flowchart and narrative). The first two blocks are provided to facilitate your accomplishing this exercise.

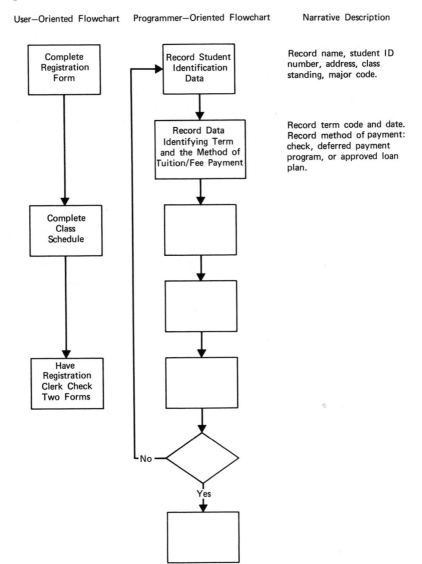

User–Oriented Flowchart   Programmer–Oriented Flowchart   Narrative Description

Preparing Decision Logic Specifications

The System Survey provided an overview of decision logic, in the form of decision symbols on user-oriented flowcharts. To enable a programmer to code decision logic, these summary level decision blocks must be detailed. Some decisions are simple and can be portrayed by the diamond-shaped decision symbol (e.g., the decision shown in the preceding exercise where the registration clerk determined if the forms were completed correctly). Many decisions are more involved and necessitate a more elaborate approach.

The technique for this activity is the decision logic table. The table is designed to depict the conditions that originate the need for a decision and the various actions which may be taken.

Figure 18–7 provides an example of the decision logic table for handling airline reservations.

Rule No. ⟶

	1	2	3	4
REQUEST IS FOR	1st CLASS	1st CLASS	TOURIST	TOURIST
1STCLASS AVAILABLE	Y	N		
TOURIST AVAILABLE			Y	N
ISSUE	1st CLASS		TOURIST	
PLACE ON WAIT LIST		X		X

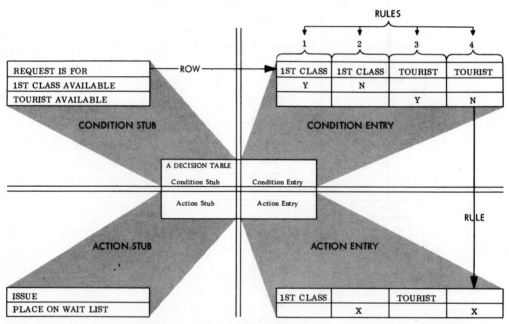

Figure 18–7. *Decision logic table. Depicts logic for handling airline reservations (courtesy IBM).*

Observing the lower portion of Figure 18–7, we can identify the components of a decision logic table: conditions, condition entries, actions, and action entries.

Conditions and actions have an "if...then" relationship (e.g., *if* a set of conditions exist *then* the following actions are to be taken).

Conditions	Conditions Entries
Actions	Actions Entries

Working through a simple illustration will demonstrate the development of a decision logic table. Table 18–2 provides a step-by-step description of development of a decision table from a narrative procedure. Read this procedure because it will be used in completing Exercise 18–5 and several problems in the chapter examination.

QUESTION: It was not obvious from reading the narrative procedure that so much duplication existed. The conditions in the narrative were reduced from _____ to 3 in the decision logic table while the actions were reduced from _____ to 4.
ANSWER: 8, 5

An important advantage of decision logic tables is their ability to be translated directly into COBOL or FORTRAN language. Special translators, called interpreters, were developed for this process. Key entry personnel punch cards for each line in the table. The resulting deck of cards is read into the computer and is translated into COBOL statements, bypassing the coding function for this portion of the system. A summary of advantages and disadvantages of decision tables is provided in Table 18–3.

501 / PREPARING DECISION LOGIC SPECIFICATIONS

TABLE 18-2
Procedure for Development of a Decision Table

The procedure the systems analyst follows in preparing a decision table may be simply to identify conditions and actions of the problem statement as he encounters them. Conditions are placed on the top half of the form; actions on the bottom half.

Consider the following problem narrative:

When the quantity ordered for a particular item does not exceed the order limit and the credit approval is "OK", move the quantity-ordered amount to the quantity-shipped field; then go to a table to prepare a shipment release. Of course, there must be a sufficient quantity on hand to fill the order.

When the quantity ordered exceeds the order limit, go to a table named "Order Reject". Do the same if the credit approval is not "OK".

Occasionally, the quantity ordered does not exceed the order limit, credit approval is "OK", but there is insufficient quantity on hand to fill the order. In this case, go to a table named "Back Order".

Note that this is not written with all conditions first, prefixed by "if", and with all actions following, prefixed by "then". The narrative was written casually with conditions and actions scrambled, much like the original baseball problem. Words like "when" and "occasionally" are used instead of the more precise "if". Such ambiguity is typical of most narratives. For illustrative purposes the problem is restated below with a solid line under conditions and a broken line under actions.

When the quantity ordered for a particular item does not exceed the order limit and the credit approval is "OK", move the quantity-ordered amount to the quantity-shipped field, then go to a table to prepare a shipment release. Of course, there must be a sufficient quantity on hand to fill the order.

When the quantity ordered exceeds the order limit, go to a table named "Order Reject". Do the same if the credit approval is not "OK".

Occasionally, the quantity ordered does not exceed the order limit, credit approval is "OK", but there is insufficient quantity on hand to fill the order. In this case, go to a table named "Back Order".

A count shows eight conditions and five actions for the problem.

C1 QTY ORDERED IS LESS THAN OR EQUAL TO ORDER LIMIT
C2 CREDIT APPROVAL IS "OK"
C3 QTY ON HAND IS GREATER THAN OR EQUAL TO QTY ORDERED
C4 QTY ORDERED IS GREATER THAN ORDER LIMIT
C5 CREDIT APPROVAL IS NOT "OK"
C6 QTY ORDERED IS LESS THAN OR EQUAL TO ORDER LIMIT
C7 CREDIT APPROVAL IS "OK"
C8 QTY ON HAND IS LESS THAN QTY ORDERED

A1 MOVE QTY ORDERED TO QTY SHIP
A2 GO TO SHIP RELEASE
A3 GO TO ORDER REJECT
A4 GO TO ORDER REJECT
A5 GO TO BACK ORDER

Notice that C1 and C2 are identical to C6 and C7, and that A3 is identical to A4. This occurs because a narrative describes rules one after another (serially). Thus two sets of two conditions common to two rules, appear in the narrative. On the other hand, a decision table aligns rules side by side (parallel). Thus a condition or action common to several rules need appear only once. Furthermore, C5 is not necessary since it is the negative of C2. Similarly C4 and C8 are the negatives of C1 and C3. Negative entries after the positive statements of C1, C2 and C3 cover the other cases.

The next step in preparing the table might be to identify and consolidate similar rows. C1, C6 and C4 are combined. C2, C5 and C7 are combined. Finally, C3 and C8 are combined.

In the action half of the decision table form, A3 and A4 are combined. After consolidation there are only three condition rows and four action rows.

Condition Stub

QTY ORDERED IS LESS THAN OR EQUAL TO ORDER LIMIT
CREDIT APPROVAL IS "OK"
QTY ON HAND IS GREATER THAN OR EQUAL TO QTY ORDERED

Action Stub

MOVE QTY ORDERED TO QTY SHIP
GO TO PREPARE SHIP RELEASE
GO TO ORDER REJECT
GO TO BACK ORDER

The stub portion of the table is now completed. In order to fill out the entry portions, the analyst must determine the rules expressed in the narrative. In this example, the first paragraph describes a single rule. The analyst enters the appropriate Y, N or X in the entry portions for rule 1. The second paragraph contains two rules. The analyst enters the appropriate Y, N, or X in the entry portion for rules 2 and 3. Finally, the last paragraph becomes rule 4 of the decision table. The final result is shown below:

	Rule	1	2	3	4
	OPEN				
1	QTY ORDER LE ORDER LIMIT	Y	N	Y	Y
2	CREDIT APPROVAL IS "OK"	Y		N	Y
3	QTY ON HAND GR QTY ORDERED	Y			N
4	MOVE QTY ORDERED TO QTY SHIP	X			
5	GO TO PREPARE SHIP RELEASE	X			
6	GO TO ORDER REJECT		X	X	
7	GO TO BACK ORDER				X

TABLE 18-3
Advantages and Disadvantages of Decision Logic Tables[a]

1. **Display situations concisely**
2. **Promote completeness and accuracy**
3. **Can have completeness and accuracy checking techniques applied to them**
4. **Permit a complex situation to be more easily grasped**
5. **Allow the study and design of systems previously too complex to be handled by other methods**
6. **Facilitate modularity**
7. **Are relatively easy to construct, modify, and read**
8. **Are not limited to computer applications**
9. **Improve user/analyst communication**
10. **Are easily understood by both business and scientific personnel**
11. **Are more easily understood than flowcharts**
12. **Document applications involving complex interactions of variables more clearly than flowcharts**
13. **Can be used as a computer source language**

Some of the disadvantages of decision tables are:
1. **People experienced in drawing flowcharts find it initially difficult to create decision tables**
2. **It would sometimes be helpful to be able to refer to a specific rule in one table while working within another rule in the same or a different table (e.g., branch to rule 2 of Table 7). However, this violates one of the current conventions of table usage.**
3. **Tables can become unwieldy if action segments are predicated on just one or two simple conditions rather than on many complex conditions. However, an alert table creator can usually prevent this situation.**

[a]From a paper by Robert Fergus in *System Analysis Techniques*, J. D. Couger and R. W. Knapp, Wiley, New York, 1974, pp. 174–176.

QUESTION: Which advantage is most important in your opinion? Why?

_____

_____

_____.

ANSWER: Although all the reasons are important, reason number 5 is the principal reason for using decision logic tables instead of other methods, such as flowcharts. The advantage of decision tables over flowcharts increases as the conditions increase. To illustrate, for expressing the logic of four binary conditions (four yes-no conditions), the possible combinations are 16 (2^4). For 9 conditions, the combinations number 512.

Exercise 18–5

Insure your understanding of this important analysis technique by developing a decision logic table for the following set of decision logic:

A. Read employees' cards with the following information:
   (1) Employee clock number
   (2) Gross pay

B. Use the following table to compute the tax and find the net pay where net is equal to gross pay, less tax:

Gross Earnings	Tax
Less than $2000	0
$2000 or more, but less than $5000	2 percent of the excess over $2000
$5000 or more	$60, plus 5 percent of the excess over $5000

C. Terminate when the employee's clock number is zero

D. Print the clock number, gross pay, tax, and net pay for each employee

Preparing Input Specifications

The final task in logical system design is definition of input. When specifications for output, processing, and decision logic have been prepared, input specifications are easily determined.

Input Descriptors, prepared in the System Survey, provide the basis for input specifications. In some cases the Input Descriptor will serve as the specification without change. An example might be the Input Descriptor for the Purchasing Order (Figure 17–6). In other cases, the input document will be redesigned to provide more information or to facilitate preparation and processing. For example, the inventory and billing subsystems for a retail clothing outlet may be combined and may use a Point-of-Sale (POS) recorder as input to both systems. When the cashier rings up a credit and a sale, the inputs for revising inventory *and* for changing the accounts receivable file are electrically transmitted to the computer.

However, rather than specify a specific form or device, the primary task of the analyst is to identify data required for input. Near completion of the physical system design, a detailed feasibility study determines the appropriate media for input. To illustrate, different analysts may be preparing the logical system design for the inventory and accounts receivable systems. During physical system design, it may be determined that combining the two inputs will justify the POS device.

Essentially, both input and output specifications are machine-independent. However, by virtue of working directly with the user, the analyst is in a better position to determine the advantages of the various media. Therefore, it is a team task for the analyst and designer to determine feasibility of input and output media. The analyst provides data on system benefits, and the designer provides data on equipment costs.

QUESTION: Input specifications will be recorded on the Input Descriptor form; however, the new system may require input not provided previously, such as input to models incorporated into the system, characteristic of Sophistication Level _____?

ANSWER: three

An example of an Input Descriptor prepared for data not previously in the system is provided in Figure 18–8. Following through on the question above, this example shows the input specification for data needed for the EOQ model imbedded in the inventory system.

QUESTION: Analyze the Input Specification for EOQ data (Figure 18–8). Although some of these data may reside somewhere in various files, most of the EOQ formula is computed by a _____ _____ and input via a _____ _____.

ANSWER: management scientist, punched card

QUESTION: Notice the frequency of updating these data, "as needed." What conditions cause a change in these data? (*Hint*: the two major components of the EOQ formula are inventory carrying cost and ordering cost.) _____

_____

_____.

ANSWER: Suppliers change prices, but not normally on a scheduled basis. Costs of handling and storing inventory change, also on irregular basis

Preparation of input specifications is not difficult, relative to the other three forms of specification. With the input specifications provided in the logical system design, the specific input forms and devices can be determined in the physical system design phase.

Summary

Logical system design is identification of the user's needs and how those needs will be satisfied. Although the elements of that task may be subdivided among several specialists, the function remains the same.

The System Survey provided the overview of the total system for the firm, gathering information on all *major* systems.

The major systems, such as the manufacturing system are subdivided into subsystems (e.g., the production planning subsystem, the final assembly subsystem, and the shipping subsystem). Logical systems are designed for each subsystem, with close coordination to insure compatibility and to reduce cost and possibility of errors due to differing definitions of input and processing procedures. For example, one set of input is used for financial inventory and another for physical inventory. However, design of these inputs is coordinated to insure compatibility, or the two inventories will never agree. Likewise, if data from one input can also serve another system, entry costs are reduced and both departments are working on the same set of data.

INPUT/OUTPUT DESCRIPTOR				
I/O Identifier			**I/O No.**	
	Data for Economic Order Quantity Determination		121	
Originator		**Media**		**Frequency**
	Management Science Unit	Punched Card		As needed
Description				
	Data for EOQ model used in inventory system.			
Method of Preparation				
	Not a production type input. Prepared by management scientist.			
Disposition				
	A copy retained in management science unit. Data resides on Inventory File Number 3.			

CONTENTS					
Data No.	*Data Name*	*Frequency*	*No. of Characters*	*Type*	*Source*
111	Demand Rate	1	5	N	Prod Control
129	Reorder Point	1	8	N	Material
130	Reorder Level	1	8	N	Material
314	Order Cost	1	6	N	Purchasing
315	Purchase Cost per Unit	1	6	N	Purchasing
095	Inventory Carrying Cost per Unit	1	4	N	Material
131	Safety Stock Quantity	1	8	N	Material
330	Order Quantity	1	8	N	Computed

Date		**Analyst**		**User Repr.**
4-1-74		C. McMillan		R. Taylor

Figure 18–8. *Input Specification Using I/O Descriptor Form*

Logical systems are typically being designed simultaneously in several areas of the firm. However, it is rare for a firm to have the resources to design a highly sophisticated system from scratch. Typically, system design is separated into stages, perhaps a year apart. Level of sophistication is increased in each stage of redesign, within the resource capability of the firm. A Level 4 system may require 12 man-years of effort (e.g., four design years and eight programming years). It is an unusual situation for a firm to decide to hire 12 people to accomplish this design in one year. By implementing the system in stages the firm will realize benefits within the first year. Benefits will increase as subsequent stages are designed and implemented *and* the firm has not used a disproportionate amount of resources for its computer activities compared to other needs of the firm. Although 12 man-years may appear to be a low cost, one must remember that systems are being designed simultaneously for several major areas of the firm. Continuing our hypothetical situation, assume each system requires resources in the neighborhood of 12 man-years for development. And—to design costs are added computer and supplies cost. Staying within the industry experience of less than 2 percent of gross sales for all computer-related expenditures requires separating a system into stages of development. Also, the capability of the firm's employees to work effectively with a fourth level of sophistication system substantiates the need for development in progressive stages.

Once subsystems have been delineated, logical system design is initiated. The analyst details the data gathered from the system survey. Effective logical design requires close coordination with the user (typically there are several users although the term has been used in its singular form for simplicity).

The resulting logical system design consists of four major components, prepared in the following sequence: output specification, processing specifications, decision logic, and input specifications. However, processing specifications are separated into file descriptors and file processing procedures.

On completion of logical system design, Phase III of the system development cycle is initiated—physical system design. That is the subject of the next chapter.

Solutions to Exercises

Exercise 18–1

1. Simplification, mechanization.
2. Expansion, reliable, responsive.
3. Management sciences, ledgers.
4. Eliminate, planning, employee motivation.

Exercise 18–2

Level 2. Cards are punched for *all* requirements.
Level 3. Utilize management science techniques like ABC, EOQ.
Level 4. Through integration and optimization, information is provided to each level of management.

Exercise 18–3

Who receives this report? Who else should receive it?
Where is the report filed? Are these files readily accessible?

Why is the report necessary?
When is it used? Daily? Weekly, etc.?
How is it used? To load production facilities or as a performance report on loading? Can it be improved?
With what level of resources is the information presently acquired?

Exercise 18–4

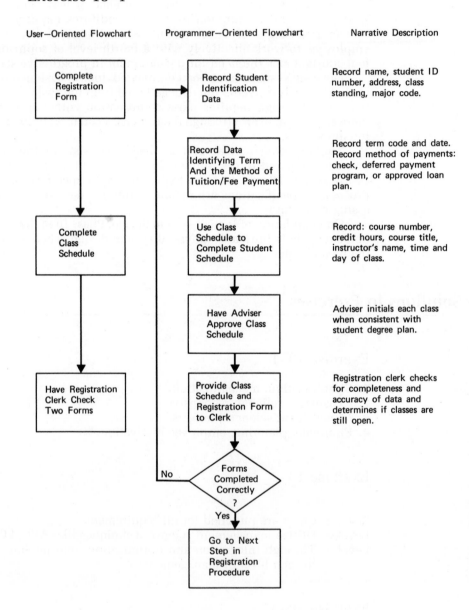

User—Oriented Flowchart	Programmer—Oriented Flowchart	Narrative Description
Complete Registration Form	Record Student Identification Data	Record name, student ID number, address, class standing, major code.
	Record Data Identifying Term And the Method of Tuition/Fee Payment	Record term code and date. Record method of payments: check, deferred payment program, or approved loan plan.
Complete Class Schedule	Use Class Schedule to Complete Student Schedule	Record: course number, credit hours, course title, instructor's name, time and day of class.
	Have Adviser Approve Class Schedule	Adviser initials each class when consistent with student degree plan.
Have Registration Clerk Check Two Forms	Provide Class Schedule and Registration Form to Clerk	Registration clerk checks for completeness and accuracy of data and determines if classes are still open.
	Forms Completed Correctly? — No / Yes	
	Go to Next Step in Registration Procedure	

Exercise 18–5

PROCEDURE TO COMPUTE PAYROLL

CONDITIONS	RULES			
	1	2	3	4
Clock Number Zero?	Y	N	N	N
Earnings:				
Less than $2000		Y	N	N
2000 < 5000			Y	N
≥ 5000				Y
Compute tax:				
Zero tax		X		
2% of excess > $2000			X	
$60 plus 5% of excess > $5000				X
Calculate net pay		X	X	X
Print clock number, gross pay,				
tax, net pay		X	X	X
Terminate program	X			

Chapter Examination

1. The four levels of sophistication in System Design are:

    Level 1 _____

    Level 2 _____

    Level 3 _____

    Level 4 _____

2. Although an organization may achieve the fourth level of sophistication in less than four stages of system of development, it is rare to achieve it in two stages. Why?

_____

_____

_____

3. What are the advantages of implementing the system in three or four stages instead of designing the fourth level of sophistication for the initial stage?

_____

_____

_____

4. Construct a chart that shows the relationship of the four levels of design sophistication (Table 18–1) to the stages of development and implementation of a system. Show this within the framework of the seven phases in the system development cycle (Figure 16–1).

Phase I   Phase VII
                          System Development Cycle

5. List the four components of the logical system design specification:

(a) _____

(b) _____

(c) _____

(d) _____

6. One of the above components (see problem 5) is subdivided, as described in the chapter summary. What are those subdivisions?

7. Develop an Input Descriptor for the input document shown in Figure 21–2, for the top two inputs only. (Use the blank form provided at the end of the chapter.)

8. Logical system design is hardware-independent. However, since the analyst works closely with the user, the media for _____ and _____ may be recommended. The detailed feasibility study near completion of physical system design will determine specific input and output _____.

9. Depending on the circumstances of the specific organization, logical and physical system design may be performed by _____ or _____ persons. Large organizations typically employ an information or system analyst, who is a liaison between the designer and the user. This person works for the user and consolidates the requirements for *all users* in a given functional organization (e.g., manufacturing).

10. Processing specifications include what factors?

(a) _____

(b) _____

(c) _____

(d) _____

(e) _____

11. The System Survey provides information to perform a general feasibility study. The detailed feasibility study requires both _____ and _____ system design.

12. Which area of an individual's needs are perceived as threatened by computerizing portions of his job? (Refer to Maslow's chart on hierarchy of needs, Chapter 2).

_____

_____

_____

_____

511 / CHAPTER EXAMINATION

13. Development of a system in stages reduces the individual's perception of threat. Why? _____

_____

_____

14. Development of a system in stages is usually required for economic as well as behavioral reasons. Explain. _____

_____

_____

15. Develop a User-Oriented flowchart to depict the fourth level of system sophistication (Table 18–1).

16. Develop Output Descriptors for the reports shown in Figure 21–3b.

17. Assume one of the systems for which you prepared O²S flowcharts in the Chapter 17 examination justifies computer processing. Prepare processing specifications for that system.

18. Develop a decision logic table to portray the following set of logic:

Personnel Selection
Given:
A. Field Names
   Employee name
   Department number
   Hourly rate
   Hours worked
   Deduction code (A, B, C, D)
   Sex (M = male, F = female)

Obtain:
A. Select all males who satisfy the following conditions:
   1. They must work in Department 47.
   2. Weekly hours not over 40.
   3. Must have a deduction code "B" or code "D."
B. Select all females that satisfy the following conditions:
   1. They must work in department 48, 49, or 50.
   2. Weekly hours not over 40.
   3. Must have a deduction under code "C" or hourly rate must be more than $2.50.
C. If section A is satisfied—go to routine 1.
   If section B is satisfied—go to routine 2.
   If neither A nor B is satisfied—go to routine 3.

INPUT/OUTPUT DESCRIPTOR

I/O Identifier

I/O No.

Originator

Media

Frequency

Description

Method of Preparation

Disposition

CONTENTS

Data No.	Data Name	Frequency	No. of Characters	Type	Source

Date

Analyst

User Repr.

19. Develop a decision table to portray the following set of logic:

Classification of Capital Gains and Losses. The phrase "short term" applies to gains and losses from the sale or exchange of capital assets held for six months or less; the phrase "long-term" applies to capital assets held for more than six months.

Treatment of capital gains and losses: Short-term capital gains and losses will be merged to obtain the net short-term capital gain or loss. Long-term capital gains and losses (taken into account at 100 percent) will be merged to obtain the net long-term capital gain or loss.

1. Given: Purchase date
Sales date
Net sales price
Net cost

2. Obtain: Total long-term result
Total short-term result
Type of long-term result (gain, loss)
Type of short-term result (gain, loss)
Net result

20. Develop a decision table to portray the following set of logic:

Stockholder Reports. From a file of stockholder records, we wish to extract the records of stockholders other than individuals and the records of individuals who hold more than 100,000 shares. With this information produce a detail listing containing the name of each stockholder, the type of stockholder (decoded), and number of shares owned. Also produce a final total of the number of stockholders and number of shares owned listed in this report.

For each stockholder we have:

1. Stockholder name
2. Stockholder type (individual -01, trust -02, bank -03, broker -04)
3. Number of shares owned

21. Under what circumstances are Programmer-Oriented flowcharts appropriate for displaying logic, instead of decision tables?

_____

_____

_____

_____

_____

_____

22. Develop a processing specification for one of the following processes.
   (a) A computer system for setting up a student record file and keeping it current with transactions occurring each term.
   (b) A computer system for tabulating library fines, parking ticket fees, and damaged laboratory equipment to flag the need to withhold diplomas until these matters are handled.

23. Develop four levels of sophistication in one of the systems you flowcharted in the examination for Chapter 17. Describe each level in one paragraph.

Chapter 19

PHYSICAL SYSTEM DESIGN

Overview

Physical system design is concerned with converting the logical system design into a form that can be processed by the computer economically and effectively.

As one expert in the computer field has stated, "The system analyst looks outward, toward the user, while the system designer looks inward, toward the computer."

Actually the interaction between logical and physical design is an iterative process rather than a sequential process as implied above. The system analyst prescribes the processing/decision rules by which input is converted to output. However, the level of sophistication desired in the logical system design may not be feasible with the presently installed computing system of the organization. The system designer will normally prepare a physical design within the constraints of the existing computing system, then the analyst/designer team will evaluate the feasibility of implementing the system. Rarely is it feasible to acquire the computing configuration for a design that produces the fourth level of sophistication. These two professionals devise a plan for designing and implementing the system in stages within the resource constraints of the organization.

The process of physical system design includes: (1) selection of a file organization and processing scheme, (2) design of the database, (3) design of the files, (4) incorporation of controls to insure processing reliability, and (5) formatting or layout of input and output.

The resulting physical system design includes specifications for computer programming and file conversion and procedures for data control and computer processing.

This is the key chapter of the book. All the previous material has prepared the student to comprehend the task of the system designer. When systems incorporate the fourth level of design sophistication, they become an integral and crucial part of the firm's operations. The computer is applied to life-stream systems that "make or break" the firm.

While all phases in system development are important, the key to success or failure is Phase III, the physical design phase.

This chapter describes the components of Phase III of the system development cycle and the relationships to the preceding and succeeding phases.

Determining the Level of Sophistication in Physical System Design

The physical system designer utilizes the following materials — the logical system design package.

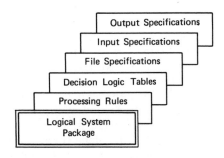

On completing analysis of this package the system designer has two options in preparing the physical system design:

1. Optimizing the system *within* the constraints of the existing computer configuration.
2. Optimizing the system *without considering* the constraints of the existing computer configuration.

For example, an optimal design for a retail marketing store may include point-of-sale I/O devices with on-line capability of responding within seconds to provide the salesperson up-to-date information on customer status. If a purchase is made, the record of the transaction is automatically input to both the inventory and the accounts receivable systems.

However, if the firm's present system is a batch-oriented system, the designer must determine the feasibility of converting to a computer configuration with on-line capability.

As the above example shows, expanded capability is rarely justified on one system alone. The on-line POS system permits improvements in both the inventory and accounts receivable systems, as well as other systems such as the sales commission accounting system.

Therefore, justification of an expanded system is a cooperative effort between designers assigned to the major systems of the firm.

Also, the firm may be considering its first computer rather than adding applications to a computer already installed. Or, it may be using a service bureau's computer or may be sharing a computer with another organization.

The physical system designer, therefore, has many options to consider. Several alternative designs are developed and evaluated. This is the detailed feasibility analysis referred to previously — evaluation of the various levels of design sophistication possible within the resource constraints of the organization. Pursuing the above illustration, the on-line POS system may be delayed until Stage II of the sales processing system, when the accounts receivable and sales commission systems are to be computerized, as is shown in Figure 19–1.

QUESTION: Observe Figure 19–1. Stage I of all six major systems is designed over an _____ month period to keep design costs consistent with the firm's _____.

ANSWER: 18-, overall budget

Figure 19–1 illustrates a firm that has the resource limitation during the first 18 months of developing only two major systems concurrently. During the first 18 months of the CBMIS Implementation Schedule, Stage I is implemented for each of six major systems. Thereafter, the benefits derived from these systems justify greater resources, and Stage II is accomplished for three systems simultaneously.

Some firms may have the resources to design the second level of sophistication into Stage I of the system. Figure 19–1 actually illustrates such a case: the sales and inventory systems are designed simultaneously and are integrated. In Stage II, accounts receivable is integrated with the sales processing/accounts receivable system. The third level of sophistication is achieved because management science techniques are incorporated to control inventory better.

The level of sophistication of each design stage will depend on the firm's ability to underwrite system development costs. Many months may elapse before the stream of benefits begins to emerge. If a firm has several design teams working on systems concurrently the resource problem is intensified.

QUESTION: The principal reasons for designing and implementing systems in stages is to stay within the resource constraints of the firm; that is, to hold costs down until _____

_____ .

ANSWER: benefits of the installed systems provide funds for further sophistication of these systems

Systems	Year 1	Year 2	Year 3
Sales Processing	I	II	
Inventory	I	II	
Accounts Receivable	I	II	
Payroll	I		II
Accounts Payable	I	II	
General Ledger	I	II	

Figure 19–1. *Implementing systems in stages consistent with the firm's resource limitations.*

A plan for implementation is developed in cooperation with the other design teams. The common objective is to move to the fourth level of sophistication for each of the major systems as soon as is possible within the resource constraints of the organization. However, the priority of development is determined by the impact of the systems on the life-stream activities of the firm.

Database Design

In first and second generation design methodology, systems were designed for independent processing. For example, although the real-life tasks of production planning and inventory planning were interdependent, the systems designed for these functions were independent. Data was collected, input, processed, and printed out with little sharing between systems. Consequently, the systems were suboptimal. Not only did duplication occur in key entry but it also occurred in storage and processing.

The third generation design approach places emphasis on capturing a data element only once, at its logical initiation point, and inputting this data element to all systems where it will be used. Likewise, files are designed for sharing information among systems. Although there are more elegant definitions, this is essentially the *database concept*, that systems are designed for integration through sharing a common database. Nor is the concept confined to individual organizations; the airline companies are now sharing a database for their flight reservation systems. Many governmental agencies share a database for information on citizens, accessed by the social security number.

Figure 19–2 depicts the computer-based information system for a manufacturing firm. The major systems are identified by the numbers in small blocks above the diagram.

QUESTION: Observe Figure 19–2; what do the arrows indicate? _____

_____ .

ANSWER: The flow of data and information between systems: that is, the sharing of information in an integrated system

QUESTION: What would be the principal data element in the database for a bank? _____ .

ANSWER: The customer record, accessed by account number

QUESTION: Figure 19–2 illustrates the CBMIS approach because all activity is initiated by _____

_____ .

ANSWER: management decisions; within the framework of the objectives of the firm

The database approach appears so obviously beneficial that it is difficult to understand why the concept was slow to be adopted. There are several reasons.

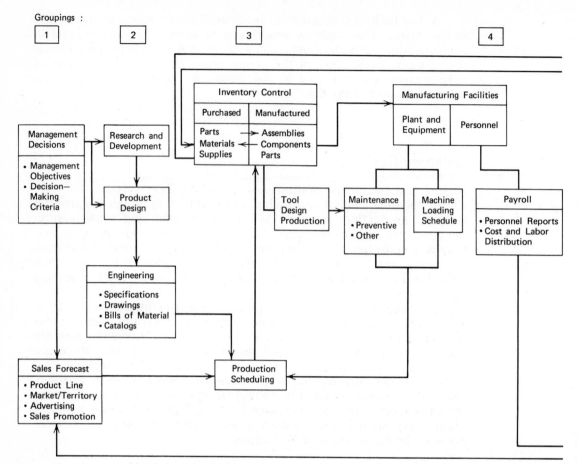

Groupings :

| 1 | 2 | 3 | 4 |

Figure 19–2. *Computer-based management information system for a manufacturing firm. (Major systems are identi-*

First, if several systems are to share a database, their development is interdependent. Implementation time is lengthened because of negotiation of the database structure by the various system teams. For example, the marketing system can be designed and implemented more quickly if its designers do not have to consider how data from marketing plans and marketing analyses might be used in other systems, such as the inventory system. To perform the marketing function, the marketing system does not require all the data from the corporation's master plan; however, it is practical to capture these data at one time, for both economic and data verification reasons. The marketing system is the logical one to assign input of these data to the database.

The designers of the marketing system, therefore, must coordinate their design with designers of the other major systems. As a result, design of the marketing system will take longer when the firm employs the database concept.

A second reason for the delay in implementing the database concept was a misunderstanding of the concept. Some widely-read writers in the field implied that adoption of the concept requires use of only one storage medium, the disk file. They also inferred that the concept required

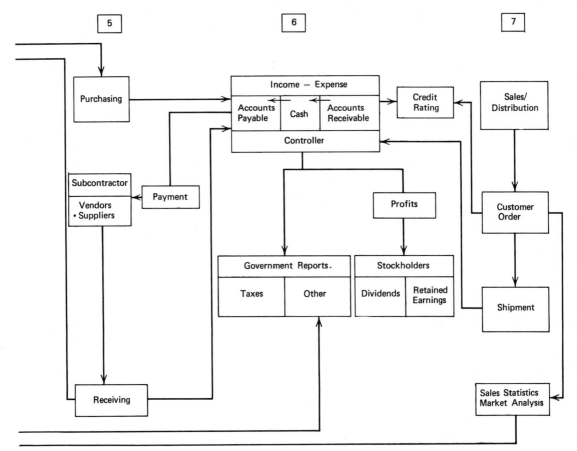

fied by numbered blocks. Courtesy IBM.)

on-line access to that storage medium. Neither is required to implement the database concept. The database approach is a concept not a physical device. The approach is to design for integrating systems and sharing of data among files rather than placing all data on one physical file. A data element used in several systems, for example, the employee record, may be on magnetic tape, or even on punched cards. The key factor is the design of that record to include all the information needed by the various systems that access it.

Even that statement may be misinterpreted, proving the problem of understanding and implementing the database concept. The database concept does not require that all data involved in an entity be stored in one master record, but generally only those data used by more than one system. For example, the product master file may reside in two, linked locations. The lengthy, space-consuming description of the product may be separated from the basic record. It is needed infrequently and would be costly to access each time the basic record is required. Only when the description is required would the linked portion of the record be accessed.

The third reason for the delay in adopting the database concept was the cost for storage of the master file. Although the database does not

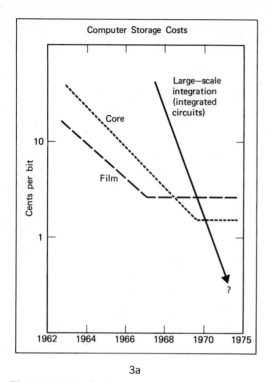

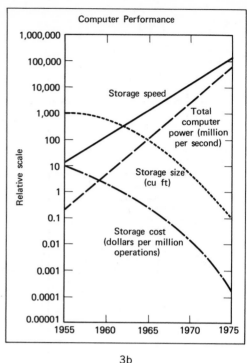

3a   3b

Figure 19–3. *Reduction of computer storage costs and improvement in computer performance (courtesy of the Conference Board).*

have to be on-line to gain the benefits of integrating systems, processing is greatly expedited when it is on-line. Cost of on-line storage of the database was prohibitive for most firms during the era of first and second generation computers. However, the cost of storage has been reduced significantly for third generation systems, as shown in Figure 19–3.

QUESTION: Observe Figure 19–3a. What was the cost per bit of storage in 1964 (film) compared to LSI for 1973? _____

_____

_____

_____.

ANSWER: The cost in 1964 = approximately 10 cents; in 1973 = approximately ½ cent. As is shown by Figure 19–3b, storage cost per million operations reduced by a factor of 1,000 from 1955 to 1970 while speed of access to storage increased by a factor of 10,000 over the same period.

The fourth reason for delay in adopting the database concept was due also to a misinterpretation of the concept. Some of the writing on the subject implies that the database must contain every conceivable item of data/information the firm might need, both present and future. As is noted in the first objective of a CBMIS (stated in Chapter 2), the goal is to capture "all data pertinent" to the firm's operation. It is a complex enough

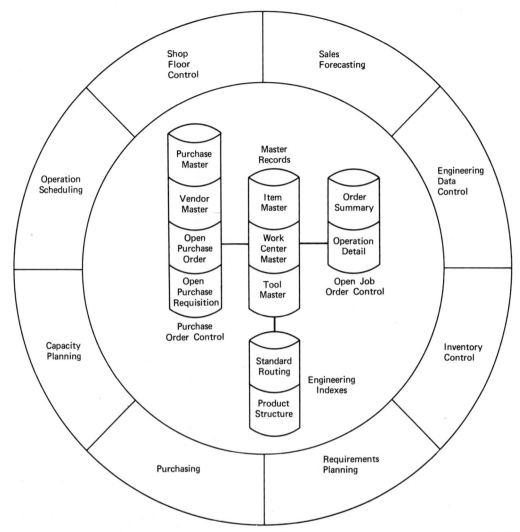

Figure 19–4. *The integrated database information is shared among all major systems (courtesy IBM).*

task to assess present and near-future needs. Files can always be expanded as new needs arise, although a cost is involved. This cost is usually less than the cost of unused storage left in each record for undefined needs. Many firms have implemented the database concept, while maintaining the objective of determining those items "pertinent" within the foreseeable future.

The four principal reasons cited above for delay in adoption of the database concept are no longer valid. Design of third generation systems includes the database concept. Figure 19–4 illustrates the database concept and shows how several major files share information to support the major systems of the manufacturing firm referred to in Figure 19–2.

QUESTION: Observe Figure 19–4. Which shared files are used for the Purchasing system? _____.

ANSWER: The four files on the left; however, these files interact with the others

523 / DATABASE DESIGN

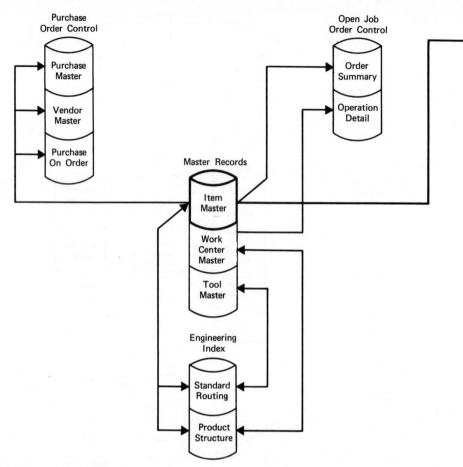

Figure 19–5. *Sharing the item master among the various files (courtesy IBM).*

Figure 19–5 shows how a record is shared among files. This record is the inventory item master, and the basic data in this record is used in all the other files depicted.

QUESTION: To make sure you understand this sharing concept, indicate the fields in the item master that would be used by the Purchase Master file, shown in the upper left-hand corner of Figure 19–5.
Fields: _____

_____.

ANSWER: Item Number, then all the fields that pertain to ordering: order policy, forecasting, lead times, unit costs, unit prices, current period inventory, inventory on hand, gross requirements, and planned and released orders

The advantages of implementing the database concept are the following.

1. Reduction of input cost through sharing of data.
2. Elimination of duplicate records.

Features of the ITEM MASTER

Type	Item Number	Description	Unit of Measure	Inventory Value Classification	Engineering Cross References	
					To Product Structure	To Standard Routing

Order Policy	Forecasting	Lead Times	Unit Costs	Unit Prices	Parts Usage History	Current Period Inventory	

Inventory On Hand (Quantity and Locations)	Gross Requirements	Planned and Released Orders	Purchasing On Order	
			Total Quantity	Cross Reference to Detail Purchase Order

Cross Reference to Other Purchasing Records			Production On Order	
Detail Requisitions	Vendor Master	Purchase Master	Total Quantity	Cross Reference to Order Summary and Operation Detail

Engineering Drawing	Engineering Change Control

3. Common definition of a data element among all systems.
4. Reduction in computer processing time.
5. Validation of data is facilitated since entered once and shared thereafter.
6. Reduction in sorting of records because fewer duplicates.
7. Reduction in the number of computer programs to be written since data will be retrieved using a standard procedure.

Exercise 19–1

Looking at the seven advantages of the database, which produce savings in computer cost and which produce savings in labor cost?

1. Computer cost reduction: _____

2. Labor cost reduction: _____

File Design Concepts

Design of the database includes determination of processing and access procedures. Basic methods of file organization were discussed in the chapter on Concepts of Data Processing. Recall that there are two fundamentally different approaches: sequential organization, and direct access. In the sequential organization, records are located in sequence according to their key. This approach facilitates file maintenance but requires extensive searching to locate individual records. On the other hand, direct access permits the location of individual records without searching, but is much less efficient for maintaining a file with high activity.

Index sequential is a technique that combines the advantages of sequential and direct access methods. This and other important file design concepts for direct access storage devices are discussed in this section.

Direct Access Design

In a direct access file, individual records are located in the file according to their key or identifier. This may be accomplished in one of two ways:

1. *Direct relation.* The record key is the same as the address in the storage device. For example, record number 12345 is stored at disk address 12345.
2. *Key transformation.* The key is operated on mathematically, yielding a number that is used as the address of the record. This technique is sometimes called *randomizing.*

The direct relation is the fastest and most straightforward method of locating records. However, it tends to be wasteful of storage space. For example, suppose an organization has 10,000 employees whose employee numbers range from one to 20,000 (many numbers are unused, corresponding to former employees who have left the organization). The employee records could be stored in locations numbered one to 20,000 using a direct relation. However, the locations would be only 50 percent used. For this reason, the direct relation approach is seldom used.

To achieve higher storage utilization, randomizing is often used. A number of techniques for transforming the record key is available. One method is to divide the record key by the number of storage addresses to be used, and to use the remainder as the address for the record. To illustrate, suppose there are seven records, numbered as follows: 4, 13, 21, 38, 42, 55, 63. The records are to be stored in 11 locations, numbered 0 to 10.

The first record, with a key of 4, is divided by 11:

$$11 \overline{)4} \begin{array}{c} 0 \\ \underline{0} \\ 4 \end{array}$$

Since the remainder is 4, the record is stored in location 4. Dividing the next record number (13) by 11 results in a remainder of 2, so record number 13 is stored at address 2. Proceeding in this manner results in the records being stored as is shown in Figure 19–6.

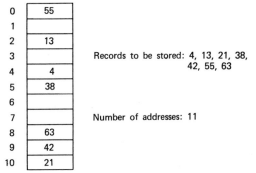

0	55
1	
2	13
3	
4	4
5	38
6	
7	
8	63
9	42
10	21

Records to be stored: 4, 13, 21, 38, 42, 55, 63

Number of addresses: 11

Figure 19–6. *Locating records using division as a randomization method.*

QUESTION: Suppose that it is desired to store record number 81 in the file shown in Figure 19–6. Using the above procedure, the record should be stored at address _____.

ANSWER: 4, the remainder when 81 is divided by 11

This example illustrates a problem that arises in using key transformation. Although record 81 should be stored at address 4, Figure 19–6 shows that record number 4 is already stored at that address. Record keys that generate the same storage addresses are referred to as *synonyms*. One method of handling synonyms is to locate a record in the next available storage location.

QUESTION: In Figure 19–6, record number 81 would be stored at address _____.

ANSWER: 6, which is the next available address after 4

The occurrence of synonyms creates problems when records must be retrieved. In the above example, when record number 81 is to be retrieved, the computer first goes to address 4. Not finding the desired record, it must then search following records until record 81 is found — in this case, at address 6. Problems of synonyms can be kept at a minimum by using these measures:

1. Keeping the file sparsely populated. As a rule of thumb, when a direct access file is 50 percent full, 20 percent of the records to be retrieved will result in synonyms. As with direct relation, this measure has the disadvantage of low file utilization.
2. Use programming techniques such as chaining.

Chaining is the use of a pointer in a record to indicate the address of the next record. To illustrate, Figure 19–7 shows the example discussed above. Record number 81 is stored at address 6, the first available location after address 4. Address 4 contains a pointer that indicates the location of this record, so that the computer need not search intervening records to retrieve record number 81.

QUESTION: Suppose it is desired to store record number 49 in the file. What changes are needed in Figure 19–7? _____

527 / FILE DESIGN CONCEPTS

	Record	Pointer
0	55	
1		
2	13	
3		
4	4	6
5	38	
6	81	
7		
8	63	
9	42	
10	21	

Address 4 contains record 4, plus a pointer that "points" to the location of record 81, a synonym.

Figure 19–7. *Chaining is used to facilitate locating records whose keys are synonyms.*

ANSWER: The record is placed at address 7, the first available location. A pointer is placed at address 5 (the computed address), pointing to address 7.

Index Sequential Organization. In some situations it is desirable to combine the abilities of sequential and direct access organizations. For example, in a payroll application the files are normally organized sequentially for the periodic payroll runs. Also, it is sometimes desired to retrieve individual records from the master file. This is much more easily accomplished with a direct access file.

With the index sequential technique, records are arranged sequentially on a direct access storage device. For direct access operation, tables are built into the file that permit looking up the address of an individual record. Often the tables are in hierarchial form, to permit rapid location of the track containing the desired record.

An example of direct access search under index sequential is shown in Figure 19–8. In the example, the search is for the record with key number 79. The computer first examines a table containing a master index of cylinders. The search is for the first cylinder whose highest key is greater than the desired record key. In this case, record number 79 is located on cylinder 2.

The search is then directed to an index of tracks for cylinder 2. Again the search is for the first track number with a number greater than the key. In the example, the record is located on track 3. Finally, the computer searches track 3 for the desired record. If the record is not found on this track because of overflow, a pointer or chained reference indicates its exact location.

QUESTION: Suppose in Figure 19–8 that it is desired to locate record number 59. On what cylinder and track should it be located? _____

_____.

ANSWER: Cylinder 2, track 1

The advantage of index sequential is that it does combine the advantages of direct access and sequential organization. The disadvantage is that extra search steps are needed to locate individual records, as compared to simple direct access. Also, index tables require additional storage capacity and must be maintained as the file is changed.

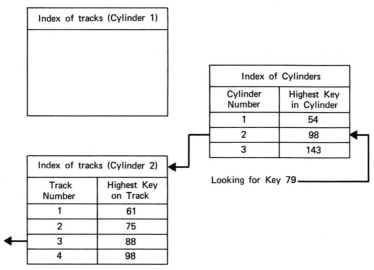

Figure 19–8. *Searching for a record under Index Sequential.*

Inverted Files. Direct access or index sequential file organization permits rapid retrieval of individual records, provided the record key is known. However, in management information systems it is often desired to search a file for records having a particular characteristic. For example, it may be desired to retrieve records for all employees having a particular skill, or for all students in a given major. Unless special provisions are made, it is necessary to search the entire file to locate records with the desired fields.

Inverted file techniques facilitate searching a file on one or more fields. To illustrate, Figure 19–9 shows a portion of a student record file. Each record contains the student number (key), class (1 = freshman, etc.), major (codes 1-4), and grade point average (GPA). It is assumed that the organization is direct access, so that any record can be retrieved, given the student number.

Student No.	Class	Major	GPA
105	2	2	2.87
113	1	4	3.42
129	4	3	1.93
134	3	1	2.33
147	4	4	3.63
163	2	3	2.69
171	1	2	3.08
182	3	1	2.74
190	2	2	3.16
198	3	4	2.44

Figure 19–9. *Portion of student record file.*

529 / FILE DESIGN CONCEPTS

Suppose that it is desired to retrieve the record for each student who is a junior (class = 3). Ordinarily it would be necessary to read the entire file (in this instance, 10 records) to locate the desired records. However, in Figure 19–10 the file has been inverted on two fields: class and major. A search of the *inverted file table* for class tells the computer it need only retrieve records with numbers 134, 182, and 198.

Class	Key	Key	Key		Major	Key	Key	Key
1	113	171			1	134	182	
2	105	163	190		2	105	171	190
3	134	182	198		3	129	163	
4	129	147			4	113	147	198
(1) Inversion by class					(2) Inversion by major			

Figure 19–10. *Inverted file tables for student file.*

QUESTION: Suppose it is desired to retrieve the records for sophomores (class = 2) who are in major 2. From Figure 19–10, what records should be retrieved? _____

_____

ANSWER: Records number 105 and 190, which appear as keys for both class = 2 and major = 2

In Figure 19–10 the student file was inverted on two of the three data fields. It would also be possible to invert the file on grade point average, using a range of GPA values for each entry in the inverted file table. A file that is inverted on each field of its records is said to be *fully inverted.*

Inverted files greatly facilitate searching on multiple fields. The disadvantage of this approach is the additional storage space and table maintenance required for the inverted file tables. Whether the technique should be used depends on the frequency and extent to which searching for record characteristics is required.

Hierarchial Organization. A recurring problem in file design is that some records are longer than others. One method of handling this is to use variable length records, as is discussed in Chapter 9. In third generation systems a hierarchial record structure is more often used.

In hierarchial organization, records are segmented into a base or root segment, followed by a series of subordinate segments. Chaining (or pointers) may be used in the base segment or in other segments to point to the location of subordinate segments.

As an example, in a student record file the base segment might contain student number, class, major, and grade point average. One subordinate segment might then contain a record of courses taken at the school, while a second subordinate segment would contain a record of courses taken at another school. The hierarchial organization for this example is shown in Figure 19–11.

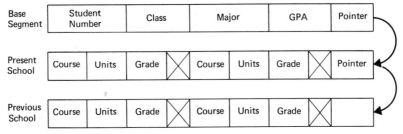

Figure 19–11. *Hierarchial organization of student record.*

Exercise 19–2

1. Locating records by operating on the key mathematically is referred

 to as _____ or _____ _____.

2. Record keys that result in the same storage addresses when trans-

 formed are called _____.

3. _____ is the use of a pointer in a record to indicate
 the address of a related record.

4. Refer to Figure 19–7. Where would record number 23 be located?

 _____ Record number 27? _____

5. Refer to Figure 19–8. On what cylinder and track should record num-

 ber 109 be located? _____

6. A technique of using tables to search for records with a given charac-

 teristic is termed _____ _____.

7. Refer to Figure 19–10. What record keys pertain to *either* seniors or

 major 3 (or both)? _____

8. In a hierarchial organization, records are segmened into a _____

 or _____ segment and _____ segments.

Providing for Data Communications

An added complexity in the physical system design process for many present-day systems is the data communications specification. A background on data communications is provided in Chapter 8. The system designer usually calls on a specialist to assist in designing the data communications portion of the system. One or more specialists are employed full-time in large companies; however, the small firm usually relies on outside expertise. The telephone company, or other organizations that provide communications, will also provide consulting aid in designing the communications portion of the system.

531 / PROVIDING FOR DATA COMMUNICATIONS

The key part played by the system designer is specifying data communications requirements for the system.

Designing Data Communications

Although detailed information is provided in the chapter on data communications, the important aspect to remember here is that such systems are rarely justified for one application alone. Design teams of the various major systems cooperatively determine the level of sophistication required to offset the cost of communication. For example the system may only provide transmission of input data from remote locations. Or, it may be designed for two-way transmission with interactive capability. The selection of facilities is based on the factors listed below.

Selection of Facilities. The class of facilities selected by a particular user depends on the volume of messages to be transmitted, and their priority or urgency. A cost/benefit analysis is required to select an optimum configuration of terminals and lines. The American Telephone and Telegraph Company suggests the following criteria be used in planning a telecommunications system.

1. *Function.* The type of information to be transmitted, and the operations to be performed.
2. *Distribution.* The number of locations involved in the transmission and receipt of information.
3. *Volume.* The total amount of information that must be transmitted over a given period of time.
4. *Urgency.* The speed with which messages must be delivered.
5. *Language.* The form in which data is received, and the code in which it is transmitted.
6. *Accuracy.* Greater accuracy can be achieved using error detection and correction techniques; however, such systems are more costly.
7. *Cost.* Total systems costs of hardware, software, and personnel must be considered.

QUESTION: Which criterion would be least important in designing a time-sharing system for college student use? _____
Why? _____
ANSWER: Volume; the amount of information transmitted would be much less than in a business application because students are primarily debugging programs, not transmitting data

Designing Input

In the process of evaluating design alternatives, input media are identified. For example, Stage I might utilize input transmittals while Stage II calls for on-line terminal input. The physical design produced the procedure for input and formatting of the input.

Figure 19–12 illustrates a set of transmittals designed to facilitate input for an inventory system. The designer would prepare an accompanying procedure explaining precisely how the data is to be recorded and under what circumstances.

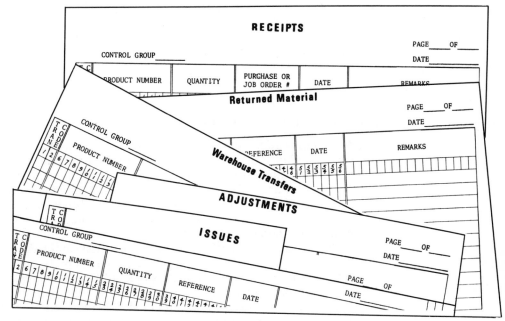

Figure 19–12. *Format specifications for input (an inventory system).*

QUESTION: In the case illustrated in Figure 19–12, the system designer chose to design separate forms for each transaction rather than have all transactions recorded on a standard transmittal and identified by transaction code (e.g., one form for receipts, one for issues, etc). What circumstances justified separate transmittals, in your opinion?

ANSWER: The volume of transactions in each category would fill several sheets each day; therefore, little was saved by having one transmittal. Also, by designing a different transmittal for each transaction type, the possibility of error in identifying type of transaction is reduced

I/O and Processing Controls

The last part of the system design task is to develop a scheme of controls to insure that the system accomplishes what it is designed to do. Three sets of controls are designed to insure:

1. Validity and completeness of data preparation.
2. Accuracy of key entry.
3. Reliability of computer processing.

T R A N E / C O D E	PRODUCT NUMBER	QUANTITY	PURCHASE OR JOB ORDER #	DATE	F R O M	T O	REMARKS
01	248 1007A2	24		15A	121273	46	
02	10C544523	5000		78		51	

Figure 19–13. *Input transmittal transaction codes.*

Controls on Data Preparation

One thing computerized systems have in common with manual systems is their dependence on completeness of input. For example, if a transaction on withdrawal of inventory is not entered to the system, the inventory is no longer accurate. Or, if a bank deposit slip is misplaced, the customer's balance is incorrect. User procedures establish controls to insure that all transactions are routed to the appropriate person for preparation of data for the key entry operation.

However, data preparation for the computer system has an additional step that makes this process more error prone than its manual system counterpart. In the manual system, a stock clerk posts receipts and withdrawals on an inventory card.

In a computer system an additional step is required. The clerk must record a code for the transaction, to cause the computer to make the addition or deletion from inventory, as is shown in Figure 19–13. In this example, transaction code 01 represents an addition to inventory while code 02 represents a deletion.

In some instances, the key entry personnel can work directly from a user document. More often, data is transcribed to an input transmittal, as shown in Figure 19–13. Although preparation of the transmittal form necessitates an activity not required in the former manual system, it is usually justified. The cost of preparing the transmittal is offset by the savings in key entry, for these reasons:

1. Personnel in key entry typically work on input for a variety of systems; it is difficult to reorient to a variety of documents.
2. Key entry is more accurate, since the operator reads only one line, from left to right, as opposed to scanning the whole form.

Therefore, the system designer concentrates on developing control procedures that simplify data preparation to reduce the possibility of error. A well-designed input transmittal reduces error possibilities—for input preparation as well as key entry. With proper training, errors in filling out transmittals are minimal.

The procedure seldom calls for verification of the transmittal by a second person. However, one of the authors worked in an atomic energy plant where input to a process control computer was visually verified before key entry, then was also machine verified by a second key entry operation. The risk associated with inaccurate input justified this approach. Procedures of this type are not typical. There are other ways to validate input, as is described in the next section.

The input procedure also provides checks and balances to insure that all transactions enter the system. Numbering forms is one approach. Another is consolidating documents into groups or batches. At each handling station the batch total is compared to the number of documents to insure that no documents have been lost.

QUESTION: The designer would specify key entry directly from the user document only when _____.
ANSWER: there is no interpretation to be done by the operator, where the entry is direct and in sequence

Controls on Key Entry

Considerable change has occurred in design of controls for insuring accuracy of key entry. Until recently, data was converted to machine-readable media by the card punch device. Many organizations still use this mechanical device, which is slow and cumbersome to operate when compared to the electronic key entry devices. The new devices also permit an improved level of controls. Previously, the accuracy of keypunching was verified by rekeying the information on a second machine, called the verifier. Instead of punching holes, this machine seeks the absence or presence of holes in a card by a device similar to a photo-electric cell. However, if an error is detected, the card has to be sent back through the keypunch operation again, even if only one of the 80 columns is mispunched.

Using the new disk-oriented or tape-oriented key entry systems reduces the requirement for verification. For example, in the disk systems multiple key entry devices are coupled to a minicomputer. Editing of data is programmed into the minicomputer so the data can be checked for logical errors as well as keying errors. Previously, editing was accomplished in the main computer, requiring recycling through the manual operations to correct the detected errors. Now, a great deal of editing is completed in the key entry system. For example, the common key entry error of transposition can be logically edited if the part numbering system is designed for certain positions to be only alphabetic or numeric. Tables can be referenced, such as zip code tables, to compare a zip code against city and state to insure its validity. The key entry operator is notified and corrects the error immediately.

A similar editing function is designed for systems where data is entered directly to the system by a user. Detection of errors occurs and is signaled back to the CRT at the entry terminal so correction can be made immediately. It is the system designer's task to determine which entry approach is feasible and to design control procedures.

Controls on Data Flow

With the large volume of data flowing into and out of the computer organization, a data control function is usually established. The system designer incorporates two kinds of controls in this operation:

1. Schedule control.
2. Completeness of input and validity of output.

Schedule control consists of monitoring flow of input to make sure it is entered on time to the proper processing run. It also insures that output is distributed on time to the various users.

Insuring completeness of input requires procedures on handling of input. Just as input may be batched prior to the preparation of data transmittals, the transmittals must be controlled to insure that all data are converted to machine-readable media. Numbering is the common control for data transmittals. When key entry occurs directly from a form, such as a customer order form, counting into batches (e.g., 25 or 50) is the common control, with dollar totals and/or hash totals also included in the batch control. The *dollar total* might be total sales dollars for orders, or total purchase commitment for purchase orders.

The *hash total* is a tally of items in certain fields, which has no value except for a control. When a bank processes deposit slips, the number of items per deposit slip might be totaled to compare with the number of checks associated with the deposit, as a double control that all input was included. That total has significance and thus is not a hash total. An example of a hash total would be the sum of all account numbers, which has no physical significance, hence, the term "hash."

The data control function is also responsible for gathering the materials necessary to process the job: the cards, magnetic tapes or disk packs containing input, and the computer program. On completion of processing, the data control group refiles these materials. Therefore, media labeling and storage is included in the control procedures for this function.

The data control procedure specifies routing of output from the computer; therefore, this group is responsible for getting output to the specified persons in accordance with schedule.

The data control procedure also specifies checks on the validity of output. For example, a computer system malfunction may have been undetected during processing. A "reasonableness" check by data control personnel controls against such malfunctions. Such controls consist of two parts. The first is random check of transactions (e.g., is the total for randomly selected invoices correct for items ordered?) The second check is on control totals (e.g., is the payroll total consistent with predetermined maximums?).

QUESTION: For input, data control operators check to insure _____ . For output the check is on _____ .
ANSWER: completeness, validity

Controls on Computer Processing

Although controls will be designed into the output analysis function, the desirable place to catch processing errors is as close as possible to the point of occurrence. Therefore, the system designer builds checkpoints into the processing cycle. One approach is to interrupt processing to print control totals on the console typewriter. The operator compares these totals to predetermined ranges for reasonableness before proceeding with the processing. For example, the total payroll might be compared to a predetermined amounts to insure processing validity before initiating the printing of payroll checks.

If a problem is detected, the operator must decide which element produced the system malfunction. It may have occurred in a tape reader or in the CPU, or the like. The procedure for isolating malfunctions is one designed by the computer manufacturer, not the system designer, and is beyond the scope of this book. However, the system designer in cooperation with the programmer determines checkpoints for processing of an application. Rather than finding at the end of the job that several hours of processing were wasted, checkpoints are provided throughout processing.

However, operator intervention to determine processing reliability is costly. Whenever possible, the check is built into the logic of the application so processing proceeds without interruption unless the check is negative. Then the operator is notified of the problem and initiates the procedure to identify the source of the error.

QUESTION: It is costly to interrupt processing to print out messages to be interpreted by operators, so the system logic specifies interruption only when the _____ check is negative.

ANSWER: reasonableness

Editing Checks

The system designer prepares a comprehensive set of controls referred to as editing checks, to insure data is validated and processing is verified. Whether accomplished by the key entry minicomputer or by the main processor, these editing checks are commonly classified in the following categories.[1]

1. Coding checks.
2. Combination checks.
3. Check digits.
4. Matching checks.
5. Composition checks.
6. Crossfooting checks.
7. Sign checks.

Coding checks reject data codes that do not conform with established coding lists. For example, suppose normally there should be only three types of entries in a given procedure — A, B, and C. If a given entry is neither A nor B, a positive test establishes whether it is C.

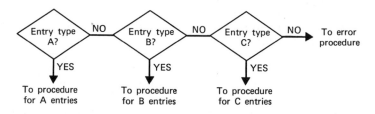

[1]From Haskins and Sells, *Internal Control in Electronic Accounting Systems*, New York, 1965, pp. 73–84.

Combination checks are an extension of coding checks. Under program control, a computer can recognize valid relationships between two fields of coded information and can reject impossible combinations. To illustrate, assume the following assignment of territories to salesmen:

Salesman	Territory
Jones	Illinois and Iowa
Smith	Illinois
Brown	Iowa and Missouri

If the coded representation of these combinations is stored internally, a computer can detect improper relationships, such as an entry that purports to credit Jones with a Missouri sale. It should be noted, too, that this lookup ability can be utilized to eliminate initial coding (and keypunching) in many situations. For instance, assume the following arrangement:

Salesman	Territory
Jones	Illinois
Jones	Indiana
Smith	Iowa
Brown	Missouri

Here the territories are exclusive, although one salesman, Jones, can sell in two states. If the input entry is coded for territory, the computer can supply the salesman's code (and name, if desired) making it unnecessary to code this information in the input operations.

A variation of this method of editing is sometimes used to verify the coding of account numbers. Where the chart of accounts is relatively complex, requiring long account numbers, the entire chart may be stored in the computer's memory. This provides a table for acceptable numbers against which the incoming record may be checked.

A *check digit* is an extra digit assigned to coded numbers, enabling the computer to perform the arithmetic needed to establish the probable correctness of the number. This would eliminate the need for the special device that otherwise is required to be attached to the card punch machine. Under this method, however, the errors would not be detected until a later stage in the processing cycle.

Matching checks detect improperly coded transaction numbers in file maintenance programs that are processed sequentially. The basic logic of the operation is shown below. If both the transaction and master file records are intended to be in ascending numerical order, a determination that the transaction number is less than the master number, followed by a determination that the transaction is not a new record for the file, is an indication of some type of error. Investigation will disclose that the transaction number is out of sequence, that a master record for the transaction should have been added to the file previously, or that the transaction number is incorrect.

Composition checks test the appropriateness of data in a variety of ways. Data fields may be tested for blanks to determine whether any significant information is missing from the input records. Numeric fields may be tested to locate extraneous alphabetic characters. Amount fields within a record may be crossfooted where it is possible to prove the accuracy of the individual fields.

Crossfooting checks prove the arithmetical accuracy of individual records or a group of records or both. Just as a clerk checks a schedule by crossfooting columnar totals, a computer can crossfoot individual rec-

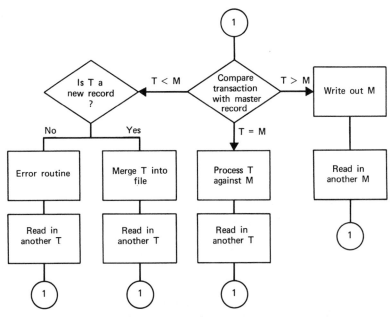

ords, such as gross pay to net pay, accumulate the respective amounts, and crossfoot the final totals. The technique is a simple way of establishing overall completeness and accuracy. It is especially effective at the conclusion of lengthy jobs, since they may be subject to interruption for mechanical or scheduling reasons and thus may be vulnerable to restart errors.

Sign checks, as their name implies, test the algebraic sign of a field of information. For example, the machines can detect a negative balance in inventory, an excess of payroll deduction over gross pay, or a change in an account balance from debit to credit. The checks frequently are used to indicate a failure to receive data. This could be the case, for example, when issues from stock are deducted before the receipt of goods is processed.

QUESTION: Which check would be appropriate for determining if a zip code were valid? _____

_____.

ANSWER: Composition check. The address could be compared with the zip code table stored in memory

Determining Level of Controls

Although 100 percent accuracy is desired by both user and system designer, it is seldom practical to design controls to achieve this kind of accuracy. The cost is often prohibitive. As we mentioned previously in the example of control over an atomic energy process, 100 percent accuracy may be necessary. In the typical business system the system design team must select controls based on the following evaluation.

1. What are the consequences of an undetected error?
2. What is the cost of achieving various levels of accuracy?
3. Where should the controls be established?

1. What are the four major categories of controls that the system designer includes in the physical system design?

(a) _____

(b) _____

(c) _____

(d) _____

2. What is the major factor in determining if data communications are justified for a system?

_____

_____

3. The following description is an example of which of the editing checks? During computer processing, a check on transaction file reveals no

corresponding master file. _____

4. The following description is an example of which of the editing checks?

The zip code check is not consistent with the city name. _____

_____

5. One hundred percent accuracy is rarely a design objective in setting

up controls. Why? _____

_____

_____

Preparing Output Formats

With the variety of output media available today, the task of preparing output formats has increased in scope. For example, a bank may provide audio output, in response to a customer's inquiry entered through a touchtone telephone device in the lobby of the bank or at another location. Many brokers' offices have visual output devices in customer lounges and at the brokers' desks. Microfiche output is becoming much less expensive. Even the granddaddy of output, the printed report, has a variety of forms: from the simple printing on blank stock to elaborate reports on pre-printed forms. Examples of the various output media are provided in the Chapter 7, "Input and Output Concepts and Devices."

The physical system design includes output formats for each of the media utilized. Figure 19–14 shows the designer's output layout for a report to be printed on standard output paper. Figure 19–15 shows the

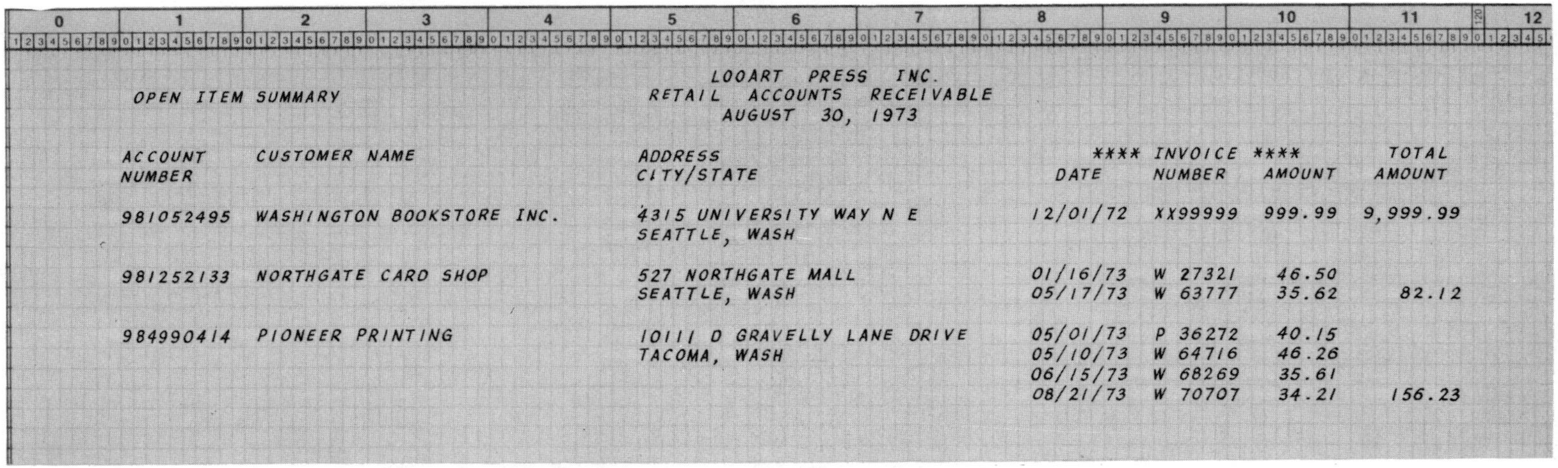

OPEN ITEM SUMMARY — LOOART PRESS INC. — RETAIL ACCOUNTS RECEIVABLE — AUGUST 30, 1973

ACCOUNT NUMBER	CUSTOMER NAME	ADDRESS CITY/STATE	**** INVOICE **** DATE	NUMBER	AMOUNT ****	TOTAL AMOUNT
981052495	WASHINGTON BOOKSTORE INC.	4315 UNIVERSITY WAY N E	12/01/72	XX99999	999.99	9,999.99
		SEATTLE, WASH				
981252133	NORTHGATE CARD SHOP	527 NORTHGATE MALL	01/16/73	W 27321	46.50	
		SEATTLE, WASH	05/17/73	W 63777	35.62	82.12
984990414	PIONEER PRINTING	10111 D GRAVELLY LANE DRIVE	05/01/73	P 36272	40.15	
		TACOMA, WASH	05/10/73	W 64716	46.26	
			06/15/73	W 68269	35.61	
			08/21/73	W 70707	34.21	156.23

Figure 19–14. *Example of a format specification for computer printout where printing is on plain output paper.*

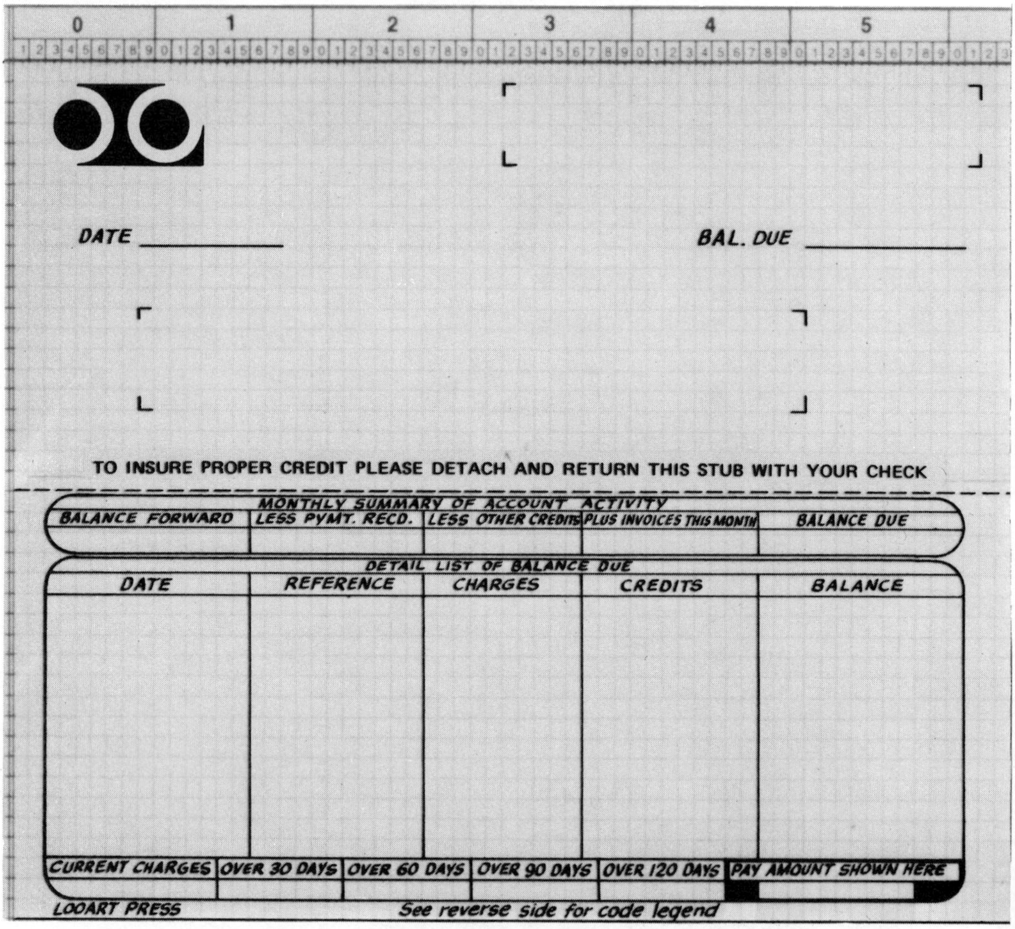

Figure 19-15. *Example of a format specification for computer printout where a preprinted form will be used.*

DATE	REFERENCE	CHARGES	CREDITS	BALANCE

CURRENT CHARGES	30 DAYS	60 DAYS	90 DAYS	120 DAYS	PAY THIS AMOUNT

LOOART PRESS   See reverse side for codes

DATE _____   BAL. DUE $_____

TO INSURE PROPER CREDIT PLEASE DETACH AND RETURN THIS STUB WITH YOUR CHECK

```
┌─────────────────────────────────────────────────────────────┐
│         PERSONNEL  SUMMARY  BLOCK   (AA)                      │
│                                                              │
│  JONES,  GERALD                                              │
│  POSITION:                    DEVELOPMENT  ENGINEER           │
│  HIRED:                       08/11/61                       │
│  SKILL  SPECIALTY  CODE:  0923A                              │
│  MAN  NUMBER:                 8610                            │
│                                                              │
│  FOR  INFORMATION  CONCERNING  THE  FOLLOWING                │
│  DATA  BLOCKS,   TOUCH  LIGHT  PEN  TO  APPROPRIATE          │
│  KEY  SYMBOL:                                                │
│              BLOCK                              KEY           │
│        PERSONAL  DATA                            A           │
│        ACADEMIC  TRAINING                        B           │
│        COMPANY  TRAINING                         C           │
│        PRIOR  JOB  EXPERIENCE                    D           │
│        COMPANY  JOB  EXPERIENCE                  E           │
│        MILITARY  SERVICE                         F           │
│        PUBLICATIONS,   AWARDS                    G           │
│        ORG.  MEMBERSHIPS                         H           │
│        JOB  AND  LOCATION  PREFERENCES           I           │
│        SALARY  HISTORY                           J           │
│        APPRAISAL  HISTORY                        K           │
│        SKILL  CODE  SUMMARY                      L           │
└─────────────────────────────────────────────────────────────┘
```

Figure 19-16. *CRT output where light pen is used to request further detail.*

layout for a preprinted form. In the latter instance, the form will be printed in a continuous sheet, exactly to these specifications so data can be printed precisely in the fields shown in the layout.

QUESTION: In the first format (Figure 19–14), the designer has provided a field size of _____ for the total amount.

ANSWER: eight positions including decimal and comma

QUESTION: In the second format (Figure 19–15), the designer has allowed _____ positions in the "Balance" field. (Count the positions at the top of the form above that field.)

ANSWER: Positions 48 to 60, or 13

When a terminal device is used for input, the procedure includes sample CRT output. Figure 19–16 illustrates CRT output that is obtained by a touch light pen input, allowing the user to obtain as much as desired. This approach implements the management-by-exception principle.

QUESTION: Designing input for a terminal device is more difficult, since the procedure must include a scheme for verifying that the input was transmitted accurately. The chapter on data communications lists several transmission checking approaches. Name one. _____

_____.

ANSWER: Any of the following: block parity check, cyclic redundancy check, retransmission, or loop checking.

Exercise 19–4

1. The system designer determines both the type of output device and the

   _____ of the output.

2. Output formats are prepared to facilitate the next phase in the system

   development process, that of _____ .

3. Although this section does not state it precisely, would you expect that the same kind of output format form would be used for printed output and for a visual display (CRT)-oriented system? _____ What differences would there be? _____

File Conversion Plan

The final activity to be completed before implementing a computerized system is file conversion. The task may be relatively simple if it is already in some computer-readable medium. If this is the case, the conversion may consist of merely restructuring the file. A simple computer program can accomplish the task, although many hours of computer time might be required. The time requirement for conversion depends on the volume of the file and the amount of restructuring.

If the file is not on machine-readable medium, the conversion may be a costly and time-consuming task. Considerable lead time may be required for the conversion if the file is voluminous.

The system designer normally prepares a file conversion plan to avoid a crash effort for conversion. However, in converting from one medium to another, the old files are needed until implementation of the new system. In this case, file conversion may occur on a weekend. Or, the old and new files may be maintained during parallel processing. Obviously this is a costly solution; therefore, parallel operation is planned for as short a time period as possible.

QUESTION: Is the file conversion plan a function of logical or physical system design? Explain. _____

_____ .

ANSWER: Physical. The logical system design specifies the information the system is to produce and provides descriptors on input, output, and files. However, the physical system design produces file and record layouts — necessary to determine a file conversion plan

SUMMARY

The physical system design prescribes specifically how the system is to be implemented on the computer available to the organization.

The physical design package provides the programmer with all

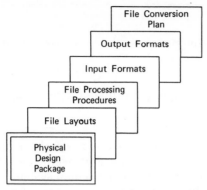

Figure 19-17. *Output of the physical design process.*

the information needed to convert the design to a machine-processable form: file layouts, file processing procedures, decision logic, input formats, and output formats.

In developing the physical design, the design team determines which level of design sophistication is feasible within existing resource contraints. This process is accomplished in cooperation with the user representative, who is most knowledgeable concerning the benefits possible through each level of sophistication.

The design teams for the various major systems of the organization are cooperatively designing their systems so that information may be shared between systems. A database is developed for the subsystems within each major system and eventually is merged into a common database for the entire organization.

Many organizations have geographically dispersed operations; hence, the physical design function includes evaluation of a data communications network.

The physical system design also includes controls to insure system reliability. Often a representative of the internal auditing organization aids in designing system controls.

A file conversion plan is the last part of the physical design package. The design team is also responsible for planning for implementation, which is described in the next chapter.

The output of the physical design process is shown in Figure 19-17. File processing procedures include design logic. Control procedures are incorporated into each of these subpackages, where appropriate (e.g., editing in the input procedure).

Solutions to Exercises

Exercise 19-1

1. 2, 4, 6.
2. 1, 3, 5, 7.

Exercise 19–2

1. Randomizing, key transformation.
2. Synonyms.
3. Chaining.
4. 1; 7 (first available).
5. Cylinder 3; an index of tracks for cylinder 3 is not shown.
6. Inverted files.
7. 129; 163; 147.
8. Base; root; subordinate.

Exercise 19–3

1. (a) Data preparation controls.
   (b) Key entry controls.
   (c) Data flow controls.
   (d) Computer processing controls.

2. Cost; selection of facilities is based on seven criteria.

3. Matching code.

4. Combination checks.

5. The cost would be prohibitive unless it were a system that involved life and death, like the computer systems controlling a space flight.

Exercise 19–4

1. Format.

2. Computer programming.

3. Yes. The manufacturer specifies how much data can be displayed, so an output format would show the precise positions on the CRT screen where the output was to be displayed.

Chapter Examination

1. What is a database? _____

_____

_____

2. Why is a database essential for implementing the computer-based management information system? _____

_____

_____

3. What are the major components of the system design package:

Logical Design   Physical Design

(a) _____   _____

(b) _____   _____

(c) _____   _____

(d) _____   _____

(e) _____   _____

4. What factors determine the level of sophistication that can be built into the initial stage of a system design? _____

_____

_____

5. What factors are considered in selecting data communication facilities?

(a) _____

(b) _____

(c) _____

(d) _____

(e) _____

(f) _____

(g) _____

6. Refer to Figure 19–8. Assume the computer is accessing record number 97. On what cylinder _____ and what track _____ should it be located?

7. The advantages and disadvantages of index sequential file access are:

Advantages   Disadvantages

(a) _____   _____

(b) _____   _____

8. Which file design concept is appropriate for the Student Record System (described in problem 13 of the Chapter Examination in Chapter 17). Explain your selection.

_____

_____

_____

9. Which file design concept is appropriate for the Checking Account System (described in problem 14 of the Chapter Examination in Chapter 17). Explain your selection.

_____

_____

_____

10. Which file design concept is appropriate for the Department Store System (described in problem 15 of the Chapter Examination in Chapter 17). Explain your selection.

_____

_____

_____

11. Which file design concept is appropriate for the Production Control System (described in problem 16 of the Chapter Examination in Chapter 17). Explain your selection.

_____

_____

_____

12. What are inverted files? What are their advantages and disadvantages? _____

_____

_____

_____

13. Refer to Figure 19–10. Assume that we are retrieving a record for seniors who are in major code 3. What records are retrieved?

_____

14. Does Figure 19–10 represent a fully inverted file? Why? _____

_____

15. Refer to Figure 19–11. What distinguishes this file as one with hierarchial organization? _____

_____

_____

16. Prepare a record layout for the Purchase Order File, detailed in the File Descriptor form of Figure 17–7, Chapter 17. Do not worry about the fields being proportional, just record the layout in the space below, identifying positions and field names; the first field is filled in for you.

File Positions	
1–6	
P.O. Number	

17. Which file organization and access method would be best for the Purchase Order File? (Figure 17–7) What additional information would you need to know to be able to choose the proper approach?

_____

_____

18. Prepare a card layout for the Input Descriptor in Figure 17–6, using the form provided at the end of the Chapter Examination.

19. Prepare a report layout for the Output Descriptor in Figure 18–2, using the form provided at the end of the Chapter Examination.

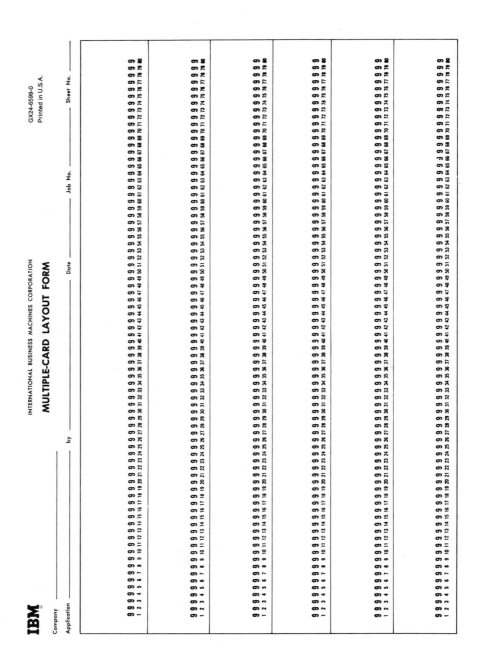

International Business Machines Corporation

GX24-6599-0
Printed in U.S.A.

MULTIPLE-CARD LAYOUT FORM

20. Which of the controls listed in the section on controls should be be included in every system, in your opinion? Explain. _____

_____

_____

MULTIPLE-CARD LAYOUT FORM

Chapter 20

SYSTEM FEASIBILITY ANALYSIS

Overview

The term *system feasibility analysis* refers to the process of evaluating the advantages versus the costs of converting a manual operation to the computer. The term *computer justification* refers to the process of evaluating the pros and cons of acquiring a computer.

Justification of a computer installation normally requires several system feasibility analyses. Rarely is a computer justified by one application. The exception would be a computer for an airline reservations system or for control of an oil refinery process. Typically, an organization first evaluates the advantages of computerization of individual systems, for instance, the inventory system or the sales analysis system. Then the combined benefits of computerization of several systems are considered to determine if computer installation is justified.

On the other hand, it is usually suboptimal to evaluate each system independently. Some systems may be marginally feasible when evaluated alone and yet be quite economical when using data captured by another system. For example, the market analysis system relies heavily on data generated by the sales order processing system.

Therefore, this chapter concentrates on the information needs of the entire organization as a basis for delineating systems and for determining system feasibility.

Chapter 16 describes procedures for documenting existing systems. Chapter 17 describes techniques for analyzing these systems as a basis for designing improved systems. Chapter 18 explains the methodology for developing the logical system design. Chapter 19 explains the methodology for developing the physical system design.

Feasibility analysis is actually a continual process rather than a one-time activity. The system designer must have some general computer configuration in mind when he prepares the physical system design. The system may ultimately be designed for on-line processing but may be limited to the batch-processing mode in Stage I, because of resource constraints. Therefore, the designer considers several possibilities.

553

Likewise, the benefits must be estimated for several system alternatives. For example, the on-line system may produce 50 percent higher saving than a batch processing system yet may not justify acquisition of an on-line computer configuration at this stage of the company's growth.

Typically, a sizable investment is involved in system development. Management needs to compare this investment with other investment opportunities. The complete feasibility package includes a cash flow analysis, a return on investment analysis, and an appraisal of the impact of the system on the Profit and Loss Statement.

Benefits of Computer Processing

In the early days of computer use, operations were converted to the computer primarily for reduction in clerical costs. For some organizations, such as insurance companies and banks, reduction of clerical costs remains a principal reason for computerizing an activity. One expert has estimated that by 1985 all women in the United States population between the ages of 18 and 36 would have been needed to work in banking activities if the computer had not been introduced.

However, reduction of clerical costs is not the principal reason for computer application in many organizations. Speed of response is a more important benefit of computer use for some organizations. For example, few of us would be content with airline reservation systems as slow and inaccurate as those in operation in the early 1950s. Today, a major airline would not be able to compete without a computerized reservation system.

Speed of response is equally important in other types of business. Consider the mail-order firm used previously to illustrate documentation and analysis techniques. In a seasonal business such as providing products for Christmas gifts, the order processing cycle is crucial to success. Not only is quick response important for competitive reasons, it can result in a higher level of reorders. The mail-order company found that reducing the order processing time from four weeks to less than a week resulted in an increase of 15 percent in reorders. The customer received the merchandise, liked it, and had time to make another catalog purchase before Christmas.

Accuracy is another important reason for converting to computer operations. Computerizing complicated procedures such as insurance policy preparation results in far fewer errors.

In summary, varied benefits are possible from computer use. Table 20–1 provides a listing of these benefits.

Exercise 20–1

Which advantages of data processing listed in Table 20–1 would *not* apply to the following applications (explain your answer):

1. Airline reservations system. _____

_____

_____

TABLE 20–1
Advantages of Data Processing Applications

1. Lower costs
   a. Reduction in clerical operations.
   b. Savings in space required for personnel, desks, and files.
   c. Reduction in redundant files.
   d. Reduction in duplication of operations.
   e. Detection of problems before they become costly.
   f. Reduction in the routine, clerical elements in high-caliber jobs.
   g. Reduction in amount of paperwork by utilizing exception principle.
   h. Reduction in inventory.
   i. Combination of like functions in several departments.

2. Faster reaction
   a. Improved ability to react to changing external conditions.
   b. Larger reservoir of information for producing realistic operating plans and forecasting market conditions.
   c. Closer monitoring of operations and utilization of feedback principle to produce corrective actions.
   d. Assessing impact of problems of one area on the other activities of the firm.
   e. Faster turnaround time for processing jobs due to less clerical activity.
   f. Ability to compare alternative courses of action more comprehensively and rapidly.

3. Improved accuracy
   a. Mechanization of operations, permitting more checks and less error possibilities.
   b. Sharing of information between files, reducing the errors resulting from manual intervention.
   c. Ability to raise confidence limits on activities due to more information for measuring performance and more information to permit more accurate forecasts.
   d. Integrity of information maintained through improved validation techniques.

4. Improved information for management
   a. Higher quality information through feasibility to employ management science techniques.
   b. Capability to utilize management-by-exception principle to a greater extent.
   c. Capability of developing simulation models for inclusion of all factors in forecasting and developing alternative management plans.
   d. Improved performance indicators through more quantitative data and faster response on performance of all functions.

2. Utility company billing system. _____

_____

_____

_____

3. University student records system. _____

_____

_____

_____

Determining the Benefits of the Proposed System

The process of determining the benefits of the proposed system is a joint responsibility of the designers and the users of the system. However, since the manager of the area where the computer is applied is ultimately responsible for both the cost and productivity of his activity, he has the major role in estimating the benefits of the system. The system designer supports the manager in data gathering and analysis to determine benefits.

In a previous chapter, the distinction was made between first and third generation approach to system analysis and design. A similar distinction is possible in system feasibility analysis. First generation approach was to separate benefits into tangible and intangible benefits. The system was usually approved if tangible benefits exceeded costs. If a system were marginally feasible, intangible benefits often weighted the decision in favor of computerization.

Third generation system feasibility analysis does not attempt to distinguish tangible and intangible benefits. Instead, each potential benefit is assessed according to its probability of occurrence.

For example, marketing management might calculate benefits of adopting a sales order processing system as follows:

1. Reduction in clerical costs: $7,950
($.53 per order x 15,000 orders per year)

2. Increase in reorders due to faster order turnaround: $23,625
(15 percent x 15,000 orders per year x $105 per order)

3. Competitive advantage of capturing sales data for marketing database: $54,300
(3 percent improvement in annual sales at $105 revenue per order)

However, each of these three benefits has a different probability of occurrence. The system designer would ask the persons most knowledgeable concerning the benefits to estimate the probability of occurrence for each benefit, producing the following information:

Benefit	Possible Annual Savings		Probability of Occurrence		Expected Return
1	$ 7,950	×	.95	=	$ 7,553
2	$23,625	×	.50	=	$11,813
3	$54,300	×	.20	=	$10,860
	Total Net Forecast of Annual Benefits				$30,226

First generation approach would have considered benefit no. 3 as an intangible. Yet, the improvement in marketing database should produce tangible results. One might wonder if there would be a tendency to overstate benefits, using the third generation approach. Two factors indicate that the approach has adequate safeguards:

1. Ultimate marketing department performance is directly dependent on the reliability of its estimates.
2. Most organizations today charge the user for computer use, providing a strong incentive for accurate forecast of benefits.

Another method used in third generation approach is to ask the user manager to forecast a range of probability estimates. The system designer calculates expected return and asks the manager to aid in determining the benefit forecast. In the following example the designer would prepare the first two columns and then would assist the user in estimating the third column, probability of occurrence.

Such an approach provides the manager with a good basis for comparing estimated benefits with costs to determine if the system should be given the go-ahead. (See table 20–2).

For example, the system designer may be urging expansion of the inventory system to include a purchasing system, to enable automatic selection of economic order quantities. The manager may decide the probability of achieving an 8 percent reduction in inventory level would be increased to 70 percent with the expanded system.

TABLE 20–2
Expected Benefit Determination

Benefit	Possible Annual Savings	Probability of Occurrence	Expected Return	Weighted Estimate of Expected Return
Reduction in inventory level (cost of carrying inventory is 25 percent on average inventory level of $650,000)				
2 percent reduction	$ 3,250	.80	$2,600	
5 percent reduction	8,125	.15	1,219	
8 percent reduction	13,000	.05	650	
		1.00		$4,469

QUESTION: Indicate True or False. The user is responsible for making the probability estimates. _____ . Explain your answer. _____ .

ANSWER: True. The system designer assists by gathering and analyzing data as input to the manager's estimates

Savings Due to Third Generation Design Approach

Third generation system design approach places emphasis on those systems that are life-stream activities of the firm, the sales order processing system, the inventory system, the production system, and the distribution system. First generation system design placed emphasis on administrative systems, such as payroll or sales statistics. Whereas the payroll application might replace several clerks, the sales order processing application could speed up the order cycle enough to gain new customers and to obtain more reorders, as well as saving clerical costs. Also, the computer's capacity makes the sales order processing operation more flexible, able to handle wide swings in volume instead of hiring and laying off clerical personnel. Also, by capturing sales information as a by-product, the marketing analysis using this data gives the company a competitive advantage that may produce more savings than any of the previously cited savings potentials. The third generation approach is to determine feasibility based on computerization of several, interrelated systems.

In summary, properly applied, the computer's main advantages are flexibility, speed of response, accuracy, capability of processing large volumes of data, and computational ability.

Exercise 20–2

1. Ms. Clair E. Cull, Manager of Operations in the Littlefield Valley Bank estimates a cost of 12 cents per check in clerical processing costs if the system is converted from manual to computer processing. A bank across town will computer process checks for Littlefield Valley for 10.5 cents each. However, it charges $5 per trip to pick up and deliver the checks each evening. The bank has a volume of 2000 checks each day. Is it feasible for Ms. Cull to utilize the computer service?

---

2. Ms. Cull would like her own computer next year. A minicomputer appropriate for this operation rents for only $300 per month. What volume of check processing will be necessary next year to justify the the minicomputer, assuming that she can process as cheaply as the

bank across town? _____ .

3. By expanding the system to handle all transactions, both deposits and withdrawals, Ms. Cull calculates that she can reduce clerical costs by $250 per month. She has also determined that an in-house computer would enable her department to process all transactions within

one hour of receipt. Ms. Cull has asked Mr. Monte Bags (the bank president) to estimate the probable increase in accounts if a depositer could have an up-to-date balance within the hour. Mr. Bags estimates a 5 percent increase in customers with a 95 percent probability of occurrence. The bank now has 2000 accounts with an average monthly income of $0.75 per customer for demand deposit accounting alone. Can Ms. Cull justify the computer on the one-hour turnaround principle, or must she find other areas of application?

_____

_____

_____

_____

4. Ever persistent, Ms. Cull asks the Loan Department Manager, Mr. Tye T. Wad, what benefits would accrue by using the computer for his department. He can't think of any. Can you?

_____

_____

_____

5. How might the demand deposit data bank be used by the Loan Department?

_____

_____

Cost of Computer Use

The three components of the cost of computerization are: (1) development cost, (2) implementation cost, and (3) operating cost.

Development costs are _one-time_ costs, consisting of:

1. Documenting the existing system.
2. Analyzing the system to determine how improvement can be made.
3. Designing a new system.
4. Programming and debugging the system.

Implementation costs are _one-time_ costs, consisting of:

1. Training the users of the system.
2. Training the computer department personnel to operate the system.
3. Installing and testing the system.

Operating costs are *recurring* costs, consisting of:

1. Preparing data for entry to the system.
2. Performing control checks on input and output.
3. Computer processing.

QUESTION: Key entry costs also occur in the development phase but there are not enough to list under that heading. Why? _____

_____ .

ANSWER: Only the test data are key entered.

Development Costs

Comparison of first and third generation costs was shown in Figure 16–1. Not only are costs higher today but more emphasis is placed on Phases I through III of the development cycle. The more sophisticated systems of today require more effort in the early phases of the development cycle. On the other hand, returns are higher because the computer is applied to lifestream systems.

The resource levels required to support the development effort for a given system might appear as is illustrated in Figure 20–1.

QUESTION: Why would the cost of user representatives jump so drastically in Phase V? _____

_____

ANSWER: The system has been installed and needs close attention during the first month of operation to work out all the kinks.

System Cost in K Dollars	Time Periods										Total
	1	2	3	4	5	6	7	8	9	10	
50											
40											
30											
20									20.0		
10					12.5						
0	4.0	4.0								7.5	
PHASES	I	II	III ◄			► III	IV ◄		► IV	V	

Cost Element											
PERSONNEL											
User Representatives	2000	2000	1000	500	500	500	500	500	500	2000	
Analyst/Designers	2000	2000	2000	3000	3000	2000	1000	1000	1000	1000	
Programmers							4000	5000	4000	500	
Key Entry							100	200	300	2500	
Operators							50	100	100	200	
COMPUTER							300	600	600	1200	
SUPPLIES							50	50	50	100	
Total	4000	4000	3000	3500	3500	2500	6000	7450	6550	7500	48,000

Figure 20–1. *Resource levels for typical system development.*

Implementation Costs

Training costs are a large part of the cost of implementing third generation systems. Often, by using first generation system design approach, systems were converted to the computer with little change in operating procedure. The computer permitted the operations to be performed more quickly. Third generation systems are designed to take full advantage of the computer's capabilities, in analysis as well as processing speed.

For example, in processing insurance applications the computer program can compare the applicant's medical examination results with a wide variety of criteria to determine if he is an acceptable risk for insuring. Similar analysis can be performed in determining the financial qualifications of the applicant. The system of processing applications may be revised substantially to permit more thorough analysis of the insurance application.

As a consequence of these increases in system complexity and changes in system philosophy, training of personnel to utilize the system becomes more complicated. Whereas training may have been quite informal for first generation systems, it is formal today. An operating procedure has been developed both for users of the system (e.g., the insurance application review department in the above cited instance) and the data processing department personnel who run the system. The training activity is designed to review this procedure in depth and to provide an understanding of system objectives for all persons involved.

The other ingredient of implementation cost is the actual installation and testing of the system. While the system logic has been thoroughly tested, using both hypothetical and actual data, the test is not concluded until the person responsible for its operation is satisfied with its performance. In the above case, the person responsible would be the head of the insurance application review department.

Typically, the new system is run in parallel with the old system for a short time, to insure comparable results. However, since third generation systems are usually very different from the previous system, it is rarely practical to run the two in parallel for more than a few days. Is it practical to expect the staff to work 16 hours per day operating the old system during the first shift and the new system during the second shift? The more common practice is to test the new system on last month's data; for example, to run last month's input through the new system to compare results.

The emphasis on shorter parallel testing periods requires more careful planning of the tests. Therefore, the users and system analyst/designers are developing operating procedures, training programs, and implementation plans and test procedures during Phase IV of the development cycle, while the system is being programmed. All persons involved in the system are trained and prepared to operate the new system when Phase V is initiated.

QUESTION: Figure 16–1 shows implementation costs are lower today than they were with first generation systems. Why? _____

_____ .

ANSWER: More work is done in the prior phases, facilitating implementation. As a result, implementation costs are reduced despite the systems being more complicated than first generation systems

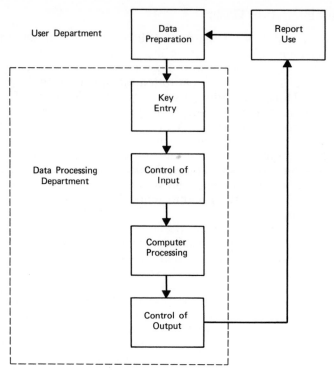

Figure 20–2. *System operating cycle.*

Operating Costs

Operating costs occur once the system is implemented. The major categories of operating costs are described below: key entry costs, data control costs, and computer processing costs.

While development and implementation costs are one-time costs, operating costs are recurring. The typical cycle is as shown in Figure 20–2.

QUESTION: Which of these costs are also occurring during system development? _____ .

ANSWER: The control function on I/O is not instituted until the system is installed. All other activities are required in developing the system, but only on an intermittent rather than a continuous basis

Key Entry Costs. The User Department prepares data in a format that can be used by Key Entry personnel. In some instances, data is transcribed from a document to a form that is designed to facilitate key entry. In other instances, the user document itself is redesigned, to permit key entry directly from the document. Figure 20–3 provides examples of both documents.

In some cases, data is entered directly to the system by the User Department, through an on-line terminal. However, this process is more expensive than off-line key entry when large volumes of data are involved. Key entry costs have been reduced by systems where the data is recorded directly on magnetic tape or disk, instead of punched into cards. See Chapter 7 for a discussion of input media.

QUESTION: Re-examine Figure 20–1. Key entry costs are high, compared to computer operators and the computer cost itself. What does this situation dictate to the system designer? _____

_____.

ANSWER: That considerable attention must be given to simplify the key entry document

Data Control Costs. As shown in Figure 20–2, in the typical system input is batched and checked before and after processing, to insure that all data was processed. Also, many systems are designed to include an editing operation, to search for key entry errors before processing. The edit program is a separate computer program that is prepared to analyze input, searching for errors to correct before the processing of the main program begins. Examples of errors that may be detected through the editing program are: (1) incorrect part numbers or account numbers, (2) omissions of data that should have been entered, (3) illogical entries, such as an invoice total inconsistent with quantity ordered multiplied by prices of items, or a zip code inconsistent with address.

The data control function has the following responsibilities: (1) control of input to insure all data is entered to the system, (2) providing data, programs, and processing procedures to computer operations for each job run, and (3) checking output to insure correct processing of the job.

Application *House List Maintenance*

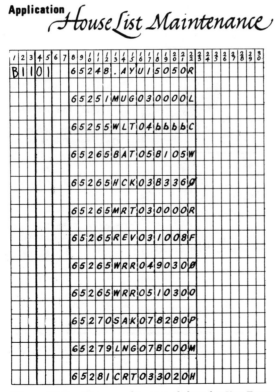

Figure 20–3a. *Form used to record data for Key Entry from User Document.*

Figure 20–3b. *Document designed for dual use by User Department and Key Entry.*

QUESTION: Data control functions did not exist for many first generation applications. What do you think may have caused this function to be developed? _____

_____.

ANSWER: Input was lost, or output was misplaced, as systems became more complex with a wider variety of input and larger numbers of users. Also, more control to reduce errors in input data was required

Computer Processing Costs. Since the editing function is accomplished by a computer program, the typical system has, at least, two passes through the computer: (1) processing of the editing program, and (2) processing of the main program.

However, the main processing may also be separated into several phases. For example, data may be input to the system daily with some processing occurring, such as updating the inventory. However, other processing steps may occur weekly, bimonthly and monthly, such as preparation of reports.

The computer operator is provided data, operating instructions, and the computer programs. Typically the input is recorded on magnetic tape, and these tapes must be mounted on the tape drives. The computer programs may be on magnetic tape or disk. The operator loads the program into the computer. A variety of media may be involved, since the master file is often on magnetic disk. The job is then processed according to the operating instructions. In preparing output, multiple media may again be involved. A printed report may be produced, or some special output documents, such as paychecks or invoices.

Output is given to Data Control for distribution, some to the User and some for storage in the Data Processing Department in preparation for the next run.

QUESTION: Although Figure 20–1 indicates that computer operations cost is low, relative to other costs, the job is error prone. Why?

_____.

ANSWER: A variety of tasks and media are involved. Procedures must be explicit to insure the reliability of operations

---

Exercise 20–3

To better understand the characteristics of development costs, answer these questions concerning the example in Figure 20–1.

1. Three major components of development costs are:

(a) _____

(b) _____

(c) _____

2. Total the costs:

(a) Personnel   _____

      User representatives   _____

      Analyst/designers   _____

      Programmers   _____

      Key entry   _____

      Operators   _____

(b) Computer   _____

(c) Supplies   =======

                                                $48,000

3. Determine the percentage of total cost allocated to each cost area:

(a) User representatives   _____

(b) Analyst/designers   _____

(c) Programmers   _____

(d) Key entry   _____

(e) Operators   _____

(f) Computer   _____

(g) Supplies   =======

                         100 percent

4. Assume programmers earn $800 per month and analyst/designers earn $1,000 per month: total man-months of effort are as follows:

      Analyst/designers   _____

      Programmers   _____

5. Analyze the costs to determine whether the following statements are true or false (you will need to refer to both Figures 16–1 and 20–1.)

_____ (a) User representatives and system analyst/designers are involved during the entire development cycle.

_____ (b) The information analysts are involved principally in analyzing the existing system and in implementing the new system.

_____ (c) Computer cost per period is doubled during implementation, compared to testing.

        (d) Since key entry costs balloon when Phase V begins, it appears that only sample transactions are keypunched during the programming/testing phase.

        (e) The cost of computer operators is approximately one fourth the cost of computer processing.

Estimating Cost of the System

Developmental Cost. Developmental costs are the most difficult component of system costs to estimate. After the Systems Survey is complete, the general scope of the system has been assessed but the degree of difficulty in system design is hard to predict.

Organizations often seek outside assistance in estimating development cost. A consultant who is experienced in the type of system to be designed is often used to provide estimates of development time and cost. Or, the design team will visit organizations with systems already implemented, to discuss the factors involved in design and implementation.

Once an organization has developed several systems of its own, it can build a reservoir of data for estimating development costs in its own special environment.

The major factor that effects system design costs is the qualification of system analysts/designers. Senior designers may complete a system design in one half the time required by a person with one year's experience, yet earn only one fourth more in salary.

The designers' tasks, spelled out in detail in the previous chapter, include: general flowcharting or decision table development, forms design and layout, report content determination and layout, file design, processing design, file conversion planning and procedure preparation, and preparation of both procedures and data processing procedures.

Cost estimating is usually separated into two phases:

1. A general estimate is made on completion of Phase II of the development cycle; at this point in time, the logical system design is complete, providing a general basis for estimating costs and benefits. Management decides if the investment warrants proceeding to the detailed design phase.
2. On approval to proceed, the team begins the physical design of the system, Phase III of the development cycle. Midway through this stage, estimates of cost and benefits can be much more precise. Management is provided a better basis for deciding to proceed or to discontinue the project. The latter decision is rarely made. Instead, the system designer provides alternatives in degree of sophistication for the system. Three or four levels of refinement of the system may be designed, as is described for the inventory system in Chapter 18 (Table 18–1) and illustrated in time-phase in Figure 20–4.

The complexity and scope of the system are the principal determinants of system development costs. The items considered in physical system design, as described in Chapter 19, affect both cost and schedule. In addition to dividing the system into stages, the designer separates

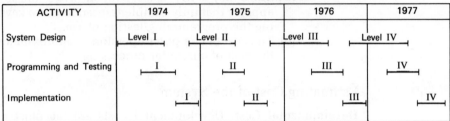

Figure 20–4. *System development plan: inventory system showing four levels of sophistication.*

the first stage of his system design into modules, facilitating estimates for programming and testing. When the detailed specifications for a system have been completed, along with separation of modules, estimates of programming and testing may be fairly accurately predicted. Rules of thumb for programming/testing estimates have been developed, such as the number of completed instructions per hour. Such an estimate takes into account all the activities of developing a finalized program: flowcharting, coding, creating test data, desk checking, and operational testing. Several cycles are necessary as the programmer organizes to utilize the special characteristics of the specific computer configuration being used: tape blocking, channel assignment, program overlays, use of subroutines, utility programs, reference tables, work areas, overlapping, file organization, file access techniques, and indexing approaches as well as other technical aspects. Automatic flowcharting and debugging packages may be used to reduce programming effort.

Once file design and access methods are determined, cost of operation can be accurately determined. Computer processing times can be determined by charts like the one in Figure 20–5. Processing time is proportional to the number of master file records that must be located, read into memory, updated, rewritten, and verified. The processing time for an IBM 360 Model 20 is shown by the curve in Figure 20–5. Such charts are readily available to facilitate the process of estimating computer costs.

QUESTION: Refer to Figure 20–5 and use the curve to determine the time to process 10K, 100 byte records on a 360/20? _____.

ANSWER: Approximately 30 minutes

Key entry costs are accurately estimated through the availability of data on the number of key strokes per hour expected of various experience levels of personnel. Given the specific record to be entered, exact estimates of key entry costs can be calculated.

Data control costs may be easily estimated, since a clerical rather than a creative activity is involved.

When estimates are completed for these three levels of cost (development, implementation, operation), and system benefits have been projected, cost/benefit analysis may be undertaken. Approaches for cost/benefit analysis, that is, system feasibility, are described in the next section.

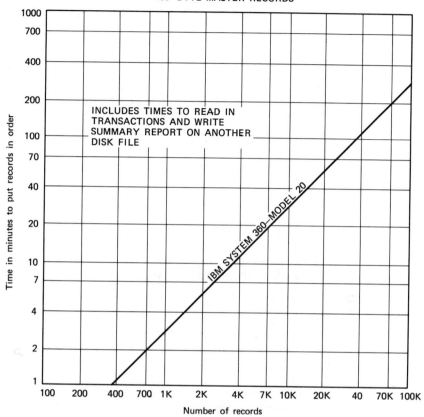

Figure 20–5. *Chart to determine computer processing time (courtesy of Aurblach).*

Exercise 20–4

1. What are the cost ingredients in system design?

_____

_____

_____

_____

_____

569 / ESTIMATING COST OF THE SYSTEM

2. What are the cost ingredients in programming?

_____

_____

_____

3. What are the specific characteristics of the computer configuration that must be considered by the programmer?

_____

_____

_____

Feasibility Analysis

When estimated benefits exceed costs of the proposed system, it still may not be feasible to proceed with development. The resources required to develop the system are always scarce resources and must be evaluated for use on an array of company projects.

Referring to the illustration in Figure 20–1, the $48,000 project may pay for itself in a year. However, let us assume that manufacturing management wants to purchase an expensive machine and that marketing management is recommending the addition of a market research organization. Both organizations have completed cost/benefit analyses to show that their recommendations are economically justified.

Company management must choose between these alternatives. Three financial analysis techniques are utilized in determining feasibility of a project, whether it is a computer project, a manufacturing project, or a marketing project. These three techniques, used in combination for evaluating projects, are:

1. Payback analysis.
2. Cash flow analysis.
3. Return on investment/present value analysis.

The use of these three financial analysis techniques is demonstrated on the system illustrated in Figure 20–1, the inventory system. In prior sections, techniques for estimating cost and benefits are described. Figure 20–1 provides the results of those estimates. Figure 20–6 represents the cost and benefit comparison for the system, providing the basis for feasibility analysis of the system.

After costs and benefits have been identified, the system analyst/designer is ready to prepare the feasibility analysis, utilizing the three financial analysis techniques described below.

Payback Analysis

As its title indicates, this technique is used to determine when the system will pay for itself, that is, when it will recover the development cost.

	Cost		Benefits	
One-Time		*Annual*		
Development Cost	$48,000	Inventory Reduction		$19,200
Annual		Purchase Order Preparation		
Operating Cost	$24,000	Simplification		7,200
		Revenue from Back Order		
		Reduction		8,400
				$34,800

Figure 20–6. *Cost/benefit comparison for inventory system.*

The system illustrated in Figure 20–1, the inventory system, will be used to demonstrate each of the three financial analysis techniques. The cost/benefit comparison (Figure 20–6) provides data for payback analysis. As is shown in Figure 20–7, the period required to recover development cost, the payback period, is 4.4 years. Most organizations have some policy on payback; frequently the policy is that a system must pay for itself in 5 years.

QUESTION: Is the period of 4.4 years a reasonable time for payback? _____ Explain: _____

_____.

ANSWER: This depends on the company's policy toward investment opportunity and on its cash flow position. Cash flow and ROI analyses provides a basis for answering that question, and are illustrated next

Cash Flow Analysis

The cash flow for the first 15 months of system development and operation is shown in Figure 20–8. The data is derived from Figure 20–1. As the name implies, cash flow analysis projects the effect of the system on the cash resources of the firm. Payback analysis projected a period of 4.4 years to recover cost but did not reveal that the firm would have a negative net cash flow until the thirteenth month after system development begins. And, although annual savings of $34,800 are forecast, savings do not accrue immediately on implementation of the system.

Observe the savings projected under the category, inventory reduction. Inventory cannot be automatically reduced with system implementation but is gradually reduced. Likewise reduction in customer back orders does not immediately produce more orders. When customers gain confidence that the firm will supply orders on time (that is, not run out

Gross Annual Savings		$34,800
Less Operating Cost		24,000
Net Annual Savings		$10,800

$$\text{Payback Period} = \frac{\text{Development Cost}}{\text{Net Savings}} = \frac{\$48,000}{\$10,800} = 4.4 \text{ years}$$

Figure 20–7. Payback analysis for inventory system.

Cash Flow Element	Time Period (Months)															24-Month Total
	1	2	3	4	5	6	7	8	9	10	11	12	13	14	15	
(in K's of $)																
Cost																
Personnel	4.0	4.0	3.0	3.5	3.5	2.5	5.6	6.8	5.8	6.2	1.1	1.1	1.1	1.1	1.1	
Computer							.3	.6	.6	1.2	.8	.8	.8	.8	.8	
Supplies							.1	.1	.1	.1	.1	.1	.1	.1	.1	
Total	4.0	4.0	3.0	3.5	3.5	2.5	6.0	7.5	6.5	7.5	2.0	2.0	2.0	2.0	2.0	78.0
Benefit																
Inventory reduction											.6	.5	.8	1.2	1.6	
PO cost reduction												.6	.6	.6	.6	
BO revenue												.1	.3	.7	.7	
Total											.6	1.2	1.7	2.5	2.9	29.2
Net cash flow	-4.0	-4.0	-3.0	-3.5	-3.5	-2.5	-6.0	-7.5	-6.5	-7.5	-1.4	-.8	-.3	+.5	+.9	-48.8
Cumulative cash flow	-4.0	-8.0	-11.0	-14.5	-18.0	-20.5	-26.5	-34.0	-40.5	-48.0	-49.4	-50.2	-50.5	-50.0	-41.9	

Figure 20–8. Cash Flow Analysis of Inventory System

of stock and place the item on back order), they will be more likely to reorder from the firm. Such confidence builds slowly. On the other hand, the reduction in purchase order preparation costs occurs immediately on implementation of the system, because the computer now performs some activities previously performed manually.

Cash flow analysis permits the officers of the firm to determine the effect on the firm's cash position if the system is undertaken. The financial officer may have to arrange for a bank loan, or may delay some expenditures in other areas during the period of heaviest cash drain.

QUESTION: Cash flow analysis provides the following information that payback analysis does not reveal: _____

_____.

ANSWER: The amount of cash required to underwrite each period of development. Also, it shows benefits versus costs on a period basis

Return on Investment (ROI) Analysis

Management must rank various investment alternatives, since there is always a limit to investments that the company can finance. Assuming it could borrow without limit, the minimum cost of capital in these additional alternatives would be the going interest rate, say, 8 percent. Therefore, 8 percent is the cutoff for return on investment. Any project that did not produce a ROI of, at least, 8 percent would be rejected by management. However, rarely does a company have unlimited borrowing capability. Management must decide which projects to approve and typically will rank projects according to projected return on investment. The ROI analysis of the inventory system is provided in Figure 20–9, using data from Figure 20–8.

Projected Benefits (in K's of $)	YEAR				Four-Year Total
	1	2	3	4	
Inventory reduction	$ .5	$18.0	$19.2	$19.2	$56.9
PO cost reduction	1.2	7.2	7.2	7.2	22.8
BO reduction	.1	8.0	8.4	8.4	24.9
Subtotals	$ 1.8	$33.2	$34.8	$34.8	104.6
Projected costs	$52.0	$24.0	$24.0	$24.0	124.0
cumulative savings	1.8	33.2	69.8	104.6	
cumulative costs	52.0	76.0	100.0	124.0	Four-Year Average
ROI =	.03	.44	.70	.84	$\frac{.84}{4} = 21$ percent

Figure 20–9 *Return on Investment Analysis (Cost and Savings Derived from Figure 20–8.)*

End of Year	Present Value per Dollar	Savings	Present Value of Savings
2	$1 \div (1. + .08)^2 = .857^a \times \$\ 7,000^b =$		$ 5,999
3	$1 \div (1. + .08)^3 = .794 \times \$10,800 =$		8,575
4	$1 \div (1. + .08)^4 = .735 \times \$10,800 =$		7,938
5	$1 \div (1. + .08)^5 = .681 \times \$10,800 =$		7,355
6	$1 \div (1. + .08)^6 = .630 \times \$10,800 =$		6,804
7	$1 \div (1. + .08)^7 = .583 \times \$10,800 =$		6,296
8	$1 \div (1. + .08)^8 = .540 \times \$10,800 =$		5,832
			$48,799

Figure 20–10. *Present Value Analysis for Inventory System*
[a]*(Figures Come from Table 20–3 at end of chapter)*
[b]*(Savings Come from Figure 20–8)*

The ROI averages 21 percent over the four-year period. However, that figure is misleading. What if the company invested the $48,000 (development cost) in another project that earned 8 percent compounded annually. For example, $1,000 invested at 8 percent and compounded annually would grow to $1,361 at the end of four years, as shown below:

$$CP = P(1. + R)^n$$

where

CP = compounded principal
P = starting principal
R = rate of interest
N = number of years of compounding

$$CP = \$1000 (1. + .08)^4$$
$$= \$1000 (1.08 \times 1.08 \times 1.08 \times 1.08)$$
$$= \$1,360.49$$

The present value of $1,361 received at the end of four years is $1,000. Applying the present value concept to the inventory system, we obtain the result shown in Figure 20-10. It takes more than seven years to produce ROI comparable to that of investing in a project that earns 8 percent compounded annually. Examine Figure 20–10 to see why this is true. At the end of two years, $7K in net savings has resulted [From Figure 20–8: savings ($35K) – cost ($28K) = $7K]. Thereafter, $10.8K net savings results. The present value of each period of savings is cumulated until the development cost of $48,000 is exceeded. Therefore, almost eight years are required to produce ROI comparable to investing the $48,000 elsewhere at 8 percent.

If the system has a life cycle of at least 8 years, the investment is a sound one, for an organization that uses 8 percent as a cutoff for investment alternatives. Most companies use a much higher cutoff, since money invested in the firm typically earns much more than the bank rate.

This project appears to be a reasonable investment. However, the company must acquire the resources to cover the first two years of cash drain. Such an analysis enables the financial officer to plan for the availability of funds to underwrite the system.

Management may decide to break the project into phases, to reduce the initial cash outlay. It may decide to proceed with the system in preference to other proposed projects that have a higher ROI, such as manufacturing machines or the marketing research function — if it determines the impact on the firm's operations is more significant than other projects.

The key to success for the system designer is preparation of a comprehensive package for the feasibility determination. If both quantitative and qualitative considerations are included in the package, management has an excellent basis for determining system feasibility.

QUESTION: What did management learn from present value analysis that was not obvious from cash flow analysis? _____

_____.

ANSWER: To equal return on other similar investment opportunities, the system must have a life of at least 8 years.

The Feasibility Decision

With the integrated set of analyses illustrated above, management has a good basis for determining the feasibility of adoption of a system.

However, the decision is rarely based on these factors alone. Other important considerations are involved:

1. The system may be necessary because of a shortage of skilled labor in that locality.
2. The system may be necessary to handle the variations in product demand that would be difficult to meet with existing facilities and labor force.
3. The system may be essential to meet competition that provides better customer service because of computerization of its operations.
4. The system may provide a database that is necessary for other functions in the firm.

Exercise 20–5

1. Why use all three analytical techniques: ROI, cash flow analysis, payback analysis? What different information is provided to management by each of these analytical techniques:

ROI/present value analysis: _____

_____

_____

Cash flow analysis: _____

_____

_____

TABLE 20-3
Present Value of $1 Received Annually for N Years

Periods until Payment	1%	2%	4%	6%	8%	10%	12%	14%	15%	16%	18%	20%	22%	24%	25%	26%	28%	30%	35%	40%	45%	50%
1	0.990	0.980	0.962	0.943	0.926	0.909	0.893	0.877	0.870	0.862	0.847	0.833	0.820	0.806	0.800	0.794	0.781	0.769	0.741	0.714	0.690	0.667
2	0.980	0.961	0.925	0.890	0.857	0.826	0.797	0.769	0.756	0.743	0.718	0.694	0.672	0.650	0.640	0.630	0.610	0.592	0.549	0.510	0.476	0.444
3	0.971	0.942	0.889	0.840	0.794	0.751	0.712	0.675	0.658	0.641	0.609	0.579	0.551	0.524	0.512	0.500	0.477	0.455	0.406	0.364	0.328	0.296
4	0.961	0.924	0.855	0.792	0.735	0.683	0.636	0.592	0.572	0.552	0.516	0.482	0.451	0.423	0.410	0.397	0.373	0.350	0.301	0.260	0.226	0.198
5	0.951	0.906	0.822	0.747	0.681	0.621	0.567	0.519	0.497	0.476	0.437	0.402	0.370	0.341	0.328	0.315	0.291	0.269	0.223	0.186	0.156	0.132
6	0.942	0.888	0.790	0.705	0.630	0.564	0.507	0.456	0.432	0.410	0.370	0.335	0.303	0.275	0.262	0.250	0.227	0.207	0.165	0.133	0.108	0.088
7	0.933	0.871	0.760	0.655	0.583	0.513	0.452	0.400	0.376	0.354	0.314	0.279	0.249	0.222	0.210	0.198	0.178	0.159	0.122	0.095	0.074	0.059
8	0.923	0.853	0.731	0.627	0.540	0.467	0.404	0.351	0.327	0.305	0.266	0.233	0.204	0.179	0.168	0.157	0.139	0.123	0.091	0.068	0.051	0.039
9	0.914	0.837	0.703	0.592	0.500	0.424	0.361	0.308	0.284	0.263	0.225	0.194	0.167	0.144	0.134	0.125	0.108	0.094	0.067	0.048	0.035	0.026
10	0.905	0.820	0.676	0.558	0.463	0.386	0.322	0.270	0.247	0.227	0.191	0.162	0.137	0.116	0.107	0.099	0.085	0.073	0.050	0.035	0.024	0.017
11	0.896	0.804	0.650	0.527	0.429	0.350	0.287	0.237	0.215	0.195	0.162	0.135	0.112	0.094	0.086	0.079	0.066	0.056	0.037	0.025	0.017	0.012
12	0.887	0.788	0.625	0.497	0.397	0.319	0.257	0.208	0.187	0.168	0.137	0.112	0.092	0.076	0.069	0.062	0.052	0.043	0.027	0.018	0.012	0.008
13	0.879	0.773	0.601	0.469	0.368	0.290	0.229	0.182	0.163	0.145	0.116	0.093	0.075	0.061	0.055	0.050	0.040	0.033	0.020	0.013	0.008	0.005
14	0.870	0.758	0.577	0.442	0.340	0.263	0.205	0.160	0.141	0.125	0.099	0.078	0.062	0.049	0.044	0.039	0.032	0.025	0.015	0.009	0.006	0.003
15	0.861	0.743	0.555	0.417	0.315	0.239	0.183	0.140	0.123	0.108	0.084	0.065	0.051	0.040	0.035	0.031	0.025	0.020	0.011	0.006	0.004	0.002
16	0.853	0.728	0.534	0.394	0.292	0.218	0.163	0.123	0.107	0.093	0.071	0.054	0.042	0.032	0.028	0.025	0.019	0.015	0.008	0.005	0.003	0.002
17	0.844	0.714	0.513	0.371	0.270	0.198	0.146	0.108	0.093	0.080	0.060	0.045	0.034	0.026	0.023	0.020	0.015	0.012	0.006	0.003	0.002	0.001
18	0.836	0.700	0.494	0.350	0.250	0.180	0.130	0.095	0.081	0.069	0.051	0.038	0.028	0.021	0.018	0.016	0.012	0.009	0.005	0.002	0.001	0.001
19	0.828	0.686	0.475	0.331	0.232	0.164	0.116	0.083	0.070	0.060	0.043	0.031	0.023	0.017	0.014	0.012	0.009	0.007	0.003	0.002	0.001	
20	0.820	0.673	0.456	0.312	0.215	0.149	0.104	0.073	0.061	0.051	0.037	0.026	0.019	0.014	0.012	0.010	0.007	0.005	0.002	0.001	0.001	
21	0.811	0.660	0.439	0.294	0.199	0.135	0.093	0.064	0.053	0.044	0.031	0.022	0.015	0.011	0.009	0.008	0.006	0.004	0.002	0.001		
22	0.803	0.647	0.422	0.278	0.184	0.123	0.083	0.056	0.046	0.038	0.026	0.018	0.013	0.009	0.007	0.006	0.004	0.003	0.001	0.001		
23	0.795	0.634	0.406	0.262	0.170	0.112	0.074	0.049	0.040	0.033	0.022	0.015	0.010	0.007	0.006	0.005	0.003	0.002	0.001			
24	0.788	0.622	0.390	0.247	0.158	0.102	0.066	0.043	0.035	0.028	0.019	0.013	0.008	0.006	0.005	0.004	0.003	0.002	0.001			
25	0.780	0.610	0.375	0.233	0.146	0.092	0.059	0.038	0.030	0.024	0.016	0.010	0.007	0.005	0.004	0.003	0.002	0.001	0.001			
26	0.772	0.598	0.361	0.220	0.135	0.084	0.053	0.033	0.026	0.021	0.014	0.009	0.006	0.004	0.003	0.002	0.002	0.001				
27	0.764	0.586	0.347	0.207	0.125	0.076	0.047	0.029	0.023	0.018	0.011	0.007	0.005	0.003	0.002	0.002	0.001	0.001				
28	0.757	0.574	0.333	0.196	0.116	0.069	0.042	0.026	0.020	0.016	0.010	0.006	0.004	0.002	0.002	0.002	0.001	0.001				
29	0.749	0.563	0.321	0.185	0.107	0.063	0.037	0.022	0.017	0.014	0.008	0.005	0.003	0.002	0.002	0.001	0.001					
30	0.742	0.552	0.308	0.174	0.099	0.057	0.033	0.020	0.015	0.012	0.007	0.004	0.003	0.002	0.001	0.001	0.001					
40	0.672	0.453	0.208	0.097	0.046	0.022	0.011	0.005	0.004	0.003	0.001	0.001										
50	0.608	0.372	0.141	0.054	0.021	0.009	0.003	0.001	0.001	0.001												

Source. Levy and Sarnat, Investment and Portfolio Analysis, Wiley, 1972.

Payback analysis. _____

_____

_____

2. Perform ROI/PV analysis, cash flow analysis and payback analysis for the following system.

| Development cost | $20,000 | (months 1–6: 50% of cost, months 7–12: 30% of cost, months 13–18: 20% of cost) |

Annual figures:

Operating cost	3,000	
Clerical savings	2,200	(all savings began immediately on implementation)
Floor-space saving	500	(all savings began immediately on implementation)
Equipment savings	1,800	(all savings began immediately on implementation)

Techniques:

(a) Payback analysis. _____
(b) ROI/PV (use 10% cutoff, see Table 20–3).

End of Year	Present Value per Dollar		Savings		PV of Savings
2	.826	×	$7250	=	5989
3					
4					

(c) Cash Flow Analysis (use the following format)

	Time Period (Months)						Three-Year Total
Period	1–6	7–12	13–18	19–24	25–30	31–36	
Cost							
Benefit							
Net Cash Flow							
Cum Cash Flow							

3. Assume the above system represents computerization of the DDA system (demand deposit accounting) of a bank. You are the bank officer deciding whether to approve the system.

577 / THE FEASIBILITY DECISION

(A) If the system must be replaced after 2 years, is it feasible? Explain your answer:

_____

_____

_____

_____

(B) What other factors would enter into your feasibility decision?

(1) _____

_____

_____

(2) _____

_____

_____

(3) _____

_____

_____

(4) _____

_____

_____

Summary

Feasibility analysis provides management with the information to determine if a system should be approved. However, in third generation system design practice, systems are not designed independently. Nor are they analyzed independently for feasibility. Integrated systems have some common input data and share common files. Therefore, the teams designing the various systems for the firm coordinate feasibility studies. The set of systems may justify the first computer for the organization or, perhaps, a more powerful one if a computer is already installed. Or, some may be processed on external computers, shared with other organizations. In any event, the procedure for determining feasibility does not vary — only the cost and benefit factors vary.

Application of the computer to life-stream operations of sales order processing, production, inventory, and distribution produces more benefit than administrative and clerical applications. On the other hand, costs may be higher than administrative applications, because backup must be provided when a life-stream operation is computerized.

Use of the techniques of payback analysis, cash flow analysis, and return-on-investment provides management the information necessary to make the decision about computerization. As is true throughout system development, the analysis/designer works with the user to determine costs and benefits. This cooperation insures that the system meets the need of users within the cost constraints of the firm.

Solutions to Exercises

Exercise 20–1

1. *Airline reservations system:* 1-f, computerized airline reservations would not reduce the routine in high-caliber jobs, but would definitely improve all other phases, for example, reduction in numbers of flights, forecasting, and response to changing situations.

2. *Utility company billing system:* 1-h, no reduction in inventory.

3. *University student records system:* 1-f, for reasons given in (1) above; 1-h, no inventory; 2-f, no alternative courses available.

Exercise 20–2

1. Ms. Cull should utilize the computer service.

	Littlefield Bank	Computer Service
[a] Check processing charge	$240	$210
Pickup cost	—0—	5
Delivery cost	—0—	5
Total cost	$240	$220

[a] $.12 \times 2000 = 240$
$.105 \times 2000 = 210$

2. X = volume of checks necessary to justify minicomputer.

$$X = \frac{\text{Monthly cost}}{\text{Cost per check}} = \frac{\$300.}{\$.105} = 2857 \text{ checks per month}$$

3. Ms. Cull can justify the computer on the one-hour turnaround principle.

Benefit	Possible Monthly Saving	Probability of × Occurrence	= Expected Return
Reduced clerical costs	$250	× 100 percent =	$250.00
Increase in number of accounts (2000 customers × 5%) = 100 × $.75	75	× 95 percent =	71.25
			$321.25

Savings to bank per month	$321.25
Rental cost per month	−300.00
Savings	$ 21.25

4. (a) The computer could provide a fast, accurate update on the status of loans his department is responsible for.
(b) A reduction of paperwork.
(c) Since data on loans would not be entered and stored on magnetic tape or disk, there would be a savings in the amount of space required for files.
(d) Information on different types of loans could be processed faster.
(e) Less errors due to mechanization of operations.
(f) Could provide an analysis of the pattern of people taking out loans.
(g) Could share information between files of different departments.
(h) There would be a capability of assessing the impact of different managerial decisions on the loan department.

5. To show cash reserve requirements due to turnover in demand deposits and thus prevent overloaning. Also, to calculate how much interest to charge for loans based on demand deposit data interest payments.

Exercise 20–3

1. The three major components of development costs are
(a) Personnel costs
(b) Computer costs
(c) Supply costs

2. Total the costs:

(a) Personnel		$45,050
Information analysts	$10,000	
Analyst/designers	18,000	
Programmers	13,500	
Key entry	3,100	
Operators	450	
(b) Computer		2,700
(c) Supplies		250
		$48,000

3. Determine the percentage of total cost allocated to each cost area:

(a) Information analysts	20.8 percent
(b) Analyst/designers	37.5
(c) Programmers	28.1
(d) Key entry	6.5
(e) Operators	1.0
(f) Computer	5.6
(g) Supplies	.5
	100.0 percent

4. Total man-months of effort are

(a) Analyst/designers	18
(b) Programmers	18.875

5. True-False:
(a) T
(b) T
(c) T
(d) T
(e) F (approximately $\frac{1}{8}$)

Exercise 20–4

1. The major factor that effects system design costs is the qualification of system designers to perform their jobs: general flowcharting or decision table development, forms design and layout, report content determination and layout, file design, processing design and file conversion planning, procedure preparation, both user procedures and data processing procedures.

2. Costs associated with programming include all the activities of developing a finalized program: flowcharting, coding, creating test data, desk checking, and operational testing.

3. The specific characteristics of the computer configuration being programmed that must be considered by the programmer include: tape blocking, channel assignment, program overlays, use of subroutines, utility programs, reference tables, work areas, overlapping, file organization, file access techniques, and indexing approaches as well as other technical aspects.

Exercise 20–5

1. ROI/PV analysis helps management rank different investment alternatives, since there is normally a limit to the alternatives that can be underwritten by company profit.

Cash flow analysis projects the effect of the system on the cash resources of a firm.

Payback analysis is used to determine when the system will recover its developmental costs, but does not consider alternative investment opportunities.

All three techniques are used in determining feasibility of a project. Payback analysis may give a period of, say, 2 years. Whether or not this period of time is reasonable depends on the company's policy toward other investment opportunities and its cash flow position.

2. *Costs*

Development ($20,000)	1–6 months	=	$10,000
	7–12 months	=	$6,000
	13–18 months	=	$4,000
Operating (annual)	Beyond 18 months	=	$3,000 per year

Savings ($14,500 per year)

Clerical at $12,200
Floor space at $500
Equipment at $1,800

(a) Payback period $= \dfrac{\text{Development cost}}{\text{Net savings}}$

Net Savings $= \$14,500 - \$3,000 = \$11,500$ per year

Payback period $= \dfrac{20,000}{11,500} = 1.7$ years

(b) *ROI/PV analysis*

Projected Benefits	Year			Three-Year Total
	1	2	3	
Clerical savings	−0−	6,100	12,200	18,300
Floor space savings	−0−	250	500	750
Equipment savings	−0−	900	1,800	2,700
Subtotals	−0−	7,250	14,500	21,750
Projected costs	16,000	5,500	3,000	24,500
ROI $= \dfrac{\text{savings}}{\text{cost}}$	$\dfrac{0}{16,000} = .00$	$\dfrac{7,250}{21,500} = .337$	$\dfrac{21,750}{24,500} = .888$	Average 29.6 percent

End of Year	Present Value per Dollar	Savings		Present Value of Savings
2	.826	× $ 7,250	=	5,989
3	.751	× 11,500	=	8,637
4	.683	× 11,500	=	7,855
				22,481

(c) *Cash Flow Analysis*

582 / SYSTEM FEASIBILITY ANALYSIS

Cash Flow Element	1–6	7–12	13–18	19–24	25–30	31–36	Three-Year Total
Cost							
Development	10,000	6,000	4,000				
Operating				1,500	1,500	1,500	
Total	10,000	6,000	4,000	1,500	1,500	1,500	24,500
Benefit							
Clerical				6,100	6,100	6,100	
Floor space				250	250	250	
Equipment				900	900	900	
Total	–0–	–0–	–0–	7,250	7,250	7,250	21,750
Net cash flow	(10,000)	(6,000)	(4,000)	5,750	5,750	5,750	
Cumulative cash flow	(10,000)	(16,000)	(20,000)	(14,250)	(8,500)	(2,750)	(2,750)

3. (A) Feasibility is questionable because:
   (1) Payback period is only 1.7 years but system life is only 2 years.
   (2) ROI exceeds going interest rates and PV analysis shows less than 4 years are required to recover development cost at an investment cutoff of 10 percent.
   (3) Cash flow: a negative cash flow will continue until the fourth year.
   Conclusion. If the system has a life of only 2 years, it is not feasible, when compared to other investment alternatives that will realize 10 percent or greater return.
   (B) Other factors in the feasibility decision:
   (1) The system may provide a database that may be necessary for other functions in the firm.
   (2) Shortage of clerical help.
   (3) The system may be necessary to handle volumes of data that would be infeasible with existing facilities.
   (4) The system may be essential for meeting competition that provides fast response because of computerization of its operations.

Chapter Examination

1. What four principal categories of benefits accrue from computerizing systems?

(a) _____

(b) _____

(c) _____

(d) _____

2. Why is the term "intangible" benefits no longer acceptable in feasibility analysis?

_____

_____

3. Why do life-stream operations produce greater savings than the kinds of applications computerized in the first generation systems era? Give an example.

_____

_____

4. Examine Table 20–1 and indicate which of those benefits could be derived by implementing a first level of sophistication for a student record system? Circle the item number below:
   Lower costs: a, b, c, d, e, f, g, h, i
   Faster reaction: a, b, c, d, e, f
   Improved accuracy: a, b, c, d
   Improved information: a, b, c, d

5. Repeat question 4, for a system designed to achieve a third level of sophistication.
   Lower costs: a, b, c, d, e, f, g, h, i
   Faster reaction: a, b, c, d, e, f
   Improved accuracy: a, b, c, d
   Improved information: a, b, c, d

6. Match the following with their proper category of cost of computerization:
   Development cost __1__ , Implementation cost __2__ , Operating cost __3__
   Computer processing ____
   Performing controls on input and output ____
   Preparing data for entry to the system ____
   Programming and debugging the system ____
   Documenting the existing system ____
   Designing a new system ____
   Training the computer department personnel to operate the system ____
   Installing and testing the system ____
   Training the users of the system ____
   Analyzing the system to determine improvements _____

7. Describe how the process of estimating system design costs is facilitated by analyzing the design tasks separately, as follows:

(a) _____

(b) _____

(c) _____

8. What special characteristics of the computer system must be considered in estimating programming costs?

(a) _____

(b) _____

(c) _____

(d) _____

(e) _____

(f) _____

(g) _____

(h) _____

(i) _____

(j) _____

(k) _____

9. How are computer processing costs estimated? _____

_____

_____

10. How are key entry costs estimated? _____

_____

_____

11. How are data control costs estimated? _____

_____

_____

12. Examine Figure 20–1. Costs are shown only for the first five phases of system development. Which cost elements continue?

For Phase VI: _____

For Phase VII: _____

13. What would be the life-stream applications for a bank? What benefits would result from computerizing these systems?

_____

_____

_____

_____

14. Feasibility analysis is not a one-time activity. During the course of development, as costs are more precisely known, feasibility is re-evaluated. Assume that system design and programming are each estimated to be 50 percent higher than the original estimates. Present Value should be computed at the 9 percent rate. Recalculate Exercise 20–5, problem 2, based on these new estimates. (Use a separate sheet for your answer).

15. Based on the results of your calculations in problem 14, what recommendations would you make to management about continuation of the project?

_____

_____

_____

16. Assume a new cost/benefit analysis has been conducted for the system illustrated in Figure 20–1. By increasing personnel the first 6 months ($1,200 per month), benefits will accrue sooner. Move the benefit schedule forward 3 months and determine feasibility, using all three feasibility analysis techniques. (Use a separate sheet for your answer)

17. Examine Figure 20–5. What is the time (in minutes) to process 40k, 100 byte records on a 360/20? _____ What processes are performed during this time?

_____

_____

18. Why is it inappropriate to designate some system benefits as intangible?

_____

_____

19. Prepare an expected benefit determination table for a college preregistration system where the admissions officer estimates that he will receive advance tuition payments as follows:

Total average tuition per semester = $235,500

Probability estimates:
  (80 percent probability that one fourth of tuition will be paid in advance)
  (15 percent probability that one half of tuition will be paid in advance)
  (5 percent probability that three fourths of tuition will be paid in advance)

The college can invest the tuition at a return of 6 percent per annum and will expect to have use of the money 2 months earlier than it would have it under the old system.

20. What recommendations would you make to the admissions officer, based on the analysis performed in completing problem 19?

_____

_____

_____

587 / CHAPTER EXAMINATION

Chapter 21

SYSTEM IMPLEMENTATION

Overview

Phase V of the system development cycle is the system implementation phase. Despite its being the shortest phase, the implementation phase is crucial to system success. Over the years some very well-designed systems have been less than successful because implementation was poorly planned.

The tasks of system implementation include: (1) testing the system, (2) development of procedures, (3) training personnel to operate the system, (4) running it in parallel with the old system to insure proper operation, (5) cutover to the new system, and (6) post-implementation audit against design criteria.

Since many activities are involved and the phasing of these activities is critical, careful planning is necessary for implementation. The Gantt and PERT planning techniques have proved applicable to implementation of computer systems.

This chapter also discusses Phases VI and VII of the system development cycle, operation of the system and maintenance of the system. Operation consists of the repetitive tasks of data preparation, key entry, data control, computer processing, and distribution of results. Maintenance consists of making minor improvements in the system.

Testing the System

Testing of a system to validate it against design criteria is separated into three parts: (1) module tests (2) system test and (3) parallel processing test.

Module Tests. During the development of their programs, programmers design test data to prove the validity of logic in each module. However, these are usually hypothetical data. For example, in testing a payroll system, the programmer will enter data for several hypothetical employees whose pay will be calculated, using all types of deductions. This approach insures proper logic for handling each payroll variation.

System Tests. When all programming modules are finished, they are assembled and a complete system test is conducted. Using the payroll example again, one programmer may have been assigned the module that handled input to the system: (1) establishing the file of employee records, with information supplied by the personnel department, (2) input on deductions, and (3) weekly input concerning hours worked, and the like. Another programmer may have been assigned the module that calculates payroll and prepares payroll checks.

When each module has been tested and proved satisfactory, the modules are assembled for the system test. Again, hypothetical data may be used for the first series of tests. It is the responsibility of the system designer to prepare system test data — working with the user to design test data representative of that which will be handled by the system after implementation.

Parallel Processing Tests. The third in the series of tests before cutover to the new system is the parallel processing of old and new systems. This procedure may appear to require excessive testing; however, experience has proved the necessity of a thorough testing approach. When companies are implementing life-stream systems, vital to the continuing success of the firm, the consequence of error is too high for less than thorough testing.

The length of parallel processing depends on the type of system. A payroll system would not require an elaborate parallel processing. The system designer could use the input for the prior month's payroll as data for the system test. The parallel processing of the entire payroll for one period should be sufficient testing of the typical payroll system.

QUESTION: Would the same approach, using last month's transactions, be appropriate for testing a personal checking-account system for a bank? Explain your answer.

ANSWER: Yes, the approach should prove the validity of system logic unless the system were changed so much that a direct comparison was difficult to make

Testing of other systems may be much more complicated than the payroll system. For example, the new inventory system may be very different from the old one. The new system undoubtedly includes new logic, such as economic order quantity determination and reorder point calculation. Or, a new system may integrate two systems, such as the inventory and purchasing systems. Therefore, system implementation may be very complicated, requiring six weeks to two months of parallel processing.

On the other hand, lengthy parallel processing is constrained by practical considerations, such as the availability of personnel to operate both the old and new systems. Nor can a manager expect his staff to operate the old system on the first shift and the new system on the second shift. Although the new system should require far fewer activities in the user department, the two systems will be enough different to complicate parallel processing using the same personnel to operate both systems.

QUESTION: What do you think would be a satisfactory approach to parallel processing for testing a student-records system?

_____

_____ .

ANSWER: Testing it over a vacation period, or a period during the term when the least difficulty could arise. The start and end of terms would be the least appropriate times

A typical industrial testing approach is to operate the old system during the week and to parallel the new system over the weekend. Since less manual activity is required with the new system, the full crew would not be needed each weekend. Most employees would be willing to work every other weekend for one month to enable a full month's parallel processing.

In summary, for more sophisticated systems the system test, rather than parallel processing, is the key to determining system reliability. However, other steps can be taken to lessen the risk associated with short-term parallel processing: (1) detailed user procedures, (2) detailed data processing procedures, (3) comprehensive data control, and (4) thorough training. These activities are discussed in the following sections.

Development of Procedures

User Procedures. A complete set of instructions for preparing input to the system is another responsibility of the system designer/user team. The system analyst has a thorough understanding of the user department while the system designer has a thorough understanding of the system requirements. Together, they develop a set of detailed input procedures.

User procedures include both narrative and graphic materials. Understanding of the procedure is facilitated if the narrative portion is supported by flowcharts, such as the one shown in Figure 21–1.

QUESTION: What information is immediately conveyed by the flowchart that is not as obvious from the narrative? _____

_____

ANSWER: Flow of paperwork

Also, less error on input will occur if each input form is included with sample input data, as is shown in Figure 21–2.

QUESTION: Step 2 of the procedure explains how each field is to be completed. Should it also describe how the data is used by the system?

_____

_____

_____ .

Graphic Procedure

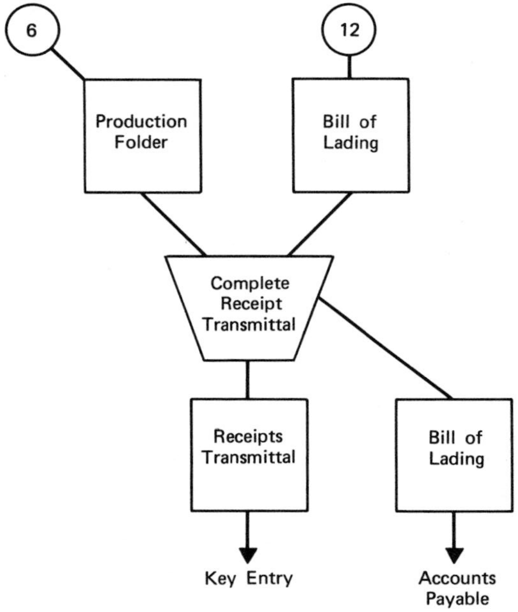

Narrative Procedure

Action Initiator: Bill of Lading or Production Folder

Procedure

1. Use Receipts Transmittal to enter data into computer inventory.
2. Enter data from Bill of Lading received from Incoming Inspection or from internal production

   Transaction Code: B/L = 40   PF = 41
   Product Number: transcribe from input document
   Quantity: transcribe from input document
   Purchase/Job Order No.: transcribe from input document
   Item: record from Stock Catalog
   Stat: check status, see if on backorder. If so record BO
   Date: date entered on Transmittal
   Reference: name of person preparing Transmittal

RECEIPTS

T C O D E	PRODUCT NUMBER	QUANTITY	PURCHASE OR JOB ORDER #	ITEM	STAT	DATE	REFERENCE	REMARKS
4 0	3 / 6 A A A	1 / 5 2 0 0	B 4 2 5 C	2 5	B O	0 4 / 9 7 3	J R M O L L Y	

CONTROL GROUP ___   PAGE ___ OF ___   DATE ___

Figure 21-1. *Excerpt from a user procedure.*

Application *Inventory Update*

(Class / Division / Std./New / Max. Buy / Sales Chan. / Cust. Serv. / M/C / Next Sea.)

TRAN CODE	GROUP NO.	PRODUCT NUMBER	DESCRIPTION			
U 1	0 0 / /		CURRENT CAPERS F73	B 2 M 0 M	2	

PROD MIX % — THIS SEASON

TRAN CODE	GROUP NO.	PRODUCT NUMBER	LEAD TIME	SFTY STOCK	SPOIL FACTOR	MAX WEEKS AVAIL	MIN ORDER	MAX ORDER	BUILD % / WK	CURR	NEXT	ORIG. PROJ.	REV.
U 2													

TRAN CODE	GROUP NO.	PRODUCT NUMBER	STOCK ON HAND	RECEIPTS	ISSUES	INVENTORY ADJ.	RELEASED FOR SHIPMENT	SHIPPED
U 3	0 0 / / A 3 2 G A		0 0 0 4 0 0 0 0					

WEEKLY SUMMARY — SEASON

TRAN CODE	GROUP NO.	PRODUCT NUMBER	PRODUCED	SOLD	RELEASED	SHIPPED	PRODUCED	SOLD
U 4								

SELLING PRICE

TRAN CODE	GROUP NO.	PRODUCT NUMBER	REG	LIST	CASH	EMP	PROD WGT	PROD VOL	DATE BO-HO	EST SHIP DATE	MISSING COMPONENT
U 5	0 0 / / A 3 2 G A		2				0 9 4 0 0 0 5				

STOCK ON HAND BY LOCATION — NON-LOOART L

TRAN CODE	GROUP NO.	PRODUCT NUMBER	PLANT (P)	NICHOLS (N)	EL PASO (E)	COWEN (C)	LOC I (X)	LOC 2
U 6	0 0 / / A 3 2 G A		0 0 0 2 0 0 0 0	0 0 0 0 0 0 0 0	0 0 0 0 2 0 0 0	0 0 0 0 0 0 0 0		

COST

TRAN CODE	GROUP NO.	PRODUCT NUMBER	MATL	LAB	FIXED	VARIABLE	DATE LAST TRANS. MM D D Y Y	DATE LAST SALE MM D D Y Y
U 7	0 0 / / A 3 2 G A		0 7 0 8 0 0	1 0 0 0 0 0	3 0 0 0 0	5 0 0		

Figure 21–2. Input forms filled-in with examples of representative data.

ANSWER: Input personnel must have an understanding of the system's operation to recognize the importance of their task. However, the explanation should precede the procedure, so as not to detract from the important single task of explaining how each field is to be completed

QUESTION: Observe the report in Figure 21–3a. The Purchasing Agent would be interested in the figures in the final column. Will these figures be used for information or will they initiate some action on his part? (Explain your answer.) _____

_____

_____

ANSWER: The report provides information on inventory; however, the action-initiating report, shown in Figure 21–3b, is the initiating report. It provides the suggested order quantity

In depth, comprehensive user procedures have a major impact on ease of conversion to the new computerized system. They also facilitate training of personnel.

(AMTS. IN THOUS.)		WK 12	WK 13	WK 14	18 WEEK BALANCE	WEEKS ON-HAND
COLONIAL STATY	PROJ	.1	.0	.0	.0	
	PLAN	.0	.0	.0	.0	
1A32AB AFP 2.0		1.9	1.9	1.9	1.9	26.0
FOLDER-NEW COLONIAL STATY						
	DEMD	.0	.0	.0	.0	
	PLAN	.0	.0	.0	.0	
122AMA AFP 16.2		16.2	16.2	16.2	39.2	26.0

MATERIALS PLANNING — WEEK 11 — DATE 03/16/73

Figure 21-3a. *Materials planning report—an informational report.*

QUESTION: One of the authors worked with a firm where the key entry employees worked in a team with the system designer in development of input procedures. What are the advantages of this approach?

ANSWER: Whether key entry personnel are involved in the preparation of procedures or in "debugging" them, the views of these employees are needed before the procedures are prepared in final form

Data Processing Procedures. Just as user personnel need procedures, personnel in data processing operation must have specific written procedures for their activities in processing the new system. Part of the design task is preparation of these procedures.

Key Entry Procedures Key entry procedures identify precisely where each field of data is to be recorded. If the input document is a form, for example, an order, the procedure must also specify where on the document each data element is to be found.

CURRENT — CURR WK 20
FIN PARTS — MASTER PURCHASING PLAN
SALES THROUGH 05/18/73 — INVENTORY THROUGH 05/18/73

PRODUCT	DESCRIPTION	FIRST ORD %	BALANCE TO SELL	QUAN OH FG+FGP	SUGGESTED ORD-QUAN
122AEA	FOLDER-CAPERS	.60	6.0	.7	10.7
122AEB	FOLDER-F73 CAPERS	.00	.0	.0	.0-
122AFA	FOLDER-CARUUSEL ELEPHANT	.60	5.3	4.6	4.5-
122AFB	FOLDER-F73 CAR ELEPHANT	.00	.0	10.0	10.0-
122AGA	FOLDER-CAROUSEL HOUSE	.60	4.7	20.0	21.2-
122AGB	FOLDER-F73 CAROUSEL HOUSE	.00	.0	.0	.0-
122AHA	FOLDER-F FLAP SUNBURST	.60	12.1	13.9	16.2
122AHB	FOLDER-F FLAP LEAVES	.60	18.1	20.0	25.1
122AHC	FOLDER-F FLAP B.BEE	.60	26.2	37.8	7.4
122AHD	FOLDER-F FLAP BUTTERFLY	.60	16.1	28.1	12.0
122AHE	FOLDER-F FLAP SANTA	.99	.0	69.7	69.7-
122AHF	FOLDER-F FLAP BELLS	.99	.0	90.9	90.9-
122AJA	FOLDER-CHILDRENS CARDS	.99	.0	42.7	42.7-
122AKA	FOLDER-HERB&SPICE	.60	70.5	86.6	23.9-
122AKB	FOLDER-BRIGHT&BREEZY	.60	221.5	39.1	462.4
122AKC	FOLDER-GARDEN GREETINGS	.60	40.3	20.8	79.4

Figure 21-3b. *Open order report—an action initiating report.*

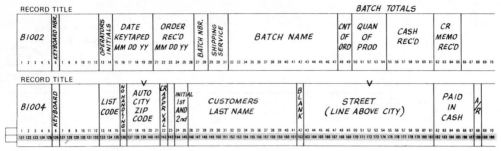

Figure 21–4. Procedure for key entry.

The importance of such procedures is illustrated by the experience of one of the authors. He was asked to assist an organization that was having considerable difficulty in detecting the source of a specific type of error that kept showing up on the computer output. He carefully traced back through each step in preparation of input for the system. The user input area was determined as satisfactory. The problem area was isolated as key entry. We finally located a third-shift keypunch operator who had a three-week accumulation of punched cards stacked on a shelf near the machine. The keypunch procedure omitted an explanation on how one type of transaction was to be handled. The keypunch operator told us, "I knew someone would come along sooner or later and explain what to do with those cards."

QUESTION: Was the keypunch operator the culprit? If not, who was at fault? _____

_____.

ANSWER: The system designer is responsible for preparing procedures for all steps in data processing: receipt of data from the user, key entry, computer processing, and distribution of output

A typical key entry procedure is shown in Figure 21–4. The procedure will indicate which items are to be verified, either visually via a CRT unit connected to the keyboard or by reentering the data at that station or at another station. The letter "V" above a field indicates need for verification.

QUESTION: Analyze the data in Figure 21–4. Why do these two fields require verification?

_____

_____

_____.

ANSWER: The payment field (columns 62–67) in the second card should be verified, because the batch totals will be checked against the sum of the individual orders. An error in customer name is undesirable but the address should be verified to make sure the order gets to the customer

Computer Operations Procedures Just as key entry personnel need procedures, computer operators require an explanation for processing each job. Figure 21–5 provides such a procedure. It identifies the units to be used, the operator actions during processing, and the output media.

```
                        OPERATIONS PROCEDURE
                           PROGRAM NAME
                              SORT

  FUNCTION:                              Follows Program:  B1035
   SORTS PICKING SLIPS                   Precedes Program: B1036


                                         Programmer: ___Billiard___

                                         Date: _____3-2-75_____


  DISK DATA:                   │  CARD READER:

  Logical drive     Name       │
                               │
      0 SOP-004                │
                               │
      1 SOP-003                │
                               │
  ──────────────────────────── │
  TAPE DATA:                    │
                               │
  Logical drive   Name   Write ring │
                               │
      1 SOP-009               │
                               │
      2                       │
                               │
      3                       │  CONSOLE:
                               │
                               │  When SORT message appears, read
                               │  logical tape drive 1 (Master file)
  ──────────────────────────── │
  PRINTER:                      │
                               │
  Paper ___STANDARD___         │
                               │
  Expected output __SORT MESSAGES__ │
```

Figure 21–5. *Computer operator procedure.*

QUESTION: The sections on disk data and tape data instruct the operator concerning the files to use in the processing of this step. What is the operator instructed to do when the console prints a message?

ANSWER: Mount another tape for the master file update step. This step occurs midway through the processing initiated by the console message. The special instructions identify which tape to use and how to handle the resulting output tape

Data Control Procedures Input sheets may be lost or misplaced, so a function is required for assuring that all data is entered to the system. Usually, input is batched. For example, sales orders may be batched in groups of 50. Or, input may be logged, to insure that all transactions enter the system. For example, inventory transaction sheets may be numbered and a log may be used to keep track of all sheets. Likewise, control of output is necessary—making sure the correct copy gets to the appropriate user.

For a small computer operation each department may have its own data control activity. When a large volume of material is passing through the computer center, a data control group is usually established in that department. This group insures that all items entering the key entry area complete that activity and that all items entering computer operations are processed. It also audits the computer output to insure that the information is reasonable and complete. For example, assume the computer operator loaded a wrong magnetic tape. Instead of using Tuesday's tape of all transactions for the week, Monday's tape was used. The data control personnel could compare output and isolate such errors.

Procedures for handling output need to be as explicit as those for input. Some output is informational, other output triggers further action. For example, one output of the Inventory system would be a report of the time span that inventory will cover (Figure 21–3a). If any person in the company needs inventory status on any item, this report would be the source of information. Another output of the Inventory system would be suggested order quantity, sequenced by date-of-delivery schedule (Figure 21–3b). This report initiates action to order additional material. Detailed procedures are required for the handling of each type of output.

For proper control, detailed procedures are required for this activity, as well as other data processing activities. The system designer prepares these procedures as a part of the implementation package.

QUESTION: In the example above, why would the magnetic tape record of Monday's transactions be retained?

ANSWER: Standard operating procedure requires that several day's data are retained. A machine malfunction might occur and might "clobber" the Tuesday tape. The operator then must reconstruct the master tape by reprocessing transactions against the Monday tape before moving onto Tuesday's transactions

1. Why would several months of parallel processing be infeasible for a fourth level of sophistication system? _____

_____.

2. What approach would be used? _____

_____.

3. Procedures for data processing are similar to user procedures in what respects? _____

_____.

File Conversion

A major activity in system implementation is file conversion—both manual and computer-media files. A company for which one of the authors serves as consultant was forced to shelve a bill-of-materials system after the cost of converting manual to computer files was determined to be more than $40,000. The system design was already completed but the feasibility study omitted assessing the impact of converting manual to machine-processable records.

Conversion of a file that is already on some machine-processable medium (punched cards, magnetic tape, etc.) is not nearly so difficult. Nevertheless, this activity requires careful planning and control. Often it occupies the computer for an extended period and must be performed over a weekend—perhaps seven shifts (Friday night third shift, and three shifts each on Saturday and Sunday).

An example of complexity in file conversion is the integration of two major systems. The production requirements system may be combined with the inventory system. A special computer program usually is required to consolidate several files. Although the computer program is rarely large or complicated, the sheer volume of the files may make the conversion time-consuming. If a manual system must be converted to machine-processable media the cost can be large—depending on the volume of records.

QUESTION: Assume a bank is implementing a banking system where all records for each customer are consolidated. A combined monthly statement is produced for the customer instead of separate statements for checking account, savings account, loans, trust funds, and the like. A computer program is written to merge these records. Would you expect the bank to implement this new system for a few customers at a time to reduce the impact of file conversion, or to cutover all at one time? Why?

_____

_____

_____

_____.

ANSWER: The answer would depend on the volume and media involved. Some activities, such as trust fund accounting may not be computerized, and that data may have to be key-entered before any consolidation is done. The consolidated statement system could be implemented over several days or weeks because it is primarily a reporting system. The other systems feeding this one are unchanged except for providing input to this reporting system as a by-product of their output. If the bank were combining all the systems into one major system, a complete cutover would be the only feasible approach

Training

When all procedures (user and data processing) have been completed, the user/system designer team can begin training personnel concerning the new system.

Most often, this training includes both formal and informal training sessions. The entire user group is brought together to explain user input procedures for the system as a whole. The overall objectives of the system are reviewed, then the detailed operation of the system is discussed, with ample opportunity for questions.

Then, informally each person is instructed on his or her specific duties associated with the system.

If this task is done thoroughly, it can serve as the final "debugging" activity prior to publication of the procedures.

QUESTION: To what extent should supervision be involved in user training? _____

_____

_____

_____.

ANSWER: If the user/designer team has done its job properly, supervision has been involved throughout the system analysis, design, and implementation activities. Otherwise, the user is tempted to regard the system as belonging to "that computer group." Obviously, the system remains the responsibility of the user. To assume responsibility, the user must have the opportunity to access and to evaluate the system *throughout* development

Training versus Education

Personnel are trained concerning the system and their specific responsibility in its operation. They should also be provided an education concerning computer uses and implications, long before the training phase.

Part of the education occurs during the feasibility phase, arising from the kinds of questions asked. When asked about volumes of transactions, flow of information, costs of operations, and the like, employees begin to comprehend the criteria for determining if a computer is potentially beneficial.

However, formal education sessions are also essential, both to provide new information and to establish a positive environment about computer use in the organization. Chapter 2 enumerates the steps required to achieve such an environment, principally that of recognizing the threat to individual needs. The basis for that analysis is Maslow's *Model of the Hierarchy of An Individual's Needs.*

Personnel are normally apprehensive about the initial installation of a computer. Chapter 2 relates Maslow's *Hierarchy of Needs* to the "perceived" threat of computer use. The goal of the education program is to correct wrong perceptions and to create an environment of honesty between management and the employee concerning the implications of computer use.

QUESTION: Would the following activity be representative of training or education? A person is given a tour of the computer operation to understand better what transpires there. _____

_____

_____.

ANSWER: If it concentrates on general computer principles, the tour would be education. If it concentrates on the flow of the specific system with which the person is directly involved, it would be considered training. Both activities are important in introducing the computer in an organization

Exercise 21–2

1. The explanation of the types of procedures should enable the student to determine whether the user representative or the system designer is primarily responsible for developing the following types of procedures. Explain your reasoning.

(a) User procedures. _____

_____

(b) Operations procedures. _____

_____

(c) Data control procedures. _____

2. The explanation about training should enable the student to suggest who should conduct the training session? Explain.

   (a) User department training. _____

   (b) Data processing department training. _____

3. Who designs the file conversion, the system designer or the programmer? (The answer is not given in the text; try to develop a logical answer on your own.)

_____

_____

_____

_____

Implementation Planning Techniques

Implementation planning and control can be facilitated through use of one or more of the techniques used in other planning activities for the firm. The Gantt chart technique is appropriate for the planning of an individual's efforts in system development, as is shown in Figure 21–6. The number of activities is small enough that the Gantt chart easily portrays the schedule for each activity.

When considering the multitude of activities for an entire system, the Gantt chart approach is inadequate. Too many interrelationships are involved to be properly depicted on the Gantt chart. Network techniques,

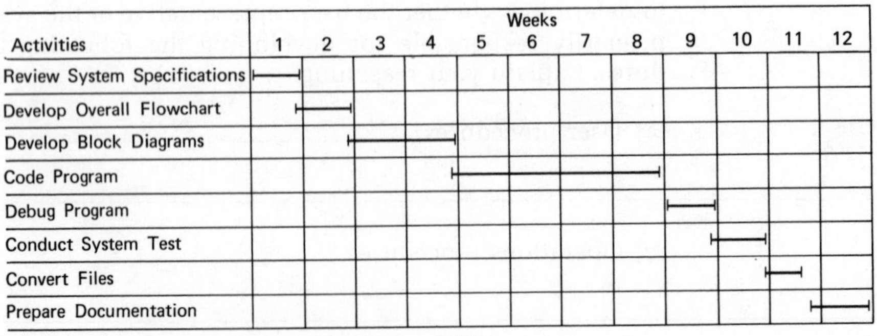

Activities	Weeks											
	1	2	3	4	5	6	7	8	9	10	11	12
Review System Specifications	├─┤											
Develop Overall Flowchart		├┤										
Develop Block Diagrams			├─┤									
Code Program					├──────			─┤				
Debug Program									├┤			
Conduct System Test										├─┤		
Convert Files										├┤		
Prepare Documentation												├──┤

Figure 21–6. *Gantt chart of programmer activities.*

such as PERT or CPM charts,[1] are more appropriate for planning and controlling development of sophisticated information systems. Figure 21–7 depicts the use of a PERT chart for planning and control of a major system. The network technique is needed to show the interrelationships of all the activities.

Both PERT and CPM techniques are based on similar logic: (1) activities required for system development and implementation are arranged according to sequence of occurrence; (2) estimates are made for the time to accomplish each activity; (3) a critical path is determined, along with alternate paths progressively less critical.

Figure 21–7 illustrates the complexity in planning and control of a major system development. Many interrelated activities are involved, and the network technique is a good approach to identify these relationships.

Computer manufacturers provide computerized network packages to enable customers to utilize this technique in system development. The system designer prepares a network as a standard part of the development package and processes it, using whichever of the network packages is available. Either PERT or CPM is appropriate. The main distinction between the two techniques is that PERT provides for three time estimates for each activity as is shown in Figure 21–8: the optimistic estimate, the most likely estimate, and the pessimistic estimate. Looking at the estimate for programming (Figure 21–8), we see the three time estimates as follows:

$$④\frac{65 - 75 - 100}{\text{Write Computer Programs}}⑦$$

QUESTION: Observe Figure 21–8. List the event numbers that define the activities of system personnel as distinguished from those involved in programming (the paths converge at event 10):

System activities: _____.

Programming activities: _____.

ANSWER: System activities: 1-2-4-5-10-12-14-15; Programming activities: 4-7-10-12-14-15. Activities 6-9-12-13-15 are also system designer responsibilities. Observe the advantage over the Gantt chart in that interdependent activities are linked in a PERT chart

QUESTION: What other differences do you see between the Gantt chart and PERT network?

1. _____.

2. _____.

3. _____.

ANSWER

1. Three times shown for each PERT activity instead of one for Gantt
2. Length of lines on PERT chart do not correspond to amount of time required
3. Parallel activities are more easily identified with PERT.

[1]PERT is an acronym for Program Evaluation and Review Technique. CPM stands for Critical Path Method.

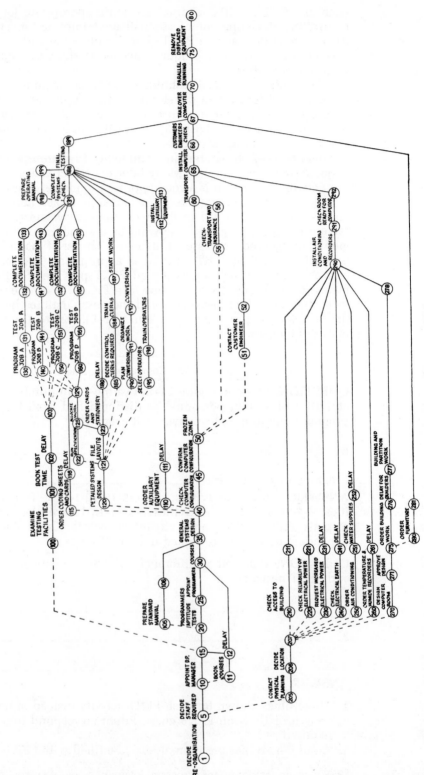

Figure 21–7. Hardware/software implementation plan, using network technique (Courtesy IBM).

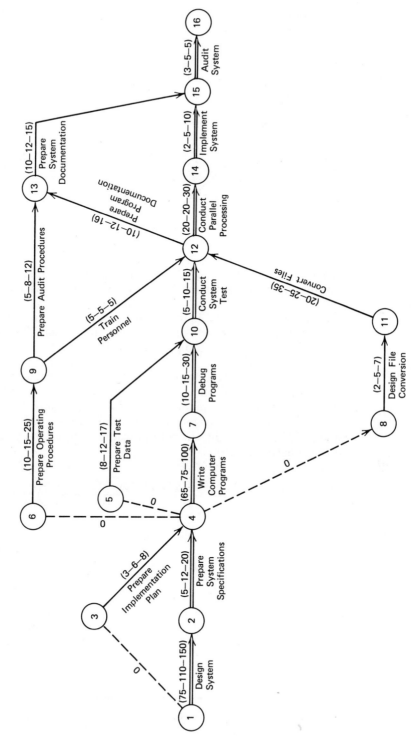

Figure 21–8. Use of a PERT network for the system development and implementation plan.

Using CPM, the designer develops a cost/time curve for each activity. As shown below: three points define the curve. Observing the curve, one sees that the time for completing the activity for programming, T, can be shortened by increasing the level of resources applied, C.

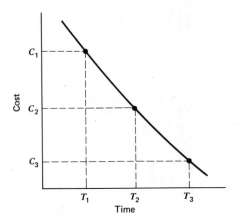

Therefore, the CPM method provides cost as well as time estimates for completing a job. However, PERT Cost packages have been developed that enable budgets to be established for each activity.

The advantage of CPM is the ability to vary the time along the critical path to determine its effect on cost, and vice versa. The advantage of PERT is the ability to develop probability estimates for each activity, and for the critical path.

CPM is used for situations where good historical data exists, such as installation of a computer. PERT is more appropriate where the activity is unique, like development of a CBMIS for a specific organization. Since this book concentrates on the latter, PERT will be explained. For the PERT activity, the three time estimates give the probability distribution illustrated below:

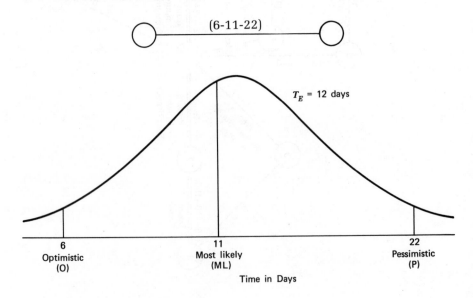

It is possible to calculate both the expected time for completing the activity t_a, and its variance, σ^2 using these formulas:

$$t_a = \frac{O + 4ML + P}{6} \qquad \sigma^2 = \left(\frac{P - O}{6}\right)^2$$

QUESTION: Calculate expected time, t_a and variance,[2] σ^2 for the programming activity shown immediately above:

$$t_a = \underline{\hspace{4cm}} \text{ days}$$

$$\sigma^2 = \underline{\hspace{4cm}} \text{ days}$$

ANSWER: $t_a = \dfrac{6 + 44 + 22}{6} = 12$ days; $\sigma^2 = \left(\dfrac{22 - 6}{6}\right)^2 = 7.11$ days

PERT Procedure for Determining the Critical Path

To determine the critical path, the following procedure is utilized.

1. Add t_a for each activity along a path until it merges with another path (e.g., in the following network paths 1-3-4 and 1-2-4 merge at event 4.)

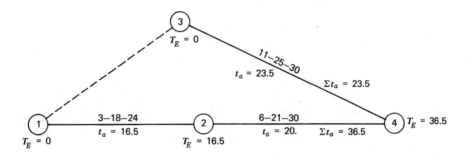

2. Obtain the expected time for completing an event, T_E, by adding all values for t_a along the path leading to the event. When paths converge, select the T_E for the path that constrains completion of the event (e.g., path 1-2-4 takes more time and, therefore, is the constraint; hence, the expected completion time for event 4 is 36.5 days. Therefore, all paths that continue from that event take on the time for that event, 36.5 days).
3. Continue until the T_E for the final event is determined. Remember, t_a represents time to complete an activity. T_E represents time to complete an event. Always use the longest time for converging paths, since the event cannot be completed until all preceding activities are completed. Record the T_E for each event below the circle, as is shown in the above example.

[2] Variance is used to calculate the probability of completing the end event, T_E, to be described in the next section.

Calculating Probability of Project Completion

Although the distribution for an individual activity may be skewed (as is shown by the probability curve illustrated previously), the probability distribution of T_E for the end event of a project comprised of a number of activities is approximated by the normal distribution. As is shown below, the T_E equally divides the area under the normal curve, that is, is the mean.

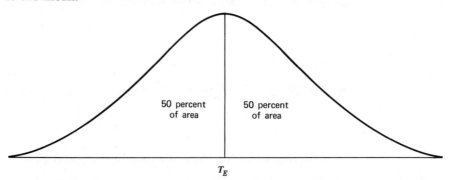

For illustration, assume that T_E for the final event is 65 weeks. To calculate the probability of meeting T_E, all the variances along the critical path are summed. Assume that the variances sum to 9 weeks. To compute the standard deviation of the mean, we take the square root of the variance, as follows:

$$\sigma_{T_E} = \sqrt{\Sigma \sigma_{T_E}^2}$$

$$= \sqrt{9} = 3$$

Since approximately 68 percent of the area under a normal curve represents one standard deviation on either side of the mean, we have a probability of 68 percent that the project will be completed sometime between weeks 62 and 68 (65 weeks ±3). The spread of weeks associated with probabilities is shown below:

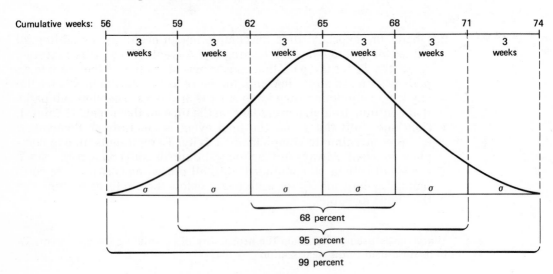

QUESTION: We have a 95 percent probability that the project will be completed between weeks _____ and _____ .

ANSWER: 59 and 71 (65 weeks ±6). A 95 percent probability represents two standard deviations on either side of the mean. We have a 99 percent probability of completing the project between weeks 56 and 74 (65 weeks ±9)

With this information, the project manager could decide what the schedule date should be; or, if a schedule were designated by management, what activities were constraining in meeting that schedule. The project manager could do any of the following to reduce the span of time along the critical path.

1. Allocate overtime to the critical activities.
2. Assign more personnel to those activities.
3. Reassign some tasks along the critical path to less critical paths.

QUESTION: Assume the task of debugging is on the critical path. How could tasks in debugging be redistributed to reduce the span of time required for debugging? _____

_____

_____

_____ .

ANSWER: (1) Less desk-checking and more use of compiler to catch errors. (2) Assign one programmer to debug while the principal programmer continues to code

To continue our illustration of how the PERT network is useful in project control, assume that the project manager holds a weekly status meeting to redetermine the probability of completing on schedule. The following calculations are involved in such a determination.

First, the time estimates are updated. As the project progresses, the persons involved have more knowledge about the job and are in a better position to estimate times.

Second, expected completion time and variances are recalculated.

Third, the normal deviate is calculated. To determine the probability of meeting a scheduled date, we measure the area under the normal curve that represents the schedule. By comparing that area with the total area under the curve, the probability of meeting the scheduled date can be ascertained. Assume the project was scheduled for completion in 36 weeks and that T_E was recalculated to be 39 weeks with a standard deviation of 2 weeks. The third step then would determine the number of standard deviations from the mean, T_E, to the scheduled date, T_S, referred to as the normal deviate.

$$\text{Normal Deviate } (Z) = \frac{T_S - T_E}{\sigma_{T_E}}$$

$$Z = \frac{36 - 39}{2} = \frac{-3}{2} = -1.5$$

Fourth, the probability of meeting schedule is obtained. The table of normal distribution (Table 21–1) is used. The normal deviate of -1.5 represents an area under the curve of only .07, that is, the probability of meeting the schedule in 36 weeks when $T_E = 39$ weeks is only 7 percent.

TABLE 21–1
Probability of Meeting Scheduled Date

Table of Normal Distribution

Normal Deviate	Area	Normal Deviate	Area
−0.0	.50	0.0	.50
−0.1	.46	0.1	.54
−0.2	.42	0.2	.58
−0.3	.38	0.3	.62
−0.4	.34	0.4	.66
−0.5	.31	0.5	.69
−0.6	.27	0.6	.73
−0.7	.24	0.7	.76
−0.8	.21	0.8	.79
−0.9	.18	0.9	.82
−1.0	.16	1.0	.84
−1.1	.14	1.1	.86
−1.2	.12	1.2	.88
−1.3	.10	1.3	.90
−1.4	.08	1.4	.92
−1.5	.07	1.5	.93
−1.6	.05	1.6	.95
−1.7	.04	1.7	.96
−1.8	.04	1.8	.96
−1.9	.03	1.9	.97
−2.0	.02	2.0	.98
−2.1	.02	2.1	.98
−2.2	.01	2.2	.99
−2.3	.01	2.3	.99
−2.4	.01	2.4	.99
−2.5	.01	2.5	.99

Exercise 21–3

Using the procedure in the four steps above, calculate the probability of completing the project on the schedule of 40 weeks, where $T_E = 39$ and $\sigma = 2$ weeks.

Comparing Alternatives for Meeting Schedule

In Exercise 21–3, the probability of completing the project by the scheduled date was determined to be 69 percent. That is, 69 percent of the area under the curve constituted the period before week 40, as is shown below.

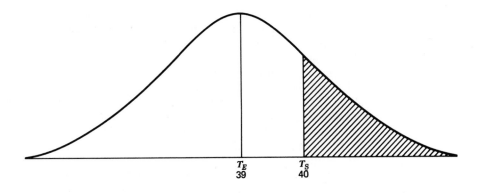

Only 31 percent of the area under the curve fell beyond week 40. Therefore, a 31 percent probability exists of completing the project beyond the scheduled date. With this information the project leader may decide to reassign one man-week of work to another project, since there now appears to be slack time of one week. However, remember that these are estimates; in all likelihood, no action would be taken unless a greater difference resulted from the calculations. A 95 percent confidence level is more generally used.

The crucial decisions arise when the project is behind schedule. The critical path determination permits management-by-exception (the project leader concentrates first on the most critical path). However, other paths cannot be ignored. There may be little difference in criticality between two or more paths.

The project manager is interested in slack time between the various paths, or in other terms, the degree of slack from the most to the least critical path.

Procedure for Calculating Slack

The following procedure is used to calculate slack.

First, determine the difference in time to complete the paths converging on the final event. In Figure 21–8, only one path goes into the final event. Two paths converge into the preceding event. These portions of the network are repeated below:

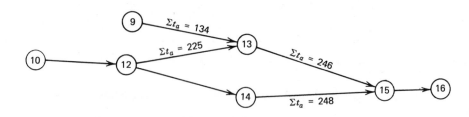

Since the path coming through event 12 took more time than the one coming through event 9, the T_E for event 13 was the longer of the two. That is why there is only two days difference between 12-13-15 and 12-14-15. The difference represents slack; that is, the upper path has two days slack. The project manager could instruct personnel working on the upper path to delay start of their work by two days without endangering the completion target date.

Second, determine the difference in time to complete all other paths. For example, two paths converge at event 13. The one coming from event 12 has $\Sigma t_a = 225$. The one coming from event 9 has $\Sigma t_a = 134$. There is a slack of 91 days (225-134) along path 1-3-4-6-9-13.

The project leader could delay start of the activities along that path. Or, these personnel could be working on other projects in addition to this one, without delaying this one.

As was mentioned previously, programs are available to perform the calculations in PERT or CPM. A rule of thumb is that networks with more than 300 activities justify computer processing; at that volume of activities the cost of computer processing is less than the cost of manual calculation. However, in addition to calculating expected time and probability of completion on schedule, these programs perform other important functions that would be quite difficult manually. For example, reports are provided showing activities sorted by slack, by schedule date, by organization responsible, and the like. Illustration of these reports is provided in Figure 21–9.

Figure 21–10 shows a report for a PERT/COST system, where budget has been allocated to each activity. Weekly reports provide performance against expected completion data and against budget.

These results demonstrate the value of the network technique for planning of implementation. Although the summarized plan in Figure 21–8 would not require networking, control of the more realistic implementation shown in Figure 21–7 would benefit measurably by use of this technique.

QUESTION: From Figure 21–10 it can be seen that a project manager is able to maintain both time and cost control on the project. For example, Event E1-D70 has 6.4 weeks slack and is underrun $2,959 in cost versus

PERT SYSTEM
ACTIVITY REPORT --- (ORDERED BY SLACK TIME)

PROJECT		CONTRACT NO.	REPORT DATE	CONTRACT DATE	RELEASE DATE
STAT REPORT | | | 10/ 4/63 | 9/ 4/63 | |

EVENT		ACTIVITY DESCRIPTION	ACTIV. TIME	DATE EXPECTED ALLOWED	DATE COMP/SCHED SLACK	REMAINING TIME	ORG.
PRED.	SUCC.						
E1	E40	ACTIVITY 102	4.2	9/27/63 A10/ 1/63	±.4		XX2
E40	E30	ACTIVITY 103	4.0	10/29/63 10/25/63 10/23/63	±.4	3.4	XX3
E40	E80	ACTIVITY 107	4.0	10/29/63 10/25/63 10/25/63	±.4	3.4	XX7
E30	E90	ACTIVITY 109A	2.0	11/12/63 11/ 8/63 11/ 8/63	±.4	5.4	XX9

E90
E80
E11

PERT SYSTEM
ACTIVITY REPORT --- (ORDERED BY PRED EVENT)

E10
E1 | PROJECT | | CONTRACT NO. | REPORT DATE | CONTRACT DATE | RELEASE DATE |
E50   STAT REPORT | | | 10/ 4/63 | 9/ 4/63 | |
E1
E20 | EVENT | | ACTIVITY DESCRIPTION | ACTIV. TIME | DATE EXPECTED ALLOWED | DATE COMP/SCHED SLACK | REMAINING TIME | ORG. |
E1 | PRED. | SUCC. | | | | | | |

E60	E1	E20	ACTIVITY 101A	2.4	10/14/63 A 9/18/63	3.6		XX1
E70	E1	E40	ACTIVITY 102	4.2	9/27/63 A10/ 1/63	±.4		XX2
	E1	E50	ACTIVITY 106A	2.8	9/27/63 A 9/20/63	1.0		XX6
	E1	E60	ACTIVITY 104A	3.4	11/ 8/63 A 9/25/63	6.4		XX4

PERT SYSTEM
ACTIVITY REPORT --- (ORDERED BY EXPECTED DATE)

PROJECT		CONTRACT NO.	REPORT DATE	CONTRACT DATE	RELEASE
STAT REPORT | | | 10/ 4/63 | 9/ 4/63 | |

EVENT		ACTIVITY DESCRIPTION	ACTIV. TIME	DATE EXPECTED ALLOWED	DATE COMP/SCHED SLACK	REMAINING TIME·	ORG.
PRED.	SUCC.						

						7.2	XX9
						11.4	XX10
						5.4	XX9
						3.4	XX3
						3.4	XX7
E1	E20	ACTIVITY 101A	2.4	10/14/63 A 9/18/63	3.6	2.0 XX1	XX6
E1	E50	ACTIVITY 106A	2.8	9/27/63 A 9/20/63	1.0	.6 XX6	XX4
E1	E60	ACTIVITY 104A	3.4	11/ 8/63 A 9/25/63	6.4	4.6 XX4	XX5
E20						8.4	XX8
E1						8.4	XX9

E60
E1
E50
E40   PERT SYSTEM
E40   ACTIVITY REPORT --- (ORDERED BY ORGAN --SLACK)
E70
E30 | PROJECT | | CONTRACT NO. | REPORT DATE | CONTRACT DATE | RELEASE DATE |
E10   STAT REPORT | | | 10/ 4/63 | 9/ 4/63 | |
E80
E90 | EVENT | | ACTIVITY DESCRIPTION | ACTIV. TIME | DATE EXPECTED ALLOWED | DATE COMP/SCHED SLACK | REMAINING TIME | ORG. |
E11 | PRED. | SUCC. | | | | | | |

E1	E20	ACTIVITY 101A	2.4	10/14/63 A 9/18/63	3.6		XX1
E20	E30	ACTIVITY 101B	1.8	10/25/63 A10/ 1/63	3.6		XX1
E1	E40	ACTIVITY 102	4.2	9/27/63 A10/ 1/63	±.4		XX2
E1	E60	ACTIVITY 104A	3.4	11/ 8/63 A 9/25/63	6.4		XX4
E1	E50	ACTIVITY 106A	2.8	9/27/63 A 9/20/63	1.0		XX6
E11	E12	ACTIVITY 110	3.0	12/24/63 12/20/63 12/20/63	±.4	11.4	XX10
E40	E30	ACTIVITY 103	4.0	10/29/63 10/25/63 10/23/63	±.4	3.4	XX3

Figure 21–9. *Reports produced by PERT computer program (Courtesy Control Data Corp.)*

budget. It is projected to underrun a total of $32,495. However, the preceding event, E40-E30 has negative slack of _____ and is projected to overrun by $ _____.

ANSWER: − .40 weeks, $8,000

Post-Implementation Audit

A recent addition to the implementation process is a post-implementation audit. Within three months of cutover to the new system, an audit is performed. System performance is compared to the original system objectives to insure the system is accomplishing what it was conceived to produce.

Since it is a violation of the concept of control to have a group audit itself, the audit is performed by a group independent of the original system development team. Some companies assign the responsibility to the internal audit department within the controller's division. Others set up a group within the computer department to perform these audits.

PERT SYSTEM
PROGRAM/PROJECT STATUS REPORT

STAT REPORT	PROJECT	CONTRACT NO.	REPORT DATE 10/ 4/63	CONTRACT DATE 9/ 4/63	CUT OFF DATE	RELEASE DATE

LEVEL / SUMMARY ITEM - 1 / ALPHA   BLOCK1

IDENTIFICATION				TIME STATUS			COST OF WORK - UNITS					
							WORK PERFORMED TO DATE			TOTALS AT COMPLETION		
CHARGE OR SUMMARY NUMBER	LEV	FIRST EVENT NO.	LAST EVENT NO.	SCHD OR ACT(A) COMPL DATE	EARLIEST -LATEST COMPL DATE	MOST CRIT SLACK (WKS)	VALUE	ACTUAL COST	(OVERRUN) UNDERRUN	PLANNED COST	LATEST REV EST.	PROJECTED (OVERRUN) UNDERRUN
BLOCK1 ALPHA	1	E1	E12	12/20/63	12/24/63 12/20/63 E12	-.40	11064	73367	(5.63) (62303)	1278651	1297118	(.01) (18467)
BLOCK2 101	2	E1	E30	A10/ 1/63	E20	-0		65840			65840	
BLOCK5 102	2	E1	E40	A10/ 1/63	E40	-0		2800			2800	
BLOCK3 GAMMA	2	E1	E30	10/23/63	10/29/63 10/25/63 E30	-.40	5464	2505	.54 2959	100000	75505	.24 24495
BLOCK3A 103	3	E40	E30	10/23/63	10/29/63 10/25/63 E30	-.40				40000	48000	(.20) (8000)
BLOCK3B 104	3	E1	E70	10/11/63	10/ 9/63 11/22/63 E70	6.40	5464	2505	.54 2959	60000	27505	.54 32495
BLOCK6 PHI	2	E10	E12	12/20/63	12/24/63 12/20/63 E12	-.40				253537	234621	.07 18916
BLOCK6A 109	3	E10	E11	11/29/63	11/25/63 11/29/63 E11	-.40				161737	126621	.22 35116
BLOCK6B 110	3	E11	E12	12/20/63	12/24/63 12/20/63 E12	-.40				91800	108000	(.18) (16200)

Figure 21-10. PERT/COST computer output (Courtesy Control Data Corp.)

QUESTION: What are the advantages and disadvantages of using the internal auditors instead of an independent system design group within the computer department?

	Advantages		Disadvantages
1.	_____	1.	_____
	_____		_____
2.	_____	2.	_____
	_____		_____

ANSWER:

Advantages	Disadvantages
1. Knowledge of standard auditing procedures	1. Less knowledgeable concerning computer systems
2. Independence from control of computer department director	2. May have "accounting" view instead of CBMIS perspective

Other Phases

Phase VI of the system development cycle is the operational phase. Once installed, the operation consists of the repetitive tasks of data preparation, key entry, data control, computer processing, and distribution of results. If procedures are detailed and if all personnel are properly trained, the operation should run smoothly.

Phase VII is the maintenance phase. Two types of changes are made to installed systems: (1) changes resulting from revision in the function that was computerized (e.g., the company sets up a new chart-of-accounts), and (2) changes to improve the efficiency of the system (e.g., reprogramming as a result of acquiring new peripheral equipment for the computer). The maintenance phase is not to be interpreted as the next stage of development. Systems are planned to be implemented in several stages, to achieve increasing levels of sophistication. However, it is inevitable that minor changes need to be made to each stage. Activities of this kind are referred to as maintenance of the system.

System Documentation

There is an axiom in the computer field, called Murphy's law: "Anything that can go wrong, will go wrong." Murphy's view was that today's systems are so complex that problems are bound to occur.

However, problems can be minimized by proper system documentation. Also, the next level of sophistication in design is greatly facilitated if each stage is properly documented. System documentation consists of the materials shown in Figure 21-11.

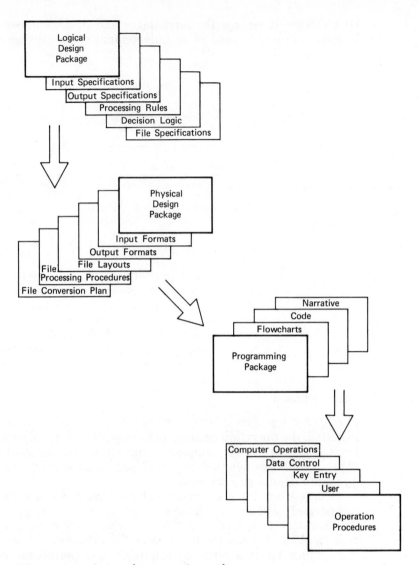

Figure 21–11. *System documentation package.*

Summary

Despite its shortness in span of time, the implementation phase consists of a number of activities that are crucial to the success of the system: testing the system, procedure development, training personnel, parallel processing, file conversion, and cutover to the new system.

Insuring system reliability involves the following series of tests: (1) module test, (2) system test, and (3) parallel processing test.

Procedures are developed for two groups: the user group and the data processing group. Within the latter group are the data control function, key entry function, and computer operations function. These same groups require training in application of these procedures.

File conversion planning is very important because a variety of files are involved in implementing life-stream systems. The time and cost to convert manual files to computer-oriented media are significant factors in meeting system cost/schedule objectives.

Because of the present-day emphasis on integrating systems into a computer-based management information system, implementation planning requires use of special techniques. The Gantt chart technique is appropriate for planning the activities for individuals. One of the network techniques is required for the complicated task of interrelating all activities in a major system implementation. Either the PERT or CPM network methods are used for this purpose. CPM is more appropriate for implementing systems where there is historical data to construct time/cost curves for each activity. When the system is unique and estimates must be made, the PERT technique is more appropriate. In both techniques a critical path is determined, permitting management-by-exception.

Post-implementation audits are required once the system is operational, to insure that the system is meeting design criteria. Some revisions might be necessary, and this activity is referred to as the maintenance phase. Maintenance is facilitated if the system is documented properly. Also, the next stage of sophistication is more readily designed and implemented when the documentation package includes the items identified in Figure 21–11.

Computerizing life-stream operations of the firm can produce significant benefits. Likewise, considerable risk is associated with computerizing such systems, since they are vital to the firm's continued success. Careful planning for implementation, using the procedures and techniques described in this chapter, can reduce that risk.

It is a dual responsibility—of the user representative and the system analyst/designer—to insure that these tasks are properly planned and implemented.

Solutions to Exercises

Exercise 21–1

1. When major systems are integrated, the activities change so much that the new system would not be similar enough to parallel the old.
2. Run the old system during the week and parallel on the weekend. More care is taken in planning a fourth-level sophistication system to insure reliability. The system test must prove the reliability of the system.
3. Instructions must be explicit to insure input is accurately prepared and processed.

Exercise 21–2

1. (a) System designer, in cooperation with the user representative. The user representative is most knowledgeable about the area of application, and the user is ultimately responsible for the system. However, the system designer is responsible for all procedures related to the system.
   (b) System designer. These are technical procedures in which the user is not expected to be knowledgeable.
   (c) System designer and user representative. User personnel interact with data control personnel in handling input and output.
2. (a) User personnel. Operation of the system is the user responsibility. Training by the user representative will reinforce that concept. Also, the user representative will be able to understand better the perspective to insure all aspects are covered in the training sessions.
   (b) System designer. Same reasoning as above, applied to the data processing functions and personnel.
3. The system designer determines what files are to be converted and the file conversion procedure. The programmer prepares a program to accomplish the conversion.

Exercise 21–3

$$\text{Normal deviate} = \frac{40 - 39}{2} = \frac{1}{2} = .5$$

Referring to Table 21-1, the area under the curve associated with this deviation is .69; probability of completion by the scheduled time is 69 percent.

Chapter Examination

1. Examine Figure 16–1. Implementation took only _____ months and was allocated approximately _____ percent of the budget. Why is this phase of the System Development cycle so important? _____

_____

_____

2. Explain the tests that are involved in validation of the system.

(a) _____

(b) _____

(c) _____

3. What determines the length of parallel processing?

(a) _____

(b) _____

(c) _____

4. User procedures and input procedures include both narrative and

graphic material. Why? _____

_____

_____

5. File conversion may be complicated when systems are integrated. Refer to Figure 18–5 and list the files and file media required to meet user output needs.

File Name	Access Needs	Medium Required
_____	_____	_____
_____	_____	_____
_____	_____	_____
_____	_____	_____
_____	_____	_____

6. What is the distinction between training and education—as is related

to implementing a major data processing system? _____

_____

_____

_____

7. Examine the network depicted in Figure 21–7, the hardware/software implementation plan, and answer these questions:
   (a) Activity 50 – 60 is entitled "Frozen Zone." Although this activity is not explained, you can logically deduce its meaning (Hint: it has something to do with additional changes once the computer configuration was established).

_____

_____

617 / CHAPTER EXAMINATION

(b) Jobs A, B, C, D are being programmed in parallel. Are they merely modules of the same system? Explain.

_____

_____

(c) Activity 101 – 102, entitled "Book Test Time," means arranging for programming test time on someone else's computer, since ours will not arrive until the first set of programs is completed. Unless the computer is a local one, the cost of transporting programmers is significant. What programming procedures could be introduced to keep transportation costs down?

_____

_____

8. Examine the network depicted in Figure 21–8, the system development and implementation plan, and answer the following questions.
   (a) What is the expected time for each activity?

Activity	t_a	σ	σ^2	Activity	t_a	σ	σ^2
1–2				6–9			
2–4				9–13			
4–7				13–15			
7–10				5–10			
10–12				9–12			
12–14				12–13			
14–15				8–11			
15–16				3–4			

(b) What is the variance for each activity? [Record next to the t_a in part (a).]
(c) Within what time span would there be a probability of 95 percent

of completing the project? _____

_____

_____

(d) Calculate the probability of completing the project by the scheduled date, 260 days from start time (i.e., compare the T_E you calculated with $T_S = 260$).

_____

_____

_____

9. With the information obtained in question 8, management control functions are possible. Answer the following questions to aid that process.

(a) Which activity is most time-consuming? _____
(b) What might be done to reduce this constraint on system development?

_____

_____

(c) What is the next most time-consuming activity? _____
(d) What might be done to reduce this time constraint? (Several possibilities are the same as for the system design constraint. However, additional possibilities exist for the programming constraint. While design could have begun sooner, programming must wait until the specifications are prepared.)

_____

_____

(e) Designers are preparing test data, operating procedures, and file conversion while programming is going on. However, both programmers and designers are involved in system tests and parallel processing. What might a manager do regarding computer availability to speed up these two activities (other than overtime or

additional manpower)? _____

_____

_____

10. Calculate slack for the network in Figure 21–8.

Path 4–8–11–12   Slack is _____

Path 4–6–9–12   Slack is _____

11. Based on the calculations in problem 10, what are your recommendations to the project manager?_____

_____

_____

12. As a project manager when would you use the Gantt technique instead of PERT?

_____

_____

_____

_____

13. Why not use CPM instead of PERT? Certainly the project manager needs to control costs as well as schedule.

_____

_____

_____

_____

14. The post-implementation audit is designed to accomplish what function?_____

_____

15. Which group should perform such an audit? Explain.

_____

_____

_____

16. The four major components of System Documentation are (refer to Figure 21–11):

(a) _____

(b) _____

(c) _____

(d) _____

17. What is the distinction between input specifications (logical design package), input formats (physical design package), and key entry procedures (operations procedures package)? _____

_____

_____

_____

18. What is the distinction between processing rules (logical system design) and file processing procedures (physical system design)?

_____

_____

_____

19. Who is responsible for preparing each of the subsections of the four documentation components (there are multiple responsibilities in some cases)?
(a) *Logical System Design*

(1) Input specs. _____

(2) Output specs. _____

(3) Processing rules. _____

(4) Decision logic. _____

(5) File specifications. _____

(b) *Physical System Design*

    (1) Input formats. ————————————————————

    (2) Output formats. ————————————————————

    (3) File layouts. ————————————————————

    (4) File processing procedures. ————————————————

    (5) File conversion plan. ————————————————

(c) *Programming Package*

    (1) Flowcharts. ————————————————————

    (2) Code. ————————————————————

    (3) Narrative. ————————————————————

(d) *Operation Procedures*

    (1) User procedures. ————————————————————

    (2) Key entry procedures. ————————————————

    (3) Data control procedures. ————————————————

    (4) Computer operations procedures. ————————————

20. What is the difference between maintenance of a system and a revision such as increasing the level of sophistication?

——

——

——

APPENDIX

COMPUTING NEWSLETTER

FOR SCHOOLS OF BUSINESS

J. DANIEL COUGER, EDITOR

PUBLISHED BY THE COLLEGE OF BUSINESS ADMINISTRATION • UNIVERSITY OF COLORADO • COLORADO SPRINGS

Vol. VII, No. 4

December, 1973

NEW CURRICULUM FOR INFORMATION SYSTEMS PROGRAMS

This month's issue of **Communications of the ACM** contains recommendations for undergraduate curriculum in information systems, prepared by the ACM Curriculum Committee on Computer Education for Management.

This newsletter summarizes the report, giving the background and philosophy. Organizations interested in the full report should request reprints from ACM, 1133 Avenue of the Americas, New York, N.Y. 10036. The complete report, entitled "Curriculum Recommendations for Undergraduate Programs in Information Systems," contains descriptions of detailed course contents and recommended references.

The need for degree programs in information systems was documented in the ACM Committee's position paper.[1] Comprehensive curriculum recommendations for a graduate-level program in information systems development were presented in a further report.[2] Formal education for computer operators and applications programmers is provided through a two-year program, such as those offered by the community colleges. Other positions such as the information analyst and the system designer require advanced education. This view is consistent with those expressed in the recommendations of the National Advisory Committee for Computer Curriculum of the American Association of Junior Colleges.[3]

The new report gives recommendations for undergraduate-level programs, based on the same general concept of the information systems specialty in organizations. Two subspecialities for undergraduate concentration are presented, the emphasis being characterized either as organizational or as technological (shown below).

Chairman of the Subcommittee on Undergraduate Curricula was J. Daniel Couger (University of Colorado). Other members of the ACM Committee who participated in the preparation of this report are: Daniel Teichroew (University of Michigan), Russell M. Armstrong (H.B.R. Singer Co.), Robert L. Ashenhurst (University of Chicago), Robert I. Benjamin (Xerox Corporation), Gordon B. Davis (University of Minnesota), John F. Lubin (University of Pennsylvania), James L. McKenney (Harvard University), Howard L. Morgan (University of Pennsylvania), and Frederic M. Tonge Jr. (University of California, Irvine). A draft version of this report was circulated for review to members of the academic and professional community. Representatives of government, industry, and educational institutions participated in a two-day review of the curriculum at the University of Colorado, Colorado Springs.

1. Teichroew, D. (Ed.) Education related to the use of computers in organizations (Position Paper—ACM Curriculum Committee on Computer Education for Management). **Comm. ACM 14**, 9 (Sept. 1971), 573-588. Reprinted in IAGJ. 4 (1971), 220-252.

2. Ashenhurst, R. L. (Ed.) Curriculum recommendations for graduate professional programs in information systems. **Comm. ACM 15**, 5 (May 1972), 365-398.

3. Brightman, R. W. (Ed.) **The Computer and the Junior College:** Curriculum, American Association of Junior Colleges, One DuPont Circle, N.W., Washington, D.C. 20036, 1970.

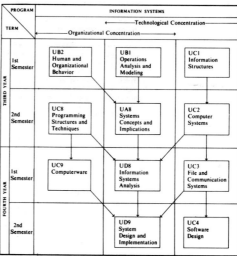

Fig. 1 – Two concentrations in Information Systems Program.

BACKGROUND ON THE INFORMATION SYSTEMS PROGRAM

The Information Systems Field

The information systems development process is viewed as consisting of analysis, design, and implementation phases, prior to the operation phase. These phases do not ordinarily take place strictly in the order given but rather exist together in a continuing pattern of interaction.

Analysis and design proceed in steps together, each affecting the other. An operation phase follows successful implementation, but analysis, design, and implementation activities generally continue as the system is modified and eventually supplanted.

Implementation involves writing and debugging programs, gathering information for data bases, training personnel who will use, operate, and maintain the system, and finally installation and checkout.

Operation involves the routine running of the system and is thereby appropriately the function of an information processing department.

The analysis and design functions, however, are pure developmental activities, and it is here that system inadequacies often have their roots. Such inadequacies may stem from failure to achieve a proper balance between organizational and technological factors, each of which is subject to continuing change.

To highlight the need for balance between these two sets of factors, the analysis and design phase of systems development is explicitly recognized as consisting of two activities: information analysis and system design.

The main emphasis in information analysis is the determination of information needs and patterns of information flow which will satisfy these needs. This requires interaction with organizational personnel and a good understanding of how the organization functions.

The main emphasis in system design is the translation of specified information requirements into a detailed implementation plan which can be realized in hardware/software. This requires interaction with the information processing department and a good understanding of computer technology.

The terms **logical** system design and **physical** system design are sometimes used to differentiate between the specification of the information system itself and its implementation in hardware/software.

Both of these phases concentrate on the system, whereas information analysis concentrates on the organization. Two phases of information analysis may also be distinguished—analysis of information needs and analysis of how they may be satisfied in terms of requirements on an information system. The two phases of information analysis are sometimes called "feasibility study" and "system specification."

The development of information systems then consists of an iterated process of information analysis, system design, and implementation. This "system life cycle" applies to other kinds of development effort as well.

Options in the Program

The recommendations for undergraduate programs for information systems specialist are presented in terms of two concentration options.

1. Organizational Concentration

This option is designed to prepare a person to be an effective computer user. The undergraduate student, therefore, combines information systems course work with the academic area of emphasis in a field of application, such as business or government. With the five-course option in information systems, the student essentially has a double major with, for example, marketing or political science or hospital administration. Upon entering a career field, the graduate will be able to participate effectively on a system development team of users and practitioners. Until recently, an additional option would have extended a student's program beyond the normal four-year requirement. Today most programs allow enough electives to accommodate easily a second area of emphasis.

2. Technological Concentration

This option is designed to prepare a person for an entry-level job in an information processing department. The graduate would typically begin as a programmer and, through practical experience and advanced education, qualify to move into the area of logical and physical system design.

Background on the Information Systems Specialty

The previously cited reports of the Committee provide the background for degree programs in information systems. The position paper[1] gives the justification for the degree programs, citing surveys on demand for such persons and the kinds of capabilities required of practitioners in the field. The second report[2] provides detailed course descriptions for graduate-level professional programs. The reader is encouraged to obtain copies of those papers as a background for the undergraduate curriculum recommendations.

Prerequisite Qualifications

The areas of prerequisite qualifications for the undergraduate program are listed in terms of five course subjects.

(1) finite mathematics, including the fundamentals of formal logic, sets and relations, and linear algebra;

(2) elementary statistics, including the fundamentals of probability, expected value, and construction of sample estimates;

(3) elementary computer programming, including problem analysis and algorithm synthesis, and competence in a higher-level language;

(4) elementary economics, including microeconomics and theory of the firm, and price theory;

(5) elementary psychology, including fundamentals of personality formation, attitudes, and motivation.

FRAMEWORK FOR THE INFORMATION SYSTEMS OPTION

The basic framework of the recommendations for graduate professional programs is used as a context for specifying undergraduate programs. There are, however, differences not only in level but in program objectives and in envisioned program implementation environments. The approach to the graduate curriculum was to present a single "standalone" program based on 13 specified courses. Using this course material as a base, modified programs were presented for adoption by business schools, computer science, or other departments which have a less comprehensive emphasis in the development area. The modified programs involved the definition of three additional courses, containing certain pairs of the 13.

Entry-level positions for people with undergraduate degrees are expected to be less demanding, in terms of the knowledge and abilities required. On the other hand, the fact that an undergraduate program is necessarily less concentrated on the "major" subject makes it more difficult to be comprehensive in the coverage of the information systems field, even in more condensed form. Accordingly, instead of a single program of information systems courses, two concentration options are distinguished, labeled "organizational" and "technological." These two terms correspond to the terms "information analysis" and "system design."

Each concentration option is specified in terms of a set of core courses (seven in the case of organizational, eight in the case of technological). The two sets of core requirements share four courses in common, so both concentrations can be offered by implementing a total of 11 courses.

The question also arises how the undergraduate program will relate to the master's level program. After the undergraduate program has been completed, only one year is required to complete the master's program. The contents of the two sets of core courses seem to fit most naturally into two different undergraduate schools—organizational into business and technological into engineering. Each concentration is regarded as essentially based on the idea of a double major covering a field of application. A university desiring to have both concentration options available for undergraduates could achieve this by having the programs separately available in the undergraduate business and engineering schools, but this would require duplication of the common core courses.

A collaborative effort would obviously be more satisfactory. It might be further argued that a most desirable solution would be to make the combined program, with both concentration options available, in a school of arts and science or equivalent, thus removing the more narrow emphasis in "business" or "engineering." Although this would undeniably make a broader set of combined application fields possible, the fact that an information systems speciality has an ultimate aim which is practical rather than intellectual should not be disregarded; and for a particular university, the compatibility of this with the rest of the arts and science curricula should be carefully considered.

Figure 2 gives a typical four-year program (assuming five courses per semester, two semesters per year) for the organizational concentration in a business school, with accounting as the parallel program field.

TERM / YEAR	1st Semester					2nd Semester				
First Year	Finite Math*	Econ*	English	Science	Elective	Psych*	English	Science	Humanities	Elective
Second Year	Computer Programming*	Intro. Acct.	Social Science	Humanities	Elective	Statistics*	Intro. Acct.	Social Science	Humanities	Elective
Third Year	UB1 Human & Organizational Behavior	UB2 Operations Analysis & Modeling	Marketing	Elective	Elective	UA8 Systems Concepts & Implications	UC8 Programming Structures & Techn.	Money & Banking	Finance	Elective
Fourth Year	UD8 System & Information Analysis	UC9 Computerware	(e.g.) Cost Acct.	(e.g.) Intermed Acct.	Elective	UD9 System Design & Implementation	(e.g.) Auditing Theory	(e.g.) Acct. Theory	(e.g.) Acct. Prob. & Cases	Elective

* Information systems prerequisite

Fig. 2—Typical course schedule for undergraduate program—organizational concentration (illustrated with accounting as parallel program).

OUTPUT QUALIFICATIONS OF PROGRAM

The output qualifications identify knowledge and abilities, grouped in six categories: (a) people, (b) models, (c) systems, (d) computers, (e) organizations, and (f) society. In addition to modifying or omitting certain of the "knowledge" and "ability" entries of the graduate report, some characterizations in terms of "understanding of the process" and "general knowledge" have been included to reflect the necessarily more modest objectives of an undergraduate program. For example, acquiring the ability to develop specifications requires considerably more course time than merely understanding the process of developing specifications. The capabilities listed are testable in the academic environment—by written or oral examinations, successfully operating computer programs, and other commonly accepted means.

A suggested list of objectives common to the organizational and technical concentrations is:

(a) **people**
ability to interact verbally with others, to listen and understand the views of others, to articulate and explain complex ideas.

(b) **models**
ability to formulate and solve simple models of the operations research type, and to recognize the kind of situations in which they apply.

(c) **systems**
ability to view, describe, define any situation as a system—specifying components, boundaries, and so forth;
ability to present in writing a summary of a project for management action (suitable to serve as a basis for decision);
ability to present in writing a detailed description of part of a project, for use in completing or maintaining same.

(d) **computers**
general knowledge of basic hardware/software components of computer systems, and their patterns of configuration;
ability to program in a higher-level language;
ability to program a defined problem involving data files and communications structures;
general knowledge of sources for updating knowledge of technology;
ability to discuss the major alternatives (assuming current technology) in specifying an information processing system, including data files and communications structures, to the level of major system components;
ability to sketch "rough-cut" feasibility evaluations (in terms of economic and behavioral variables) of proposed new techniques or applications of current technology, identifying critical variables and making estimates and extrapolations;
ability to sketch an economic analysis for selecting among alternatives above, including identification of necessary information for making that analysis, and also to identify noneconomic factors;
understanding of the process of developing specifications for the computer-based part of a major information system, with details of task management and data base management components.

(e) **organizations**
general knowledge of the function of purposeful organizational structure, and of the major alternative for that structure;
knowledge of how information systems are superimposed on organizational patterns, on the operational, control, and planning levels;
general knowledge of techniques for gathering information;
ability to gather information systematically within an organization, given specified information needs and/or specified information flows;
ability to outline, given information needs and sources, several alternative sets of information transfers and processing to meet needs;
ability to sketch "rough-cut" feasibility evaluations of such alternatives;

understanding of the process of developing specifications for a major information system, addressing a given organizational need, and determining the breakdown into manual and computer-based parts.

(f) **society**
ability to articulate and defend a personal position on some important issue of the impact of information technology and systems on society (important, as defined by Congressional interest, public press, semitechnical press, etc.).

The above should be achieved, in more or less similar degree, by information systems graduates in either the organizational or technological concentration. The former group should have in addition the following, originally listed under the "organizations" heading:

knowledge of the functional areas of an organization—operations, finance, marketing, product specification and development;
knowledge of typical roles and role behavior in each functional area;
ability to suggest possible short-term and long-term effects of a specified action on organizational goals;
ability to discuss information needs appropriate to issues and roles above;
understanding of the process of developing positive and negative impacts of a specified information system on specified parts of an organization.

The undergraduate in the technological concentration, however, is not expected to be supplied the background in either organizational functions or organizational behavior except to attain a very general notion of the foregoing. The same can be said of the following entry originally listed under the "people" heading:

ability to describe individual and group behavior and to predict likely alternative and future behavior in terms of commonly used variables of psychology and economics.

On the other hand, the technological option gives the student considerably more in-depth exposure to computer and programming techniques. Therefore, the following three abilities, originally listed under the "computers" heading, are appropriate for the technological option graduate:

ability to develop several logical structures for a specified problem;
ability to develop several different implementations of a specified logical structure;
ability to develop specifications for a major programming project, in terms of functions, modules, and interfaces.

The student in the organizational concentration is only expected to have some general acquaintenance with the process of performing these tasks.

One of the primary limitations an undergraduate program has that a concentrated graduate program does not have is in the amount of exposure to prototype "real world" situations that can be included. Nevertheless, it is desirable that the undergraduate have at least some of the experience listed as desirable for the graduate, in particular:

having gathered information in "real" or hypothetical organization;
having served as a member of a project team outlining an information system, then programming a module of that system;
having participated in planning and conducting an oral presentation of the results of a team project.

COURSE OBJECTIVES AND DESCRIPTIONS

Course group UB

Course UB1. Operations Analysis and Modeling

Objectives. To introduce and exercise a range of analytical and simulation modeling techniques useful in decision making in the system design environment. To consider the function of such models as guides for data collection, structures for data manipulation, and as systems for testing assumptions and generating a variety of alternatives. To identify the problems of data collection, maintenance, and accuracy when using models to assist decision-making activities.

Description. Characterization of scheduling situations. Analysis of allocation problems with mathematical programming. Queuing models. Inventory models. Use of simulation models. *Prerequisites:* finite mathematics, elementary statistics, elementary computer programming.

Course UB2. Human and Organizational Behavior

Objectives. To introduce the student to the principles governing human behavior, particularly as they relate to organizations and to the introduction and continued operation in organizations of computer-based information systems.

Description. Individual behavior. Interpersonal and group behavior. Organizational structure and behavior. The process of organizational change. The implementation and introduction of information systems. *Prerequisite:* elementary psychology.

Course group UC.

Approach to the UC Courses. In the undergraduate program more emphasis is placed on programming skills than in the graduate-level program. In particular, since it is likely that graduates will take entry-level programming positions, the student should have written programs to:

    perform data entry, editing, and validation
    update master files (sequential and random)
    generate reports
    perform error checking and handling
    search and sort

As part of course UC4, the student should participate in a team programming project, with emphasis on how to decide on the subdivision of the programming task.

Course UC1. Information Structures

Objectives. To introduce the student to structures for representing the logical relationship between elements of information, whether program or data, and to techniques for operating upon information structures. To examine the methods by which higher-level programming languages implement such structures and facilitate such techniques.

Description. Basic concepts of information. Modeling structures—linear lists. Modeling structures—multilinked structures. Machine-level implementation structures. Storage management. Programming language implementation structures. Sorting and searching. Examples of the use of information structures. *Prerequisite:* elementary computer programming.

Course UC2. Computer Systems

Objectives. To provide a working view of hardware/software configurations as integrated systems, with (possibly) concurrently functioning components.

Description. Hardware modules. Execution software. Operation software. Data and program handling software. Multi-programming and multi-processing environments. *Prerequisite.* UC1.

Course UC3. File and Communication Systems

Objectives. To introduce the basic functions of file and communication systems, and to current realizations of those systems. To analyze such realizations in terms of the tradeoffs among cost, capacity, responsiveness. To examine some systems integrating file and communication functions, such as the organizational data base system or the computer utility.

Description. Functions of file and communication systems. File system hardware. File system organization and structure. Analysis of file systems. Data management systems. Communication system hardware. Communication system organization and structure. Analysis of communication systems. Examples of integrated systems. *Prerequisite:* UC2.

Course UC4. Software Design

Objectives. To examine how a complex computer programming task can be subdivided for maximum clarity, efficiency, and ease of maintenance and modification, giving special attention to available programming and linking structures for some frequently used interface programs, such as file and communication modules. To introduce a sense of programming style into the program design process.

Description. Run-time structures in programming languages. Communication, linking, and sharing of programs and data. Interface design. Program documentation. Program debugging and testing. Programming style and aesthetics. Selected examples. *Prerequisite:* UC3.

Course UC8. Programming Structures and Techniques

Objectives. To introduce the student to structures for representing the logical relationship between elements of information, whether program or data, and to techniques for operating upon information structures. To examine how a complex computer programming task can be subdivided for maximum clarity, efficiency, and ease of maintenance and modification.

Description. Basic concepts of information. Storage management. Programming language implementation structures. Examples of the use of information structures. Searching and sorting. Communication linking, and sharing of programs and data. Interface design. Program documentation, debugging and testing. *Prerequisite:* elementary computer programming.

COURSE OBJECTIVES AND DESCRIPTIONS (cont'd.)

Course UC9. Computerware

Objectives. To provide a working view of hardware/ software configurations as integrated systems. To introduce the basic functions of file and communication systems, in terms of the tradeoffs among costs, capacity, responsiveness. To examine some systems integrating file and communications functions, such as the organizational data base system or the computer utility.

Description. Hardware modules. Execution software, multi-programming and multi-processing. Operation software. Data and program handling software. Functions of file and communication systems. File systems. Review of data management systems and analysis. Review of communication systems. Examples. *Prerequisite:* UC8.

Course group UA

Course UA8. System Concepts and Implications

Objectives. To introduce the student to the information analysis and system design curriculum. To identify the basic concepts that subsequent courses will draw upon: the systems point of view, the organization as a system, its information flows, and the nature of management information systems. To explore the current and projected social and economic effects of information systems in organizations.

Description. The systems concept. Defining a system. Systems analysis. Management systems. Management information systems. Historical perspective of the computer industry. Effects on organizational practice. Privacy and the quality of life. *Prerequisite:* UB1.

Course group UD

Course UD8. Information System Analysis

Objectives. To identify the decision requirements for the management of an organization. To analyze the design of an information gathering and processing system intended to facilitate decision making and planning and control. To analyze the concept of an information system. To review the approaches and techniques available to evaluate existing systems. To examine the concept of common data base for all functional modules.

Description. Nature of the decision-making process. Operational, tactical, and strategic-level systems. System life cycle management. Basic analysis tools. Defining logical system requirements. Determining economics of alternative systems. *Prerequisites:* UA8, and UC2 or UC8.

Course UD9. System Design and Implementation

Objectives. To provide the knowledge and tools necessary to develop a physical design and an operational system from the logical design. To provide students with supervised and structured practical experience in the development of computer-based systems.

Description. Basic design tools and objectives. Hardware/software selection and evaluation. Design and engineering of software. Data base development. System implementation. Post implementation analyses. Long-range system planning. System development projects. *Prerequisites:* UD8, and UC3 or UC9.

RELATIONSHIP TO GRADUATE PROGRAM

A further question which naturally arises is how the undergraduate work prepares the student for a professional master's level program. The undergraduate preparation would be adequate to cover some but not all of the corresponding graduate components. In particular, the D group courses should be taken in their entirety at the graduate level, despite the condensed coverage already afforded by UD8 and UD9.

Figure 3 shows two one-year graduate programs, one for each of the undergraduate concentration options. This approach enables the graduate program to be completed in one year and is consistent with the second year of the graduate program specified in the earlier report.[*]

Figure 3 — One-year graduate programs for students who completed undergraduate options.

1st Semester				2nd Semester			
A3 Information Systems for Operations and Management	D1 Information Analysis	C3 File and Communication Systems	Elective	A4 Social Implications of Information Systems	D2 System Design	D3 Systems Development Projects	C4 Software Design

Undergraduate program had organizational concentration.

1st Semester				2nd Semester			
A3 Information Systems for Operations and Management	D1 Information Analysis	B2 Human and Organizational Behavior	A2 Organizational Functions	A4 Social Implications of Information Systems	D2 System Design	D3 Systems Development Projects	Elective

Undergraduate program had technological concentration.

GLOSSARY

Absolute value An integer or whole number, represented by a symbol such as 0, 1, 2, 3, etc. For example, the decimal number system has ten absolute values, viz 0 thru 9; the octal number system has eight absolute values, viz 0 thru 7.

Access motion time In accessing a disk, it is that time necessary for the access arm to move in or out to the correct track location.

Accumulator A register which is used to accumulate the results of arithmetic operations. In some computers the accumulator cannot be referenced directly while in others several addressable accumulators are available.

Adder A set of logical circuitry that receives data from two sources, performs addition, and stores the result.

Address A label, name, or number identifying a register, location, or unit where information is stored. Also, the operand part of an instruction.

Addressable register A register which may be specifically referenced by the programmer.

Administrative application See Business application.

ALGOL ALGOrithmic Language. A data processing language used to express problem-solving formulas for machine solution.

Algorithm A procedure for solution of a problem in a finite number of steps.

Analog computer A device which measures relatively tractable data. An electronic analog computer solves problems by translating physical conditions, such as temperature, pressure, speed, or voltage into related electrical quantities and uses electrical-equivalent circuits as an analog for the physical phenomenon being investigated.

Analyst See System analyst.

Application See Computer application.

Application in the humanities Computer application which pertains to the humanities, i.e., literature, philosophy, art, etc. For instance, computer art design, music composition, historical research, and harmonics analysis.

Argument The known reference factor necessary to find the desired item (function) in a table.

Arithmetic/logic unit A major component of the CPU which performs all arithmetic and logical operations under the direction of the control unit.

Arithmetic overflow That condition which exists when the outcome of an arithmetic operation exceeds the storage space made available for the results. When this condition occurs, core is generally dumped (contents printed) and processing is terminated.

Array An organized collection of data in which the argument is positioned before the function.

Assembler A computer program that directs a computer to operate upon a symbolic language program and produce a machine language program which then may be directly executed by the machine. The assembler thus serves as a translating routine, which accepts or selects required subroutines, assembles parts of a routine, and usually makes the necessary adjustments required for cross-referencing.

Assembly language A machine-oriented language designed to be used to write or express statements of an assembly program. The instruction code written in an assembly language is often a mnemonic code for assembling machine language computer instructions.

Asynchronous data transmission In this type of data transmission, additional bits are included with each character to indicate the beginning and end of the character.

Auxiliary storage See Secondary storage.

Bandwidth In data transmission, it refers to the frequency range that can be accommodated by a transmission line, which in turn determines the rate at which data can be transmitted.

Base In a number system, the base is the value which indicates how many absolute values are used in the system, e.g., the binary number system has base 2, octal has base 8, hexidecimal has base 16.

BASIC Basic All-purpose Symbolic Instruction Code. A data processing language developed at Dartmouth College as an instructional tool for the teaching of fundamental programming concepts. It has since gained wide acceptance as a time-sharing language and is considered to be perhaps the easiest programming language to learn.

Batch processing system Data processing in which a number of similar input data items are grouped together before they are processed. Used extensively in applications with high input volume, where there is no great need for fast response times.

Batch terminal A terminal oriented to high input volume and relatively low response time. A batch terminal often includes high speed card readers, line printers, and magnetic tape units.

Baud In data transmission, it is a unit of measurement often used to specify transmission speeds. A baud, or a bit can be numerically the same (in the case of narrowband transmission), or may be numerically different (as in broadband transmission). That is, in narrowband transmission, a baud is equivalent to one bit per second. In broadband transmission, a baud is equivalent to a "bit set" per second. Therefore, if a "bit set" consists of eight bits, one baud is equivalent to eight bits per second.

Binary coded decimal representation (BCD) A system of representing decimal numbers, in which each decimal digit is represented by a combination of four digits (bits). For example, the decimal value 6 is represented by 0110 in BCD, the decimal value 15 is represented by 0001 0101.

Binary digit (bit) A numeral in the binary scale of notation. This digit may be zero (0), or one (1), which is equivalent to an off or on position, respectively. Often abbreviated to "bit".

Binary number system The number system which has base 2, i.e., 2^0, 2^1, 2^2, 2^3, etc., and uses binary coded decimal representation to indicate the desired positional value.

Bit A single character in a binary number. Often used as an abbreviation for binary digit.

Block One or more records considered or transferred as a unit, particularly with reference to input and output.

Block parity check In data transmission, it is an error detection technique, which is used in addition to parity checks. That is, in addition to parity bits, one or more check characters are added to each message transmitted. When received, if these characters match the ones transmitted, the message is assumed correct, otherwise an error is noted.

Branching A computer operation where a selection is made between two or more possible courses of action depending upon some related fact or condition.

Branch instruction A computer instruction that enables the programmer to instruct the computer to choose between alternative subprograms depending upon the condition and outcome of some arithmetic or logic operation, or on the state of some indicator.

Broadband In data transmission, it is used to denote facilities capable of transmitting ultra-high data rates (up to several million bits per second). Broadband facilities generally use coaxial cable or microwave transmission.

Buffer A temporary storage device used to compensate for a difference in rate of flow of data, or time of occurrence of events when transmitting data from one device to another.

Business application Computer application that pertains to the functions of a business, such as invoicing, accounting, payroll, and scheduling.

Byte A group of binary digits usually operated on as a unit.

Card punch A device that will make holes in cards in certain patterns so as to represent data. The holes are punched at specific locations in accordance with signals received by the punch. Usually, provisions are made to automatically remove a card from a feeder hopper, move the card along a track as a pattern of holes are punched to represent characters, in accordance with coded signals received, and then place the card in a stacking hopper.

Card reader A device that reads, or senses, holes in cards, transforming the data from patterns of holes to patterns of electrical pulses. Usually, a card reader has facilities for holding a deck of cards, feeding the cards past sensing stations, generating pulse patterns corresponding to the data on the cards, and stacking the cards that have been read.

Cash flow analysis An analysis that projects the specific effect of an investment, on the cash resources of a firm. The cash flow analysis typically delineates the period-to-period effect of an investment on cash resources.

Cathode-ray tube (CRT) A vacuum tube (similar to a television picture tube), with a screen and a controlled beam of electrons, that may be used as a display or a storage device, or both.

CBMIS See Computer-based management information system.

Centralized processing A system that consists of a central computer facility interconnected to a system of remote data terminals. All data is transmitted to the central computer, which maintains and updates the data base. Results of processing data and inquiries are transmitted to the remote locations.

Central processing unit (CPU) Controlling center of a digital computer system which processes data, supervises and coordinates the various functional units of the computer system, and provides primary storage capacity. Major components of the CPU are: a control unit, an arithmetic/logic unit, and a storage unit.

Chaining The use of a pointer in a record to indicate the address of another record that is logically related to the first.

Character One symbol of a set of elementary symbols. The symbols include the decimal digits 0 to 9, the letters A to Z, punctuation marks, operation symbols, and any other single symbols that a computer may read, store, or write.

Character printer A printer in which a single character at a time is selected, or composed, and determined within the device prior to its being printed.

Check digit A means of verifying data through the assignment of an extra digit to coded numbers, enabling the computer to perform the arithmetic needed to establish the probable correctness of the number.

Classifying The grouping of data into categories or classes.

Closed subroutine A subroutine that is not stored in the main path of the routine. Such a subroutine is entered by a jump operation, and provision is made to return control to the main routine at the end of the operation.

COBOL Common Business Oriented Language. A business data-processing language developed by CODASYL, designed to express data manipulation and processing problems in English narrative form, in a precise and standard manner.

CODASYL A committee organized and sponsored by the United States Department of Defense and responsible for COBOL.

Coding The act of writing a sequence of computer instructions to accomplish a desired task.

Coding check A means of verifying data to insure that it conforms with established codes.

Combination check A means of verifying relationships between two fields of coded information to insure that an acceptable relation exists.

Communications control unit (CCU) In a data communications system, the CCU is the means by which the central CPU communicates with various input-output devices. The CCU is connected to the CPU by means of data channels that coordinate the flow of information into and out of the computer.

Communication link The physical equipment used to connect one location to another for the purpose of transmitting and receiving information.

Compiler A computer program that prepares a machine-language program from instructions or subroutines written in a high-level language. A compiler usually generates more than one machine instruction for each symbolic instruction.

Composition check A means of verifying data to insure that appropriate characters are in the appropriate fields or that hash totals are correct.

Computer A device capable of solving problems by accepting data, performing prescribed operations on the data under the direction of a stored program, and supplying the results of these operations.

Computer application The specific problem or job to be solved or accomplished by automatic data-processing devices.

Computer-based management information system (CBMIS) The set of computerized systems that undergird the management process. In CBMIS, data is captured as close as possible to the point of origin, then is shared with all those systems where it is used.

Computer justification The process of evaluating the pros and cons of acquiring a computer.

Computer network Two or more interconnected computers that individually perform local processing tasks as well as transmitting messages to a central computer for updating central files or processing inquires.

Computer output microfilm (COM) Microfilm that is produced by the use of a COM device. That is, a COM device displays data on a CRT screen, and the data is exposed to microfilm. Output is a microfilm copy of the data, either in roll or microfiche form. The computer than produces an index to locate the proper roll and frame for a given output. The device may display data on-line from the computer, or off-line from magnetic tape.

Computer simulation The simulation of physical systems or real-world phenomena through the use of a computer by means of mathematical or physical models that are designed to represent the particular phenomena being investigated.

Computer system An organized collection of hardware and software, whose interaction is designed to accomplish specific functions, such as process computer applications.

Computing Consists of arithmetic operations performed on data and logical operations necessary for program control.

Conditional branch instruction An instruction that is taken only if a specified condition or set of conditions is satisfied. If the condition is not satisfied, the computer performs the next instruction in sequence.

Console The part of a computer that is used for communications between the operators or service personnel and the system. The console contains lights, keys, switches, and related circuits for man-machine communication. The console may be used to control the machine manually, correct errors, determine the status of machine circuits, registers, and counters, determine the contents of storage, and manually revise the contents of storage.

Constant The quantity or message that will be present in the computer and available as data for the program, and which usually are not subject to change with time.

Control unit A major component of the CPU that directs the activities of the computer by interpreting a set of instructions, called a program.

Coordinate Refers to the way data is visualized as being spread out. For example, in an array, if the data (function) is spread over a single row or column, there is one coordinate. Correspondingly, if the data is spread over both rows and columns, there are two coordinates.

Core See Magnetic core.

Counter A device for storing a number and allowing the number to be increased or decreased as directed by the computer instructions.

CPM See Critical path method.

Critical path method A graphical management tool for defining and interrelating on a time scale the jobs and events that must take place to accomplish desired objectives. The interdependency of tasks establishes a network in which the longest path through the network is the critical path that determines the duration of the overall project. In contrast to PERT, CPM has the ability to vary the time along the critical path to determine its effect on cost, and vice versa.

Cross-footing check A means of verifying data to insure that arithmetical accuracy of individual records and/or a group or records is attained.

Cybernetic The scientific study of those methods of control and communication that are common to living organisms and machines. For example, the comparative study of complex electronic calculating machines and the human nervous system to explain the nature of the brain.

Cycle One iteration or loop through a set of logical steps.

Cylinder In disk units with multiple read-write heads, a cylinder constitutes all of the data tracks under the read-write heads. This data can be accessed without mechanical movement of the read-write heads.

Database An integrated set of files, tables, arrays, and other data structures. In a database, separate files may exist, but they are linked together to facilitate providing the information needed by a segment of an organization or, ultimately, the organization as a whole.

Database concept A concept in data-processing that emphasizes integration of data, information, and files. Data elements are captured at the earliest possible source and are made available to all systems and subsystems.

Data channel A physical path along which data may be transferred or transmitted. A channel is essentially a minicomputer, contained near or in the CPU, which permits input-output operations to be controlled independently of the central processing unit (CPU).

Data communication system A system of terminals, communications equipment and channels, and software that links together the various elements of data-processing systems.

Data control Those procedures necessary to control the flow of data or information.

Data management system A comprehensive software system to store, retrieve, and update data. It provides for the definition and creation of files or databases or both, the maintenance of indexes, and for file security.

Data set In a data communications system, it is the device that modulates (dc signal to tones) and demodulates (tones back to dc signals) data between two or more input-output devices and a data transmission link.

Data structure A systematic method of organizing or visualizing data.

Data throughput The rate in messages per minute at which data is transmitted from source to destination.

Debugging The process of identifying and correcting mistakes in a computer program.

Decision criteria Identified conditions or actions that are necessary before a decision is made.

Decision function The process of evaluating criteria and selecting alternatives.

Decision logic table A table of possible courses of action, alternatives, or contingencies to be considered in the description of a problem, with the actions to be taken. Decision tables are often used in place of flowcharts for problem description, analysis, and accompanying documentation.

Demodulation The process of converting tones to a direct current signal. The conversion process is performed by a data set.

Design logic The set of logic used in developing an improved system.

Desk checking Manual checking of a program before it is keypunched.

Development costs One-time costs of system development, consisting of: analyzing and documenting the existing system, designing, programming, debugging, and implementing a new system.

Diagnostics Computer output designed to provide the programmer with information of maximum utility and convenience in checking out programs.

Dialed service In data transmission, dialed service is the intermittent use of communication facilities. When a message is to be transmitted, the user dials the destination number (either computer or remote terminal), just as for a telephone call. With dialed service, the user must compete with other users for an available line, and he may encounter a busy signal at any given time. The user is charged only for the time used, with rates depending on the time of day, day of the week, and distance involved.

Digital computer Basically, a counting device that operates on discrete or discontinuous data or numbers. More specifically, it is a device for performing sequences of arithmetical and logical operations, not only on data but also on its own program.

Dimension In an array, the number of elements that comprise each coordinate. For example, an array that has two rows and three columns, would be of dimension (2,3).

Direct access Addressable storage locations in which each storage location is in no way dependent on the location of the previously obtained data. Thus each particular record can be accessed (by its identifier) and operated on without the need for sequential searching.

Direct-entry system System oriented to direct entry of data from a keyboard. The system typically includes a disk storage unit for mass storage of data files. Output may be by means of a line printer or a visual display device or both.

Diskette A small magnetic disk (resembles a 45-rpm record), which is sealed in a plastic jacket about 8 inches square and weighs less than 2 ounces.

Distributed processing A system in which the processing workload is spread out through the teleprocessing network.

Documentation Organization and communication or recorded knowledge to maintain a complete record to facilitate changes in conditions.

Echo checking See Loop checking.

Effective error rate In data transmission, it is the rate at which undetected errors occur in transmission. Effective error rates depend on the nominal error rates, quality of transmission facilities used, and on the sophistication of the error detection and correction techniques used.

Elementary item A data item or field containing no subordinate items. In other words, elementary items are data items or fields that are not subdivided.

Error correction codes In data transmission, it is a code containing redundant data to assist in error correction and detection.

E-time See Execution time.

Execution time (E-time) The time necessary for the computer to execute an instruction. Several machine cycles are often required for execution time, depending on the instruction.

Extended binary coded decimal interchange code (EBCDIC) A system of representing data (alphabetic, numeric, and special characters), in which each character is represented by a combination of eight-bit positions (excluding parity bit position). The eight positions consist of four zone bits and four numeric bits.

External storage A storage device or medium outside the computer that can store information in a form acceptable to the computer. External storage devices usually have larger capacities and lower access speeds than internal and secondary storage. External storage consists of punched cards, magnetic tape, and documents encoded with magnetic ink characters, or optical characters.

Fading In data transmission, fading refers to temporary loss of signal that occurs primarily in microwave transmission and may be caused by atmospheric conditions, severe rainstorms, or even a bird flying between towers.

File descriptor A document used to describe and provide detailed information for each file in the system, whether or not computerized.

File maintenance The activity of keeping a file up to date by adding, changing, or deleting data.

First generation system design approach A systems development approach that placed emphasis on administrative functions and concentrated on individual systems rather than integrated systems.

Fixed word length A computer word in which there is always a constant number of bit position. The size of a fixed word depends on the particular computer.

Floating point (FORTRAN) The mode that utilizes decimal numbers and/or variable names beginning with the letters A to H, and O to Z. These variables are called floating point or real mode variables, because the computer "floats" numbers into proper decimal alignment before computing.

Flowchart A schematic or graphic presentation of the logic required to solve a problem.

Flying spot scanner In optical character recognition (OCR), a device employing a moving spot of light to scan a sample space, the intensity of the transmitted or reflected light being sensed by a photoelectric transducer.

Forms flowchart A chart that depicts the flow of paperwork and forms.

FORTRAN FORmula TRANslator. A compiler language developed by the IBM Corporation, originally conceived for use on scientific problems but sometimes adapted for commercial problems as well.

Front-end processor In distributed computer networks, the front-end processor is a computer (typically a minicomputer) that is attached to and facilitates the host processor. When a front-end processor is used, all communications control functions are removed from the host (central) processor to the front-end processor.

Full duplex In data transmission, full duplex is a transmission mode that permits transmission of data in both directions simultaneously.

Function In a table, a function is the relation of one item from a set of items with each item from another set.

Gantt chart The predecessor to network analysis, in which the representation of tasks and their relationship is shown via time scale.

General-purpose flowchart A flowchart designed for a general purpose. That is, the terminology utilized is of a general nature and is applicable to a number of situations.

GPSS General Purpose System Simulation. A simulation language that is suitable for representing and experimenting with the essential elements of a large system of a computer.

Graphics Pertaining to visual display in which three-dimensional objects may be displayed via a CRT device. Some graphic units use a light pen or other device that permits an operator to input data in graphical form.

Graph plotter A device capable of representing data in graphic form, such as two-dimensional curves or line drawings, either as direct computer output or from magnetic tape. Graph plotters are often used as a computer output device to display the results of computation.

Group item An item that is further subdivided.

Half duplex In data transmission, half duplex is a transmission mode that permits transmission of data in both directions, but only one direction at a time.

Halographic memory A reuseable storage medium that is a high-resolution photographic plate embedded in a heat sensitive plastic.

Hardware Physical equipment, such as the mechanical, electronic, and magnetic units in a computer.

Hash total An account, total, or tally of items in certain fields, used for control of input, processing, and output operations.

Hexadecimal number system The number system that has base 16, that is 16^0, 16^1, 16^2, 16^3, etc., and uses characters representing the absolute values 0 to 15.

High-order languages The programming languages that tend toward being independent of the limitations of a specific computer, such as COBOL, FORTRAN, and PL/I.

History file An obsolete master or transaction file, retained for historical use or reference.

Hollerith code An alpha-numeric punched-card code invented by Dr. Herman Hollerith in 1889, in which the top three positions in a column are called "zone" punches (12, 11, and 0, from the top downward), and are combined with the remaining punches, or digit punches (1 to 9) to represent alphabetic, numeric, and special characters.

Horizontally-oriented systems Operational systems that handle the basic operations of the organization, for example, a checking account system, and a demand deposit account system.

Host processor In a data communications system, there may be several computers, some of which may be assigned specialized functions such as message switching and local processing. In such a system, there is generally a large central computer that performs the major data-processing tasks. This computer is often referred to as the "host processor."

Hybrid computer A combination analog and digital computer. An integration that permits dynamic simulation and high-speed differential-equation solution to be performed (analog side), plus static and algebraic computations (digital side). Overall computational economy and efficiency are thereby maximized through hybrid computers.

Identifier One or more characters utilized in the identification or location of an item or record.

Impact printer A printer that forms characters by the use of print hammers that press the paper and ribbon against selected type characters as they pass in front of the paper. Type characters are commonly mounted on a moving chain or are engraved on the face of a rotating drum. Typical speeds range from 500 to 2,000 lines per minute.

Implementation costs In system development, they are one-time costs that consist of: training personnel to operate the system, plus the cost of installing and testing the system.

Index sequential organization A file organization combining the efficiency of sequential organization with the ability to rapidly access records out of sequence. It may be used only on direct-access devices.

Information analyst See System analyst.

Information system The network of all communication methods within an organization.

Initialize The establishment of an initial value for a counter.

Input-output control system (IOCS) Various library routines that a programmer can select by means of macro-instructions for input and output of data.

Input-output descriptor A document used to describe and provide detailed information for each system input and output.

Input specification A document, prepared by the system analyst, that delineates the appropriate input, content, and media required for the system.

Instruction A coded program step that tells the computer what to do and where to find or store data for a single operation in a program. Basically, an instruction consists of two parts: operation code and operand.

Instruction counter A special purpose register that contains the address of the next instruction to be executed.

Instruction time (I-time) The time necessary for a computer to move an instruction from main memory to the storage register. During this time the operation code is routed to the operation-code register, and the address portion to the address register. Total instruction time generally requires one machine cycle.

Integer mode (FORTRAN) The mode that utilizes integer numbers or variable names or both beginning with the letters I to N.

Integration The sharing of data or information among subsystems and systems.

Intelligent terminal Essentially, a minicomputer with an input keyboard and often a CRT display. An intelligent terminal can perform checking, editing, and formatting on input data; error control; message routing and switching; and stand alone computing, that is, performing small-scale processing tasks.

Interblock gap An interval of space between recorded portions of data or physical records that permits tape stop-start operations.

Interface A common boundary between automatic data-processing systems or parts of a single system. For example, the connection between a data channel and the control unit.

Internal storage See Primary storage.

Interrecord gap See Interblock gap.

Inverted files A method of file organization in which a data item, field, or keyword identifies a record instead of the original identifier or key.

Interation One loop or cycle through a set of logical steps.

I-time See Instruction time.

Job control cards Cards that contain program names, parameters, or special instructions for a specific application. The data on the control cards usually represent information for executing a computer program other than the actual input data or the actual program to be run.

Job control language The specific data processing language used for a particular set of job control cards.

Job deck See Job control cards.

Key See Identifier.

Keyboard printer A device that permits a versatile means of transmitting messages and data between a remote user and the computer at speeds related to the common-carrier service available.

Key-disk system A system in which data is entered from a keyboard device (similar to a typewriter) and is recorded directly onto a magnetic disk. Often, this approach is facilitated through the use of a minicomputer. That is, data is entered through keyboards, is processed by the systems-shared computer and then is stored on a magnetic disk.

Keypunch machine A special device to record information in cards or tape to represent letters, digits, and special characters.

Key-tape system A system in which data is entered from a keyboard device (similar to a typewriter) and is recorded directly on magnetic tape. Generally, the data being keyed is stored in a buffer (or small memory device) and is displayed on a CRT, so that the operator can see what is being recorded. In the event of an error, the operator merely backspaces and retypes the data. When the record is completed, it is then released to the magnetic tape.

Key transformation A scheme, usually mathematical, which is utilized to determine a number that is used as the address of a record.

Large-scale integrated (LSI) circuitry An ultra-high speed storage device that uses miniature semiconductors (such as transistors) to form very small, compact memory arrays.

Latency See Rotational delay time.

Leased service In data transmission systems, leased service refers to the use of communication facilities through a lease arrangement. The user may lease a line from a common carrier on a fulltime basis, permitting 24-hours-a-day availability. A flat rate is charged for the service, depending on the distance.

Libraries An organized collection of standard, checked-out routines that may be incorporated into larger routines as the need arises.

Lifestream activities Those activities that are key to the life of an organization.

Linear programming The analysis of problems in which a linear function of a number of variables is to be maximized (or minimized) when those variables are subject to a number of linear constraints.

Line printer A printer in which an entire line of characters is composed and determined within the device prior to printing.

Links See Pointer.

LISP A high-order data-processing language that is suitable for "symbol manipulation." LISP was designed for language translation, information retrieval, text editing, and other areas where manipulation of alphabetical data and words was necessary.

List A data structure in which logical records are connected by means of pointers.

Location In a computer, it is an addressable area in main memory or auxiliary storage where a unit of data may be stored or retrieved.

Logic The science that deals with the principles of correct or reliable inferences.

Logical design Phase II of the system development process that is essentially hardware-independent. In this phase, the system analyst works with the user, or his representative, to define precisely what the system is intended to perform.

Logical errors Errors in the logic of a particular program.

Logical file A complete set of related records for a specific area or purpose that may occupy a fraction or all of a physical file, or may require more than one physical file, for example, an inventory master file that may require one or more reels of magnetic tape (i.e., physical files).

Logical operation The examination of data to determine relationships, such as comparing, selecting, referencing, matching, sorting, merging, and the like.

Logical record A collection or an association of data items, fields, or records on the basis of their content instead of on their physical location. For example, all data relating to a given person forms a logical record regardless of where or how the data may be located, dispersed, or distributed.

Loop An interation or cycle through a set of logical steps.

Loop checking An error detection and correction technique used in data transmission. In loop checking, when an operator strikes a key on the typewriter terminal, it is transmitted to the computer where it is received and checked. The character is then transmitted back to the terminal and printed. If the character that is printed is the same as the key that was struck, the operator is insured that the message has been properly received by the computer.

Low-order language Those programming languages that most closely resemble machine language. Generally, each instruction is equivalent to one machine instruction.

Machine language A programming language or instruction code used directly by the computer. The code (binary-based notation) is in a form directly acceptable to a computer and requires no translation.

Machine-readable Pertaining to the characteristic of being able to be sensed or read by a device, usually by a device that has been designed and built specifically to perform the reading or sensing function. Thus data on tapes, cards, drums, disks, and similar media are machine readable.

Macro-instruction An instruction that programmers can write in a source program to call for special or library routines that perform wanted functions as open, seek, close, and the like. Macro-instructions result in one-for-many instructions and are extensively used.

Magnetic core A tiny doughnut-shaped element about the size of a grain of salt, which is capable of being polarized in one of two directions (i.e., ON or OFF).

Magnetic disk A storage device of magnetically coated disks, on the surface of which information is stored in the form of magnetic spots arranged in a manner to represent binary data. These data are arranged in circular tracks around the disks and are accessible to reading and writing heads on an arm that can be moved mechanically to the desired disk, and then to the desired track on that disk. Data from a give track is read or written sequentially as the disk rotates.

Magnetic drum A cylinder with a magnetic surface on which data can be stored by selective magnetization of portions of the curved surface. Data is written and sensed by a set of read-write heads positioned close to the surface of the drum while it is rotating at high speed.

Magnetic ink character recognition (MICR) A technique in which characters are inscribed on documents with magnetic ink containing particles of iron oxide. The document reader senses the magnetic pattern, permitting sorting, summing, and control. Only 14 characters are used in MICR (the 10 digits 0 to 9, plus 4 special characters). MICR was pioneered, developed, and is currently in wide-spread use among American banks.

Magnetic ledger card A card with a magnetic surface on which data can be stored by selective magnetization of portions of the card. The cards are read by a ledger card reader, and results are printed on the card and also are recorded on magnetic strip. Magnetic ledger cards are confined to low-volume applications, however, the cards are relatively low in cost and are easily interpreted by humans without computer processing.

Magnetic strip storage Consists of a number of addressable small oxide-coated plastic strips or cards mounted on a cartridge holder. When referenced, the strip drops out of the holder, moves under a read-write head for storage or retrieval, and then is replaced in the holder. Magnetic strip storage is relatively inexpensive and provides very large storage capacity.

Magnetic tape An external storage medium in the form of a ferrous oxide coating on a reel of metallic or plastic tape on which bits may be recorded magnetically as a means of retaining data.

Main storage See Primary storage.

Management-by-exception The management principle that is concerned with exceptional conditions, that is, when actual results differ from planned results. When results occur within a normal range they are not reported.

Management information system (MIS) The complete set of business techniques designed and operated to assist in decision making at various levels of management. A management information system may or may not be computerized.

Master file A set of relatively permanent records containing identifying, statistical, and historical information, used as a source of reference for an application.

Matching checks A means of varifying data through the matching of identifiers or coded transaction numbers.

Merging The combining of two or more files into a single file in the same sequence.

MICR See Magnetic ink character recognition.

Microcomputer Relatively small but powerful computer mounted on a single semiconductor chip or printed circuit board.

Microprogram A machine-language instruction causes a single functional step to be performed. Each instruction is actually a composite of a number of still more elementary steps, called micro-instructions. Each micro-instruction is coded as several bits, one bit for each functional unit or data path in the computer hardware. The program that transforms each machine language instruction into a series of micro-instructions is called "microprogram."

Microsecond A measurement used in determination of cycle time, typically used in second generation systems, that is, one millionth of a second.

Millisecond A measurement used in determination of cycle time, typically used in first generation systems, that is, one thousandth of a second.

Minicomputer A computer usually weighing less than 50 pounds, that contains a relatively small internal memory and that can accept peripherals such as disk storage, magnetic tape units, and line printers.

Mixed mode (FORTRAN) An expression that contains a combination of integer and real constants and/or variable names. In evaluating a mixed mode expression the FORTRAN compiler usually converts integer quantities to floating-point quantities and performs the arithmetic in floating-point mode.

Modem See Data set.

Modular programming The segmentation of a large program into a number of small, self-contained subprograms or subroutines.

Modulation The process of converting a direct current (dc) signal to tones for transmission via a communications link. The conversion process is performed by a data set.

Module A separate and distinct (yet, integral) part of a system that can be compiled independently.

Module tests Those individual tests performed on the separate programs, subroutines, or parts of a system, for purposes of assuring accuracy, capability, and adequacy of each unit.

Monitor See Supervisor.

Multiplexor channel A channel that permits the transmission of two or more messages on a single channel by use of an interleaving process. That is, the multiplexor channel receives a message from an input unit one character at a time in its usual operation. In between these characters the multiplexor channel sandwiches a character from each of the other units that also want to communicate with the processing unit.

Thus, the multiplexor channel resolves the high speed of the processor with slower input and output equipment by permitting many input or output devices to communicate simultaneously with the processor.

Multiprogramming A technique by means of which a digital computer can appear to process several programs at once, and yet still operate in a strictly sequential manner. For example, if two or more different programs reside in main memory at the same time, the computer performs a number of instructions of the first program, then switches to the second program, performs a set of its instructions, then switches to the next program, and eventually comes back to the first program again until all the programs are completed.

Nanosecond A measurement used in determination of cycle time, typically used in third generation systems, that is, one billionth of a second.

Narrowband Facilities capable of transmitting data at rates from 45 to 300 bits per second. Narrowband facilities are typically limited to applications with low volumes.

Network See Communications link.

Noise In data transmission, noise refers to random signals that interfere with the transmitted signal. There are two basic types of noise: background noise and impulse noise. Impulse noise, which is the greater source of error, is caused by electrical storms (or other disturbances) that cause a burst of short-duration pulses.

Nominal error rate In data transmission, nominal error rate is the rate which is inherent in the transmission link that is used. This rate depends on a number of factors such as type of equipment, distance, transmission speed, and weather.

Nondestructive read A reading process that does not destroy or change the data in the source.

Nonimpact printer A printer that forms characters by transferring electrical charges to the paper. Some nonimpact printers can print more than 5,000 lines per minute; however, they are not appropriate for producing carbon copies.

Nonoverlapped processing A process in which the typical cycle, that is, read, process, and write, is performed serially (i.e., in sequence). Thus the total cycle time is the sum of the read time, plus the process time, plus the write time.

Object computer The computer that accepts the object program to thus execute the instructions, as contrasted to a computer that might be used to merely compile the object program from the source program.

Octal number system The number system that has base 8, that is, 8^0, 8^1, 8^2, 8^3, etc., and uses characters representing the absolute values 0 to 7.

Off-line communication system A system in which data is recorded on a machine-readable medium, instead of being transmitted directly to or from the computer.

One-address instruction See Single-address instruction.

On-line batch system A system in which data is accumulated in batches and transmitted directly to the computer for processing.

On-line processing system The operation of terminals, files, and other auxiliary equipment under direct and absolute control of the central processor to eliminate the need for human intervention at any stage between initial input and computer output.

On-line real-time system An on-line system that provides near-instantaneous responses to inquires from a terminal. Typically, such a system has immediate access to all necessary data, which often permits a response within seconds.

Op code See Operation code.

Open subroutine A subroutine inserted directly into the linear operational sequence rather than by a jump. Such a subroutine must be recopied at each point that it is needed in a routine.

Operand The second part of an instruction that tells the computer "where" to find or to store data to be processed, or the location of the next instruction. It is the address of a storage location where the desired data or instruction is found.

Operating costs In system development they are recurring costs, consisting of (1) preparing report, (2) entering data on machine processible media, (3) performing control checks on input, and output, and (4) computer processing.

Operating system An integrated set of programs and subroutines that controls the execution of programs and provides services such as language translation, input-output control, and job scheduling.

Operation code The first part of an instruction that tells the computer "what" operation to perform, such as add, multiply, compare, and read.

Optical character reader This unit reads numerical data printed in widely used type styles on paper or card documents. The printed data automatically is translated into machine language for direct input to the processor.

Optical character recognition (OCR) The identification of graphic characters, directly from a printer or handwritten document, by use of photosensitive devices. Thus, OCR eliminates the need for data conversion.

Optical mark reader An optical mark reader senses data recorded by an ordinary pencil in the form of marks (such as "X's" or slashes (/)) on cards or other documents. The sensed data may be transmitted directly to a computer for processing, or may be automatically recorded on another medium such as punched card or magnetic tape.

Organization-oriented system flowchart (O²S flowchart) A flowchart in which organizational responsibility is identified for each activity performed, each major system within the organization has a flowchart, and the resources required in each organization in the system are delineated.

Output specifications Those documents produced through in-depth discussions with users of the system. Output specifications identify precisely what the system should provide the user.

Overlapped processing A process in which the typical cycle, that is, read, process, and write, is performed simultaneously. The total cycle time is determined by that event which takes the most time to perform (either read time, or write time, or processing time).

Packed decimal A decimal format in EBCDIC in which the zone portions of numerical digits are removed and two decimal digits are packed into each eight-bit set. The sign of the number is stored in the rightmost portion of the character string.

Pages In the concept of virtual storage, it is the segmentation of a program into modules called "pages." This is accomplished by a combination of software and hardware in which only those pages that are actually being used are contained in primary storage.

Parallel processing tests The processing of the new system and the old system with the same input and time period to verify that the new system satisfactorily meets design criteria.

Parity checking A summation check in which the binary digits, in a character or word, are added, and the sum is checked against a single, previously computed parity digit. The check tests whether the number of ones (bits in "on" position) in a word is odd or even, depending on the particular parity check.

Payback analysis An analysis to determine the period of time necessary to recover the costs of an investment or project.

Peripherals Input-output and secondary storage devices that represent the means by which data is input, stored, retrieved, and output from the computer.

Peripheral storage See Secondary storage.

PERT Program Evaluation and Review Technique. A graphical management tool for defining and interrelating on a time scale the jobs and events that must take place to accomplish desired objectives. The interdependency of tasks establishes a network in which the longest path through the network is the critical path that determines the duration of the overall project. In contrast to CPM, PERT has the ability to develop probability estimates for each activity, and for the critical path.

Photodigital storage Consists of the permanent recording, by an electron beam, of binary data on small film chips. The film is read by a flying spot scanner.

Physical design Physical system design is concerned with the conversion of the logical system design into a form that can be processed by the computer economically and effectively. Generally, physical system design takes place in Phase III of the system development process and determines the organization of files and the devices to be used.

Physical file A physical unit such as a reel of magnetic tape.

Physical record A collection of related data elements, items, or fields, treated as a unit.

PL/I A general purpose data processing language that is suitable for both scientific and business applications. PL/I combines many of the features of FORTRAN and COBOL, and has a wide range of possible applications; however, it is relatively complex and not universally used.

Pointer A field in a record which gives the address (identifier) of another record that is logically related to the first.

Point of sale recorders A device that is used to input sales data at the time when a sale is executed. Generally, a point of sale recorder uses optical or magnetic reading techniques.

Positional value The value that is found by raising the base of the number system used to the power of the position. For example, in the decimal system the zero (or units) position has positional value 10^0 or 1, and the first (or tens) position has positional value 10^1, etc.

Present value analysis An analysis that takes into account the time value of money. Present value is the equivalent value *now* of future dollars discounted back from a specified future date to the present date at a given rate of compound interest.

Primary storage The storage that is considered an integral part of the CPU. It contains both the computer program(s) and the data to be processed by the program(s).

Problem-oriented flowchart A flowchart in which the terminology used is expressed in terms commonly used in the activity to be computerized.

Problem-oriented language A programming language designed for ease of problem definition and problem solution for specific classes of problems.

Procedure-oriented flowchart Synonymous with problem-oriented flowchart.

Procedure-oriented language A programming language designed for convenience in expressing the technique or sequence of steps required to carry out a process or flow. It is usually a source language and is usually not machine oriented.

Process flowchart A flowchart used in the early 1900s to portray physical flow of materials, products, and often clerical activities.

Processing specification A document, prepared by the system analyst, that delineates appropriate procedures for computer processing data.

Program An explicit set of steps or instructions that directs the computer and coordinates the operation of the various hardware components.

Program evaluation and review technique See PERT.

Programmer-oriented flowcharts Those flowcharts that use the terminology, symbols, and terms generally required by a programmer in developing a computer application.

Punched card A card that is punched with a pattern of holes to represent information. The punched card is commonly used as an input-output medium for digital computers. The punched holes are sensed electrically by wire brushes, mechanically by metal feelers, or photoelectrically.

Punched paper tape Paper tape on which a pattern of holes or cuts is used to represent data.

Punch unit See Card punch.

Radix See Base.

Random access See Direct access.

Randomizing See Key transformation.

Random processing The processing of transactions in the order in which they occur. Used in direct access file organization.

Reasonableness check A means of verifying data to insure that it does not exceed the limit prescribed by reason.

Record A set of related data items of fields, pertaining to a particular item, unit, or entity.

Record key See Identifier.

Recording density The number of characters or symbols recorded or stored in a unit of length, area, or volume.

Redundancy In data transmission, it refers to parity bits and checks added to the message to assist in determining the accuracy of transmitted digits or words.

Register A device for the temporary storage of data or instructions to facilitate arithmetical, logical, or transferral operations.

Report file Set of records extracted from data in master files, used to prepare reports.

Return on investment analysis An analysis to determine the expected return on monies invested. It is derived by dividing savings (income) by the cost of an investment. Return on investment is a useful management tool utilized in the ranking of various investment alternatives.

Rotational delay time In accessing a disk, it is that time necessary for the disk to rotate until the desired sector (or record) is positioned at the read-write head.

RPG Report Program Generator. A data processing language designed for relatively simple business applications in which there is a need for generating routine business reports.

Run manual The complete documentation of a specific program used in a particular run.

Scalar In an array, a scalar is a single element of data, usually a number.

Scientific application Computer application which pertains to the sciences, that is, primarily deals with facts or truths. For instance, airframe stress analysis, guidance and flight control, matrix inversion, and blood count analysis.

Secondary storage A storage that principally supplements primary storage. Secondary storage devices include magnetic disk units, magnetic drums, and magnetic tape. Secondary storage is characterized by slower speed of operation and correspondingly lower cost than those related to primary storage.

Sector A portion of a track (from a magnetic disk) whose shape is similar to a slice of pie. Each track is equally divided into sectors, in which each sector may have its own distinct address.

Selector channel A channel that is used where high-speed devices are to be attached to a system. A single channel can operate only one input-output device at a time. Two or more channels connected to any computer system provide the ability to read, write, and compute from multiple input-output devices.

Sequential access A file organization in which items of information become available only in a one after the other sequence, whether or not all the information or only some of it is desired. That is, it is necessary to start at a given reference point and to examine each record in sequence until the desired record is located.

Sequential file A file in which records are arranged in ascending or descending order according to a key that may be numeric, alphabetic, or alphanumeric. To locate a specific record it is necessary to start at a given reference point and to examine each record in sequence until the desired record is located.

Sign check A means of verifying data to ascertain the appropriateness of the algebraic sign.

Simple parity check In data transmission, it is an error detection technique, in which a bit is added to each character to make the total number of one bits in each character transmitted either odd or even. Each character is then checked for correct parity at the receiving end. Simple parity check will not detect errors involving an even number of bits, and does not permit error correction.

Simplex In data transmission, it is a transmission mode that permits transmission of data in one direction only.

SIMSCRIPT A simulation language that is suitable for representing and experimenting with the essential elements of a large system on a computer.

Single-address instruction An instruction consisting of an operation and exactly one address.

Small business computers Basically, a minicomputer central processing unit, with peripherals and software especially designed for data processing applications. Main storage capacity typically ranges from 4,000 to 32,000 positions or more. Utilized primarily by small businesses, that is, businesses with less than $10 million in sales per year.

Software Computer programs and related techniques that bridge the gap between a user's problems, on one hand, and strictly hardware functions and requirements, on the other. Software includes programming languages and translators, operating systems, and applications programs.

Sorting The arranging of a list (or file) of data into a desired sequence.

Source computer The computer that is utilized to translate source programs into object programs for computer execution.

Special-purpose flowchart A flowchart designed for a specific function. The terminology utilized restricts its use to a special purpose.

Standard binary coded decimal representation A system of representing data, in which each character is represented by a combination of six-bit positions (excluding parity bit position). The six positions consist of two zone bits and four numeric bits. To represent a numerical value, the zone bits are set to zero. For example, in standard BCD, the decimal value 6 is represented by 000110, and the alphabetic character A is represented by 110001.

Storage device See Storage unit.

Storage unit A device into which data may be inserted, in which it may be retained, and from which it may be retrieved.

Stored program A set of instructions contained in main memory that directs the operation of a computer without human intervention.

Subprogram A part of a larger program that can be compiled independently.

Subroutine The system or sequence of machine instructions inserted in response to a macro-instruction. Also, a routine that is part of another routine.

Subscript Coordinate "postions" used to reference individual elements within an array.

Supervisor A routine that controls and coordinates all operations in the computer system. The supervisor organizes and regulates the flow of work, and provides translations among languages, diagnoses of human mistakes, priority assignments, equipment malfunctions, and opens and closes files, as well as other housekeeping details.

Switched service See Dialed service.

Symbolic addresses An address, or label chosen for convenience by a programmer to specify a storage location in the context of a particular program.

Synchronous data transmission In this type of data transmission, the sending and receiving terminals are kept in constant synchronization by data sets. Synchronizing information is transmitted in the modulated signal, and special timing circuitry is used in the receiving station.

Synergism The concept that the whole is equal to more than the sum of its parts. For example, man and computer together can produce more than either can produce alone.

Synonyms Record keys or identifiers that generate the same storage addresses. In other words, synonyms require a search of two or more areas before location of the desired record is attained.

Syntax error An error in the usage of the programming language utilized.

System An organized collection of parts or elements united by regulated interaction and designed or required to accomplish a specific purpose or objective. Every system involves (1) input, (2) processing, and (3) output.

System analysis The delineation of resources (personnel, equipment, materials, and facilities) required for proper operation of the system.

System analyst An individual who analyzes a system to determine where improvements can be made.

System designer An individual who converts system requirements into a set of specifications which allow it to be computer-processed.

System feasibility analysis The process of evaluating the advantages versus the costs of converting a manual operation to computer processing.

System survey The initial phase of the system development cycle which documents company history, external environment, objectives and policies, and delineates the master plan.

System tests Actual running of all applications (modules) on the complete system, using actual or hypothetical data and analyzing the results. System tests are designed for purposes of testing the accuracy, capability, and adequacy of an entire system.

Table An organized collection of data, usually arranged in an array where each item in the array is uniquely identifiable by some label or by its relative position. Items in a table are easier to locate or identify, and thus provide a ready reference.

Tabulating operation flowchart A modification of the process flowchart to meet the special characteristics of punched card processing.

Telecommunications See Data communication system.

Teleprocessing See Data communication system.

Terminal In data communication systems, a terminal is a point at which data can enter or leave the communication network.

Thin film An ultra-high-speed storage device consisting of a molecular deposit of material on a suitable plate, usually silicon or glass. Common sizes are one twentieth of an inch square that may contain entire etched circuits replacing thousands of transistors, and the like.

Third generation system design approach A systems development approach that concentrates on studying the organization as a whole, giving priority to the life-stream activities of the firm.

Three-address instruction A computer instruction that makes a reference to three addresses. The addresses may specify the location of operands, results, or other instructions.

Time-sharing system An on-line system in which many users share availability of a remote central computer.

Trace routine A routine used to observe how the object program operates while it is being executed.

Track The portion of a moving memory medium (such as tape, disk, or drum) which passes beneath, and is accessible to a particular read-write head position. In a disk or drum, tracks run in a circular manner whereas tracks in tapes run lengthwise.

Transaction file Set of records resulting from transactions that affect the status of items in the master file. It is used to update the master file.

Translator A routine, program, or device capable of directing the translation or transformation of statements or their equivalent codes in one language to equivalent statements or their equivalent codes in another language.

Two-address instruction A computer instruction that makes a reference to two addresses. The addresses may specify the location of operands, results, or other instructions.

Unconditional branch instruction An instruction that is always executed each time the computer encounters it. The unconditional branch instruction causes the computer to branch to another location in the program—either a higher or lower address.

User-oriented flowchart Those flowcharts that use the terminology, symbols, and terms that permit verification of logic by the user.

Utility program A general-purpose program, supplied by a manufacturer with his equipment, for executing standard or typical operations, such as sorting, indexing, translating, assembling, compiling, or merging.

Variable A symbol whose numeric value changes from one repetition of a program to the next, or changes within each repetition of a program.

Variable word length A computer word in which the number of characters in a given word is variable and subject to the discretion of the programmer. Each character is addressable, which permits control of word lengths.

Vertically oriented systems Management systems that provide pertinent information to various levels of management, for example, a market forecasting system.

Video display A device that uses a cathode-ray tube (CRT) and permits on-line visual display of data. Display units are widely used where it is necessary to provide direct access to computer files.

Virtual storage A concept applicable whenever primary storage is so vast that a programmer is not limited to storage addresses corresponding to the range of actual storage capacity.

Visual display See Video display.

Voiceband In data transmission, it is used to denote facilities capable of transmitting data at rates up to 2,400 bits per second, or more.
with some noncommon carrier data sets).

Voice response unit A unit that permits audio response. That is, an inquiry is made to the computer by means of a keyboard. The computer transmits the response to an audio response unit that contains a magnetic drum. The unit selects words and phrases from a prerecorded vocabulary stored on the drum, and forms a verbal reply.

Wideband See Broadband.

Word A set of characters that occupies one storage location and is treated by the computer circuits as a unit and is transported as such. Word lengths are fixed or variable, depending on the particular computer and program.

Zoned decimal A decimal representation in EBCDIC in which each character is encoded as an eight-bit character, utilizing both the zone and numeric bits for each decimal digit. The zone bits represent the sign of the number, that is, a bit pattern of 1111 in the zone portion represents an unsigned number, 1100 represents a positive number, and 1101 represents a negative number.

INDEX